TALKING ABOUT PEOPLE

TALKING ABOUT PEOPLE

Readings in Contemporary Cultural Anthropology

Second Edition

William A. Haviland
UNIVERSITY OF VERMONT

Robert J. Gordon
UNIVERSITY OF VERMONT

Mayfield Publishing Company
Mountain View, California
London • Toronto

Library of Congress Cataloging-in-Publication Data
Talking about people : readings in contemporary cultural anthropology
/ [edited by] William A. Haviland, Robert J. Gordon.—2nd ed.
    p.   cm.
    Includes index.
    ISBN 1-55934-524-1
    1. Ethnology.   I. Haviland, William A.   II. Gordon, Robert J.
GN316.T34   1995
306—dc20   95-39143
                                                            CIP

Manufactured in the United States of America
10 9 8 7 6 5 4 3 2 1

Mayfield Publishing Company
1280 Villa Street
Mountain View, California 94041

Sponsoring editor, Janet M. Beatty; production, The Book Company; manuscript editor, Ellen Silge; text designer, Wendy LaChance; cover photographer, © Robert Holmes; cover designer, Donna Davis; art director, Jeanne M. Schreiber; manufacturing manager, Randy Hurst. The text was set in 10/12 Palatino by Thompson Type and printed on 50# Butte des Morts by The Banta Company.

To all the women in our lives

Preface

This anthology is designed as a supplement for introductory cultural anthropology courses. It consists of thirteen chapters with three to five articles each, and each chapter has a short introduction written by the editors that relates the articles to each other and to the topic of the chapter. The chapters themselves are arranged to complement the chapter topics and order found in most introductory texts and courses.

In the second edition, eighteen articles are new, and we've introduced an appendix, "Using the Internet," by David Houston, that we hope will be useful in helping readers explore the global arena in anthropology.

FEATURES AND BENEFITS OF THIS BOOK

Freshness and Originality

Most anthologies reproduce with some regularity "old chestnuts." While we have nothing against the classics, we do feel that it creates the impression that nothing new has happened in anthropology. We want to introduce students to some of the more recent and provocative works of anthropologists. We want students to read provocative articles, for one of the aims of the introductory course should be to shake up the students' comfortably ethnocentric beliefs about the world in which they live.

Focus on Contemporary Global Concerns

It is no secret that North Americans are surprisingly ignorant about the nature of the "global society" of which they are a part. In an era when North Americans constitute a small minority of the world's people and are increasingly dependent on the rest of the world for vital raw materials, manufactured goods, and markets for those products still made at home, reliable information about other peoples and the ways in which they live has become ever more important for the survival of North Americans themselves. Because anthropology has always been in the forefront of efforts to learn about other peoples, it has a special role to play in combating the insularity and provincialism that sometimes accompany students to college. Thus, the majority of articles in this anthology focus on common global interests. From William Klausner's examination of the question "Can One Really Go 'Native'?" in Chapter 1 to Gernot Köhler's analysis of global apartheid in Chapter 13, the volume highlights global concerns.

At the same time, this anthology seeks to show the exotic in the familiar by suggesting new and provocative ways of looking at the student's own society. We feel this closer examination is an essential way to combat racism and other invidious distinctions that North Americans like to draw between "us" and "them." From articles such as Alan Dundes's on American football in Chapter 4 and James Brain's "Ugly American Revisited" in Chapter 12, readers will gain fascinating insights into their own cultures and societies.

International Authorship

In keeping with the global perspective of this anthology, we include a significant number of articles by authors from outside the United States. Anthropology is not, after all, an exclusive American preserve (and how arrogant we are to call ourselves Americans!). It is an exciting international discipline whose members are not all white middle-class males. We have tried to reflect the profession more closely by increasing the representation of not only foreign (British, Canadian, Danish, French, Mexican, Nigerian, Philippine, South African, Zairean) but also female contributors, including a number of nonanthropologists. About 40 percent of the authors come from outside the United States, and 40 percent are female.

Incorporation of Gender Issues

Because anthropology is the study of women as well as men, we have deemed it important that gender issues be well represented by the articles here. Considerations of gender enter into virtually everything that people do, so we chose to spread the material on gender throughout the book. Notable examples of articles that deal with gender are Alma Gottleib's "The Anthropologist as Mother" in Chapter 4; Dirk Johnson's "Polygamists Emerge From Secrecy," John Coggeshall's "'Ladies' Behind Bars," and Regina Smith Oboler's "Is the Female Husband a Man?" in Chapter 7; Brett Williams's "Why Migrant Women Feed Their Husbands Tamales," Margery Wolf's "Uterine Families and the Women's Community," and Alice Schlegel's "Male and Female in Hopi Thought and Action" in Chapter 8; Abigail Adams's "Dyke to Dyke" in Chapter 9, Elizabeth A. Eames's "Why the Women Went to War" in Chapter 10, and Sylvia Rodgers's "Feminine Power at Sea" in Chapter 11.

Abundant Student Learning Aids

An annotated table of contents offers students previews of the various articles, and chapter introductions provide some contextual "glue" for the points made by the articles. Brief biographical sketches of the authors of each article further enhance the international flavor of the volume and contribute further insights into what anthropology is all about. The references and notes for each article will appeal to the student who wants to know more, and the glossary and map showing the location of peoples and places discussed will be helpful to all students. Finally, the index contributes further to making this a user-friendly book.

A NOTE ON THE ARTICLES

While many of the articles are reprinted here in their entirety, some have been edited in order to keep the book to a reasonable length. For the most part, the cuts have involved details of methodology so as not to adversely affect either the substance or the spirit of the article.

We have compiled an anthology with authors from many countries to provide a global anthropological perspective. We retained the spellings from the original texts to give students the experience of reading other versions of the English language and learning to distinguish between British and U.S. spellings; we thought this would help students learn something about the frames of reference of the authors. That was our theory, but in practice the book is a bit more complicated than that.

We have included authors, North American and British-style (includes all non-U.S. anthropologists), who were educated all over the world. They wrote for United States publications with editors who liked "North American" spelling and for British-style publications with editors who liked "British" spellings. And finally, they moved from one country to another. As anthropologists, we are a global community who often spell in both styles, switching from one to another without realizing it. To the utter horror of all copyeditors, we leave with you this evidence of our international lives, a bit of linguistic anthropological research on the anthropologists themselves!

ACKNOWLEDGMENTS

Lots of people have contributed in one way or another to this volume. Those behind the scenes who have made vital contributions include Anita de Laguna Haviland who, besides riding herd on both editors to meet deadlines, put everything into the computer, caught numerous errors, tracked down a variety of information, and assisted in writing the Instructor's Manual. Rinda Gordon kept one of the editors in line and helped with the Instructor's Manual. We acknowledge Ken Marty's assistance with the manual as well.

The changes in this new edition in part reflect the reactions in Gordon's introductory anthropology course at the University of Vermont in the fall of 1994. To the students in that class, as well as in all the other classes we have taught through the years (Haviland has been teaching introductory students since 1965, Gordon in the United States since 1979 and before that in Papua, New Guinea), we are grateful for all we have learned about teaching and the kinds of material students find effective.

We'd like to thank the anonymous instructors who returned questionnaires about the first edition, as well as the following reviewers for their comments on the first edition and suggestions for the second; their advice proved enormously helpful in selecting articles: Albert A. Dekin, Jr., SUNY, Binghamton; Nicholas Honerkamp, University of Tennessee at Chattanooga; Susan Russell, Northern Illinois University; Charles Rutheiser, Georgia State University; Edwin S. Segal,

University of Louisville; R. Daniel Shaw, Fuller Theological Seminary; Richard L. Warms, Southwest Texas State University; and Michael James Winkelman, Arizona State University.

Many people at Mayfield Publishing Company have helped bring this project to fruition. First of all, we are grateful to Jan Beatty, who has kept us posted on user reactions to the first edition and provided numerous valuable suggestions. We appreciate the interest she has shown in our ideas from the outset and the

ideas and advice she has contributed along the way. We are no less grateful to the others at Mayfield who have seen this volume through production, particularly April Wells-Hayes.

Hats off to you all!

William A. Haviland
Robert J. Gordon
Burlington, Vermont

Contents

1   THE NATURE OF ANTHROPOLOGY   1

Some anthropologists do fieldwork in their own countries. By making the everyday exotic, they develop double-vision, the ability to see issues from different perspectives.

The task of understanding a culture other than one's own is fraught with difficulty; not only are there all sorts of unsuspected things to be discovered, but the anthropologist may also be fed all sorts of misinformation. The difficulties are compounded as one tries to write up one's material in a way that will be comprehensible to an audience with a different cultural background without doing violence to ethnographic reality.

Is it possible to "go native"? William Klausner suggests that it is difficult.

2   CULTURE   13

3   LANGUAGE AND COMMUNICATION   40

4 PSYCHOLOGICAL ANTHROPOLOGY 52

Amparo B. Ojeda

Growing up American: Doing the Right Thing   54

In North America, children are usually raised to become independent, assertive, and self-reliant. In other places, behaviors like compliance and respect for authority are emphasized. For a person raised in one way, the other may seem "bizarre," but each pattern fits its particular culture's overall design.

Alma Gottlieb

The Anthropologist as Mother: Reflections on Childbirth Observed and Childbirth Experienced   57

In spite of the value North Americans set on personal independence and self-reliance, they often find themselves in situations where they are forced to submit to authority. Yet authorities are not always aware that there are other ways of doing things. For someone who is aware, having one's own way is not always easy.

Alan Dundes

Into the Endzone for a Touchdown: A Psychoanalytic Consideration of American Football   64

Adopting a psychoanalytical approach, anthropologist Alan Dundes likens football in North America to non-Western adolescent initiation rites involving acts of homosexuality.

5 SUBSISTENCE 71

Daniel Stiles

Nomads on Notice   73

Across the arid lands from West Africa to Mongolia, pastoral nomadic people have prospered for millennia in spite of droughts and raids. How they have done so is illustrated by the Gabbra of Kenya. But can they survive the threats posed by postcolonial states and their economists?

Baird Straughan

The Secrets of Ancient Tiwanaku Are Benefiting Today's Bolivia   76

Knowledge of ancient intensive agricultural techniques shows promise of doing what Western systems of farming cannot: dramatically increasing the crop yields of peasants living in the Bolivian Andes.

10   POLITICAL ORGANIZATION AND SOCIAL CONTROL   176

11 RELIGION AND MAGIC 193

Tanya Luhrmann

The Goat and the Gazelle: Witchcraft 195

Magic and witchcraft are phenomena with a wide distribution, including the contemporary United States and Europe. Luhrmann provides a first-hand ethnography of witchcraft in England.

Silvia Rodgers

Feminine Power at Sea 204

Far from being cold-hearted, rational individuals, English sailors and their officers have some important superstitions and beliefs that guide their actions.

J. D. Lewis-Williams

Reality and Non-Reality in San Rock Art 208

Because all humans, wherever they live, have the same kind of nervous system, all are capable of entering trance. Although some cultures regard such behavior as "abnormal," others—like the Bushmen—regard it as central to encountering the supernatural.

Carolyn Nordstrom

Treating the Wounds of War: The Culture of Violence 217

In Zambia the violence of war has created a culture of violence, which traditional healers now seek to overcome.

12 CULTURE CHANGE 221

A. L. Spedding

Coca Eradication: A Remedy for Independence?—With a Postscript 223

Reagan and Bush's War on Drugs has unintended reverberations in Bolivia.

James L. Brain

The Ugly American Revisited 230

Why is so much of the Third World prone to violent anti-American feelings? Jim Brain, who tried to work for an American aid agency, explains his disillusionment and provides important clues.

Appendix   276

David Houston
An Anthropologist's Guide to the Internet

TALKING ABOUT PEOPLE

1

The Nature of Anthropology

Most anthropologists define **anthropology** as The Study of Man, claiming that it was derived from the Greek words *anthropos* and *logos* meaning "man study," and many introductory texts bear pretentious titles like "The Study of Mankind, or Humanity." However, if one probes deeper into the Greek lexicon, *anthropos* and *logos* can also be glossed as "bearer of scandals or tales." This is why pioneering British social anthropologist Lucy Mair, to whom we pay tribute in titling this anthology, modestly defined her discipline in her lectures as simply "talking about people." Talking about people, or gossip, is not only a pleasantly informal activity (and the fodder of the ubiquitous TV talk shows!), but, as this anthology shows, it can be a disciplined, engrossing, and enriching experience leading to important personal and social insights. Indeed, "talking about people" is a basic social and cultural activity in which we humans engage in order to educate and place ourselves in the world and to make sense of our beings and universe.

We feel that this more modest stance has contributed substantially to the increasing popularity of anthropology in recent years. There are of course other reasons as well. Some attribute its popularity to the fact that, of the various social sciences, anthropology has the least amount of jargon—a situation derived in part from the fact that the people researchers have studied do not read their studies. This has changed, however, in a world that is increasingly becoming a global village—which may also account for anthropology's new-found status, as there are many more opportunities for cultural misunderstanding and thus more need for an understanding of other cultures. This process of **globalization** has resulted in many of us realizing the

importance of the interrelationships between our part of the world and people in other parts of the planet, most graphically illustrated by our concern for the Amazonian rain forest and how deforestation there will affect our own well-being. Graphic TV images of drought, famine, and pestilence in the Third World have made us sense an impending crisis. A growing disillusionment with "development" and the fact that more and more people are asking penetrating questions about why development has failed have also propelled anthropology to prominence (see readings in Chapters 5 and 12). "Development experts" are starting to realize that possibly one reason for the failure of development has been that they have not understood or talked to local people. Anthropology is the academic discipline that makes it its business to talk to such folks.

Indeed, it is precisely this emphasis on the "Other" that makes the study of anthropology attractive to many. In essence, anthropology is concerned with the study of alternative lifestyles and cultures. It looks at how other people solve common human problems. On a more personal level, people who are interested in alternative lifestyles and cultures tend to be dissatisfied with their own society. In short, they suffer from various degrees of alienation; this gives rise to the old saw about the definition of anthropologists: those who reject their own society before that society rejects them. There is merit in this joke in that anthropology has a distinguished record of attracting far more women and minorities than any other social science. Most first-year students can name some prominent female anthropologists like Margaret Mead, Ruth Benedict or the British Lucy Mair, Audrey Richards or Monica Wilson. This tradition still continues—over half of all presidents of the

2 THE NATURE OF ANTHROPOLOGY

American Anthropological Association since World War II have been women. Other social sciences and humanities like sociology, political science, psychology, and history are hard-pressed to even halfway replicate such a distinguished record.

There is nothing deviant or abnormal about being alienated from one's society. On the contrary, some would argue that it is inevitable given the present condition of modernity. Disciplining one's alienation and using it as a way of seeing can lead to important insights. Indeed, we would argue that this alienated perspective is crucial. When one of the authors was first coming to the United States, he asked a native what books he should read to understand his new country. He was surprised to be told to read de Tocqueville's *Democracy in America* and Gunnar Myrdal's *An American Dilemma*. In retrospect, what they have in common, apart from providing original and synthetic insights into the workings of the United States, is that both authors were clearly outsiders to the United States.

Perhaps the most important characteristic of anthropology is that it self-consciously takes an outsider perspective on society and culture. In Robert Burns's immortal words, "Aye wad the giftie gie us, tae see ourselves as others see us." As such, anthropology can be a wonderful antidote to **ethnocentrism** and its associated myths of **cultural arrogance**. This disciplined outsider perspective is typically acquired by travel, either geographical or imaginary. But, as we all know, travel does not necessarily broaden the mind; that only happens if one is predisposed to let it happen, and this is where the anthropological perspective comes in.

A concern with the Other, either real or imagined, leads directly and inevitably into a consideration of difference. What are the implications of difference? Is difference largely in the eye of the beholder? For example, a Papua New Guinean village would obey the District Commissioner's instruction to "tidy up the Village" by assiduously sweeping up all the dog and pig droppings but leaving all the papers and cans. To them, papers and cans are not dirty but a sign of affluence and status. Here is an example of the important role played by culture in defining difference. Culture is one of the key concerns of anthropology, and in Chapter 2 we concentrate exclusively on the concept. A concern with difference also raises a host of issues such as how much difference should be tolerated. This issue manifests itself in many ways, ranging from the young New Yorker in Papua New Guinea who rationalized wearing a scanty bikini among bare-breasted women despite their disapproval because in New York she would not object to what *they* wore, to the explosive issue of **multiculturalism** that is gripping U.S. campuses.

The issue of the Other and cultural differences is the focus of the article by Marion Benedict. She relates her experiences as an ethnographer in the Seychelles, struggling to understand the islanders' lives as *they* live them, yet finding it impossible to be a mere "fly on the wall" herself. Her article demonstrates not only the difficulties of getting to know Others, but also the difficulties of accurately writing about a particular culture for an audience with a different background. How does one do this, without the description becoming a caricature? At the same time, as Klausner points out, it is exceedingly difficult to "Go Native."

For the novice a quick look at any anthropology department would appear to reveal a bewildering array of diverse individuals who appear to have nothing in common with one another, except perhaps a department secretary. This is illusionary, however, because what relates the **linguist,** the **social anthropologist,** the **ethnologist,** the **prehistorian,** and the **physical anthropologist** is precisely an appreciation for the role of culture in the construction of difference. Historically, this arose out of a shared concern for what were originally "tribal people," but the focus is now increasingly on contemporary changes. Anthropologists are increasingly studying segments of their own society, using a distinctive **anthropological perspective.** The article by Judith Okely is a good example of this. Although anthropologists will debate the smaller details, most agree that the following constitute some of the defining characteristics:

1. **Fieldwork** is perhaps the characteristic of which anthropologists are most proud. According to Seligman (quoted in Lewis 1976:27), "What the blood of the martyrs was to the Early Church, Fieldwork was to anthropology." He was perhaps exaggerating, but only slightly. Indeed, many give this distinctive characteristic the status of a tribal initiation rite: One is not an anthropologist unless one has done fieldwork for an extended period of time.

2. Extended fieldwork leads almost naturally to a focus on local communities and a feel for grass-roots issues.

3. Fieldwork immersion and the breadth of anthropological training emphasize the **holistic perspective,** examining social relationships in the full context of their interrelationships. While other social scientists might spend all their time examining the beauty of the flowers, anthropologists pause from this task to take in the beauty of the entire fields from the top of the mountain and thus see a broader pattern.

It is from these holistic perspectives that anthropologists can engage in the increasingly important task of debunking myths about the Other and themselves.

REFERENCE

Lewis, I. M. 1976. *Social Anthropology in Perspective,* Harmondsworth, England, Penguin.

Fieldwork in the Home Counties

Judith Okely

Judith Okely has done extensive fieldwork on Gypsies and lectures in anthropology and sociology at the University of Edinburgh in the United Kingdom.

Malinowski's advice on fieldwork included the famous pleas to learn the indigenous language and to avoid contact with white men. Such advice would have been inappropriate for my fieldwork. Granted, Gypsies in England are respectably exotic as non-literate nomads, not found in the conventional typologies. Yet we shared the same language, apart from the occasional Romani word inserted into English sentences. Fieldwork did not require progress through grammar books, interpreters and mental translations. This apparent concordance with one's own culture masked other differences.

We are always reassuring ourselves that anthropology highlights the contrasts between cultures. These contrasts are rarely experienced within the same space and time as they are during fieldwork at home. Long-term fieldwork in my own country made explicit the contrast with my customary life. The anthropologist abroad has a different relationship with the society within which the group studied is embedded. He or she is usually a stranger to all contexts. By contrast, in my case, I was moving from a specific experience defined by class, gender, race and education into a stigmatized minority about whom I knew almost nothing, beyond the non-Gypsy (Gorgio) stereotypes and representations. Until a community worker drove me to a cluster of modern caravans and lorries just off the M1, I should not have recognised them as members of the exotic category vaguely associated with horses and waggons. Previously, I should have thought I was looking at the caravans of temporary road workers.

You experience the sudden absence of basic amenities like water and a W.C. on a camping holiday, but usually in a depopulated, rural setting. The Gypsies did not live in the woods of the nursery rhyme. The camps were bordered by major roads and sometimes housing estates, lorries thundered along the elevated

"Fieldwork in the Home Counties," by Judith Okely, from *Royal Anthropological Institute News*, 1984, Royal Anthropological Institute. Reprinted with permission.

dual carriageway a few yards away. On one camp we nestled beneath a factory floodlit at night. A costly new site was built on a former sewage farm. Cannibalized car bodies, piles of scrap and smoking tyres were my palm trees and coral strand.

To the Travellers I did not appear as an eccentric foreigner but as a member of the dominant persecuting society, albeit a well-meaning student. In this context, Malinowski's and later Powdermaker's suggestions for a preliminary census were inadvisable at any stage. The Trobriand Islanders may on the face of it have been complimented by attention to their way of life, or perhaps a colonized people has learned to submit to censuses, but nomads everywhere have learned how to evade them. I was warned by one Gypsy friend that I could be burned for writing down a genealogy. Evans-Pritchard and Chagnon have also known difficulties in getting mere names.

Unlike anthropology abroad, fieldwork at home is not a matter of memorizing a new vocabulary; only slowly did I realise that I had to learn another language in the words of my mother tongue. I unlearned my boarding school accent, changed clothing and body movements. Dropping my 'aitches and throwing in swear words, I was doing an Eliza Dolittle in reverse and without Professor Higgins to supervise me. After some months a Traveller said "Judith your speech has improved." Washing and eating became different procedures with the same utensils and food from the same shops up the road (see Okely, 1983). My past identity was slowly dismantled in the home counties I had inhabited since childhood.

The view of a famous provincial town, from the cab of a lorry crammed with Traveller parents and children, looked both familiar and alien. As we drove through districts I had known before, the Travellers would show me another landscape stamped by their past: "That's where I stopped as a kid with our waggon and horses," "we tarmacced that forecourt," "years ago we got loads of scrap from that air base," "Billy rents this field for his horses."

One summer, I was calling for scrap and rags in a sleepy village with my regular Traveller work mate: "Lovely houses these," she said as we passed a desirable Georgian residence. The lilac hung heavy over a white garden seat. I dreamed of a Grantchester tea and imagined the view from a top window; it would make a lovely study, I was thinking. My daydream was fractured by my Traveller companion; "Lovely houses for calling—those rich people'll have a lot to throw out." She had rightly seen them as a resource, a place for acquiring goods not for habitation. If she had pressed her face against the window pane, it would not be with any longing to enter.

Despite my change in clothing, when calling for "any old iron, scrap, batteries or rags," I still couldn't get the demeanour right. The housewives would invariably ask me, but not my Traveller mates, what it was for. Eventually, I found it simpler to say it was for charity than reveal that I was an anthropologist doing participant observation as a Gypsy on Gorgio doorsteps. Some of the Gorgio women looked like myself in another life. I was looking in a distorted mirror. In the company of Travellers, I did experience abuse as a Gypsy at garden gates and in shops, and was chased away where previously I would have been welcome.

An anthropologist abroad does not experience the double knowledge I felt, for example in the following case. My mate Reena persuaded one woman on a private estate to part with an old battery. As it was leaking acid, Reena wrapped it in newspaper. After loading up, Reena's mother Aunt Doll stuffed the newspaper in the hedge, thinking she was being "tidy." The Gorgio woman had been watching us from her gravel drive. Her views on rubbish disposal were as intimately known to me as those of my head-mistress. I shrank at her scorn: "What have you done with that newspaper?" she called out: "It's alright," said Aunt Doll, "I've put it in the hedge." "That's typical of you Gypsies, you like to live among old car bodies in a dust bowl!" Aunt Doll drew herself up to her full height. "Madam. I'm not a Gypsy and I don't live in no dust bowl. If you want to know I give up my time for this work, I'm working for charity." This time it was the Gorgio woman's turn to shrink away. Whereas Aunt Doll was detached from the criticism about rubbish disposal, she resented the stigma attached to the word Gypsy. I was, on the other hand, inwardly free of such identification, but I felt her pain. At the same time, I felt it "wrong" to shove newspaper in that hedge.

The one or two unexpected visits to my camp by Gorgio friends brought into sharper focus the contrast between my two existences and double vision in the same country. Anthropologists abroad may also risk intrusions from friends back home, but at least the visitors have been partially sobered by the extended journey and the obvious strangeness. My friends, however, drove the same roads as the Travellers.

One afternoon, after an especially dramatic confrontation between Travellers and the police on the camp, a small mini van pulled in. We wondered if this was another "pig" in disguise. Out stepped my college friend Mike in chic Kings Road shirt, tight Levis and dark glasses. I had to emerge from the cluster of confused Travellers and identify myself. I switched to a fellow intellectual tone and became ungainly in my loosely hung attire. Despite his desire to hang around or sit gossiping in my caravan, I told him to drive me to a tea shop in the town. Mike had been given my exact ordnance survey location by a secretary at my London Research Centre.

The other male visitor, well over 60, caused a sensation by greeting me with a slight peck on the cheek. He also anticipated a free and easy conversation in my caravan. Soon we were joined by six children and three women, two of whom had never deigned to visit me before. Their presence was actually a useful protection against any accusation that I fitted the Gypsy stereotype of a free-wheeling Gorgio woman, something I needed to dissociate myself from. My grey-haired "uncle" (the only acceptable category) continued his Hempstead flavoured literary discussion, naively complaining to me later of the "immaturity" of the Travellers' uncontrollable shrieks and giggles. My Gorgio visitors found my prudish demeanour both comical and unnecessary. It was hard to explain that mixed gender encounters are treated as sexual liaisons.

Anthropologists abroad both today and in the past have had to work under the shadow of officials and their policies towards subordinate groups. In my own case, government intervention occurred even before the research began. A senior civil servant wrote to the governor of our independent research centre reminding them of their partial state funding. He then objected to the centre's proposed Gypsy research, all of which he insisted should be conducted within Whitehall. Fortunately a charitable trust had already offered funding. Anthropologists have to negotiate for permits and visas. Similarly, I depended on some official consent to living on a temporary site. In all cases, there is a risk of identification with the officials, whether or not you study them.

Malinowski was also troubled on occasions by a "double vision." He could see the white administrator's view of the Trobriand landscape while he was attempting to understand the Islander's experience of it, or at least while he was attempting to isolate his own view. When accompanied unwillingly by two officials, he wrote "I saw and felt the utter drabness of the Kiriwana villages; I saw them through their eyes (it's fine to have this ability), but I forgot to look at them with my own" (1967:163). Malinowski, like many other anthropologists, responded to this dilemma by cutting white men out of his research (see Okely 1975). Fieldwork in one's own country may make this separation of suitable research fields even less tenable. Apart from the theoretical and historical necessity of including the wider context, the effects of those same policymakers are lived with daily in the anthropologist's country both before and after fieldwork.

The research project to which I was originally attached included a study of legislation and government reports. Research into officials entering the camps was as problematic as in colonial times. First, because I had had to negotiate with them for my own entry and secondly because they assumed I would identify with their view of the "Gypsy problem." The Travellers also tended at first to identify me with the officials. This identification was hard to throw off. An Officer giving me a lift from the County Hall suddenly stopped the car to ask a Traveller family on the roadside to move on. Predictably, that family never trusted me and spread a story that I collaborated with the police.

I was given free access to files at County Hall because it was assumed, despite my explanations to the contrary, that my research centre was attached to the Ministry and also that my write-up would be wholly favourable. My boarding school accent was useful again. This called for another change of clothing. As a female, I was also seen as harmless. The files proved to be a Pandora's box and when my guarded queries betrayed a lack of consensus, some of the files were mysteriously withdrawn. My double identity had become apparent. Later, official controls operated in gentlemanly ways, unique to anthropological fieldwork at home. My research centre insisted on sending drafts of our report to the council who sanitized it and inserted a final paragraph which made nonsense of the rest. It was never considered appropriate to send similar drafts to Gypsy representatives.

When publication is in the same country as fieldwork, the anthropologist cannot escape being read or misread by a wide range of interested parties beyond the usual academic constituency. The text will therefore bear the marks of such future scrutiny. If the study includes a minority group, the publication will be read more easily by some of its members. This development is to be welcomed, for the anthropologist cannot avoid the political consequences of his or her research. These consequences remain on the anthropologist's door step. Any latent tendency to treat people as objects or distant curios has to be confronted, not left repressed in a secret diary. The double vision has to be focussed correctly. The fieldworker at home cannot split identities between countries.

REFERENCES

Malinowski, B. 1967. *A Diary in the Strict Sense of the Term.* London: Routledge.

Okely, J. 1975. "The Self and Scientism." In *Journal of the Anthropological Society*, Oxford, Trinity Term.

Okely, J. 1983. *The Traveller-Gypsies.* Cambridge, England: Cambridge University Press.

Fact Versus Fiction

An Ethnographic Paradox Set in the Seychelles

Marion Benedict

Marion Benedict and her husband went to the Seychelles with their young children to do ethnographic fieldwork. She is at present a freelance author living with her anthropologist husband and her family in Berkeley, California.

The Seychelles are islands in the middle of the Indian Ocean, where my husband and I went for six months in 1960 and five months in 1975 to do anthropological fieldwork. Once we had decided to go there, I asked about the islands among my friends in London where we then lived. Everyone who had ever heard of the Seychelles had three things to say about them, and these were recited with remarkable agreement of thought and phrasing. First, the islands were breathtakingly beautiful, glittering like a necklace in a sunsplashed sea. Second, it was a land of free love where dark beauties, happy and carefree, all longed for white babies; and third, it was riddled with superstition and black magic.

Right away I wanted to look into that black magic, but my friends warned me not to. It was illegal, they said, and dangerous. Furthermore any investigations into such a subject would be construed as spying for the government, which would queer our fieldwork for good.

So I decided to take a sociological census. I had a notebook, a list of questions to ask, and an informant who could translate the local Creole for me and help me find my way around—and who might drop a few secrets along the way. My aim was to contribute to the world bank of ethnography and ultimately, to get to know people unlike myself—the "not me," the "Other."

Once in the field, in the confusion of new sights, sounds, smells and ways of thinking, I clung to that notebook and those questions as to a lifebelt. It represented the objective truth I was recording. It represented order and system; counting and measurement; collation and comparison; and objective observation.

"Fact Versus Fiction: An Ethnographic Paradox Set in the Seychelles" by Marion Benedict, from *Anthropology Today,* Vol. 1, no. 5, October 1985. Reprinted by permission of the Royal Anthropological Institute of Great Britain and Ireland.

The notebook defined my progress; it promised completion; it rationalized and legitimized my presence in that strange place among those strange people. It connected me to other collectors of ethnography and was a reassuring reminder of my own values, my own logical categories, the way I and my kind think—and, indeed, who I was.

But the facts I was trying to collect by asking questions tended to slide away. It had seemed an easy matter of question and answer, but the answer never came simply and directly, and sometimes never came at all, even after a long discussion of the topic. Lengthy digressions were the rule, and after my frustration wore off, I began to see that the important information lay in those very digressions, and not in the answers I was seeking. Important, I mean, in that my overall purpose was to comprehend these people in their own terms and not in terms of how they answered my questions, or of how they fitted into any ready-made logical categories.

Furthermore, I suspected that many answers to my questions were inventions, and that the more directly the people answered me the more thoroughly they were lying. The vexed problem of what and whom to believe loomed larger and larger until I was forced to consider my own part in the dialogue. Upon what grounds did I decide what was true and what false? Sheerly on intuition, my own gut response based on some private mental/emotional grid far beyond the reach of any available logic.

And on what grounds had I chosen to record some things and not others? How did I sort out the significant from the insignificant? Again, it was on the seemingly illogical basis of intuition. And so the process of altering the text, or tampering with reality—that is, fictionalizing—had begun.

My intuition was at work in other ways, too. For instance, I had begun to think that one informant was paranoid in her fantastic suspicions that people were out to "get" her. But how could I know for sure? And when I began to suspect that people were lying to me and laughing at me, how could I know that I was not catching her paranoia? Although I was able to check up on some facts and some of the answers given me, mostly I had to rely on guesswork.

I felt that the people were laughing at me and my concern with the tedious exercise of filling my notebook with their lies. I recall, during those first few weeks, bending my head constantly over the pages of my notebook, fingers smudged with ink, shooing away flies, writing up endless little facts that died as I pinned them down while the people around me nudged and winked and whispered and giggled, carrying on their real lives over my head . . . I was confronting head-on the difficulty of knowing the "Other." There was also the difficulty of how to write up the material and make it readable. How to begin, and what form to use? It seemed evident that the first step was to determine exactly what I wanted to say and then find the appropriate form in which to say it. In practice, however, there was a constant interchange between those two steps. Considering the form threw me back to reappraising the content, and considering the content threw me back to reappraising the form.

At first I tried the form of the anthropological monograph with its third person narration. That has the benefit of concentrating the reader's attention on the people by eliminating the "I" (except, of course, insofar as the author is always implied). But then I encountered the same difficulty as when collecting the material—without the personal, perceiving "I" the material was dull. In pursuing objectivity I had pushed out the felt life. So the "I" was moved in. But I still wanted to keep out the self: I wanted to write about them, not about me. So I thought of shaping the diary that I had kept in the field into readable form and presenting the material in that way.

The diary form had many advantages. In the first place, it was easy. Keeping my eye on the relations between the people and myself, I had only to shuffle around some times and places, cut irrelevancies, invent some transitions and the job was done. I could thus get rid of distracting disclaimers like "it seemed to me" and "or so I thought" because the personal point of view inhered in the diary form itself. The "I" was squeezed into the form, and so the reader's attention could fix itself upon the people.

The diary form also had the merit of accuracy, in that it was as exact an account of my activities in collecting the material as I could give in a readable form. It gave the sense of the present tense in all its immediacy, and transmitted my response to daily events as I saw them, and left it to the reader to do the work of fitting them into his own mental grid—that is, the work of interpretation.

But the diary had one big disadvantage; it did not have an organizing theme. It was anecdotal, episodic, and didn't go anywhere. There was nothing to carry the reader along; no build up, no suspense. Ultimately there was not enough meaning to make it interesting. It did not lead to any generalizations or argue any theory. So I shoved it into a drawer and did not look at it for several years.

When I did take it out again, I saw clearly that I had not sufficiently digested the material at the time I had written it. It was entertaining—amusing, even—but it didn't explain anything. I had not sufficiently engaged with what, all along, had been my underlying preoccupation.

But now I had digested the material. Now I saw a pattern emerging in my fieldnotes and a theme for my writing up. I saw that, in recording household compositions, behaviour, jokes told by fishermen and priests, schoolteachers and washerwomen, in noting down rituals and even the cost of raising pigs—I had been gathering an understanding about the nature of witchcraft. I had been recording evidence of how it works, and how that working radiates out to illuminate the most intimate and sensitive—and trivial—relations among the people of the Seychelles.

This new theme required a new form. I now saw that the ordering principle of my writing up must be the process of my understanding of witchcraft. In this way the search for content recapitulated the search for form. And the form required that the "I" be moved to centre stage.

This "I" had to be fictionalized. For the sake of coherence and emphasis on the important issues, I pretended to be a more naive observer than I really was. I took the reader by the hand and demonstrated, piece by piece, the evidence I had collected that led to my theory of witchcraft. I didn't actually *say* so, however, because I wanted the reader to go through the process of discovery for himself or herself. Sometimes I even planted clues so that the reader could see what was happening before I did.

Further fictionalizing was done in order to protect my informants. For that, I falsified names and put one person's words into another's mouth. For the sake of clarity and simplification I compressed several people into one. For instance, I really went to four fortunetellers, but I telescoped them into two. My main character herself is a composite of several women whom I had interviewed at length.

In order to clarify the narration I discarded material about whole families who, although they provided complexities and insights that my diary had included, nevertheless would distract the reader from the theme of witchcraft. The insights, however, helped to inform my final conclusions as I rearranged the actual process of discovery.

In order to show rather than to tell, I invented scenes of transition and thus imposed an order upon my narration that was never present in the field.

All this was done in the name of telling the truth and it resulted in a fiction. I had written a continuous narrative with suspense, a plot, fictional characters, a climax and a point—that is, a *novella*.

Fictionalizing continued as I invented another language to convey the rhythm and structure of my informants' diction. Their logic was roundabout; they told the middle first, then left me scrabbling for the subject and the message, so that it seemed a long and meaningless ramble until sometime later when I might have the good fortune to seize the point. But when my favourite informant spoke to her people she did not sound long-winded and tedious. The lilt of her Creole carried the knotty and treacherous structure along in an easy and natural flow that died when literally reproduced in my English on the printed page. Also, there was a freshness in her choice of words and a slyness in her digressions which alerted me to the calculated art that lay behind her kind of organization. But in order to convey the sense of this to my reader, I had to impose my own kind of organization as well as employ a free translation.

Witchcraft was a subject shrouded in secrecy and fraught with hysteria. Asking about it was like asking somebody to take hold of a live wire. The only way to approach it was indirectly. I had to go around in circles, pretending not to be interested in it to get close to it at all.

So my notebook is full of everything from very specific observations related to witchcraft—like accounts of my visits to witches—to the most conjectural. I recorded bits of gossip heavy with innuendo; half-guesses about oblique hints gleaned from informants; conversations with people describing their experiences with witches (or *bonhommes* or *bonnefemmes de bois*, as they called them). I noted behaviour that might be related to witchcraft and kept my eyes and ears open for signs of this hidden but ubiquitous phenomenon.

I was lucky to have, among my informants, an apprentice witch—not that she admitted it until the very end of my stay, by which time I already knew it. But the fieldnotes about my experiences with her became very valuable. They helped me to see, later on, how witchcraft works. I came to see that a witch can do harm simply because people believe that she can. People create the reality of spirits and magic simply by believing in them. They also believe that gossip can hurt them and so give it the power to do so. Gossip then takes on a life of its own, apart from being thoughts in people's minds and words on their tongues, and becomes what I have called gossip power. Gossip, when applied, becomes black magic. And conversely, black magic becomes applied gossip. I go to great pains to demonstrate that in my narration.

It was only through mulling over the material later that these generalizations sprang to mind. I also saw that the phenomenon of witchcraft is a prime example of how one's mental set shapes the world one sees. If somebody expects to see a spirit he will very likely do so. If he believes that his neighbour hates him and is practising black magic against him, he will then act in such a way that the neighbour will do just that. If he believes a fortuneteller's prediction that he will fall ill, he probably will. Thus subjective beliefs become objective reality.

This brings us back to the difficulties of objective truth, in this case of knowing what I now thought of simply as "others." I had wanted to keep myself out of the picture, to watch people interacting while I stood aside, just looking. But that simply did not work. If I stood aside I was ignored; nobody told me anything. It was like being erased. That nearly happened at first, when one of my informants pushed me aside and pursued her own ends at the beginning of my fieldwork. I accepted that for a while and watched from the sidelines, catching what attitudes and words I could as they flew by. But I was missing more than I was catching. Had I been part of their lives—able to help with their illnesses, or with getting jobs, I might have achieved a greater understanding. But as it was, their real lives eluded me because I was not sharing them. I could only achieve a deeper level of understanding through participating in the details and complexities of their everyday lives.

But how could I participate in their lives? The practical difficulties were too many: insufficient time; inadequate grasp of the language; not knowing enough about the people's pasts; not having been there when the important things had happened to them. All these played a part. But most important was the fact that I was an outsider. I was not one of them. I was richer and whiter and I could get out. They were there for life.

Even getting to know one person, as I tried to get to know my favourite informant, turned out to be difficult in a way I had not anticipated. She was watching me as closely as I was watching her. To be her friend required tact, respect, and reciprocity. She was very sensitive to anything I might do that could be construed as a slight. If she caught me in an insincerity she retaliated instantly with some egregious affectation of her own. Any suggestion of patronization maddened her and she would punish me by long absences. I don't think she ever resorted to witchcraft to take revenge upon me, as she did upon others, because she thought white people were not susceptible to black magic. But she could always get her own back by making me, foreigner that I was, a laughing-stock among her people.

She was suspicious of circumspection on my part—perhaps because she herself was so expert at it and knew what it concealed. She despised a doormat and ethnography was, to her, just another name for self-interest. She knew all about trade-offs and was determined to exact her quids-pro-quo.

She would walk all over anyone who let her. She tried it with me, and I called her bluff. It was only then, when I cared enough to show my spite and to pit my wits against hers, only then that I touched the quick of her life as she touched the quick of mine. I had to stand up to her, to talk back in order to win her respect. I could not beg it, or buy it—I had to earn it by becoming vulnerable myself, which involved, among other things, telling her my secrets as she had told me hers. It took my heart as well as my head, my intuition as well as my logic, my whole personality—that watchful, self-concealing ethnographer would never have uncovered her inner life.

There were also epistemological difficulties in knowing others. I had wanted an understanding distinct from self—but what could I know about others except what I could perceive through my own eyes and interpret through my own mental grid? The very cognitive process itself involved an "I" to observe and to know. How could I know anything that was "not me" when my very method of knowing was all me?

It was a paradox. Even though I came back to self when reaching out for the other, nevertheless something of the other did emerge in the process. That is, even though knowing may reside only in the knower, nevertheless some objective knowledge resides in my fictional *novella*.

Going Native

William J. Klausner

William J. Klausner teaches law and anthropology, in both Thai and English, at Chulalongkorn University, Bangkok, and other Thai universities. Born in New York City, he graduated from Yale and has worked in Thailand since 1955. He has written extensively on law, culture, and popular Buddhism.

In a recent personal letter, the Editor of *Anthropology Today* referred obliquely to the ambivalence of my persona. He wondered aloud as to the pros and cons of becoming closely identified with the country of one's study and the possible loss of detachment in the process.

For the past forty years, I have been on a continuous pilgrimage seeking to fathom the intricate patterns of Thai culture. During this decades-long hegira, I didn't have to—and couldn't—forsake my western heritage, but I could and did conveniently subject it to a traditional Thai massage. New intellectual and emotional pressure points were discovered. New dimensions to my nature emerged and hitherto familiar ways of thinking, acting and speaking were altered.

I remember being cautioned in Yale Graduate School not to forget that the anthropologist's very presence in the field can itself change the atmospherics and alter the very reality one seeks to capture. Actually, my experience, living for a year in a fairly remote northeastern Thai village, did not validate such an admonition. Very quickly, I found myself swept up into the rhythms of daily village life. Any impressions my footprints may have made on the village paths were quickly erased. If there was any meaningful alteration, it was in my own perceptions and perspectives. However, there was no wholesale change. In taking off my Rayban glasses and trying on Thai shades, did I lose my detachment? I would hope not. Since I finished fieldwork almost four decades ago and began my teaching and foundation careers, I have been interpreting Thai culture and trying to bridge cultural chasms through lectures to and essays written for audiences of western diplomats, businessmen and foreign aid workers and volunteers. Despite my close identification with and commitment to Thailand, I do not feel I have lost the detachment necessary for objective scholarship. Identification has led to empathy and sympathetic understanding; but, hopefully, intellectual distance has largely been preserved. The challenge has been to maintain my psychological equilibrium as a new identity, merging the newly acquired Eastern and the more familiar Western elements of my persona, has been shaped and formed.

Buddhism has had a profound influence in the development of my new identity. Despite my academic background, it was not its philosophical tenets that first drew me to the Buddhist faith. Rather, it was my introduction to village Buddhism in practice. Living within the confines of the temple for the first few months of my year's stay in the village, I soon found myself under the spell of the charismatic resident monks. They exuded an aura of serenity, equanimity and compassion as they fulfilled their daily religious and secular community service responsibilities. They, as well as their village parishioners, taught me to avoid confrontation and maintain a "cool heart." It was only in later years that I studied the Buddhist texts and found myself, as a humanist, attracted to what I felt was the quite compatible intellectual content of Buddhism.

On reflection, I believe the often stated contradiction between a close identification with a culture and the preservation of one's detachment is a false one. Of course, some may argue that subjectivity is not totally negative and that total objectivity is unattainable. I would agree that subjectivity can have a certain value at times, especially in instilling some passion into a foreign scholar's analysis and commentary. I would also accept that objectivity should be measured in terms of degree rather than in absolute terms. However, given the limitation of space, I hope I may be forgiven for treating the issues involved in this essay in more general and absolute terms. I am convinced

"Going Native," by William J. Klausner, from *Anthropology Today*, Vol. 10, No. 3, June 1994, pp. 18–19. Reprinted by permission of the Royal Anthropological Institute of Great Britain and Ireland.

that one can, for the most part, be both identified and detached. Those foreign scholars who deny completely their own heritage, their cultural roots, in their attempts to take on the coloration and hues of another culture, are fated to live in a fool's paradise. Such an expatriate does not—and I believe cannot—fully change his or her persona and become Thai, Japanese or Indonesian. Those that believe they have fully assumed the cultural identity of the country they have studied and identified with are, I would contend, deluding themselves. They have denied and lost one identity and yet not truly found a new one. They remain in limbo. For these cultural alchemists who have convinced themselves that such a total conversion has been achieved, objectivity and detachment are inevitably lost.

There are limitations to culture conversion, no matter how close one's identification, engagement, attachment and empathy. As in religious conversion, one often becomes more Papal than the Pope and loses one's perspective and objectivity. However, loss of detachment and objectivity does not mean one has actually assumed the essence, as well as the form, of a new cultural identity. One can study and grasp the intellectual meaning of a country's literature and history; of its language; its proverbs; its fairy tales; its religion and world view. However, unlike a child's enculturation process wherein literature, language, history, morality and appropriate behaviour are learned, largely uncritically, and impressed on a veritable cultural *tabula rasa*, the alien anthropologist, at a later stage in life, inevitably studies and learns through the lens of his or her own cultural and intellectual background; often rather heavy baggage.

For example, reading Thai literature and poetry of the past with its unmistakable hierarchical, patriarchal and male chauvinist bias can give one an appreciation of Thai social structure and gender bias. However, can such study for the scholar in his or her twenties, thirties, forties and beyond have the same emotional impact and intellectual meaning as for the native child whose received knowledge at a most impressionable age is constantly reinforced by his or her peers? One can record the prevalent practice of urban Thai schoolboys visiting prostitutes in one time-honoured *rite de passage* to manhood and note the double sexual standard involved. However, how can the adult foreign scholar ever internalize the emotional charge of participating in the above ritual passage encouraged, sustained and fortified by one's peers? The scholar can read of the extra-territorial courts in Thailand in the latter half of the 19th and early 20th centuries during the period of colonial influence, if not total control. One can intellectually appreciate the fixation of the Thai judiciary on preserving its integrity and independence and the extreme sensitivity to any outside interference. However, can the foreign scholar ever truly expect to comprehend the emotional intensity of the older generation of Thai judges concerning the above without having experienced such judicial domination and intimation or been regaled about such interference on one's father's knee? How can the mature Western scholar, reading the skewed and biased historical accounts of relationships with the neighbouring countries of Laos, Burma and Cambodia, appreciate the building blocks of prejudice and stereotypes set and reinforced in primary and secondary Thai schools? Likewise, the rational and scientific mind and tools of the foreign scholar can be brought to bear in analysing the function of spirit worship in maintaining social harmony and communal solidarity and order in rural Thailand. However, can one ever expect to experience the fear and dread of and, at the same time, sense of reliance on spirits inculcated in the earliest years of childhood?

The above examples indicate the difficulty of truly "going native" in substance, rather than just form. In almost all cases, the end result is a shadow play, not reality. If in that process, one loses a sense of objectivity and detachment, the individual scholar must be faulted. One becomes, at that stage, a translator producing often beautifully crafted literal translations, but ones devoid of inner meaning. On the other hand, it is not impossible to achieve a sense of empathy and understanding after years of intimate and close identification with an alien culture and, in so doing, to interpret judiciously and objectively the essence of the culture with a close, if not absolute, approximation to emotional and intellectual certitude.

In the diminishing eyesight of this expatriate, I, thus, only see the positive side of close identification with an alien culture over a long period of time. Detachment and objectivity do not have to be sacrificed. If they are, then one loses the ability to interpret, to be a bridge between cultures. One retires, often in silence. One recalls the perhaps apocryphal anthropologist whose empathy and attachment to the Native American society he was studying were so compelling that he was accorded the rare honour of being initiated into the tribe's secret society. Alas, bound by oath, he never revealed its secrets and, thereafter, was forever reticent about writing about the tribe which had adopted him.

I believe governments, foundations and businesses have largely accepted the conventional wisdom of the contradiction between close identification and detachment. Thus, they continue to arbitrarily limit the duration of one's employment abroad in any one country to three, four or five years. Headquarters pride themselves on their success in avoiding their employees' close identification with the society in which they are working. Alas, a high price has been paid—unnecessarily so—for what is mistakenly assumed would be the commitment and concomitant loss of objectivity and detached judgment. What these institutions have actually lost is the insight and the unrivalled, informed analysis that can only come with many years of language study and the intimate identification with and engagement in the society and its culture.

Someday, perhaps, anthropologists, from whatever continent, about to venture into the field for the first time will be adequately advised by their university mentors to be prepared for their own ordeal by fire as their familiar ways of thinking and acting are tested. In the challenge and response of their first field experience, their intellectual and emotional horizons will expand. Whether one returns or remains, one may look forward to enhanced and enriched personas being forged. In these altered states, new identities emerge.

As for my own personal quest, my reflections on my sixtieth birthday are apposite: ". . . my fifth cycle is the continuation of a struggle to ensure the tensions of the Eastern and Western elements of my persona remain creative and that parallel paths ultimately merge into a single road of productive contemplation, which, supported by virtue, will lead to wisdom."

2

Culture

What would happen if a student went into a North American supermarket during rush hour and tried to haggle over the price of a 79-cent tube of toothpaste? Apart from causing considerable embarrassment and probable ejection from the store, the student would be illustrating the dangers of culturally inappropriate behavior. In many parts of the world, haggling is culturally appropriate.

As befits its centrality, the notion of **culture** is problematic and means many different things to different people, even to anthropologists—A. L. Kroeber and Clyde Kluckhohn's discussion of different anthropological definitions of culture, published in 1952, is a thick book! It is easier, however, to give examples of culture than to define it.

Culture, in brief, is what gives meaning to the world. It provides the lens through which people interpret and make sense of what they perceive the world to be. As such, it consists largely of knowledge and, like other resources, is not distributed equitably. By "making sense," it gives us a sense of patterning and thus of predictability, which allows us to anticipate events and actions. The importance of people being able to anticipate one another's social behavior is well illustrated in Luke Rinehart's novel *The Dice Man*. This book is about a psychotherapist who adopts a decision-making method of assigning odds and rolling dice. He literally "gets away with murder" because his decisions are all random and no "motive" can be assigned to his behavior.

Making sense of behavior becomes particularly problematic when one is in a foreign milieu, as are most anthropologists. Indeed, as Sir Raymond Firth recalled:

Even with the pages of my diary before me it is difficult to reconstruct the impressions of that first day ashore— to depersonalize the people I later came to know so well and view them as merely a part of the tawny surging crowd. . . . In his early experience in the field the anthropologist is constantly grappling with the intangible. The reality of native life is going on all around him, but he himself is not yet in focus to see it. He knows that what he at first records will be useless: it will be either definitely incorrect, or so inadequate that it must be later discarded. Yet he must make a beginning somewhere. He realizes that at this stage he is incapable of separating the patterns of custom from the accidentals of individual behavior, he wonders if each slight gesture does not hold some meaning which is hidden from him. . . . At the same time, he is experiencing the delights of discovery, he is gaining an inkling of what is in store; like a gourmet walking round a feast that is spread, he savors in anticipation the quality of what he will later appreciate in full. (Peacock and Kirsch 1980)

Culture, in short, provides the patterns for behavior, whereas **society** is the product of patterns of behavior. Perhaps the safest way to define culture is by emphasizing some of its most striking characteristics. Following Roger Keesing (1976), it can be seen as a resource consisting of the sum total of learned, accumulated experience that is shared in varying degrees. As an abstraction it is a generalization—that is, no one has the exact same version. It is also a composite, in so far as no one knows all of it. Finally, it is dialectical— that is, it consists invariably of a number of **subcultures.**

Culture, then, is an interpretive dimension and knowledge; in making the world we experience more "predictable," it also creates categories. Implicit in such an exercise is the creation of boundaries of class, ethnicity, race, and gender. Boundaries are created when people learn the appropriate **rituals** and habits of speech and eventually become taken for granted and unproblematic (except for people with a probing anthropological perspective). State borders are a good example, as Robert Thornton, an anthropologist from South Africa, explains:

> In crossing an "international boundary" we involve ourselves in a complex political ritual which includes elaborate signposts, people wearing austere uniforms with obscure insignia . . . gates and narrow corridors. There is always an element of risk, of interference with personal freedom, even death if the formalities of this particularly powerful political ritual are not acknowledged and complied with. The boundaries between countries in fact, exist only in the imagination. They are created through speech, text and gesture, and are enabled by the complex calculation of latitude and longitude which accurate clocks have made possible. We may see the power of culture in the political boundaries of states—a special kind of cultural category-making—for which most of us today are willing to risk all in modern warfare. (1988:27)

David Maybury-Lewis's article heads this chapter quite deliberately. He brings forth the ethics and passion vital in conveying the message that when a culture dies, a whole people die with it. He also introduces the important concept of **cultural relativism,** the proposition that one cannot understand another culture without suspending judgment to see how it works in its own terms. Although some people mistakenly take this to mean that one must accept uncritically the worth of any custom no matter how reprehensible—human sacrifice among the Aztecs, for example, or warfare in modern industrial society—Maybury-Lewis points out that this is not so. One can take a critical stance toward any custom, but only *after* understanding it in its cultural context. And for that, cultural relativism is mandatory.

The reading that follows, by Lynn Morgan, deals with the theme of how culture defines what we are, in this case the distinction between "human" and "person." The final article takes as its point of departure the **cargo cults** of Melanesia—religious **revitalization movements** that represent deliberate attempts to transform a culture perceived as being unsatisfactory into a new, more satisfying one. These cults are a response to oppressive European domination; typically a native prophet outlines a series of practices that, if followed, will result in the return of dead ancestors in ships (or planes) laden with European goods. The ancestors will drive the Europeans out, ushering in a new golden age. Lamont Lindstrom likens cargo lists to the shopping lists of Europeans and analyzes them to see what they reveal about both Melanesian and Western culture.

REFERENCES

Keesing, Roger. 1976. *Cultural Anthropology*. New York: Holt, Rinehart and Winston.

Kroeber, A. L., & C. Kluckhohn. 1952. *Culture: A Critical Review of Concepts and Definitions*. Cambridge, MA: Harvard University Press (Papers of the Peabody Museum of American Archaeology and Ethnology).

Peacock, James, & A. Thomas Kirsch. 1980. *The Human Direction: An Evolutionary Approach to Social and Cultural Anthropology* (3d ed.). Englewood Cliffs, NJ: Prentice-Hall.

Thornton, Robert, 1988. "Culture: A Contemporary Definition," in *South African Keywords*, ed. by Boonzaier Emiole & John Sharp. Cape Town: Philip.

A Special Sort of Pleading

Anthropology at the Service of Ethnic Groups[1]

David H. P. Maybury-Lewis

David H. P. Maybury-Lewis received his D.Phil. degree from Oxford University in 1960. He has carried out fieldwork among the Shavante and Sherente of central Brazil, whose experience he has followed from independence to their current status as minorities within the Brazilian state. A professor of anthropology at Harvard, he is also president of Cultural Survival, Inc., an organization he founded to defend the interests of indigenous peoples and to help them retain their identity within countries in which they exist.

COMMON MISCONCEPTIONS

Advocacy has a distinctly dubious reputation in the United States and, I suspect, elsewhere. It conjures up images of lobbyists and lawyers and of people whose ethics leave much to be desired. So, if anthropologists are to be cast in the role of advocates, it is important to emphasize the peculiar nature of their advocacy. It has little in common with the hallowed tradition of Anglo-American jurisprudence, according to which truth emerges from the efforts of skilled pleaders who make themselves available to argue the cases of any who can afford their fees. By contrast, anthropologists normally do not possess special skills in advocacy which they can put at the disposal of the peoples they try to assist. In the case of tribal societies and underprivileged ethnic groups, anthropologists usually try to help because of their conviction that such societies are being wronged, often with no very clear idea of how to set about righting a wrong.

The ethical stance is important. It is what impels us to get involved in this work in the first place: but it is not enough. It needs to be supplemented by a rigorous analysis of the nature of the injustices against which we inveigh and the possible strategies for fighting them. Such issues may not be part of the usual anthropological curriculum, although they are increasingly being included in it: but they are directly related to what I consider to be fundamental anthropological precepts. I shall demonstrate this by referring to data

from the Americas, but the argument is applicable to other parts of the world as well.

It is well known that the original conquest of the Americas by European invaders had traumatic consequences for the autochthonous inhabitants of the New World. Many indigenous societies with low population densities were annihilated altogether. Others were driven into remote areas or survived as small pockets of population in regions dominated by aliens. The larger Indian populations of Central and Andean America were decimated, then enslaved, and survive today in a state of virtual peonage in countries which they can hardly call their own.

The conquerors offered justifications for this terrible history. They suggested at first that the indigenous peoples were perhaps not fully human. They did not possess souls. Their barbarous customs placed them beyond the pale. At the very least there were circumstances which made it legitimate to wage just wars on them and to enslave them.[2] Later the mission of conquest tended to be justified in the name of a higher civilization, which would impart peace, scientific thinking and rational institutions to the war-like and illogical natives (Merivale 1861).

These old arguments may seem preposterous, but I repeat them here in order to show their relationship to the modern versions of them that still persist in our conventional wisdom and in much contemporary theorizing. There is something like a second conquest taking place in the Americas today, powered by the world-wide search for resources. This new conquest threatens the Indians with the expropriation of their remaining lands and the total destruction of their way of life. This conquest too has its justification. It is carried out in the name of development. Indigenous

"A Special Sort of Pleading: Anthropology at the Service of Ethnic Groups" by David Maybury-Lewis, from *Advocacy and Anthropologies*, Robert Paine, ed. 1985, pp. 135–490. Reprinted by permission of the publisher.

peoples are thus stigmatized for clinging to a backward way of life and thereby "standing in the way of development." To the extent that they are reluctant or unable to abandon their separate identities and disappear into the mainstream of the states in which they live, they are also condemned as obstacles to nation-building and therefore to modernization. Hence, the argument runs, they should give up their archaic cultures and join the mainstream. This would not only make development much easier for all concerned but would conveniently remove "ethnic cysts" (to borrow the phrase once used by a Brazilian minister to refer to his country's Indians) from lands which they occupy and which other people covet. Meanwhile the world is assured that this doubtless regrettable disappearance of Indian cultures is inevitable and therefore should not be artificially or sentimentally delayed. This corresponds to the neo-Darwinian view which permeates the thinking of much of what we are pleased to call the developed world, according to which stronger societies are bound to extinguish weaker ones; this is coupled with the implication that there is not much that can be done about this, since it is some sort of natural law.

Such arguments are, of course, the direct descendants of those used by the conquistadors. They are self-serving justifications for the convenient use of power against the relatively powerless and they obscure the fact that indigenous cultures are not extinguished by natural laws so much as by political choices. Moreover, since such arguments make the destruction of indigenous cultures seem not only natural but even beneficial, they preempt any discussion of possible alternatives and thus contribute to the inevitability of that destruction.

Any advocacy of indigenous rights must therefore begin by countering such arguments and reopening the discussion of possible futures for indigenous cultures. We need to remember that it was seriously argued until recently that slavery was a natural part of the human condition. Scholars based their arguments on Aristotle, the Justinian codes and the writings of the French *philosophes* of the eighteenth century as they maintained that the differences in the natural endowments of individuals and races, coupled with the unavoidable differences of power in human affairs, rendered slavery inevitable.[3] We have seen this contention demonstrated as false and we no longer take seriously the nineteenth and even twentieth century arguments about the natural superiority or inferiority of certain races. Pro-indigenous advocates must work to create a similar climate of opinion in which we can look back with bemusement at the plausible falsehoods that were generally and conveniently believed by those who condemned indigenous cultures to extinction.

That is why I have elsewhere (Maybury-Lewis 1984) criticized the mesmeric fascination with which the modern world regards the nation-state. I showed that the divisive effects of ethnic attachments have been systematically over-emphasized and contrasted with the hypothetical benefits of the idealized nation-state. This is done equally by high-minded reformers trying to better the lot of the Indians and by oligarchs trying to break up their communities. The one thing that Simon Bolivar and General Pinochet have in common is the belief that Indians should abandon their traditional ways, should in effect abandon their Indianness, and become solid (preferably property-owning) citizens of their states. For quite different reasons both leaders concluded the persistence of Indian cultures was undesirable, since they weakened the state. If, however, we re-examine the role of ethnic subcultures, particularly in Third World countries, we find that allegations of ethnic divisiveness, backwardness or separatism are often used by governments as cloaks for exploitation, authoritarianism and hegemonic privilege. The cry of "One nation, indivisible" with perhaps added imprecations hurled against tribalists and separatists is all too often used as an ideological weapon against those who wish to alter the *status quo* and to share fully and equally the privileges of citizenship. This is particularly ironic, since our modern fascination with the needs of the state derives from the French revolutionary idea of the state, based on equality and fraternity. Nowadays, in many parts of the world, people are resorting to their ethnicity as a sort of civil rights movement, to achieve the equality of treatment which had previously been denied them in the name of modernization. Yet people do not cling to their cultures merely to use them as inter-ethnic strategies. They cling to them because it is through them that they make sense of the world and have a sense of themselves. We know that when people are forced to give up their culture or when they give it up too rapidly, the consequences are normally social breakdown and personal disorientation and despair. The right of a people to its own culture is therefore derived from a fundamental human need, yet it receives less protection, even in theory, than other human rights because it concerns groups rather than individuals.

The United Nations, for example, has declared its intent to protect the rights of individuals and in practice is most solicitous of the rights of states. But it skirts the issue of the rights of peoples, preferring to assume that peoples who are not part of the mainstream culture of their state should assimilate to it (Claude 1955 and Kuper 1984). There is in fact a world-wide tendency to deny the rights and sometimes even the very existence of ethnic minorities, in order to protect the nation-states. Advocacy of indigenous rights must therefore expose this tendency and develop the arguments for the desirability and viability of multi-ethnic polities.

The right of a people to its own culture is however a complex matter and insistence on it is frequently misunderstood. Let me dispose quickly of two common misunderstandings. The first of these is that the advocacy of the right of peoples to their own cultures entails a total moral and cultural relativism. Anthropologists are sometimes accused of such a relativism, according to which we are supposed to defend the right of any people to engage in any practice, however reprehensible, simply because it is "part of their culture." The charge is absurd but it serves to distract attention from the comfortable and unreasoning ethnocentrism and prejudice of those who make it. It needs therefore to be stressed that what is taken for anthropological relativism is in reality an anthropological insistence on suspending judgment on other peoples' practices; not forever, but only until those practices have been understood in their own cultural terms. This injunction sounds simple enough, but most people (and that includes the majority of the world's planners) find it extremely hard to follow. They tend to pass judgments on other cultures and their practices long before they have any understanding of them and in fact those often unthinking judgments frequently prevent understanding of other cultures in their own terms. An important part of the discipline of an anthropological training is to teach people to recognize and avoid premature judgment on other cultures. It is only where this is done systematically that we can hope to incorporate other people's values into our own thinking, or at least to mediate between our values and theirs. This is a critical matter when our thinking is about the life or death of their cultures. The anthropological stance then is that one does not avoid making judgments, but rather postpones them in order to make informed judgments later.

Another common misconception is that those who defend the right of a people to its own culture are arguing that other societies should remain true to their own traditions. Anthropologists are accused, for good measure, of wanting to keep traditional societies in their backward state in order to study them. The second suggestion is merely a malicious variation on the first, which implies that cultural survival is an antiquarian matter of clinging to tradition and resisting change. It is important to stress therefore that both of these perceptions are quite false. For instance, Cultural Survival, the organization of which I am president, defends the right of tribal societies and ethnic groups to maintain their own cultures, but we do not see this as a matter of maintaining folkways, but rather as a question of a society's having a say in its own affairs and its own future. Our advocacy and our projects therefore aim to create the conditions under which such societies can retain the largest measure of autonomy and power of decision over their own affairs. Ideally we believe

that this is best achieved through the creation of appropriate mechanisms in multi-ethnic states. Furthermore, the advocacy of self-determination for indigenous peoples within such states is often a politically more viable strategy, for it cannot be opposed on the usual grounds that any recognition of the rights of ethnic groups leads inevitably to separatism and the undermining of the state. Nevertheless, we understand the pessimism about multi-ethnic solutions which has led many native peoples to demand that they be recognized internationally as sovereign nations. Independence and separation may be the only solution where justice is denied within the state, which is why it is particularly important to make multi-ethnic solutions work.

It is worth stressing that the sort of cultural survival for which we work is defined in the last analysis by the societies which we assist. We do not urge them to be true to their traditions; partly because such a stance would be intolerably paternalistic, but also because we assume that all societies are constantly changing and some are abandoning their traditions of their own accord. We therefore offer our help to tribal societies and ethnic groups who need it to maintain those aspects of their culture which they consider important.

This brings me at last from theory to the practicalities of advocacy in action. I make no apology for spending so much of this short paper on theoretical questions, for I am convinced that useful action must flow logically from a clear understanding of theoretical issues. Much project action, in the Americas and elsewhere, revolves around land and access to material resources. These issues are particularly acute in the Americas since it was the invading Europeans who set up the systems of law and land titling which everywhere form the basis of valid claims to land ownership. The indigenous inhabitants were outside these systems, which were then manipulated to their detriment, so that they have been engaged in a constant struggle to force or persuade their unsympathetic conquerors to grant them title to any part of the lands which they originally considered theirs.

This continues to be extremely difficult for most indigenous peoples. Although most nations in the Americas recognize in theory that their aboriginal inhabitants have some rights to land, the gap between that theoretical recognition and actual granting of title is wide and all too often permanent. Most native land claims are disputed by interests with the power to block them. Even when they are not, the process of demarcating, registering and titling lands has often proved impossible for indigenous groups to complete.

Such a situation recently posed a cruel dilemma for pro-Indian organizations in Paraguay. In the late 1970s few Indian societies in Paraguay had legal title to the lands they occupied and Paraguayan law did not recognize collective title to land, even for indigenous peoples. The two major organizations working for the Indians in Paraguay responded to this problem in different, even conflicting ways. AIP (the Paraguayan Indigenist Association) insisted that Indians had inherent rights of ownership in their lands and was lobbying to persuade the government to recognize this, by passing a law enabling Indian societies to hold lands collectively, and by putting this law into effect. Meanwhile, API (the Association of Indian Peoples) also insisted on Indian rights to land; but it had concluded that the situation of many Indian groups was so desperate that it had begun to buy lands for them from Paraguayans. AIP complained that their campaign to get the government to recognize Indian land rights was being undercut by the willingness of their sister organization to buy lands for the Indians. API responded that it was trying to help groups which would starve or disband or both if they waited for the success of AIP's strategy (see Maybury-Lewis and Howe 1980).

PROBLEMS OF LAND

Land is the key to the cultural and often even the physical survival of indigenous peoples. Tribal societies that have traditionally supplied their own wants from their own environment can be physically annihilated if forced off their own lands. Cast adrift, with no marketable skills, to fend for themselves in an alien society, whose language they do not speak and whose economy they do not understand, such peoples face a grim future or no future at all. It is their plight, as the nations of the Americas have stepped up their efforts to explore and exploit their own hinterlands, that has recently been arousing world-wide concern. Yet peoples who are long settled and have centuries of contact with settler society are still traumatically threatened by the prospect of losing their lands.

Such losses are a constant threat, because the indigenous society's title is usually unclear and because it is usually unable to protect its holdings against powerful interests in settler society. Meanwhile there is constant pressure on indigenous societies to break up their communal lands and to treat them as individual (and saleable) holdings. A variety of factors combine to produce this pressure. The laws of most American countries do not recognize communal land holdings or make it extremely difficult to register them. Meanwhile, even liberal reformers have traditionally thought that the individual ownership of land was the means by which indigenous peoples could modernize and join the mainstream. At the same time, those who wish to eliminate Indian societies altogether find that insistence on individual landholding is an effective way to

do it and one which does not incur the opprobrium which is occasionally visited nowadays on nations that resort to genocide. So Chile's new land law, making it obligatory to subdivide the lands left to the Mapuche Indians if only one person living on them requests such subdivision, may achieve the final elimination of Mapuche society and culture which has survived incredible pressures for more than four hundred years.[4] Meanwhile, in an entirely different spirit, the Alaskan Native Claims Settlement Act, which is regarded as a reasonably generous settlement of indigenous land claims may have similar results. In the 1990s Alaskan native communities will legally become joint stock corporations, in which individuals who received shares at the time of the act will hold stock. This is an entirely different notion of community from the one the indigenous peoples are accustomed to and the one which most of them still live by. It is becoming clear that the majority of them have not realized the implications of what is likely to happen in ten years time when individuals can sell their stock in the "community," and shares in the "community" can be bought on the open market (see Arnold 1976).

Here then is one of the critically important aspects of pro-indigenous advocacy. The advocate can help native communities to analyze not only the consequences of their own actions, but also the possible effects of processes which affect them. This is a vital matter in the negotiation of land rights. A normal and natural reaction on the part of tribal communities whose land is threatened for the first time is to insist that they should be left alone to enjoy what has traditionally been theirs. Advocacy in such a case involves helping the indigenous community realize that it is unlikely to be left alone, that it will have to fight (but not physically) for its lands and that it is unlikely to be able to hold onto all of them. At the same time it involves persuading the powers-that-be that native rights should be taken seriously and, if necessary, creating administrative or public pressure to see that this is done. In the Pichis-Palcazu area of Amazonian Peru, for example, advocacy involved persuading the Peruvian government which was sponsoring a scheme of massive colonization for the area and US AID (Agency for International Development) which was about to finance it, that the valleys were already occupied by native peoples and that the project would be a disaster. Cultural Survival took a leading role in this campaign, which ultimately succeeded in changing the original colonization scheme into the Central Selva Resource Management project. The new project is more sensibly designed to protect not only the Indian inhabitants of the area but also the local environment and the interests of the future occupants, both Indian and non-Indian, of the region as a whole. As a preliminary to the implementation of the project, survey teams were sent out and they enabled the Amuesha Indians to gain formal title to their lands for the first time. This is no more than a reprieve, however. The project as originally designed has yet to be put into effect and it is not clear whether it will be, now that the economic and political climate in Peru is becoming more and more uncertain.[5]

Ideally, native lands should be titled and guaranteed before development projects are planned for their areas but, as we have seen, the native land situation in the Americas is far from ideal. There are therefore twin strategies which should be followed by pro-Indian organizations. One is to exert constant pressure for the regularization of all native land titles. The other is to try and turn the threat posed to native peoples by development projects into an opportunity to create pressure for the protection of indigenous lands. Cultural Survival used the latter strategy when the Brazilian government asked the World Bank for a loan to improve the road system in its northwestern region and thus encourage colonization of a vast area where scores of small Indian tribes are known to live. Cultural Survival urged the bank to make the demarcation of Indian lands and the protection of their cultures a condition of the loan. In response to years of pressure the bank finally adopted, prior to the signing of the loan agreements, its own policy guidelines making it mandatory in the future to insist on guarantees for tribal peoples and ethnic minorities in areas where loans are contemplated (World Bank 1981). I believe that these are the only such guidelines at present contained in the policies of any international lending agency. Naturally, the policies are only as effective as their enforcement and the preliminary reports from Brazil indicate that this leaves much to be desired, but having such policies and laws on the books is not unimportant as I shall argue in a moment.[6]

The defence of native land rights is a complex matter, even when they are not threatened by ruthless and unscrupulous interests. The view that native peoples have a dubious claim to land if other people can make better (i.e., more productive) use of it is very common in developmental circles. The moral and legal absurdity of such a view is readily exposed if one asks the earnest planner whether he or she would be willing to apply the same precepts to his or her own piece of property. Does another person have a superior claim to that property to plant vegetables on it, if the present owner manages only flowers and crab-grass? Yet governments regularly use such arguments when moving to take native lands by eminent domain. They act, they insist, for the greater good of the greatest number, to make better use of the land and they imply that it is somehow selfish of native peoples to want to sit on resources which should rightfully be distributed through-

out the entire populace. Such arguments can usually be exposed as flimsy justification for exploitation.

PROBLEMS OF DEVELOPMENT

In Brazil, for example, this type of argument has regularly been used by successive military governments, all claiming to give development the highest priority and insisting that small Indian tribes should not be allowed to stand in the way of it. The argument only holds, however, if development promotes equity and Indian peoples are obstacles to it. Yet neither contention is true. The Brazil model of development, which was so highly touted in the sixties and seventies (though not by those of us who were working at the grass roots) is no longer regarded as a miracle. In fact it is closer to being regarded as a disaster for the entire Western banking system. This is not due to bad luck, like the rise in the price of oil, which Brazil has still been unable to find within her own capacious land, but rather to a policy which has paid insufficient attention to structural change and modernization within Brazilian society. The years of the "Miracle" produced enormous profits for some but they did little to solve the problems of Northeastern Brazil (the largest pocket of poverty in the western hemisphere) or of the increasing numbers of urban poor or of the landless rural labourers. The latter are constantly moved off their patches of land in much the same way as the state has intermittently sought to move the Indians off theirs. The argument from equity thus breaks down.[7] Hypothetically, such an argument could be made in other places, but it would in any case come down to a question of what compensation should be made to native peoples (or others) who are asked to give up a resource for the common good.

At the same time it is important to insist that native peoples are not inherently "obstacles to development." This is only true if "development" is defined in such a way to exclude their participation. There are innumerable examples to show that indigenous peoples whose land base and cultural survival are guaranteed can make productive contributions to the local economy. Advocacy here becomes a matter of persuading the powers-that-be that this is so, and getting them to include indigenous representatives in the development planning for a given region. Cultural Survival has recently succeeded in doing this, for example, in Ecuador. There the Ecuadorian government established a commission consisting of representatives from Cultural Survival, the National Agrarian Reform Institute, the Forestry and National Parks Department, a regional development agency and 22 Indians representing three groups. The commission studied the land needs of Ecuador's most seriously threatened Indian groups, the Siona-Secoya, Cofan and Huaorani. It documented their land requirements and recommended specific borders to satisfy their needs. It also recommended that Indian lands should be titled at the borders of national parks. The Indians would have access to the parks for subsistence hunting and fishing and their lands would act as buffers to protect the parks from settler incursion. Meanwhile these newly titled Indian lands were incorporated into a large forestry development and management project (see Macdonald 1980 and in press, and Uquillas 1982).

Another dramatic example of such a project is one which I have recently been observing in Brazil. This is the project sponsored in the midst of bitter controversy by the Brazilian Indian Agency (FUNAI) and which has transformed many communities of Shavante Indians into extensive, tractor-driven rice farmers. The project was put into effect over the violent protests of the local landowners who complained to the President of the Republic that FUNAI was trying to turn the State of Mato Grosso into a vast Indian reserve. This was hyperbole, even by settler standards, considering that Mato Grosso was so large—larger than Bolivia or Colombia and only slightly smaller than Peru—that it has now been divided into two states; moreover its population is still tiny. The project was finally put into effect because the Shavante were tough enough to threaten the local landowners and force them off Indian lands and astute enough to visit Brasilia regularly to present their demands to the government. These visits also served to rally their supporters among anthropologists and the Brazilian public at large and received great publicity. The publicity reached its peak when a delegation of Shavante chiefs threatened to defenestrate the general in charge of FUNAI, and escaped reprisals since the threat was carried out with the cameras of the major TV networks waiting to record the consequences (Maybury-Lewis 1983a and 1985).

PROBLEMS OF REPRESENTATION

The Shavante affair highlights another dilemma of pro-Indian advocacy. Whom do pro-Indian advocates represent and how do they relate to the Indians who are being their own advocates? Initially, of course, such advocates may not represent any more than their own consciences. They are people who are willing to speak out to denounce what they perceive as injustice. The pro-Indian commissions which were formed all over Brazil at the end of the 1970s came into existence because of the outcry raised by anthropologists over the government's proposal to "emancipate" the Indians. It was concerned anthropologists who pointed out that

such emancipation would abolish the FUNAI and its tutelary role towards the Indians. It would thus do away with the legal requirement to demarcate and defend Indian lands and the agency which was supposed to carry it out. The newly "emancipated" Indians would then be able to take their chances on their own and as individuals against whichever interests happened to be threatening them in their part of the country. When these consequences were pointed out to the Indians, they themselves opposed emancipation unreservedly and, backed by the newly formed pro-Indian commissions, insisted that the government, rather than abolish FUNAI, should press it to do its job on behalf of the Indians (see Maybury-Lewis 1979 and Comissão Pro-Indio 1979).

Later the pressure and publicity generated by such commissions were instrumental in helping the Shavante gain their objectives. The campaign on behalf of the Shavante launched one of their number into national prominence. Mario Juruna, the chief of a small Shavante community, had spent years in his youth traveling and working his way around Brazil and learning the ways of the white man. He endeared himself to the Brazilian media as "the Indian with the tape-recorder," because he carried around his own recording machine and insisted on recording the promises made to him and his people, so that they could not later be blandly forgotten or denied. In 1982 he was elected to Congress as the first Indian ever to become a federal deputy. Needless to say he was elected to represent Rio de Janeiro, not his native Mato Grosso, a state which is hardly ripe yet for an Indian candidacy. It is not even clear that he would have been elected in a solely Shavante constituency, if such a one were to exist. He has nevertheless become a leader who speaks for Brazilian Indians in general and is recognized by most of them as their spokesman (Maybury-Lewis 1983b).

The question of who really represents indigenous peoples has led to some confusion among those who deal with them or seek to assist them. It is of course a question which is often debated with reference to other societies as well. When the representative of a nation state speaks on behalf of its people, we know that he or she is unlikely to represent the views of all of them; but we also know how he or she came by his or her credentials and we normally have a good deal of information about which groups are represented by the official view and which groups are not. It is precisely this kind of information which is usually lacking for indigenous societies. The world at large does not normally know much about their internal politics, nor does it know whom their representatives do and do not speak for, nor how the representatives came to be chosen in the first place. Indeed, the situation is so fluid that individuals can and do appear at international gatherings and claim to represent indigenous societies, without those societies being aware that they are being so represented and in some cases without those societies even knowing the individuals who claim to represent them. Obviously this makes for considerable misunderstanding and political manipulation (see Richard Chase Smith 1982).

Even when there are no such uncertainties concerning the leaders or representatives of an indigenous group, there is no guarantee that its leadership will speak with a single voice. It is a form of naive romanticism to believe that political disagreements do not exist among indigenous peoples or to suppose that they always achieve consensus on every issue, even though such claims are sometimes made on their behalf, especially when their way is being contrasted with the white man's way. Both the record and ordinary common sense would lead us instead to expect a certain amount of politicking in indigenous societies. One deals with this in much the same way as one does with politicking in any other society, by being as well informed as possible about the divisive issues and how people stand on them. Cultural Survival, for example, tries hard to get opinions from its own network of contacts on the politics of indigenous societies in order to discover which leaders enjoy a sufficient base of support for them to represent their peoples with some legitimacy. Where a people or a community is so badly divided that they cannot be so represented, then Cultural Survival would not normally consider collaborating with them on a project. Since all of our field projects are designed and carried out in collaboration with the people they are intended to help, this means in effect that we would not consider a project to assist these people until the political situation was clarified.

PROBLEMS OF DISAGREEMENT

A more difficult question is what to do when the indigenous society and its recognized leaders insist on pursuing a course of action which we, as advocates, believe to be disastrous. Let me give two examples to illustrate this sort of dilemma. In southern Brazil an Indian society was offered what seemed to them to be a vast sum of money by lumber companies in return for the right to cut down trees on Indian land. The Indians, who had no idea of the ecological devastation which uncontrolled lumbering can cause, felt that they were being offered a small fortune for the depletion of an essentially inexhaustible resource. They were anxious to accept. Anthropologists from the University of Santa Catarina, who have been very active in the pro-Indian cause, tried hard to dissuade them. In the

meantime they also worked to prevent the start of the lumbering operation. Eventually however they failed to convince the Indians, abandoned their active opposition to the lumbering project, and withdrew as advisers to these particular Indians. It seems to me that that was the correct thing to do. The lumbering project was being carried out with the informed consent of the Indians and the anthropologists had done what they could to make the harmful consequences of it known to the people it was going to harm. It would have been the worst sort of paternalism to try to prevent the project from being put into effect over the wishes of the Indians themselves.

Even more difficult is the issue of what to do when indigenous leaders espouse what we consider to be the harmful rhetoric of settler society. Mario Juruna, the Shavante deputy in the Brazilian congress, learned for example that Brazilian farmers could raise money by mortgaging their land. He therefore argued at one time that Indians should be allowed to do the same. They are normally unable to do so because their land (when it is legally theirs at all) is held in trust for their communities by FUNAI. Juruna wanted the government to get off the backs of the Indians by making it possible for them to own their own land individually and to do what they like with it. Here again there is only one course of action open to an advocate who believes, as I do, that such a policy would be disastrous for the Indians. That is to try and persuade both Juruna himself and the Indians in general of the reasons why this is so and to encourage them to support a different point of view. This may not be so difficult. I have heard many Indian leaders lecture me eloquently about their people's attitude to land as a common and sacred good and their revulsion against the white man's insistence on treating it as a commodity that may be individually owned, bought and sold. The Mapuche, for example, are desperately aware of what individual land holding is likely to do to their way of life and have requested help to try and hold their society together in what they see as a last do or die effort. Yet if it came to the point that an Indian people was fully aware of the likely consequences of dividing up the land and still wanted to do it, then it should have the right to do so.

ADVOCACY IN A SUPPORTING ROLE

It follows from this that I see no particular problem posed for pro-Indian groups by the fact that Indians are increasingly doing their own advocacy. On the contrary, it should be the desired aim of such groups to assist indigenous peoples to conduct their own advocacy. The form of this assistance will change as a function of the relations between the Indians being assisted and the outside world. A tribal society which has had little contact with settler society needs advocates to speak for it in the nation at large. It also needs people who are able to help its members understand the national and regional forces with which it must henceforward cope. Eventually, one hopes, such a society will be able to negotiate on its own behalf or at least to join with others in indigenous associations which can do such negotiating. Even at this stage, however, indigenous associations which speak for their own people can be well served by friendly advocates in the world at large. Such advocates can provide them with expertise which it is difficult and unnecessary for them to acquire on their own. Cultural Survival can, for example, document what happens to Indian societies whose land is divided into individually owned parcels and make this information available to the Indians themselves. We can tell Indians in Brazil about the techniques used in successful projects that have benefitted Indians in, say, Ecuador. We can put Indian societies in touch with each other both at a national and international level. Above all, indigenous advocacy normally depends for its success on a favourable or at least not resolutely hostile climate of opinion in the country concerned. The role of national and international advocates of the indigenous cause, in creating this climate and keeping up the pressure to maintain it, should not be underestimated.

This brings me back to the point I made earlier about the importance of good laws and policies, even when they are ineffectively enforced. Settler societies are everywhere unscrupulous about the rights of the autochthonous peoples whom they dispossess. The frontiersmen and their supporters in the metropolis can always be relied upon to be resolutely anti-Indian or anti any other native people. It is when these elements receive the wholehearted support of the metropolis that indigenous peoples suffer most. It is no accident that the tribal Indians of Brazil suffered most acutely in the late sixties, at a time when the military regime in power was at its most repressive and was insisting on development without regard to human costs. When liberal elements gain a hearing in the metropolis, they are unlikely ever to eliminate the anti-Indian factions and are certainly unlikely to change the minds of the frontiersmen. But they can and do provide a counterweight to the sentiments of the frontiersmen, and it is this tension that provides indigenous peoples with the opportunity to have their rights respected and to establish themselves in the wider society. It is thus critical to keep up the pressure for good laws. They represent the conscience of the society and can thus be appealed to when they are not being properly enforced. The link between good laws and effective enforcement has to be the focus of advocacy efforts on behalf of indigenous peoples.

UNUSUAL ADVOCACY: ORDINARY ANTHROPOLOGY

I hope these comments have served to show that although work on behalf of tribal peoples and ethnic groups may be a peculiar form of advocacy it is not a very strange sort of anthropology. It only seems strange at times because it abandons old anthropological habits that were once so much part of anthropological practice that they acquired ritual, if not actually canonical status. Anthropologists used to see themselves as lone scientists who dissected exotic cultures and presented the truth of their systems to a scholarly audience. They now know that they are not alone in their work, that the truth of another culture is never monolithic, that better and better approximations to it emerge from rigorous analysis and vigorous debate, in which the members of the cultures studied increasingly participate. Anthropologists used to think that advocacy was "unscientific" and would undermine their scholarly credibility. Many of us now believe that it is precisely the most rigorous anthropological analysis which impels us toward advocacy and provides us with the tools to engage in it. Indeed the credibility of anthropologists and their work in many parts of the world is nowadays more threatened by an unwillingness to engage in any form of advocacy than the reverse.

The kind of advocacy discussed in this paper requires the classic skills of anthropology. It requires the ability to suspend judgment while analyzing societies very unlike our own. It also requires the ability to study our own society (or other "modern industrial societies") with a detachment similar to that we strive for in studying the exotic. It requires the ability to analyze national policies, developmental ideologies and the workings of bureaucracies with a detachment that enables us to see beyond their familiar obfuscations and self-deceptions. It then requires the advocate to combine these analyses dialectically in order to understand and eventually influence the complex processes which affect underprivileged ethnic groups. The rest is politics and the extent to which the advocate is willing or effectively able to get involved in that depends very much on temperament, circumstance and opportunity. Even at the political stage of advocacy an anthropological training is not a bad preparation, though an anthropological temperament may well be. Above all, this type of advocacy is intimately related to what I consider to be perhaps the most important impulse behind anthropology itself—the interest in social theory and moral philosophy. Boas and Durkheim, to mention the apical ancestors of what used to be thought of as the American and British styles of anthropology, did not devote themselves to their professions just to do science. This misreading of their efforts was a distortion introduced by their disciples, one that reduced anthropology to a kind of functionalist trick which was soon proclaimed not to work. In fact, Boas and Durkheim, while extremely concerned that their work should be properly scientific, both felt strongly that they were engaged in researches which would help to improve the human conditions. They practised, as Boas once put it, "science in the service of a higher tolerance." Boas devoted his science to the fight against racism. We could do worse than to devote ours to the battle against ethnocentrism in the struggle to shape a world where people can live together in multi-ethnic societies on the basis of mutual tolerance and respect.

NOTES

1. I wish to acknowledge the assistance of Dr. Theodore Macdonald and Dr. Jason Clay, my colleagues in Cultural Survival, in preparing this paper. It should be clear to the reader that in writing about the advocacy undertaken by our organization, I am describing something which is very much a collective effort.
2. See Hanke 1959 for a discussion of the famous debates on these issues at the Spanish court between Las Casas and Sepulveda.
3. For a discussion of these ideas, see D. B. Davis 1966.
4. See the report of the Interchurch Committee on Human Rights in Latin America (1980) and Barreiro and Wright (1982:60–63).
5. See Cultural Survival 1981a and Richard Chase Smith 1979, 1982.
6. For a discussion of the World Bank project in northwestern Brazil, see Cultural Survival 1981b.
7. There is voluminous literature on the Brazilian "miracle," but especially relevant to the points made here are Furtado 1982, Fishlow 1973, Foweraker 1981 and Velho 1976.

REFERENCES

Arnold, Robert. 1976. *Alaska Native Land Claims.* Anchorage: The Alaska Native Foundation.

Barreiro, Jose, and Robin Wright (eds.) 1982. *Native Peoples in Struggle: Russell Tribunal and Other International Forums.* Boston: Anthropology Resource Center, Inc.

Claude, Inis L. 1955. *National Minorities: An International Problem.* Cambridge: Harvard University Press.

Comissão Pro-Indio. 1979. *A Questão da Emancipação.* São Paulo, Brazil: Comissão Pro-Indio. Caderno No. 1.

Cultural Survival. 1981a. "Development Planning in Peru's Amazon—the Palcazu." *Cultural Survival Newsletter,* 5(3).

Cultural Survival. 1981b. *In the Path of Polonoroeste: Endangered Peoples of Western Brazil.* Cambridge: Cultural Survival Occasional Paper No. 6.

Davis, David Brion. 1966. *The Problem of Slavery in Western Culture.* Ithaca: Cornell University Press.

Fishlow, Albert. 1973. "Some Reflections on Post-1964 Brazilian Economic Policy." In Alfred Stepan (ed.), *Authoritarian Brazil.* New Haven: Yale University Press.

Foweraker, Joe. 1981. *The Struggle for Land: A Political Economy of the Pioneer Frontier in Brazil from 1930 to the Present Day.* Cambridge: Cambridge Latin American Studies No. 39.

Furtado, Celso. 1982. *Analise do "Modelo" Brasileiro.* Rio de Janeiro: Civilização Brasileira.

Hanke, Lewis. 1959. *Aristotle and the American Indians: A Study in Race Prejudice in the Modern World.* Bloomington: University of Indiana Press.

Interchurch Committee on Human Rights in Latin America. 1980. *Mapuches: People of the Land.* Toronto: ICCHRLA.

Kuper, Leo. 1984. "International Protection Against Genocide in Plural Societies." In David Maybury-Lewis (ed.), *The Prospects for Plural Societies.* Washington, D.C.: Proceedings of the American Ethnological Society (1982).

Macdonald, Theodore. 1980. "Ecuador Land Demarcation." *Cultural Survival Newsletter,* 4(4).

Maybury-Lewis, David (ed.). 1979. *Brazil.* Special Report No. 1. Cambridge: Cultural Survival.

Maybury-Lewis, David. 1983a. "The Shavante Struggle for Their Lands." *Cultural Survival Quarterly,* 7(1).

Maybury-Lewis, David. 1983b. "Brazilian Indians Find Their Voice." *Cultural Survival Quarterly,* 7(1).

Maybury-Lewis, David. 1984. "Living in Leviathan: Ethnic Groups and the State." In David Maybury-Lewis (ed.), *The Prospects for Plural Societies.* Washington, D.C.: Proceedings of the American Ethnological Society (1982).

Maybury-Lewis, David. 1985. "Brazilian Indianist Policy: Some Lessons from the Shavante Project." In Theodore Macdonald, Jr. (ed.), *Native Peoples and Economic Development: Six Studies from Latin America.* Cambridge: Cultural Survival Occasional Paper No. 16.

Maybury-Lewis, David, and James Howe. 1980. *The Indian Peoples of Paraguay: Their Plight and Their Prospects.* Cambridge: Cultural Survival Special Publication No. 2.

Merivale, Herman. 1861. *Lectures on Colonization and Colonies.* London: Green, Longman and Roberts.

Smith, Richard Chase. 1979. *The Multinational Squeeze on the Amuesha People of Central Peru.* Copenhagen: International Work Group for Indigenous Affairs, Document No. 35.

Smith, Richard Chase. 1982. *The Dialectics of Domination in Peru: Native Communities and the Myth of the Vast Amazonian Emptiness.* Cambridge: Cultural Survival Occasional Paper No. 8.

Uquillas, Jorge E. (ed.). 1982. *Informe para la Delimitacion de Territorios Nativos Siona Secoya, Cofán y Huaorani.* Quito: Ediciones INCRAE #039.

Velho, Otavio. 1976. *Capitalismo Autoritário e Campesinato.* São Paulo, Brazil: DIFEL.

World Bank 1981. *Economic Development and Tribal Peoples: Human Ecologic Considerations.* Washington, D.C.: World Bank.

When Does Life Begin?

A Cross-Cultural Perspective on the Personhood of Fetuses and Young Children

Lynn M. Morgan

Lynn M. Morgan has a Ph.D. in medical anthropology, awarded jointly by the University of California, Berkeley, and the University of California, San Francisco. An associate professor at Mount Holyoke College, she has carried out fieldwork in Latin America; besides medical anthropology, her interests include development and political economy.

Participants in the U.S. abortion debate have argued about life and personhood from philosophical, religious, moral, biological, and political points of view, yet very few have examined the cultural dimensions of when life begins. Because they have overlooked the relevance of comparative cultural information, it has been difficult for participants in the debate to acknowledge the extent to which human life and personhood are culturally constructed. Perhaps a reflexive, cross-cultural perspective on personhood is an unaffordable luxury now, with the 1973 landmark *Roe v. Wade* Supreme Court decision legalizing abortion under fire from anti-abortion groups. Because the legality of abortion is seriously threatened, the subtleties and ambiguities about abortion are rarely acknowledged for fear of muddying the central policy issue.[1] In spite of the political stakes, however, I will argue that the discourse on personhood should be expanded to include perspectives from other cultures, thus encouraging Americans to confront and challenge the myriad culture-bound assumptions which permeate the U.S. debate over reproductive health policy.

The social recognition of fetuses, newborns, and young children is embedded within a wider social context. This observation is not new: a burgeoning literature illuminates the links between abortion, childrearing, women's status, social stratification, child welfare, ethnic and gender discrimination, and changing relations between the sexes. The process through which young human lives come to be valued is derived in part from these factors, but personhood is also a function of cultural divisions of the life cycle, attitudes toward

death, the social organization of descent and inheritance, and social systems of authority and achievement. Anthropologists such as Mauss, Fortes, and La Fontaine[2] have documented a rich and remarkable range of variation showing the relationship among notions of self, body imagery, social organization, and ideational features such as consciousness and individuality. The cross-cultural evidence shows that the early thresholds of human life and personhood are just one issue in the larger question of whom society allows to become a person, under what circumstances, and why.

Every human being is potentially at risk of being aborted, miscarried, stillborn, or killed by natural cause or human agency before being accepted into a social community and labelled a person, yet there has been no recent systematic attempt to examine when other cultures come to value human life. . . .

Viewing the issue of personhood from a cross-cultural perspective helps to illustrate inconsistent and contradictory features of reproductive ethics debates in the United States. The ethnographic data show that the parameters of the U.S. abortion debate as presently constituted do not exhaust the realm of possibilities found among the earth's inhabitants. A close reading of the ethnographic evidence shows that killing neonates is often not regarded as murder, especially when the killing occurs before an infant is recognized as a human or person. Infanticide, then, with all the moral repugnance it evokes in the West, is a cultural construct rather than a universal moral edict. Apart from Tooley's influential *Abortion and Infanticide*,[3] few theorists have seriously considered the moral justifications for infanticide, yet the comparative cultural data indicate that this question deserves far more attention than it receives.

The cross-cultural evidence reveals two culturally constructed concepts used widely to divide the human life cycle continuum at its earliest stages: human-ness and personhood. In order to be granted status as a person, a fetus or neonate must first be recognized as a member of the human species. In some societies the decision to call a fetus "human" is not made until biological birth when the newborn's physical attributes can be assessed. Personhood, in contrast, is a socially recognized moral status. Neonates may not be labelled as persons until social birth rites are performed, often several days or months after biological birth. Social birth gives the neonate a moral status and binds it securely to a social community. Biological and social birth are not recognized as separate events in Western societies, even though they structure the onset of personhood in many non-Western societies. The U.S. abortion debate thus replicates Western divisions of the life cycle, overlooking the fact that even the human developmental cycle is socially patterned.

The attribution of personhood is a collective social decision, for the legal and ethical boundaries of personhood can only be negotiated within social settings. The limits of personhood are not decided by individuals, but by the entire society acting on shared cultural beliefs and values. For this reason, personhood—the value placed on human life—is not a concept which will be altered by religious mandate, nor by radical legislation by either the Right or the Left. Yet consensus is obviously eluding us, and seems destined to elude us as long as North Americans feel personal ambivalence and the compulsion to engage in increasingly polarized struggles over the issues surrounding abortion. Perhaps by reflecting on the social context of personhood and the value of fetuses and young children in other cultural contexts, we will be better able to understand how they are valued in our own.

"HUMAN" VERSUS "PERSON"

The furor over abortion in the United States has been waged in part through the manipulation of highly emotional symbols, resulting in a great deal of semantic confusion (a fetus may be called a "baby," an "unborn child," or "the product of conception"[4]). I will make only one semantic distinction while examining the cross-cultural evidence: between the concepts of "human," and "person.". . .

Although "human" generally refers to a biological designation, the term is still subject to cultural influence and negotiation. In the United States, most people assume that the product of a human pregnancy will be human, yet the cross-cultural evidence shows greater variety. Among the Arunta of Central Australia, "[if] a child is born at a very premature stage, nothing will persuade the natives that it is an undeveloped human being, for it is nothing like a *Kuruna* [spirit] or a *re-*

tappa [newborn]; 'they are perfectly convinced that it is the young of some other animal, such as a kangaroo, which has by mistake got inside the woman.'"[5] In Bang Chan, Thailand, women related episodes of "giving birth to 'gold,' 'jewels,' 'a monkey,' 'a fish's stomach,' and a mouse-like 'Golden Child.'"[6] In aboriginal Australia and Thailand, the products of conception are not assumed *a priori* to be human, for human status must be empirically verified.

In societies where humanity and personhood are defined separately, the determination of humanity always precedes the determination of personhood. On the island of Truk, for example, people waited until biological birth to see whether the newborn could be categorized as human. They did not take for granted the anthropomorphic character of the creature which would emerge from the womb. Abnormal or deformed infants were labelled as ghosts and burned or thrown into the sea: "Culturally this is not defined as infanticide and the suggestion of infanticide horrified the Trukese; a ghost is not a person and cannot be killed in any case."[7] This case, in which humanity itself was denied, is characteristic of the justification given for killing twins in some societies. Among the Tallensi in Africa, Fortes reports that twins were regarded suspiciously, because they may have been "malicious bush spirits" in human guise. After the first month of birth, a twin would be treated as any other child, but "only when it reaches the age of about four, and is placed under the spiritual guardianship of an ancestor spirit, is a twin definitely regarded as a complete social being."[8] A turn-of-the-century account of childhood in southern Africa noted that twins were regarded as more animal than human, and thus dangerously unpredictable: "No woman would care to marry a twin, for she would say that he was not a proper human being, and might turn wild like an animal, and kill her."[9] In these societies the neonate is not assumed to be born human, but is "anthropomorphized" after birth on the basis of physical characteristics which may or may not subsequently be endowed with moral significance. The criteria used to anthropomorphize newborns in different cultural contexts vary with caretakers' perceptions of the status of neonates.

DEFINING PERSONHOOD

Personhood is contingent on social recognition, and a person is recognized using established sociocultural conventions. Persons possess a special moral stature within their societies, yet in specific historical circumstances this status has been denied to certain groups, including women, children, slaves, prisoners of war, lepers, countless subordinate ethnic groups, and the insane. In all cultures, persons are living human entities whose killing is classed as murder; that is, the killing invokes some degree of moral condemnation and social retribution. The social construction of personhood varies according to the environmental, cosmological, and historical circumstances of different societies. What this means, in sum, is that "people are defined by people."[10] There can be no absolute definition of personhood isolated from a sociocultural context.

Burial customs may provide one source of data on cultural definitions of personhood, since only "persons" are buried. The data show a range of variation sufficient to highlight some of the contradictions in current U.S. policy. For example, on one extreme, a Chippewa Amerindian woman:

> knew her baby was two or three months along when she lost it . . . You could tell that it was just beginning to form. They cleaned it just like a child that is born and wrapped it. They gave a feast for it just like for a dead person and buried it in the same way. They believe that a child is human when it is conceived.[11]

Such behavior contrasts strikingly with burial practices in the United States, where fetuses weighing less than 500 grams are not buried, even in Roman Catholic hospitals where stated policy professes to respect human life from the time of conception.[12] On the other extreme, Ashanti children of Ghana who died before adolescence were reportedly thrown on the village midden heap,[13] indicating that burial rites and the full status of personhood were adult perquisites. In the U.S., "fetuses ex utero over 500 grams are considered premature newborns, and therefore birth certificates must be issued for them and they must be buried,"[14] yet U.S. burial customs for children depend on more than the weight or size of the body. In New York City, a study revealed that many indigent children under one year of age were buried in unmarked graves in Potter's Field, where parents were not permitted to visit the gravesites.[15] Apparently child burial customs and the parents' right to graveside grieving are at least in part a function of social class in the U.S., suggesting that the lives of poor children are valued less than those from wealthier families.

SOCIAL BIRTH

In Western industrialized societies, people generally believe that biological birth marks the entrance of a new being into the social community. The tenacity of this belief results from the cultural conviction that biological events have social significance. Unconsciously but relentlessly, Westerners have imbued that biological act of birth with profound importance, to the extent that legal and civil institutions confer personhood in-

stantly when an infant is born alive. The social status of personhood is thus granted concurrently with a biological act: emerging from the womb. In several non-Western societies, however, members observe a period of transitional, liminal time between biological birth—when the infant can be seen, inspected, and evaluated—and social birth, when the infant is formally accepted into its social community. This is a stage of the life cycle which acknowledges and reinforces the cultural and cognitive divisions between the marginal, uncertain status of the fetus and the secure, protected status of a person. As a clearly bounded life cycle division, this period between biological and social birth so characteristic of many non-Western societies is unknown in 20th century Western societies.

Until abortion became such a contentious issue, most people in the United States rarely stopped to question whether the social status of an infant could be separated from its biological status. It would be thought inappropriate to refer to the unborn fetus as a person complete with social identity (in part because the sex of the individual is essential to the construction of an individual's social identity). At birth the healthy child was automatically endowed with a social identity: as soon as the umbilical cord was cut, the neonate became a person. Biological birth was the major moral dividing line along the life cycle continuum: every individual who had passed the line was granted the rights and social status of persons,[16] while every individual shy of the line was not. Biological and social birth were inextricably intertwined in legal and medical institutions as well as in popular consciousness. This has changed only recently. In 1973, for example, *Roe v. Wade* established "viability" as the moral dividing line between fetuses which could be legally aborted and those which merited the protection of the State. Amniocentesis and other advances in medical technology have also altered the idea that persons could be distinguished from non-persons only at birth.

Many non-industrial societies, on the other hand, do not endow biological facts with the same degree of social importance. They separate the purely physiological act of birth from the social acceptance of the newborn. Social birth is marked by a ritual held sometime after biological birth, during which the newborn is granted a place in the social world. Social birth rituals often introduce the newborn formally for the first time to significant members of the community such as parents, siblings, godparents, other relatives, and community elders. The infant may also be presented to non-human entities considered important by the community, for example, sacred animals, natural entities, or supernatural beings. Social birth may be the occasion for some symbolically important event such as naming, hair cutting, depilation,[17] ear piercing,[18] removing incisor teeth,[19] or circumcision. Social birth may take place anywhere from a few days to several years after biological birth. It can be a one-time occurrence or it may be a gradual process involving a number of socially significant events: crying, suckling, or weaning for the first time, or learning—as a small child—to perform certain chores.[20] Long, gradual transitions to personhood, sometimes lasting an entire lifetime, are common in non-Western societies,[21] yet a crucial induction into personhood often occurs early in life, with social birth. In a society where social birth rites are essential to personhood, an infant who dies before social birth has died before it was born.

DIVIDING THE LIFE CYCLE

Models of an individual life cycle, from the moment of conception to death and afterlife, are constructed differently from one society to the next. Societies divide the developmental cycle into segments, and mark transitions from one stage to the next by birthdays, marriage, parenthood, and religious rites of passage. Life cycle divisions are one way in which societies categorize their members. Life stages allow status to be monitored and evaluated by other members of society who look for age- and status-related cues to determine their attitudes and behavior toward those around them. Stages of life which North Americans take for granted, such as childhood, adolescence, and middle age, are in fact cultural constructions which have evolved in response to demographic, economic, and social factors. Anthropologists have been acutely aware of the social nature of the life cycle since Margaret Mead wrote about the nature of adolescence in Samoa. In the 20th-century United States, she said, adolescence had become known "as the period in which idealism flowered and rebellion against authority was strong, a period during which difficulties and conflicts were absolutely inevitable."[22] In Samoa, however, teenagers did not pass through an analogous period of turmoil. Mead used the ethnographic evidence to show that adolescence was a phase of life unique to Western culture, specifically to the United States.

Childhood is another stage of life with a discernible social history, as Aries demonstrates for Western Europe. By analyzing European literature and iconography, Aries shows that children were not accorded the unique status they now occupy in the West until well after the advent of institutionalized schooling in the 16th and 17th centuries. Around that time, moralists began to argue that children needed to be trained, reformed, and subjected to "a kind of quarantine" before they would be fit company for adults.[23] The concept of infancy did not arise in western Europe until much later. British vital statistics did not distinguish among miscarried, stillborn, or infant deaths until late in the

19th century.[24] Until the mid-19th century, the French had no word for "baby."[25] During the first few months of life, when an infant could not interact with or respond to adult stimuli, it "simply 'did not count.'"[26] As the concept of childhood evolved in modern Europe, so did parents' ideals of the number and quality of children they desired, and society's expectations of the appropriate behaviors characterizing ideal adults and children.

Middle-age, in addition to adolescence and childhood, is also a socially constructed life stage category. Brandes has shown that the American mid-life crisis (often associated with the fortieth birthday) is not a biological or developmental phenomenon, but cultural.[27] The turmoil and anxiety one feels on approaching the fortieth year is a reflection of our society's success in continuing the process of socialization through the adult years. Adults as well as children internalize society's popular wisdom and myths, one of which is that mid-life crisis is inevitable, natural, and almost genetically programmed. This relentlessly repeated message is deeply encoded in many realms of social life, including Western number symbolism. As a result, the American mid-life crisis has become a self-fulfilling prophecy: "the expectation of change at certain key times along the life course—especially if such expectation is elevated to the position of a shared, transmitted cultural norm—is likely actually to produce a change that might not otherwise occur."[28]

If the ethnographic evidence shows that the human developmental cycle is divided differently according to cultural and historical contingencies, then non-Western cultures can be expected to have divisions of the life cycle unfamiliar to Westerners. One well-known example is the clearly marked transition from childhood and adulthood celebrated by adolescent initiation rites in parts of Africa and Melanesia. Another such stage occurs early in life, during the period between biological birth and social birth.

PERSONHOOD, A CROSS-CULTURAL VIEW

When viewed in cross-cultural perspective, the criteria for personhood are widely divergent: in one society personhood may be an ascribed status, conferred automatically when an infant is born alive or given a name; in another society the status may be achieved only through a very long, gradual process of socialization. In Java "the people quite flatly say, 'To be human [i.e., a "a person" in my terms] is to be Javanese.' Small children, boors, simpletons, the insane, the flagrantly immoral, are said to be *ndurung kjawa*, 'not yet Javanese'" and hence, not yet persons.[29] Evans-Pritchard reported that among the Nuer of the Nilotic Sudan, the death of a small child was not considered the death of a person:

People do not mourn for a small child, for "a small child is not a person (*ran*). When he tethers the cattle and herds the goats he is a person. When he cleans the byres and spreads the dung out to dry and collects it and carries it to the fire he is a person." A man will not say he has a son till the child is about six years of age.[30]

A 1950s ethnographic account of Korea reported that the death of a newborn would receive "scarcely more deference than any other animal. If it lives only through a long course of learning and ceremonies will it obtain the position of a recognized personality."[31] Personhood is not a "natural" category or a universal right of human beings, but a culturally and historically constructed assemblage of behaviors, knowledge, and practices. For societies which observe social birth rites, biological birth and the recognition of humanity are only early indications of what an individual may become. Biological birth acknowledges potential, but carries no guarantee of eventual acceptance into the social community. . . .

LIMINALITY, DANGER, AND THE FATE OF THE NEONATE

In many societies, the period between biological and social birth is treated socially and symbolically as an extension of being in the womb. The newborn is kept in seclusion, sheltered indoors away from the view of all save its mother (and perhaps a midwife or other female caretaker). Danger is minimized by recreating and maintaining a womb-like environment in which the infant resides until social birth. In the rural Philippines, for example, the newborn must be kept in strict seclusion for two weeks after biological birth, behind closed windows and above a well-sealed floor.[32] An ethnographer reporting on the Yavapai Amerindians of central Arizona wrote that mother and newborn stayed isolated and immobile for six days after parturition, resting on a bed of warm coals and earth and covered with grass.[33]

In society's terms none of these children have yet been born. They have emerged from their mother's uterus to a womb-like waiting room for pre-persons; their liminal status is perhaps analogous to a transitory phase at the other end of the life cycle known to Christians as purgatory.

Seclusion of infants is sometimes justified by citing the many perceived threats to their existence. Peoples of the Ghanaian Northern Territories told ethnographers that the infant may be reclaimed by spirits during the first seven days after biological birth:

[A] newborn baby may in fact be a spirit-child, and not a human child at all. If it is a spirit, it will return to the world of spirits before a week is out, so for the first seven days after the birth the mother and child are confined to the room in which the birth took place, or at any rate to the house. If the child dies during that time, it is assumed that it was in fact a spirit-child. The body is mutilated and buried in a pot, to prevent its return in similar circumstances. The parents are not allowed to mourn its loss, but should show signs of joy at being rid of such an unwelcome guest.[34]

If the infant survives its first seven days outside the biological womb, it will be allowed to emerge from the symbolic social womb as well. At that point, "it is considered that the child is human, and it is 'out-doored,' or brought into the open for the first time."[35] Supernatural threats to the newborn also justify an eight-day hiatus between biological and social birth among the Ashanti of western Africa. Ashanti beliefs about conception and early infancy are known to anthropologists because of the *ntoro* concept, a spiritual bond passed from father to child in a society structured around matrilineal descent. At biological birth the Ashanti question whether the newborn is meant to stay in the human world or whether it is a wandering ghost who will soon return to the spirit world. For eight days the mother and child remain indoors, with no special efforts made to bind the child to the human world: "It is given any kind of old mat or old rag to lie upon; it is not addressed in any endearing terms; water or pap, if given to it, is administered out of an old banana skin or ground-nut husk. It is true it is permitted to feed at the mother's breast, but it is hardly encouraged."[36] If the child is still alive after eight days, a *Nteatea* rite is performed, "when the child is named for its senior *ntoro* relative, and it is then for the first time regarded as a member of the human family."[37]

Similar "out-dooring" ceremonies have been recorded in other parts of the world. In the Nilgiri hills in south India, the Toda keep the newborn indoors for three months after biological birth. The sun is not allowed to touch the child's face. One morning after three months have passed, a "face opening" ceremony is held at dawn. The infant is brought outdoors with its face covered, and unveiled when the first bird sings. During this social birth rite the infant is introduced to the temple, to nature, to buffaloes, and to its clansmen. The infant is not considered a person until the ceremony has been performed.[38] Greeting the sun was also a feature of social birth among the Hopi Amerindians a century ago. On the twentieth day after birth, a ceremony was held to purify the new mother, name the baby, and present the child to the sun. Great care was taken by the father to announce the precise moment the sun rose above the horizon. At that instant, the "godmother throws the blanket from the face of the baby" and presents a cornmeal offering to the sun.[39]

All those present, including the newborn, then ate a ritual breakfast marking the entrance of a new person into the community.[40]

The above are quintessential examples of social birth rites: the newborn is kept indoors and out of sight for a specified period of time while the larger society remains symbolically unaware of its presence. This is a period of trial. The infant must "prove" it is worthy of personhood; first by managing to survive, then by exhibiting the vigor, health, and affect of one destined to become a functioning member of the community. If it survives and thrives, it is ready to pass through the social birth canal, to be ceremoniously welcomed as a person into the community. Completion of social birth rites ties the individual to the kin group and to the mortal world, granting it a moral status designed to protect it from harm by placing it under the protection of the group. If any of these criteria are not satisfied, the infant is classed as a non-person (and may in fact be labelled as non-human and hence not eligible for personhood, as with witches, ghosts and spirit-children). If it does not die of its own accord, it may be neglected until it does die, or it may be killed.

Infanticide is murder by definition, but most societies punish only the killing of human persons. It is problematic, then, to apply the label of infanticide to killing neonates before they are recognized as human or granted personhood. We might rather think of this as post-partum abortion, an image more applicable to the American experience. Induced abortion in the U.S. is rationalized (in part) by regarding the fetus as a pre-person, not yet accorded the same sanctity of life applied to "babies." Societies without safe and effective means of inducing abortion at early gestational stages may delay valuing the infant until well after biological birth. During this interim between biological and social birth the unwanted fetus (and it *is* still regarded as a fetus by that society) can be killed while its caretakers remain immune from punishment. Infanticide is condemned in most societies, but only after the newborn has been accorded human status or recognized as a person:

> [I]nfanticide is most readily condoned if it occurs before the infant is named and has been accepted as a bona fide member of its society. It seems that the primary and fundamental restriction in most societies is the taboo on murder, i.e., killing a member of the ingroup. The less eligible a child is for membership in the group, the less seriously the act of killing the child is viewed.[41]

Thus the Bariba of Benin believe that some babies will be born witches, who may endanger their mothers' health and bring misfortune to the entire community. Witch babies can be identified at biological birth and should ideally be killed at that time to prevent

future havoc.[42] In many societies the decision to expose or kill a neonate is made immediately at biological birth or within a few hours afterward. Among the Mohave Amerindians, if a newborn "was permitted to live long enough to be put to the breast, it was no longer subject to being killed."[43]

Post-partum abortion becomes infanticide if it is practiced after social birth rites are performed: "Thus in Athens the child could be exposed before the Amphidromia, a family ceremony at which the child was carried by its nurse around the hearth and thus received the religious consecration and its name."[44] In England during the 17th and 18th centuries, infanticide was practiced even though newborns were socially recognized as persons.[45] In those cases, however, personhood was granted incrementally, and infants were considered to be less significant persons than older children and adults. Under civil and religious law, killing a baby was a sin and a crime, but as practiced by the populace infanticide was less heinous than murdering an adult.

Becoming a person sometimes involves a long period of nurturing and socialization by the mother. This makes the infant's right to personhood in some societies contingent on the mother's survival and well-being. For example, an ethnographer reported that, among the Toba Amerindians of the Bolivian Gran Chaco, if a woman died in childbirth the newborn would be buried alive with her body. If both lived, personhood was granted only when the infant gained physical autonomy from the mother after weaning. Before that time, neither abortion nor infanticide was considered immoral: "A new-born child is no personality and has not an independent existence; its parents, and particularly the mother, have full right to decide over its life."[46] Yanomamo infants, also living in lowland South America, were considered appendages of their mothers until weaned at the end of their third year. When nursing ended, "the child, which hitherto belonged to the flesh and blood of the mother, has become an independent human being."[47] The personhood of the newborn in these two societies was predicated, at least in part, on attaining physical independence from the mother.

Ethnographic accounts cite a wide range of socially significant events which mark the end of liminality and the beginning of personhood. Weaning is one example, but naming is by far the most common. A nameless infant, in many cases, is not considered a person. The social function of naming is discussed in Ford's cross-cultural study of reproductive behavior:

> Naming probably has derived its extremely widespread acceptance from the manifest advantages which result from the practice. A name facilitates social intercourse. . . .

Naming a child helps to pull him into the framework of his society as an accepted member of the group. By virtue of being named the infant becomes a person like everyone else in the society; he is no longer a nameless outsider.[48]

Killing a child prior to naming was acceptable among certain societies, while killing a child after it was named would be tantamount to murder.[49] This was apparently the case among the Atayal aborigines of Formosa, where an early ethnographer reported "there is no punishment for the killing of an as yet nameless— i.e., less than two-or-three-year-old—child."[50] Among Arctic coast peoples, an ethnographer noted that infants were named after the deceased, thereupon reincarnating their ghosts: "naming may have restrained infanticide . . . because killing a named child could offend the reincarnated ghost."[51] Countless similar cases are found in the literature, where the name is a symbol of having become a person, and where a child who died prior to receiving a name was not regarded as a person.[52] Cherokee Amerindian babies were generally named a few days after birth. If the birth were prolonged or difficult, however, the child would be named during birth "so as to have something 'material' by which to exercise an influence upon it."[53] In the contemporary United States, where biological and social birth occur simultaneously, most newborns have names already chosen for them, which allows them to move directly from the womb into a permanent social identity.

Not everywhere, however, is a name the dominant symbol of the value placed on a newborn's life. Naming is delayed in many societies, but this behavior can have completely different meanings according to the social and environmental context. In northeast Brazil, where infant mortality is high, delayed naming is one of the emotional defenses which poor mothers use to shield themselves from the devastating psychological impact of frequent infant death. These Brazilian women view their children "as human, but [as] significantly less human than the grown child or adult."[54] Extreme poverty, widespread hunger, and high infant mortality rates affect the mother's emotional investment in her children: emotional deprivation is, in this context, a product of material scarcity.[55] Conversely in the Himalayas, where infant mortality is also high, children are not called their names precisely because their vulnerable young lives are highly valued. There Hindu children are named by a Brahmin priest on the tenth day after birth, but no one calls a child by this name for fear of making the child susceptible to the perils of "evil eye." Although not calling a child by its name may correspond with a denial of personhood in some societies, among the Hindus it is a "strong expression of the value and vulnerability placed on early lives, already begun but somehow requiring more protection."[56]

DISCUSSION

The ethnographic literature offers no universal consensus about who or what constitutes a person, for personhood is evaluated and bestowed on the basis of moral criteria which vary tremendously among and within different sociocultural contexts. The value placed on the lives of fetuses, neonates, and young children is determined according to a complex constellation of cultural factors, and cannot be determined simply by asking, "When does life begin?" Without a more general understanding of what it means to be a person in a given society, the beginnings of personhood can never be fully understood. An awareness of beginnings affords us only rudimentary insights into the social construction of personhood, which depends on the social relevance of gender, age, and material conditions and is in many contexts a gradual process. An example from West Africa will illustrate the point.

The Ashanti were mentioned earlier in connection with social birth rites which occur eight days after birth, but apparently these rites did not complete the transition to personhood. According to Rattray personhood was sometimes not solidified until adolescence: "In times not so very remote, persons dying before they reached adolescence were in no case accorded the ordinary funeral rites, and were often merely buried on the village midden heap. They were classed with the 'ghost children' who had not even survived eight days."[57] Not until passing through adolescent initiation rites did an Ashanti youngster become a complete person. As reflected in burial rites, children were not as highly valued as adults. This can be understood by examining the context and significance of personhood within Ashanti society. Among the Ashanti, differentiation between the sexes was an essential feature of adulthood, but sexual differentiation was insignificant until a child reached puberty and acquired the capacity to reproduce. Because reproduction was crucial to the perpetuation of the socio-political order, adolescent initiation rites symbolized the growth not only of the individual physical body but of the collective social body as well. Adolescents embodied society's hopes for its future. This point is made in Comaroff's discussion of healing among the Tshidi; there adolescent initiation rites "linked the natural maturation of the physical body to the reproduction of the socio-political system."[58] The importance of continuing the social formation is underscored by rites which grant personhood to adolescents: in La Fontaine's terms, "The concept [of person] serves to fuse the finite span of a human life with the unlimited continuity of social forms, by identifying personhood with self reproduction."[59] For the Ashanti child, to be a person meant to enjoy bodily autonomy with few corresponding social obligations, but to be an adult person meant that one's social responsibilities were multiplied, intensified, and enmeshed more tightly within the body politic.

So far we have been concerned with the valuation of fetuses and children cross-culturally, yet societal norms affect the personhood of the mother as well as the fetus, newborn, and young child. The mother's status as a person depends in most societies on her reproductive condition, the reproductive choices she makes, and her society's attitudes toward childbearing and childrearing. Feminist scholars writing in the United States argue that the abortion debate has focused too exclusively on fetal rights, virtually ignoring the role of women in society.[60] Recent attempts to reverse this trend include books by Luker, who demonstrates that U.S. women's opinions about abortion are conditioned by their life circumstances and perceived career options,[61] and Petchesky, who argues that the reproductive choices available to women must be understood within the broad socio-economic and political framework affecting the role of women.[62] Certainly these insights are applicable cross-culturally as well. Throughout the world women are primarily responsible for decisions affecting the lives and well-being of fetuses, neonates, and young children, and the choices women make in this regard are contingent on their own assessments of available options. The options change with the social tides, alternately restricting and expanding women's responsibilities for their born and unborn offspring. Such changes can be seen in a California lawsuit where a woman was charged with the wrongful death of her newborn child because she took illicit drugs and had sexual relations late in pregnancy, disregarding her doctor's orders. If this trend continues, American women will be increasingly held responsible for prenatal child abuse and neglect, even though fetuses have not been granted the rights of persons under the U.S. Constitution.

The ethnographic and historical literature is filled with accounts illustrating that a woman's status—even her claim to personhood and life itself—is contingent on her reproductive choices. In 15th-century England, for example, mothers known to have destroyed their newborn children were punished by death while wet nurses guilty of the same crime were not punished.[63] Piers argues that the reason for differential treatment was class bias, since wealthy women could afford to hire wet nurses for their children while poor women could not. Wet nurses were not executed for infanticide because breast milk was a rare and valuable commodity and wet nurses were scarce: "society simply could

not have afforded to kill her."[64] Indigent natural mothers, in contrast, were relatively expendable, and these were the women most often found guilty of murdering their babies. The 15th-century criminal sentence for murdering an infant depended not on the value of the infant's life, but on the social class of the accused. The hierarchy of values ranked the lives of wet nurses above the lives of "natural" mothers, obscuring the fact that wet nurses were themselves natural mothers. While Christian moralists railed against child murder, society's response reflected how certain classes of women were so devalued and oppressed that their execution was condoned. Their crime was in reality the inability to afford a wet nurse.

A woman's status within society can be heightened, undermined, or made ambiguous by pregnancy. Generally if the pregnancy results in a healthy newborn (in some patrilineal societies only a healthy newborn boy is satisfactory) her status will be enhanced, but, if the pregnancy outcome is viewed as negative, she may suffer irreparable damage or even death. Devereux cites at least two societies where women could reportedly be killed with impunity for inducing an abortion.[65] The mother's status in such cases was rendered ambiguous by the liminal status of the fetus. Whereas before the pregnancy her murder would have been a punishable crime, in pregnancy her life was valued less than that of the fetus she carried.

Most often the woman making reproductive decisions is held directly responsible for her own actions, as interpreted through societal mores and prejudices. In some cases, though, the lives of several people may be affected by a woman's decision. The Azande of central Africa have a polygamous, patrilocal social structure which allowed a woman's reproductive decisions to have far-reaching repercussions:

> If the husband learns that his wife has used an abortifacient plant, he considers this tantamount to the assassination of his child. He therefore asks his father-in-law for a second wife, or else, in vengeance, he kills the wife of his father-in-law or one of his father-in-law's children.[66]

In this case, the woman's relatives paid the consequences of her actions, demonstrating the links between fetal status, female status, and the status of other members of society. A similar issue can be seen in the United States abortion debates: should the decision to induce abortion be made in private between a woman and her physician, or should the permission of the father also be required? To what extent is the personhood of the woman contingent on her relationship to others in her sphere of social relations? Anthropologists have shown that in some societies one's social identity and personhood [are] completely, inextricably embedded in the social structure, to the point where individuals cannot envision having relationships not dictated by social structural roles and statuses.[67] The very essence of personhood is negotiated, manipulated, bestowed, and denied in accordance with the tacit or considered approval of society's members.

In the United States, the abortion debate has been foreshortened by a culture-bound discourse on personhood. The discussion of fetal personhood and abortion legislation has been limited almost exclusively to the period between conception and biological birth, largely as a result of a shared, cultural belief that biological birth is the event which distinguishes persons from non-persons. Consequently, the only space left to negotiate the boundaries of personhood is prior to biological birth. We have framed the debate over abortion in such a way that we argue whether it would be defensible to push the dividing line earlier, toward conception, but not later, toward early childhood. In the process of limiting debate to this realm, we have largely ignored the expansive, multiple meanings of personhood in American society, including the implications for adult women and men of the social context which determines our life decisions.

How can the range of cultural variability discussed here affect the U.S. abortion policy debates? In spite of the relativist stance presented here, I will not argue that Americans should weigh the merits of post-partum abortion—that would be ignoring a fundamental U.S. cultural reality which gave us the term "infanticide." Nonetheless Americans have felt forced to construct convoluted philosophical justifications for their positions on these issues, even when contorted logic theoretically could be avoided by admitting the existence and relevance of cultural variation. Debates over fetal personhood would be more honest, although undoubtedly more agonizing, if it were easier to admit that the moral dividing of life between persons and non-persons at biological birth or "viability" is a cultural construction. The question is whether we can tolerate knowing that our beliefs and values are remarkably malleable, arbitrary products of our cultural milieu.

NOTES

1. Daniel Callahan, "How Technology Is Reframing the Abortion Debate," *Hastings Center Report* (February 1986): 33–42, esp. 41.
2. Marcel Mauss, "A Category of the Human Mind: The Notion of Person, The Notion of Self," in *The Category of the Person,* ed. M. Carrithers, S. Collins, and S. Luke (Cambridge: Cambridge University Press, 1985), 1–25; Meyer Fortes, "On the Concept of the Person Among the Tallensi," in *La Notion de la Personne en Afrique Noire,* ed. G. Dieterlen (Paris: Editions du Centre National de la Recherche Scientifique, 1973); J. S. La Fontaine, "Person and Individual: Some Anthropological Reflections," in *The Category of the Person,* ed. M. Carrithers, S. Collins, and S. Luke (Cambridge: Cambridge University Press, 1985), 123–140.
3. Michael Tooley, "Abortion and Infanticide," *Philosophy and Public Affairs* 2 (1972): 37–65.
4. Leonard Kovit, "Babies as Social Products: The Social Determinants of Classification," *Social Science & Medicine* 12 (1978): 347–351.
5. Ashley Montagu, *Coming Into Being Among the Australian Aborigines* (London: Routledge & Kegan Paul, 1974), p. 31.
6. Jane Richardson Hanks, *Maternity and Its Rituals in Bang Chan* (Ithaca: Cornell Thailand Project, 1963), esp. 34–35.
7. Thomas Gladwin and Seymour B. Sarason, *Truk: A Man in Paradise* (New York: Wenner-Gren Foundation, 1953), p. 133; quoted in George Devereux, *A Study of Abortion in Primitive Societies* (New York: International University Press, 1955), p. 344.
8. Meyer Fortes, *The Web of Kinship Among the Tallensi: The Second Part of an Analysis of the Social Structure of a Trans-Volta Tribe* (London: Oxford University Press, 1949), p. 271.
9. Dudley Kidd, *Savage Childhood: A Study of Kaffir Children* (London: Adam and Charles Black, 1906), p. 45.
10. Andie L. Knutson, "The Definition and Value of a New Human Life," *Social Science & Medicine* 1 (1967): 7–29.
11. Devereux 1955, pp. 207–208.
12. Caroline Whitbeck, "The Moral Implications of Regarding Women as People: New Perspectives on Pregnancy and Personhood," in *Abortion and the Status of the Fetus,* ed. William B. Bondeson et al. (Dordrecht, Holland: D. Reidel Publishing Company, 1983), 247–272, esp. 258.
13. Robert S. Rattray, *Religion and Art Among the Ashanti* (Oxford: Clarendon Press, 1927).
14. Whitbeck, p. 258.
15. Peter Kerr, "Groups Fault City Policy on Burial of Poor Infants," *New York Times* (May 25, 1986), p. 30.
16. H. Tristram Engelhardt, Jr., "Viability and the Use of the Fetus," in *Abortion and the Status of the Fetus,* ed. William B. Bondeson et al. (Dordrecht, Holland: D. Reidel Publishing Company, 1983), 183–208, esp. 191.
17. Among the Siriono of eastern Bolivia, see Allan R. Holmberg, *Nomads of the Long Bow* (New York: Natural History Press, 1969).
18. Among the Argentine Araucanians, see M. Inez Hilger, *Araucanian Child Life and Its Cultural Background* (Washington: Smithsonian Miscellaneous Collections, Volume 133, 1957).
19. Performed among the Nuer when a child reached seven or eight years of age, see E. E. Evans-Pritchard, *Nuer Religion* (Oxford: Clarendon Press, 1956).
20. See Mead and Newton, p. 154, for examples.
21. La Fontaine, p. 132.
22. Margaret Mead, *Coming of Age in Samoa* (New York: American Museum of Natural History, 1928).
23. Philippe Aries, *Centuries of Childhood* (New York: Vintage Books, 1962), p. 412.
24. David Armstrong, "The Invention of Infant Mortality," *Sociology of Health and Illness* 8 (1986): 211–232, p. 214.
25. Aries, p. 29.
26. Aries, p. 128.
27. Stanley H. Brandes, *Forty: The Age and the Symbol* (Knoxville: University of Tennessee Press, 1985).
28. Brandes, p. 126.
29. Clifford Geertz, *The Interpretation of Cultures* (New York: Basic, 1973), p. 52.
30. Evans-Pritchard, p. 146.
31. Cornelius Osgood, *The Koreans and Their Culture* (New York: Ronald Press, 1951).
32. J. Landa Jocando, *Growing Up in a Philippine Barrio* (New York: Holt, Rinehart and Winston, 1969).
33. E. W. Gifford, "Northeastern and Western Yavapai," *University of California Publications in American Archaeology and Ethnology* 34 (1937): 247–354, esp. 300.

34. Barrington Kaye, *Bringing Up Children in Ghana* (London: George Allen & Unwin Ltd., 1962), pp. 56–57.

35. Kaye, p. 57.

36. Rattray, p. 59.

37. Edith Clarke, "The Sociological Significance of Ancestor Worship in Ashanti," *Africa 3* (1930): 431–470, esp. 431.

38. David G. Mandelbaum, Department of Anthropology, University of California, Berkeley, personal communication.

39. J. G. Owens, "Natal Ceremonies of the Hopi Indians," *Journal of American Ethnology and Archaeology 2* (1892): 163–75, esp. 170–73.

40. See Tilly E. Stevenson, "The Religious Life of a Zuni Child," *Fifth Annual Report of the Bureau of Ethnology* (1883–84): 539–555, esp. 546, for an account of a similar social birth rite which took place among the Zuni of western New Mexico.

41. Clelland S. Ford, "Control of Contraception in Cross-Cultural Perspective," *Annals of the New York Academy of Sciences 54* (1952): 763–768; cited in Mildred Dickeman, "Demographic Consequences of Infanticide in Man," *Annual Review of Ecology and Systematics 6* (1975): 107–137, esp. 115.

42. Carolyn Fishel Sargent, *The Cultural Context of Therapeutic Choice* (Dordrecht, Holland: D. Reidel Publishing Company, 1982), esp. 89–91.

43. George Devereux, "Mohave Indian Infanticide," The *Psychoanalytic Review 35* (2, 1948): 126–139, esp. 127.

44. Glanville Williams, *The Sanctity of Life and Criminal Law* (New York: Knopf, 1957), p. 14.

45. Peter C. Hoffer and N. E. H. Hull, *Murdering Mothers; Infanticide in England and New England 1558–1803* (New York: New York University Press, 1981).

46. Rafael Karsten, *The Toba Indians of the Bolivian Gran Chaco* (Oosterhout N. B., The Netherlands: Anthropological Publications, 1967 [1923]), pp. 24–25; thanks to Beth Ann Conklin for providing me with this reference.

47. Hans Becher, *Die Surara und Pakidai, swei Yanomami Stamme in Nordwestbrasilien* (Hamburg: Mirseum fur Voklerkinde, Mitteilunger 26, 1960).

48. Clelland S. Ford, *A Comparative Study of Human Reproduction* (New Haven: Human Relations Area Files Press, 1964), p. 77.

49. Clelland S. Ford, *Field Guide to the Study of Human Reproduction* (New Haven: Human Relations Area Files Press, 1964).

50. O. Wiedfeldt, "Wirtschaftliche, rechtliche, und soziale Grandtatsachen und Grandformen der Atayalen auf Formosa," *Deutsche Gesellschaft fur Natur—und Volkerkunde Ostasiens*, Witteilungen 15 (Teil C, 1914): 1–55, esp. 23.

51. Asen Balicki, "Female Infanticide on the Arctic Coast," *Man 2* (1967): 615–25, esp. 619.

52. Devereux 1955, p. 232; Mead and Newton, p. 154; and Gerald T. Perkoff, "Toward a Normative Definition of Personhood," in *Abortion and the Status of the Fetus*, ed. William B. Bondeson et al. (Dordrecht, Holland: D. Reidel Publishing Company, 1983), 159–166, esp. 162.

53. James Mooney and Frans M. Olbrechts, "The Swimmer Manuscript: Cherokee Sacred Formulas and Medicinal Prescriptions," *Smithsonian Institution Bureau of American Ethnology 99* (1932): 127.

54. Nancy Scheper-Hughes, "Culture, Scarcity and Maternal Thinking: Maternal Detachment and Infant Survival in a Brazilian Shantytown," *Ethos 13* (1985): 291–317, esp. 312.

55. Scheper-Hughes, p. 292.

56. Lois McCloskey, School of Public Health, University of California, Los Angeles, personal communication.

57. Rattray, p. 61.

58. Jean Comaroff, "Medicine: Symbol and Ideology," in *The Problem of Medical Knowledge*, eds. P. Wright and A. Treacher (Edinburgh: Edinburgh University Press, 1982), 49–68, esp. 52.

59. La Fontaine, p. 132.

60. See Whitbeck, 1983.

61. Kristin Luker, *Abortion and the Politics of Motherhood* (Berkeley: University of California Press, 1984).

62. Petchesky, Rosalind P., *Abortion and Women's Choice: The State, Sexuality and Reproductive Freedom* (Boston: Northeastern University Press, 1985).

63. Maria W. Piers, *Infanticide* (New York: W. W. Norton & Company, 1978).

64. Piers, p. 51.

65. Devereux, 1955, pp. 58, 248.

66. Devereux, 1955, p. 188.

67. La Fontaine, 1985, p. 129.

REFERENCES

Aries, Philippe. 1962. *Centuries of Childhood*. New York: Vintage Books.

Armstrong, David. 1986. "The Invention of Infant Mortality," *Sociology of Health and Illness* Vol. 8: 211–232.

Balicki, Asen. 1967. "Female Infanticide on the Arctic Coast," *Man* Vol. 2: 615–25.

Becher, Hans. 1960. *Die Surara und Pakidai, swei Yanomami Stamme in Nordwestbrasilien*. Hamburg: Mirseum fur Voklerkinde, Mitteilunger 26.

Brandes, Stanley H. 1985. *Forty: The Age and the Symbol*. Knoxville: University of Tennessee Press.

Callahan, Daniel. 1986. "How Technology Is Reframing the Abortion Debate," *Hastings Center Report* (February 1986): 33–42.

Clarke, Edith. 1930. "The Sociological Significance of Ancestor Worship in Ashanti," *Africa* Vol. 3: 431–470.

Comaroff, Jean. 1982. "Medicine: Symbol and Ideology," in *The Problem of Medical Knowledge*, ed. by P. Wright & A. Treacher. Edinburgh: Edinburgh University Press.

Devereux, George. 1948. "Mohave Indian Infanticide," The *Psychoanalytic Review* 35 (2): 126–139.

Engelhardt, H. Tristram, Jr. 1983. "Viability and the Use of the Fetus," in *Abortion and the Status of the Fetus*, ed. by William B. Bondeson et al. Dordrecht, Holland: D. Reidel.

Evans-Pritchard, E. E. 1956. *Nuer Religion*. Oxford: Clarendon Press.

Ford, Clelland S. 1952. "Control of Contraception in Cross-Cultural Perspective," *Annals of the New York Academy of Sciences* Vol. 54: 763–768; cited in Mildred Dickeman, "Demographic Consequences of Infanticide in Man," *Annual Review of Ecology and Systematics* Vol. 6 (1975): 107–137.

Ford, Clelland S. 1964. *A Comparative Study of Human Reproduction*. New Haven, CT: Human Relations Area Files Press.

Ford, Clelland S. 1964. *Field Guide to the Study of Human Reproduction*. New Haven, CT: Human Relations Area Files Press.

Fortes, Meyer. 1949. *The Web of Kinship among the Tallensi: The Second Part of an Analysis of the Social Structure of a Trans-Volta Tribe*. London: Oxford University Press.

Fortes, Meyer. 1973. "On the Concept of the Person among the Tallensi," in *La Notion de la Personne en Afrique Noire*, ed. by G. Dieterlen. Paris: Editions du Centre National de la Recherche Scientifique.

Geertz, Clifford. 1973. *The Interpretation of Cultures*. New York: Basic.

Gifford, E. W. 1937. "Northeastern and Western Yavapai," *University of California Publications in American Archaeology and Ethnology* Vol. 34: 247–354.

Gladwin, Thomas, & Seymour B. Sarason. 1953. *Truk: A Man in Paradise*. New York: Wenner-Gren Foundation; quoted in George Devereux, 1955. *A Study of Abortion in Primitive Societies*. New York: International University Press.

Hanks, Jane Richardson. 1963. *Maternity and Its Rituals in Bang Chan*. Ithaca, NY: Cornell Thailand Project.

Hilger, M. Inez. 1957. *Araucanian Child Life and Its Cultural Background*. Washington, DC: Smithsonian Miscellaneous Collections, Vol. 133.

Hoffer, Peter C., & N. E. H. Hull. 1981. *Murdering Mothers; Infanticide in England and New England 1558–1803*. New York: New York University Press.

Holmberg, Allan R. 1969. *Nomads of the Long Bow*. New York: Natural History Press.

Jocando, J. Landa. 1969. *Growing Up in a Philippine Barrio*. New York: Holt, Rinehart and Winston.

Karsten, Rafael. 1967 [1923]. *The Toba Indians of the Bolivian Gran Chaco*. Oosterhout N.B., The Netherlands: Anthropological Publications.

Kaye, Barrington. 1962. *Bringing Up Children in Ghana*. London: Allen & Unwin.

Kerr, Peter. 1986. "Groups Faults City Policy on Burial of Poor Infants," *New York Times* (May 25), p. 30.

Kidd, Dudley. 1906. *Savage Childhood: A Study of Kaffir Children*. London: Black.

Knutson, Andie L. 1967. "The Definition and Value of a New Human Life," *Social Science & Medicine* Vol. 1: 7–29.

Kovit, Leonard. 1978. "Babies as Social Products: The Social Determinants of Classification," *Social Science & Medicine* Vol. 12: 347–351.

La Fontaine, J. S. 1985. "Person and Individual: Some Anthropological Reflections," in *The Category of the Person*, ed. by M. Carrithers, S. Collins, & S. Luke. Cambridge, England: Cambridge University Press.

Luker, Kristin. 1984. *Abortion and the Politics of Motherhood*. Berkeley: University of California Press.

Mandelbaum, David G. Department of Anthropology, University of California, Berkeley, personal communication.

Mauss, Marcel. 1985. "A Category of the Human Mind: The Notion of Person, The Notion of Self," in *The Category of the Person*, ed. by M. Carrithers, S. Collins, & S. Luke. Cambridge, England: Cambridge University Press.

McCloskey, Lois. School of Public Health, University of California, Los Angeles, personal communication.

Mead, Margaret. 1928. *Coming of Age in Samoa*. New York: American Museum of Natural History.

Mead, Margaret, & Niles Newton. 1967. "Cultural Patterning of Perinatal Behavior," in *Childbearing: Its Social and Psychological Aspects*, ed. by S. A. Richardson & A. F. Guttmacher. New York: Williams and Wilkins, p. 153.

Montague, Ashley. 1974. *Coming into Being among the Australian Aborigines*. London: Routledge & Kegan Paul.

Mooney, James, & Frans M. Olbrechts. 1932. "The Swimmer Manuscript: Cherokee Sacred Formulas and Medicinal Prescriptions," *Smithsonian Institution Bureau of American Ethnology* Vol. 99: 127.

Osgood, Cornelius. 1951. *The Koreans and Their Culture*. New York: Ronald Press.

Ovens, J. G. 1982. "Natal Ceremonies of the Hopi Indians," *Journal of American Ethnology and Archaeology* Vol. 2: 163–175.

Perkoff, Gerald T. 1983. "Toward a Normative Definition of Personhood," in *Abortion and the Status of the Fetus*, ed. by William B. Bondeson et al. Dordrecht, Holland: Reidel.

Petchesky, Rosalind P. 1985. *Abortion and Women's Choice: The State, Sexuality and Reproductive Freedom*. Boston: Northeastern University Press.

Piers, Maria W. 1978. *Infanticide*. New York: Norton.

Rattray, Robert S. 1927. *Religion and Art among the Ashanti*. Oxford: Clarendon Press.

Sargent, Carolyn Fishel. 1982. *The Cultural Context of Therapeutic Choice*. Dordrecht, Holland: Reidel.

Scheper-Hughes, Nancy. 1985. "Culture, Scarcity and Maternal Thinking: Maternal Detachment and Infant Survival in a Brazilian Shantytown," *Ethos* Vol. 13: 291–317.

Stevenson, Tilly E. 1883–84. "The Religious Life of a Zuni Child," *Fifth Annual Report of the Bureau of Ethnology*: 539–555.

Tooley, Michael. 1972. "Abortion and Infanticide," *Philosophy and Public Affairs* Vol. 2: 37–65.

Turner, Victor. 1964. "Betwixt and Between: The Liminal Period in Rites of Passage," in *Symposium on New Approaches to the Study of Religion*, ed. by J. Helm. Seattle: American Ethnological Society.

U.S. Senate Subcommittee on Separation of Powers. (1981). *Report to the Committee on the Judiciary*. The Human Life Bill—S. 158. 97th Congress. Washington, DC: U.S. Government Printing Office, p. 12.

Van Gennep, Arnold. 1960 [1908]. *The Rites of Passage*. Chicago: University of Chicago Press.

Whitbeck, Caroline. 1983. "The Moral Implications of Regarding Women as People: New Perspectives on Pregnancy and Personhood," in *Abortion and the Status of the Fetus*, ed. by William B. Bondeson et al. Dordrecht, Holland: Reidel.

Wiedfeldt, O. 1914. "Wirtschaftliche, rechtliche, und soziale Grandtatsachen und Grandformen der Atayalen auf Formosa," *Deutsche Geselschaft fur Natur—und Volkerkunde Ostasiens*, Witteilungen 15 (Teil C., 1914): 1–55.

Williams, Glanville. 1957. *The Sanctity of Life and Criminal Law*. New York: Knopf.

Cargo Inventories, Shopping Lists, and Desire

Lamont Lindstrom

Lamont Lindstrom is chair of anthropology at the University of Tulsa and author of *Knowledge and Power in a South Pacific Society* and more recently *Cargo Cult: Strange Stories of Desire from Melanesia and Beyond*. He has published on kava, Pacific War ethnohistory, the politics of tradition, and Pacific sociolinguistics.

Let's begin with an inspirational message from Norman Vincent Peale:

> The happiness habit is developed by simply practicing happy thinking. Make a mental list of happy thoughts and pass them through your mind several times every day. . . . Every morning before arising, lie relaxed in bed and deliberately drop happy thoughts into your conscious mind. Let a series of pictures pass across your mind of each happy experience you expect to have during the day. Savor their joy. Such thoughts will help cause things to turn out that way. (1952:75)

Peale's technique, the "mental photograph" posed as a wish list for the future, was, and is, tremendously popular. Numerous prophets of self-fulfillment and of worldly and heavenly salvation counsel the composing of lists. They command: "Write down everything you want, everything you want to be; now, read and reread this list every day until it all comes true." I list myself driving a lime-green Miata; I write down a house with two chimneys; a job by a beach; 160 pounds on the scale; a Democratic Congress.

Diligent observers of the cargo cult have likewise compiled cargo lists, or shopping lists, of the merchandise that Melanesians desire. One of the first such anthropological inventories was Francis Williams's 1923 catalog of the goods coveted by the cultic residents of Vailala village: "tobacco, calico, knives, axes, food-stuffs" (1977:341). Even earlier inventories appear in mission literature. In 1882, for example, Agnes Watt listed the wares that a Tannese spirit medium claimed to fetch from her ghostly ancestors: "beads, turkey-red, tobacco, pipes, knives" (1896:214). A century later, in 1980, a second Tanna cargo inventory listed "refrigerators, televisions and washing machines" (Shears 1980:105).

Luckily, the cultural history of the list doesn't occupy much library space. This permits me room to speculate about the several purposes of Melanesian cargo lists, and of wish lists in general. The shopping list, the mental photograph, the cargo inventory, the wish list, the Christmas list have a common genealogy. They also share a serious function. The list, as a recipe for the future, constructs and reconstructs images of the identity of list-maker. Lists are a technique of personal invention—an invention informed by the broader, cultural imagination of personhood. The wish list operates as a mediator of self, of desire, and of the future.

Jack Goody, writing on the history of lists, distinguished three types: the retrospective list (e.g., the catalogs of names and places that epic poetry offers); the lexical list (which matured into dictionaries and encyclopedias); and the shopping list "which serves as a guide for future action, a plan" (1977:83). The cargo inventory, as a list of goods to be acquired, is a sort of shopping list.

Shopping lists are both aides-memoire and wish lists (J. Carrier, personal communication). As an aide-memoire, they jog shopper memory and, perhaps, help derail the provocative seductions of the market, at least for those who stick firmly to their lists. As a plan, shopping lists work to shape the future. They are wish lists of things desired, whether or not purchases get made. Goody focuses on a list's structuring effects on social action. The initial item on the list, for example, perhaps dictates where one goes first seeking the desired good:

> The shopping list is a way of constructing the future schedule of an individual or group, a schedule of movement in space and in time, relative to the requirements of the household economy; it is not simply a statement of what one wants, for writing permits a person to

"Cargo Inventories, Shopping Lists, and Desire" by Lamont Lindstrom, paper presented at the 93rd Annual Meeting of the American Anthropological Association, Atlanta, GA, 1994. Printed with permission.

re-order the items in relation to the source of supply. (1977:135)

I am concerned, here, more with the *content* of lists. This content, too, is both a plan and an image of the future. It models what will be when I return home from the store, or what will be when cargo ships land on Melanesian islands. Francis Spufford, who edited a collection of literary lists, suggests that lists of goods and definitions of personal identity fused in the seventeenth century:

> Because the seventeenth century was the first great age of *things*, when the expansion of national and international trade brought a large proportion of the European population into possession of manufactured goods for the first time, it became possible, too, for individual preferences to be registered in the individual choice of actual possessions, rather than in a selection of ideal future benefits. A character would be recorded, in literature, by itemising the contents of a house or a room or a cabinet or a bag as the projection of a self. (1989:15)

Here is where cargo inventories and shopping lists converge. For Melanesians, cargo lists are supposed to report the desired future—they detail the cargo inventories of the ships and planes to come. But we, like Spufford's litterateurs, read lists of goods as also projections of the character and predicaments of a self. The question is whose self?

Whose lists are these? Do we take them to be reports from the field—the actual testimony of cultists as recorded by investigative anthropologists? Or are they the constructions of anthropologists, journalists, and others who have attempted to represent Melanesian desire? Goody (1977:108) suggests that listing *per se*, as a technique, is less common in oral societies. And even in European tradition, the list, especially the shopping list that projects personality, may be a modern device. Spufford suggests that lists "have a structural affinity . . . with modernism, and with some other renovating movements which see the reinvention of forms as both compelling and compelled by new kinds of observation" (1989:6).

The social history of the shopping list has yet to be written. But this practice perhaps only dates back to the early years of this century when shoppers confronted an increasingly anonymous yet increasingly seductive marketplace (J. Carrier, personal communication).

The cargo inventory is, at the least, a joint production of Melanesian and anthropological shoppers. Cargo lists reflect the changing desires and perspectives of cultic observers as much as they do those of cargo cultists. Even granting some testimonial reality for Melanesian desire, clearly cargo lists have been selected, arranged, and written up by outside observers. Whatever the actual range of desire might be, the list-maker chooses just a handful of goods to compose an inventory of desire, the rest remaining an unsaid "and so forth, and so on, and the like, etc." And once composed, these lists continue to circulate, regularly repeated and rephrased, in the minor but still significant and popular literature of the cargo cult (see Lindstrom 1993).

Let's look with some suspicion at Melanesian cargo inventories. Here are a few examples:

- "Highly exciting things like calico and electric torches and refrigerators" (Priday 1950:67)
- "Enough food for everybody, prefabricated houses, washing machines, refrigerators, and blondes for the chief men" (Cameron 1964:224)
- "Icebox, a pair of trousers, and sewing machine" (Illich 1971:50)
- "Fabulous shiploads of refrigerators, jeeps, bulldozers, bottles of Coca-cola" (Hermann & Bonnemaison 1975:92)
- "Canned food, axes, cameras, and refrigerators (Hamilton 1983:1)
- "Bulk supplies of European goods (cargo)—civilian stock, such as tinned meat, cotton cloth, steel tools and motor vehicles, and military equipment, especially rifles and ammunition" (Lawrence 1987:74)
- "The liberating cargo of trucks, jeeps, houses, fridges, tables, chairs and cigars" (Evans 1992: 130)

Table 1 summarizes some 63 cargo lists published between 1922 and 1993. (This sampling of lists is not randomly selected, but rather reflects material that I have at hand; 23 come from descriptions of Tanna's John Frum movement.) This list of lists groups together goods that to my eyes (although perhaps not Melanesian) cluster together; it also counts the various goods specified in the inventories; and it lists these desires roughly by the frequency of their appearance. Food, especially processed food; cloth and clothing; tools; weapons; and refrigerators top the list. Neon advertising, American jargon, jobs, and blondes follow someway behind. But is this what cultic Melanesia desires?

Or perhaps this is how we desire them to desire. The cargo cult is a strange mirror. This is the curious, fervid desire of distant islanders to be like us, or at least so the cargo story goes. They want our Western clothing, Coca-cola and pickles, pointed shoes, modern implements, ammunition, Toyota trucks, and prefabricated houses. Or, on a less material plane, cultists desire—just as we do—cognitive consonance, personal salvation, national independence, reunited selves and undivided bodies.

Cargo stories in general, and cargo lists in particular, project a doubled identity. On one face, cargo lists suppose a desirous Melanesian who wants what we

Table 1 "List of Lists"

food	10	refrigerators	19	beer	2
tinned (canned)		ice boxes	2	wine	1
foods	11			whiskey	1
rice	8				
tinned meat	5	tobacco	12		
flour	4	cigarettes	4		
tinned fish	1	cigars	1	wristwatches	2
Coca-Cola	2			books	2
tinned salmon	1	means of conveyance	1		
tinned beef	1	motor vehicles	1	hospitals	1
tea	1	jeeps	7	stores	1
sugar	1	cars	4	new roads	1
milk	1	trucks	4		
ice cream	1	Toyota trucks	2	horses	1
candy	1	permit for truck	1	dogs	1
pickles	1	motorcycles	2	swarms of fish	1
		bicycles	1		
		bicycle clips	1		
clothes (clothing)	11	aircraft	6	modern luxury goods	1
Western clothing	1	ships	3	trade articles	1
cloth	5	boats	2	mosquito nets	2
calico	6	canoes	1	ornaments	1
loin cloths		outboard motors	1	razor blades	1
(laplaps)	3	bulldozers	1	mirrors	1
cotton cloth	2	tractors	1	colored beads	1
bolts of cloth	1			skin lightening	
textiles	1	machines	3	creams	1
handkerchiefs	3	sewing machines	3	wigs	1
socks	1	washing machines	2	red dye	1
shoes	1	machines for		plastic combs	1
pointed shoes	1	making electric		hydrogen peroxide	1
pair of trousers	1	light	1	china plates	1
		houses	2	china teacups	1
tools	5	prefabricated		saucepans	1
metal tools	1	houses	2	toilet paper	1
modern		houses of man-		aspirin	1
implements	1	made materials	1		
axes	9	metal houses	1	tables	1
tomahawks	2	building materials	1	pingpong tables	1
knives	9	corrugated iron	1	chairs	1
scout knives	1	iron	1		
pocket knives	1	steel	1	Neon advertising	1
bush knives	1			American jargon	1
scissors	1	radios	4		
tin opener	1	portable radios	2	jobs	1
fishhooks	1	television sets	1		
fishline	1	cameras	1	blondes	1
barbed wire	1				
		lamps	2		
military equipment	2	hurricane lamps	1		
firearms (weapons)	9	oil lamps	1		
guns	7	electric torches	2		
rifles	7	flashlights	1		
ammunition	1				
		money	7		

Cargo inventories as shopping lists, thus, tell us who we are or, perhaps, who we should be. They police the modern. Melanesians must want tinned food, handkerchiefs, guns, and television sets because we want these things too. Their desire warrants and certifies the correct nature and the appropriate range of our desire. Certainly, we are the intended audience of these enumerations. Reading the lists and inventories of Melanesian wanting, we thereby naturalize our own desires.

Since 1923 various desired items have moved onto and off, and up and down, cargo inventories. These shopping list fluctuations reveal shifting interpretations of Melanesian desire as well as commodity replacement and innovation within the global marketplace. The bicycle, for example, lists briefly in the 1950s; the radio first appears in 1960; ice cream in 1974; Coca-Cola in 1975; the wristwatch in 1978; television in 1980; and the camera in 1983. These goods serve as metonyms of modernity. For those who buy the wonders of progressive technological development, cargo inventories naturally change over time as Melanesians catch up with what the world's marketplace offers. Their constant but creeping desire for televisions and cameras assures us that these goods, indeed, represent the rolling pinnacle of modern technological accomplishment. Or, alternatively, in an inverted storyline, helpless Melanesian desire for American jargon, neon advertising, and skin lightening creams signifies the depths of our modern degradation. Either way, we can suspect that cargo shopping lists speak to us and about us as much as they reveal the truth of Melanesian desire. By locating desire for particular goods within Melanesian hearts, and thereby universalizing this desire, we soothe and make sense of our own urges.

I want to focus, very briefly, on four items that most frequently appear, decade by decade, on cargo lists: clothing and cloth; weapons; food—notably processed foods; and refrigerators.

CLOTH

Cloth and clothing of various sorts appear 37 times in my selected lists. The representation of status and identity through practices of clothing the body is a fundamental characteristic of European constructions of human civility. We might recall, here, Todorov's comments on Columbus's first impressions of Native Americans:

> The first characteristic of these people to strike Columbus is the absence of clothes—which in their turn symbolize culture . . . physically naked, the indians are also, to Columbus's eyes, deprived of all cultural property: they are characterized, in a sense, by the absence of customs, rights, religion (which has a certain logic, since for a man like Columbus, human beings wear clothes following their expulsion from Paradise, itself at the source of their cultural identity). (1984:34–35; see Mason 1990:171)

have—who, perhaps, desires deeply to become us. But these stories and lists construct a second face—our own face (see Lindstrom 1995). If the cultist desires to be modern, we thereby must also recognize ourselves as the focus of this reputed desire. We perceive in the cult images of who we are and of what our modernity consists. Cargo lists are the projection of *two* selves—ourself as well as that of the cultist. Lists of desires signify a Melanesian and a Western character both. They suggest a Melanesian future that is to be fashioned according to a supposed Western present.

Melanesians, so it makes sense, desire to dress themselves as do all civil humans. And the peculiar clothes, textiles, and pointed shoes with which we decorate our own bodies wear more comfortably on us when we see them featured prominently in cargo shopping lists.

WEAPONS

Listed Melanesian desires for guns, rifles, and ammunition, which appear 26 times in the inventories, might partially reflect colonialist fear and projected guilt. Melanesians are feared to desire the same firearms that Europeans used to dominate, and to yearn to turn these weapons against the colonial oppressor. Thus, a cargo list recorded in the 1933/34 Annual Report of the Territory of New Guinea specified "cases of meat, tobacco, loin cloths, rice, lamps and rifles. The rifles would be far more powerful than those used by the Administration" (1935:27).

However, one might also recall on-going metamorphoses in the image of the civil human during the 20th century—surely the bloodiest of times ever. Millions of men and women shouldered rifles and guns during two world wars and they took up arms again to kill one another in thousands of more limited conflicts. Powerful, if not always altogether convincing, political discourses of freedom and manhood have worked overtime to identify a man with his piece. The image of the firearm, today, oddly floats somewhere between that of common household utensil and icon of potency, individual authority and control. In effect, the location of firearms on cargo shopping lists serves the NRA project. Of course cargo cultists desire weapons. Nowadays, who doesn't?

FOOD

The 49 listings of food include 39 citations of tinned or otherwise packaged edibles (e.g., rice, flour, tea, sugar, milk, candy). The increasing urbanization and factory agriculture of our century have required that all of us—not just cultists—must often witlessly desire to eat tinned fish, bottled milk, Coca-Cola, and boxed sugars and teas. Although a variety of counter-discourses impugn the health and nutritional value of store-bought food, nearly all of us nowadays must go to market to eat. It is no surprise, then, that cultists likewise crave to leave their gardenstuffs behind for the packaged delights of the supermarket. As we swallow down what plops from tins, what pours from boxes, small worries might occasionally darken our alimentary pleasures. But we are relieved, perhaps, to learn that these same manufactured and packaged foods count among the most fervent desires of exotic cultists, heading their shopping lists as well as our own.

REFRIGERATORS

The 21 listings of refrigerators, at first glance, might appear to be one of the most curious ambitions of cultic desire. But, for us, the 20th-century refrigerator has a powerfully doubled impact as both metonym of technological progress and the focus of sociability and commensalism within the modern household. Solid white refrigerators concatenate a variety of images: the wonders of mass production; modernity and progress; the cleanliness of white enamel; and the psychological security of tomorrow's dinner. Joined, but not replaced, in recent years only by the television set, the refrigerator marks the bounds of the family unit, and the patterns of its depletion and replenishment mirror household economy and organization.

Melanesians also remark the existence of important social relationships with an exchange of food. But this food is in no manner refrigerated, nor do most people wish it to be so. Melanesians are farmers. They appreciate the agricultural origins of food. We are the ones who seek sustenance and comfort behind the white enameled door. Refrigerators, in Melanesia, have yet to come to symbolize human relations. Their frequent enumeration on Melanesian cargo shopping lists, however, naturalizes the peculiar status that they occupy within our own system of desire. (And the same, of course, might be said of the motor vehicle and the television.)

The imagined shopper who comes to mind, reading through this wonderful archive of cargo inventories and shopping lists, is an arm-toting, Coca-Cola drinking, flour-eating dreamer who stands in front of his refrigerator in pointed shoes. But is this a Melanesian cultist? Or is it me? Or you?

REFERENCES

Cameron, Roderick. 1964. *The Golden Haze: With Captain Cook in the South Pacific.* Cleveland and New York: World.

Evans, Julian. 1992. *Transit of Venus: Travels in the Pacific.* New York: Pantheon Books.

Goody, Jack. 1977. *The Domestication of the Savage Mind.* Cambridge, England: Cambridge University Press.

Hamilton, John. 1983. "The Cargo-Cult Chief and the Letters from a God." *Brisbane Courier-Mail*, 1 December, pp. 1–2.

Hermann, Bernard, & Joël Bonnemaison. 1975. *New Hebrides.* Papéete: Les Editions du Pacifique.

Illich, Ivan. 1971. *Deschooling Society.* New York: Harper and Row.

Lawrence, Peter. 1987. "Cargo Cult." In *The Encyclopedia of Religion*, Vol. 3, ed. by Mircea Eliade. New York: Macmillan.

Lindstrom, Lamont. 1993. *Cargo Cult: Strange Stories of Desire from Melanesia and Beyond.* Honolulu: University of Hawaii Press.

Lindstrom, Lamont. 1995. "Cargoism and Orientalism." In *Occidentalism: Images of the West*, ed. by J. Carrier. Oxford: Oxford University Press.

Mason, Peter. 1990. *Deconstructing America: Representations of the Other.* London: Routledge.

Peale, Norman Vincent. 1952. *The Power of Positive Thinking.* Englewood Cliffs, NJ: Prentice-Hall.

Priday, H. E. L. 1950. "'Jonfrum' Is New Hebridean 'Cargo Cult': Interesting History of this Native Movement on the Island of Tanna." *Pacific Islands Monthly* Vol. 20 (6, Jan): 67–70; Vol. 20 (7, Feb): 59–65.

Shears, Richard. 1980. *The Coconut War: The Crisis on Espiritu Santo.* Sydney: Cassell Australia.

Spufford, Francis. 1989. *The Chatto Book of Cabbages and Kings: Lists in Literature.* London: Chatto & Windus.

Territory of New Guinea. 1935. *Report to the Council of the League of Nations on the Administration of the Territory of New Guinea, from 1st July 1934, to 30th June, 1935.* Canberra: Australian Government Printer.

Todorov, Tzvetan. 1984. *The Conquest of America: The Question of the Other.* New York: Harper and Row.

Watt, Agnes C. P. 1896. *Twenty-five Years Mission Life on Tanna, New Hebrides.* Paisley: Parlane.

Williams, Francis E. 1977 [1923]. *"The Vailala Madness" and Other Essays.* Honolulu: University of Hawaii Press.

3

Language and Communication

One of the things that people spend a great deal of time doing is talking to one another. The reason they do so is simple—they have a great deal to communicate. For one thing, as social creatures, they need to let one another know how they are feeling and what they are up to at a given moment, so they can adjust their behavior in appropriate ways so as not to antagonize each other or operate at cross-purposes. For another, because they rely so heavily for survival on the learned body of knowledge we call culture, there is an extraordinary amount of information that must be passed from one person to another, and from one generation to the next. Of course, humans are not alone in their need to communicate, nor are they the only animals for whom learning plays an important role in their survival. In the past few decades, for example, studies of both captive and free living monkeys and apes have shown the importance of learned behavior in their lives and revealed hitherto unsuspected communicative abilities among them. Indeed, so highly developed are these abilities that several captive apes have been taught to converse with humans using such systems as American Sign Language, and some have even taught this to others of their kind. Yet, the sheer complexity of what humans must learn in order to function adequately requires some means of **communication** surpassing those normally used by monkeys and apes. Although the latter can be taught to "talk" in a variety of nonverbal ways, their language skills (so far) do not progress beyond those of a 2- to 3-year-old human child (Miles 1994:46). Furthermore, they do not normally develop to this point on their own. Humans, by contrast, are "programmed" by their biology to talk, and it is virtually impossible to prevent them from doing so. All normal individuals growing up in appropriate social environments will learn to talk at the proper time; precisely which language they learn to speak depends upon what is spoken by the people among whom they live.

Although spoken **language**—a system of sounds that, when put together according to certain rules, conveys meanings intelligible to all its speakers—is the primary means by which humans communicate, it is not their sole means of communication. Two others that accompany language are **paralanguage,** a system of extralinguistic noises that have meaning, and **kinesics,** a system of body motions used to convey messages. Both represent survivals of the gesture-call systems relied upon by other primates, such as monkeys and apes, to communicate their current states of being (contented, irritated, uncomfortable, sleepy, restless, and so forth) as well as their immediate intentions. Among humans, kinesics, or "body language," has received much attention and even popular interest. Paralanguage has received less attention in spite of our awareness of its importance, as signified by the phrase "It's not so much what she said as how she said it." As anthropologists O'Barr and Conley point out in their article, in courtroom proceedings *how* things are said is often more important than *what* is said.

Naturally enough, since humans rely primarily on language to communicate their hopes and aspirations, their upsets and concerns, and to transmit their accumulated wisdom from one generation to the next, specialists in the field of **linguistic anthropology** have devoted a great deal of time to its study. In addition to analyzing the structure of languages **(structural linguistics)** and their historical development **(historical linguistics),** they have investigated the important relationship between language and culture; for instance, how social variables such as class, gender, and status of the speaker will influence his or her use of a language **(sociolinguistics).** Such interests are represented in this chapter by the article by Salikoko S. Mufwene, a native of Zaire, who describes his reaction to the different usage of forms of address in the United States, as compared with his central African homeland. As he puts it: ". . . coming from my Third World background, there was more to be overwhelmed by than space-age technology."

The example of forms of address introduces another important point: Besides enabling us to communicate with one another, language serves other purposes as well. For one thing, it establishes boundaries between **social groups,** the members of which speak different languages or dialects of a particular language. Conversely, the imposition of one group's language or dialect upon another group has been a means by which one people has asserted its dominance over another.

The importance of language as an ethnic marker cannot be overestimated, and raises important issues of human rights. The fact is, to deprive a people of their language does more than rob them of their identity, for a people's language is uniquely tailored to express their particular culture's view of the world and to facilitate their customary ways of thinking. These issues are discussed in the article by the Mexican scholar Rodolfo Stavenhagen, excerpted from a presentation at a 1989 Geneva seminar organized by the United Nations Centre for Human Rights. Professor Stavenhagen is coordinator of a UN project on ethnic minorities and human social development.

REFERENCE

Miles, H. Lynn White. 1994. "Language and the Orang-utan: the Old Person of the Forest." In *The Great Ape Project,* ed. by Paola Cavalieri & Peter Singer. New York: St. Martins Press.

When a Juror Watches a Lawyer

William M. O'Barr and John M. Conley

William M. O'Barr has a joint professorship in the departments of cultural anthropology and sociology at Duke University and is adjunct professor of law at the University of North Carolina. He received his Ph.D. from Northwestern University in 1969. His research has involved peoples of Africa as well as the United States, and his interests include legal anthropology, sociolinguistics, and discourse analysis. He also researches the anthropology of advertising.

John M. Conley is a professor of law at the University of North Carolina, where he currently holds the Ivey Research Chair. He is also an adjunct professor in anthropology at Duke and practiced trial law for a number of years. His recent book, *Fortune and Folly,* is an anthropological look at institutional investors on Wall Street. Conley received his J.D. from Duke in 1977 and his Ph.D. in anthropology from Duke in 1980.

How things are said in court, as any successful trial lawyer knows, may be much more important than what is actually said.

Not only in the court, but in our everyday language, all of us have an intuitive notion that subtle differences in the language we use can communicate more than the obvious surface meaning. These additional communication cues, in turn, greatly influence the way our spoken thoughts are understood and interpreted. Some differences in courtroom language may be so subtle as to defy precise description by all but those trained in linguistic analysis. No linguistic training is necessary, however, to sense the difference between an effective and an ineffective presentation by a lawyer, a strong and a weak witness or a hostile versus a friendly exchange. New research on language used in trial courtrooms reveals that the subliminal messages communicated by seemingly minor differences in phraseology, tempo, length of answers and the like may be far more important than even the most perceptive lawyers have realized.

Two witnesses who are asked identical questions by the same lawyer are not likely to respond in the same way. Differences in manner of speaking, however, are usually overlooked by the court in its fact-finding quest. Once an initial determination of admissibility has been made, witnesses may follow their own stylistic inclinations within the broad bounds of the law of evidence.

"When a Juror Watches a Lawyer" by William M. O'Barr and John M. Conley, from *Barrister*. Reprinted with permission.

Scrutinize carefully the following pairs of excerpts from trial transcripts, and consider whether, as the law of evidence would hold, they are equivalent presentations of facts.

EXAMPLE 1

Q. What was the nature of your acquaintance with her?

A_1. We were, uh, very close friends. Uh, she was even sort of like a mother to me.

A_2. We were very close friends. She was like a mother to me.

EXAMPLE 2

Q. Now, calling your attention to the 21st day of November, a Saturday, what were your working hours?

A. Well, I was working from, uh, 7 a.m. to 3 p.m. I arrived at the store at 6:30 and opened the store at 7.

Compare this answer to the following exchange ensuing from the same question.

A. Well, I was working from 7 to 3.

Q. Was that 7 a.m.?

A. Yes.

Q. And what time that day did you arrive at the store?

A. 6:30.

Q. 6:30. And did, uh, you open the store at 7 o'clock?

A. Yes, it has to be opened.

EXAMPLE 3

Q. Now, what did she tell you that would indicate to you that she . . .

A. (interrupting) She told me a long time ago that if she called, and I knew there was trouble, to definitely call the police right away.

Compare the above with the slightly different version, where the lawyer completes his question before the witness begins answering.

Q. Now, what did she tell you that would indicate to you that she needed help?

A. She told me a long time ago that if she called, and I knew there was trouble, to definitely call the police right away.

Two years of study of language variation in a North Carolina trial courtroom, sponsored by the National Science Foundation, have led us to conclude that differences as subtle as these carry an impact which is probably as substantial as the factual variation with which lawyers have traditionally concerned themselves.

POWER LANGUAGE AND GETTING POINTS ACROSS

The three examples of differences in testimony shown here are drawn from separate experiments which the team has conducted. The study from which Example 1 is taken was inspired by the work of Robin Lakoff, a linguist from the University of California at Berkeley.

Lakoff maintains that certain distinctive attributes mark female speech as different and distinct from male styles. Among the characteristics she notes in "women's language" are:

- A high frequency of *hedges* ("I think . . . , It seems like . . . ." "Perhaps. . . ." "If I'm not mistaken . . .")
- *Rising intonation* in declarative statements (e.g., in answer to a question about the speed at which a car was going, "Thirty, thirty-five?" said with rising intonation as though seeking approval of the questioner)
- *Repetition* indicating insecurity
- *Intensifiers* ("very close friends" instead of "close friends" or just "friends")
- High frequency of *direct quotations* indicating deference to authority, and so on

We studied our trial tapes from the perspective of Lakoff's theory and found that the speech of many of the female witnesses was indeed characterized by a high frequency of the features she attributes to women's language. When we discovered that some male witnesses also made significant use of this style of speaking, we developed what we called a "power language" continuum. From powerless speech (having the characteristics listed above), this continuum ranged to relatively more powerful speech (lacking the characteristics described by Lakoff).

Our experiment is based on an actual ten-minute segment of a trial in which a prosecution witness under direct examination gave her testimony in a relatively "powerless" mode. We rewrote the script, removing most of the hedges, correcting intonation to a more standard declarative manner, minimizing repetition and intensifiers, and otherwise transforming the testimony to a more "powerful" mode.

From the point of view of the "facts" contained in the two versions, a court would probably consider the two modes equivalent. Despite this factual similarity, the experimental subjects found the two witnesses markedly different. The subjects rated the witness speaking in the powerless style significantly less favorably in terms of such evaluative characteristics as believability, intelligence, competence, likability and assertiveness.

To determine whether the same effects would carry over for a male witness speaking in "power" and "powerless" modes, we took the same script, made minor adjustments for sex of witness, and produced two more experimental tapes. As with females, subjects were less favorably disposed toward a male speaking in the powerless mode.

These results confirm the general proposition that how a witness gives testimony may indeed alter the reception it gets. Since most juries are assigned the task of deciding upon relative credibility of witnesses whose various pieces of testimony are not entirely consistent, speech factors which may affect a witness's credibility may be critical factors in the overall chemistry of the trial courtrooms.

These findings are not limited to a single study. Similar patterns have been discovered with other kinds of variation in presentational style.

Example 2 comes from a study of differences in the length of answers which a witness gives in the courtroom. Treatises on trial practice often advise allowing the witness to assume as much control over his testimony as possible during direct examination. Implicit in such advice is an hypothesis that relative control of the questioning and answering by lawyer versus witness may affect perception of the testimony itself.

To test this hypothesis we again selected a segment of testimony from an actual trial. The original testimony was rewritten so that, in one version, the witness gave short attenuated answers to the lawyer's probing questions. In the other version, the same facts were given by the witness in the form of longer, more complex answers to fewer questions by the lawyer.

BUT THEN, HOW LONG SHOULD A WITNESS SPEAK?

Contrary to our expectations, the form of answer did not affect the subjects' perception of the *witness*, but it did have a significant influence on the judgments about the *lawyer*. When the lawyer asked more questions to get the same information, subjects viewed him as more manipulative and allowing the witness less opportunity to present evidence.

The subjects' perceptions of the lawyer's opinion of his witness were also colored by the structure of the witness's answers; however, the differences were significant only when the witnesses were male. When more questions were asked by the lawyer, subjects believed the lawyer thought his witness was significantly less intelligent, less competent and less assertive.

On this point, then, standard trial practice theory is confirmed indirectly. The lawyer who finds it necessary to exert tight control over his witness will hurt his presentation by creating a less favorable impression of himself and suggesting that he has little confidence in the witness.

A LOT DEPENDS ON WHO INTERRUPTS WHOM

Example 3 is part of a study of interruptions and simultaneous talk in the courtroom. We wanted to know what effect a lawyer's interrupting a witness or a witness's interrupting a lawyer would have. Preparing a witness for a courtroom examination often includes an admonishment against arguing with the opposition lawyer during cross-examination, and a lawyer often advises his own witness to stop talking when he interrupts what the witness is saying.

To study some aspects of this complex phenomenon, we focused on the relative tendency of the lawyer and the witness to persist in speaking when the other party interrupts or begins to speak at the same time. This is one of the most subtle factors of language variation in the courtroom which we have studied, but, like the other differences, this too alters perception of testimony.

Working from the same original testimony, four experimental tapes were prepared: one in which there were no instances of simultaneous talk by lawyer and witness, one in which the witness primarily yielded to the lawyer during simultaneous talk by breaking off before completion of his statement, one in which the lawyer deferred to the witness by allowing the witness to talk whenever both began to talk at once, and finally one in which the frequency of deference by lawyer and witness to one another were about equal.

All four tapes are clearly "hostile" and "unfriendly" in tone. The three containing simultaneous speech, or overlaps between lawyer and witness, would be difficult to distinguish by a person untrained in linguistic analysis of sequencing of questions and answers. Yet these subtle differences in patterns of deference in overlapping speech can be and are perceived differently by experimental subjects.

Findings from this study, like those from the second experiment, show significant effects on the perception of the lawyer. Subject-jurors rate the lawyer as maintaining most control when no overlapping speech occurs. The lawyer's control over the examination of the witness is perceived to diminish in all those situations where both lawyer and witness talk at once.

Comparing the situation in which the lawyer persists to the one in which the witness persists, interesting results also emerge. When the lawyer persists, he is viewed not only as less fair to the witness but also as less intelligent than in the situation when the witness continues. The lawyer who stops in order to allow the witness to speak is perceived as allowing the witness significantly more opportunity to present his testimony in full.

The second and third experiments thus show speech style affecting perceptions of lawyers in critical ways. Modes of speaking which create negative impressions of lawyers may have severe consequences in the trial courtroom. In all adversarial proceedings, lawyers assume the role of spokesmen for their clients. Impressions formed about lawyers are, to some degree, also impressions formed about those whom they represent.

The implications of these findings may be most severe in those criminal trials where the defendants elect not to testify, but they apply as well to all situations where lawyers act as representatives of their clients.

THE FACT IS: A FACT MAY BE MORE THAN A FACT

While the results of these particular experiments are undoubtedly important for the practicing lawyer, we feel that the true significance of the project lies in its broader implications. In a variety of settings, we have shown that lay audiences pay meticulous attention, whether consciously or unconsciously, to subtle details of the language used in the trial courtroom.

Our results suggest that a fact is not just a fact, regardless of presentations; rather, the facts are only one of many important considerations which are capable of influencing the jury.

As noted earlier, the law of evidence has traditionally concerned itself primarily with threshold questions of admissibility. The guiding principles have always been held to be ensuring the reliability of evidence admitted and preventing undue prejudice to the litigants. If it is true that questions of style have impact comparable to that of questions of fact, then lawyers will have to begin to read such considerations into the law of evidence if they are to be faithful to its principles.

As judges and lawyers become increasingly sensitized to the potentially prejudicial effects of speech style, one remedy might be to employ cautionary instructions in an effort to control jury reactions. For example, might it not be appropriate for a court confronted with a witness speaking in an extreme variant of the powerless mode to instruct the jury not to be swayed by style in considering the facts?

Additionally, lawyers themselves might begin to give greater recognition to stylistic factors while addressing the jury during voire dire, opening statement and closing argument.

Lawyers are already accustomed to calling jurors' attention to such presentational features as extreme emotion in urging on them particular interpretations of the evidence. What we suggest is merely an extension of a familiar technique into newly explored areas. . . .

REFERENCES

Lakoff, Robin T. 1976. *Language and Woman's Place*. New York: Octagon Books.

Lakoff, Robin T. 1990. *Talking Power: The Politics of Language in Our Lives*. New York: Basic Books.

Forms of Address: How Their Social Functions May Vary

Salikoko S. Mufwene

Salikoko S. Mufwene, a native of Zaire, came to the United States in 1974 as a graduate student at the University of Chicago. He received his Ph.D. in linguistics in 1979 and is now professor of linguistics at his old alma mater. Previously he taught at the University of the West Indies in Jamaica and at the University of Georgia. Among his research interests are the relationship between language and culture, as well as pidgin and Creole speech.

The point of view presented in this essay is primarily Bantu, one of the several groups of sub-Saharan Africans typically characterized as black. Moreover, the outlook is that of a person who grew up in the transition from colonial Zaire (then the Belgian Congo, in central Africa) to postindependence Zaire, in an education system that fosters an interesting coexistence of colonial European and local African cultures. From a sociolinguistic point of view, French, inherited from the colonial days as the official language and the medium of education from the fourth grade up to higher education, has been adapted to convey this marriage of African and colonial European cultures heavily anchored in the African tradition.

In this essay, I show how this background affected my reaction over fifteen years ago to English forms of address, as used at a major midwestern American university. With time, I have also learned that the customs described in this essay do not apply universally to the overall American society. However, I think that these first impressions reflect best my then unacculturated perception of a facet of American culture.

The term "form of address" is used in this essay as much for names, like *Peter, Mary,* and *Bob,* as for titles, like *Mr., Mrs., Dr.,* and *Professor,* which are normally used before last or full names, for example, *Mr. (Paul) Simon* or *Dr. (Alice) Rosenfeld.* The term is also used for other titles such as *sir* and *ma'am,* normally used without a name; for kinship terms such as *Dad, Mom,* and *son* used to address relatives; for pet names such as *buttercup* and *cupcake;* or for any word used to address

"Forms of Address: How Their Social Functions May Vary" by Salikoko S. Mufwene, from *Distant Mirrors: America as a Foreign Culture,* ed. by Philip R. DeVita & James D. Armstrong. Belmont, CA: Wadsworth. Reprinted by permission of the author.

a person. Ethnographically, these forms of address specify the relation between the speaker and the addressee (for example, pals, professionals, parent-child, lovers) and the terms of their interaction (for example, distant, close, intimate), depending sometimes on the specific circumstances of the communication. To take an American example, a person named *Alice Rosenfeld* may be addressed in various ways, depending on context. She may be addressed as *Dr. Rosenfeld* in formal professional interaction, as *Mrs.* or *Ms. Rosenfeld* in situations where she is not well known, as *Mom* by her children, as *Alice* by her husband and colleagues in places where professional relations are not formal, and as *dear, darling,* or *honey* by her husband in intimate interaction.

I will restrict my observations on the American system to the usage of forms of address after the first time people have been introduced to each other. I will ignore those situations where preestablished relationships might allow usage of pet names and kinship titles, for instance, the title *uncle* extended to friends of the speaker's parents or blood uncles. However, it will help to provide more general background information about myself at this point, so that the reader may understand my original shock at how Americans address each other, at least at the university I attended.

In my Bantu background, addressees' names are often avoided in quite a variety of situations in order to express deference and/or intimacy. For instance, in the Bantu vernacular languages, people of the same age as one's parents are addressed by the same titles as the parents of the same sex, with the terms *papa* or *tata* (father) or *mama* (mother) prefixed to their names to express deference, for example, *Papa Kaniki* or *Mama Moseka.* These honorifics (that is, special forms of address for respect) are also used alone, without a name, to express both deference and intimacy when the speaker knows the addressee closely. For instance, in Kikongo-Kituba (my regional lingua franca), a close relation of the speaker's family who is of approximately the same age as, or older than, his or her father may be addressed as follows: *Papa, ebwe?* (Papa, how are you?).

When used alone to address strangers, the honorifics *papa* and *mama* are simple markers of politeness corresponding to the English honorifics *sir* and *ma'am,* used without a name, or to the honorifics *Mr., Mrs., Ms., Dr.,* and the like prefixed to the last names in formal interaction. These honorifics also are often used for addresses of the age group of the speaker's children as affective forms of address, corresponding to, for instance, the use of *son* by a nonkin. Thus, the sentence *Papa, ebwe?* used by an adult to a child is affective and may be translated idiomatically as "How are you, son/darling/dear?" All these Bantu forms of address fit in a system in which addressees' names are generally avoided, a practice to which I return below.

People of the age group of the speaker's older siblings are addressed in Kikongo-Kituba either by prefixing the kinship honorific *yaya* (older sibling) to their names for deference or by using the title alone for both deference and intimacy, for example, *Yaya Kalala.* Ethnographically, this corresponds in American English to addressing such a close relation by his or her first name or nickname.

A number of older male persons are assimilated to uncles and are addressed on the same pattern as above with the kinship honorific *noko* (uncle), for example, *Noko Mukoko.* However, note that many of the people addressed with this honorific would not be addressed with the honorific *uncle* in American English, since they may not be close friends of the speaker's parents or blood uncles.

Adult close friends often address one another by their professional titles, if these are considered as achievements (for example, *Munganga ebwe?* [Dr. (MD), how are you?]), or by their nicknames or play names (for example, *Mbongo mpasi, ebwe?* [Hard Money, how are you?]). This custom is to express intimacy. In the case of professional titles, close associates bear the responsibility of setting up examples for others to follow; deference starts at home. Once more, usage of addressees' names is generally restricted to situations where it is absolutely necessary to make clear which person is being addressed, for instance, when more than one person in the same setting may be addressed by the same honorific.

Much of the same behavior is carried on in local French, except that the honorifics *monsieur* (sir), *madame* (ma'am), and *mademoiselle* (miss) are generally substituted for the traditional honorifics derived from kin terms. More recently, the honorifics *citoyen* (male citizen) and *citoyenne* (female citizen) were used by a political-ideological decree from the government in 1971 to distinguish the natives from foreigners.[1] Like the Bantu honorifics based on kin terms, they are generally used alone without the addressees' names. In all such cases, it is generally thought that only deference, not social distance, is expressed. Thus, translations with western European honorifics generally distort the ethnographic meaning somewhat, since they suggest social distance where none is suggested in either the Bantu forms of address with honorifics for deference or the local French adaptations to the system. For instance, the translation of the local French sentence *Suivez-moi, citoyen(ne)* (Follow me, citoyen(ne)) either becomes odd if *citoyen(ne)* is also translated as *citizen* or distorted if it is translated idiomatically as *sir* or *ma'am.* In the latter case, the idiomatic translation assigns higher status to the addressee, whereas the honorific *citoyen(ne)* does not.

Last, aside from the fact that names are generally avoided, it matters little in the Bantu system whether the first name or the surname is used. In any case, to make up for the tradition, speakers of local French often use the traditional Bantu honorifics, the kind of thing that is done less comfortably in a native French setting, unless all the interactants are from the same Bantu background. Note also that, as a rule, French requires that the polite pronoun *vous,* rather than the intimate pronoun *tu,* be used to address people concomitantly with the above titles. In fact, *vous* in the construction *Vous pouvez partir, monsieur/madame* (You may leave, sir/ma'am) assigns high status to the addressee. Using the traditional Bantu honorifics makes allowance for the intimate or status-free pronoun *tu,* which in a construction such as *Tu peux partir, papa* (You may leave, father) conveys both deference and intimacy or lack of status, depending on the case. Using *vous* together with *papa* makes explicit either the higher status of the addressee or the speaker's decision to establish social distance in the interaction.

In my American experience, I had to learn new norms of conduct. Honorifics based on age, and often even on rank, are commonly avoided.[2] My shock started in my first class, when the professor asked to be addressed as Jerry. Most of the other professors did likewise, regardless of age.[3] I found out that generally people do not give their titles when introducing themselves. More often than not, they either give only the first name or ask to be addressed by the first name. Further, the first names have usually been clipped to monosyllabics or disyllabics; for example, *Fred* is short for *Frederick* and *Ed* is short for *Edward.* Sometimes first names have been replaced by seemingly unrelated short nicknames; for example, *Bob* and *Bobby* are short for *Robert* and *Ted* is short for *Edward.* The native French transitional address system according to which persons are addressed by their honorifics and the pronoun *vous,* until there is a tacit or explicit agreement to convert to an intimate and informal mode of address, does not exist in America.

There is more to this American system of address. Foreigners are rebaptized, so to speak! The often long and "complicated" first names are replaced by nicknames. Ever since my first class, I have usually been addressed as *Sali*. The few Americans that say "Salikoko" either find the name "musical" or want to show off their familiarity with foreign names, in contrast with the regular reaction "I can't say that one."

However, addressing people by their first names does not necessarily mean a close relationship or intimacy. As suggested above, there are ways of expressing closeness or intimacy, but these will not be discussed here. The American system of address is basically a sign of informality, which is created from the onset of a social relationship, much sooner than I would have expected in the mixed cultural background I came from.

I also learned something else about names. As noted above, it makes little difference in the Bantu system whether one is addressed by one's first name or by one's surname, whenever names must or can be used. Names are typically avoided when addressing some relations, such as close friends, and names are taboo in addressing or referring to one's own parents. In the case of friends, professional titles or descriptive nicknames dealing with events in one's life are normally used. Name avoidance is a sign of closeness or intimacy. It is considered disrespectful to address ascending and descending in-laws by their names. Their kinship titles must be used not only to express deference but also to reassert the close social bond of the extended family by marriage. The expectation to use kinship honorifics in this case applies even to spouses' relatives when they interact among themselves, for instance, when the wife's cousin interacts with the husband's cousin.

The Bantu custom is in sharp contrast with the American custom of using first names or nicknames between close friends and with most in-laws.[4] In the beginning, I found it bizarre to see ascending and descending in-laws (fathers- and mothers-in-law and sons- and daughters-in-law, respectively) address each other by their first names and to see them interact casually with each other. (In my background, ascending and descending in-laws maintain avoidance relationships.) The new custom gave me the impression that Americans did not care much about these special, affined ties and that all social relations were of the same kind. I also assumed then that Americans did not distinguish between acquaintances and friends. In addition, I thought that Americans became personal with people they had just met rather quickly. (This impression was due essentially to the stereotypical French address system I had learned in school in Zaire.) As noted above, acculturation to American ways has now taken the original shock away. However, coming from my Third World background, there was more to be overwhelmed by than space-age technology.

ACKNOWLEDGMENTS

I am grateful to James Armstrong, Kathleen MacQueen, and Jennifer Eason for feedback on drafts of this essay. I alone assume full responsibility for its shortcomings.

NOTES

1. This custom was patterned on the French system during Napoleon Bonaparte's regime in the nineteenth century to suggest an egalitarian revolution in the way Zaireans interact with each other. The corruption and the socioeconomic discriminatory system it was meant to eradicate have grown stronger, starting from the political leadership, and a reactionary trend has now reverted to the current French forms of address with *monsieur* (sir), *madame* (ma'am), or *mademoiselle* (miss) when formality is required.

2. I will disregard here professional titles such as *Dr.* (for medical doctors) that act as part of the name in professional settings. Constraints are more complex here regarding when the title may be dropped.

3. There are apparently some exceptions to this observation. In my graduate school experience, I knew of some professors in their sixties that most students addressed as Mr. _____ , though their much younger colleagues still addressed them by their first names.

4. I do not wish to ignore cases of assimilation where in-laws are addressed by the same kinship titles the spouse uses for them. However, coming from my background, another peculiarity here is that the assimilation applies almost only to the speaker relative to his or her spouse's relatives; his or her own relatives do not assimilate and show intimacy or closeness by using first names.

Language and Social Identity

Rodolfo Stavenhagen

Rodolfo Stavenhagen, who has an international reputation as a development anthropologist, is on the faculty of El Colegio de Mexico. He is also coordinator of the United Nations university project on ethnic minorities and human and social development.

Languages shape culture and society in many important ways. They are, for example, the vehicles for literary and poetic expressions, the instruments whereby oral history, myths and beliefs are shared by a community, and transmitted from generation to generation. Just as an Indian without land is a dead Indian (as the World Council of Indigenous Peoples states), so also an ethnic community without a language is a dying community. This was well understood by the romantic nationalists of the 19th and 20th centuries who strove for a revival of "national" languages as part of the politics of nationalism.

On the other hand, language has always been an instrument of conquest and empire. Nebrija, a 15th-century Castillian grammarian and adviser to Queen Isabella I of Spain, published his Spanish grammar the same year Columbus reached America, and he advised his queen to use the language as an instrument for the good government of the empire. Both the Spanish Crown and the Church took the advice to heart—and Spanish became one of the universal languages of the modern world. So did English, of course, for the British Empire knew well the power of the word as an instrument of world power.

In the process of colonization, the languages of the colonized peoples—especially if unwritten—were usually downgraded to mere "dialects," a term which connotes something less than a full-fledged structured language, and therefore casts doubt on the status of the culture which uses it. Thus indigenous and tribal peoples are still widely considered today to speak only dialects and not languages—a position frequently shared by government bureaucrats.

This is, of course, linguistic nonsense, but it carries a political message. As some anonymous wit has expressed it: a language is a dialect with an army. Or, to put it in another way, a dominant group is able to impose its language on subordinate groups. Linguistic dominance is more often than not an expression of political and economic domination. To be sure, there are exceptions: in Africa, Asia and the Caribbean, there are a number of *linguae francae,* vehicular languages used for trade and commerce which do not necessarily denote political domination.

In the predominant statist view, stressing national unity, assimilation and development, the languages of indigenous and tribal peoples have usually been destined to disappear. Government policies have generally been designed to help this process along. In most countries, indigenous languages are not given legal recognition, are not used in official administrative and judicial dealings, and are not taught in schools. The people who do use them are discriminated against and treated by the nonindigenous as outsiders, foreigners, barbarians, primitives, and so on.

Very often, the men of a tribe or indigenous community, who move around in the outside world for economic reasons, learn the official or national language of a country and become bilingual. Women tend to be more monolingual, which increases their isolation and the discrimination which they suffer. Small children, before school age, speak the maternal language—but often, as soon as they start school, are not allowed to speak it in class. Observers have noted that this can create serious psychological and learning problems among the school-age children of many indigenous and tribal peoples. Indeed because of language and other forms of discrimination, families sometimes avoid sending their children to official or missionary schools at all.

A United Nations examination of language practices noted that the policies followed by a great many governments were based on earlier assumptions that "indigenous populations, cultures and languages would

"Language and Social Identity" by Rodolfo Stavenhagen, from United Nations *Work in Progress,* Vol. 13, No. 2, December 1990.

disappear naturally or by absorption into other segments of the population and the national culture." Now, however, judging by their effects, such policies are beginning to be recognized as not well grounded; public schooling directed toward the achievement of these policies has been severely questioned.

As a result of policies of persecution and general attitudes of discrimination against them, many indigenous peoples have internalized the negative attitudes of the dominant society against their languages and cultures. Particularly when they leave their communities, they tend to deny their identity and feel ashamed of being "aboriginal," or "native" or "primitive."

But hiding an identity is not always possible, given that many ethnic and cultural differences are accompanied by biological distinctions. This has been particularly the case in European settler societies where the biological differences between the upper classes and the indigenous populations are particularly visible. It is less so in societies which have undergone a process of racial intermarriage and mixing, as in many Asian and Latin American countries.

In recent years, indigenous and tribal peoples have begun to resist the forced disappearance of their languages and cultures. And there has been a slow but growing awareness among social scientists, humanists, educators and even politicians that the maintenance of indigenous languages within the concept of cultural pluralism is not necessarily undesirable for a given country.

One of the questions being debated currently among linguistic specialists is whether language rights should be considered human rights. Article 27 of the International Covenant on Civil and Political Rights establishes that persons belonging to ethnic, religious or linguistic minorities shall not be denied the right to use their own language. However, organizations of indigenous peoples around the world refuse to be categorized among "ethnic minorities." This is one of the reasons why a specific declaration of indigenous rights is being prepared in the specialized UN bodies.

Language rights certainly seem to be a major issue among indigenous organizations. At the regional level, for example, periodic inter-American indigenist congresses (which are affiliated with the Organization of American States) have reaffirmed for several years the linguistic rights of the indigenous populations in the Western Hemisphere. UNESCO has also underlined the importance of the use of vernacular languages as an integral part of the cultural policies of states, particularly as regards education for minority groups. A number of countries have recently changed their traditional postures of discrimination against, and the neglect of, indigenous and tribal minority languages, and have designed policies to protect and promote these languages.

In a number of countries, indigenous organizations—and sometimes sympathetic governments—are experimenting with new linguistic and educational policies which take indigenous claims into account. In order to teach the vernacular language, however, many unwritten indigenous languages have had to be turned into written tongues. Alphabets have had to be prepared; educational materials in the vernacular have had to be provided, and teachers have had to be trained.

But this can be a lengthy and complicated process, and among educators and government officials the debates continue as to the relative merits of one or another kind of educational system—monolingual or multilingual. In countries where there exist myriad small indigenous linguistic groups, governments argue that such educational innovations are costly and basically inefficient. In addition, it is often feared that fragmenting the educational systems along linguistic lines is a potential threat to national unity. In these countries, if a majority national language exists, government policy tends to favour teaching only the national or official language.

In other countries, where the indigenous communities are large—and particularly if they have a certain amount of political clout—the education in indigenous languages is more likely to become accepted. In most countries where indigenous language schooling is taking root, bilingual education tends to be the norm. The indigenous language is taught together with the official or national language.

Just what the pedagogical mix between the various languages is depends on local conditions. Some authors consider formal schooling in an indigenous language as merely a step towards the appropriation of the official or national language. Others consider it as an end in itself—which is what the indigenous peoples themselves claim. In most countries, the teaching of an indigenous language is carried out only at the lower levels of elementary schooling. In others it also covers up through secondary levels and higher technical schools.

A linked, but much more complicated, educational problem is making bilingual schooling truly bicultural or intercultural. School children in urban industrial environments formally learn about their own larger "national" culture. Children in indigenous schools must take the reverse path: learning about their own particular cultures and identities, along with what they are taught about their "total society." This poses a formidable task for educational planners as to curriculum development, preparation of textbooks, reading and audio-visual materials, and so forth.

Indigenous peoples have been claiming the right to establish and control their own educational institutions, which means exercising control over their own curriculum, and educational contents. In some countries this is being achieved, and, in many areas, interesting educational experiments are taking place. In other countries—and particularly in the poorer third world countries—this must be the government's responsibility. But, as I have noted, governments are not always eager to undertake such innovation, particularly because they have been identified so long with assimilationist approaches.

The individual human rights spelled out in the Universal Declaration of Human Rights are now, forty years after their proclamation, generally accepted as international *customary* law. Obviously, indigenous peoples enjoy these same rights. There is a growing consensus, however, that the various international human rights instruments are not enough to guarantee the survival and protection of indigenous peoples around the world—particularly in the face of accelerated economic, social and cultural change. Thus the need for the definition of *collective* economic, social and cultural human rights is now becoming increasingly recognized.

4

Psychological Anthropology

In 1925, a young anthropology graduate student named Margaret Mead set out for Samoa to test a theory widely accepted at the time: that the biological changes of adolescence could not be accomplished without a great deal of psychological and social stress. Three years later, she published a book that was to become a classic, *Coming of Age in Samoa: A Study of Primitive Youth for Western Civilization.* Although the work later was subjected to some criticism, it is generally credited as establishing culture and personality as a specialty within **cultural anthropology.** Originally concerned with the effects of different child-rearing practices on the formation of adult personalities, the specialty has since developed into the broader one of **psychological anthropology.**

Since culture is learned, rather than biologically inherited, it is only natural that anthropologists should have become interested in *how* culture is learned. Initially, anthropologists thought that the different ways in which societies raised their children ought to result in adult personalities that differed distinctively from one culture to another. Perhaps the most famous (and extreme) statement of this point of view was Ruth Benedict's attempt to categorize whole cultures in terms of certain personality types. In her best-selling book *Patterns of Culture,* published in 1934 (and still in print), she characterized the Kwakiutl Indians of North America's northwest coast as "Dionysian," the Zuni Indians of the southwestern United States as "Apollonian," and the Dobuans of New Guinea as "Paranoid." Aside from the fact that her labels reflect the biases of Western culture, what she overlooked was the range of variation to be seen in any culture. For example, to characterize the Zuni as "Apollonian," she focused on their distrust of individualism and rejection of excess

and disruptive psychological states, while ignoring such seemingly "Dionysian" practices as sword swallowing and walking over hot coals.

What we now know is that no culture can be characterized in terms of a single personality structure exhibited by all or even a majority of adults. Because each individual is born with a particular genetic potential, and because no two individuals have *precisely* the same childhood experiences, as adults their personalities show considerable variability. On the other hand, it is true that each culture does hold up a particular ideal toward which individuals should aspire. That these ideals may vary considerably from one culture to another is illustrated in the article by Amparo B. Ojeda. In her own Filipino culture, children are raised to be obedient to authority, to respect elders, to recognize the primacy of the family over the individual, and to strive for harmony and "togetherness." This **dependence training,** which promotes compliance and dependence on one's domestic group, contrasts with the **independence training** that is stressed in the United States, which promotes independent, assertive behavior on the part of children, as they are taught to be self-reliant and able to look out for their own self-interests. Needless to say, it is difficult for people raised in one way not to regard the other as somehow "bizarre."

Greatly though a society may value one set of ideals in the abstract, its practices do not always live up to the ideal. In the United States, for example, in spite of the great value set on personal independence, authority often takes precedence in particular situations, as illustrated by Gottlieb's paper on childbirth. Although pregnancy and childbirth are not diseases, in the United States people generally behave as if they were.

In pregnancy an emphasis is often placed on suffering, and, just as sickness prevents one's full participation in ordinary daily activities, so are pregnancy and motherhood often considered incompatible with everyday work. In fact, expectant mothers are expected to submit to the authority of the medical establishment and do as they are told. Moreover, the birth itself typically takes place in a hospital, an institution otherwise dedicated to treatment of people who have genuine illnesses. As Gottlieb shows, pregnancy and childbirth do not have to be seen as "sickness," nor does a mother-to-be necessarily have to assume the status of "passive victim" even in the United States. To assert her independence in the face of medical authority, however, is no easy thing.

Given their interest in the relationship between childhood experiences and personality, it was inevitable that anthropologists early on would develop an interest in **psychoanalytic theory,** with its emphasis on the importance of early childhood experiences. One problem with psychoanalytic theory, however, is that

its concepts have often been based in assumptions of Western culture. Another is that, clinical studies to the contrary notwithstanding, psychoanalytic theorists have done little systematic testing through recourse to cross-cultural data. Many of the early culture and personality studies carried out by anthropologists were explicit tests of psychoanalytic theory. Among some anthropologists, interest in a psychoanalytic approach continues today. It is represented in this chapter by anthropologist/folklorist Alan Dundes's article on football, which he sees as a kind of ritual **homosexuality** in which sexual acts are carried out in symbolic form by males against other males. Thus, he likens the game to adolescent **male initiation rites** in many non-Western cultures that involve homosexual activity.

REFERENCES

Benedict, Ruth. 1934. *Patterns of Culture*. Boston: Houghton Mifflin.
Mead, Margaret. 1928. *Coming of Age in Samoa: A Psychological Study of Primitive Youth for Western Civilization*. New York: Morrow.

Growing Up American: Doing the Right Thing

Amparo B. Ojeda

Amparo B. Ojeda is a native Filipina who is now associate professor of anthropology and linguistics at Loyola University, Chicago. After completing an MA in English literature from the University of San Carlos in the Philippines, she came to the United States for an MS in linguistics from Georgetown University. Her Ph.D. in anthropology was earned at San Carlos in 1975. She has carried out fieldwork in the Philippines and in Chicago, where she is studying the adjustment of Filipino immigrants in the metropolitan area.

The earliest and closest encounter that I had with Americans, and a most superficial brush with their culture, goes back to my childhood days when an American family moved into our neighborhood. I used to gaze at the children, a boy and a girl, who were always neatly dressed and who would romp around their fenced front yard. Not knowing their names, I, together with a cousin, used to call them, *"Hoy, Americano!"* (Hey, American!), and they themselves soon learned to greet us with "Hey Filipino!" That was as far as our "acquaintance" went because in no time at all they were gone, and we never again heard about them.

That brief encounter aroused my curiosity. I wanted to know something more about the "Americanos." What kind of people are they? What food do they eat? Where is America? As time passed, I learned about America—about the people and about some aspects of their lifestyle—but my knowledge was indirect. The opportunity to experience the world of the "Americano" directly was long in coming, and when it did I was gripped with a sense of ambivalence. How would I fare in a strange and foreign land with an unfamiliar culture? That was how I finally found myself on the plane that would bring me on the first leg of my cultural sojourn to Hawaii.

Excited as I was, I could hear my heart thumping, and apprehension came over me. Suddenly, the thought hit me: I have journeyed far from home, away from the comforts and familiarity of my culture. You see, in this trip, my first outside of my homeland, I did not come as an anthropologist to do fieldwork. I came

"Growing Up American: Doing the Right Thing" by Amparo B. Ojeda, from *Distant Mirrors: America as a Foreign Culture*, ed. by Philip R. DeVita & James D. Armstrong. Belmont, CA: Wadsworth, 1993. Reprinted by permission Amparo B. Ojeda.

as a graduate student to study linguistics. Seven years later I would be an anthropologist. But I am getting ahead of myself.

My host family during my brief two-week stay in Honolulu was waiting at the airport. The whole family was there! The children's beaming faces and the family's warm and gracious greetings gave me a sense of assurance that everything was going to be fine. "There's nothing to it," we Fulbright scholars were reassured during a briefing on aspects of adjustment to American life and culture. So there I was in Hawaii, the first leg of my cultural sojourn (I stayed in the Midwest for another four weeks of orientation, before proceeding east to do graduate work), equipped with a theoretical survival kit designed and guaranteed to work. I would later discover that there were discrepancies between the ideal procedures and techniques and day-to-day behavior.

The differences between my culture and American culture became evident in the first few hours after my arrival. On our way out of the air terminal, the children began to fuss: "I'm hungry," "I'm tired," "I'm thirsty," "I want to go to the bathroom!" Over the whining and fidgeting of the children, my hosts and I tried to carry on a conversation but to no avail. Amazingly, despite the constant interruptions, the adults displayed considerable tolerance and patience. No voice was raised, nor harsh words spoken. I vividly recall how, as children, we were reminded never to interrupt while adults were talking, and to avoid annoying behavior, especially when in the company of adults, whether these people were kin, friends, or strangers.

We left the main highway, drove on a country road, and eventually parked by a Howard Johnson restaurant. The children did not need any bidding at all. They ran inside the restaurant in search of a table for us. I was fascinated by their quite independent and assertive behavior (more of this, later). I had originally been feeling dizzy and drowsy from the long plane ride, but I wasn't anymore. My "cultural" curiosity was aroused by the children's youthful showmanship, or so I thought. As soon as we were all seated, a young man came to hand us menus. The children made their own choices. Not feeling hungry at all, but wanting to show appreciation, I settled for a cup of soup. When the food finally came, I was completely shocked by the portions each child had. I wondered if they could eat it all. Just as I feared, they left their portions only partially eaten. What a waste, I thought. I remembered one of my father's gems of thought: "Take only what you can eat, and make sure to eat the last morsel on your plate." I must confess that I felt very bad looking at mounds of uneaten food. How can so much food be wasted? Why were children allowed to order their food themselves instead of Mom and Dad doing it for them? Was it a part of independence training? Or were Mom and Dad simply indulgent of their children's wants? I did not have any answers, but I surmised that it wasn't going to be easy understanding the American way. Neither would it be easy accepting or adjusting to American customs. I realized later that my difficulty was brought about by my cultural bias and naïveté. Given the situation, I expected my own familiar behavioral/cultural response. For instance, in the Philippines, as well as in many other Asian countries, children are rarely allowed, if at all, to "do their own thing" without the consent of their parents. Consultation with parents, older siblings, aunts and uncles, or grandparents is always sought. In America, I found out that from an early age, a person is encouraged to be independent, to make up his or her mind, and to stand up for his or her rights. Individualism is encouraged among the American youth, whereas among Asians, including Filipinos, group unity, togetherness, and harmony are valued.

Values such as obedience to authority (older people are vested with authority) and respect for elders are seriously observed and practiced. The young address their elders using terms of respect. Among the Tagalog, the particle *po* (sir, ma'am) or *opo* (yes sir, yes ma'am) is always used. Not to do so is considered rude. Children do not call anybody older by their first names. This deference to age contrasts sharply with the American notions of egalitarianism and informality.

American children, I observe, are allowed to call older people by their first names. I recall two interesting incidents, amusing now but definitely bothersome then. The first incident took place in the university cafeteria. To foster collegiality among the faculty and graduate students, professors and students usually ate lunch together. During one of these occasions, I heard a student greet a teacher, "Hey Bob! That was a tough exam! You really gave us a hard time, buddy!" I was stunned. I couldn't believe what I heard. All I could say to myself was, "My God! How bold and disrespectful!"

Not long afterward, I found myself in a similar scenario. This time, I was with some very young children of new acquaintances. They called to say hello and to ask if I could spend the weekend with the family. At their place, I met more people, young and not so young. Uninhibited, the children took the liberty of introducing me to everybody. Each child who played the role of "introducer" would address each person by his or her first name. No titles such as "Mr.," "Mrs." or "Miss" were used; we were simply introduced as "Steve, this is Amparo" and "Amparo, this is Paula." Because I was not acquainted with the sociolinguistics of American communicative style, this took me quite by surprise. I was not prepared for the reality of being addressed as the children's equal. In my own experience, it took me some time to muster courage before I could call my senior colleagues by their first names.

A somewhat similar occurrence happened many years later. I had impressed on my little girl the proper and polite way to address older people, that is, for her always to say "Mr." or "Mrs." before mentioning their first names and family names. I used to prod and remind her often that it was the right thing to do. Imagine my surprise and embarrassment when one day I heard her greet our next-door neighbor saying "Hi Martha!" I asked her why she greeted her that way. She readily answered, "Mommy, Martha told me not to call her Mrs. _____, just Martha!" What could I say? Since then, she was always called Martha, but I had qualms each time I heard my daughter greet her. In the Philippines, older people, regardless of their status in life, whether they are relatives or strangers, are always addressed using respectful terms such as *mang* (title for an elderly man), *iyo* (abbreviated variant for *tiyo*, or uncle, a title for a male relative but also used to address someone who is elderly), *aling* (respectful title for an older or elderly woman), and *manang* (a regional variant for *aling*). However, one gets used to doing things in a certain way after a while. So did I! After all, isn't that what adaptation is all about? But my cultural adventure or misadventure did not end here. This was only a prelude.

I was introduced into American culture from the periphery, which provided me with only a glimpse of the people's life-style, their passing moods and attitudes, and their values and ideas. I did not have the time, effort, or desire to take a long hard look at the cultural environment around me. I returned to the Philippines with some notions about American culture. If I have another chance, I told myself, I want to check it out judiciously and with objectivity. Seven years later, an opportunity presented itself. I was back in the "good old U.S.A.," this time to stay. I humored myself with the thought that I was smarter, wiser, and better prepared for challenges. I did not expect any serious problems. If there were problems, they would be inconsequential and therefore less stressful. This was far from the truth, however!

This time I was not alone against a whole new world. I had become a mother and was raising my child while virtually swimming against the current of cultural values that were not my own. True, there are clusters of universal human values to which everybody adheres. But it is likewise true that certain values are distinctive to a culture. Here lay the crux of an important problem that I needed to resolve. How was I going to bring up my child? Did I want her to grow up American, or did I want her to be a reflection and/or extension of myself, culturally speaking? The longer I pondered on these nagging questions, the more I began to realize that they were rather unfair questions. There were no easy answers.

There was, however, one thing of which I was certain: I wanted the best for my child, that is, the best of two worlds, America and my own. To do this, there were choices to be made. Predictably, I found myself straddling between two cultures, my right hand not knowing what my left hand was doing. At times, I found myself engaged in a balancing act in an effort to understand American culture without jeopardizing my cultural ways. Thus, alternatively, I would be strongly assertive and modestly defensive when my peculiar beliefs and actions were questioned.

Two incidents remain fresh in my mind. Briefly, someone made her observations very clearly to me by her remarks: "I see you always walk your daughter to and from school every day. . . . You know, many children in the neighborhood walk to school unaccompanied by adults. Why don't you let your daughter walk with them to school? She will learn to be on her own if you let go."

Another woman, some years later, asked me whether my daughter had started to drive, to which I answered "No." Surprised, she asked how my daughter could get around (to parties, movies, and so on). She remarked, "It would be easy for her and for you if she started taking driving lessons and got her own car." Forthright remarks! Fair criticism?

These two incidents bring into sharp focus the contrast between Filipino culture and American culture in the area of socialization. It is plain to see that in these instances, I am perceived as controlling and reprimanding, whereas the other person (American) is viewed as sociable, egalitarian, and indulgent. Because of the American emphasis on self-reliance and inde-

pendence, relationships between the children and the (Asian) Filipino mother are often interpreted as overdependent. Mothers are often perceived as overprotective. This observation results from unfamiliarity with the traditional family dynamics of the (Asian) Filipino family. In order to avoid a distorted perception of one culture by another, it is extremely important that the uniqueness and cultural distinctiveness of a culture be explored, recognized, and respected for what it is. Otherwise, that which is not familiar, and therefore not clearly understood, would be viewed as "bizarre," although it is completely meaningful to members of another culture.

Among the Filipinos, life is governed by traditions that do not stress independence and autonomy of the individual. The family surpasses the individual. Hierarchical roles define each member's position in the network of relationships. These relationships are strictly prescribed, such as the relationship between children and parents, between father and children, and between mother and children. For instance, the mother plays a paramount role in the nurturance of the children. The burden of the child's well-being rests on the mother.

Going back to the heart of the problem—that is, the issue of childrearing values—I have made a conscious choice, and in doing so, my values, beliefs, and actions have been brought into question. I have reassured myself that there is no need to worry as long as my child benefits from the quality of life I have prayerfully sought and arduously worked for.

At this point, I come full circle to the question: How am I doing as a parent, as a mother? Did I do the right thing? Is my daughter growing up American? My answer would have to be: "It depends. Let's wait and see!"

NOTE

I wrote this article not to discredit or minimize the significance of American childrearing ideas, attitudes, and practices. I simply want to emphasize that there are cross-cultural differences in outlook, values, customs, and practices. Certainly, the socialization of the young is no exception.

SUGGESTED READINGS

McGoldrick, Monica, John Pearce, & Joseph Giordano (Eds.). 1982. *Ethnicity and Family Therapy.* New York: Guilford Press.
Mead, Margaret, & Martha Wolfenstein (Eds.). 1955. *Childhood in Contemporary Cultures.* Chicago: University of Chicago Press.
Whiting, Beatrice B., & Carolyn P. Edwards. 1988. *Children of Different Worlds.* Cambridge, MA: Harvard University Press.

The Anthropologist as Mother

Reflections on Childbirth Observed and Childbirth Experienced

Alma Gottlieb

Alma Gottlieb is associate professor of anthropology at the University of Illinois, Urbana-Champaign, having received her Ph.D. at the University of Virginia in 1983. She has carried out fieldwork in West Africa, and her research interests include such diverse topics as interpretive theory, religion, gender issues, kinship, and epistemology of fieldwork.

While conducting fieldwork among the Beng people of Côte d'Ivoire in 1979–80 and again in 1985, whenever I gave small presents to people, I was often thanked with the phrase, *"Eci mi gba lɛɳni kpekpeàà"* ("May god give you a healthy child") or *"Eci mi gba lɛɳni bamaà"* ("May god give you an enormous child") or *"Eci mi gba lɛɳni kpáɳ kpáɳ kpáɳ"* ("May god give you many, many, many children"). Clearly, our Beng hosts and hostesses wanted me, a young woman already married, to grow up and become a mother; as elsewhere in rural Africa, adulthood for the Beng is very much a relative rather than absolute concept, and parenting is integral to its definition. My husband, Philip Graham, and I had our reasons for sticking to our own parenting schedule—but these reasons made far more sense in our own society than they did in Bengland, and so while in Africa we kept these to ourselves.

In 1986, back in the U.S. after two stints of fieldwork, we decided we were ready to become parents. One morning I awoke and knew I was pregnant—though we decided we might as well participate in the confirmatory rituals of our culture to watch the E.P.T. dipstick turn from white to blue. But of course no medical knowledge is authoritative in the United States if it is not confirmed by a specialist with an advanced degree.[1] As an anthropologist who had seen firsthand how medical knowledge can be defined in radically different ways depending on local cultural context, I had more than a passing skepticism concerning the system of medical knowledge as it is defined by my society; but somehow, when it came to my own bodily experiences, I was ensconced enough in the medical system of my childhood to seek the legitimation of its specialists. So we scheduled the mandatory visit with my gynecologist . . . who, to our surprise, simply echoed my diagnosis without even ordering a urine test—he was that rarest of species in the panoply of American medicine: a doctor, and an OB-GYN at that, who actually believed his patient.[2] Still, I wasn't sure how many more of these medically authoritative offerings of knowledge I would want to seek out—in fact, I wasn't even sure I wanted an obstetrician to preside at my delivery. Clearly Philip and I had a lot of thinking—and research—to do.

Despite our elation, I wanted to keep the news private for as long as possible. The usual reason in our social circle concerns the increased likelihood of first-trimester disasters. My motivation was different. I knew that women-as-mothers and women-as-professionals are often seen as two different species in the middle-class slice of North American culture in which I live much of my life, and as a female professor I wasn't yet ready to deal with that perceived bifurcation of my future self. Having lived in West Africa, I'd been impressed by Beng women who had no trouble working while surrounded by their children. I couldn't imagine how they would respond to a Western survey question of the type that women in the U.S. are inundated with: "On a scale of 1 to 10, how torn do you feel between your career and your children?" or "How much do you have to juggle between home and work?" In most regions of rural Africa, such questions would simply make no sense: it is inconceivable for adults—both men and women—*not* to work while surrounded by little people. For one thing, children in such settings represent the future—and to some extent, even the present—labor force that will ultimately be trained to take over an adult's job. Even though most work days in the industrial West are

"The Anthropologist as Mother: Reflections on Childbirth Observed and Childbirth Experienced" by Alma Gottlieb, from *Anthropology Today* June (1995). Reprinted by permission of the Royal Anthropological Institute.

arranged quite differently, due to a host of factors—including the ascendancy of the nuclear family, the rise of the public school system, and the extreme division of labor brought on by industrialization—nevertheless, I was very much affected by what I saw in Bengland. Without romanticizing our Beng hosts and hostesses, without ignoring the extraordinary hardships attendant on their grinding poverty, I still felt I had much to learn from the integrated nature of their daily working lives.

Soon, another part of Africa asserted itself: the urge to relish rather than conceal my impending motherhood. After only a month, my waistline swelled with the slightest hint of a bulge. In celebration, I bought my first installment of maternity clothes. At a party, someone teased me: "It's only a month, and already you're wearing baggy shirts? Come on, you're just showing off!"

"No, I really *have* gained a couple of pounds!" I protested, laughing through my embarrassment—for of course my friend was right: my pride in my pregnancy, rarely spoken of in the U.S., was unmasked. Indeed I came to hear the phrase *You're showing*, repeated more frequently as my pregnancy advanced, as ambivalent, with more than a touch of implicit criticism. In American women's lives, other bodily items that "show" are not meant to: bra straps, slip hems should all be concealed with great effort. If my pregnancy were "showing," was I supposed to somehow tuck it in like underwear?

Luckily my pregnancy was easy—no morning sickness; no lower back pain; not even any weird, midnight food cravings; and if anything, I felt more energetic than usual. But anytime I revealed my fortunate situation—especially to my pregnant friends, and to fellow classmates in a pregnancy aerobics class (and, later, a pregnancy yoga class)—I instantly regretted it, for in their awkward and resentful silences, I found that the discourse of pregnancy in my home country is a discourse of suffering: Eve all over again. Having nothing to lament meant I lacked anything legitimate to discuss.

During this time, my husband and I tried to imagine how our lives—which we had shared as a couple for some thirteen years—would be transformed by becoming a trio. It was hard, for we simply didn't see children very often. While lacking the formal age grades for which, for example, many East African societies are known, American society nevertheless segregates people by age quite systematically. Not only do children inhabit different social spaces from those populated by adults, but children are separated from each other by increments of only a year once they join nursery school or day care settings. I did begin to notice little people in public places where I'd previously over-

looked them: restaurants, malls, waiting rooms. But their new visibility only confirmed what I'd already noticed after our first return from Côte d'Ivoire: even when older people and children inhabit the same places, they rarely intermix. Instead, parents spend much public time disciplining their young sons and daughters to conform to adults' rules of politeness—"Don't shout!" "Don't run!" "Don't play!" were incantations I now heard regularly from exasperated mothers and fathers in public places clearly never intended for children. Why were there no indoor playgrounds in shopping centers, airports, office buildings, I wondered. Why were children almost never invited to the parties we attended, whether among academic colleagues, at artists' get-togethers, or fund-raising soirées for our favorite political candidates?

At the same time, I started observing how the things we use daily are manufactured with adults in mind, causing children no end of frustration as they endeavor, often unsuccessfully, to negotiate oversized spaces and giant objects. Parenting books warned that before our baby started to crawl, we must get down on hands and knees and look up to imagine our rooms from the infant's perspective, anticipating heavy chairs that might be toppled, hot stove burners that might scald a child's curious fingers, food processor blades that could prove lethal. I compared all this with the lives of Beng village children. Their days are hardly idyllic, but a high, unreachable world isn't one of their troubles. Hand-carved, low wooden stools allow even young toddlers to sit comfortably, feet touching the ground; women cook over campfires, allowing the youngest children to have a peek in the pot without fear of overturning it, or to help stir the sauce without having to balance precariously on a shaky stepladder; small mortars and pestles permit even two-year-old girls to begin to master the techniques of pounding that are essential to Beng cuisine. I was discouraged to think that already, my culture's architects had planned for our as-yet-unborn child's exclusion.

Pondering all this led me to push away my fears and consider my inevitable labor. Because I'd encountered in Africa a medical system that emphasized personal rather than technological connections, I was tempted to have the birth at home. Curious about such alternatives, I turned to Brigitte Jordan's path-breaking book on childbirth in several cultural settings (1983), midwife Ina Mae Gaskin's journeys into the spiritually uplifting aspects of birth (1978), Robbie Davis-Floyd's developing work offering devastating critiques of American hospital births (e.g., Davis-Floyd 1988), as well as my own field notes—for I had also seen and heard much of births while conducting fieldwork among the Beng.[3]

The more I considered the anthropological documentation of childbirth in other places, the more I thought that, in theory, there was much to recommend a home birth. I'd feel at home in our bedroom, could assume any delivery position I found comfortable—maybe lean back into the comforting arms of a birthing companion, as I'd seen my laboring Beng friend Amenan do; listen to soothing music; even moan and scream without embarrassment if the pain gripped me. And I could avoid all those machines that measure a laboring woman's bodily events while ignoring her state of mind (Davis-Floyd 1990, 1992; Jordan 1992). In short, I could relocate birth from an event defined by sickness and danger to one that sees it as an intensely emotional experience that might encompass anything from terror to joy.

While Western medical textbooks monotonously emphasized all that could go wrong during childbirth, other books and articles suggested that a normal birth could easily avoid the sophisticated technologies that modern medicine has compulsively developed. Moreover, some researchers were now documenting how, ironically, a reliance on the sophisticated Western technology of fetal monitors actually increases the likelihood of medical complications, including unnecessary Caesarean-section deliveries.[4] And the more I heard friends' and colleagues' hospital birth stories, so often marked by frustration and disappointment, the more convinced I was that, except in unusual circumstances, Western hospitals are a poor choice for the ritual moment of birth.

I thought back to Lévi-Strauss's marvellous article (1963) on Cuna Indian childbirth chants, which I'd long admired for its poetics. If a Cuna woman of Panama does not make sufficient progress during labor, he wrote, an attending shaman undertakes a dangerous, invisible journey to the underworld of the woman's uterus that is inhabited by Muu, the goddess that formed the fetus. Travelling "Muu's way," Lévi-Strauss wrote, the shaman recounts to the woman how he is embarking on "a complicated itinerary that is a true mythical anatomy, corresponding less to the real structure of the genital organs than to a kind of emotional geography" (p. 195). Along the way, the shaman battles the powerful uterine forces that stole the woman's soul, and he emerges to inform the woman that her soul has been regained; then, the delivery can proceed normally. If a Cuna woman could have her blocked labor eased by such a song, I thought, surely there should be some other, equally noninvasive means to help birthing Western women in trouble.

Still, I was bothered that Lévi-Strauss failed to mention one important detail: what proportion of difficult labors were indeed helped by this mythic treatment? Conversely, what was the rate of death during childbirth for Cuna women? Confronting this frightening question forced me to consider the tragedy of my Beng friend, Kouakou Nguessan. One day her husband had come to fetch me while I was working in another village, imploring me to return immediately to drive Nguessan to the dispensary in town, almost an hour away, because she was having difficulty in her labor. Of course I agreed, and soon Philip and I found ourselves racing down the gravelly road, Nguessan screaming her agony in the back seat. Perhaps the bumps in the road helped advance the baby down the birth canal, or perhaps the massaging that the midwife's assistant and I soon administered to Nguessan helped, but whatever it was, Nguessan delivered her baby soon after settling into the delivery bed. Still, the tiny infant was clearly in distress—she emerged green, and she wasn't breathing. Only extraordinary efforts by the midwife's assistant revived the child.

At the time, I felt blessed to have been able to help in this event. But a few years later, I learned that the little girl born from that fateful ride, frail ever since her traumatic birth, had died, and Nguessan herself, once again pregnant and having no access to medical screening or transportation to town, had died in labor.

Nguessan's tragedy warned me not to romanticize: childbirth could indeed be dangerous. I thought back to the slow, mournful dance I'd seen of pregnant Beng women commemorating the loss of one of their compatriots in childbirth (Gottlieb & Graham 1993: 150–151), and I recalled that the Asante, among others, liken childbirth to war (Rattray 1927:58–59).

I decided I'd better do some preliminary research into home birth in my own part of the world. As long as women considered at medical risk for a safe delivery were excluded, a home birth with a trained midwife presiding seemed to be at least as safe as a hospital birth. Yet I was surprised to find that 99% of all childbirths in the U.S. take place in hospitals, and of these, over 97% have doctors presiding.[5] One of the major explanations for this situation, I discovered to my dismay, is that most states in the U.S., including Illinois, place midwifery and/or home birth on an extremely shaky legal footing, and have done so since 1920 (Whitby 1986:992–93; Wolfson 1985–86:958–67). In many situations involving a birth at home, if the newborn or birthing mother were to have a medical complication, the attending health specialist—whether midwife or doctor—could be held legally liable—up to and including imprisonment.[6] Thus in most states, including ours, there was no publicly available listing of midwives willing to attend home deliveries—one discovered their identities through hush-hush conversations conducted amidst oaths to keep the names secret. Through the pregnant women's rumor mill, I even heard of a recent home birth tragedy not far away, with the attending midwife having been sued by the state. It was a sobering story.

With not a little ambivalence—and anger that we lived in a country whose leaders could think to make giving birth at home a crime—Philip and I decided to have a hospital birth . . . but only if we could together recast the hospital's vision of birth to our own. After all, having seen a very different system in action, we no longer accepted our culture's constructed set of knowledge as having a *unique* claim to authority. We vowed to compel the medical system operating in our local hospital to accommodate our vision of birth. But would it be possible?

We took tours of our town's two maternity wards. The nurse in the first hospital showed off their new intensive care unit, new fetal monitors, ordinary beds that "broke down" to classic delivery beds complete with metal stirrups, and an array of miscellaneous items of shiny steel—in this post-industrial age, such items of raw industry are oddly enough still meant to convey authority. When I asked about the possibility of a less technological birth, the nurse remembered that they owned one birthing chair; she rummaged around until she found the key to a closet in which the molded plastic chair was stored. But when questioned further, our tour guide admitted that not many women use the chair because the semi-circle cut out of the seat was too narrow, causing larger-headed newborns to get stuck. It was depressing to see how industrial production only executes its high standards for efficiency when the goals of the product in question are in synch with those of the culture (Davis-Floyd 1990, 1992). And why hadn't anyone in the hospital—say, a maintenance crew member—remedied the deficiency with a low-tech solution such as a saw? Perhaps that wouldn't be deemed appropriate—too imprecise for such a precise subject as medical supplies.

In the second hospital, the head nurse also showed off their latest equipment, concluding her sales pitch by saying that it's a competitive environment, and her hospital wanted to do everything possible to accommodate the desires of the birthing couple. I wasn't enthralled with her capitalist's analogy of birthing-mother-as-consumer, but at least this nurse seemed a bit more flexible than the other. Still, my husband and I began to realize that we would have to make serious efforts to shape our birth experience—otherwise the normal routines of the technology-crazy hospital would certainly take over.

We needed someone at the delivery who could serve as an advocate, fend off the monitor-wielding nurses, challenge the authority of this medical system's medically unnecessary practices. I thought back to the Beng women's births I knew about. They'd always had one kinswoman to lean against, another to catch the baby, another to dispose of the placenta. How nice it would be if I had female relatives who could do this for me. But with my family aging, fragmented and dis-

persed even more than the usual American middle-class family, this wasn't possible. Who could I find in their place?

Happily, my identities as professor and as mother-to-be converged when I stumbled upon the idea of asking a then-graduate student named Laura O'Banion to serve as my birth attendant. Laura was completing both an M.D. degree and a brilliant master's thesis in anthropology on American midwives: she was perfect. Together, we devised a strategy: once my labor started, I'd stay home as long as possible. The less time spent in the hospital, we reasoned, the less I'd have to reject the nurses' inevitable offers of drugs or fetal monitors.

———————

My waters broke late at night. I looked in the mirror: after tomorrow, that image would forever be that of a mother.

"I can't believe it, we're about to become parents!" Philip said. "Do you think we should pack the suitcase?"

"Not yet," I said. "I'm afraid if we pack now, I'll be tempted to leave for the hospital right away. But I wonder how far along I am. Maybe we should call Laura."

After sleepily grilling me on the timing of my contractions, Laura said I was still in early labor, but she graciously offered to spend the rest of the night in our guest room. Philip and Laura caught a few hours of sleep; massaging my cramping stomach, changing positions every few minutes to settle into the quickening contractions, I was too pained—and too excited—to do anything but lie, wide-eyed, in our dark bedroom, trying to recall the signs that Indian women use to predict the sex of the unborn baby, or the name of the herb that Beng women use to hasten the delivery.

At the first light of dawn, feeling the need for company and sympathy, I roused Philip. He obligingly massaged my back and shoulders, but those contractions had already surpassed the intensity of menstrual cramps and his kneading hands could do nothing to soften them. When Laura woke, Philip said he thought he'd take a short break to mail a note he'd dashed off to his literary agent early last night—in which he'd written that this would be his last letter before becoming a father.

"How far is the mailbox?" Laura asked.

"Oh, just two blocks," Philip said, "I'll be back in a few minutes."

Laura turned to me. "Why don't you go along? You know, walking helps move the baby down the birth canal."

"Hmmm—okay," I said, eager for anything to distract me from those relentless pangs.

It was 7 a.m.—the hour of joggers and dog-walkers. Those two blocks possessed me, a Turnerian time out of time. I stared at the few people we passed, at once proud and, unfairly, a little annoyed that they'd stumbled on my private ritual; they stared back, no doubt appalled at the strangely un-American spectacle of a woman obviously in labor walking the streets. All I need, I thought, is to reach that mail box—if only we were there, if only I could drop that letter down the chute, if only this baby would be born. Under an especially glistening turquoise sky, those pains so gripped me that I stopped to rest against every tree; finally, an hour later, we were back home.

We found Laura cheerfully making breakfast. The medical books had advised me to fast; the midwifery books had advised me to eat. I didn't know what Beng women ate or didn't eat during the hours of their labors. In any case, I wasn't the remotest bit hungry, so I watched disinterestedly as Philip sipped our usual Pep-Up milk-shake and Laura cooked herself some eggs.

I paced and moaned through our house as the contractions intensified and I thought of my laboring Beng friend Amenan, sitting on her dirt floor, leaning back slightly against her mother, legs outstretched, forehead sweating, saying to me in her fine French, *"Je souffre un peu"* ("I'm suffering a little"). Her stoicism shamed me.

The day dragged on, the space between contractions shortened, but still Laura charted only the barest progress. I began to despair. Maybe I needed a fast, bumpy ride on a dirt road, like the one we'd offered Nguessan. Or was there something seriously wrong?

"How much longer?" I pestered Laura. If only she could throw cowry shells as the Beng diviner Lamine might, to see the outcome of this day. I thought of Nguessan suffering in her bedroom, I thought of Amenan's mother getting stuck in her labor for several hours before her sorcerer cousin who was bewitching her was finally killed by a falling tree sent by an avenging Earth, I thought of Amenan herself almost dying during her delivery of her son Kouadio, I thought of Nguessan finally succumbing during her next delivery. Had my Beng friends ever lost hope, imagining they might never emerge from their ordeals, or were they always confident that their bodies would cooperate, that the witches could be kept at bay, that a healthy baby would eventually be born?

Finally it was time to assemble our baggage for the hospital. A Beng woman would have laughed at all the gear we toted. But if I wasn't having a baby at home, I wanted to bring large chunks of home with me: we carried reading pillows covered with our own patterned sheets; some tapes and a boom box to play them on; and a pair of birthing stools now covered with a pink and white tie-dyed *pagne* from Côte d'Ivoire—a piece of another home.

Once inside the hospital, my first act was to decline a wheelchair ride to the maternity ward; my second

was to decline the offer of an ugly hospital gown—no need to play the invalid, or to occupy an anonymous predecessor's birthing garments. Indeed, the theme of my hospital stay became refusal: No, I didn't want to be hooked up to machines, or take painkillers, or lie down in bed. The head nurse was unnerved by my constant rebuffs—after all, she was offering the best of what both her training and her years of experience had assured her was the right way to have a baby; who was I, a first-time not-yet-mother, to turn down all these nuggets of wisdom? Hoping for female solidarity, I was disappointed to find myself at odds with the woman before me, each of us sure of what we believed, eager for the other to convert. At least the young nurse-in-training was solicitous, especially when her boss left the room. Still open-minded, she hadn't yet settled on a single version of authoritative knowledge. How many births would she attend before that would happen?

——————

My most serious resistance occurred when it was time to prepare for the delivery. The head nurse was adamant about resituating me in bed; in too much pain to have an opinion about anything any longer, I was about to capitulate when Laura gently suggested I try the birthing stool. Lacking the will to disagree with anyone, I limped over to the stool, which Laura set up in front of a love seat, so that Philip could sit behind me and massage my shoulders. The head nurse panicked: it seemed the baby would be born onto the carpeted floor, and what about all the germs? The idea was intolerable. I was too distracted to mention that during the delivery of my Beng friend Amenan that I had partially witnessed, not only was the baby born onto the floor, but it was a dirt floor at that—no attempts at sterility anywhere—and the baby didn't seem to suffer any from the experience. But to accommodate the nurse, Laura suggested they spread one of the many available clean sheets on the carpet in front of me. The nurse gazed at us as if we were insane, but Laura—an M.D.-in-training, after all—prevailed.

Soon my obstetrician entered the room. He took one look at the odd scene in front of him and exchanged glances with the head nurse—who, according to Philip, gave him an imploring look that Philip interpreted to mean: "At last! Can you please take charge and get this crazy woman up on the bed?" But my doctor, showing himself to be even more aberrant than I'd dared hope, walked casually over to the rocking chair in the corner and proceeded to watch as Philip and Laura helped me through my contractions.

Like the nurse in a birth story documented by Brigitte Jordan (1992), Laura discouraged me from pushing when I had the urge to do so. But unlike that nurse, Laura explained the reason and offered me a choice: if I decided I could accept an episiotomy, she'd perform it and I could push now. Otherwise, I could try to resist the urge to push—she'd help me breathe in a way that accomplished this—and wait until I was effaced enough to avoid a tear or an episiotomy. Offered these two alternatives, I mustered my last bit of strength and chose to delay the delivery. And so Laura and my husband puffed and massaged, the young apprentice nurse cooled my sweaty forehead with ice, the doctor rocked and smiled, and the birth proceeded— very slowly.

Looking back on that day over seven years ago, when our son Nathaniel emerged triumphantly— from a dark wet world to a new, and very different one—I am struck by the concatenation of power relations that encased both me and my medical team. As a laboring woman, I should have been structurally placed in the position of disempowered and frustrated patient, as Robbie Davis-Floyd and Emily Martin, among others, have so painfully demonstrated is usually the case in American hospitals. Yet lucky enough to have had an advanced education, I was motivated to read widely on the subject of birth and so was able to offer Facts and Case Studies to my doctor ahead of time in order to present my own case for a birthing style that was certainly unusual by American hospital standards. In other words, I confronted my physician with a different system of authority, but one that was nonetheless premised on evidence to which he could relate. Impoverished women in inner-city hospitals do not partake of this conceptual system, and thus are not so graciously accorded the opportunities I was of recasting their birthing experiences (Martin 1987). Yet even most middle-class American women who yearn for a "natural" birth emerge from their hospital experiences disappointed at least to some degree, and often profoundly so (Davis-Floyd 1992).

But perhaps this should not be surprising, for as Brigitte Jordan has written, authoritative knowledge is just that. Like religion, it takes on an "aura of factuality," as Geertz would put it (1973:90), to make it seem "really real" (ibid.:112). My own modest and partial resistance to the locally dominant system of medicine was inspired by my exposure to a radically different system of authoritative knowledge in another part of the world—another system of "really real" that focuses on the laboring woman rather than machines as a reliable source of information; that accommodates the woman in a familiar setting surrounded by kinswomen and neighbors; and that looks to disturbances in social and spiritual relations as causes of obstructed deliveries.

In these days of widespread American discontent with the medical system in general and the practices of modern obstetrics in particular, one wonders what it will take to change our all-too-often unsatisfying system of hospital births in any significant and meaningful way. In recent years, feminists in a variety of disciplines have begun to contemplate the roles, responsibilities and choices open to them, and to speculate on the impact, both practical and theoretical, of feminism on their own disciplinary practices, and on the newfound sense of taking seriously the personal, the domestic and the emotional (e.g., Harding 1987). In accord with this move, it may be that feminist anthropologists can seize a unique opportunity to contribute to the growing debate on the particular subject of childbirth by sharing their invaluable comparative perspectives. After all, the past two decades or so have seen an upsurge of the "practice" approach to social life which, among other things, offers the possibility of *multiple layers* of knowledge forms even within so-called simple societies (Ortner 1984). Perhaps the next wave of anthropological analyses of childbirth experiences cross-culturally will provide us with the intellectual tools to consider a significant slice of the multiplicity of knowledge forms available in post-industrial, Western society (cf. Davis-Floyd & Sargent, n.d.). Anthropologists, I suggest, have something important to contribute to this growing international conversation.

ACKNOWLEDGMENTS

This article was first presented as a paper at the Annual Meeting of the American Anthropological Association (San Francisco, 2–6 December 1992). I am grateful to Robbie Davis-Floyd for the invitation to join the session, and to Rayna Rapp for her illuminating comments.

I acknowledge with gratitude the following agencies that have supported my research into Beng society over the years: the Social Science Research Council; the Wenner-Gren Foundation for Anthropological Research; the National Endowment for the Humanities; the Woodrow Wilson Foundation; the American Association of University Women; the United States Information Agency; and the Center for African Studies, the Research Board, International Programs and Studies, and the Department of Anthropology, all at the University of Illinois at Urbana-Champaign.

On a more personal note, I am grateful to those Beng women, some of whom are mentioned in this essay, who allowed me to participate in their lives as mothers, farmers, and everything else; and to Laura O'Banion, Larry Lane, my husband Philip Graham, and our son Nathaniel Gottlieb-Graham, who each in their own way contributed to my own birth experience.

I dedicate this essay to the memory of Kouakou Nguessan.

NOTES

1. I borrow the notion of "authoritative knowledge" from Brigitte Jordan, who developed it with reference to technical and business settings (e.g., Jordan 1992), but it has proven quite useful in the anthropological analysis of childbirth (Davis-Floyd & Sargent, n.d.).
2. For a depressing array of U.S. obstetricians who have either ignored or actively challenged the observations and insights of their female patients, see, for example, Martin (1987) and Davis-Floyd (1992).
3. For descriptions of some Beng childbirths, see Gottlieb and Graham (1993).
4. For references to critiques of hospital-based birth techniques, see Whitby (1986:987, N. 10; 988, N. 15; 995, N. 70; 1025).
5. These statistics are derived from: U.S. Dept. of Health and Services (1987): Sect. 2, Table 2-1, p. 1, and Sect. 2, Table 2-2, p. 87.
6. For a listing of such cases nationally, see Wolfson (1985–86: 929–33); on the problematic legal status of midwifery in Illinois as of 1986, see Whitby (1986:999, N. 89).

REFERENCES

Davis-Floyd, Robbie. 1988. "Birth as an American Rite of Passage." In *Childbirth in America: Anthropological Perspectives*, ed. by Karen Michaelson. South Hadley, MA: Bergin & Garvey.

Davis-Floyd, Robbie. 1990. "The Technological Model of Birth." In *Annual Editions 89/90*, ed. by Elvio Angeloni. Guilford, CT: Dushkin.

Davis-Floyd, Robbie. 1992. *Birth as an American Rite of Passage*. Berkeley: University of California Press.

Davis-Floyd, Robbie, & Carolyn Sargent (Eds.). In press. *Childbirth and Authoritative Knowledge: Cross-cultural Perspectives*. Berkeley: University of California Press.

Gaskin, Ina Mae. 1978. *Spiritual Midwifery* (rev. ed.). Summertown, TN: The Book Publishing Company.

Geertz, Clifford. 1973 [1966]. "Religion as a Cultural System." In *The Interpretation of Cultures*. New York: Basic Books.

Gottlieb, Alma, & Philip Graham. 1993. *Parallel Worlds: An Anthropologist and a Writer Encounter Africa*. New York: Crown/Random House.

Harding, Sandra (Ed.). 1987. *Feminism and Methodology: Social Science Issues*. Bloomington: Indiana University Press.

Jordan, Brigitte. 1983. *Childbirth in Four Cultures* (3d ed.). Montreal: Eden Press.

Jordan, Brigitte. 1992. *Technology and Social Interaction: Notes on the Achievement of Authoritative Knowledge in Complex Settings*. Palo Alto, CA: Institute for Research on Learning. Unpublished ms.

Lévi-Strauss, Claude. 1963 [1949]. "The Effectiveness of Symbols." In *Structural Anthropology*, trans. by Claire Jacobson & Brooke Grundfest Schoepf. New York: Basic Books. (Original: *L'anthropologie structurale*, Paris, 1958).

Martin, Emily. 1987. *The Woman in the Body*. Boston: Beacon Press.

Ortner, Sherry. 1984. "Theory in Anthropology since the Sixties." *Comparative Studies in Society and History*, Vol. 26, No. 1: 126–166.

Rattray, R. S. 1927. *Religion and Art in Ashanti*. Oxford: Clarendon Press.

U.S. Department of Health and Human Services. 1987. *Vital Statistics of the United States, 1986. I: Natality*. Washington, DC: U.S. Dept. of Health and Human Services.

Whitby, Kathleen M. 1986. "Choice in Childbirth: Parents, Lay Midwives, and Statutory Regulation." *St. Louis University Law Journal* Vol. 30, No. 3:985–1028.

Wolfson, Charles. 1985–86. "Midwives and Home Birth: Social, Medical, and Legal Perspectives." *Hastings Law Journal* Vol. 37:909–976.

Into the Endzone for a Touchdown

A Psychoanalytic Consideration of American Football

Alan Dundes

Alan Dundes received his Ph.D. in 1962 from Indiana University and is now professor of anthropology at the University of California in Berkeley. Best known as a folklorist, he is interested in structural analysis, symbolism, worldview, and psychoanalysis.

In college athletics it is abundantly clear that it is football which counts highest among both enrolled students and alumni. It is almost as though the masculinity of male alumni is at stake in a given game, especially when a hated rival school is the opponent. College fund raisers are well aware that a winning football season may prove to be the key to a successful financial campaign to increase the school's endowment capital. The Rose Bowl and other postseason bowl games for colleges, plus the Super Bowl for professional football teams have come to rank as national festival occasions in the United States. All this makes it reasonable to assume that there is something about football which strikes a most responsive chord in the American psyche. No other American sport consistently draws fans in the numbers which are attracted to football. One need only compare the crowd-attendance statistics for college or professional baseball games with the analogous figures for football to see the enormous appeal of the latter. The question is: what is it about American football that could possibly account for its extraordinary popularity?

In the relatively meager scholarship devoted to football, one finds the usual array of theoretical approaches. The ancestral form of football, a game more like Rugby or soccer, was interpreted as a solar ritual—with a disc-shaped rock or object supposedly representing the sun[1]—and also as a fertility ritual intended to ensure agricultural abundance. It had been noted, for example, that in some parts of England and France, the rival teams consisted of married men playing against bachelors.[2] In one custom, a newly married woman would throw over the church a ball for which married men and bachelors fought. The distinction between the married and the unmarried suggests that the game

might be a kind of ritual test or battle with marriage signifying socially sanctioned fertility.[3]

The historical evolution of American football from English Rugby has been well documented,[4] but the historical facts do not in and of themselves account for any psychological rationale leading to the unprecedented enthusiasm for the sport. It is insufficient to state that football offers an appropriate outlet for the expression of aggression. William Arens has rightly observed that it would be an oversimplification "to single out violence as the sole or even primary reason for the game's popularity."[5] Many sports provide a similar outlet (e.g., wrestling, ice hockey, roller derby), but few of these come close to matching football as a spectacle for many Americans. Similarly, pointing to such features as a love of competition, or the admiration of coordinated teamwork, or the development of specialists (e.g., punters, punt returners, field-goal kickers, etc.) is not convincing since such features occur in most if not all sports.

Recently, studies of American football have suggested that the game serves as a male initiation ritual.[6] Arens, for example, remarks that football is "a male preserve that manifests both the physical and cultural values of masculinity,"[7] a description which had previously been applied, aptly it would appear, to British Rugby.[8] Arens points out that the equipment worn "accents the male physique" through the enlarged head and shoulders coupled with a narrowed waist. With the lower torso "poured into skintight pants accented only by a metal codpiece," Arens contends that the result "is not an expression but an exaggeration of maleness." He comments further: "Dressed in this manner, the players can engage in hand holding, hugging, and bottom patting, which would be disapproved of in any other context, but which is accepted on the gridiron without a second thought."[9] Having said this much, Arens fails to draw any inferences about possible ritual homosexual aspects of football. Instead, he goes on to note that American football resembles male rituals in other cultures insofar as contact with females is discouraged if not forbidden. The argument usually given is one of "limited good."[10] A man has only so much energy and if he uses it in sexual activity, he will have that much less to use in hunting, warfare, or in this case, football. I believe Arens and others are correct in calling attention to the ritual and symbolic dimensions of American football, but I think the psychological implications of the underlying symbolism have not been adequately explored.

Football is one of a large number of competitive games which involve the scoring of points by gaining access to a defended area in an opponent's territory. In basketball, one must throw a ball through a hoop (and net) attached to the other team's backboard. In ice hockey, one must hit the puck into the goal at the opponent's end of the rink. In football, the object is to move the ball across the opponent's goal into his endzone. It does not require a great deal of Freudian sophistication to see a possible sexual component in such acts as throwing a ball through a hoop, hitting a puck across a "crease" into an enclosed area bounded by nets or cage, and other structurally similar acts. But what is not so obvious is the connection of such sexual symbolism with an all-male group of participants.

Psychologists and psychoanalysts have not chosen to examine American football to any great extent. Psychologist G. T. W. Patrick, writing in 1903, tried to explain the fascination of the game: "Evidently there is some great force, psychological or sociological, at work here which science has not yet investigated"; but he could offer little detail about what that great force might be.[11] Similarly, psychoanalyst A. A. Brill's superficial consideration of football in 1929 failed to illuminate the psychodynamics of the game.[12] Perhaps the best-known Freudian analysis of football is the parody written originally in 1955 in the *Rocky Mountain Herald* by poet Thomas Hornsby Ferril, using the pseudonym Childe Herald, but the essay is more amusing than analytic. Actually his interpretation tends to be more inclined towards ritual than psychoanalytic theory. He suggests: "football is a syndrome of religious rites symbolizing the struggle to preserve the egg of life through the rigors of impending winter. The rites begin at the autumn equinox and culminate on the first day of the New Year with great festivals identified with bowls of plenty; the festivals are associated with flowers such as roses, fruits such as oranges, farm crops such as cotton and even sun-worship and the appeasement of great reptiles such as alligators."[13] While he does say that "football obviously arises out of the Oedipus complex," he provides little evidence other than mentioning that college games are usually played for one's alma mater, which he translates as "dear mother."

Actually, a more literal translation would be "nourishing mother" (and for that matter, *alumnus* literally means nursling.)

A more conventional psychoanalytic perspective is offered by Adrian Stokes in his survey of ball games with special reference to cricket. Stokes predictably describes football (soccer) in Oedipal terms. Each team defends the goal at their back. "In front is a new land, the new woman, whom they strive to possess in the interest of preserving the mother inviolate, in order, as it were, to progress from infancy to adulthood: at the same time, the defensive role is the father's; he opposes the forward youth of the opposition."[14] Speaking of Rugby football, Stokes proposes the following description: "Ejected out of the mother's body, out of the scrum, after frantic hooking and pushing, there emerges the rich loot of the father's genital." According to Stokes, both teams fight to possess the father's phallus, that is, the ball, in order to "steer it through the archetypal vagina, the goal."[15] Earlier, Stokes had suggested the ball represented semen though he claimed that "more generally the ball is itself the phallus."[16] Folk speech offers some support for the phallic connotation of a ball. One thinks of "balls" for testicles. A man who has "balls" is a man of strength and determination. To "ball" someone is a slang expression for sexual intercourse.[17] On the other hand, while one might agree with the general thesis that there might be a sexual component to both soccer and American football, it is difficult to cite concrete evidence supporting Stokes's contention that the game involves a mother figure or a father surrogate. If psychoanalytic interpretations are valid, then it ought to be possible to adduce specific details of idiom and ritual as documentation for such interpretations. It is not enough for a psychoanalyst to assert ex cathedra what a given event or object supposedly symbolizes.

I believe that a useful way to begin an attempt to understand the psychoanalytic significance of American football is through an examination of football folk speech. For it is precisely in the idioms and metaphors that a clear pattern of personal interaction is revealed. In this regard, it might be helpful first to briefly consider the slang employed in the verbal dueling of the American male. In effect, I am suggesting that American football is analogous to male verbal dueling. Football entails ritual and dramatic action while verbal dueling is more concerned with words. But structurally speaking, they are similar or at least functionally equivalent. In verbal dueling, it is common to speak about putting one's opponent "down." This could mean simply to topple an opponent figuratively, but it could also imply forcing one's adversary to assume a supine position, that is, the "female" position in typical Western sexual intercourse. It should also be noted that an equally humiliating experience for a male would be to serve as a passive receptacle for a male aggressor's phallic thrust. Numerous idioms attest to the widespread popularity of this pattern of imagery to describe a loser. One speaks of having been screwed by one's boss or of having been given the shaft. Submitting to anal intercourse is also implied in perhaps the most common single American folk gesture, the so-called *digitus impudicus,* better known in folk parlance as "the finger." Giving someone the finger is often accompanied by such unambiguous explanatory phrases as "Fuck you!" "Screw you!" "Up yours!" or "Up your ass!"

Now what has all this to do with football? I believe that the same symbolic pattern is at work in verbal dueling and much ritual play. Instead of scoring a putdown, one scores a touchdown. Certainly the terminology used in football is suggestive. One gains yardage, but it is not territory which is kept in the sense of being permanently acquired by the invading team. The territory invaded remains nominally under the proprietorship of the opponent. A sports announcer or fan might say, for example, "This is the deepest *penetration* into (opponent's team name) territory so far" [my emphasis]. Only if one gets into the endzone (or kicks a field goal through the uprights of the goalposts) does one earn points.

The use of the term *end* is not accidental. Evidently there is a kind of structural isomorphism between the line (as opposed to the backfield) and the layout of the field of play. Each line has two ends (left end and right end) with a "center" in the middle. Similarly, each playing field has two ends (endzones) with a midfield line (the fifty-yard line). Ferril remarked on the parallel between the oval shape of the football and the oval shape of most football stadiums,[18] but I submit it might be just as plausible to see the football shape as an elongated version of the earlier round soccer or Rugby ball, a shape which tends to produce two accentuated ends of the ball. Surely the distinctive difference between the shape of a football and the shape of the balls used in most other ball games (e.g., baseball, basketball, soccer) is that it is not perfectly spherical. The notion that a football has two "ends" is found in the standard idiom used to describe a kick or punt in which the ball turns over and over from front to back during flight (as opposed to moving in a more direct, linear, spiraling pattern) as an "end over end" kick.

The object of the game, simply stated, is to get into the opponent's endzone while preventing the opponent from getting into one's own endzone. Structurally speaking, this is precisely what is involved in male verbal dueling. One wishes to put one's opponent down; to "screw" him while avoiding being screwed by him. We can now better understand the appropriateness of the "bottom patting" so often observed among football players. A good offensive or defensive play deserves a

pat on the rear end. The recipient has held up his end and has thereby helped protect the collective "end" of the entire team. One pats one's teammates' ends, but one seeks to violate the endzone of one's opponents!

The trust one has for one's own teammates is perhaps signalled by the common postural stance of football players. The so-called three-point stance involves bending over in a distinct stooped position with one's rear end exposed. It is an unusual position (in terms of normal life activities) and it does make one especially vulnerable to attack from behind, that is, vulnerable to a homosexual attack. In some ways, the posture might be likened to what is termed *presenting* among nonhuman primates. *Presenting* refers to a subordinate animal's turning its rump towards a higher-ranking or dominant one. The center thus presents to the quarterback—just as linemen do to the backs in general. George Plimpton has described how the quarterback's "hand, the top of it, rests up against the center's backside as he bends over the ball—medically, against the perineum, the pelvic floor."[19] We know that some dominant nonhuman primates will sometimes reach out to touch a presenting subordinate in similar fashion. In football, however, it is safe to present to one's teammates. Since one can trust one's teammates, one knows that one will be patted, not raped. The traditional joking admonitions of the locker room warning against bending over in the shower or picking up the soap (thus presumably offering an inviting target for homosexual attack) do not apply since one is among friends. "Grabass" among friends is understood as being harmless joking behavior.

The importance of the "ends" is signalled by the fact that they alone among linemen are eligible to receive a forward pass. In that sense, ends are equivalent to the "backs." In symbolic terms, I am arguing that the end is a kind of backside and that the endzone is a kind of erogenous zone. The relatively recently coined terms *tight end* and *split end* further demonstrate the special emphasis upon this "position" on the team. The terms refer to whether the end stays close to his neighboring tackle, e.g., to block, or whether he moves well away from the normally adjacent tackle, e.g., to go out for a pass. However, both *tight end* and *split end* (cf. also *wide receiver*) could easily be understood as possessing an erotic nuance.

I must stress that the evidence for the present interpretation of American football does not depend upon just a single word. Rather, there are many terms which appear to be relevant. The semantics of the word *down* are of interest. A down is a unit of play insofar as a team has four downs in which to either advance ten yards or score. A touchdown, which earns six points, refers to the act of an offensive player's possessing the ball in the opponent's endzone. (Note it is not sufficient for the player to be in the endzone; it is the ball which must be in the zone.) In a running play, the ball often physically touches the endzone and could therefore be said to "touch down" in that area. However, if an offensive player catches a pass in the endzone, the ball does not actually touch the ground. The recent practice of "spiking" the ball, in which the successful offensive player hurls the ball at the ground as hard as he can, might be construed as an attempt to have the football physically touch down in the endzone. In any case, the use of the word *touch* in connection with scoring in football does conform to a general sexually symbolic use of that term. The sexual nuances of *touch* can even be found in the Bible. For example, in I Corinthians 7:12, we find: "It is good for a man not to touch a woman. Nevertheless to avoid fornication, let every man have his own wife" (cf. Genesis 20:6; Proverbs 6:29). Touching can be construed as an aggressive act. Thus to be touched by an opponent means that one has been the victim of aggression. The game of "touch football" (as opposed to "tackle" football) supports the notion that a mere art of touching is sufficient to fulfill the structural (and psychological) requirements of the basic rules. No team wants to give up a touchdown to an opponent. Often a team on defense may put up a determined goal-line stand to avoid being penetrated by the opponent's offense. The special spatial nature of the endzone is perhaps indicated by the fact that it is not measured in the one hundred yard distance between the goal lines. Yet it is measured. It is only ten yards deep; a pass caught by an offensive player whose feet are beyond the end line of the endzone would be ruled incomplete.

Additional football folk speech could be cited. The object of the game is to "score," a term which in standard slang means to engage in sexual intercourse with a member of the opposite sex. One "scores" by going "all the way." The latter phrase refers specifically to making a touchdown.[20] In sexual slang, it alludes to indulging in intercourse as opposed to petting or necking. The offensive team may try to mount a "drive" in order to "penetrate" the other team's territory. A ball carrier might go "up the middle" or he might "go through a hole" (made by his linemen in the opposing defensive line). A particularly skillful runner might be able to make his own hole. The defense is equally determined to "close the hole." Linemen may encourage one another "to stick it to 'em," meaning to place their helmeted heads (with phallic-symbolic overtones) against the chests of their opposite numbers to drive them back or put them out of the play.

A player who scores a touchdown may elect to "spike" the ball by hurling it down towards the ground full force. This spiking movement confirms to all assembled that the enemy's endzone has been penetrated. The team scored upon is thus shamed and humiliated in front of an audience. In this regard, football is similar to verbal

dueling inasmuch as dueling invariably takes place before one or more third parties. The term *spike* may also be germane. As a noun, it could refer to a sharp-pointed, long, slender part or projection. As a verb, it could mean either "to mark or cut with a spike" (the football would presumably be the phallic spike) or "to thwart or sabotage an enemy." In any event, the ritual act of spiking serves to prolong and accentuate the all-too-short moment of triumph, the successful entry into the enemy's endzone.

The sexual connotations of football folk speech apply equally to players on defense. One goal of the defensive line is to penetrate the offensive line to get to the quarterback. Getting to the offensive quarterback and bringing him down to the ground is termed "sacking the quarterback." The verb *sack* connotes plunder, ravage, and perhaps even rape. David Kopay, one of the few homosexuals in professional football willing to admit a preference for members of the same sex, commented on the nature of typical exhortations made by coaches and others:

> The whole language of football is involved in sexual allusions. We were told to go out and "fuck those guys"; to take that ball and "stick it up their asses" or "down their throats." The coaches would yell, "knock their dicks off," or more often than that, "knock their jocks off." They'd say, "Go out there and give it all you've got, a hundred and ten per cent, shoot your wad." You controlled their line and "knocked" 'em into submission. Over the years I've seen many a coach get emotionally aroused while he was diagramming a particular play into an imaginary hole on the blackboard. His face red, his voice rising, he would show the ball carrier how he wanted him to "stick it in the hole."[21]

The term *rape* is not inappropriate and in fact it has been used to describe what happens when an experienced player humiliates a younger player: "That poor kid, he was raped, keelhauled, he was just *destroyed*. . . ."[22] Kopay's reference to *jock* as phallus is of interest since *jock* is a term (short for *jockstrap*, the article of underapparel worn to protect the male genitals) typically used to refer generally to athletes. Calling an athlete a *jock* or a *strap* thus tends to reduce him to a phallus. A *jocker* is used in hobo slang and in prison slang to refer to an aggressive male homosexual.[23] (The meaning of *jock* may well be related to the term *jockey* insofar as the latter refers to the act of mounting and riding a horse.)

Some of the football folk speech is less obvious and the interpretation admittedly a bit more speculative. For example, a lineman may be urged to "pop" an opposing player, meaning to tackle or block him well. Executing a perfect tackle or block may entail placing one's helmet as close as possible to the middle of the opponent's chest. The use of the verbs strongly suggests defloration, as in the idiom "to pop the cherry" referring to the notion of rupturing the maidenhead in the process of having intercourse with a virgin."[24] In Afro-American folk speech, "pop" can refer to sexual penetration.[25] To "pop" an opponent thus implies reducing him to female-victim status. Much of the sexual slang makes it very clear that the winners are men while the losers are women or passive homosexuals. David Kopay articulates this when he says, "From grade school on, the curse words on the football field are about behaving like a girl. If you don't run fast enough to block or tackle hard enough you're a pussy, a cunt, a sissy."[26] By implication, if a player succeeds, he is male. Thus in the beginning of the football game, we have two sets or teams of males. By the end of the game, one of the teams is "on top," namely the one which has "scored" most by getting into the other team's "end zone." The losing team, if the scoring differential is great, may be said to have been "creamed."

It is tempting to make something of the fact that originally the inner portion of the football was an inflated animal bladder. Thus touching the enemy's endzone with a bladder would be appropriate ritual behavior in the context of a male homosexual attack. However, it could be argued that the bladder was used simply because it was a convenient inflatable object available to serve as a ball.

If the team on offense is perceived in phallic terms, then it is the quarterback who could be said to be nominally in charge of directing the attack. In this context, it may be noteworthy that a quarterback intending to pass often tries to stay inside of the "pocket," a deployment of offensive players behind the line of scrimmage designed to provide an area of maximum protection.[27] A pants pocket, of course, could be construed as an area where males can covertly touch or manipulate their genitals without being observed. "Pocket pool," for example, is a slang idiom for fondling the genitals,[28] an idiom which incidentally may suggest something about the symbolic nature of billiards. The quarterback, if given adequate protection by his "pocket," may be able to "thread the needle," that is, throw the ball accurately, past the hands of the defensive players, into the hands of his receiver. The metaphor of threading the needle is an apt one since getting the thread through the eye of the needle is only preparatory for the act of "sewing." (Note also that "to make a pass" at someone is a conventional idiom for an act of flirtation.) Once the ball is in his possession, the receiver is transformed from a passive to an active role as he tries to move the ball as far forward as possible.

While it is possible to disagree with several of the interpretations offered of individual items of folk speech cited thus far, it would seem difficult to deny the overall sexual nature of much of football (and other sports) slang. The word *sport* itself has this connotation

and has had it for centuries. Consider one of Gloucester's early lines in *King Lear* when he refers to his bastard son Edmund by saying "There was good sport at his making" (I,i,23) or in such modern usages as "sporting house" for brothel"[29] or "sporting life" referring to pimps and prostitutes.[30] In the early 1950s, kissing was commonly referred to by adolescents as a "favorite indoor sport" presumably in contrast to outdoor sports such as football. It should also be noted that *game* can carry the same sexual connotation as *sport*.[31]

I have no doubt that a good many football players and fans will be skeptical (to say the least) of the analysis proposed here. Even academics with presumably less personal investment in football will probably find implausible, if not downright repugnant, the idea that American football could be a ritual combat between groups of males attempting to assert their masculinity by penetrating the endzones of their rivals. David Kopay, despite suggesting that for a long time football provided a kind of replacement for sex in his life and admitting that football is "a real outlet for repressed sexual energy,"[32] refuses to believe that "being able to hold hands in the huddle and to pat each other on the ass if we felt like it" is necessarily an overt show of homosexuality.[33] Yet I think it is highly likely that the ritual aspect of football, providing as it does a socially sanctioned framework for male body contact—football, after all, is a so-called body contact sport—is a form of homosexual behavior. The unequivocal sexual symbolism of the game, as plainly evidenced in folk speech, coupled with the fact that all of the participants are male, make it difficult to draw any other conclusion. Sexual acts carried out in thinly disguised symbolic form by, and directed towards, males and males only, would seem to constitute ritual homosexuality.

Evidence from other cultures indicates that male homosexual ritual combats are fairly common. Answering the question of who penetrates whom is a pretty standard means of testing masculinity cross-culturally. Interestingly enough, the word *masculine* itself seems to derive from Latin *mas* (male) and *culus* (anus). The implication might be that for a male to prove his masculinity with his peers, he would need to control or guard his buttocks area while at the same time threatening the posterior of another (weaker) male. A good many men's jokes in Mediterranean cultures (e.g., in Italy and in Spain) center on the *culo*.

That a mass spectacle could be based upon a ritual masculinity contest should not surprise anyone familiar with the bullfight. Without intending to reduce the complexity of the bullfight to a single factor, one could nonetheless observe that it is in part a battle between males attempting to penetrate one another. The one who is penetrated loses. If it is the bull, he may be further feminized or emasculated by having various extremities cut off to reward the successful matador. In this context, we can see American football as a male activity (along with the Boy Scouts, fraternities, and other exclusively male social organizations in American culture) as belonging to the general range of male rituals around the world in which masculinity is defined and affirmed. In American culture, women are permitted to be present as spectators or even cheerleaders, but they are not participants. Women resenting men's preoccupation with such male sports are commonly referred to as football widows (analogous to golf widows). This too suggests that the sport activity is in some sense a substitute for normal heterosexual relations. The men are "dead" as far as relationships with females are concerned. In sport and in ritual, men play both male *and* female parts. Whether it is the verbal dueling tradition of the circum-Mediterranean[34] in which young men threaten to put opponents into a passive homosexual position, or the initiation rites in aboriginal Australia and New Guinea (and elsewhere) in which younger men are subjected to actual homosexual anal intercourse by older members of the male group,[35] the underlying psychological rationale appears to be similar. Professional football's financial incentives may extend the playing years of individuals beyond late adolescence, but in its essence American football is an adolescent masculinity initiation ritual in which the winner gets into the loser's endzone more times than the loser gets into his!

NOTES

1. W. Branch Johnson, "Football, A Survival of Magic?" *The Contemporary Review* 135 (1929):228.
2. Johnson, 230–31; Francis Peabody Magoun, Jr., "Shrove Tuesday Football," *Harvard Studies and Notes in Philology and Literature* 13 (1931):24, 36, 44.
3. Johnson, 230.
4. David Riesman & Reuel Denney, "Football in America: A Study in Cultural Diffusion," *American Quarterly* 3 (1951): 309–25.
5. William Arens, "The Great American Football Ritual," *Natural History* 84 (1975):72–80. Reprinted in W. Arens & Susan P. Montague, eds., *The American Dimension: Cultural Myths and Social Realities* (Port Washington, 1975), 3–14.
6. Arnold R. Beisser, *The Madness in Sports* (New York, 1967); Shirley Fiske, "Pigskin Review: An American Initiation," in *Sport in the Socio-Cultural Process*, ed. M. Marie Hart (Dubuque, 1972), 241–58; and Arens, 72–80.
7. Arens, 77.
8. K. G. Sheard & E. G. Dunning, "The Rugby Football Club as a Type of 'Male Preserve': Some Sociological Notes," *International Review of Sport Sociology* 3–4 (1973):5–24.
9. Arens, 79.
10. George M. Foster, "Peasant Society and the Image of Limited Good," *American Anthropologist* 67 (1965):293–315.
11. G. T. W. Patrick, "The Psychology of Football," *American Journal of Psychology* 14 (1903):370.
12. A. A. Brill, "The Why of the Fan," *North American Review* 228 (1929):429–34.
13. Childe Herald [Thomas Hornsby Ferril], "Freud and Football," in *Reader in Comparative Religion,* eds. William A. Lessa and Evon Z. Vogt (New York, 2d ed., 1965), 250–52.
14. Adrian Stokes, "Psycho-Analytic Reflections on the Development of Ball Games, Particularly Cricket," *International Journal of Psycho-Analysis* 37 (1956):185–92.
15. Stokes, 190.
16. Stokes, 187.
17. Bruce Rodgers, *The Queens' Vernacular: A Gay Lexicon* (San Francisco, 1972), 27; Dennis Wepman, Ronald B. Newman, & Murray B. Binderman, *The Life: The Lore and Folk Poetry of the Black Hustler* (Philadelphia, 1976), 178.
18. Herald, 250.
19. George Plimpton, *Paper Lion* (New York, 1965), 59.
20. Kyle Rote & Jack Winter, *The Language of Pro Football* (New York, 1966), 102.
21. David Kopay & Perry Deane Young, *The David Kopay Story* (New York, 1977), 53–54.
22. Plimpton, 195, 339.
23. Harold Wentworth & Stuart Berg Flexner, *Dictionary of American Slang* (New York, 1967), 294; Rodgers, 155.
24. Vance Randolph, *Pissing in the Snow & Other Ozark Folktales* (Urbana, 1976), 9.
25. Wepman, Newman, & Binderman, 186.
26. Kopay & Young, 50–51.
27. Rote & Winter, 130.
28. Rodgers, 152.
29. Wentworth & Flexner, 511.
30. Wepman, Newman, & Binderman, *The Life.*
31. Rodgers, 92; Wepman, Newman, & Binderman, 182.
32. Kopay & Young, 11, 53.
33. Kopay & Young, 57.
34. Cf. Alan Dundes, Jerry W. Leach, & Bora Özkök. "The Strategy of Turkish Boys' Verbal Dueling Rhymes," *Journal of American Folklore* 83 (1970):325–49.
35. Cf. Alan Dundes, "A Psychoanalytic Study of the Bullroarer," *Man* 11 (1976):220–38.

REFERENCES

Arens, Williams. 1975. "The Great American Football Ritual," *Natural History* Vol. 84: 72–80. Reprinted in *The American Dimension: Cultural Myths and Social Realities*, ed. by W. Arens & Susan P. Montague. Port Washington.

Beisser, Arnold R. 1967. *The Madness in Sports*. New York.

Brill, A. A. 1929. "The Why of the Fan," *North American Review* 228: 429–34.

Childe, Herald [Thomas Hornsby Ferril]. 1965. "Freud and Football," in *Reader in Comparative Religion* (2d ed.), ed. by William A. Lessa & Evon Z. Vogt. New York.

Dundes, Alan. 1976. "A Psychoanalytic Study of the Bullroarer," *Man* Vol. 11:220–38.

Dundes, Alan, Jerry W. Leach, & Bora Özkök. 1970. "The Strategy of Turkish Boys' Verbal Dueling Rhymes," *Journal of American Folklore* Vol. 83:325–49.

Fiske, Shirley. 1972. "Pigskin Review: An American Initiation," in *Sport in the Socio-Cultural Process*, ed. by M. Marie Hart. Dubuque, IA.

Foster, George M. 1965. "Peasant Society and the Image of Limited Good," *American Anthropologist* Vol. 67:293–315.

Johnson, W. Branch. 1929. "Football, A Survival of Magic?" *The Contemporary Review* Vol. 135:228.

Kopay, David, & Perry Deane Young. 1977. *The David Kopay Story.* New York.

Magoun, Francis Peabody, Jr. 1931. "Shrove Tuesday Football," *Harvard Studies and Notes in Philology and Literature* Vol. 13, No. 24:36, 44.

Patrick, G. T. W. 1903. "The Psychology of Football," *American Journal of Psychology* Vol. 14:370.

Plimpton, George. 1965. *Paper Lion*. New York.

Randolph, Vance. 1967. *Pissing in the Snow & Other Ozark Folktales*. Urbana, IL.

Riesman, David, & Reuel Denney. 1951. "Football in America: A Study in Cultural Diffusion," *American Quarterly* Vol. 3:309–25.

Rodgers, Bruce. 1972. *The Queens' Vernacular: A Gay Lexicon*. San Francisco.

Rote, Kyle, & Jack Winter. 1966. *The Language of Pro Football*. New York.

Sheard, K. G., & E. G. Dunning. 1973. "The Rugby Football Club as a Type of 'Male Preserve': Some Sociological Notes," *International Review of Sport Sociology* Vol. 3–4:5–24.

Stokes, Adrian. 1956. "Psycho-Analytic Reflections on the Development of Ball Games, Particularly Cricket," *International Journal of Psycho-Analysis* Vol. 37:185–92.

Wentworth, Harold, & Stuart Berg Flexner. 1967. *Dictionary of American Slang*. New York.

Wepman, Dennis, Ronald B. Newman, & Murray B. Binderman. 1976. *The Life: The Lore and Folk Poetry of the Black Hustler*. Philadelphia.

5

Subsistence

With images of famine and drought very much at the forefront of the media, the question of how people subsist takes on an added urgency. The United States has ritually affirmed the importance of this issue by proclaiming World Food Day on October 16 and Earth Day on April 22. **Subsistence** at its most elementary entails the production of food and other necessities, requiring the application of human labor, techniques, and technologies to natural resources. In sum it is a process in which energy is expended to produce energy in different forms. The way in which a society produces energy—preeminently in the form of food, but including fire, animal power, and fossil fuels—obviously has a significant impact on the way people live, since neither features of the environment nor technology can be changed limitlessly. At the same time the environment will obviously impose constraints upon the type of subsistence people will practice.

Most anthropology textbooks discuss the different types of subsistence practices globally; they will thus not be discussed in depth here. Typically they include:

1. Foraging
   a. Pedestrian
   b. Equestrian
   c. Aquatic
2. Swidden/Slash and Burn/Extensive Agriculture
3. Pastoralism
   a. Transhumance
   b. Nomadism
4. Intensive/Large-Scale Agriculture

There is much debate about which of these systems are the most "energy-efficient," an issue dramatized during the regular "energy crises" the United States undergoes. It is important to emphasize that these are generally ideal types and that in reality most people, especially in the current world society, practice a mix of these strategies. Even the most isolated **hunter-gatherers** like the Bushmen have been part of the world system for a long time. Much of the ivory used in the manufacture of pianos that were prized possessions in many late nineteenth-century households in the United States, for example, was supplied by the Bushmen of Southwest Africa (Gordon, 1992). The important point is that in the current world situation more and more people are locked together in ties of interdependence. While officially the United States became involved in removing Iraq from Kuwait because of international law, most people realized that the need for Middle Eastern oil was a major unspoken factor. We have also begun to realize how one form of subsistence—for example, large-scale agriculture as practiced in the United States—can have an irreversible impact on people practicing, say, **foraging** in the Amazon, and vice versa. At the same time, these types of subsistence can interpenetrate or encapsulate each other. What, for example, is homelessness in the United States but a form of foraging? Or, for that matter, commercial fishing? These are in sharp contrast to some of the ideal types of subsistence where people had a larger degree of autonomy and were not so dependent upon other people. As people believe that they can produce energy and goods more cheaply by specialization, ties of interdependence increase. One can see this even in the case of a traditional people like the Gabbra, pastoral nomads of East Africa. Even in the absence of much specialization, the importance of redistribution of livestock for peoples' survival is indicative of their interdependence.

People like the Gabbra are often looked upon today with disapproval for their nomadic ways. In East Africa, postcolonial states see their disregard of political boundaries as a threat to their authority and so try to curtail their nomadism by encouraging more sedentary ways. Development economists regard their traditional ways as an inefficient method of raising livestock; to them, the rational approach is to drill wells to provide permanent water sources, permitting more livestock to be raised for sale, with less need to move around. The result of this combined impetus from politicians and economists to settle down is often massive environmental degradation, which leads to criticism from environmentalists, who all too often blame the nomads themselves for their plight. What they fail to recognize is that they supported themselves successfully for millennia without destroying their environment. The keys to their success were that they kept no more animals than were sufficient for their own needs and that they were able to move about as necessary so as not to overgraze any one place.

Daniel Stiles's article on the Gabbra depicts a successful adaptation that is now threatened by outside interests. Baird Straughan's article on the raised fields of Tiwanaku shows us another kind of adaptation, a form of intensive agriculture. In this case, although the system failed a thousand years ago, probably for political reasons, discovery of how this ancient system works holds promise of doing what modern agriculture has failed to do: provide a means by which Bolivian peasants can produce abundant food for themselves and their families as well as for sale. Not only will this be good for the Bolivians, but it may be good for the United States as well. If the peasants make

a decent living for themselves in the highlands, there is less incentive for them to move to the lowlands to grow coca, the source of cocaine. In the long run, reviving ancient agricultural technology in the Titicaca basin may do more to slow the production of cocaine than the various other (largely unsuccessful) techniques that have been tried (see Spedding's article in Chapter 12).

Pastoralism and agriculture (both intensive and extensive) are both forms of food production in which people rely on a relatively narrow range of domestic plants and animals for their subsistence. Up until about 12,000 years ago people were exclusively food foragers, relying on a wide variety of wild plants and animals for survival. Although food production developed independently in several different parts of the world, it is interesting that in all cases people hit upon the same combination of plant foods—what Sidney Mintz refers to as core (complex carbohydrates), legumes (protein-giving) and fringe (flavor-giving) plants, regardless of the specific varieties of plants involved. After serving us well for several years, as Mintz notes, this "core-legume-fringe" pattern is now being altered in a revolutionary way as humans have added (or are adding) high amounts of fats and processed sugars to their diets. The reasons for this change have as much to do with the symbolic meanings people assign to food as with anything else. For, as Mintz notes, food is not merely a source of nutrition but is loaded with symbolic meanings of all sorts.

REFERENCE

Gordon, Robert J. 1992. *The Bushman Myth: The Making of a Namibian Underclass.* Boulder, CO: Westview Press.

Nomads on Notice

Daniel Stiles

Daniel Stiles received a Ph.D. from the University of California at Berkeley for work on prehistoric cultures of eastern and southern Africa and is now a consultant to the United Nations Environmental Programme. He is also a research associate at the British Institute in East Africa. He first met the Gabbra in 1971 when working as a student archaeological assistant at Richard Leakey's research site on Lake Turkana. His current interest is in food foragers of Kenya, Madagascar, and India who are suppliers of forest products; his hope is to use this economic importance as a means for saving biological and cultural diversity.

Northern Kenya is a land of extremes, with wind-blasted volcanic wastes in the lowlands and lush tropical forests on isolated mountains. The territory is divided among several tribes that vigilantly defend their domains. The Gabbra pastoralists, who number about 35,000, cluster around the cracked, salt-encrusted mud flats of the Chalbi Desert and along the eastern shore of Lake Turkana. Because rainfall is sporadic and localized, water sources and vegetation are scattered and unpredictable. (Oases near the lake often provide fresh water, but the jade-colored lake itself is bitter with accumulated salts.) The Gabbra must move periodically, often splitting up their camps to take advantage of nature's meager offerings.

The keys to the Gabbra's survival are mobility, hard work, and cooperation. During their lives, married men go through various life stages, becoming at different times "political elders" and then "ritual elders." Along with those chosen for specific leadership roles, these elders control Gabbra life and also provide moral guidance.

The Gabbra separate their herds of camels, cattle, sheep, and goats by species, age, and whether or not they are giving milk. Milk is the traditional staple, followed by meat and then blood, but the Gabbra now commonly buy cornmeal through the sale of small livestock. They keep milk-giving animals at the main settlements (*ola*) and, to avoid overgrazing, send the dry ones and most males off to distant locations. Because of the danger of raiding by other tribes,

young warriors usually run the satellite camps, called *fora*. The zones separating enemy tribes are sparsely inhabited.

One of the insecure zones is around Koobi Fora, paleontologist Richard Leakey's research site. In 1971, while I was there on my first trip to northern Kenya, a raiding party of a neighboring nomadic group, the Dassenech, came across the border from Ethiopia, sending the Gabbra running and scaring the wits out of the researchers and camp crew. The Dassenech had guns; the Gabbra didn't.

In a few hours, the Gabbra can pack a settlement, tents and all, on the backs of their camels and be on their way to an area where rain has fallen. The household effects are simple: aluminum cooking pots; wooden and woven fiber containers for storing milk, meat, and fat; bed poles and sleeping skins; and various ritual sticks that symbolize status (for a young man, a married man, a father, a married women, an elder, and so on). Between 6:30 and 11:30 one morning, I observed four women in an area called Bubissa pack up their four families' skin tents, along with their pole frameworks and assorted contents, and load them onto the backs of groaning camels. The four households then set off on camels across the stony plains to go to Maikona, a two-day walk. A settlement may move up to ten times a year, depending on grazing conditions and security.

The Gabbra define four seasons, according to temperature and rainfall. Although conditions vary from year to year, generally the long, heavy rains come between late March and early June, followed by the cool dry season from June to September. Short rains arrive in October and last until early December, when the hot dry season sets in. During the dry periods, the Gabbra tend to live in small settlements grouped around permanent water sources, while in wetter times they occupy larger, more widely scattered settlements. When water becomes available in rain pools, for example, the otherwise dry Huri Hills become a favored pasture area. Three times a year, as many family members as possible, together with their livestock, gather at the *ola* for a *sorio,* a ceremony to bless the community and the livestock and to pray for rain and fertility.

Camels make up the bulk of the tribe's holdings, and without them the Gabbra could not live where they do. As beasts of burden, camels enable the Gabbra to move the *ola* rapidly to find fresh pasture after a cloudburst. Camels also transport water to the settlement, permitting an *ola* to be situated in good pasture as much as thirty miles from water. The Gabbra prefer to have female camels, with as many lactating ones as possible. In dry lands, camels provide much more milk than cattle do, lactating on average for at least a year after bearing a calf. A good camel can give more than two and a half gallons of milk a day during the rainy season and two to five quarts during the dry season. In contrast, a typical cow lactates only seven to nine months, giving two quarts of milk a day when pasture is lush and just a pint a day—and eventually none at all—during the dry times.

Camels also do less damage to the environment than other livestock. Their soft feet do not scuff up topsoil, causing it to blow or wash away, as hoofs do; and they feed on various types of vegetation, particularly leaves, so that the land does not lose the soil-conserving grass. Owing to the camel's relatively varied diet, its milk is higher in vitamin C and certain other nutrients than cattle milk.

Despite their sense of separate identity, the Gabbra are of mixed origins, in part derived from neighboring peoples. Arriving in the region in the late nineteenth century, mainly from Ethiopia and from farther east in Kenya, they took the land they now occupy from the Rendille and Samburu, who were squeezed to the south. They have since defended their territory successfully against invasions by the Turkana, who live west of Lake Turkana, and the Masai, who once occupied much of central and southern Kenya.

The Gabbra retain a reputation as fierce warriors. In greeting and prayer, however, they often use the word *nagaya*—"peace"—a cultural trait they share with Semitic peoples of western Asia, who are members of the same Afro-Asiatic language family. They particularly abhor strife within the tribe. I once witnessed two children, a boy and a girl, get into a fight. The boy hit the girl on the head with a rock and knocked her down. While I was treating her wound with antiseptic, several adults ran around seemingly in

a panic. By the time I had finished and calmed the girl down, the parents had organized an expiation ceremony on the spot. They recited prayers and sacrificed a sheep offered by the boy's parents. I received a goatskin bracelet made from the sacrificed animal, signifying welcome and peace.

Water is critical for survival in the desert, but the Gabbra carefully avoid fighting among themselves over access to the few wells and water holes. At the height of the dry season, hundreds of thirsty camels, cattle, sheep, and goats may bellow for water and kick up clouds of dust around a well as their herders struggle to keep them at bay and await their allotted turn. The "father of dividing," selected by the political elders (and almost always one himself), schedules each herd by species and ownership. He must be a man of fairness and iron will.

A chain of six or eight men position themselves in the well on dug-out ledges, projecting rocks in the wall, or scaffolding and pass the traditional giraffeskin containers up and down. The wells are often called "singing wells" because the men keep up a rhythmic chant as they draw the water up by hand from a depth of as much as fifty feet. The animals drink from a trough of molded mud, which needs constant repair from the damage caused by their jostling.

One of the biggest problems the Gabbra face is fulfilling labor needs. Averaging the wet- and dry-season regimes, researchers have calculated that nine people must work nine hours a day, every day, to mind one family herd and take care of the various household chores. To find the necessary labor, the Gabbra draw on a network of kinship and other social ties to look after the subdivided herds at the *ola* and the outlying camel, cattle, and small livestock camps.

In doing censuses, I learned that many more people are attached to a household than mom, dad, and the kids. For example, Wario Guyo, his wife, Shanu, and their young daughter slept in their house, while Wario's two nephews and an unmarried brother-in-law slept behind a thorn-branch windbreak out by the camel corral. A man belonging to a lower-status subgroup, the Wata, not allowed by tradition to sleep in the *ola,* lived to the west in the shade of an acacia tree. These additional household members each had a different herd of Wario's to care for and were paid in kind by food and stock offspring. Away from the *ola,* which was located on the eastern margin of the Chalbi Desert, two of Wario's sons looked after a *fora* near Lake Turkana, and the third was in school at Mount Marsabit, about sixty miles away.

To discover how many animals people owned, I had to unravel various types of loans and ownership arrangements. One young married man, Dub Boru, explained that most of his animals still belonged to his father, and that he had received them as an advance on his inheritance. He also had three camels and several sheep and goats that his *abuya*, a special uncle, had given him on important occasions, such as his circumcision. Dub also managed several milk camels obtained on loan. In exchange for taking care of the animals, he was entitled to their milk and their offspring, but had to give all subsequent generations of animals to the owner. Counting all the animals at Dub's *ola* and out at the *fora*, I estimated that he controlled at least eight lactating camels, two lactating cows, ten other adult camels, seven camel calves, four other cattle, and about sixty sheep and goats (small livestock reproduce quickly and are often sold or slaughtered, so exact figures are hard to come by). These animals provided food for six adults and adolescents and eight children.

Dub also exchanged animals. When his second child was born, for example, he traded one of his transport camels for a lactating cow; and when he needed money for cloth for his wife and school fees for a sister's son, he traded a heifer camel for ten goats, which he then sold. (Gabbra do not sell camels directly for money, for they fear this would bring misfortune.) Even with these maneuverings, Dub's animals weren't always sufficient to feed his family, owing to fluctuations in milk supply. So he pooled his herd with that of his brother-in-law, who was in a similar situation. The combined herds provided a more reliable source of milk.

The right of personal ownership does not, in the Gabbra's view, permit a man to monopolize more animals than he and his dependents need for survival. Through loans and gifts, excess animals are redistributed to the needy, allowing the whole community to survive. The secular authority of political elders and the moral authority of ritual elders ensure that these mechanisms of social cooperation are respected. One old man, Guracha Galgallo, is famous for owning about one thousand camels and many cattle and small livestock. Yet he dresses as all other Gabbra do, lives in the same style house, and eats the same food as the poorest Gabbra (although probably more regularly). Most of his animals are out on loan to those who have need of milk or transport or a bull for mating. His reward is respect.

The redistribution of livestock maximizes their use for food, transport, and cash. When there is a real surplus of animals, more than needed to meet the food requirements for the community as a whole (a rare occurrence), they are sacrificed and consumed at special ceremonial occasions to thank Waqa, the supreme be-

ing. As a result, the burden placed on the fragile environment is kept to a minimum. In contrast, many cattle pastoralists with more restricted systems of redistribution accumulate great numbers of animals. While their herds serve as insurance against drought and other calamities, they can cause serious land degradation.

Because food is usually in short supply, the Gabbra store little, although they have the technology to do so. For example, milk is soured and made into a kind of yogurt that lasts for weeks. And pieces of meat, stored with fat in small woven or wooden containers, can keep for more than a year. With food resources fluctuating from season to season and year to year, a group must manage enough animals to survive the worst conditions. To get by, an average family of six needs about twenty-eight camels, including six to eight that are lactating, or the equivalent in other cattle. Unfortunately, in 1991 drought and an undiagnosed camel disease reduced the herds below this level.

When the Gabbra and other northern Kenya pastoralists experienced hard times in the past, they always managed to endure. But now they are receiving food relief, and foreign relief agencies and other Westerners are exerting great influence on them. Because of the scarcity of livestock—and deteriorating security due to the troubles in Somalia and Ethiopia—raiding has also become much more frequent. Some Gabbra have moved to refugee camps to escape armed bandits.

If the neighboring countries regain political stability, and if the rains return, the Gabbra's traditional life should improve. But the last time I visited Gabbra country, I was not encouraged. Outsiders—famine relief workers, development-aid workers, missionaries, teachers, and government officers—are telling the Gabbra that they are backward and primitive. They are urging some to move to settlements on nearby Mount Marsabit and learn how to grow crops. There they would join Ethiopian immigrants, mission-settled refugees, southern Kenyan traders and administrators, and others who are encroaching on a "protected" national park forest.

Most Gabbra I know are horrified at the thought of taking up cultivation. One man, a ritual elder named Elema Arbu, told me that becoming a farmer was equivalent to becoming an outcast. "Without livestock, how can I provide bride price for my sons? How can I pay my stock debts? How can I make *sorio* and other sacrifices? How can I give the stock gifts at my nephews' circumcisions? Without herds, how can I hold my head up?"

The Secrets of Ancient Tiwanaku Are Benefiting Today's Bolivia

Baird Straughan

Baird Straughan is a journalist who does radio reports from La Paz and writes about Latin American politics. Currently he is working on behalf of the environmental movement in Bolivia. Alan Kolata ("El Doctor" to the Aymara) and Oswaldo Rivera, about whom he writes, are professor of anthropology at the University of Chicago and director of Bolivia's National Institute of Archaeology, respectively. They have been working at the archaeological site of Tiwanaku since 1978.

In 1987, Roberto Cruz didn't know his ancestors had built a civilization that lasted for nearly a thousand years. If you had told him their capital had been the nearby town of Tiwanaku, or that new research indicates they exercised control over a vast territory from Peru to Argentina, from the Pacific to the eastern slope of the Andes, he probably wouldn't have cared.

Cruz, an Aymara Indian living at 12,500 feet near the southern shores of Lake Titicaca in Bolivia, had enough trouble just surviving. His lands on the lake's floodplain, the Pampa Koani, were useless. Frosts there killed the crops, and boggy conditions rotted potatoes in the ground. His small fields on the hillside were exhausted, and he had no time to think about "the grandfathers," as he calls them.

That was before they reached out from the centuries and touched his life. They reached him through two outsiders whom Cruz met one day in 1987 walking across the pampa, over the strange pattern of parallel ridges and depressions that stretches for miles across the floodplain. He knew that they had been working for years among the ancient ruins nearby. But the two men told him some things he found hard to believe: that a thousand years ago his boggy lands had been fertile; that the ridges and depressions were the remains of a system of raised planting surfaces separated by canals; that if he redug the canals, the raised fields would produce again.

Cruz called together his neighbors. Could this be true? No, the Aymara concluded, the strangers probably just wanted to steal the land. No, they would continue farming the hillsides, where they had been as

"The Secrets of Ancient Tiwanaku Are Benefiting Today's Bolivia" by Baird Straughan, from *Smithsonion Magazine* Vol. 21, No. 11 (1991) pp. 38–43, 46, 47. Reprinted with permission.

long as anybody could remember. The frosts were milder there. But Cruz was curious. He told the two they could redig the canals on his lowland fields.

His neighbors were incensed. They called him to a meeting, and when he wouldn't go willingly, they trapped him, gathered the villagers and castigated him. Outsiders were bad luck, digging up "virgin earth that had never seen the light of the sun." That disturbed the weather. It was why the region was suffering a severe drought. Thanks to Cruz, they said, the whole town would starve. They threatened banishment.

Cruz wouldn't back down. He planted a crop on the raised platforms between the canals and watched his potato plants grow taller than he'd ever seen. Then, just before harvest, came his worst fear—frost. That whole night the villagers stood watch in their fields, Cruz with them. By early morning 90 percent of the crop on the hillsides was lost. Cruz walked down toward his fields on the pampa, knowing he'd made a terrible mistake. He could feel the coldest air flowing downhill to gather on the floodplain, where it would kill everything. The community had been right. The strangers had tricked him.

But when Cruz arrived at his land he saw with surprise that a mist had formed over it, a low white cloud that covered his fields "like a blanket." It lasted until the first rays of the morning sun, then vanished. Cruz walked out onto the platforms and was amazed to find his plants virtually undamaged.

Shortly thereafter he took in a record harvest. Today the edge of the Pampa Koani near Cruz's home is lined with raised fields dug by his neighbors. Cruz is a respected member of the community again.

He still thinks back to that one particularly bitter frost, and how his crop was miraculously saved. In fact, he now knows that what he saw rising from his fields that freezing night was the genius of Tiwanaku, a powerful state built by some of the greatest hydrologists the world had ever known.

The altiplano gets a great deal of heat from the sun during the day, but at night that heat escapes from the soil. Because the canals, which make up about 30 percent of the surface area, retain heat, they remain at least tepid and create a large temperature gradient. Water begins to evaporate and produces a fine mist that covers the fields, creating an artificial microclimate. In addition to the fog blanket, water drawn up into the soil platform by capillary action conducts heat to the plants' root systems.

One of the outsiders Roberto Cruz met on the pampa in 1987 was Alan Kolata.... He had come to Tiwanaku in 1978 through "a bit of serendipity," as he puts it. Given the opportunity to collaborate on a new archaeological project in Bolivia shortly after receiving his doctorate from Harvard, he flew to La Paz and was met by Oswaldo Rivera, a rising archaeologist from Bolivia's National Institute of Archaeology. Robert West, chairman of the board of Tesoro Petroleum Company of San Antonio, was setting up the Tiwanaku Archaeological Foundation to explore the ruins of the pre-Inca civilization on the altiplano bordering Lake Titicaca. Kolata and Rivera were to be in charge of it. "Dr. West has generously supported the project—and our work—with research funds ever since," Kolata says.

He began by surveying the Akapana Pyramid, Tiwanaku's most sacred temple. For the next four years the two archaeologists concentrated on excavation, finding fragments of Tiwanaku pottery and other artifacts among the ruins of the ancient city or on the nearby Pampa Koani.

A pattern of ridges and depressions on the floodplain intrigued them. They knew that similar topography had been reconstructed into raised fields and irrigation canals in Maya and Aztec jungle areas of Central America. Could it be done here?

Soon after beginning their collaboration, Kolata and Rivera identified 43 square miles that were the remains of raised fields separated by interconnected irrigation canals linked to the Katari River. They were beginning to suspect that Tiwanaku had been a far larger civilization than had been thought, one that would have needed excess crop yields to sustain conquests, crafts, a complex social hierarchy. But Western agronomists consider the altiplano at best marginal land, beset as it is by frequent frosts and exhausted soils.

Could the ancient Tiwanakans have succeeded where modern mechanized agriculture has failed? Would these fields have produced enough to sustain such a civilization? Kolata and Rivera decided there was only one way to find out: rehabilitate a field and plant a crop. A similar project, led by a colleague, Clark

Erickson of the University of Pennsylvania, was beginning across the lake in Peru.

In 1981, long before they met Cruz, they approached the community of Lacaya. Their presentation was well received. But as did the people of Cruz's village of Chokara several years later, the Lacayans soon blamed Kolata and Rivera for the severe drought. On one occasion campesinos stoned the two. "We were lucky to escape," Kolata recalls. It was not until 1987 that the reclamation project was back on track, first with Cruz and then at Lacaya. "We received major funding from the Inter-American Foundation. We put a lot of people to work and reintroduced the concept."

In April 1988, as Cruz was confounding his neighbors with his success, the first crop in the Lacaya fields yielded 20 metric tons of potatoes per hectare (about 2.5 acres): some were the size of grapefruit. It was seven times the average altiplano yield. There were also good crops of quinoa (a local grain), barley, oats, and vegetables such as lettuce and onions. Based on these yields, Kolata estimates that the Pampa Koani alone could have fed half a million people.

The new technique yielded another dividend: algae and aquatic plants began to grow, and with them, colonies of nitrogen-fixing bacteria. In several months a thick ooze formed at the bottom of the canals. When the harvest was in, the campesinos drained the canals and shoveled excellent organic fertilizer onto their fields.

There has been a complete turnabout in the reception the archaeologists receive. Kolata is now a welcome figure on the southern shores of Lake Titicaca. Clad in jeans and cowboy boots, his lanky 6-foot-2-inch frame towers above the Aymara, short people with broad torsos that house lungs big enough to cope with the thin air. Despite his appearance, he is completely at home among the campesinos in the fields or supervising the careful work of uncovering the secrets of the once glorious city called, according to legend, Taypi Kala, "The Stone in the Center."

A LEGACY FROM "THE GRANDFATHERS"

Harvests such as those now being reaped on Tiwanaku's ancestral fields give hope for the future. About 1,200 compesinos are using raised fields. Oswaldo Rivera ... has requests for assistance from another 50 villages eager to apply the same principle. Some units of the Bolivian Army have begun a Plan Verde (Green Plan), teaching conscripts the raised-field technology. And the Bolivian government is looking for $40 million to spread the technique throughout the country. Large-scale development projects have a bad record in Bolivia, but if the government is successful in this one it would be in a better position to confront the country's burgeoning problems.

U.S. Ambassador Robert Gelbard, an enthusiastic supporter of and fundraiser for the project, urges that it be expanded as quickly as possible. "We are finding that nutritional levels have improved dramatically in these areas," he explains, "and not just because of the potato harvest. There are fish in the canals, the ducks lay eggs—protein levels have gone up considerably."

The potential benefits for Bolivia are tremendous. Chronic malnutrition afflicts nearly half of all Bolivian children, and the country must import food even though most of its citizens work in agriculture. Large numbers of farmers are abandoning their exhausted land on the altiplano and migrating to the Amazon basin, where they can grow coca or clear new farms in the rain forest by the slash-and-burn method.

"The good thing about the system," according to Kolata, "is that it functions almost anywhere there's a secure source of water." As to the archaeologists' role, he says simply. "We're only giving back to the Aymara what their ancestors developed thousands of years ago."

A Taste of History

Sidney Mintz

Sidney W. Mintz, who is professor of anthropology at Johns Hopkins University, received his Ph.D. from Columbia University in 1951. In addition to the anthropology of food, his theoretical interests include economic anthropology and peasant society. His regional interests lie in Latin America and the Caribbean.

Eating unites all living things; but not all living things eat in the same manner, nor even with the same intentions. Our species stands alone, having resolutely created regimens of diet, and manners of eating, ludicrously remote from its animal nature. Not all members of our species eat the same things, any more than they speak the same language, wear the same clothes, or pray to the same god.

As a species that deals continuously in things that stand for something else, in "representations," we have burdened the food we eat with a backbreaking symbolic load. Food represents us; it sends our distinctive messages. Hence eating, like fasting, serves many purposes. "I'm not hungry," can be a signal of great potency, as every anxious mother knows. Only of us human beings may it be said that when we are hungry, we may act sated. The same cannot be said of my cat, or your dog; when they act unconcerned about food, they've really had enough to eat.

There is more to this matter of eating mysteries. In her pioneering studies of food and taboo, Mary Douglas, drawing upon Claude Lévi-Strauss, has called our attention to the ways that human groups categorise social reality. In Douglas's view, much of the mystery of food inheres in the structure of the abstract categories that society has created. She has offered her readers a vision of tabooed foods as foods that straddle categories—the absence of scales, the presence of cloven hoofs—creatures with mixed traits, that will not fall into place, and so their flesh is deemed unclean. Though her views have been challenged, they have, I think, a convincing ring.

The strong feelings of other cultures about certain foods, as revealed in their taboos, are not likely to surprise us, as long as we find the prohibited items repulsive. If, however, we are enthusiastic eaters of some of these tabooed foods ourselves, we may be somewhat hurt—or perhaps just condescending—when confronted with the visible disgust of others. The tabooing of pork by Moslems, like the tabooing of milk by many Asians, may appear to westerners as regrettable but excusable benightedness. But sincere revulsion at the sight of a food we care about can seem to us unfeeling—indeed, insulting. Whatever else we are about food, we humans are touchy, deeply affected by its colours, smells, and contexts.

That food can excite strong positive feelings we all know and recognise. The tastes, smells, colours and textures of foods are among our earliest memories. Reawakened by association, they can take us back to our infancy: dependent, fragile, busily soaking up emotional and bodily nourishment in the arms or on the laps of those who made us human by teaching us to like the foods our culture deemed proper for humans.

People everywhere are certain that they not only know what is good for real humans to eat, but that their being human is somehow connected to their food habits. Why else do members of one culture so often find the food habits of another odd; or mildly unpleasant; or downright disgusting? Yet if we know nothing of the culture, we have no way of knowing what food its folk will consider delicious, and what repulsive.

Eating habits, in other words, are not only acquired habits but also historically derived habits, uninscribed in our natures. But what people eat actually pales to near-insignificance alongside why people eat—and why they do not. Classical scholars tell us of those people who overate, and then made themselves vomit, simply in order to be able to eat more. Others starved themselves in order to get close to their gods. How arresting is this aspect of our nature, that so fundamental

"A Taste of History" by Sidney W. Mintz, from *The Higher Perspective*, May 8, 1992, pp. 15, 18. Reprinted with permission of the author.

a need of our physical selves may be stifled, at will, for some other perceived good!

In my country, the United States, there were those who formed picket lines and boycotted restaurants, to fight for the right to eat in the company of people they did not like. That was because breaking bread together—or, at any rate, next to each other—was correctly understood to be a powerful and nearly universal marker of equality. In certain highly stratified societies, such as India, the whole domain of food is deeply embedded in considerations of social, economic, political and religious identity, such that food and status are practically inseparable sociologically. No wonder that the eating behaviour of our species reminds us of no other animal—it is so unlike that of any other.

Indeed it may be said of this biological bedrock activity that human eating in culturally specific terms—and it always is culturally specific—is but barely connected to human biology at all.

This aspect of our behaviour has to do with the uniquely human capacity to create a symbolic world, and then both to call it reality and to treat it as real. But each symbolic world—Aymara, Bemba, American—is a different symbolic world. It is precisely this staggering diversity of worlds of meaning, carried by members of one single species, that makes the human animal so special.

Though human beings have been seeking and successfully finding their food for perhaps three million years or more now, only in the past 12,000 or so have they learned how to domesticate plants and animals, so that they could control the growth of their own food supply. It was not something invented just once, but many different times, and with different living things. Rice and soyabeans and pigs in Asia; potatoes and llamas and guinea pigs in the Andes; maize and tomatoes and chocolate and chili and turkeys in Mexico and Central America; millet and okra and coffee and pussycats in Africa; olives and cabbage in Europe—all domesticated by nameless ordinary folk, and bequeathed to all of us by a posterity that culture made possible.

Domestication is the single greatest technical achievement in the human record, more important than the internal combustion engine or nuclear energy. Like these others, it was from the beginning a remarkable way to capture and control energy. But those other accomplishments were culminations of millennia of prior technical achievement—achievement made possible because of the benefits once arising from domestication.

In spite of the tremendous variety of plants and animals domesticated by humankind, over time it became clear that a relatively small number had become the subsistence mainstay of our species. Animals will not concern us here; plants will. Among the plants upon which our species gradually became dependent

there figured less than a dozen grasses and perhaps an equal number of rhizomes or tubers. The grasses would include wheat, barley, oats, rye, maize, rice, sorghum and the millets—not many more ever became truly important. The tubers include manioc (cassava), yams, taro, sweet potatoes, and potatoes—again, few others ever became truly important. Around this array, most of the important societies in world history built their food supply. Moreover, the increase in world population occurring in the very period when domestication was mastered makes it likely that the majority of human beings who have ever lived subsisted primarily on this rather small number of foods.

Everywhere that one finds these plants with lots of "starch" in them—the so-called "complex carbohydrates"—one also finds one or more legumes. The legumes or pulses are protein-carrying plants: peas, beans, groundnuts, chickpeas. They "go with" the starchy goods, the complex carbohydrates.

Finally, everywhere that people eat one or more complex carbohydrates with one or more legumes, they also have flavours for their food. They are what Audrey Richards called "relish" and I shall call fringe. Every cuisine has it. It "helps the food go down." It differs in lots of ways from the basic starchy food, and some of those differences show up provocatively. The important thing is to see these three food types as types, as categories, not as particular foods. The starchy centre of the cuisine I call the "core"; the flavour-giving foods I call "fringe"; the protein-giving food I call "legume" (because that is what they are): core-fringe-legume. Together they form a pattern, and I call that pattern the CFLP. Of course the pattern is not apparent to the eaters—they are interested in eating, not in some observer's devices for explaining things to himself. The particular foods are immensely important to the eater. Imagine convincing the Chinese to replace rice with black bread—or the Russians to replace black bread with rice! Eaters do not care about the words of others, but about food, and they all have startlingly specific and explicit notions of what a good meal is. Like language, in that sense food is "democratic." Everybody speaks, but knows and cherishes his own or her own language. Similarly, everybody has strong opinions on food, but those opinions are about specific foods, familiar foods, the "right" foods. Yet from the picture of a pattern I am trying to develop here, the Chinese rice and the Russian black bread are to some degree interchangeable.

Let us imagine three different meals, to see how this might work. In the first, a broth or soup is made, using various fringe elements as well as one or more legumes. Into the soup at serving is ladled a substantial quantity of a precooked starchy meal or flour, to make a kind of soupy stew or porridge. The dish is then eaten with a spoon. In the second cuisine, some kind of bread is baked or otherwise cooked from the flour of a cereal. Once it is baked, there is inserted into it—as if it were an envelope, a sheath, or other container—a quantity of fringe foods and legumes. The resulting dish, rather like a large sandwich, can be eaten with one's hands. Or the core food can form a "plate" for the fringe and legume. In the third cuisine, a thick porridge or gruel is made from the rhizome of a starchy vegetative plant. It is then sprinkled with, or has stirred into it, additional foods, probably including some fringe elements; a legume may also be added, or it may be eaten separately instead. The flavoured gruel is then folded within an inedible leaf container, and in this form may be boiled, steamed or baked. It is unwrapped to be eaten. The appearance of these principal dishes varies greatly; but their composition may be quite similar.

The difference between core and fringe seems always to be enshrined in the language itself, and in the way food is eaten. That a Chinese banquet has no rice is, among other things, a way of declaring that it is a banquet. That the proportion of fringe to core increases on ritual occasions is a way of saying it is a ritual occasion. That core without fringe would be tedious most of the time is understood; that fringe without core would be "rich"—even nauseating—is just as well understood. People seem often to be left wanting a "little more" of some part of the fringe; but they do not normally imagine making a meal of the fringe. In other words, the formal distinctions which follow should not blind us to the fact that this difference is a living part of the way the world of food is organised for most people.

Perhaps the most striking difference between core and fringe is botanical: the core is always a complex carbohydrate; the fringe is probably never one. Another striking difference is likely to be texture: the core is always cooked, and always relatively soft and chewy (bread, rice, potatoes, tortillas, couscous, boiled and mashed yams, taro, manioc "bread," sorghum "mealies," and so on. Texture is another customary difference: the core is almost always soft, if the fringe is solid; but the fringe may be mainly liquid in some cuisines. Cooking normally transforms the core into a softer substance with homogeneous taste and texture. The fringe may also be soft, but it may also be hard and chewy, or of any intermediate texture. Perhaps the most dramatic difference will be colour. The fringe is almost invariably more coloured than the core, and may even be quite violently coloured (red, golden, bright green; many-coloured, with special dyes, black or dark purple or grey). The core is usually white or beige, or cream-coloured or some shade or shades of brown. This is merely the beginning of the contrast, because the real difference is taste. The fringe always has "more taste" than the core; the core "tastes better" with fringe; the fringe "helps" one eat more core; the

fringe by itself (like the core by itself, except under special ritual conditions) is less appetising than the two combined. The ingredient(s) in the fringe may be from a cultivated or a wild source—to pick an example, wild dandelion leaves versus cultivated watercress. It may be plant (garlic) versus animal (cheese). It may be liquid (broth) versus solid (mushrooms).

A classification as simple as this one cannot by any means serve to describe cuisines. That is not its purpose. But it can serve to make major cuisines comparable, at a simple level. It has certain nutritional implications—but again, these are only of the simplest sort. And it has historical implications, too, because it is based on the idea that certain parallels in cuisine emerged after the mastery of plant and animal husbandry. I believe that these parallels were standardised to some extent, as complex political systems emerged, and territorial control was extended over large and ecologically different zones.

To discuss meaning in the context of the cuisines of specific civilisations and cultures is beyond my purpose here. But anyone who has read of the mystical significance of maize in the case of American Indian peoples, of rice in the case of Asia, or of wheat in the case of the West knows well how the imagery of particular foods can provide a governing idiom for life itself. Here, I would like to turn to quite another sort of meaning.

A few hundred years ago, the ancient and widespread centre-fringe-legume pattern, diverse in detail but similar from case to case in its broad outlines, began to crumble. This happened first in western Europe. Its deterioration came at about the same time as the Industrial Revolution. During the ensuing two centuries, the CFLP has decayed at ever-faster rates, over more and more of the Earth's surface.

The main alternative foods, which have served to hasten the destruction of the ancient CFLP itself, fall into two principal categories. Both are typified by high caloric concentrations. Both stand in dramatic contrast to the starchy cores. Both can be consumed in varied fashion with the core foods. Indeed both, in one form or another, have certain very ancient associations with human appetite.

One of these two food categories consists of fats—animal fats such as lard and butter, and nonanimal (seed, nut and vegetable) oils, such as corn (maize), palm, cottonseed, peanut (groundnut) safflower, rapeseed and sesame oil. There are great differences between these two sorts of fats, "animal" and "vegetable," both in terms of their nutritive and health meanings for humans, and in terms of the nature and economy of their production. Yet there are reasons for classifying them together here. The most important modern example of these fats for our purposes is oleomargarine, a hydrogenated fat product now most commonly from vegetable oils.

The other such alternative food category consists of sugars—but so-called "processed sugars," such as sucrose from cane, dextrose and (isomerised) fructose from maize, and so on, rather than the unprocessed sugars to be found in fruits and vegetables.

Together, fats and sugars—both in the ways that they are extracted, and in the ways that they are conceived and combined—have modified in some ways our human relationship to nature, while playing a special role in the remaking of the food habits of the entire world. That remaking, however, has been uneven and, as noted earlier, it happened first in the West, particularly in western Europe. It happened next in the European (or "white") colonies or erstwhile colonies—such as the US, Canada, Australia, Argentina, South Africa, and so on. It has now begun to happen in much of the world at large, including the old colonial areas of the West (such as Africa, the Caribbean and South East Asia), and in what once was called the socialist world. This massive change, whereby sugars and fats have gradually begun to replace the complex carbohydrates of the centre and thereby to erode the structure of the meal itself, I refer to as the "second revolution." If the first revolution was domestication, perfected 12,000 years ago, then the second revolution is now much less than five centuries old.

The way CFLP eaters become big consumers of fats and sugars is not some single, undifferentiated vector, but many different ongoing processes, some not yet well understood, that I have lumped together here under one messy term. Our understanding of how food habits change, both historically and at the present time, remains incomplete. Hardly anywhere, apparently, is the value of a change from one way of eating to another carefully weighed or questioned by consumers, who often seem to be "thinking about something else" besides eating and drinking when they are learning to consume a new product. A good illustration of a modern new food that has wrought great changes in a short time, almost unnoticed, is the so-called "soft drink," usually a carbonated, heavily sweetened, flavoured drink served cold. A trivial product consumed by a tiny minority of the world's population 75 years ago, the soft drink is now almost as widely diffused as salt. In the US, we now drink more soft drinks than water.

I return to the matter of meaning. Consider the increases in the consumption of sugar in the United Kingdom in the period from about 1650 to 1900, especially in association with the hot stimulant beverages. It seemed to me that there was no single convincing reason why Britons and their neighbours had so enthusiastically taken up the consumption of heavily sweetened tea. But poor nutrition, a difficult climate, and the appeal of a hot, stimulating, heavily sweetened beverage made this change highly probable, once sugar and tea became known and affordable. What might be said about meaning in this connection?

In trying to answer the question, I did not think it enough to talk about the structure of the meal, or the symbolic significance of the contrasts within it, in explaining what food meant. Such analyses of meaning can proceed without recourse to history or economics, because meaning is defined as embodied in the foods themselves.

But the way British food habits changed—the replacement of home baking with store-bought breads, of home-brewed ale with tea, of butter with jam—suggests the usefulness of analysis that takes into account change, prices, advertising and the social conditions under which a new food is added, including the intentions of producers, retailers and the state. I want to know where these new foods came from, why they succeeded, who benefited from their production and sale, how their prices had changed. The answers to such questions are clearly quite different from those concerned with the internal symbolic structure of the meal.

In effect, I suggest that the cultural materials, such as food, which people employ in creating systems of symbols, are not givens, but are themselves the precipitate of economic, social and political processes. Sugar was a relatively new substance for the British people, one which percolated down the class system from royalty to the people, meanwhile acquiring all sorts of particular symbolic weight. These creations of "inside" meaning occurred within a field of larger forces: the interests of the planters, the slave traders and the merchants; the taxing and military power of the state; the medical and political/economic arguments that were made in favour of sugar. It seemed to me that all properly enter into a broader discussion of what sugar came to mean to those who eventually became its consumers. To decode fully the meaning of the meal, one might try decoding the process of codification as well. Of course such a view is arguable. It is another sort of meaning of foods that might be worth thinking about.

6

Economic Systems

Generally two meanings are attached to the word **economics.** On the one hand, it refers to maximizing behavior, as when we have to "economize"; on the other hand, it also refers to a system of how production is organized, exchanged, or distributed and consumed. While we like to think of economic behavior as rational, values, tastes, fads, and other idiosyncrasies play a role in our decision making in such a way as to bedevil any apparent rationality. How many parents would charge their children interest for a loan? Why do we grow our own vegetables when it would be much cheaper to purchase them at the local supermarket?

At the same time, we have an institution known as the national economy in which we feel as if we are passive recipients of forces beyond our control. While these two economies seem to be disparate and distinct, they share a number of common characteristics; most importantly, since very few people directly consume what they produce, both of them have to do with **exchange.**

Marshall Sahlins (1972), who defined the various types of exchange, distinguishes between reciprocal, redistributive, and market exchanges. There are three types of reciprocity. First is **generalized reciprocity,** where there is no expectation of an immediate counterflow of equal value. Two typical examples are the following:

- Bushmen foragers share the spoils of a hunt with other camp followers in the expectation that their generosity will be reciprocated in some distant time.
- Parents will spoil children in the hope that when the parents are old, the children will feel obligated to help them. In these types of exchanges the participants will deny that they are economic and will couch them in terms of kinship or friendship obligations.

Second, there is **balanced reciprocity,** or trade, where one has a direct obligation to reciprocate in order to continue the social relationship. Again, it need not be a single commercial transaction. For example, it might be cheaper for me to buy groceries at the supermarket, but I often prefer to use my local corner store, even though it is more expensive, because on occasion they will provide me with credit and other favors. Similarly, as most members of a social drinking group know, when one buys a round, everyone reciprocates. If one member does not drink beer, however, but prefers whiskey, very soon that person gets left out or changes his or her taste because the reciprocity becomes unbalanced and this somehow "spoils the atmosphere." Finally, there is **negative reciprocity,** which is impersonal, barter-based, and centered on one's own ends. In terms of economic behavior, it is the "most economic" and ranges from theft to exploitation. It has very little morality in it and is typically practiced on people separated by great social distance.

All types of reciprocity can be found in one relationship, as in the case of a marital relationship in which one's spouse is unfaithful. Even socially frowned-upon practices like corruption can be analyzed in terms of exchange, as is made clear by Sean McNamara's case study of how to bribe a policeman.

The second type of exchange that Sahlins mentions is **redistributive,** which is more coercive and entails the produce of labor from several individuals being brought to a central place where it is sorted, counted, and reallocated. Such forms of redistribution can take two forms: egalitarian or stratified. A good example of **egalitarian redistribution** would be among the Yanomami where the headman/redistributer simply has to work harder than anyone else and gets nothing in return immediately except perhaps admiration. In **stratified redistribution** the redistributer withholds his or her own labor, retains the largest share, and ends up with more material wealth. Typically these exchanges are clothed in a rhetoric of kinship obligations.

Market exchange, the final type, is by far the most dominant; its most important form of exchange is buying and selling. Closely related to the capitalist system in which the idea of a market is central, market exchange is not, however, the sole mechanism for exchange in a capitalist system. Prices on the market are determined by supply and demand. In the market, loyalties and values are not supposed to enter in, but they often do.

One of the great contributions of anthropology has been in the discovery of the informal sector, or dual economy, of the market. This notion, first pioneered by the anthropologist Keith Hart in 1973, has had a major impact on our understanding of how people survive economically. It refers essentially to people's innumerable economic activities that are not recorded in government statistics as tax returns or licenses. In many parts of the world this vibrant sector was usually ignored by economists, principally because it is so difficult to track. Philippe Bourgois's study, "Crack in Spanish Harlem," is representative of this type of economic activity. In many parts of the world the informal sector is more important than the formal sector.

Another contribution anthropologists have made is in their "discovery" of the obvious, an example being the economic importance of used clothing in Zambia. In Karen Hansen's article we see how used clothing has become a "hot item" of market exchange, and how the West's discarded items are transformed into desired garments that are distinctively Zambian, and symbolic of hope and progress.

REFERENCE

Sahlins, Marshall. 1972. *Stone Age Economics*. Chicago: Aldine.

Learning How to Bribe a Policeman

Sean Cush McNamara

Sean Cush McNamara is a British anthropologist who has carried out fieldwork in Bolivia.

There has been some discussion by social scientists interested in development studies on the use of public office for private gain. Although this question has had general interest for me, I never thought I would have any experience to contribute to the discussion. Indeed, as for many law-abiding people in Britain, such interests appear rather exotic. It was therefore rather a surprise, during a recent visit to Bolivia, to find myself inside a prison and bribing my way out again. What was immediately interesting was that I did not know how to bribe someone. This does not seem to have been part of my education in life skills and I had to learn about the process.

How did I find myself in this situation? Well, with a friend I had just arrived in Santa Cruz from La Paz. Santa Cruz is of interest as one of the last remaining "frontier" regions of the world. This frontier has been created first of all by discovery of oil and the subsequent immigration this has stimulated. The sleepy town surrounded by forest of the early 1970s is now a bustling centre from which the forest has receded. It has the feel of the Wild West to match its situation but with new pick-up trucks, not horses, in the streets. Two hours after arrival in Santa Cruz we were in the central plaza looking at an exhibition of handicrafts, and about a quarter of an hour later we were in the police station. Later, out again and back in our hotel, we overheard an American couple talking of their brush with the law and of their near-imprisonment. So this was not an isolated incident. In order to understand the system which gives rise to harassment of foreigners in Santa Cruz there is a need to describe the most salient features of the local economy.

THE CONTEXT

In Bolivia there is an inflation rate variously estimated between 500 and 2,000% per year. This means salaries

erode rapidly and rises granted every quarter or even every month cannot keep pace. Daily paid workers obtain rises daily. There are two exchange rates in operation: in early June 1985 the official rate was 75,000 pesos to the dollar while the parallel rate was rising rapidly from about 300,000 to 400,000 pesos. This means that there is a great desire among salaried people, including the police, to obtain dollars in order to retain the value of "savings" (i.e., cash that has not been spent today but which will be needed tomorrow). The general importance of these factors in the bribery of policemen will be seen later. I should stress that these are not sufficient conditions: there are special features of Santa Cruz which make it different from the rest of the country. Whilst the national economy is struggling, the economy of Santa Cruz is buoyant. Santa Cruz is the area where oil, cocaine, and contraband play major roles in the economy. The resultant dollar wealth has two consequences which are relevant here. First, there is an extremely unequal distribution of dollars. Second, every foreigner is a potential supply, as are street money changers and small-time cocaine dealers.

THE PROTECTION OF THE LAW

The general objective for a salaried policeman is to ensure his subsistence for the whole month. In June 1985 it was reckoned that his salary of approximately $28 would last about a fortnight. Other cash must be obtained from other sources. The operational problem to be resolved by many policemen (without access to other funds) is how to ensure a reasonable flow of cash. Here the policeman's duty of upholding the law is very useful as it can be used to generate further funds.

Dealing in cocaine or contraband is illegal. There is mounting international pressure to reduce the flow of cocaine from Bolivia, and the Bolivian government is itself concerned about increasing domestic drug

"Learning How to Bribe a Policeman" by Sean Cush McNamara, from *Anthropology Today,* Vol. 2, No. 2, 1986. Royal Anthropological Institute. Reprinted with permission.

addiction. However it is common knowledge in Santa Cruz that some drug dealers are very wealthy and powerful and manage to evade the law. The same cannot be said of small-time dealers with few connections. Such small-timers populate the local prison.

Currency transactions in the street are also illegal but can be considered almost a necessity if the illegal dollar earnings are to be used within the Santa Cruz economy. Perhaps in recognition of this, money changers continue to operate in the street but have been moving away from the central plaza to the ring road.

Because of the intense interest in drugs there is a justification for taking an interest in foreigners: every one is a potential drug smuggler. However there must usually be some pretext for questioning a foreigner. Such pretexts are easy to find: talking to a known money changer; not carrying passports; driving a foreign vehicle. Once contact has been established, the game plan is as follows:

- Talking to someone *is* changing money illegally.
- Not carrying passport *is* being a suspected drug smuggler.
- Parking a vehicle *is* parking illegally.

All these pretexts enable the law to be used to gain a top-up of salary. In our case we were talking in the plaza when a policeman asked for proof of identity. Our passports were in the hotel—theft of passports is quite common—and a driving licence was not considered sufficient.

At this point there are three options for a foreigner:

1. Walk away immediately and with determination.
2. Pay bribe on the spot.
3. Accompany officer to the police station.

The problem of the second option is that foreigners do not know how to do it, and the first option does not come to mind. The third option has the consequence that a senior officer is involved and he wishes to receive the bribe. However, in front of many people in the outer offices of the police station it will probably appear even more difficult to bribe a policeman. The opportunity is offered by the senior officer requesting all pockets to be emptied. Having cash in pesos and dollars is further "evidence" of illegal money changing. We had the impression that confiscation of dollars was possible at this stage, except that since we were carrying travellers' cheques in the main this was less likely.

Not resolving the issue at this stage brings about an escalation in police pressure. The protest of innocence to the first policeman is now interpreted as "threatening behaviour," and the suspect is removed to the inner courtyard. This is inhabited by minor drug dealers and others serving a range of sentences or simply being held in custody. The economy of this part of the prison involving sale of clothing to buy food, negotiations between guards and women also held there—would be an interesting study in its own right.

Once in the courtyard the charge is rumoured to have increased again to assaulting a policeman, and an even more senior officer (who never appears in person) is involved. The immediate prospect seems to be a few hours or days in this courtyard; this is clearly designed as a softening up until the bribe is paid.

LEARNING HOW TO PAY A BRIBE

In the courtyard the minor drug dealers know the rules. One, who had been in the main prison elsewhere, had secured his own transfer to the relative comfort of the courtyard. A laid-back character who has now kicked his own habit but with 20 years still to serve officially (having completed 5), he makes himself useful talking to newcomers and passing on information received. We had the feeling our story was being checked informally and we heard how the charges were escalating. Through this intermediary it was made known that a bribe could be made and initial negotiations began over the amount. At the same time a CID man was sent to the hotel to collect the passports. Also the police heard that it was difficult for us to give a "bribe."

The final arrangements were made by the officer from the outer offices. The charges about hitting a policeman were forgotten but a "fine" was to be paid for keeping the passports safely in the hotel. We were asked how much we would like to pay. Working on the basis that $1 would have probably been acceptable to the very first policeman and that $50 obtains an internal transfer for a drug dealer according to our new friend, a sum of approximately $15 was offered in pesos to compensate for the inconvenience we had caused the police. This was agreed. Possibly a lower "fine" would have been acceptable in dollars.

As a sidelight on the affair, the CID man who had collected the passports had to accompany us back to the hotel where the staff had made him sign a receipt for the passports. He asked for $2 for his inconvenience.

CONCLUSIONS

The experience brings out a number of points:

1. If a bribe is a "fine," cross-cultural difficulties are resolved.

2. The amount increases as the centre of the prison is approached, and more senior officers are involved. A visitor should avoid accompanying the officer to the police station.

3. The police require their own justifications—for making the first contact and for raising the "fine" and these are found by reference to the law.

4. Police harassment is determined in this situation by economic factors; the incidence of harassment increases as the month progresses (and the salary diminishes in value).

5. The contempt with which local people treated the local police almost amounted to counter-harassment, except that locals were very aware of how and when to walk away from confrontation.

Ironically we had been trying to obtain cash dollars in order to pay the airport tax but were not able to find any legally so on the way to the airport the ring road money changers proved useful—though they were reluctant to buy pesos. This was an illustration of how a system of law not founded in economic reality— i.e., having to pay airport tax in dollars but there being none offered legally for purchase—creates a necessity for illegality.

Finally, although the experience is unique, I hope it adds some local colour to the recent debate on the use of public office for private gain.

Crack in Spanish Harlem
Culture and Economy in the Inner City

Philippe Bourgois

Philippe Bourgois, an associate professor at San Francisco State University, was awarded the Ph.D. by Stanford University in 1985. Bourgois has carried out fieldwork in the Caribbean and Central America as well as in Spanish Harlem and has research interests in political economy, ethnicity, immigration, and the work process.

The heavy-set, white undercover policeman pushed me across the ice-cream counter, spreading my legs and poking me around the groin. As he came dangerously close to the bulge in my right pocket I hissed in his ear "It's a tape recorder." He snapped backwards, releasing my left hand's grip on my neck and whispering a barely audible "Sorry." Apparently, he thought he had clumsily intercepted an undercover from another department because before I could get a close look at his face he had left the *bodega* grocery-store cum numbers-joint. Meanwhile, the marijuana sellers stationed in front of the *bodega* that Gato and I had just entered to buy 16-ounce cans of Private Stock (beer), observing that the undercover had been rough with me when he searched through my pants, suddenly felt safe and relieved—finally confident that I was a white drug addict rather than an undercover.

As we hurried to leave this embarrassing scene we were blocked by Bennie, an emaciated teenager high on angel dust who was barging through the door along with two friends to mug us. I ran to the back of the *bodega* but Gato had to stand firmly because this was the corner he worked, and those were his former partners. They dragged him onto the sidewalk surrounding him on all sides, shouting about the money he still owed, and began kicking and hitting him with a baseball bat. I found out later that Gato owed them for his share of the supply of marijuana confiscated in a drug bust last week. . . . After we finished telling the story at the crack/*botanica*[1] house where I had been spending most of my evening hours this summer, Chino, who was on duty selling that night with Julio (pronounced Jew-Lee-oh), jumped up excitedly calling out, "What street was that on? Come on, let's go, we can still catch

them—How many were they?" I quickly stopped this mobilization for a revenge posse, explaining that it was not worth my time, and that we should just forget about it. Chino looked at me disgustedly sitting back down on the milk crate in front of the *botanica's* door and turned his face away from me, shrugging his shoulders. Julio, whom I knew better and had become quite close to for a number of weeks last year, jumped up in front of me raising his voice to berate me for being "pussy." He also sat back down shortly afterwards feigning exasperated incredulity with the comment "Man you still think like a *blanquito*." A half dozen spectators—some of them empty-pocketed ("thirsty!") crack addicts, but most of them sharply dressed teenage drug-free girls competing for Chino's and Julio's attentions—giggled and snickered at me.

CULTURE AND MATERIAL REALITY

The above extract from sanitized fieldwork notes is merely a personalized glimpse of the day-to-day struggle for survival *and for meaning* by the people who stand behind the extraordinary statistics on inner city violent crime in the United States. These are the same Puerto Rican residents of Spanish Harlem, New York City, that Oscar Lewis in *La Vida* declared to be victims of a "culture of poverty" enmired in a "self-perpetuating cycle of poverty" (Lewis 1966:5). The culture of poverty concept has been severely criticized for its internal inconsistencies, its inadequate understanding of "culture" and ethnicity, its ethnocentric/middle class bias, its blindness to structural forces, and its blame-the-victim implications (cf. Leacock 1971; Valentine 1968; Waxman 1977; Stack 1974). Despite the negative scholarly consensus on Lewis's theory, the alternative discussions either tend towards economic reductionism (Ryan 1971; Stein-

"Crack in Spanish Harlem: Culture and Economy in the Inner City" by Philippe Bourgois, from *Anthropology Today*, Vol. 5, No. 4, 1989. Royal Anthropological Institute. Reprinted with permission.

berg 1981; Wilson 1978) or else ultimately minimize the reality of profound marginalization and destruction—some of it internalized—that envelop a disproportionate share of the inner city poor (cf. Stack 1974; Valentine 1978; see critiques by Maxwell 1988; Wilson 1987). More importantly, the media, public policy-makers and a large proportion of inner city residents themselves continue to subscribe to a popularized blame-the-victim/culture of poverty concept that has not been adequately rebutted by scholars.

The inner city residents described in the ethnographic vignette above are the pariahs of urban industrial US society. They seek their income and subsequently their identity and the meaning in their life through what they perceive to be high-powered careers "on the street." They partake of ideologies and values and share symbols which form the basis of an "inner city street culture" completely excluded from the mainstream economy and society but ultimately derived from it. Most of them have few direct contacts with non-inner city residents, and when they do it is usually with people who are in a position of domination: teachers in school, bosses, police officers, and later parole or probation officers.

How can one understand the complicated ideological dynamic accompanying inner city poverty without falling into a hopelessly idealistic culture of poverty and blame-the-victim interpretation? Structural, political economy reinterpretations of the inner city dynamic emphasize historical processes of labour migration in the context of institutionalized ethnic discrimination. They dissect the structural transformations in the international economy which are destroying the manufacturing sector in the United States and are swelling the low wage, low prestige service sector (cf. Davis 1987; Sassen-Koob 1986; Steinberg 1981; Tabb & Sawers 1984; Wilson 1978, 1987). These analyses address the structural confines of the inner city dynamic but fall prey to a passive interpretation of human action and subscribe to a weakly dialectic interpretation of the relationship between ideological processes and material reality, or between culture and class.

Although ultimately traceable directly to being products of international labour migrations in a transnational world economy, street-level inner city residents are more than merely passive victims of historical economic transformations or of the institutionalized discrimination of a perverse political and economic system. They do not passively accept their fourth-class citizen fate. They are struggling determinedly—just as ruthlessly as the railroad and oil robber-barons of the previous century and the investment-banker "yuppies" of today—to earn money, demand dignity and lead meaningful lives. Tragically, it is that very process of struggle against—yet within—the system which exacerbates the trauma of their community and which destroys hundreds of thousands of lives on the individual level.

In the day-to-day experience of the street-bound inner city resident, unemployment and personal anxiety over the inability to provide one's family with a minimal standard of living translates itself into intra-community crime, intra-community drug abuse, intra-family violence. The objective, structural desperation of a population without a viable economy, and facing systematic barriers of ethnic discrimination and ideological marginalization, becomes charged at the community level into self-destructive channels.

Most importantly, the "personal failure" of those who survive on the street is articulated in the idiom of race. The racism imposed by the larger society becomes internalized on a personal level. Once again, although the individuals in the ethnographic fragment at the beginning of this paper are the victims of long-term historical and structural transformations, they do not analyse their difficult situation from a political economy perspective. In their struggle to survive and even to be successful, they enforce on a day-to-day level the details of the trauma and cruelty of their lives on the excluded margins of US urban society.

CULTURAL REPRODUCTION THEORY

Theorists of education have developed a literature on processes of social and cultural reproduction which focus on the ideological domination of the poor and the working class in the school setting (cf. Giroux 1983). Although some of the social reproduction approaches tend towards an economic reductionism or a simple, mechanical functionalism (cf. Bowles & Gintis 1977), the more recent variants emphasize the complexity and contradictory nature of the dynamic of ideological domination (Willis 1983). There are several ethnographies which document how the very process whereby students resist school channels them into marginal roles in the economy for the rest of their lives (cf. Willis 1977; Macleod 1987). Other ethnographically based interpretations emphasize how success for inner city African-American students requires a rejection of their ethnic identity and cultural dignity (Fordham 1988).

There is no reason why these theories of cultural resistance and ideological domination have to be limited to the institutional school setting. Cultural reproduction theory has great potential for shedding light on the interaction between structurally induced cultural resistance and self-reinforced marginalization at the street-level in the inner city experience. The violence, crime and substance abuse plaguing the inner city can be understood as the manifestations of a "culture of resistance" to mainstream, white racist, and economically exclusive society. This "culture of resistance," however, results in greater oppression and self-destruction. More concretely, refusing to accept the outside society's racist role playing and refusing to accept low wage, entry-level jobs, translates into high crime rates, high addiction rates and high intra-community violence.

Most of the individuals in the above ethnographic description are proud that they are not being exploited by "the White Man," but they feel "like fucking ass-holes" for being poor. All of them have previously held numerous jobs in the legal economy in their lives. Most of them hit the street in their early teens working odd jobs as delivery boys and baggers in supermarkets and *bodegas*. Most of them have held the jobs that are recognized as among the least desirable in US society. Virtually all of these street participants have had deeply negative personal experiences in the minimum-wage labour market, owing to abusive, exploitative and often racist bosses or supervisors. They see the illegal underground economy as not only offering superior wages, but also a more dignified work place. For example, Gato had formerly worked for the ASPCA cleaning out the gas chambers where stray dogs and cats are killed. Bennie had been fired six months earlier from a night shift job as security guard on the violent ward for the criminally insane on Wards Island; Chino had been fired a year ago from a job installing high altitude storm windows on skyscrapers following an accident which temporarily blinded him in the right eye. Upon being disabled he discovered that his contractor had hired him illegally through an arrangement with a corrupt union official who had paid him half the union wage, pocketing the rest, and who had not taken health insurance for him. Chino also claimed that his foreman from Pennsylvania was a "Ku Klux Klanner" and had been especially abusive to him as he was a black Puerto Rican. In the process of recovering from the accident, Chino had become addicted to crack and ended up in the hospital as a gunshot victim before landing a job at Papito's crack house. Julio's last legal job before selling crack was as an off-the-books messenger for a magazine catering to New York yuppies. He had become addicted to crack, began selling possessions from out of his home and finally was thrown out by his wife who had just given birth to his son, who carried his name as Junior the IIIrd, on public assistance. Julio had quit his messenger job in favour of stealing car radios for a couple of hours at night in the very same neighbourhood where he had been delivering messages for ten-hour days at just above minimum wage. Nevertheless, after a close encounter with the police Julio begged his cousin for a job selling in his crack house. Significantly, the sense of responsibility, success and prestige that selling crack gave him enabled him to kick his crack habit and replace it by a less expensive and destructive powder cocaine and alcohol habit.

The underground economy, consequently, is the ultimate "equal opportunity employer" for inner city youth (cf. Kornblum & Williams 1985). As Davis (1987: 75) has noted for Los Angeles, the structural economic incentive to participate in the drug economy is overwhelming:

> With 78,000 unemployed youth in the Watts-Willowbrook area, it is not surprising that there are now 145 branches of the rival Crips and Bloods gangs in South L.A., or that the jobless resort to the opportunities of the burgeoning "Crack" economy.

The individuals "successfully" pursuing careers in the "crack economy" or any other facet of the underground economy are no longer "exploitable" by legal society. They speak with anger at their former low wages and bad treatment. They make fun of friends and acquaintances—many of whom come to buy drugs from them—who are still employed in factories, in service jobs, or in what they (and most other people) would call "shitwork." Of course, many others are less self-conscious about the reasons for their rejection of entry-level, mainstream employment. Instead, they think of themselves as lazy and irresponsible. They claim they quit their jobs in order to have a good time on the street. Many still pay lip service to the value of a steady, legal job. Still others cycle in and out of legal employment supplementing their bouts at entry-level jobs through part-time crack sales in an almost perverse parody of the economic subsidy of the wage labour sector by semi-subsistence peasants who cyclically engage in migratory wage labour in third world economies (cf. Meillassoux 1981; Wallerstein 1977).

THE CULTURE OF TERROR IN THE UNDERGROUND ECONOMY

The culture of resistance that has emerged in the underground street-level economy in opposition to demeaning, underpaid employment in the mainstream economy engenders violence. In the South America context of extreme political repression and racism against Amerindians and Jews, anthropologist Michael Taussig has argued that "cultures of terror" emerge to become ". . . a high powered tool for domination and a principal medium for political practice" (1984: 492). Unlike Taussig's examples of the 1910s Putumaya massacres and the 1970s Argentine torture chambers, domination in the case of the inner city's culture of terror is self-administered even if the root cause is generated or even imposed externally. With the exception of occasional brutality by policemen or the bureaucratized repression of the social welfare and criminal justice institutions (cf. Davis 1988), the physical violence and terror of the inner city are largely carried out by inner city residents themselves.

Regular displays of violence are necessary for success in the underground economy—especially at the street-level drug dealing world. Violence is essential for maintaining credibility and for preventing rip-off by colleagues, customers and hold-up artists. Indeed, upward mobility in the underground economy requires a systematic and effective use of violence against one's colleagues, one's neighbours and, to a certain extent, against oneself. Behaviour that appears irrationally violent and self-destructive to the middle class (or the working class) outside observer can be reinterpreted, according to the logic of the underground economy, as a judicious case of public relations, advertising, rapport building and long-term investment in one's "human capital development."

The importance of one's reputation is well illustrated in the fieldwork fragment at the beginning of this paper. Gato and I were mugged because Gato had a reputation for being "soft" or "pussy" and because I was publicly unmasked as *not being* an undercover cop: hence safe to attack. Gato tried to minimize the damage to his future ability to sell on that corner by not turning and running. He had pranced sideways down the street, though being beaten with a baseball bat and kicked to the ground twice. Significantly, I found out later that it was the second time this had happened to Gato this year. Gato was not going to be upwardly mobile in the underground economy because of his "pussy" reputation and he was further cementing his fate with an increasingly out of control addiction to crack.

Employers or new entrepreneurs in the underground economy are looking for people who can demonstrate their capacity for effective violence and terror. For example, in the eyes of Papito, the owner of the string of crack franchises I am currently researching, the ability of his employees to hold up under gunpoint is crucial as stick-ups of dealing dens are not infrequent. In fact, since my fieldwork began in 1986, the *botanica* has been held up twice. Julio happened to be on duty both times. He admitted to me that he had been very nervous when they held the gun to his temple and had asked for money and crack. Nevertheless, not only did he withhold some of the money and crack that was hidden behind the bogus *botanica* merchandise, but he also later exaggerated to Papito the amount that had been stolen in order to pocket the difference.

On several occasions in the midst of long conversations with active criminals (i.e., once with a dealing-den stick-up artist, several times with crack dealers, and once with a former bank robber) I asked them to explain how they were able to trust their partners in crime sufficiently to ensure the longevity and effectiveness of their enterprise. To my surprise I was not given any righteous diatribes about blood-brotherhood trustworthiness or any adulations of boyhood loyalty. Instead, in each case, in slightly different language I was told somewhat aggressively: "What do you mean how do I trust him? You should ask 'How does he trust me?'" Their ruthlessness is their security: "My support network is me, myself and I." They made these assertions with such vehemence as to appear threatened by the concept that their security and success might depend upon the trustworthiness of their partner or their employer. They were claiming—in one case angrily— that they were not dependent upon trust: because they were tough enough to command respect and enforce all contracts they entered into. The "How can they trust me?" was said with smug pride, perhaps not unlike the way a stockbroker might brag about his access to inside information on an upcoming hostile takeover deal.

At the end of the summer Chino demonstrated clearly the how-can-I-be-trusted dynamic. His cocaine snorting habit had been degenerating into a crack addiction by the end of the summer, and finally one night he was forced to flee out of state to a cousin's when he was unable to turn in the night's receipts to his boss Papito following a binge. Chino also owed Papito close to a thousand dollars for bail that Papito had posted when he was arrested for selling crack at the *botanica* a few months ago. Almost a year later when Papito heard that Chino had been arrested for jumping bail he arranged through another associate incarcerated in the same prison (Rikers Island) to have Chino beaten up before his trial date.

My failure to display a propensity for violence in several instances cost me the respect of the members of the crack scene that I frequented. This was very evident when I turned down Julio and Chino's offer to search for Bennie after he mugged Gato and me. Julio had despairingly exclaimed that I "still [thought] like a *blanquito*," genuinely disappointed that I was not someone with common sense and self-respect.

These concrete examples of the cultivation of violent public behaviour are the extreme cases of individuals relying on the underground economy for their income and dependent upon cultivating terror in order to survive. Individuals involved in street activity cultivate the culture of terror in order to intimidate competitors, maintain credibility, develop new contacts, cement partnerships, and ultimately to have a good time. For the most part they are not conscious of this process. The culture of terror becomes a myth and a role model with rules and satisfactions all its own which ultimately has a traumatic impact on the majority of Spanish Harlem residents—who are drug free and who work honestly at poorly remunerated legal jobs, 9 to 5 plus overtime.

PURSUING THE AMERICAN DREAM

It is important to understand that the underground economy and the violence emerging out of it are not propelled by an irrational cultural logic distinct from that of mainstream USA. On the contrary, street participants are frantically pursuing the "American dream." The assertions of the culture of poverty theorists that the poor have been badly socialized and do not share mainstream values is wrong. On the contrary, ambitious, energetic, inner city youths are attracted into the underground economy in order to try frantically to get their piece of the pie as fast as possible. They often even follow the traditional US model for upward mobility to the letter by becoming aggressive private entrepreneurs. They are the ultimate rugged individualists braving an unpredictable frontier where fortune, fame and destruction are all just around the corner. Hence Indio, a particularly enterprising and ambitious young crack dealer who was aggressively carving out a new sales point, shot his brother in the spine and paralyzed him for life while he was high on angel dust in a battle over sales rights. His brother now works for him selling on crutches. Meanwhile, the shooting has cemented Indio's reputation and his workers are awesomely disciplined: "If he shot his brother he'll shoot anyone." Indio reaffirms this symbolically by periodically walking his turf with an oversized gold chain and name plate worth several thousand dollars hanging around his neck.

The underground economy and the culture of terror are experienced as the most realistic routes to upward mobility. Entry-level jobs are not seen as viable channels to upward mobility by high school dropouts. Drug selling or other illegal activity appear as the most effective and realistic options for getting rich within one's lifetime. Many of the street dealers claim to be strictly utilitarian in their involvement with crack and they snub their clients despite the fact that they usually have considerable alcohol and powder cocaine habits themselves. Chino used to chant at his regular customers "Come on, keep on killing yourself; bring me that money; smoke yourself to death; make me rich."

Even though street sellers are employed by the owner of a sales point for whom they have to maintain regular hours, meet sales quotas and be subject to being fired, they have a great deal of autonomy and power in their daily (or nightly) routine. The boss only comes once or twice a shift to drop off drugs and pick up money. Frequently, it is a young messenger who is sent instead. Sellers are often surrounded by a bevy of "thirsty" friends and hanger-oners—frequently young teenage women in the case of male sellers—willing to run errands, pay attention to conversations, lend support in arguments and fights and provide sexual favours for them on demand because of the relatively large amounts of money and drugs passing through their hands. In fact, even youths who do not use drugs will hang out and attempt to befriend respectfully the dealer just to be privy to the excitement of people coming and going, copping and hanging; money flowing, arguments, detectives, and stick-up artists—all around danger and excitement. Other non-users will hang out to be treated to an occasional round of beer, Bacardi or, on an off night, Thunderbird.

The channel into the underground economy is by no means strictly economic. Besides wanting to earn "crazy money," people choose "hoodlum" status in order to assert their dignity at refusing to "sling a mop for the white man" (cf. Anderson 1976: 68). Employment—or better yet self-employment—in the underground economy accords a sense of autonomy, self-dignity and an opportunity for extraordinary rapid short-term upward mobility that is only too obviously unavailable in entry-level jobs. Opulent survival without a "visible means of support" is the ultimate expression of success and it is a viable option. There is plenty of visible proof of this to everyone on the street as they watch teenage crack dealers drive by in convertible Suzuki Samurai jeeps with the stereo blaring, "beem" by in impeccable BMWs, or—in the case of the middle-aged dealers—speed around in well-waxed Lincoln Continentals. Anyone can aspire to be promoted to the level of a seller perched on a 20-speed mountain bike with a beeper by their side. In fact, many youths not particularly active in the drug trade run around with beepers on their belts just pretending to be big-time. The impact of the sense of dignity and worth that can accompany selling crack is illustrated by Julio's ability to overcome his destructive addiction to crack only after getting a job selling it: "I couldn't be messin' up the money. I couldn't be fucking up no more! Besides, I had to get respect."

In New York City the insult of working for entry-level wages amidst extraordinary opulence is especially painfully perceived by Spanish Harlem youths who have grown in abject poverty only a few blocks from all-white neighbourhoods commanding some of the highest real estate values in the world. As messengers, security guards or xerox machine operators in the corporate headquarters of the Fortune 500 companies, they are brusquely ordered about by young white executives who sometimes make monthly salaries superior to their yearly wages and who do not even have the time to notice that they are being rude.

It could be argued that Manhattan sports a *de facto* apartheid labour hierarchy whereby differences in job category and prestige correlate with ethnicity and are often justified—consciously or unconsciously—through a racist logic. This humiliating confrontation with New York's ethnic/occupational hierarchy drives the street-bound cohort of inner city youths deeper into the confines of their segregated neighbourhood and the underground economy. They prefer to seek out meaning and upward mobility in a context that does not constantly oblige them to come into contact with people of a different, hostile ethnicity wielding arbitrary power over them. In the underground economy, especially in the world of substance abuse, they never have to experience the silent subtle humiliations that the entry-level labour market—or even merely a daily subway ride downtown—invariably subjects them to.

In this context the crack high and the rituals and struggles around purchasing and using the drug are comparable to the millenarian religions that sweep colonized peoples attempting to resist oppression in the context of accelerated social trauma—whether it be the Ghost dance of the Great Plains Amerindians, the "cargo cults" of Melanesia, the Mamachi movement of the Guaymi Amerindians in Panama, or even religions such as Farrakhan's Nation of Islam and the Jehovah's Witnesses in the heart of the inner city (cf. Bourgois 1986, 1989). Substance abuse in general, and crack in particular, offer the equivalent of a millenarian metamorphosis. Instantaneously users are transformed from being unemployed, depressed high school dropouts, despised by the world—and secretly convinced that their failure is due to their own inherent stupidity, "racial laziness" and disorganization—into being a mass of heart-palpitating pleasure, followed only minutes later by a jaw-gnashing crash and wide-awake alertness that provides their life with concrete purpose: get more crack—fast!

One of the most dramatic illustrations within the dynamic of the crack economy of how a cultural dynamic of resistance to exploitation can lead contradictorily to greater oppression and ideological domination is the conspicuous presence of women in the growing cohort of crack addicts. In a series of ten random surveys undertaken at Papito's crack franchises, women and girls represented just under 50% of the customers. This contrasts dramatically to the estimates of female participation in heroin addiction in the late 1970s.

The painful spectacle of young, emaciated women milling in agitated angst around crack copping corners and selling their bodies for five dollars, or even merely for a puff on a crack stem, reflects the growing emancipation of women in all aspects of inner city life, culture and economy. Women—especially the emerging generation which is most at risk for crack addiction—are no longer as obliged to stay at home and maintain the family. They no longer so readily sacrifice public life or forgo independent opportunities to generate personally disposable income. This is documented by the frequent visits to the crack houses by pregnant women and by mothers accompanied by toddlers.

A more neutral illustration of the changed position of women in street culture outside the arena of substance abuse is the growing presence of young women on inner city basketball courts. Similarly, on the national level, there are conclusive statistics documenting increased female participation in the legal labour market—especially in the working-class Puerto Rican community. By the same token, more women are also resisting exploitation in the entry-level job market and are pursuing careers in the underground economy and seeking self-definition and meaning through intensive participation in street culture.

Although women are using the drug and participating intensively in street culture, traditional gender relations still largely govern income-generating strategies in the underground economy. Most notably, women are forced disproportionately to rely on prostitution to finance their habits. The relegation of women to the traditional street role of prostitution has led to a flooding of the market for sex, leading to a drop in the price of women's bodies and to an epidemic rise in venereal disease among women and newborn babies.

Contradictorily, therefore, the underlying process of emancipation which has enabled women to demand equal participation in street culture and to carve out an expanded niche for themselves in the underground economy has led to a greater depreciation of women as ridiculed sex objects. Addicted women will tolerate a tremendous amount of verbal and physical abuse in their pursuit of a vial of crack, allowing lecherous men to humiliate and ridicule them in public. Chino, who is married and is the father of nine children, refers to the women who regularly service him with oral sex as "my moufs" [mouths]. He enjoys calling out to these addicted women from across the street. "Yo, there goes my mouf! Come on over here." Such a public degradation of a cohort of women who are conspicuously present on the street cannot be neutral. It ultimately reinforces the ideological domination of women in general.

DE-LEGITIMIZING DOMINATION

How can one discuss and analyse the phenomenon of street-level inner city culture and violence without reproducing and confirming the very ideological relationships that are its basis? In his discussion of the culture of terror, Taussig notes that it is precisely the narratives about the torture and violence of the repressive societies which ". . . are in themselves evidence of the process whereby a culture of terror was created and sustained" (1984: 279). The superhuman power that the media has accorded to crack serves a similar mythical function. The *New York Times* has run articles and interviews with scientists that portray crack as if it were a miraculous substance beyond the power of human beings to control (cf. 25 June, 1988: 1). They "prove" this by documenting how quickly rats will ecstatically kill themselves when provided with cocaine upon demand. Catheterized rats push the cocaine lever to the exclusion of the nutrient lever until they collapse exhausted to die of thirst.

The alleged omnipotence of crack coupled with even the driest recounting of the overpowering statistics on violence ultimately allows US society to absolve itself of any real responsibility for the inner city phenomena. The mythical dimensions of the culture of terror push economics and politics out of the picture and enable the US to maintain in some of its larger cities a level of ethnic segregation and economic marginalization that are unacceptable to any of the other wealthy, industrialized nations of the world, with the obvious exception of South Africa. Worse yet, on the level of theory, because of the continued domination—even in their negation—of the North America–centered culture of poverty theories, this discussion of the ideological implications of the underground economy may take readers full circle back to a blame-the-victim interpretation of inner city oppression.

NOTE

1. A *botanica* is a herbal pharmacy and *santeria* utility store.

REFERENCES

Anderson, Elijah. 1976. *A Place on the Corner*. Chicago: University of Chicago Press.

Bourgois, Philippe. 1986. "The Miskitu of Nicaragua: Politicized Ethnicity." *Anthropology Today* Vol. 2:2: 4–9.

Bourgois, Philippe. 1989. *Ethnicity at Work: Divided Labour on a Central American Banana Plantation*. Baltimore, MD: Johns Hopkins University Press.

Bowles, Samuel, & Herbert Gintis. 1977. *Schooling in Capitalist America*. New York: Basic Books.

Davis, Mike. 1987. "Chinatown, Part Two? The 'Internationalization' of Downtown Los Angeles." *New Left Review* Vol. 164: 65–86.

Davis, Mike, with Sue Ruddick. 1988. "Los Angeles: Civil Liberties Between the Hammer and the Rock." *New Left Review* 1970: 37–60.

Fordham, Signithia. 1988. "Racelessness as a Factor in Black Students' School Success: Pragmatic Strategy or Pyrrhic Victory?" *Harvard Educational Review* Vol. 58:1: 54–84.

Giroux, Henry. 1983. "Theories of Reproduction and Resistance in the New Sociology of Education: A Critical Analysis." *Harvard Educational Review* Vol. 53, No. 3: 257–293.

Kornblum, William, & Terry Williams. 1985. *Growing Up Poor*. Lexington, MA: Lexington Books.

Leacock, Eleanor Burke (Ed.). 1971. *The Culture of Poverty: A Critique*. New York: Simon & Schuster.

Lewis, Oscar. 1966. "The Culture of Poverty." In *Anthropological Essays*. New York: Random House.

Macleod, Jay. 1987. *Ain't No Makin' It*. Boulder, CO: Westview Press.

Maxwell, Andrew. 1988. "The Anthropology of Poverty in Black Communities: A Critique and Systems Alternative." *Urban Anthropology* Vol. 17, No. 2 & 3: 171–191.

Meillassoux, Claude. 1981. *Maidens, Meal and Money*. Cambridge, England: Cambridge University Press.

Ryan, William. 1986 [1971]. "Blaming the Victim." In *Taking Sides: Clashing Views on Controversial Social Issues*, ed. by Kurt Finsterbusch & George McKenna. Guilford, CT: Dushkin.

Sassen-Koob, Saskia. 1986. "New York City: Economic Restructuring and Immigration." *Development and Change* Vol. 17, No. 1: 87–119.

Stack, Carol. 1974. *All Our Kin: Strategies for Survival in a Black Community*. New York: Harper & Row.

Steinberg, Stephen. 1981. *The Ethnic Myth: Race, Ethnicity and Class in America*. New York: Atheneum.

Tabb, William, & Larry Sawers (Eds.). 1984. *Marxism and the Metropolis: New Perspectives in Urban Political Economy*. New York: Oxford University Press.

Taussig, Michael. 1984. "Culture of Terror—Space of Death, Roger Casement's Putumayo Report and the Explanation of Torture." *Comparative Studies in Society and History* Vol. 26, No. 3: 467–497.

Valentine, Bettylou. 1978. *Hustling and Other Hard Work*. New York: Free Press.

Valentine, Charles. 1968. *Culture and Poverty*. Chicago: University of Chicago Press.

Wallerstein, Emanuel. 1977. "Rural Economy in Modern World Society." *Studies in Comparative International Development* Vol. 12, No. 1: 29–40.

Waxman, Chaim. 1977. *The Stigma of Poverty: A Critique of Poverty Theories and Policies*. New York: Pergamon Press.

Willis, Paul. 1983. "Cultural Production and Theories of Reproduction." In *Race, Class and Education*, ed. by Len Barton & Stephen Walker. London: Croom-Helm.

Willis, Paul. 1977. *Learning to Labor: How Working Class Kids Get Working Class Jobs*. Aldershot, England: Gower.

Wilson, William Julius. 1978. *The Declining Significance of Race: Blacks and Changing American Institutions*. Chicago: University of Chicago Press.

Wilson, William Julius. 1987. *The Truly Disadvantaged: The Inner City, the Underclass and Public Policy*. Chicago: University of Chicago Press.

Dealing with Used Clothing

Salaula and the Construction of Identity in Zambia's Third Republic

Karen Tranberg Hansen

Karen Tranberg Hansen, a Danish anthropologist, teaches at Northwestern University, where she is an associate professor. She earned her Ph.D. at Washington University in 1979 and has carried out fieldwork in southern Africa. Her theoretical interests include colonial culture, gender relations, political economy, and urban anthropology.

The juxtaposition of Lusaka's highrise skyline with a major market in used clothing imported from the West gives graphic expression to the power of the world system to make everything over in its own image. Yet the mirror has cracks. A young male trader with a walkman wears what looks like an orderly's white hospital uniform topped with a pink peignoir. Other young male traders wear women's knit-skirts as headgear and what might have been women's shorts. Mature women wear men's dust coats over their dresses and men of all ages wear what once were women's coats. There is also the tall trader in an animal print topee who could be in a *Banana Republic* catalog.

The master narrative that regards Lusaka's booming secondhand clothes markets as just another example of exchange relations that continue to link countries like Zambia to the West in dependency terms is inadequate. It reduces all that is African, and in this case Zambian and local, to mass capitulation to western-type consumption and trivializes the active engagement between people and clothing into a warped imitation of the West. By simply assuming that clothing has been moved physically from its place of origin, such narratives treat clothing as things without histories and meanings, and above all, hide the power of objects to structure and transform relationships. Rather than being a trivial topic, I suggest that used clothing and the changing external and local relations that inform its usage offer a rich research context in which to unravel changing meanings of the entangled encounter between the West and the rest.[1]

Markets scenes like the one just described are products of complex processes that unsettle the flow of power entailed in conventional notions of center-periphery relations.[2] Much of this clothing is not manufactured in the West, but in Third World locations by foreign firms and multinational companies some of which invest in offshore banks and move their goods under flags of convenience. When shipped from the West to Zambia, used clothing already has several biographies behind it.[3] Recommodified at the point of resale, the transformation of the West's cast-off clothes into "new" garments in Zambia involves distribution and sales practices in local markets and subsequent incorporations into clothing practices that reflect and engage everyday experiences in spite of the recognizable western imprint of the garments. As such, Lusaka's markets in used clothing certainly speak of a world in Creolisation, of tensions between extensification and intensification, or even of heteroglossia, but not, I argue, of a thoroughly deterritorialized world where anything goes.[4] Just what do we make of this jostling between western imprints and local expressions? How, in short, do we deal with these ensembles of the West's discarded clothes?

The evolving story of secondhand clothes usage in Zambia is encompassed by histories of much broader encounters. Relevant actors include slavers, explorers, missionaries, African, Indian and European traders, colonial administrators and white settlers, who first introduced cloth, and later the tailor- and ready-made clothes that Africans so eagerly and rapidly restyled to suit themselves. The relative attraction and necessity of used as compared to new clothing also relates to shifting textile manufacturing policies and import regulations.

During most of the colonial period, preferential tariffs on imports from Southern Rhodesia and South Africa restricted local textile manufacturing.[5] Postcolonial policies have not helped the textile industry to expand significantly. Expansion has been limited during the economic decline Zambia experienced since the early 1970s, when foreign exchange restrictions curtailed imports of manufacturing technology and raw materials, causing frequent closings at the country's two major textile factories. In the structural adjustment efforts during the late 1980s and the atmosphere of liberalization of the early 1990s, most of the locally produced cotton is exported. Most cotton cloth, synthetic fibres, and manufactured textile goods for sale in local shops in 1992 were imported and expensive.

Clothing consumption practices are thus shaped by income and by availability and price of factory-produced cloth and ready-made items. Such practices are also influenced by ideas about what to wear and why. These ideas actively engage fragments of new lifestyle scripts provided by the West's culture industries. Given the limited availability of affordable clothing in the past, it is not surprising that in 1992 Zambians were aggressively sifting through piles of used clothing in local markets, in order both to satisfy basic clothing needs and to pursue individual desires.

In the discourse of the world system, the West's discarded items are transformed at the point of resale: from decommissioned use values to exchange values. But in the language of Zambian purchasers, the semantics shift. No longer referred to as used or secondhand, since at least 1988 such clothing has been spoken of as *salaula*, which means "to select from a pile" in Bemba, or *kaunjika*, which means "to pick" in Nyanja. The commodity has been transformed, not by sleight-of-hand, but in meaning.[6] I suggest that the transformation in meaning of the commodity can be understood in terms of recent Zambian history. In effect, while Zambians have known, dealt in, and worn used clothes throughout most of this century, the meanings they associate with such clothing have not remained the same.

This paper explores how Zambians use the West's discarded clothing and what this may tell us about the construction of identity and of difference in our late twentieth-century world.[7] Offering detailed descriptive information about the organization and actors involved in this trade in Zambia, and suggesting that local appropriations of used clothing demand the same scholarly attention as fashion, I encourage further research on interactions involving used clothing in Africa.[8]

TRANSNATIONAL BIOGRAPHIES

Used clothing is enjoying a renaissance in the West. According to an article in the April 1993 issue of *Vogue*, "scouring the flea markets [has become] increasingly chic."[9] Famous and less famous people are browsing used clothing racks for vintage or retro looks.[10] Established fashion houses and makers of New Wave looks are following suit.[11] In 1993 spring fashion shows

"thrift shop chic" was "the hottest trend on and off the international runways."[12] Some of these new fashions borrow features from past designs, combining them in innovative ways; others put parts of used clothes together into new outfits; and still others make new garments over to look old.[13]

Used clothing has attracted the attention of fashion-conscious consumers, the news media and scholars of cultural studies and popular culture.[14] Their focus has been on the upscale side and the creation of alternative lifestyles and not the needy and thrifty dimensions of practices involving used clothing, that is to say, its charitable guise. These studies also note the incorporation of fragments of "ethnic" clothing into garments produced for Western tastes.[15] But there is little substantive work on either the incorporation of the West's discarded garments into clothing practices in the Third World or the commercial involvement of charities with the exporters of such clothing.[16]

The contours of these ongoing interactions may be traced through newspaper coverage which speaks dramatically about the boom and about entanglements between charities and textile salvage dealers (rag traders). Briefly, charities in the United States gather an enormous amount of used clothing: about 100 million tons annually. About half of this clothing reaches the racks of charity retail stores. The other half is purchased by around 300 U.S. firms in the textile recycling business.[17] Resorting the clothes for a largely export business in the Third World (and increasingly in Eastern Europe)—keeping old clothes out of landfills—these firms boost U.S. export figures and earn excellent profits. For instance, the New York–based exporter, Domsey Trading Corporation, has extensive African and Zambian contacts and grosses $15 million annually.[18] Some reports estimate that one-third of sub-Saharan Africans are wearing cast-off European and American clothing.[19] U.S. exports to sub-Saharan Africa increased from $35 million in 1989 to over $72 million in 1992, and used clothing is currently the eighth largest U.S. export to sub-Saharan Africa. Used clothing exports from the U.S. to Zambia increased from $76,000 to $3,453,000 between 1988 and 1991.[20] Canada has been involved in this trade with Zambia since the mid-1980s with export values growing from C$115,000 in 1985 to C$877,000 in 1991.[21] Several European countries also export used clothing to Zambia.

In urban and rural areas across Zambia the used clothing sections of markets have expanded dramatically over the last five years. This trade is not new but its present scale is unprecedented.[22] By the inter-war years, if not before, the used clothing trade reached Zambia from Zaire, and Zambians crossed the border to Zaire to buy imported used clothes which they subsequently hawked in the copperbelt and in settlements along the railway lines.[23] The name of Mokambo, a busy Zambia–Zaire crossing point, became a common term for the clothes and the traders. It had a negative connotation and people did their best to hide that they were wearing *mokambo*. The flow of used clothing also included garments that missionaries brought and either gave away or resold in areas where they worked, as well as clothing European employers gave to African domestic servants.[24]

In the early 1970s some Zambians purchased used clothing directly from expatriate households. This practice still existed in the mid-1980s but was surpassed by the bales of secondhand clothing imported from the West. Most bales entered Zambia via Zaire, legally and illegally. Used clothing traders in Lusaka bought most of their merchandise from Zaireans in the Kamwala market (the "African" market established during the colonial period) or from a few importers located in the light industrial area. Today, Zambians have no qualms about buying salaula; they will stop you on the street to ask if your skirt is "from salaula or from the shops."

IMPORTING SALAULA

While trade in secondhand clothes is of long standing in Zambia, political and economic developments in Zaire and Zambia have altered this trade. Between 1989 and 1992 the direction of the flow of merchandise into Zambia changed. In Lusaka in 1992 hardly anyone imported used clothing from Zaire. Although a few long-term Zairean residents of Lusaka still sell salaula from market stalls at Kamwala and Soweto (the largest market in Lusaka, established in the late 1970s), for now the Zaire supply route seems to have dried up. The reduction of the Zairean trade may be attributed to a combination of factors, including restrictions on Zairean traders in Zambia, the change of political regime in Zambia, and recent upheavals within Zaire.

Most of the used clothing currently sold in local markets in Zambia is imported by fifteen to twenty trading firms and their up-country outlets. Charitable organizations also import used clothing and are exempt from customs and duties if their goods are not sold for profit. The volume of secondhand clothing imported by charitable organizations and the extent to which donated clothing is sold for profit is difficult to estimate. The longest-standing importers of secondhand clothes whom I met in Lusaka had begun selling used clothing in 1986 and 1987. One firm is owned by a Chagga man from Tanzania, and the other by two Mambwe brothers. The owners were familiar with the brisk trade of secondhand clothes in Tanzania and their enterprises in Lusaka had modest beginnings. Both now have big warehouses and import used clothes and other goods.

In the late 1980s, several other firms started importing used clothing. Among them was an enterprise owned by a group of Lebanese, who had been involved in this business in Tanzania and had recently started a firm in Lusaka. Aside from these larger dealers, a number of small enterprises have entered this business by importing or subcontracting from larger firms. They include Zambians and Indians; some have established links with the textile manufacturing, dry goods, and transport businesses. These importers purchase used apparel from dealers in the U.S., Canada, the United Kingdom and several countries in Europe which includes not only garments but also shoes, handbags, towels, sheets, blankets and draperies. A small proportion is new, mostly factory overruns and cancelled orders, but most of it is used clothing, bought by textile salvagers at bulk rates from charities in the West. A good deal of clothing that does not sell in charity shops is purchased cheaply by dealers, fumigated, sorted, packed into bales and shipped to Third World destinations.

Used clothing is exported in standard containers which hold 200 or 400 bales weighing 45 kg. Most dealers use 45 kg bales but some prefer 150 kg or 300 kg bales. The containers are shipped to Zambia via Dar es Salaam, Durban and Beira. Importers and clearing agents complain of pilferage at Dar, the red tape involved in port clearance, and port storage charges. In 1992, Durban was the preferred port of entry. Used clothing is competitively priced. The figures vary from $0.44 per pound c.i.f. (cost, insurance, freight) to a designated port from a Canadian dealer (May 1991) to U.S. $2.77 per kg c.i.f. to a designated port from an Australian dealer (July 1992). Port clearance fees, port storage, transportation charges, a variety of fees, sales tax, and customs duties considerably increase the cost.

Although importers of used clothing complain of rising costs and uneven quality of merchandise, they recognize that demand and competition are increasing. Several importers hope to find new suppliers of quality goods and complain about uneven quality, especially of the U.S. merchandise—particularly faded, torn, and cut jeans. They also noted that the West's cold-weather clothing only sells well during June and July, the cold months in Zambia. Some considered Australia a potential source of clothing suitable for a warm climate.

Importers pass their risks on to local buyers who have no guarantee of the quality of the bale's contents. When purchasing a bale from an importer's warehouse outlet, the buyer selects the type of fabric (cotton, polyester, or "wool") and clothing: for example, *changa changa* (mixed children's wear); girls' or women's dresses, skirts, jackets, or trousers.[25] There are also bales with mixed fabrics as well as bales with assorted items, e.g., women's wear. The bales are sold unopened but some dealers allow buyers to inspect the plastic wrap and the metal straps to determine if the bale has been tampered with. Looking through the plastic wrap at the variety of color and prints, the buyer makes a selection. After the buyer has decided, some dealers open the plastic cover to allow the buyer a closer look and feel. Of course this does not guarantee quality and buyers complain of the many damaged, torn, faded and worn clothes in the bales.

The price of a 45 kg bale in 1992 ranged between K15,000 (jerseys), K30,000 (blouses) and K45,000 (jackets), depending on the type of garment and fabric.[26] Prices increase steadily as importers adjust their prices in response to higher costs and Zambia's rapid inflation. Toward the end of June, for instance, a 45 kg bale of women's "silk" (polyester) blouses cost K34,000. It soon increased to K36,000 and then to K40,000 and by mid-August, the same importer charged K42,000 for a 45 kg bale of women's "silk" blouses.

SALAULA IN THE MARKETS

Trade in used clothing is large and growing in local markets, village shops, and with itinerant traders on bicycles. The salaula section in markets is many times larger than the food section in Lusaka and provincial towns. Every township in Lusaka has its salaula market and the busiest are at Kamwala and Soweto. Each of these markets has an inside and outside salaula section. The inside section consists of covered stalls or small shops; the outside section consists of demarcated plots on which traders build intricate displays for their goods or sell them from a pile on the ground. The outside section is the larger and busier place.

Salaula traders are young and old, women and men with different educational and employment histories and from many ethnic groups. Women slightly outnumber men. Traders can be grouped into three categories according to their length of involvement with the used clothing business. The most established traders have been in the business since the early 1980s, if not before. The second and larger category entered the business after the mid-1980s. The vast majority forming the third category had begun within the last one to two years.

The old-timers entered the used clothing business in two different ways. Some had purchased used clothing from expatriate households by calling directly at the door or identifying sellers—mostly departing expatriates—from newspaper advertisements. For example, a fifty-seven-year-old Bemba woman, the first in Mtendere to deal in used clothes in the early 1980s, still obtained most of her supplies in that way as late as 1988. She said that she started buying bales at Kamwala when "the Europeans began charging too much; just like Zambians." In 1992, her stand displayed the contents of three bales (jerseys, jackets, dresses) and she was planning to buy another bale soon. One of her daughters, whom I remember as a teenager helping her mother, also has a stand at the Mtendere market.

Her husband is studying in the United States and she is selling salaula to finance more lucrative trading trips abroad.

The second avenue through which well-established traders entered the used clothing business is a northern connection. Those who have pursued this line of work the longest were Mambwe and Chokwe as well as persons of Bemba and Lunda background. This route is exemplified by the career of a Chokwe trader in his fifties who came to Lusaka in 1972. He now owns a shop in the inside section of Kamwala's salaula market where he sells clothing from four bales, but he began by traveling to Lubumbashi in Zaire to buy bales to bring back to Lusaka. He had not been to Zaire recently because bales now are readily available from importers in Lusaka. His wife sells vegetables at the market in Lilanda where they live with their eight children in their own house. Like many well-established traders who are also employers, this man employed three young men.

Many traders who have remained in this business since the mid- to late-1980s have pursued diversified strategies. Among these traders are university lecturers, a woman doctor and a nurse, for whom the used clothing business is a sideline and they employ young relatives or others to supervise sales. This category also includes persons who have given up wage labor for salaula, such as a thirty-four-year-old Bemba woman who had worked as a social worker for thirteen years. When explaining how she had begun by taking unpaid leaves to go to Tanzania to buy used clothing and other goods (e.g., *kanga* [printed cloth] and enamel plates) for resale in Zambia, she said that holding a job was "a waste of time; there is no money in it." She quit her job in 1986. On her return from trips to Tanzania, she washed and ironed the clothes and took them around office buildings for sale. In those days people "looked down" on used clothes and she would say that "her sister in the U.K. had sent her things to sell." She has had an outside stand at Soweto market for the past year and a half where she sells women's clothing. Her husband is a self-employed electrician and they live at Makeni with their four children.

The category of traders who began selling salaula in the mid-1980s include a young Tumbuka man, educated through the twelfth grade. When he was declared redundant in 1987 after three years of work as a bricklayer at Minestone Contractor, he used his severance pay to purchase secondhand clothes from Zairean suppliers within Kamwala market. Like several other men in their early twenties, he was unmarried and lived with his mother and retired father. He contributes to household expenses with earnings from sales and occasional building contracts.

The third and largest category, those who launched their trade in the last couple of years, consists of many people in particularly difficult economic circumstances. Among them are recent widows and widowers, divorcees, young persons, especially young men with basic education but no formal jobs. This group also includes married women and men who sell salaula to ease strained household budgets. A few young men hoped that their earnings would finance a training course and a few young women were selling salaula while waiting for admission into nursing school or teacher's training college.

Not all of these recent traders remain in business. They all complain about rapidly increasing prices of bales, slow sales, and competition. A twenty-four-year-old married Chewa man educated through the seventh grade considered salaula preferable to his former livelihood, selling "rocco" (rock) buns and bread from his bicycle. During the past year he has traded from a stand in Kamwala's outside section, specializing in men's coats and jackets. But a thirty-five-year-old Chokwe widower who started selling salaula a year ago said he soon would return to his former job as a tailor for a shopkeeper within Soweto market. He complained about losses from a bale of men's trousers, but wanted to try a bale of men's shirts, hoping that they might sell better and faster. A twenty-two-year old recently divorced Soli woman educated through tenth grade turned to salaula as a way of supporting herself and her child. In her first three months she purchased a total of four bales and was in the process of selling the contents of the two last bales. The slow turnover made her reluctant to consider the salaula business as a viable long-term strategy for making a living.

Earnings from salaula sales differ widely and depend on factors such as location, volume, type of clothing, business practices and competing demands on the trader's time and labor. Consider the example of Mrs. Zulu who bought a bale of cotton blouses for K30,000. The bale contained around 300 pieces of acceptable quality and fifty damaged items. If Mrs. Zulu sells 200 of these blouses at a price of K300, she will make K60,000. She might even charge higher prices for better quality blouses. After the better blouses are sold, she reduces the price. Business is best when she buys bales regularly, thus adding new stock rather than selling the contents of each bale before buying again. In this way, the trader's profits from a good bale and quick sales may balance losses.

The odds against realizing profit at the rate suggested in this example are high: the quality of clothing may be poor, sales may be slow, and other claims on the earnings make it difficult to set aside sufficient capital to purchase another bale. Most traders keep books to record when they bought bales, the number of good and damaged items and the amount of daily sales. But many explained that there is "no use in keeping books because we don't see the money," which is to say that earnings from salaula readily disappear into the daily consumption budget.

BUYING SALAULA

People from all walks of life explore salaula markets. Some come with a view to buy in order to resell; others are on the lookout for that special item to complement their wardrobe. But the majority come to purchase the bulk of their household's clothing. Buying for the purpose of reselling occurs in at least two ways. The method of "one–one" involves selecting individual items that are priced separately, usually after a bale has been opened. At that point a crowd of customers fight for the best items and some select particular garments to resell.

Buying with a view to reselling is also done "on order," especially by rural visitors who subsequently sell their goods in the villages. Buying "on order" means buying several garments at a reduced rate. Often these are items that do not sell well in town. During the winter season Zimbabwean women and men travel to Lusaka to purchase cold-weather clothing—coats, jackets, "wool" skirts, and jerseys. To finance their trips and obtain Zambian currency, they bring Zimbabwean products that are of better quality or scarce in Zambia, such as blankets, bath soap, tennis shoes, and fashion knitwear. They sell their Zimbabwean goods to traders in Kamwala and Soweto markets and purchase salaula with the Zambian currency earned by these sales. Or they exchange their goods directly for salaula without any cash transaction.

Items that do not sell well in the city are bought by rural people or taken to the countryside by urban traders for sale or exchange. Such items include crimplene (polyester knit) garments, men's trousers in bright colors like red, green, and yellow, men's trousers and jackets of fabrics with large checks, and faded, torn and damaged items. Some traders make occasional rural trips and bring back chickens, fish, or produce. For instance, one young Soweto trader sold the chickens he obtained on such trips to a colleague in the market's poultry section.

As mentioned earlier, villagers go to town particularly to purchase salaula for resale in rural areas. Local traders in rural Chiawa hawk their salaula in villages, displaying them at the small trading center or near the workshops at Masstock, an Irish-financed commercial agricultural project that draws on wage labor from the region. With the exception of one recently widowed woman, all these traders were men, ranging in age from twenty-three to fifty-three. They all had been wage laborers in different places along the railway line and began to sell salaula after returning to Chiawa. The fifty-nine-year-old man (married with three wives), who had been in business longest, has sold salaula since 1988, whereas the twenty-three-year-old man (recently married) with the largest enterprise had sold salaula only for half a year. These traders purchase salaula only on order. The fifty-nine-year-old man makes monthly trips to Soweto market in Lusaka to buy salaula items worth K15,000; the twenty-three-year-old man was planning to purchase salaula worth K25,000, the largest sum he had ever had available, on his next trip to Lusaka.

Some of these traders have turned to salaula to raise money for specific purposes. The recently widowed woman had gone to Lusaka to buy salaula in order to earn money to travel to Zimbabwe where cleansing rituals for her deceased husband were to be conducted. She was uncertain if she would continue to trade after her return. In comparison, the fifty-nine-year-old man's profits from salaula sales added significantly to the household's income from farming. The twenty-three-year-old man and his wife were in the process of establishing themselves. They lived with the man's parents and as yet had no fields of their own. This young man praised salaula when speaking enthusiastically of his desire to improve his earnings; he hoped to set up a shop with his savings.

TRANSFORMING VALUE

The recommodification of used clothing involves several phases during which it is transformed into new objects.[27] Transactions between external suppliers and local importers initiate the process through which the decommissioned value of the West's discarded clothing is reactivated. Subsequent transformations of used garments into new clothes are achieved by a variety of processes that begin at the point of resale and are made public by how clothing is put to use. Transformations that involve recycling are obvious while others have to be teased out of interactions. We may reveal some of the meanings produced by these transformations by looking more closely at a variety of informal practices that have evolved around the selling and buying of salaula.

These meanings hinge on the implication of the term *salaula*—selecting from a pile. Some of the informal practices that express it concern the purchasing of a bale and its subsequent opening. Customers evaluate their merchandise when purchasing a bale from a dealer by scrutinizing the plastic wrap and the metal straps to ensure that the bale has not been tampered with. Dealers who import bales larger than the standard ones open, sort, and rebale items into 45 kg bales. Some Indian dealers are said to remove choice items in the process of rebaling; clothing presorted in this way

is said to end up in shops. The customer's scrutiny in the dealer's warehouse reflects the preference for bales whose contents are fresh from their western source, untouched by dealer interference, and thus offering a range of "new" items.

The concern with "newness" is particularly evident on "opening day," when a bale is broken up for resale. At this point, it is important that garments have not been meddled with and traders and customers prefer to open a bale publicly, enabling customers to select on the spot. A bale that is opened in the market is considered to contain new clothes. If it is opened privately the trader might put aside choice items causing customers to suspect that they are being presented with a second cut and not new clothing.

Both traders and customers are concerned with quality and style. These concerns prompt extensive recycling. Items made of fabrics that do not sell easily, for example crimplene, are turned into a variety of new garments. Crimplene trousers are remade into boys' shorts and girls' dresses. Sweaters are unravelled and the yarn reused to crochet or knit baby blankets, jerseys, and rugs. Curtain material with colorful prints is made into women's dresses and suits, draperies with metallic sheen become men's trousers, and curtain lace ends up as trains on wedding gowns. The small-scale tailors who used to sew everyday garments have recouped lost business by repairing and altering salaula. Traders and customers bring men's trousers in large sizes to the tailor to alter and restyle with pleats at the waist, back pockets, and pegged bottoms. Tailors also sew up vents on men's jackets and turn single-breasted jackets into double-breasted *chilubas*.

Some salaula is sold in more exclusive shops such as the Caroussel Botique [sic] at Soweto market. Operated by two young Chokwe men inside the market, this shop advertises its line of "Imported Cloths" in styles of "London Wise." These young men have traded in used clothes from Zaire for several years. They said that they stopped going to Lubumbashi in 1991 because of "the confusion" in Zaire. They now purchase their goods in the Soweto market. After salaula traders open their bales they select a range of choice clothing. Named after Lusaka's newest shopping mall, the Caroussel Shopping Centre, their shop features cleaned, pressed and restyled clothing at prices slightly higher than elsewhere in the market. According to the owners everyone knows this shop and customers come from all over town to buy "the latest," especially nicely restyled *chilubas*. Emblematic of changes following president Frederick Chiluba's takeover from Kenneth Kaunda, the *chiluba* suit's replacement of Kaunda's rigid Mao-inspired uniform tells a story of the opening up of society, of new opportunities, and above all, of the common man's access. The common man was the previous regime's term for the masses. In short, salaula implies choice and possibility, of better lives being within reach.

Customers demand a wide selection of new salaula items. Their needs and wants shape their selections and are influenced by age, gender, class, and by rural or urban residence. Regardless of occupation and residence, the accepted notion of how to dress makes men insist on suits, long-sleeved shirts, ties and—when of a certain age—hats for their public ensemble, even if trousers and jacket are not matched in color, fabric, print and styling; shoes, not boots, tennis shoes, or sandals, mark the man, and men go to great length and expense to find "presidential shoes" (dress moccasins). Irrespective of occupation and location, women insist on skirts below the knee, short-sleeved loose blouses or plain dresses, on top of which a *chitenge* (printed cloth) can be worn, if necessary and, when of a certain age, on headscarves; and high heels are part of their ensemble in public. Some young women and men are less conventional. Such women buy trousers, mini skirts, and tight blouses (*sheke sheke* [the name of a beer]), and men buy jogging suits and shorts. Finally, the desire to be smartly turned out, even if the garments are shabby, makes clothes-conscious Zambians insist on immaculate ensembles whose elements are laundered and ironed. Thus, detailed care for clothing helps to transform old clothes into new ensembles.

Customers, traders, and tailors work hard to make salaula into their own creation. Their preferred styles are not the outcome of the manipulating hand of the advertisement industry; local media do not pay much attention to clothing. Still, syndicated television shows, CNN, foreign magazines, mail order catalogs and old pattern books offer fragments of western styles to sections of society much broader than the television-viewing and magazine-subscribing public. Zambians combine these fragments and re-fashion them into ensembles that achieve the effect of "the latest" in ongoing interaction. Evidence of this dynamic is found on the street and in social gatherings, in what people wear and how, and in their commentary about ensembles and the scrutiny with which they examine styling— "Where did you buy that? Which tailor can do this pattern? Who sells Zairean prints? And where can I find 'silver' buttons?"

The overall combination of the ensemble's elements is always in process. In the very act of appropriating them into "the latest" Zambians undercut their western imprint. The combination of elements that constitute local ensembles may represent what Hannerz calls creolisation.[28] As used clothing consumption increasingly extends across all social strata, certain clothing practices become particularly meaningful. In Mintz's terms, they are intensified in specific contexts and events.[29] Bakhtin's notion of heteroglossia suggests how diversity in distinct clothing practices both questions and contributes to accepted notions of how to dress.[30]

The rapid increase of salaula since the late 1980s has made affordable clothing available to a broad spectrum of people. This contributes toward satisfying the need for clothing and the desire for style. The wide range of salaula give shoppers a welcome opportunity to browse and choose and avoid being bothered or ignored by unfriendly Indian shopkeepers. A dress from salaula is cheaper than one made by the local tailor who must be paid for his labor and supplied with material. Fashion-conscious shoppers add salaula to their store-bought wardrobes which they dress up with the new African-styled outfits made by tailors for prices ranging from K2,000 to K5,000. The price of between K500 and K800 for a cotton salaula dress compares favorably, especially in quality, not only with the K800 crimplene tailor-made dress sold in markets like Kamwala and Soweto, but also with the dresses on display at state shops like *Mwaiseni* or the imports at Cha-ChaCha Fashions which cost ten to twenty times more than salaula dresses. A domestic servant who earns K8,000 a month might buy his wife and children new clothes "from salaula" for Christmas; and, if he is lucky to get a Christmas bonus, he might purchase a restyled *chiluba* for himself. Entering social relations in this way, salaula is implicated in personal projects of improving lives.

CAROUSSEL BOTIQUE

Throughout the 1980s urban and rural Zambians increasingly relied on salaula because of the deterioration of the local textile industry, rapid inflation, and overall economic decline during the last years of Kaunda's Second Republic. The growing availability and acceptability of used clothing was the theme of a 1988 record, "Salaula," by popular singer Teddy Chilambe. The lyrics told of the time now past when the salaula market was only for the household servant and maid. Now even the most fashionable office workers wear secondhand suits. The song praised Zaireans for bringing salaula to Zambia and blamed those who shunned it for wasting money they should use to feed their children.[31] Zambians no longer look down on salaula or hide the fact that they wear it. Few traders or shoppers whom I interviewed had questions or concerns about why or how the West's discarded clothing ends up as a desirable commodity in Zambia. When prompted, a couple of people asked if salaula really is "dead men's clothing." Some others said that they had heard that salaula had "something to do with AIDS." The vast majority were not interested in the provenance of salaula. They explained its presence as a result of "donations" from the West, as is the case with so much else in Zambia. What they most cared about was the availability of affordable clothing.

Thus, I disagree with Teddy Chilambe's changed tune on salaula. In his 1990 "Mukonka Ifya Basungu," ("You Follow the Ways of the Whites"), Chilambe blamed epidemics in Zambia on certain patterns of consumption, including salaula. The song held second-hand clothes responsible for uncommon ailments now afflicting Zambians such as herpes and AIDS.[32] The changing appropriation of used clothes does tell a story with political and economic implications about problems affecting everyday life in Zambia. But a world-systems, dependency-thesis interpretation of unilineal transfer and blame is clearly out of tune with popular Zambian sensibilities and reactions. These reactions, I suggest, celebrate salaula. *Chokako Weka* means "move yourself" in Nyanja. Written on the sign of the Caroussel Botique, it captures some of the popular attractions of salaula in Zambia. Salaula implies progress; the ability to dress tells of improvement. In the popular view, after years of standing in queues and ending up empty handed, when people had little money, and clothing was not piled up waiting to be bought, salaula means that ordinary people can now afford to wear clothes rather than rags. It also means that more consumers than ever before can make choices in a booming clothing market. The salaula trade offers work and therefore hope about new opportunities to young women and men who might not find formal jobs.

Salaula is celebrated in urban and rural areas alike. Rural areas, which used to be characterized with statements like "there is nothing there—they don't know sugar, tea, bread, clothes, what it is like," were described in 1992 with some optimism: "there is even salaula now." After the long, hard years of the Kaunda regime's austerity programs and deteriorating terms of trade between both rural and urban areas and between Zambia and the world economy, commentaries on the recent rapid increase in salaula availability and consumption express not only disenchantment with the previous government and its state but also the attainability of future hopes and aspirations.

CONCLUSION: IDENTITY AND DIFFERENCE

Zambians have been wearing "western clothes" for a good part of this century and have made such clothing their own. We need to acknowledge these facts and thus address how their dealings with clothing involve both history and meaning. Given this perspective, the argument I have presented here may only apply to a specific historical moment. I suggest that the meanings

which Zambians at the beginning of the Third Republic attributed to salaula, and with which they proudly and aggressively defended their individual rights to "move themselves," represent a relatively new phenomenon that is a product of recent political and economic events in their country. The meanings they construct in their everyday dealings with clothing thus reflect local and distinctly Zambian experiences, in spite of the recognizable western imprint about which the inscriptions "Imported Cloths" and "London Wise" on the sign of Caroussel Botique so obviously speak.

This recent celebration of salaula might be a relatively unsteady phenomenon which because of future developments in Zambia's changing political economy barely may have time to establish itself before salaula becomes subject to new interpretations. When explained in this way, we grant used clothing a history in which what becomes of it does not inhere in its commodity status as a western cast-off. Instead, we view it as a result of what people subsequently make of it and with it, investing or divesting it with meanings. And such meanings, I suggest, are implicated in startling ways with the making and changing of local Zambian experiences in our late twentieth-century world.

While Zambians' widespread enthusiasm about salaula may reflect momentary improvement over previous years of austerity, it is also tinged with ambivalence about longer-term economic developments. The popularity and availability of used clothing in Zambia must not be explained as a romanticization of poverty but rather as its democratization. The disparity and difference of the young salaula trader's ensemble introduced at the article's outset—his hospital whites topped by pink peignoir—evoke a disparity that has to do with the unenviable position of Africa in global terms, and a difference that has to do with the peculiarities of economics and politics in Zambia. As long as the new regime maintains its liberalization of foreign imports, including used clothing, and does not empower the local textile and clothing industries, the western distinction between rags and clothing will be redefined in local terms that transform cast-offs into desired garments. The disparities inherent in this process fuel the West's multi-million dollar export business in used clothing whose chief beneficiaries, western rag dealers and local importers, are more concerned with extracting profit than with supporting local initiative.

NOTES

1. See Jean and John Comaroff, *Of Revelation and Revolution: Christianity, Colonization, and Consciousness in South Africa*. Volume 1 (Chicago: University of Chicago Press, 1991) and especially Volume 2 (in preparation) which contains a chapter about the missionary influence on clothing practices among the Tswana; and Nicholas Thomas, *Entangled Objects: Exchange, Material Cul-*

ture, and Colonialism in the Pacific (Cambridge, Mass.: Harvard University Press, 1991).

2. Ulf Hannerz, *Cultural Complexity: Studies in the Social Organization of Meaning* (New York: Columbia University Press, 1992), 217–267; and Anthony D. King, ed., *Culture, Globalization and the World System* (London: Macmillan, 1991).

3. Igor Kopytoff, "The Cultural Biography of Things: Commoditization as Process," in *The Social Life of Things: Commodities in Cultural Perspective,* A. Appadurai, ed. (Cambridge: Cambridge University Press, 1986), 64–91.

4. Ulf Hannerz, "The World in Creolisation," *Africa* 57 (1987): 546–559; Sidney W. Mintz, *Sweetness and Power: The Place of Sugar in Modern History* (New York: Viking penguin, 1985), 172–174; Mikhail M. Bakhtin, *The Dialogic Imagination: Four Essays,* ed. M. Holquist (Austin: University of Texas Press, 1982).

5. See Richard E. Baldwin, *Economic Development and Export Growth: A Study of Northern Rhodesia 1920–1960* (Berkeley: University of California Press, 1969), and M. R. Bhagavan, *Zambia: Impact of Industrial Strategy on Regional Imbalance and Social Inequality* (Uppsala: Scandinavian Institute of African Studies, 1978).

6. Arjun Appadurai, "Introduction: Commodities and the Politics of Value," in *The Social Life of Things: Commodities in Cultural Perspective,* A. Appadurai, ed. (Cambridge: Cambridge University Press, 1986), 3–63.

7. The research was undertaken between mid-June and mid-August 1992. It included interviews of secondhand clothes traders in several markets in Lusaka and in rural Chiawa, interviews of tailors, long-distance lorry drivers, clearing agents in freight companies and importers of secondhand clothing. My assistants, Mrs. Norah Rice and Mr. Jonas Phiri, and I also sampled price ranges of ready-made clothing and consumer attitudes of, among others, Zambian and Zimbabwean shoppers in markets, at the bus terminal and the railway station in Lusaka.

8. It seems that many Africanists "know about" this trade in an anecdotal manner. While bits and pieces of evidence are available in the form of offhand remarks in studies of markets, little substantive work has been done, either on questions pertaining to the international political economy of the used clothing business, or on its changing local appropriations. Deborah Heath ("Fashion, Anti-Fashion, and Heteroglossia in Urban Senegal," *American Ethnologist* 19, no 2 [1992]: 19–33) is an exception that casts interesting light on the place of used clothing in Senegambian fashion. Steven Haggblade ("The Flip Side of Fashion: Used Clothing Exports to the Third World," *Journal of Development Studies* 29, no 3 [1990]: 505–521) examines some of the economic effects of this import on the textile industry in Rwanda. Barth van Groen and Piet Lozar ("La Structure et l'organisation de la friperie à Tunis." Groupe d'Etudes Tunis, Universite Libre d'Amsterdam, 1976) offer insights into the local organization of this trade in Tunisia close to twenty years ago. These studies and my informal inspections of markets in Ibadan in Nigeria, Accra and Kumasi in Ghana in 1989, in Kampala, Uganda in 1992 as well as of used clothing sales from the roadside in towns in the Eastern Cape in South Africa in 1992 tell of diverse marketing practices that do not replicate what I describe for Lusaka.

9. *Vogue,* April 1993, 147; 152.

10. *Chicago Tribune,* Style Magazine, 24 March 1993, 17–18.

11. *Chicago Tribune,* Tempo Section, 21 March 1993, 5.

12. *New York Times,* The Living Arts Section, 22 March 1993, 3.

13. The Paris "Prince of Pieces" is Malian Lamine Kouyaté whose couture is "a patchwork of rough-hewn, castoff and factory surplus clothing—rent, dismembered and then sutured together like field wounds with coarse thread." See Amy M. Spindler, "Prince of Pieces," *New York Times,* Styles of the Times, 2 May 1993; 1; 13.

14. See for example Stuart Cosgrove, "The Zoot Suit and Style Warfare," in *Zoot Suits and Second-Hand Dresses,* A. McRobbie, ed.

(Boston: Unwin Hyman, 1988), 3–22; Caroline Evans and Minna Thornton "Fashion, Representation, Femininity," *Feminist Review* 39 (1991): 48–66; Gail Faurschou, "Fashion and the Cultural Logic of Postmodernity," in *Body Invaders: Panic Sex in America,* A. and M. Kroker, eds. (New York: St. Martin's Press, 1987) 78–93; Angela McRobbie, "Second-Hand Dresses and the Role of the Ragmarket," in *Zoot Suits and Second-Hand Dresses,* A. McRobbie, ed. (Boston, Unwin Hyman 1988), 23–49; and Kim Sawchuk, "A Tale of Inscription: Fashion Statements," in *Body Invaders: Panic Sex in America,* A. and M. Kroker, eds. (New York: St. Martin's Press, 1987), 61–77.

15. B. Bull, "L.A. International," *Vogue,* February 1989, 332–335.

16. I conducted library searches with very minimal results into Business Periodical Abstracts; Historical Abstracts; Sociological Abstracts; and various newspaper indexes. Labor unions, especially the ILGWU, have criticized charities for their involvement in this export for two main reasons: the export of used clothing is destructive to the textile industries of poor nations; and the companies exporting used clothing make hefty profits in Africa and other Third World countries and pay employees poor wages and virtually no benefits. Some of this criticism has been prompted by complaints of textile unions in South Africa and Zimbabwe about the unfair competition import of used clothes poses to local production.

17. *Los Angeles Times,* Part J, 29 October 1992, 16.

18. *Newsday,* City edition, 19 March 1991, 7.

19. J. Brooke, "International Report: Used U.S. Clothes a Best Seller in Africa," *New York Times,* Section 1,16 February 1987, 48; and R. Reinhold, "Used Clothes sell by the Pound in Texas City, Offering a Way to Scrape by," *New York Times,* 22 July 1984.

20. International Trade Association, Office of Africa, "Used Apparel Markets in Africa: Market Notes and Contacts" (Washington, D.C.: U.S. Department of Commerce, 1993), 2; 4.

21. The Canadian figures are taken from Statistics Canada, International Trade Division, Exports by Country. My research on the used clothes export from Europe to Zambia is ongoing.

22. Merle J. Davis, *Modern Industry and the African* (London: Macmillan and Co., 1933), 42.

23. On the Zairean connection, see Kenneth Kaunda, *Zambia Shall be Free* (London: Heinemann, 1962), 39; and Mwelwa C. Musambachime, Development and Growth of the Fishing Industry from Mweru-Luapula 1920–1964 (University of Wisconsin, Ph.D. Dissertation, 1981), especially chapters 4 and 7.

24. Elizabeth Colson (personal communication, Lusaka, September 1992); see Karen Tranberg Hansen, *Distant Companions: Servants and Employers in Zambia, 1900–1985* (Ithaca: Cornell University Press, 1989), 161–166.

25. "Wool," "silk," and "crimplene" are among the categories into which textile salvagers sort used clothing. "Wool" includes garments with a mixture of wool and artificial fibre. Garments of pure wool are sorted for export to Italy, a chief recycler of wool products in today's textile world economy. "Silk" refers to garments made mainly of polyester and other man-made fibres, and "crimplene" refers to polyester knits.

26. The *kwacha* equivalents of one U.S. dollar changed during the duration of this research from K155 in June of 1992, K174 in July of 1992, and K186 in September 1992.

27. Kopytoff, 73.

28. Hannerz, 1987.

29. Mintz, 172–174.

30. Bakhtin, 1982.

31. Geoff Zulu, "Between the Lines," *Zambia Daily Mail* 21 April 1989.

32. B. Katongo, "Chilambe Goes Anti-Salaula," *Zambia Daily Mail* 26 January 1990.

7

Sex and Marriage

Why is it that the worst swearwords in our society are utterances like "Motherfucker," or, even when one is being creative, always refer to reproduction or the sexual organs and incest? While there are no ready answers to this question, it does underline the importance we attach to sexual activity and the rules attached thereto, in particular incest.

The literature on **incest** is voluminous and cannot be summarized here. Suffice to say that there are at present two main camps, the Freudians and the evolutionary theorists. The psychoanalytically oriented Freudian interpreters try to explain how individual development blocks the possibility of incest. Freud argued that the child normally represses erotic feelings toward the opposite-sex parent or sibling out of fear of reprisal from the same-sex parent (the **Oedipus complex**). In short, familiarity breeds attempt, and thus the incest taboo came into being to prevent this rivalry.

The evolutionary theorists take as their founding father Edward Westermarck, the Finnish anthropologist who in 1891 suggested that **natural selection** had endowed humans with a tendency to avoid inbreeding and its harmful effects on offspring. It was, in effect, a question of familiarity breeds contempt or "Marry out or die out."

Obviously the last word on incest has not been said, and anthropologists bedevil the discussion by pointing out the large degree of variations in cultural practices, even those as basic as incest and marriage. Indeed, anthropology goes further. If there is one thing that we have shown, it is how even the most basic behavior of those whom we define as "male" and "fe-male" is very much a cultural production. John Coggeshall clearly brings this out in "'Ladies' Behind Bars." Biology is not necessarily destiny, as Regina Smith Oboler further underlines. Moreover, even sexual practices are culturally constructed and can change over time.

Theories and explanations of procreation, incest, marriage, and sex are interrelated and closely related to people's wider worldviews. From such a broader perspective the power of women has been substantially underestimated in many societies. Consider, for example, this statement by Nisa, a Bushman woman:

Women are strong; women are important. Zhun/twa men say that women are the chiefs, the rich ones, the wise ones. Because women possess something very important, something which enables men to live: their genitals. A woman can bring a man life even if he is almost dead. She can give him sex even if he is almost dead. She can give him sex and make him alive again. If she were to refuse, he would die! If there were no women around, their semen would kill men. Did you know that? If there were only men, they would all die. Women make it possible for them to live. (Shostak 1981)

Reproduction involves more than just sex; it also includes **marriage,** the **family,** and kinship. Marriage provokes many questions. Why do different arrangements occur and why and how are they socially recognized? Marriage does not have a single function. It ties a bundle of rights and obligations into one of several packages creating economic units, relating the individual to other kin groups, defining social status. It is a political instrument, as royal marriages in Europe or even the once popular soap "Dynasty" show; it regulates sex and creates a social security network. Seen from such a broad perspective, sex might have nothing to do with marriage, as every teenager knows! It is for this reason that one can find woman-woman marriages and even ghost marriages. The range of marriage types is indeed extraordinary, as Dirk Johnson shows in his article on **polygamy.** Nor is marriage a simple matter of merely "falling in love." As Nanda shows in her article, many societies regard marriage as too impor-

tant to leave entirely to the whims of young people. Accordingly, experienced adult kin of brides- and grooms-to-be play active roles in arranging marriages. Although North Americans tend to react negatively to the idea, such arranged marriages have their advantages.

REFERENCE

Shostak, Marjory, 1991. *Nisa*. McGraw-Hill: New York.

Arranging a Marriage in India

Serena Nanda

John Jay College of Criminal Justice

Serena Nanda, who earned her Ph.D. at New York University in 1973, is now a professor at John Jay College of Criminal Justice of The City University of New York. Her field research includes the study of tribal development in India, and her book, *Neither Man Nor Woman: The Higras of India*, won the 1990 Ruth Benedict Prize. She also has published on ethnicity, gender, and law in the United States, and her interests also include urban and visual anthropology.

Sister and doctor brother-in-law invite correspondence from North Indian professionals only, for a beautiful, talented, sophisticated, intelligent sister, 5' 3", slim, M.A. in textile design, father a senior civil officer. Would prefer immigrant doctors, between 26–29 years. Reply with full details and returnable photo.

A well-settled uncle invites matrimonial correspondence from slim, fair, educated South Indian girl, for his nephew, 25 years, smart, M.B.A., green card holder, 5' 6". Full particulars with returnable photo appreciated.

—*Matrimonial Advertisements*, India Abroad

In India, almost all marriages are arranged. Even among the educated middle classes in modern, urban India, marriage is as much a concern of the families as it is of the individuals. So customary is the practice of arranged marriage that there is a special name for a marriage which is not arranged: It is called a "love match."

On my first field trip to India, I met many young men and women whose parents were in the process of "getting them married." In many cases, the bride and groom would not meet each other before the marriage. At most they might meet for a brief conversation, and this meeting would take place only after their parents had decided that the match was suitable. Parents do not compel their children to marry a person who either marriage partner finds objectionable. But only after one match is refused will another be sought.

As a young American woman in India for the first time, I found this custom of arranged marriage oppressive. How could any intelligent young person agree to such a marriage without great reluctance? It was contrary to everything I believed about the importance of romantic love as the only basis of a happy marriage. It also clashed with my strongly held notions that the choice of such an intimate and permanent relationship could be made only by the individuals involved. Had anyone tried to arrange my marriage, I would have been defiant and rebellious!

At the first opportunity, I began, with more curiosity than tact, to question the young people I met on how they felt about this practice. Sita, one of my young informants, was a college graduate with a degree in political science. She had been waiting for over a year while her parents were arranging a match for her. I found it difficult to accept the docile manner in which this well-educated young woman awaited the outcome of a process that would result in her spending the rest of her life with a man she hardly knew, a virtual stranger, picked out by her parents.

"How can you go along with this?" I asked her, in frustration and distress. "Don't you care who you marry?"

"Of course I care," she answered. "This is why I must let my parents choose a boy for me. My marriage is too important to be arranged by such an inexperienced person as myself. In such matters, it is better to have my parents' guidance."

I had learned that young men and women in India do not date and have very little social life involving members of the opposite sex. Although I could not disagree with Sita's reasoning, I continued to pursue the subject.

"But how can you marry the first man you have ever met? Not only have you missed the fun of meeting a lot of different people, but you have not given yourself the chance to know who is the right man for you."

From *The Naked Anthropologist*, Wadsworth, 1992, pp. 34–35. © 1992 by Serena Nanda. Reprinted by permission.

"Meeting with a lot of different people doesn't sound like any fun at all," Sita answered. "One hears that in America the girls are spending all their time worrying about whether they will meet a man and get married. Here we have the chance to enjoy our life and let our parents do this work and worrying for us."

She had me there. The high anxiety of the competition to "be popular" with the opposite sex certainly was the most prominent feature of life as an American teenager in the late fifties. The endless worrying about the rules that governed our behavior and about our popularity ratings sapped both our self-esteem and our enjoyment of adolescence. I reflected that absence of this competition in India most certainly may have contributed to the self-confidence and natural charm of so many of the young women I met.

And yet, the idea of marrying a perfect stranger, whom one did not know and did not "love," so offended my American ideas of individualism and romanticism, that I persisted with my objections.

"I still can't imagine it," I said. "How can you agree to marry a man you hardly know?"

"But of course he will be known. My parents would never arrange a marriage for me without knowing all about the boy's family background. Naturally we will not rely only on what the family tells us. We will check the particulars out ourselves. No one will want their daughter to marry into a family that is not good. All these things we will know beforehand."

Impatiently, I responded, "Sita, I don't mean know the family, I mean, know the man. How can you marry someone you don't know personally and don't love? How can you think of spending your life with someone you may not even like?"

"If he is a good man, why should I not like him?" she said. "With you people, you know the boy so well before you marry, where will be the fun to get married? There will be no mystery and no romance. Here we have the whole of our married life to get to know and love our husband. This way is better, is it not?"

Her response made further sense, and I began to have second thoughts on the matter. Indeed, during months of meeting many intelligent young Indian people, both male and female, who had the same ideas as Sita, I saw arranged marriages in a different light. I also saw the importance of the family in Indian life and realized that a couple who took their marriage into their own hands was taking a big risk, particularly if their families were irreconcilably opposed to the match. In a country where every important resource in life—a job, a house, a social circle—is gained through family connections, it seemed foolhardy to cut oneself off from a supportive social network and depend solely on one person for happiness and success.

Six years later I returned to India to again do fieldwork, this time among the middle class in Bombay, a modern, sophisticated city. From the experience of my earlier visit, I decided to include a study of arranged marriages in my project. By this time I had met many Indian couples whose marriages had been arranged and who seemed very happy. Particularly in contrast to the fate of many of my married friends in the United States who were already in the process of divorce, the positive aspects of arranged marriages appeared to me to outweigh the negatives. In fact, I thought I might even participate in arranging a marriage myself. I had been fairly successful in the United States in "fixing up" many of my friends, and I was confident that my matchmaking skills could be easily applied to this new situation, once I learned the basic rules. "After all," I thought, "how complicated can it be? People want pretty much the same things in a marriage whether it is in India or America."

An opportunity presented itself almost immediately. A friend from my previous Indian trip was in the process of arranging for the marriage of her eldest son. In India there is a perceived shortage of "good boys," and since my friend's family was eminently respectable and the boy himself personable, well educated, and nice looking, I was sure that by the end of my year's fieldwork, we would have found a match.

The basic rule seems to be that a family's reputation is most important. It is understood that matches would be arranged only within the same caste and general social class, although some crossing of subcastes is permissible if the class positions of the bride's and groom's families are similar. Although dowry is now prohibited by law in India, extensive gift exchanges took place with every marriage. Even when the boy's family do not "make demands," every girl's family nevertheless feels the obligation to give the traditional gifts, to the girl, to the boy, and to the boy's family. Particularly when the couple would be living in the joint family—that is, with the boy's parents and his married brothers and their families, as well as with unmarried siblings—which is still very common even among the urban, upper-middle class in India, the girl's parents are anxious to establish smooth relations between their family and that of the boy. Offering the proper gifts, even when not called "dowry," is often an important factor in influencing the relationship between the bride's and groom's families and perhaps, also, the treatment of the bride in her new home.

In a society where divorce is still a scandal and where, in fact, the divorce rate is exceedingly low, an arranged marriage is the beginning of a lifetime relationship not just between the bride and groom but between their families as well. Thus, while a girl's looks are important, her character is even more so, for she is being judged as a prospective daughter-in-law as much as a prospective bride. Where she would be living in a joint family, as was the case with my friend, the girl's ability to get along harmoniously in a family is perhaps the single most important quality in assessing her suitability.

My friend is a highly esteemed wife, mother, and daughter-in-law. She is religious, soft-spoken, modest, and deferential. She rarely gossips and never quarrels, two qualities highly desirable in a woman. A family that has the reputation for gossip and conflict among its womenfolk will not find it easy to get good wives for their sons. Parents will not want to send their daughter to a house in which there is conflict.

My friend's family were originally from North India. They had lived in Bombay, where her husband owned a business, for forty years. The family had delayed in seeking a match for their eldest son because he had been an Air Force pilot for several years, stationed in such remote places that it had seemed fruitless to try to find a girl who would be willing to accompany him. In their social class, a military career, despite its economic security, has little prestige and is considered a drawback in finding a suitable bride. Many families would not allow their daughters to marry a man in an occupation so potentially dangerous and which requires so much moving around.

The son had recently left the military and joined his father's business. Since he was a college graduate, modern, and well traveled, from such a good family, and, I thought, quite handsome, it seemed to me that he, or rather his family, was in a position to pick and choose. I said as much to my friend.

While she agreed that there were many advantages on their side, she also said, "We must keep in mind that my son is both short and dark; these are drawbacks in finding the right match." While the boy's height had not escaped my notice, "dark" seemed to me inaccurate; I would have called him "wheat" colored perhaps, and in any case, I did not realize that color would be a consideration. I discovered, however, that while a boy's skin color is a less important consideration than a girl's, it is still a factor.

An important source of contacts in trying to arrange her son's marriage was my friend's social club in Bombay. Many of the women had daughters of the right age, and some had already expressed an interest in my friend's son. I was most enthusiastic about the possibilities of one particular family who had five daughters, all of whom were pretty, demure, and well educated. Their mother had told my friend, "You can have your pick for your son, whichever one of my daughters appeals to you most."

I saw a match in sight. "Surely," I said to my friend, "we will find one there. Let's go visit and make our choice." But my friend held back; she did not seem to share my enthusiasm, for reasons I could not then fathom.

When I kept pressing for an explanation of her reluctance, she admitted, "See, Serena, here is the problem. The family has so many daughters, how will they be able to provide nicely for any of them? We are not making any demands, but still, with so many daughters to marry off, one wonders whether she will even be able to make a proper wedding. Since this is our eldest son, it's best if we marry him to a girl who is the only daughter, then the wedding will truly be a gala affair." I argued that surely the quality of the girls themselves made up for any deficiency in the elaborateness of the wedding. My friend admitted this point but still seemed reluctant to proceed.

"Is there something else," I asked her, "some factor I have missed?" "Well," she finally said, "there is one other thing. They have one daughter already married and living in Bombay. The mother is always complaining to me that the girl's in-laws don't let her visit her own family often enough. So it makes me wonder, will she be that kind of mother who always wants her daughter at her own home? This will prevent the girl from adjusting to our house. It is not a good thing." And so, this family of five daughters was dropped as a possibility.

Somewhat disappointed, I nevertheless respected my friend's reasoning and geared up for the next prospect. This was also the daughter of a woman in my friend's social club. There was clear interest in this family and I could see why. The family's reputation was excellent; in fact, they came from a subcaste slightly higher than my friend's own. The girl, who was an only daughter, was pretty and well educated and had a brother studying in the United States. Yet, after expressing an interest to me in this family, all talk of them suddenly died down and the search began elsewhere.

"What happened to that girl as a prospect?" I asked one day. "You never mention her any more. She is so pretty and so educated, what did you find wrong?"

"She is too educated. We've decided against it. My husband's father saw the girl on the bus the other day and thought her forward. A girl who 'roams about' the city by herself is not the girl for our family." My disappointment this time was even greater, as I thought the son would have liked the girl very much. But then I thought, my friend is right, a girl who is going to live in a joint family cannot be too independent or she will make life miserable for everyone. I also learned that if the family of the girl has even a slightly higher social status than the family of the boy, the bride may think herself too good for them, and this too will cause problems. Later my friend admitted to me that this had been an important factor in her decision not to pursue the match.

The next candidate was the daughter of a client of my friend's husband. When the client learned that the family was looking for a match for their son, he said, "Look no further, we have a daughter." This man then invited my friends to dinner to see the girl. He had already seen their son at the office and decided that "he liked the boy." We all went together for tea, rather than dinner—it was less of a commitment—and while we were there, the girl's mother showed us around the house. The girl was studying for her exams and was briefly introduced to us.

After we left, I was anxious to hear my friend's opinion. While her husband liked the family very much and was impressed with his client's business accomplishments and reputation, the wife didn't like the girl's looks. "She is short, no doubt, which is an important plus point, but she is also fat and wears glasses." My friend obviously thought she could do better for her son and asked her husband to make his excuses to his client by saying that they had decided to postpone the boy's marriage indefinitely.

By this time almost six months had passed and I was becoming impatient. What I had thought would be an easy matter to arrange was turning out to be quite complicated. I began to believe that between my friend's desire for a girl who was modest enough to fit into her joint family, yet attractive and educated enough to be an acceptable partner for her son, she would not find anyone suitable. My friend laughed at my impatience: "Don't be so much in a hurry," she said. "You Americans want everything done so quickly. You get married quickly and then just as quickly get divorced. Here we take marriage more seriously. We must take all the factors into account. It is not enough for us to learn by our mistakes. This is too serious a business. If a mistake is made we have not only ruined the life of our son or daughter, but we have spoiled the reputation of our family as well. And that will make it much harder for their brothers and sisters to get married. So we must be very careful."

What she said was true and I promised myself to be more patient, though it was not easy. I had really hoped and expected that the match would be made before my year in India was up. But it was not to be. When I left India my friend seemed no further along in finding a suitable match for her son than when I had arrived.

Two years later, I returned to India and still my friend had not found a girl for her son. By this time, he was close to thirty, and I think she was a little worried. Since she knew I had friends all over India, and I was going to be there for a year, she asked me to "help her in this work" and keep an eye out for someone suitable. I was flattered that my judgment was respected, but knowing now how complicated the process was, I

had lost my earlier confidence as a matchmaker. Nevertheless, I promised that I would try.

It was almost at the end of my year's stay in India that I met a family with a marriageable daughter whom I felt might be a good possibility for my friend's son. The girl's father was related to a good friend of mine and by coincidence came from the same village as my friend's husband. This new family had a successful business in a medium-sized city in central India and were from the same subcaste as my friend. The daughter was pretty and chic; in fact, she had studied fashion design in college. Her parents would not allow her to go off by herself to any of the major cities in India where she could make a career, but they had compromised with her wish to work by allowing her to run a small dress-making boutique from their home. In spite of her desire to have a career, the daughter was both modest and home-loving and had had a traditional, sheltered upbringing. She had only one other sister, already married, and a brother who was in his father's business.

I mentioned the possibility of a match with my friend's son. The girl's parents were most interested. Although their daughter was not eager to marry just yet, the idea of living in Bombay—a sophisticated, extremely fashion-conscious city where she could continue her education in clothing design—was a great inducement. I gave the girl's father my friend's address and suggested that when they went to Bombay on some business or whatever, they look up the boy's family.

Returning to Bombay on my way to New York, I told my friend of this newly discovered possibility. She seemed to feel there was potential but, in spite of my urging, would not make any moves herself. She rather preferred to wait for the girl's family to call upon them. I hoped something would come of this introduction, though by now I had learned to rein in my optimism.

A year later I received a letter from my friend. The family had indeed come to visit Bombay, and their daughter and my friend's daughter, who were near in age, had become very good friends. During that year, the two girls had frequently visited each other. I thought things looked promising.

Last week I received an invitation to a wedding: My friend's son and the girl were getting married. Since I had found the match, my presence was particularly requested at the wedding. I was thrilled. Success at last! As I prepared to leave for India, I began thinking, "Now, my friend's younger son, who do I know who has a nice girl for him . . . ?"

"Ladies" Behind Bars

A Liminal Gender as Cultural Mirror

John M. Coggeshall

John M. Coggeshall, an assistant professor of anthropology at Clemson University in South Carolina, has carried out fieldwork in two medium-security prisons in Illinois. He received his Ph.D. in 1984 from Southern Illinois University.

"You here to see the show?" the inmate leered. The focus of attention was the tall blond then receiving her food in the prison cafeteria. The workers filled her plate with polite deference, and as she walked between the tables her fine blond hair bounced over her shoulders. "Make you want to leave home?" the guard next to me teased. His joke clarified the significance of the episode I had just witnessed. The object of attention was genetically a male, reconstructed as female according to the perception of gender within the cultural rule system of prison. Behind bars, certain males become redefined as "ladies." I have not been able to discern any correlation between assigned gender and the type of crime for which an inmate was sentenced. The process by which this transformation occurs reveals not only clues about gender construction in prison culture, but also suggests perceptions of gender identity in American culture in general.

Prison culture involves one predominant theme: control. To establish identity, males profess a culturally defined image to defend themselves from oppression by guards and other inmates. Men define themselves as males by juxtaposing maleness with femaleness, fabricating gender identity from the reflection. For inmates, the concept of female emerges from the concept of male. To borrow a well-known metaphor, the rib for Eve's creation is taken from Adam's side, and draws both its cultural significance and social status from the extraction. Woman is defined in contrast to man, and takes a lesser place at his side. In prison, males create females in their image, and by doing so, dominate and subjugate them.

The fieldwork upon which this study is based was conducted in two medium-security prisons in southern Illinois between 1984 and 1986. Within that time span I

taught three university-level courses to about thirty adult inmates, constituting a range of racial group and criminal record diversity representative of the overall prison population. Their perceptions provided a portion of the field data, supplemented by my observations of and conversations with guards and staff. After having received some instruction on ethnographic data collection, a former student and then resident inmate, Gene Luetkemeyer, volunteered to collect additional information on "ladies" behind bars. His nine detailed interviews of various categories of inmates, identified in the text by pseudonyms, significantly enhanced the scope and detail of the study.

Prison culture is extremely complex, and deserves much more detailed study by anthropologists (see for example the treatment by Goffman 1961, Davidson 1983, and Cardozo-Freeman 1984).[1] Even my relatively brief "incarceration" has suggested numerous leads for future research. Gender identity in prison could be explored in much greater detail, describing for example the abusive context whereby young males might become pawns by an administration concerned with pacifying gangs. Another productive line of inquiry might explore the overall cultural context of gender identity in prison culture, for themes of sexuality pervade prison, indicating its cultural significance for staff as well as inmates.

GENDER PERCEPTIONS OF CONVICTS

Here the research concentrates on the gender perceptions of convicts, i.e., the long-term residents (Davidson 1983). Convict attitudes toward homosexual behaviour vary considerably from one individual to the next. Not all participate, and not all do so with the same self-perception or with the same purposes. A subtle distinction is made by many inmates between indi-

"'Ladies' Behind Bars: A Liminal Gender as Cultural Mirror" by John M. Coggeshall, from *Anthropology Today*, Vol. 4, No. 4, 1988. Royal Anthropological Institute. Reprinted with permission.

viduals who engage entirely in submissive, recipient homosexual intercourse, and those who participate in mutual exchange of pleasure. Further distinctions also exist. Certain types or categories of homosexuals, some of which are discussed below, provide a ranking of these attitudes. Despite intra-cultural variation, widespread agreement prevails on cultural definitions of masculine and feminine gender identities.

Inmates have provided various estimates for the amount of homosexual activity in prison.[2] All agree that long-timers are more likely to engage in such practices, for they have less of a future to anticipate, more opportunities for sexual pleasure to utilize, and relatively lenient punishments for violations. For example, Paul and Sandy, homosexual lovers, and Frank, Paul's straight friend, believe that about 65% of their prison population engages in homosexual activity, an estimate supported by Dr. B, an incarcerated medical doctor. While such numbers reveal the amount of control and coercion in prisoner culture, they also reveal the "need for love, affection, [and] intimate relationships" denied by the system, another inmate observes. Some ties are based on affection, but these are relatively rare.[3] Homosexual behaviour fulfills numerous functions in the social and cultural system of prison. Thus most inmates see it as at worst a repugnant necessity and at best a tolerable alternative.

Despite varying views on prevalence, prisoners agree on the general gender constructs in prisoner culture. Males in prison adopt a "masculine role," inmates assert. Robert describes "a big . . . macho weight-lifting virile Tom Selleck type guy" as typical of the stereotype. Weight lifters, in fact, seem to predominate in the category, for strength suggests masculinity. Real men vigorously protest sexual advances from other males by exhibiting a willingness to fight. Men are also seen as preoccupied with sexual gratification, and will obtain it at all costs.

Real men in prison are perceived as those who can keep, satisfy, and protect "women." The dominant sex partner is termed a "daddy," who watches out for and protects his "kid" or "girl." For some men, the acquisition of sex partners strongly resembles courting, where the pursuer flirts with and purchases commissary (snack foods, cosmetics, and similar items) for the object of his interest. Others acquire submissive sex partners by force. Ultimately, with either type, sexual partnerships are based on power and control, the complete domination of one person and one gender by another. In fact, domination defines the structure of the relationship which distinguishes the genders in prison.

However, in prison, since the culturally defined females had been males at one time, this presents "real" men with a gender identity problem: reconciling having sexual intercourse with males while maintaining a masculine self-concept. This adjustment is accomplished by

means of a unique folk explanation of the origins of gender development and orientation. Basically, males in prison redefine selected males as females.

In direct contrast to these self-perceptions of males, men portray women in a painting of their own creation. Males see females as passive, subordinate, sexual objects. According to Robert, women are "sweet and charming," "fluid of movement," with "seductive gestures." Dr. B believes that he himself exhibits such effeminate qualities as "mild manners" and a "passive demeanour." Women are also viewed as attractive, and they use that allure to their advantage by feigning helplessness; this allows women to maintain a "certain power" over men, Paul feels. A woman might "use her charms" to "get what she wanted," while at the same time she might not "put out" sexually, according to Dr. B. Women often tease to coerce men, and sometimes withhold what had apparently been promised, he adds.

Of course, nearly all female staff in prison culture do not meet these stereotypes. By inmate definition, then, they must not be women. Such "non-women" do not challenge gender constructs but reinforce them further. Female guards and staff occupy positions of power and authority over inmates, decidedly atypical for women from a prisoner's perspective. Moreover, most of these women dress in ways to deliberately de-accentuate anatomical differences and to resemble their male counterparts uniformly. Because these women dress as "non-women" and control men, they cannot be women and must therefore be homosexuals or "dykes," as the convicts term them. To inmates, this can be the only explanation for women who do not act like women. Cultural reality persists as potentially disruptive anomalies disappear through redefinition.

TRAPPED BETWEEN MALE AND FEMALE ROLES

The process by which certain males become redefined as females in prison provides an example of Victor Turner's (1969) concept of liminality. Prisoner culture perceives certain males as being trapped in between male and female, thus necessitating the release of their true gender identities. The period of incarceration provides the "time out of time" necessary for the transfiguration to occur. In fact, inmate terms for the metamorphosis reveal this gender ambiguity: males "turn out" these non-males, transforming them into the cultural equivalent of females. The liminal gender is actually "male as female," betwixt and between both. Such individuals figuratively "turn out" to be females, reconstructed according to the prisoner cultural stereotypes of "female." They thus become their "true" selves at last.

This duality creates additional complications in self-identity for such men. Goffman (1961) noted the struggle inmates have in reconciling the staff's perception of them with their own self-concept. Inmates readjusting a sexual orientation share a similar problem. Dr. B explains that individuals who make the transition from male to female must reconcile past heterosexual behaviour with their present homosexual identity. The homosexual in prison must convince herself that this new self-perception had been her true identity all along. Thus she now has adapted the normal role befitting her identity and gender adjustment.

Vindication for the transformation comes as those forced to become homosexuals remain as such. The acceptance by the homosexual of her new gender identity and associated behaviour justifies the conversion in the eyes of the rest of the prison population. If the "male becoming female" had no natural proclivity or had not been submissive by nature and thus also female, she would never have agreed to have adopted a feminine identity. As Frank (an inmate) explains, those who surrender are weak, and females are weak. Therefore those who surrender must be female by nature.

Folk conceptions of the origins of gender further support this perspective. Tommy (another inmate) notes that all humans are "conceived as female, then either, as foetuses, develop genitalia or not." Some individuals perpetuate, even unconsciously, this dualistic foetal identity into adulthood: they can be transformed or "turned out." Not resisting, or not resisting aggressively enough, merely validates this gender liminality. In a sense, it is only appropriate that those trapped betwixt and between be released, to unfetter their true natures. Even coercive gender conversion restores the natural order.

Prisoner culture divides homosexuals into several types, each defined on the basis of degree of sexual promiscuity, amount of self-conceptual pride, and severity of coercion used to turn them out. Generally, status declines as sexual promiscuity increases, self-concept decreases, and the types and intensity of coercion used in the conversion process increase.

The highest status category of homosexuals in prison is that of "queens" or "ladies," those who had come out both voluntarily and willingly. Prisoner cultural belief suggests that these individuals had been homosexual on the outside but may have lacked the freedom to have been themselves. Prison has provided them with a treasured opportunity to "come out," and they have accepted the freedom gratefully. Such individuals maintain a high status by remaining in control of their own lives and of their own self-concept.

Other individuals volunteer to be females, transforming themselves in order to acquire material comforts or social prestige. Terms for this general category vary, depending on the amount of coercion or force needed to "turn out" the female image. "Kids," "gumps," or "punks" describe individuals who in effect have sold their male identities, surrendering their cul-turally defined masculinity to be redefined as females.

Many other inmates, however, are forced to become homosexuals against their initial will. According to Wadley (another inmate): "[E]veryone is tested. The weak—of personality, personal power, willingness to fight, physical frailty, timidity—are especially susceptible. . . . Respect is given to one who can control the life of another," he adds. Those unwilling or unable to control others are thus themselves controlled. According to the cultural rules of gender identity in prison, those who dominate, by natural right, are males, and those who submit, by natural temperament, are females.

A FORCED FEMALE ROLE

Individuals forced to adopt a female role have the lowest status, and are termed "girls," "kids," "gumps," or "punks." Kids are kept in servitude by others, as a sign of the owner's power and prestige. Gumps are generally owned or kept by a gang, which collects money by prostituting the sexual favours of the unfortunate inmate. A gump may at one time have volunteered to come out to her feminine identity, but due to lack of personal status or power she has been forced to become sexually promiscuous for money or her physical survival. A punk, most agree, initially hesitates, and is turned out by coercion.

However transformed, most homosexuals in prison take on a feminine persona and appearance, even assuming a feminine name and requesting feminine pronouns as referents. The external transformation from male to female often is remarkable. Despite the formal restrictions of a dress code in prison, clothing styles may be manipulated rather patently to proclaim gender identity. Hair is often styled or curled and worn long. Even cosmetics are possible: black felt-tip pens provide eye liner and shadow; kool-aid substitutes for blush; and baby powder disguises prominent cheekbones. The personal appearance of homosexuals enhances their identity by demarcating them as obviously different from men.

Homosexuals perform numerous functions depending upon their status and relative freedom. Generally, the higher the status the more control one has over one's activities and one's life. High-status individuals such as Sandy select their own lovers. These couples live as husbands and wives, with the "little woman" providing domestic services such as laundry, cell cleaning, grooming, and sex.

Those with less status perform much the same tasks, but less voluntarily and with less consideration from their daddies. Once an inmate has been forced to adopt a submissive lifestyle, the nightmare of domination becomes more intense. For example, gumps might be forced to pleasure a gang chief, or may be passed down to soldiers in the gang for enjoyment. A particularly attractive kid might be put "on the stroll," forced to be a prostitute, for the financial benefit of the gang. Business may prove to be so lucrative that some homosexuals must seek protective custody (solitary confinement) to get some rest.

According to Dr. B, some homosexuals actually prefer to be dominated. The prevalent value system in prison suggests that those "females" who resist sexual attacks vicariously enjoy being dominated physically and sexually by more powerful individuals.

Hated and abused, desired and adored, ladies in prison occupy an important niche: they are the women of that society, constructed as such by the male-based perception of gender identity. In prison, females are termed "holes" and "bitches," reflecting the contempt which Dr. B believes to be characteristic of society's view of lower-class women in general. In prison, he adds, a homosexual "is likely to receive much of the contempt [and] pent-up hostility that would otherwise be directed at women." Herein lies the key to unlocking the deeper significance of gender construction in prisoner culture.

GENDER CONSTRUCTION IN PRISON

Recall the general inmate perception of this liminal gender in prisoner culture. Homosexuals are owned and protected by daddies, who provide for their material and social comfort. In exchange, they provide sexual gratification. They often sell themselves and their bodies for material objects, promiscuously using their allure to manipulate men and to improve their social status. They feign helplessness in order to control their men. Ladies are emotional, helpless, and timid, while at the same time petulant, sassy, and demanding, nagging their men for attention. Best suited for certain tasks, homosexuals provide domestic and personal services for their daddies, serving their every whim.

Most fundamentally, homosexuals are sexual objects, to be used, abused, and discarded whenever necessary. Passive recipients of male power, they even enjoy being dominated and controlled. Males do them favours by releasing their "true" female identities through rape. In prison, sexuality equals power. Males have power, females do not, and thus males dominate and exploit the "weaker sex."

Ultimately, in whose image and likeness are these "males as females" created? Genetically female staff and administrators do not fit the stereotypical view, and thus provide no role models for ladies in prison. Males themselves draft the image of female in prison, forming her from their own perceptions. Males "turned out" as females perform the cultural role allotted to them by males, a role of submission and passivity. In actuality, males produce, direct, cast, and write the script for the cultural performance of gender identity behind bars.

In prison, woman is made in contrast to the image and likeness of man. Men define women as "not men," establishing their own self-identity from the juxtapositioning. Gender as a cultural construct is reflexive; each pole draws meaning from a negation of the other. As in Monteros (Brandes 1980), folk concepts reinforce the differences, emphasizing maleness at the expense of femaleness and the powerful at the expense of the powerless. By means of sexual domination, women remain in a culturally defined place of servitude and submission.

PRISON CULTURE AS A DISTORTING MIRROR

It is precisely this concept of gender identity that has proven most disquieting about the status of homosexuals in prison. Granted, prison culture fosters a terribly distorted view of American culture.[4] Nevertheless, one sees a shadowy reflection in the mirror of prisoner culture which remains hauntingly familiar. As ladies are viewed by males in prison culture, so are females perceived by many males in American culture. Gender roles and attitudes in prison do not contradict American male values; they merely exaggerate the domination and exploitation already present. In prison gender constructs, one sees not contrasts but caricatures of gender concepts "on the street." Thus, the liminal gender of ladies behind bars presents, in reality, a cultural mirror grotesquely reflecting the predominant sexism of American society in general, despite initiatives by women to redefine their position and change gender relationships.

NOTES

1. In my other writings I have discussed various ways in which inmates successfully retaliate to maintain a sense of identity. Much more could be explored, but space constrains discussion.
2. There are obvious implications for study of the spread of the AIDS virus. From my research it seems that most inmates had not yet thought about acquiring AIDS, probably on account of a low self-concept paralleling that of intravenous drug users. Since homosexual behaviour in prison cannot be eliminated, education and protection should be stressed.
3. I do not mean to suggest that homosexual relationships in society at large are similar. In this article, I do not deal with homosexuality outside of prison, nor with affectional homosexuality inside prison, which does exist.
4. Racial distinctions become exaggerated in prison. Some research indicates that prison administrations sometimes deliberately exacerbate racial antagonism to "divide and conquer" gangs by rewarding leaders with homosexuals of the opposite "race."

REFERENCES

Brandes, Stanley. 1980. *Metaphors of Masculinity: Sex and Status in Andalusian Folklore*. Publications of the American Folklore Society (n.s.) Vol. 1, Philadelphia: University of Pennsylvania Press.

Cardoza-Freeman, Inez. 1984. *The Joint: Language and Culture in a Maximum-Security Prison*. Springfield, IL: Thomas.

Davidson, R. Theodore. 1983. *Chicano Prisoners: The Key to San Quentin*. Prospect Heights, IL: Waveland Press.

Goffman, Erving. 1961. *Asylums: Essays on the Social Situation of Mental Patients and Other Inmates*. Garden City, NY: Anchor Books.

Turner, Victor. 1969. *The Ritual Process*. Chicago: Aldine.

Is The Female Husband a Man?

Woman/Woman Marriage among the Nandi of Kenya

Regina Smith Oboler

Regina Smith Oboler has taught at Temple University in Philadelphia, where she earned her Ph.D. in 1982, and has been a research associate of the Institute for Development Studies, University of Nairobi, Kenya. She is known for her fieldwork among the Nandi of highland Kenya. She is currently assistant professor of anthropology at Ursinus College.

No, I don't (carry things on my head). That is a woman's duty and nothing to do with me. I became a man and I am a man and that is all. Why should I assume women's work anymore?

—Taptuwei, a Nandi female husband

The institution of woman/woman marriage as practiced by the Nandi of western Kenya presents an example of how one society deals with a problem of sexual classification. In a cultural system in which certain important attributes of the category "man" versus the category "woman" are well defined, a woman who functions in certain ways as only a man can (e.g., exchanging cattle for a wife, transmitting property to heirs) represents an anomaly. In the Nandi case, the anomaly is resolved by the frequently reiterated public dogma that the female husband is a man. I will show that in specified sociocultural domains it is crucial that the female husband adopt male gender. Within these domains, she makes every attempt to conform to male role behavior and informants go out of their way to rationalize any deviation therefrom by a female husband. Within other sociocultural domains, the assertion that the female husband is a man masks the fact that the role adopted by the female husband is sexually ambiguous and occupies an intermediate position between male and female roles.

A female husband is a woman who pays bridewealth for, and thus marries (but does not have sexual intercourse with) another woman. By so doing, she becomes the social and legal father of her wife's children. The basic institution of woman/woman marriage is

widespread in African patrilineal societies, although the way it functions varies from society to society. In Nandi, a female husband should always be a woman of advanced age who has failed to bear a son. The purpose of the union is to provide a male heir.

The argument presented here is that the key to the question of the female husband's gender lies in her relationship to the property that is transmitted through her to the sons of her wife.[1] The exact status of this property will be discussed in greater detail below. For now, let it be said that it is an extremely important canon of Nandi ideology that the most significant property and primary means of production—livestock and, in the modern setting, land—should be held and managed exclusively by men. I will argue that the strength of the female husband's identification as a male is dependent on the social context in which the identification is made. In contexts which directly implicate the issues of property and heirship, Nandi informants are unanimous in considering it of the utmost importance to insist that the female husband is a man and behaves in exact accordance with the ideal model of the male role. Such areas are the management of family property, legitimate authority over the wife and children and the responsibility to provide for the wife and children in a material sense. The further one moves away from these issues into other aspects of the cultural definition of the male role the weaker become both the female husband's own attempts to conform to male role behavior and informants' dogmatic insistence that they in fact do so. To say that a female husband is a man in certain contexts but not in others lends a degree of clarity to the situation which is not present in fact.

The cultural definition of the category "man" is not limited to the relation to property. Once the ideological

"Is the Female Husband a Man? Woman/Woman Marriage among the Nandi of Kenya" by Regina Smith Oboler, from *Ethnology*, Vol. 19, No. 1, pp. 69–88. Reprinted with permission.

statement that the female husband is a man has been made, Nandi informants feel that they have to carry through on this idea in terms of the total cultural definition of this category. This leads them to make assertions about female husbands' behavior that observation shows to be untrue: that female husbands completely adopt the male role in the sexual division of labor, that they participate in public political discussions, that they do not carry things on their heads, and that they attend men's circumcision rites as a result of their male status. In fact, most female husbands do attend male initiation, but not because they are now considered to be men. The situation is one of rationalization and selective perception such as is typical of defensive strategies attempting to maintain important but precarious dogmas.

WOMAN/WOMAN MARRIAGE IN AFRICA

The question of the gender of the female husband has been raised, but hardly resolved, in recent publications.[2] Its resolution bears on the problem of the conditions under which sex role barriers may be transcended, and a cross-culturally valid definition of marriage. Is the role of female husband an instance of some individuals crossing sex role boundaries and, as it were, changing sex? Or is the cultural role "man" not an inevitable concomitant of the husband role, in which case marriage cannot be defined as a transaction between the categories male and female? Riviere (1971) asserts that female husbands are invariably culturally recoded as male and take on other aspects of the male role; husband is a sub-category of male, and marriages in all societies must be viewed as transactions between the male and female cultural categories. Krige (1974) rejects this view, at least for the Lovedu, and argues that the husband role in Lovedu society may be either male or female. Moreover, she maintains, Riviere's formulation reflects a misunderstanding of the nature of African marriage, in which relationships created by a marital union other than those of husband and wife may be of paramount importance. According to Krige, it is the intrinsic right of a woman (the mother of the "female husband") to the services of a daughter-in-law that is the basis of Lovedu woman marriage. O'Brien (1977) has examined accounts of woman marriage in southern Bantu societies and concluded that where female husbands may also be political leaders they are regarded as social males. The Nandi female husband is clearly culturally recoded as a man, though it is by no means clear that this is the case in all African societies (Huber 1969). Her assignment to the male gender does not mean that she easily and automatically assumes male role behavior in all spheres, however. Her position, as will be shown, is far from unambiguous and unproblematic.

The data reported here result from a study of nine woman/woman marriages in one Nandi community.[3] Nine of ten known cases of female husbands living in the community, and wherever possible their wives, were interviewed extensively. A few female husbands and wives from other communities were also interviewed with varying degrees of thoroughness. Information was also obtained through observation, and a large number of informants who were not participants in woman/woman marriages were interviewed on the subject.

THE ETHNOGRAPHIC SETTING

The Nandi are a section of Kenya's Kalenjin-speaking peoples, whom Sutton (1970) calls Highland Nilotes. Huntingford (1953) classifies them as a pastoral people. They are well known for their military organization and aggressive cattle raiding practices and their culture during the nineteenth and early twentieth centuries was marked by a pastoral ideology. Cultivation, however, has always played a major role in their economy (Gold 1977). The Nandi at present are prosperous mixed economy farmers producing maize, milk, tea and a variety of vegetables for the national market as well as for home consumption. Maize is the staple subsistence crop.

The research community is located in the north-central part of Nandi District, where elevation varies between 6,200 and 6,800 feet and rainfall, distributed over the entire year, averages between 60 and 75 inches annually. Selected for its typicality, the community is neither the most traditional nor the most modernized in Nandi District. The average household (based on a random sample community census)[4] contains 8.1 people and 9.1 adult cattle and holds 20.6 acres of land; 76.4 per cent of households grow tea, and 61.9 per cent hire a tractor for at least part of their annual plowing. Over 60 per cent of household heads are at least nominal Christians; most of them adherents of the Africa Inland Church, a fundamentalist body. Almost 51 per cent have had some primary education, 33.9 per cent perform some sort of part-time cash-gaining activity, and 16.8 per cent of ever-married male household heads are polygynous.

Traditional Nandi social organization was crosscut by a system of seven rotating age-sets (*ibinwek*) for men, localized military units (*pororosiek*), patrilineal clans (but not corporate patrilineages), and patrilocal extended families. While land was plentiful, every Nandi man was entitled to move with his family and herds to reside effectively wherever he wished. The most important unit was the local community (*kokwet*). It was the unit within which ceremonies were performed and disputes settled in most cases and within which day-to-day interaction took place. Today these functions take place at the level of the sublocation, an administrative unit made up of several traditional local communities and presided over by a government-appointed chief. It is the locus of political interaction. At its center is a group of shops, businesses, public buildings, and a community gathering place (the settlement pattern is otherwise one of scattered homesteads). The sublocation is overwhelmingly endogamous, whereas the *kokwet* is not. Patrilocal extended families are still important in today's social organization. Married couples reside patrilocally unless the husband buys a farm away from his father's homestead. The sole (but weak) function of patrilineal clans is the regulation of marriage.

THE PROPERTY SYSTEM AND WOMAN/ WOMAN MARRIAGE

In Nandi ideology, women's rights in land and cattle are very limited. A girl may be given a heifer by her father if she is a virgin at her initiation and a woman may keep one cow as bridewealth for each of her daughters. Animals held by either spouse form the family estate but the bulk of the herd consists of animals a man receives from his father through inheritance or as gifts. This is augmented by cattle the family acquires through proceeds from their cash crops, as bridewealth for their daughters, etc. Husband and wife should jointly control those cattle in which the wife's rights predominate, though the husband has the right to control independently those cattle in which his rights predominate. If a woman leaves her husband, she has no right to take any animals with her. Many informants say that it is also better that she take no property with her to her husband so that this can never be a bone of contention between them.

Management of land and cattle is a male prerogative, although informants will admit that when the husband is incapable of administering the family estate it would not be wrong for the wife to assume responsibility. The exception to the rule that women do not manage property is the case of widows. Widows can hold property in their own right and make decisions regarding the property which they hold in trust for their minor sons. The lack of congruence with public ideology that this fact presents is dealt with by the typical male claim (contrary to observable events) that effective control of the family estate is held not by the widow but by the deceased man's brother. This man may or may not be the woman's levirate husband.

Women—wives and mothers—though supposedly barred from administering the family estate are critical in its transmission. A woman's "house" (patrilineal descendants) is automatically endowed with a share of her husband's property at the time of her marriage. The system is that which Gluckman (1950) has called the house-property complex. All property held by a polygynous family is ideally divided evenly among sets of full siblings, each set receiving exactly the same share regardless of how many children the mother has. A man can marry only by using those of his father's cattle which were allotted to his mother's house, or those which came as bridewealth for his own full sisters; he should not use his half-sister's bridewealth cattle, nor may his father allot him cattle from the herd of one of his mother's co-wives. Although the effective share of the family estate to which each wife's house is entitled obviously changes as each additional wife is added to her husband's menage, the basic principle that her house is entitled to an equal share is never abrogated. Marriage is considered to be a once in a lifetime event for a Nandi woman. Though a traditional divorce proceeding existed, and while it is possible now to obtain a legal divorce through the courts, both these options are so rarely invoked that divorce may be said to be absent. Separation, however, does occur. A woman may leave her husband for a period of many years or even for life. She may live with a man in the meantime and have children by him. She may go to a town and become a prostitute. All this does not change her marriage and property rights. She remains the legal wife of the man who first married her, and her children remain his legal heirs. She can return, with children, after an absence of many years, and her husband will take her back. She can even return and take up her rights to her husband's property after his death. A woman retains throughout her life a right to live on the land of her father and brothers, but she can in no way transmit any rights to this land. A woman is incorporated into her husband's family at marriage, she takes his clan identity, and her children's only legitimate rights to filiate are with his family. Illegitimacy is a new phenomenon in Nandi, and though it would seem that there must be cases on record of children affiliating matrilaterally in exceptional circumstances, I found none in the course of the research. It is possible, however, for women to transmit to their sons property which they themselves have acquired.

Traditionally, the property of a woman's house could only be transmitted to male heirs. As it was inappropriate for a woman to hold property, it could not be passed to daughters. If an heir was completely lacking, the property would have to revert to a man's sons by other wives or to his brothers, but it was considered wrong and very unfortunate if this should happen. The demographic reality is that not every woman gives birth to a son. Woman/woman marriage is one solution to this problem. The intention is that the wife of a female husband should bear sons who will become their female father's house's male heirs in the property system.

A woman who has taken a wife is said to become a man. It is said that she has been promoted to male status (*kagotogosta komostab murenik*). She can no longer have sexual intercourse with a man (nor with a woman). She has all the nonsexual prerogatives of a male husband with regard to her wife, and is supposed to abandon all women's work. She theoretically acquires certain public prerogatives of men; for example, the right to speak in public meetings. In the past, she would also be expected to adopt to some extent male dress and adornment. She normally stops attending female initiation and in most cases will already have been admitted to male initiation in hopes of curing her infertility or inability to bear a son. (In Nandi, an infertile person of either sex is admitted to the opposite sex's initiation rituals in the hope that the infertility will thereby be cured.) Female husbands, like their male counterparts, are required to observe procedures for avoiding contamination by ritual pollution with regard to their wives and children.

Although property is the crux of the institution of woman/woman marriage, and although informants cite the advantages of being married to a wealthy woman rather than a poor man, female husbands are not exceptionally rich. In fact, those on whom data are available are not as wealthy as the community average, with average land holdings of 15.8 (versus 20.6) acres and herds of 7 (versus 9.1) adult cattle.

MOTIVATIONS OF THE PRINCIPALS IN WOMAN/WOMAN MARRIAGES

The motivation of a woman who becomes a female husband is fairly clear-cut; it is the acquisition of a male heir for her property. But why does she choose this means to her end rather than another?

There are two options other than woman/woman marriage available to a woman whose house has no heir. First, she may adopt or "buy" a male child by the payment of a large sum (these days, normally, money) to the parents of the child, who relinquish all ties to him. The children bought by Nandi women usually come from the neighboring Abaluhyia. It is difficult to find any child, particularly a Nandi child, available for sale. In the past, children born to unwed mothers were killed unless requested for adoption by a barren woman who happened to be present at the birth. Thus it was easier to adopt a child in the past than presently, as barren women would be sure to know of the approaching confinement of any pregnant girl. Today, although infanticide has been eliminated, unwed mothers usually raise their own children. Moreover, by the time a woman resigns herself to the fact that she will not bear a son, she is often too old for adoption to be a realistic option. Thus, adoption is relatively rare.

Another option is the institution known as "marrying the house" or "marrying the center post" (*tunisiet ab got, kitunis toloita*). In this form of marriage, the sonless woman's youngest daughter is retained at home and her "husband" is said to be the house or its center post. This daughter will have children by self-selected sexual partners and her sons will inherit the house's property. The custom is said to be a recent innovation but has not gained much popularity relative to woman/woman marriage.

It seems that woman/woman marriage is the most commonly adopted of these options in the case of lack of a male heir but only a minority of women who are eligible to become female husbands actually do so. From a large-scale survey of marital and fertility histories, it was found that among women over 40 years of age, only 4.3 per cent of those ever married and 24.5 per cent of those who bore no sons ultimately became female husbands. This includes women of the youngest age cohort over 40, among whom many who are candidates to be female husbands have not yet made the decision to marry. For the older two age cohorts, 39 per cent and 27 per cent, respectively, of women with no male heir married; 6.8 per cent and 6 per cent, respectively, of ever-married women ultimately became female husbands. In the community intensively studied, at least ten out of a total of 286 households were headed by female husbands. The rate for female husbands as household heads, then, is just under 3 per cent.[5]

Several factors may prevent a sonless woman from becoming a female husband. First, her house's property may not be large enough to warrant an heir, especially if her house lacks enough bridewealth cattle to acquire a wife. Second, a woman who is prepared to take a wife may have difficulty in finding one. This was the reason most commonly given by women who were prime candidates for becoming female husbands. They point out that they will not marry anyone and maintain that they will marry as soon as they find willing girls who are hard-working, well-mannered, and from good families. Occasionally sonless old women who have not become female husbands cite personal reasons for their failure to marry; e.g., the difficulty of adjusting to another person in the household. It has been suggested to me that some women may resist becoming female husbands because of the prohibition on sexual intercourse which the role entails.

Why should a woman choose to marry a wife in favor of other options? Two female husbands said that they would have adopted sons but could find no available male children. Two did adopt sons but both children were sickly. One died in infancy and the other turned out to be simple-minded and thus not a suitable heir to the property. Another female husband explained that it is bad economics to pay money equivalent to a bridewealth payment for just one infant son who might not even survive to reproductive age when, for the same amount, one can acquire a grown woman who will reproduce herself several times over in a few years. Three female husbands have daughters who wished to marry their boyfriends and refused to "marry the house." Still others provided various personal and idiosyncratic reasons for choosing woman/woman marriage. Over and above all these explanations, there is the general reason that woman/woman marriage entails a rise in status for the female husband.

Why do women become wives of female husbands? They are usually girls who for one reason or another—for example, a physical or mental defect—fail to attract a male husband. These days, the most common reason why a girl is considered unmarriageable by men is that she already has a child or is pregnant by a man who refuses to marry her. Such girls quite often become the wives of female husbands.

Some informants maintain that a girl will always prefer marriage to a man if it is possible, while others claim that there are many girls who choose to be married by female husbands as a matter of preference. The wives of female husbands are themselves divided on this score. Several said that they had received offers of marriage from men but they and their families preferred to accept an offer for woman/woman marriage. Most informants agree that it is better to be married by a wealthy woman than by a poor man. As one informant put it, "When you actually live with a man the love may fade, but the property will always be there." Second, informants cite greater sexual and social freedom for the wife as a reason to prefer woman/woman marriage. Female husbands are said to be less likely to question their wives' comings and goings. Third, informants say that female husbands are less likely than men to quarrel with their wives and beat them. Another possible motivating factor is the slight tendency of female suitors, being very anxious to marry, to give bridewealth of higher value than that given by men. Males in my sample who married between 1970 and 1977 gave bridewealth ranging between four and six adult cattle, one sheep or goat, and money ranging between none and 500 shillings. During the same period, out of seven cases of woman/woman marriage, the amounts given in five cases fell within the range of the amounts given by the men, but one female husband gave seven cattle and 500 shillings, and another gave seven cattle, 600 shillings and three sheep; an extremely high amount for Nandi bridewealth.

DOMESTIC RELATIONS IN FEMALE HUSBAND–HEADED HOUSEHOLDS

Female husbands, their wives and children are real people living together in actual household situations. What, then, are the typical patterns of interaction in these female husband–headed households? Besides the hus-

band, wife and children, other parties—such as the female husband's male husband, her co-wives and their children—are frequently significant in these interactions. Another significant party is the wife's consort, who may or may not be a regular visitor in the compound.

The wife and her children ideally occupy a separate dwelling from that of the female husband to facilitate the wife's relationship with her consort.[6] The dwellings of the female husband and wife should, however, be within the same compound and in close proximity. I know of at least one case in which both a barren woman and her husband married young wives at the same time, divided their plot, and lived side by side with their new families as brothers might. In several cases, female husbands and their wives are found living together in a common dwelling. The female husband, in these cases, maintained that she had not yet had an opportunity to provide separate housing arrangements for the wife but would do so soon.

The division of labor is said by informants to be much the same as in male husband–headed households. Cooking, washing utensils, carrying water and collecting firewood, sweeping, plastering the house, and washing clothes are supposed to be exclusively female chores. Jobs technically reserved for men include plowing, inoculating cattle, clearing bush, digging drainage ditches, fencing, house-frame building, thatching, and slaughtering. Both sexes engage in herding [and] cultivation . . . (see Oboler 1977 for a detailed description of the division of labor by sex). In the main, female husbands avoid female tasks, although with less rigidity than do men. Because of their advanced age, they are not often observed doing heavy work reserved for men but employ men to do such work for their households. Most female husbands take an active role in tasks which are not sexually coded.

Informants maintain that, except for the absence of the sex act, the relationship between a female husband and her wife should be no different from that between a male husband and his wife. They should go to the fields together in the morning, like any other married pair, and in the afternoon the female husband is free to "go for a walk" while the wife takes care of household chores. Female husbands do typically behave as men in reserving most of their afternoons for socializing but they differ little from other old women in this respect. Female husbands and their wives also behave exactly as male husbands and their wives when entertaining visitors. As one informant put it, "When a visitor comes, I sit with him outside and converse with him. My wife brings out maize-porridge, vegetables, and milk. When we have finished eating I say, 'Wife, come and take the dishes.' Then I go for a walk with the visitor." Observation confirms this description.

The wife of a female husband probably has more opportunity than the wife of a male husband to be relieved of her domestic responsibilities such as in the case of illness or a family crisis which causes her to return temporarily to her parents' home. The female husband is more able and willing to fend for herself in the domestic domain than is the typical male husband. If the two women are on good terms, the female husband will usually sympathize with the problems of her wife, having been a wife herself. Women often cited the tendency of female husbands to be less harsh and demanding as one of the advantages of woman/woman marriage.

In terms of informal interaction, it seems that female husbands and their wives enjoy more casual companionship than do ordinary couples. More opportunities for friendly and companionable conversation between female husband and wife arise since the female husband spends more time in her compound than a male husband. This is partly the result of preference and partly the result of habit. Female husbands are supposed to spend most of their time socializing with men and most of them claim that they do, but observation does not support this claim. One informant confided what is probably true for many other female husbands as well, "Men like fighting, and I don't like being with them most of the time."

No female husband would admit that she is not totally in charge of important household decisions (e.g., farm management and money allocation) but several women stated that another advantage of marriage to a female husband is the opportunity to participate more equally in household decisions.

The female husband is technically in the same position of authority over her wife as a male husband. All wives agreed that they must ask permission from their female husbands to go away from the compound, except for local, short-term activities such as marketing and visiting neighbors. The husband supervises the wife's behavior and has the right to beat her if she errs. It is agreed, however, that female husbands rarely invoke this right. This is not to say that female husbands never beat their wives, but on the whole wives of female husbands see their domestic situations as atypically harmonious. "A man who finds a mistake with his wife only wants to beat her. A woman just scolds and that is enough."

Traditionally, the female husband appointed a man to act as consort to her wife. This man would most likely be a younger clan-mate of the female husband's husband—possibly his younger brother, his brother's son, or the son of one of his other wives. It could never be the female husband's husband himself nor could it be any of her own patrilineal kin.[7] These days, however, wives are insistent on choosing their own consorts, and usually make sure that the female husband agrees in advance to this arrangement before consenting to the marriage. Where the female husband tries to appoint a consort for her wife against the wife's will, the latter remains adamant. The wife sees her sexual

autonomy as one of the chief advantages to her of woman/woman marriage and will not surrender it lightly.

Nevertheless, the wives of female husbands and other observers confirm that they are not promiscuous, but have one long-standing relationship with a male friend (*sandet*). This man visits the wife in her house on a more or less regular basis. His responsibility is to give her children and nothing else. He may occasionally give her a gift of friendship, but he is not obligated to do so. The consort may or may not be acquainted with the rest of the household, including the female husband. Some informants implied that it would be bad form for the latter to acknowledge him, while others said that he could visit the compound openly and be treated as a friend of the family. The consort has no rights of any kind in the wife or her children. He cannot demand her sexual fidelity or any wifely services, although she usually cooks for him when he visits her. He has no right to beat her if she displeases him. If he should do so, she can have him fined by the village elders. Most female husbands vigorously denied that they would ever request money or services from the wife's consort in times of difficulty. Agreement is complete that pollution connected with the wife's child cannot harm her consort, the biological father, because he is not the legal father.

Female husbands assume the formal role of father to their wive's children. The relationship between fathers and their young children is normally reserved and distant and the relationship between female fathers and their children is no different.[8] Female husbands believe that they can be harmed by pollution connected with the wife's children and treat them with the same cool aloofness displayed by male fathers. In relation to their other kin, for example, their daughters' children, they maintain the same kinship role behavior as before. It is quite remarkable to watch a female husband treat her daughter's child in the warm affective style of a grandmother at one moment and her wife's child with the reserve of a father at the next.

Female fathers, like male fathers, are responsible for the discipline of their wives' children and children reportedly respect and fear female fathers as much as they would male fathers. One of the most important areas of significance of the father role is the father's responsibility to care for the wife's children materially. That they meet this requirement was constantly stressed by female husbands.[9]

Cases of separation and estrangement occur between female husbands and their wives, just as they occur in ordinary marriages. In the beginning of my inquiries on this subject, some highly acculturated informants told me that girls do not want to be married by women and usually run away if such a marriage is arranged for them. Subsequent contacts and interviews with the principals in woman/woman marriages have convinced me that this is not the case. The usual pattern in woman/woman marriage is one of harmony and mutual respect between husband and wife which, as in ordinary marriages, often develops into real affection. As one wife said, "I respect Kogo as I would have respected a man if he had married me."

Both the female husband and her wife gain status in the community through a stable marriage. The female husband gains descendants and promotion to male status, after spending years in the unenviable status of a barren or sonless wife. The wife is likely to be a girl for whom getting married has been difficult. If she already has children, she gains inheritance and clan status for them. Otherwise, she is licensed to bear legitimate children. If she has made the mistake of premarital pregnancy and thus lost face in the community and the chance to make a good marriage with a man, she is able to recoup her position through marriage with a woman. Most wives of female husbands believe that their situation compares favorably with that of ordinary wives in many respects. . . .

IS THE FEMALE HUSBAND A MAN?

Nandi informants know very well that the female husband is not a man in the sense that she has changed her physiological sex or all her sex-typed behaviors. The impossibility of completely changing the habitual actions of a lifetime is recognized. Everyone is of course aware that the female husband is not really a man but it is a grave insult for anyone to call attention to this fact. What, then, is the claim that the female husband is a man intended to encode? What does the female husband have in common with a man that makes it essential for her to be defined as such? The oft reiterated statement of the female husband's masculine identity is a cultural dogma (Leach 1969). It is an ideological assertion which masks the fact that the female husband is an anomaly: she is a woman who of necessity behaves as no woman in her culture should. Her situation forces her to assume male behavior in certain areas that are crucial to the cultural definition of the differences between the sexes. These areas have to do with the management and transmission of the family estate.

Behaviors associated with men are not all equally important in the attempt to maintain the ideological fiction that the woman who has taken a wife is now a man. Some are essential, and the female husband insists that for these her behavior conforms to the masculine ideal. Others can be more or less ignored. Female husband is thus a category which, in some sense, occupies an intermediate position between male and female.

Unanimity about the norms to which the female husband's behavior must conform is greatest in those areas that are closest to her role in the management and transmission of the family estate: her role in the domestic division of labor, as husband to her wife and father to the wife's children, and the cessation of sexual intercourse. There is less agreement regarding other aspects of the male role such as conversing primarily with men, speaking in public meetings, attending men's initiation, refraining from carrying things on the head, and the manner of relating to children other than those of the wife and other women.

Female husbands tend to avoid such feminine chores as household maintenance, laundry, and wood and water carrying, although typically with less rigidity than do men. Several female husbands said that they can help with the milking, as many young men do nowadays. Cooking is the most indispensable domestic job and ideally should be done by the wife. Even informants who say that it is possible for a female husband to cook under unusual circumstances insist that she should never do so at her wife's hearth, which she may not approach for any purpose. This is an example of the contextuality of the female husband's gender status; in relation to female symbols connected with her wife she is quintessentially a man.

A female husband should not see her wife naked because in relation to her she is a husband and therefore a man, but she may see any other woman naked. A female husband is never present during her wife's labor. It is generally believed that the female husband can be affected by feminine/child pollution (*kerek*) due to close contact with the wife's child. The effect is reportedly at least partly the result of magic performed during the traditional wedding ceremony. This explains why it is not felt by the genitor. Since *kerek* is believed to have a negative effect on those manly qualities which ensure success as a warrior, some informants say that this is naturally of little concern to a female husband and that she can therefore take these prohibitions less seriously than do men. Others assert that female husbands take *kerek* very seriously because it can induce rapid aging and skin disease.

If the male husband of a female husband is still alive, and does not have another wife living in the compound, the wife of the female husband may be responsible for providing nonsexual domestic services to both of them, or the female husband may continue to provide some or all of these to her male husband while herself being provided them by her wife. She will not wash her own clothes because in relation to her wife she is a man (husband); but she can still wash clothes for her male husband because in relation to him she is a wife and therefore a woman. In this situation it is perhaps easiest to see the ambiguity and contextuality of the female husband's gender position.

Female husbands are rarely observed doing work that is technically reserved for men. This they rationalize, when challenged, on the grounds that they are old and no longer able to engage in such strenuous activity. Female husbands are active in types of work appropriate to both sexes—cultivation and herding—but reinterpret it as male work in order to affirm their male status. Since female husbands were occasionally observed fencing, the claim that they do male tasks is not a complete fallacy. In general, however, this is a situation in which people now conceptually defined as men have never learned to perform certain aspects of the male role and it is now too late to change the behavior patterns of a lifetime. In spite of this, female husbands are considered to have assumed the male role in the division of labor. On the one hand, informants make it a point to argue that female husbands are doing the work of men when they are in fact doing work that is equally appropriate to men or women. On the other, their taking responsibility for having male tasks done is coded as the equivalent of personally doing them.

In extradomestic contexts it is less important that female husbands conform to male role behavior. Nevertheless, since female husbands are said to be men, many informants find it necessary for the sake of logical consistency to insist that they behave as men in areas important to the cultural definition of this category. This leads people to make claims that are sometimes contrary to observation. For example, female husbands say they typically converse with men rather than women, but the observational evidence is to the contrary. All say they can participate in public meetings and political discussions but admit that they have never done so. All but one attend men's initiation. It was revealed, however, that in all cases this is due to the woman's barrenness or failure to bear a son and preceded her decision to marry a wife. Yet female husbands all implied that they attend male initiation as the result of their status as female husbands, therefore men. There is disagreement as to whether it is possible for female husbands to continue attending female initiation but it is agreed that it is at least not usual, since they are now regarded as men. Neither is there unanimity as to whether a female husband can carry things on her head, act as midwife to women other than her wife, or hold another woman's baby. Many informants say that there is nothing wrong in the latter two behaviors but some deny that a female husband should ever be present at a birth or hold any young baby because she is a man. Thus in many areas of action the female husband's gender position is ambiguous.

The female husband makes her greatest attempt to conform to male behavior, and informants rationalize any deviation from such behavior, in contexts that are closely connected with the management of the heirship to the family estate. Though issues such as avoidance of *kerek* and close physical contact with the wife's children are not immediately relevant to the management of property, they are relevant to the issue of heirship.

They are the categories of thought and action through which the relationship between the property holder and heir is acted out. With regard to heirship, the insistence that the female husband abandon her sex life is also noteworthy. Though she is presumed to be unable to conceive, there is still the danger that the impossible will somehow occur. If she should conceive, both the issue of inheritance and the dogma that she is a man would be too thoroughly confounded to be withstood.

The issue of heirship and property is also relevant to the strength with which informants maintain the ideology that the female husband is a man in the area of kinship terminology. It has been shown above that there is a great deal of ambiguity about the female husband's gender as encoded in the kinship terminology appropriately used between principals in woman/woman marriages and their respective relatives. Most uniformity exists in the areas where property transmission within patrilineal families and property exchange between patrilineal families are involved. Thus the major factor which distinguishes a female husband from a woman and makes her the same as a man is the legitimate right to hold and manage land and livestock and transmit them to heirs.

Particularly in contexts less immediately relevant to issues of property and heirship, female husband is an intermediate category between man and woman. While this is not made explicit in the cultural ideology, the recognition of this situation is often implicit. An old man explained it this way: "It is just like getting a promotion. Always when you are promoted there is still that person who does the promoting, which means that you are still under somebody. So women who have married wives have limited prerogatives. They are more nearly equal to men than are other women, but men are always ahead of them."

CONCLUSION

Among the Nandi, only men can hold and manage land and livestock, the means of production, but these are transmitted through women and rights therein devolve to a woman's house at marriage and can never be revoked. The argument developed in the preceding pages is essentially that woman marriage is the outcome of this contradiction between men's and women's rights in the house-property complex. Moreover, some of the most important attributes of the category "man" in Nandi culture have to do with management of the family estate.

These two facts taken together explain why the female husband is culturally conceptualized as a man. She must manage property because of her special circumstances, but a female holder, manager, and exchanger of property is an extremely anomalous being. Thus she is culturally recoded as a man to reduce the contradiction implicit in her role with regard to property. This explains why informants insist that the female husband is a man, and why her attempts to behave as a man are most pronounced in the areas of life that have most bearing upon the family estate and heirship to it. The degree to which the status, role, and behavior of a female husband approximates that of an actual man in various areas of ideology and activity has been reviewed in an attempt to show that the closer one gets to issues of property and heirship the stronger is the dogma that the female husband is a man; the further the remove from these issues the more this dogma is diminished.

Once articulated, the ideology that the female husband is a man has an independent existence. Informants strive for logical consistency and thus extend this ideology, which is so important in the domain of property relations, into other domains. In some senses, the female husband becomes an intermediate category between male and female. In areas removed from the realm of property relations, thus not crucial to the female husband's male status but generally important to the cultural construct man, the ambiguity is greatest. It is in these areas (e.g., political participation, male initiation) that the dogma that the female husband is a man comes to be defended with an impressive edifice of evasion, rationalization, and selective perception.

NOTES

1. For assistance in arriving at this interpretation, I am indebted to Cathy Small, Lorraine Sexton, Denise O'Brien and Diane Freedman, although I remain solely responsible for any errors of logic in its development. I am further indebted to Jennifer Jeptoo Kosut, who assisted in the collection of the data.

   The term "woman marriage" is commonly used in the anthropological literature to denote the institution I am discussing. This term is somewhat confusing, since all marriages involve women. O'Brien (1977: 110) prefers to drop the term "woman marriage" in favor of "female husband." The Nandi institution clearly belongs in the context of the entire range of institutions found in African societies in which a woman can pay bridewealth to acquire predominant rights in a wife. In some of these societies, the relationship between the two women is not that of "husband" and "wife." Therefore, I choose to use "woman/woman marriage" as a general term for the institution, and "female husband" as the term for a woman who takes a wife and is considered to stand as "husband" to her according to the rules of their culture.

2. Although the existence of woman/woman marriage in a large number of African societies has been briefly noted in various ethnographic sources (summarized by O'Brien 1972), it has received very little detailed anthropological study. A handful of ethnographic accounts by Herskovits (1937) on Dahomey; Krige and Krige (1943) and Krige (1974) on Lovedu; van Warmelo and Phophi (1948) on Venda; Evans-Pritchard (1951) on Nuer; Huber (1969) on Simbiti; and Obbo (1976) on Kamba contain more than passing references to woman/woman marriage. The most complete accounts are those of Krige (1974) and Huber (1969).

3. This study was funded by grants from the National Institute for Mental Health, the National Science Foundation, and the Woodrow Wilson National Fellowship Foundation. It was carried out during my tenure as a Research Associate of the Institute for Development Studies, University of Nairobi, Kenya. To all of the above, I wish to express my appreciation for making the research possible.

4. The census included 116 households, or a 40 per cent sample of the approximately 286 households in Kaptel sublocation. The list of 286 households from which the random sample was selected was compiled from lists provided by sublocation Chief Paulo arap Lelei and *kokwei* elders. This was the most accurate information available.

5. Woman/woman marriage is not declining in popularity at present, but several factors may ultimately work against it. For example, there are the opposition of Christians and the growing idea that daughters as well as sons should be eligible to inherit family property. Woman/woman marriage will probably continue as an option for completely childless women and girls with children who have not inherited property. The institution of woman/woman marriage is in the process of diffusing from the Nandi to other Kenyan societies.

6. In Nandi, dwelling structures are of two kinds, *got* and *sigiroinet*. The former is traditionally the dwelling of a family, with cooking hearth, overhead storage compartment, and a room for sheep and goats. The latter is usually a smaller one-room dwelling which traditionally served as sleeping quarters for warriors and their girlfriends and now houses adolescent boys and unmarried men or a man who wishes a place to sleep away from the family. The most significant distinction is that the fireplace of the *sigiroinet* is not generally used as a cooking hearth. The wife's house is consistently referred to as *got*, the female husband's fairly consistently as *sigiroinet*.

7. Langley (1979) says that the female husband "raised children either to her own or her husband's clan," that some of her informants believed that the wife's consort should belong to the female husband's own kin group and that the consort had to be approved by the female husband's own kin group as well as that of her male husband. All these points are vehemently and unanimously denied by the scores of informants I interviewed about woman/woman marriage in various areas of Nandi District and other areas of Nandi settlement.

8. The distance between father and child stems to a large degree from traditional pollution beliefs. *Kerek* is the Nandi word for a polluting substance believed to emanate from newborn infants and from women due to their close association with babies. Its effect on a man, particularly the child's own father, is to weaken his *murenotet*, or manly qualities. He loses his prowess in warfare and becomes stupid, weak, and indecisive. At the birth of a child, a husband leaves his wife's house and is not completely reincorporated into the household until the child is eight to twelve months old. Today, the period of avoidance has been shortened to about a month, in most cases, and most young people do not admit to believing in *kerek*.

9. Readers may wonder whether a male child raised in a female husband–headed household will not have a gender identity problem as the result of lacking a male role model. This concern is needless on two grounds. First, the father's relationship with the child is ordinarily distant. Second, some male adult relative is always living in or in close proximity to the female husband's compound and this man, be he the female husband's brother-in-law, the son of her co-wife, or whoever, serves as a male role model. The question of the absence of a male role model is specifically restricted to a nuclear family socialization context.

REFERENCES

Evans-Pritchard, E. E. 1951. *Kinship and Marriage among the Nuer*. Oxford.

Gluckman, M. 1950. "Kinship and Marriage among the Lozi of Northern Rhodesia and the Zulu of Natal," in *African Systems of*

Kinship and Marriage, ed. by A. R. Radcliffe-Brown & D. Forde. London.

Gold, A. E. 1977. *Cultivation and Herding in Southern Nandi ca. 1840–1914.* University of Nairobi staff seminar paper.

Herskovits, M. 1937. "A Note on 'Woman Marriage' in Dahomey." *Africa* Vol. 10: 335–341.

Huber, H. 1969. " 'Woman Marriage' in Some East African Societies." *Anthropos* Vol. 63/64: 745–752.

Huntingford, G. W. B. 1953. *The Nandi of Kenya: Tribal Control in a Pastoral Society.* London.

Krige, E. J. 1974. "Woman Marriage with Special Reference to the Lovedu—Its Significance for the Definition of Marriage." *Africa* Vol. 44: 11–36.

Krige, E. J., & J. D. Krige. 1943. *The Realm of a Rain Queen.* London.

Langley, M. S. 1979. *The Nandi of Kenya: Life Crisis Rituals in a Period of Change.* New York.

Leach, E. R. 1969. "Virgin Birth." *Genesis as Myth and Other Essays.* London.

Obbo, C. 1976. "Dominant Male Ideology and Female Options: Three East African Case Studies." *Africa* Vol. 46: 371–389.

Oboler, R. S. 1977. "Work and Leisure in Modern Nandi: Preliminary Results of a Study of Time Allocation." Working Paper No. 324. Institute for Development Studies, Nairobi.

O'Brien, D. 1972. "Female Husbands in African Societies." Paper presented at the 71st Annual Meeting of the American Anthropological Association, Toronto.

O'Brien, D. 1977. "Female Husbands in Southern Bantu Societies." *Sexual Stratification: A Cross-Cultural View,* ed. by A. Schlegel. New York.

Riviere, P. G. 1971. *Marriage: A Reassessment. Rethinking Kinship and Marriage,* ed. by R. Needham. London.

Sutton, J. E. G. 1970. "Some Reflections on the Early History of Western Kenya," in *Hadith 2: Proceedings of the 1968 Conference of the Historical Association of Kenya,* ed. by B. Ogot. Nairobi.

van Warmelo, N. J., & W. N. D. Phophi. 1948. "Venda Law." Ethnological Publication No. 23. Department of Native Affairs. Pretoria.

Polygamists Emerge from Secrecy, Seeking Not Just Peace but Respect

Dirk Johnson

Dirk Johnson received his BA from the University of Wisconsin in 1981 and went to work for the *New York Times*. He served first in New York City, then went on to become a national correspondent in Chicago. Since January 1991, he has been regional bureau chief of the Rocky Mountain Bureau, which handles everything in the West, except for the coast.

COLORADO CITY, ARIZ.—With arms full of groceries, three women in long, flowered dresses emerged from the general store here on a sun-splashed afternoon. After rounding up their playful children, they climbed into a car and headed back down the gravel road to the house, and the husband, they share.

Until recently theirs was a world that shunned outsiders, who were often stopped on the outskirts of town by police officers from the community who protected their legally forbidden way of life. The practice of polygamy has thrived quietly for generations in places like this small desert town, where fundamentalist Mormons settled after their church turned away from the practice of plural marriages a century ago.

But in recent years, as state law-enforcement officials have adopted an unwritten policy of leaving them alone, polygamists have gone public.

Indeed, they have begun a virtual public relations campaign to achieve tolerance, respect, a greater following, and ultimately legal protection. They are speaking at university forums, granting interviews to reporters and forming alliances with groups they once condemned. One such group, the state branch of the American Civil Liberties Union, has petitioned its parent organization to make legal recognition of polygamy a national cause like gay and lesbian rights.

"In this liberal age, with all the alternative life styles that are condoned," said Mayor Dan Barlow, who has five wives, "it is the height of folly to censure a man for having more than one family."

In an official endorsement of such arguments, the Utah Supreme Court ruled in March that polygamy,

while still illegal, did not by itself make a family ineligible for adoption.

About 50,000 people in the Rocky Mountain states live in households made up of a man and two or more wives, and experts believe that the number of these households has been growing. Around Colorado City, a town of about 6000 people in northwest Arizona, the population has roughly doubled in every decade since it was founded in the 1930's. Most of the people in the area are polygamists or believe in the practice.

"Without any real threat from the law, these communities have begun to feel much freer about opening a public dialogue," said Martha Bradley, a professor at Brigham Young University who studies the polygamy movement. "It's really been apparent in the last three years or so. It's almost like a P.R. campaign. They want the world to know they're not a threat. And they want to continue to attract new people."

Most of the polygamists consider themselves fundamentalist Mormons, many of them descendants of people who split from the Church of Jesus Christ of Latter-day Saints.

According to early Mormon teaching, Joseph Smith, the founder of the church, learned in a revelation from God that he should take more than one wife, as some prophets in the Old Testament had done.

"The only justification was that it was commanded by God," said Ronald K. Esplin, the director of the Joseph Fielding Smith Institute for Church History, which studies the history of Mormonism.

The Mormon Church officially abandoned polygamy 101 years ago after it was forbidden by Utah law in a deal required by Congress for the territory to become a state. The church now excommunicates members for polygamy.

Among polygamists and their wives, the degree of religious influence varies significantly.

"I see it as the ideal way for a woman to have a career and children," said Elizabeth Joseph of Big Water, a Utah town near the Arizona border. She is a lawyer and one of the nine wives of Alex Joseph. "In our family, the women can help each other care for the children. Women in monogamous relationships don't have that luxury. As I see it, if this life style didn't already exist, it would have to be invented to accommodate career women."

Her husband takes a more biblical view. "Every writer in the Old Testament, except for Daniel, was a polygamist," said Mr. Joseph, 54 years old. "The way I see it, if you're going to get a degree in electrical engineering, then you have to learn a little something about engineering. And if you're going to understand the Bible, you have to adopt the life style of those who wrote it."

SHIFT BY LAW OFFICIALS

The position among legal authorities toward polygamy has changed drastically in the past generation. In 1953, the Governor of Arizona ordered the National Guard to raid this community. Many men were jailed for bigamy, and some children were taken from their mothers and placed in foster homes.

Today law-enforcement officials generally take a "live and let live" attitude toward polygamists. Except in a few celebrated cases recently in which polygamists have committed violent acts, law-enforcement officials do not intervene.

"We all know what's going on," said Paul Van Dam, Utah's Attorney General. "But trying to do anything about it legally would be opening one Pandora's box after another."

It is a matter of legal interpretation whether this way of life technically constitutes polygamy, since the men do not typically take out more than one marriage license. In the eyes of the law, the men would be considered to be legally married to one woman, and cohabitating with one or more others.

And although laws against cohabitation or adultery may be applicable against such families, prosecutors are very reluctant to use them. "Once you start going after people for cohabitation, or adultery, where do you stop?" Mr. Van Dam asked.

Indeed, the fundamentalists, who have long rejected being grouped with other people who have adopted nontraditional living arrangements, like homosexual couples, now see society's greater tolerance as grounds to call for their own legitimacy.

It was the desire to live a more open life that led Don Cox and his wives, Katie and Earlean, to settle in Colorado City. Nearly 25 years ago, they were living in Salt Lake City and keeping their family arrangement a secret. "We told people that I was a friend of the family," Katie said.

When Katie's first child reached school age, the family moved to the polygamous community here, but they have since split with the fundamentalist church, which they feel restricts their lives too greatly. Although Mr. Cox built the family house, he does not have the property deed. It belongs to a trust controlled by the fundamentalist Mormon sect in Colorado City.

"It's a cult," Mr. Cox, a large white-haired man in suspenders, said bitterly. "They own a lot of property and they own a lot of people."

The Coxes and several other dissidents have filed a Federal suit in Salt Lake City to win the deeds for their homes. And in another sign of new openness here, the church authorities in Colorado City welcomed the suit as a way to settle the differences.

NO CHOICE IN A MARRIAGE

The Coxes live in an 11-bedroom home with a dining table long enough to accommodate them and most of their 19 children. But compared with some households here, the Cox family is relatively small. One man in town has 80 children.

In Colorado City, which straddles the Utah-Arizona border, the church faithful are expected to adopt a modest manner. Girls and women wear dresses that cover their knees, and shirts that cover their necks. They use no makeup.

Marriage partners are not a matter of choice. When individuals decide to marry, they "turn themselves in" to the church president. He is regarded as a prophet with powers of divine revelation. And he decides who marries whom. In some cases, the people have never met.

The Coxes said they did not advise their children to enter plural marriages, but left the choice to them. Only one of the children, a daughter, has chosen the polygamous way.

"It's a difficult life," Mr. Cox said. "You get competition between the sets of kids and their mothers. And you sometimes get jealousy between the wives."

In Kane County, Utah, which has a land mass as large as Connecticut and a population of about 5000 people, some polygamists found a place where they could live undisturbed.

One town in the county is Big Water, a tiny isolated settlement of weather-beaten houses and dirt roads on the Colorado Plateau. Mr. Joseph, the mayor, lives there with his 9 wives and 20 children. He shares a rambling house with 7 wives and their children; 2 other wives and their children live in a smaller house across the road.

Like Elizabeth Joseph, the lawyer, most of Mr. Joseph's wives have careers. One is a graphic designer. Another is a real estate broker.

"The only hassle I get is from men who cheat on their wives and get outraged about my life style," he said. "Sexual variety is part of it, I guess. But I know a dozen men who have more interesting sex lives than I do."

Mr. Joseph and his wives say their children experience no problems with the living arrangement. They never get teased about it at school, they said, in part because they account for about 10 percent of the enrollment. And it helps that their father is the Mayor.

One of the children, Stonewall, 11 years old, said he referred to the other women in the family as aunts, if asked where they fit in the family. But he said he did not give it much thought.

DREAMS OF BEING THIRD WIFE

Stonewall's mother, Margaret Joseph, was the only one of the wives who was raised in a polygamous family.

As a child, she said, she had always dreamed that she would grow up to be a man's third wife.

"The first wife doesn't like it when the second wife comes along," she explained. "And the second wife doesn't care for the wife who came first. So you can get some fighting and bad feeling. But the third wife, she's the tie that holds it all together."

When she met Mr. Joseph, who had only two wives at the time, she was delighted to be able to become the third.

"The hard part of this arrangement is measuring up," said another wife, Bodicca Joseph, the real estate broker. "You're surrounded by all these intelligent, successful women. So you feel like you always have to be your best."

"Since you only spend a limited amount of time with Alex, things always stay fresh," she added. "In this house, things never get boring."

8

Family and Kinship

Like apple pie, everyone, especially politicians on the stump, is in favor of The Family, yet few people specify what they mean by it and why they believe it to be the bedrock of North American society. Many anthropologists have also exhibited this belief. For example, George Murdock (1965), after surveying some 250 societies that all had a form of **nuclear family** (a married couple with dependent offspring), claimed that the family served a number of functions such as preventing disruptive sex, being essential for enculturation and the sexual division of labor, and protecting females during their reproductive years. In short, the family is seen as providing the domestic sphere in which the focus is on such essentials as food preparation, discipline, sex, and grooming. Of course, all these activities can be and are undertaken in some societies by other institutions; for example, among the Mae Enga of Papua New Guinea, men and women sleep in separate men's and women's houses. Sex is frequently a matter of coupling in the fields. In some societies where the household is organized around a group of related women, men eat at their sister's house. Similarly, in British society, much **enculturation** of boys takes place away from home at "exclusive public schools" like Eton and Harrow.

Recently the conventional approach has been increasingly questioned, and some anthropologists are now arguing that the family is not a concrete institution designed by God or even people to satisfy human needs; rather, it is an ideological construct tied up with the development of the state. Ideologically we feel that what happens in the family is of no concern of the state. Yet, as a number of observers have pointed out, domestic violence is tolerated to a far greater extent than

other forms of violence. Indeed, whereas most of us would not hesitate reporting a theft by a stranger to the police, we probably would have doubts about reporting the same theft if it were committed by a family member. When the chips are down, even though we might personally dislike family members, we feel a sense of obligation to help them.

Revisionist thinking is evident in Brett Williams's article on migrant farm workers. In the United States we hear a great deal about the breakdown of families among the poor; yet among Hispanic migrants, marital relationships show a strength that is often lacking in middle- and upper-class families. Looking at the wives in migrant communities, who are quite submissive to their husbands, one might conclude that they are oppressed and without power; yet the same women are sisters, mothers, grandmothers, aunts, and godmothers, all of whom in fact have considerable authority over men. Hence, the glib stereotype of the "oppressed woman" in migrant families needs rethinking.

Williams's paper also challenges another stereotype held by many North Americans: that families constitute independent social units. As she shows, the women in migrant Hispanic communities work long and hard at gathering and binding relations so that their families are firmly embedded in a wider network of kin—what anthropologists would call a **kindred.** These are the relatives on whom an individual can call in time of need, and in migrant communities they are crucial in helping people cope with the exigencies of life.

In most human societies, families (where they exist) are likewise embedded within larger networks of kin. In **agrarian societies** there often exists a whole hierarchy of groups based on descent, with some form of extended, multigenerational family at the base. In traditional China, for example, upon marriage a woman would leave the family into which she had been born to go live with her husband in the family into which he had been born. Thus, all men in the family shared a common male ancestor, and as older members died off, younger members were born into the family. Several families together whose men could trace their descent through men back to a more distant common male ancestor constituted a larger male descent group that anthropologists would call a **lineage.** Finally, lineages sharing a common ancestry—**clans** in anthropological parlance—were also recognized.

The Chinese case constitutes an example of patrilineal descent, a common device for specifying group membership in societies in which men perform the bulk of productive work and hold political authority. In societies without centralized political organization, in which much of the productive work is done by women, descent is apt to be reckoned matrilineally, exclusively through women. The Hopi people of the U.S. Southwest (and the subject of Alice Schlegel's article) are one example. An important correlate of how descent is reckoned is the way the family relationships are structured. As Margery Wolf shows in her article, in **patrilineal societies** a woman is apt to be isolated from her kin and must defer to the dictates of the men in her husband's family, in which she is something of an outsider. Under such conditions, women must show great resourcefulness if they are to find ways to protect their own self-interests. By contrast, although patrilineal societies are generally patriarchal, **matrilineal societies** are not matriarchal. As Schlegel's essay shows, relations between men and women are apt to be less skewed in favor of one sex over the other. In Hopi society, for example, men are not isolated from their blood kin as women are in a patrilineal society. But while they cannot be dominated by women, neither can they do anything of which women disapprove.

Why Migrant Women Feed Their Husbands Tamales

Foodways as a Basis for a Revisionist View of Tejano Family Life

Brett Williams

Brett Williams is professor of anthropology and director of American studies at American University, Washington, DC. She received her Ph.D. from the University of Illinois in 1975. Her fieldwork has been done in the United States, among migrant workers of Mexican descent from Texas, in a mixed ethnic neighborhood of a northeastern city (see Chapter 9), and among waitresses. She has written on all of these topics, as well as on Southern folklife, and on the African-American hero John Henry. Her research interests include poverty, the media, folklore, and politics and culture.

In the array of artifacts by which Tejano migrant farmworkers identify themselves, the tamale has no serious rival.[1] It is a complicated culinary treat demanding days of preparation, marking festive—sometimes sacred—occasions, signalling the cook's extraordinary concern for the diners, and requiring a special set of cultural skills and tastes to appreciate and consume appropriately. Tamales are served wrapped in corn husks which hold a soft outer paste of *masa harina* (a flour) and a rich inner mash prepared from the meat of a pig's head.

Only women make tamales. They cooperate to do so with domestic fanfare which stretches through days of buying the pigs' heads, stripping the meat, cooking the mash, preparing the paste, and stuffing, wrapping, and baking or boiling the final tamale. Women shop together because the heads are very bulky; they gather around huge, steaming pots to cook together as well. Tamales are thus labor-intensive food items which symbolize and also exaggerate women's routine nurturance of men. The ritual and cooperation of tamale cookery dramatically underscore women's shared monopoly of domestic tasks.

For middle-class women, such immersion in household affairs is generally taken as a measure of a woman's oppression. We often tend to equate power and influence in the family with freedom from routine family tasks and find such tamale vignettes as those below disconcerting:

- At home in Texas for the winter, an elderly migrant woman, with her daughters-in-law, nieces, and goddaughter, spends several weeks preparing *200 dozen* tamales to distribute to friends, relatives, and local taverns for Christmas. The effort and expense involved are enormous, but she regards this enterprise as a useful and rewarding way to commemorate the holiday, to obligate those she may need to call on later, and to befriend the tavern owners so that they will watch over her male kin who drink there.

- In Illinois for six months a year, migrant women take precious time out from field labor to prepare elaborate feasts, with many tamales, commemorating the conclusion of each harvest (in asparagus, peas, tomatoes, pumpkins, and corn) as well as dates of biographical significance to others in the camp. An especially important day is the *quinceñiera* or fifteenth birthday, on which a young girl who will most likely spend her life in field labor is feted with tamales, cakes, and dancing all night, just as though she were a debutante.

- A young migrant, with the full support of his wife's kin as well as his own, sues his wife for divorce in a smalltown Illinois court. His grounds are that she refuses to cook him tamales and dances with other men at fiestas. A disconcerted Illinois judge refuses to grant a divorce on such grounds and the migrant community is outraged: women argue with special vehemence that to nurture and bind her husband a proper wife should cook him tamales.[2]

Incidents like the last, focused on women, their husbands, elaborate domestic nurturance, and the jealous circumscription of sexuality in marriage, again seem to reveal the most repressed and traditional of females. Because migrant women are so involved in family life and so seemingly submissive to their husbands, they have been described often as martyred purveyors of rural Mexican and Christian custom, tyrannized by excessively masculine, crudely domineering, rude and petty bullies in marriage, and blind to any world outside the family because they are suffocated by the concerns of kin.[3] Most disconcerting to outside observers is that migrant women seem to embrace such stereotypes: they argue that they *should* monopolize their foodways and that they should *not* question the authority of their husbands. If men want tamales, men should have them. But easy stereotypes can mislead; in exploring the lives of the poor, researchers must revise their own notions of family life, and this paper argues that foodways can provide crucial clues about how to do so.[4]

The paradox is this: among migrant workers both women and men are equally productive wage earners, and husbands readily acknowledge that without their wives' work their families cannot earn enough to survive. For migrants the division of labor between earning a living outside the home and managing household affairs is unknown; and the dilemma facing middle-class wives who may wish to work to supplement the family's income simply does not exist. Anthropologists exploring women's status cross-culturally argue that women are most influential when they share in the production of food and have some control over its distribution.[5] If such perspectives bear at all on migrant women, one might be led to question their seemingly unfathomable obsequiousness in marriage.

Anthropologists further argue that women's influence is even greater when they are not isolated from their kinswomen, when women can cooperate in production and join, for example, agricultural work with domestic duties and childcare.[6] Most migrant women spend their lives within large, closely knit circles of kin and their work days with their kinswomen. Marriage does not uproot or isolate a woman from her family, but rather doubles the relatives each partner can depend on and widens in turn the networks of everyone involved. The lasting power of marriage is reflected in statistics which show a divorce rate of 1 percent for migrant farmworkers from Texas, demonstrating the strength of a union bolstered by large numbers of relatives concerned that it go well.[7] Crucial to this concern is that neither partner is an economic drain on the family, and the Tejano pattern of early and lifelong marriages establishes some limit on the whimsy with which men can abuse and misuse their wives.

While anthropology traditionally rests on an appreciation of other cultures in their own contexts and on their own terms, it is very difficult to avoid class bias in viewing the lives of those who share partly in one's own culture, especially when the issue is something so close to home as food and who cooks it. Part of the problem may lie in appreciating what families are and what they do. For the poor, public and private domains are blurred in confusing ways, family affairs may be closely tied to economics, and women's work at gathering and obligating or *binding* relatives is neither trivial nor merely a matter of sentiment. Another problem may lie in focusing on the marital relationship as indicative of a woman's authority in the family. We too often forget that women are sisters, grandmothers, and aunts to men as well as wives. Foodways can help us rethink both of these problematic areas and understand how women elaborate domestic roles to knit families together, to obligate both male and female kin, and to nurture and bind their husbands as well.

THE SETTING FOR FAMILY LIFE

To understand migrant family foodways, it is important to explore first the economic circumstances within which they operate. The two thousand Tejano migrants who come to Prairie Junction, Illinois, to work in its harvest for six months a year are permanent residents of the Texas Rio Grande Valley, a lush and tropical agricultural paradise.[8] Dominating that landscape are great citrus and truck farms, highly mechanized operations which rely on commuters from across the Mexican border for whatever manual labor they need. Lacking jobs or substantial property at home, Tejanos in the valley exit for part of each year to earn a living in the north. Agricultural pay is low and employment is erratic, guaranteeing no income beyond a specific hourly wage and offering no fringe benefits in the event of unemployment or disability.[9] As a consequence, migrant workers must be very flexible in pursuing work and must at the same time forge some sort of security on their own to cushion frequent economic jolts. Migrants use kinship to construct both the security and the flexibility they need to manage a very marginal economic place.

In extended families, all members are productive workers (or at the very least share in childcare duties), and migrants find a great deal of security within families whose members are mutually committed to stretching scarce resources among them. Kin call on kin often for material aid, housing, and emotional support; they cooperate in field labor and domestic tasks and freely share food, money, time, and space. Because resources are only sporadically available to individuals, depending on kin eases hard times. In turn, most persons are sensitive to their relatives' needs not only because they care about them but also because they recognize the great value of reciprocity over time.

Migrant families are not easily placed in a convenient anthropological category for they implicate relatives in binding ways while allowing husbands and wives a great deal of freedom to move and settle when they need to, and to return whenever they like. This relative independence of nuclear families allows them to scatter and regroup when pursuing erratic opportunities to work, but always underlying their travels is a sense of a long-term place within a wider circle of kin. I call migrant families *convoys,* for they should be conceptualized as a process rather than a structure; they literally join persons in travel, in work, and through the life course, sharing food as well as the most intimate of concerns.

In the rural Texas settlements (*colonias*) where most migrants spend jobless winters, and in the stark barracks of Prairie Junction where they work each summer, convoys come together (1) to produce and share food for economic survival, (2) to surround food with ritual in order to save one another's dignity in degrading situations, (3) to reaffirm their cultural identity through marking and crossing boundaries with outsiders, and (4) to gather and bind kin, including spouses, to accompany them through life.

STRATEGIES FOR SURVIVAL: ROUTINE

Just as tamales ritually underscore women's domestic commitments, the everyday preparation and sharing of food routinely reaffirms family ties and allows families to work as efficiently and profitably as possible. Especially in emergencies, the sharing of food attests to migrants' visions of their lives as closely, mutually intertwined. The discussion which follows explores the foodways of the Texas *colonias* and the Prairie Junction migrant camps, the routines which surround them, and the ways they mobilize in crisis.

A newcomer to the Texas *colonias* is struck first by the appalling poverty in which migrants live there. Most are too far from the valley's urban centers to share in such amenities as running water, sewage disposal, or garbage collection. Hand-constructed shacks usually surround a primitive central area where fruits and vegetables grow, goats and chickens roam, and children play. The homes have many hastily constructed additions and ill-defined rooms, attesting to the mobility of the individual family members and seemingly indicating an impermanence to domestic life. This feeling of impermanence is belied, however,

by the ongoing family-scale agricultural and pastoral system through which kin produce and share their own food over the Texas winters. Individuals may come and go; but through the extended family migrants adapt as peasants to those times when there is no income. The *colonias* offer evidence of creative domestic cooperation in stretching and sharing food within families and in the continuing migration of family members north from Mexico and back and forth to Illinois to work. These kin know that they can always find food from the winter gardens in Texas.

It is in this context that one can appreciate Sra. Compartida's great Christmas feasts of 200 dozen tamales for relatives, friends, and people she considers resources or contacts. She has worked for most of her life to allow her relatives in Mexico to join her, and in her old age she finds herself surrounded by kin who help her and whom she can count on. She feeds them still and is known especially for the beans and flour tortillas which she always cooks for those she welcomes home. She is clearly at the center of a convoy of cooperating kin whom she has organized and continues to remind of their obligations to one another.[10]

Sra. Compartida has worked for wages throughout her life and continues to do part-time housework when it is available. But, like other migrant women, she is a wife who appears much too submissive to her husband: she offers him extraordinary care, cooks everything he eats, and quietly abides his beer-drinking although she disapproves of it. On the other hand, her efforts on behalf of her family have compelled Sra. Compartida to learn English and cultivate respectable skills at negotiating bureaucracies such as immigration service. Her husband clearly depends on her as his ambassador, not only among kin but also with the outside Anglo world. They cooperate in setting their particular relationship apart through constructing roles in which he pretends to be boss, proclaiming extreme jealousy and expecting that she nurture him in elaborate ways. Yet one cannot dismiss their interaction by stereotype, for Sra. Compartida's authority and influence as mother, aunt, god-mother, sister, and grandmother are so definite that she simply will not fit a category. Tamales help her maintain that influence, and she uses them to express affection and obligate others, as well as gather a network of tavern owners who watch out for her husband when she cannot be there.

Domestic cooperation extends to the Illinois migrant camps, long barracks of small single rooms originally designed to accommodate prisoners of war. The camps offer domestic convoys highly inappropriate living situations, for they allot these single rooms to conjugal families, and through separating kin dramatically defy their routine commitment to shared domestic tasks. Because observers often prefer that each family convene in a tidy still-life world, migrant family life in the camps has been portrayed by some as very chaotic.[11] Kin realign in this inappropriate space to share domestic duties, care for children, cook cooperatively, allow husbands and wives conjugal privacy, and meet recurring emergency needs. While a conjugal family might remain basically committed to a particular room, kin move in and out of one another's rooms throughout the day, often carrying pots of food or other supplies. Children gather with elderly caretakers in a central outdoor spot (for the small rooms are stifling), and it is sometimes difficult to identify their mothers and fathers. Other kin who have settled temporarily in town visit the camp frequently, bringing food and children back and forth with them.

Women cook together routinely, sharing and stretching short supplies, combining scarce ingredients to preserve what they can of traditional Tejano tastes. They transport clay pots, tortilla presses, and chilies from their homes to the camps each year, and replenish short supplies throughout the summer as kin travel back and forth to Texas. Thus, surrounded by Illinois cornfields, women simmer beans in the barracks, save tomatoes from the fields for sauces when they can, and do their best to stretch the family's wages to support a large group of relatives.

STRATEGIES FOR SURVIVAL: CRISIS

If the tamale symbolizes elaborate celebration and nurturance, the tortilla is probably the most symbolic of the last bit of food a woman has to share. Simply, quickly, expertly made by migrant women, tortillas are treated very much like bread. Women roll a dough from *masa harina* or plain white flour, lard, salt, and water, flatten it with a press or by hand, and fry it on a dry griddle for just a few minutes. It is the least expensive and most basic of their food items, and when women worry (as they often do) that their supplies have dwindled to the ingredients for tortillas, they are speaking of real want. Tortillas stand for emergencies and it is through such crises that one can see perhaps most clearly how migrant family foodways work.

One family which has weathered many crises typical of migrant life is the Gomas. Their domestic convoy stretches through four generations and across several marriages, and their members are dispersed in Texas and Illinois but remain closely involved in one another's lives. The woman most central to this family is middle-aged and lives with her husband and their teenaged children off-and-on in Prairie Junction. Joana Goma and her husband have never been able to last for long in Illinois, for it is difficult for them to find work there, and they move back and forth to Texas

often, sometimes leaving one of their children there for a time or returning with other young relatives so, as she puts it, "I won't have to be lonesome for them all winter." Each summer some two dozen of the Gomas' relatives arrive to work through the migrant season, and during that time Sra. Goma mobilizes on their behalf the resources of her Illinois networks—legal aid, public assistance, transportation, and a less formal example, a service station owner who will cash paychecks. She has worked hard to stretch and secure this network, often initially obligating friends through food. By sharing her locally famous taco dinners, Illinois residents act as though they are kin, and through time she finds that she can call on them for help as if they really were.

Although Joana Goma's marriage also appears quite traditional, with food and sex recurring metaphors for conjugal loyalty, she is the center of a world on which her husband and his kin depend.[12] When her sister-in-law was disabled because her hands were poisoned by pesticides, Sra. Goma saw to it that her own sister assumed the woman's cooking and housekeeping tasks. When her sister's nephew was stricken with hepatitis, Sra. Goma untangled the complicated legal procedures whereby a local hospital was compelled to provide free medical care for indigents, secured his bus fare to Texas from Traveler's Aid, and organized an investigation of the camp's drinking water. But these smaller, frequent emergencies are less telling than a more dramatic tortilla crisis in which the Gomas powerfully affirmed the importance of family to migrant workers.

One summer, Joana Goma's husband's brother, his wife, and their five children could not find work. They were penniless and planned to stay for several months, hoping there might be employment in a later crop. Joana brought her husband's employer to their home in the middle of the night to see for himself all those little children sleeping on the floor, thinking that she might persuade him to offer her brother-in-law a job. The employer stalled, and she worked at securing public aid for the family. This process is a lengthy one, and she soon found her household with no money or food left but tortillas, which they lived on for several days while Joana visited local ministers to ask for loans. On the day the welfare check at last arrived, her father and mother were critically injured in an automobile accident in Texas; and Joana and her children traveled there immediately, financed by this check.

Migrant family life may appear chaotic as kin realign inside and outside the camps, travel when they need to give support, and share what they have down to the last tortilla. Joana and her husband will never be rich, for they are unwilling to cast off the demands of kin. They love them, and they also seem to know that they are happier and more secure in the long run if they embed their marriage in a larger family circle. Again, Joana appears the most submissive of wives, but as a sister, daughter, and in-law she is the most highly regarded member of the family.

RITUAL AND AFFIRMATION

Beyond the routine domestic order and beyond using food in emergencies as a metaphor for the ways in which person's lives are intertwined, migrants give food special significance in ritual. Some observers have noted that migrants' rituals seem both wasteful and tawdry, at best a mere release of tension for the poor.[13] From a certain perspective migrant ritual seems absurd: women waste valuable working time preparing a feast to commemorate a harvest which is not really theirs and which in fact signals a slack time between crops; or women cook extravagantly to celebrate a young girl's birthday in what appears to be a tragic display of false consciousness about the course of her future life. Further, migrant rituals are tainted by the unavailability in Illinois of their preferred foods and crops: sometimes women must substitute barbecued chicken and potato chips for the tamales, chili, and beans which have for centuries marked such occasions and are deeply rooted in an oral tradition shared by women through recipes. Even so, such feasting seems to testify to migrants' involvement with kin in ways that reach far beyond the ritual moment.

Susana Sangre is the youngest of five sisters dispersed throughout Texas and Illinois. She stays fairly permanently with her mother, father, and small nephews, whom she cares for when she is not working in the fields. As her fifteenth birthday approached, her sisters gathered in the camp bringing tamales from Texas. With the help of their mother and other women, the Sangre sisters spent almost a week digging great barbecue pits, soaking pinto beans to cook, and purchasing items such as cakes and potato chips in local stores. On the evening of Susana's birthday, almost everyone in the camp gathered to kiss and congratulate her, present her with inexpensive storebought gifts (most often handkerchiefs or jewelry), and feast and dance all night. She wore a long pink bridesmaid's dress, while the guests remained in their work clothes. Although her outfit seemed incongruous, it clearly reflected her honored status at the event, as did the great whoops and cheers which surrounded her as she opened each gift, initiated the dancing with her father, and graciously endured the evening's jolly courting. The effort and expense incurred by Susana's family were enormous, and one might argue that they should not delude her through such feasts about the significance or possibilities of her life.

The *quinceñiera* feast does signal the importance of her life to *them*, and the lavish ritual expressions which surround occasions such as this work to bind kin, recreate obligations, and promise reciprocity. Most persons know that they too will be commemorated at the appropriate times, and that their lives are significant to others as well. Further, through ritual, migrants dramatically defy the degrading "total institutions" in which they spend half their lives: the monotonous surroundings and crowded, unsanitary conditions which tacitly proclaim their worthlessness.[14] Celebrating the harvest proclaims their part in it and denies that they are its slaves. And to prepare their own foods when possible is to reaffirm the dignity of Tejano identity in an Anglo world which offers it little respect, as well as to root the celebrants in a long and great tradition mediated—made present—by the family.

STRANGERS AND FRIENDS

Tamales are distinct and unique by place: Texans prepare them differently from Californians; Salvadorian migrants to this country often disdain those made in Mexico. Tamales testify to rich oral tradition, for the most part women's tradition, about how to buy and cook them. Although many Anglos in the Southwest enjoy Mexican food and have in part transformed the tamale into a regional artifact, for Tejano migrants the real thing is deeply theirs, rooted in their homes, and kept alive by the women who prepare, distribute, and teach others about it.[15]

In Prairie Junction this distribution is critical not only in knitting together families, but in negotiating relations with outsiders as well. Such negotiations may be crucial to family life—as, for example, when migrants befriend Anglos who have the skills, power, or resources to help their kin in various ways. In these negotiations it is evident how misleading it is to proclaim family life an isolating, stultifying, belittling activity for women, as women use food to make friends and allies as well as to identify outsiders who will or will not commit themselves to the Tejano family's concerns. Women ply prospective friends with tamales and tacos, taking an acceptance of the hospitality they offer both as a show of respect for Tejano culture and as a tentative commitment to kin-like relations.

Ethnic boundaries, of course, remain important.[16] Migrant workers do not expect that prospective Anglo friends will relish these foods as Tejanos do. Migrants joke that "gringos' stomachs are too weak" and claim that they must smuggle chilies into Illinois restaurants so that they can season Anglo food properly. Many appreciated the respectful, self-deprecating remarks of a young poverty program lawyer who found that he could not eat the tacos women offered him without a healthy dose of ketchup. While potential friends should be open to traditional Tejano food, it is best appreciated by Tejanos themselves. Significantly, those Tejanos who ingratiate themselves to Anglos are labelled "Tio Tacos," the Spanish equivalent of Uncle Toms: thus, food becomes a metaphor for those who seem untrue to their ethnic identity.[17] Migrants use foodways to preserve a sense of who they are in an alien cultural setting just as they mobilize foodways to approach and appraise friends, and, again, it seems that women purposefully monopolize those skills necessary for plying and obligating others and for keeping ethnicity alive.

The most active cook in Prairie Junction is also married to the president of a self-help organization whose goal is to help those migrants who wish to "settle out," or leave the migrant stream and try to build a life in Illinois. Although Sra. Mezclado's husband wields the official community action power among Prairie Junction's Tejanos, she is the one who mobilizes several dozen women to cook the large benefit dinners on which the organization depends for funds. Sr. Mezclado's networking philosophy is consistent with the mutual assistance tenets of Tejano family life: he and his organization hold that no conjugal family can "settle out" without aid in procuring furniture, housing, and employment. Yet even in this context of outreach beyond the family, Sra. Mezclado continues to monopolize the foodways, and, with other women, to use food to identify and enlist the support of friends. Although she seems obsequious in the home, her husband acknowledges her authority and often speaks of women generally as living representations of the Lady of Guadalupe.[18] Sr. Mezclado is especially obedient to his own mother who, when she visits, rouses him early every day for church and insists that he keep a large statue of the Lady enshrined on his television set. Other men mock these traditional religious activities because they see Sr. Mezclado as an otherwise thoroughly modern man, but he argues that his mother is "*la jefa* [the boss]. I just can't say no to her." Again the marital paradox: while acknowledging the influence of women like Sr. Mezclado's mother, both spouses insist upon constructing a marital relationship which severely circumscribes sexual nuances, grants the husband seemingly whimsical authority, and offers the wife an unchallenged monopoly over domestic life.

GATHERING KIN: MEN, WOMEN AND MARRIAGE

Families and family foodways must be worked at, and among migrants it is women who most vigorously do so. Women are much more likely than men to be involved as liaisons among kin, in stretching networks to draw in kin-like persons who can be helpful, providing the props which allow persons to preserve their dignity in demeaning situations, and negotiating ethnic boundaries.

While young, women begin to build domestic convoys whose members will accompany and sustain them through life. Marriage is a crucial step in that process wherein women find both husbands and many more kin who will share their lives. Even very young and seemingly modern women uphold traditional roles when they marry. One such woman, Dolores Abierta, works in the migrant children's educational program as a teacher's aide. She feels flattered that her husband circles the school in his pick-up truck to watch over her when he can and that he forbids her to swim or wear shorts in public. He also "presses on my stomach when my period is late," "holds me in his lap and lets me cry like a baby," and "loves my cooking." Dolores takes great pride in the fact that "when we got married he was skinny and I was fat. Now it is the other way around." She also respects the limits he places on conjugal life and appreciates his concern that sexuality be confined by marriage: "Before we got married my brother-in-law's cousin used to come into my room and bother me. Now he leaves me alone."

Dolores makes it very clear that she will not allow any of her four brothers to marry women who will not obey them, cook their meals for them, and be ever ready for their sexual overtures. She polices her brothers accordingly, and she is especially wary of Anglo women, "who don't know how to be a good wife." At the same time, she gathers her kin around her, bringing her crippled mother from Texas to live in the migrant camp, giving her husband's cousin the car so "he'll have wheels," arranging for her husband's mother to change rooms so that they can be closer together and so that Dolores can learn from her how to cook tamales.

Within their convoys of kin, women's special nurturance of their husbands makes a good deal of sense. Not only do they bind men more and more closely, but also both women and men cooperate in setting marriage apart as something special within a wide circle of people sharing resources as well as the most intimate of concerns. Sexuality is no longer a larger issue. And while women cook often for many people, in marriage the obligation is immediate and forthright and binding: their husbands must have tamales.

NOTES

1. There is a great deal of ambivalence among scholars and the people themselves about the appropriate ethnic label for migrant workers from Texas and of Mexican descent. Many migrants refer to themselves as "Tejanos" (or Texans), others prefer the term "Mexicans," others "Mexican Americans," still others "Chicanos." "Tejano" is used here, because it seems to capture

the migrants' sense of themselves, as bicultural with the caution that some migrants might prefer to be identified in other ways.

2. These incidents are reported from the author's personal participant-observation in Texas and Illinois.

3. Cf. Leo Grebler, Joan Moore, and Ralph Guzman, *The Mexican-American People* (New York: Free Press, 1970); William Madsen, *The Mexican-Americans of South Texas* (New York: Holt, Rinehart and Winston, 1973); Harlan Padfield and William Martin, *Farmers, Workers, and Machines* (Tucson: Univ. of Arizona Press, 1965).

4. Recently a number of scholars have begun to revise earlier views which held that the poor were virtually without culture, that the family life of the poor in particular was dysfunctional; cf. Carol Stack, *All Our Kin* (New York: Harper and Row, 1974), and Stanley West and June Macklin, eds., *The Chicano Experience* (Boulder, Col.: Westview Press, 1980). However, few scholars have used foodways to focus on the culture of the poor.

5. Cf. Judith K. Brown, "A Note on the Division of Labor by Sex," *American Anthropologist* 72 (1970): 1073–78; Louise Lamphere and Michelle Rosaldo, eds., *Woman, Culture, and Society* (Stanford, Calif.: Stanford Univ. Press, 1974); Peggy Sanday, "Toward a Theory of the Status of Women," *American Anthropologist* 75 (1973): 1682–1700.

6. See note 5 above.

7. Cf. W. Eberstein and W. P. Frisbee, "Differences in Marital Instability Among Mexican-Americans, Blacks, and Anglos: 1960 and 1970," *Social Problems* 23 (1976): 609–21; *Census of the US Population* 19 (Washington, D.C.: U.S. Department of Commerce, Bureau of the Census, 1970).

8. The name of the town and personal names are pseudonyms.

9. For more on this subject, see Ernesto Galarza, Herman Gallegos, and Julian Samora, *Mexican-Americans in the Southwest* (Santa Barbara, Calif.: McNally and Loftin, 1969); Lamar Jones, *Mexican-American Labor Problems in Texas* (San Francisco: R&E Research Associates, 1971); John Martinez, *Mexican Emigration to the US.: 1919–1930* (San Francisco: R&E Research Associates, 1971); Carey McWilliams, *North from Mexico* (New York: Greenwood Press, 1968); David North, *The Border Crossers* (Washington, D.C.: Department of Labor, 1970); Brett Williams, *The Trip Takes Us: Chicago Migrants on the Prairie* (Ph.D. diss. Univ. of Illinois at Urbana, 1975); Brett Williams, "Chicano Farm Labor in Eastern Illinois," *Journal of the Steward Anthropological Society 7* (1976); Dean Williams, *Political and Economic Aspects of Mexican Immigration into California and the U.S. Since 1941* (San Francisco: R&E Research Associates, 1973).

10. Sra. Compartida has fostered almost a dozen children, most of whom were separated from their parents as infants. Recently, she has taken both her six-year-old grandniece and her very old and dying mother to live with her. One example of her kin-gathering activities occurred when she saw a young man in an orchard with, as she put it, "my husband's face," convinced him that he was her husband's nephew who had been separated from the family as a small child, took him home and reincorporated him in the family with great celebration and a tamale dinner.

11. See especially William Friedland and Dorothy Nelkin, *Migrant* (New York: Holt, Rinehart and Winston, 1971), treating Black migrants on the east coast.

12. He frequently threatens to "run off with a little 'mojadita!' (the diminutive female term for 'wetback')," she, to "throw him out and let him cook for himself, just like he did my cat." She also likes to boast about the time her doctor "played my legs, right in front of Pedro."

13. Friedland and Nelkin.

14. "Total institution" is a term used by Erving Goffman in *Asylums* (Garden City, N.J.: Doubleday, 1961). It refers to those institutions which are qualitatively more encompassing than most, segregating and degrading their inmates in dramatic ways, often by denying them ordinary access to the props and routines by which they build their lives.

15. For example, Gerald Ford was ridiculed by the San Antonio, Texas, press when, during his presidential campaign there, he attempted to eat a tamale without first removing the corn husk.

16. Cf. Frederik Barth, *Ethnic Groups and Boundaries* (Boston: Little, Brown, 1969), who argues that ethnic identity is realized most dramatically in the negotiation of boundaries among groups.

17. One such "Tio Taco" is criticized by others for avoiding his Tejano friends and trying very hard to align himself with his fellow (Anglo) factory workers. That he does this by taking big plates of tacos to the factory every day is especially offensive, for this is women's work. And that the Anglo workers do not reciprocate by attending the migrant organization's benefit dinners seems to indicate that "they don't care enough about our food to pay for it."

18. The Lady of Guadalupe is Tejanos' most beloved folk saint. She emerged in Mexico at the time of the Spanish Conquest, appears faintly Indian, and has been carried all over the world by Mexican migrants who turn to her frequently for help with many varied matters. As a saint, she is much like an earthly woman: she has no direct power of her own, but she has a great deal of influence as a liaison with Christ and because of this is both loving and approachable.

REFERENCES

Barth, Frederik. 1969. *Ethnic Groups and Boundaries.* Boston: Little, Brown.

Brown, Judith K. "A Note on the Division of Labor by Sex," *American Anthropologist* Vol. 72 (1970): 1073–78.

Census of the US Population 19. 1970. Washington, DC: U.S. Department of Commerce, Bureau of the Census.

Eberstein, W., & W. P. Frisbee. 1976. "Differences in Marital Instability Among Mexican-Americans, Blacks, and Anglos: 1960 and 1970," *Social Problems* Vol. 23: 609–21.

Friedland, William, & Dorothy Nelkin. 1971. *Migrant.* New York: Holt, Rinehart and Winston.

Galarza, Ernesto, Herman Gallegos, & Julian Samora. 1969. *Mexican-Americans in the Southwest.* Santa Barbara, CA: McNally and Loftin.

Goffman, Erving. 1961. *Asylums.* Garden City, NJ: Doubleday.

Grebler, Leo, Joan Moore, & Ralph Guzman. 1970. *The Mexican-American People.* New York: Free Press.

Jones, Lamar. 1971. *Mexican-American Labor Problems in Texas.* San Francisco: R&E Research Associates.

Lamphere, Louise, & Michelle Rosaldo (Eds.). 1974. *Woman, Culture, and Society.* Stanford, CA: Stanford Univ. Press.

Madsen, William. 1973. *The Mexican-Americans of South Texas.* New York: Holt, Rinehart and Winston.

Martinez, John. 1971. *Mexican Emigration to the US.: 1919–1930.* San Francisco: R&E Research Associates.

McWilliams, Carey. 1968. *North from Mexico.* New York: Greenwood Press.

North, David. 1970. *The Border Crossers.* Washington, DC: Department of Labor.

Padfield, Harlan, & William Martin. 1965. *Farmers, Workers, and Machines.* Tucson: Univ. of Arizona Press.

Sanday, Peggy. 1973. "Toward a Theory of the Status of Women," *American Anthropologist* Vol. 75: 1682–1700.

Stack, Carol. 1974. *All Our Kin.* New York: Harper and Row.

West, Stanley, & June Macklin (Eds.). 1980. *The Chicano Experience.* Boulder, CO: Westview Press.

Williams, Brett. 1975. "The Trip Takes Us: Chicago Migrants on the Prairie." Ph.D. diss. Univ. of Illinois at Urbana.

Williams, Brett. 1976. "Chicano Farm Labor in Eastern Illinois," *Journal of the Steward Anthropological Society* Vol. 7.

Williams, Dean. 1973. *Political and Economic Aspects of Mexican Immigration into California and the U.S. since 1941.* San Francisco: R&E Research Associates.

Uterine Families and the Women's Community

Margery Wolf

Margery Wolf is professor of anthropology and women's studies at the University of Iowa and is known especially for her fieldwork in Taiwan. Her research interests include feminist theory and gender studies, and she has published extensively on China.

Few women in China experience the continuity that is typical of the lives of the menfolk. A woman can and, if she is ever to have any economic security, must provide the links in the male chain of descent, but she will never appear in anyone's genealogy as that all-important name connecting the past to the future. If she dies before she is married, her tablet will not appear on her father's altar; although she was a temporary member of his household, she was not a member of his family. A man is born into his family and remains a member of it throughout his life and even after his death. He is identified with the family from birth, and every action concerning him, up to and including his death, is in the context of that group. Whatever other uncertainties may trouble his life, his place in the line of ancestors provides a permanent setting. There is no such secure setting for a woman. She will abruptly leave the household into which she is born, either as an infant or as an adult bride, and enter another whose members treat her with suspicion or even hostility.

A man defines his family as a large group that includes the dead, and not-yet-born, and the living members of his household. But how does a woman define her family? This is not a question that China specialists often consider, but from their treatment of the family in general, it would seem that a woman's family is identical with that of the senior male in the household in which she lives. Although I have never asked, I imagine a Taiwanese man would define a woman's family in very much those same terms. Women, I think, would give quite a different answer. They do not have an unchanging place, assigned at birth, in any group, and their view of the family reflects this.

When she is a child, a woman's family is defined for her by her mother and to some extent by her grandmother. No matter how fond of his daughter the father may be, she is only a temporary member of his household and useless to his family—he cannot even marry her to one of his sons as he could an adopted daughter. Her irrelevance to her father's family in turn affects the daughter's attitude toward it. It is of no particular interest to her, and the need to maintain its continuity has little meaning for her beyond the fact that this continuity matters a great deal to some of the people she loves. As a child she probably accepts to some degree her grandmother's orientation toward the family: the household, that is, those people who live together and eat together, including perhaps one or more of her father's married brothers and their children. But the group that has the most meaning for her and with which she will have the most lasting ties is the smaller, more cohesive unit centering on her mother, that is, the uterine family—her mother and her mother's children. Father is important to the group, just as grandmother is important to some of the children, but he is not quite a member of it, and for some uterine families he may even be "the enemy." As the girl grows up and her grandmother dies and a brother or two marries, she discovers that her mother's definition of the family is becoming less exclusive and may even include such outsiders as her brother's new wife. Without knowing precisely when it happened, she finds that her brother's interests and goals have shifted in a direction she cannot follow. Her mother does not push her aside, but when the mother speaks of the future, she speaks in terms of her son's future. Although the mother sees her uterine family as adding new members and another generation, her daughter sees it as dissolving, leaving her with strong particular relationships, but with no group to which she has permanent loyalties and obligations.

When a young woman marries, her formal ties with the household of her father are severed. In one of the rituals of the wedding ceremony the bride's father or brothers symbolically inform her by means of spilt water that she, like the water, may never return, and when her wedding sedan chair passes over the threshold of her father's house, the doors are slammed shut behind her. If she is ill-treated by her husband's family, her father's family may intervene, but unless her parents are willing to bring her home and support her for the rest of her life (and most parents are not), there is little they can do beyond shaming the other family. This is usually enough.

As long as her mother is alive, the daughter will continue her contacts with her father's household by as many visits as her new situation allows. If she lives nearby she may visit every few days, and no matter where she lives she must at least be allowed to return at New Year. After her mother dies her visits may become perfunctory, but her relations with at least one member of her uterine family, the group that centered on her mother, remain strong. Her brother plays an important ritual role throughout her life. She may gradually lose contact with her sisters as she and they become more involved with their own children, but her relations with her brother continue. When her sons marry, he is the guest of honor at the wedding feasts, and when her daughters marry he must give a small banquet in their honor. If her sons wish to divide their father's estate, it is their mother's brother who is called on to supervise. And when she dies, the coffin cannot be closed until her brother determines to his own satisfaction that she died a natural death and that her husband's family did everything possible to prevent it.

With the ritual slam of her father's door on her wedding day, a young woman finds herself quite literally without a family. She enters the household of her husband—a man who in an earlier time, say fifty years ago, she would never have met and who even today, in modern rural Taiwan, she is unlikely to know very well. She is an outsider, and for Chinese an outsider is always an object of deep suspicion. Her husband and her father-in-law do not see her as a member of their family. But they do see her as essential to it; they have gone to great expense to bring her into their household for the purpose of bearing a new generation for their family. Her mother-in-law, who was mainly responsible for negotiating the terms of her entry, may harbor some resentment over the hard bargaining, but she is nonetheless eager to see another generation added to *her* uterine family. A mother-in-law often has the same kind of ambivalence toward her daughter-in-law as she has toward her husband—the younger woman seems a member of her family at times and merely a member of the household at others. The new bride may find that her husband's sister is hostile or at best condescending, both attitudes reflecting the daughter's distress at an outsider who seems to be making her way right into the heart of the family.

Chinese children are taught by proverb, by example, and by experience that the family is the source of their security, and relatives the only people who can be depended on. Ostracism from the family is one of the harshest sanctions that can be imposed on erring youth. One of the reasons mainlanders as individuals are considered so untrustworthy on Taiwan is the fact that they are not subject to the controls of (and therefore have no fear of ostracism from) their families. If a timid new bride is considered an object of suspicion and potentially dangerous because she is a stranger, think how uneasy her own first few months must be surrounded by strangers. Her irrelevance to her father's family may result in her having little reverence for descent lines, but she has warm memories of the security of the family her mother created. If she is ever to return to this certainty and sense of belonging, a woman must create her own uterine family by bearing children, a goal that happily corresponds to the goals of the family into which she has married. She may gradually create a tolerable niche for herself in the household of her mother-in-law, but her family will not be formed until she herself forms it of her own children and grandchildren. In most cases, by the time she adds grandchildren, the uterine family and the household will almost completely overlap, and there will be another daughter-in-law struggling with loneliness and beginning a new uterine family.

The ambiguity of a man's position in relation to the uterine families accounts for much of the hostility between mother-in-law and daughter-in-law. There is no question in the mind of the older woman but that her son *is* her family. The daughter-in-law might be content with this situation once her sons are old enough to represent her interests in the household and in areas strictly under men's control, but until then, she is dependent on her husband. If she were to be completely absorbed into her mother-in-law's family—a rare occurrence unless she is a *simpua*—there would be little or no conflict; but under most circumstances she must rely on her husband, her mother-in-law's son, as her spokesman, and here is where the trouble begins. Since it is usually events within the household that she wishes to affect, and the household more or less overlaps with her mother-in-law's uterine family, even a minor foray by the younger woman suggests to the older one an all-out attack on everything she has worked so hard to build in the years of her own loneliness and insecurity. The birth of grandchildren further complicates their relations, for the one sees them as new members for her family and the other as desperately needed recruits to her own small circle of security.

In summary, my thesis contends . . . that because we have heretofore focused on men when examining the Chinese family—a reasonable approach to a patrilineal system—we have missed not only some of the system's subtleties but also its near-fatal weaknesses. With a male focus we see the Chinese family as a line of descent, bulging to encompass all the members of a man's household and spreading out through his descendants. With a female focus, however, we see the Chinese family not as a continuous line stretching between the vague horizons of past and future, but as a contemporary group that comes into existence out of one woman's need and is held together insofar as she has the strength to do so, or, for that matter, the need to do so. After her death the uterine family survives only in the mind of her son and is symbolized by the special attention he gives her earthly remains and her ancestral tablet. The rites themselves are demanded by the ideology of the patriliny, but the meaning they hold for most sons is formed in the uterine family. The uterine family has no ideology, no formal structure, and no public existence. It is built out of sentiments and loyalties that die with its members, but it is no less real for all that. The descent lines of men are born and nourished in the uterine families of women, and it is here that a male ideology that excludes women makes its accommodations with reality.

Women in rural Taiwan do not live their lives in the walled courtyards of their husbands' households. If they did, they might be as powerless as their stereotype. It is in their relations in the outside world (and for women in rural Taiwan that world consists almost entirely of the village) that women develop sufficient backing to maintain some independence under their powerful mothers-in-law and even occasionally to bring the men's world to terms. A successful venture into the men's world is no small feat when one recalls that the men of a village were born there and are often related to one another, whereas the women are unlikely to have either the ties of childhood or the ties of kinship to unite them. All the same, the needs, shared interests, and common problems of women are reflected in every village in a loosely knit society that can when needed be called on to exercise considerable influence.

Women carry on as many of their activities as possible outside the house. They wash clothes on the riverbank, clean and pare vegetables at a communal pump, mend under a tree that is a known meeting-place, and stop to rest on a bench or group of stones with other women. There is a continual moving back and forth between kitchens, and conversations are carried on from open doorways through the long, hot afternoons of summer. The shy young girl who enters the village as a bride is examined as frankly and suspiciously by the women as an animal that is up for sale.

If she is deferential to her elders, does not criticize or compare her new world unfavorably with the one she has left, the older residents will gradually accept her presence on the edge of their conversations and stop changing the topic to general subjects when she brings the family laundry to scrub on the rocks near them. As the young bride meets other girls in her position, she makes allies for the future, but she must also develop relationships with the older women. She learns to use considerable discretion in making and receiving confidences, for a girl who gossips freely about the affairs of her husband's household may find herself labeled a troublemaker. On the other hand, a girl who is too reticent may find herself always on the outside of the group, or worse yet, accused of snobbery. I described in *The House of Lim* the plight of Lim Chui-ieng, who had little village backing in her troubles with her husband and his family as the result of her arrogance toward the women's community. In Peihotien the young wife of the storekeeper's son suffered a similar lack of support. Warned by her husband's parents not to be too "easy" with the other villagers lest they try to buy things on credit, she obeyed to the point of being considered unfriendly by the women of the village. When she began to have serious troubles with her husband and eventually his family, there was no one in the village she could turn to for solace, advice, and, most important, peacemaking.

Once a young bride has established herself as a member of the women's community, she has also established for herself a certain amount of protection. If the members of her husband's family step beyond the limits of propriety in their treatment of her—such as refusing to allow her to return to her natal home for her brother's wedding or beating her without serious justification—she can complain to a woman friend, preferably older, while they are washing vegetables at the communal pump. The story will quickly spread to the other women, and one of them will take it on herself to check the facts with another member of the girl's household. For a few days the matter will be thoroughly discussed whenever a few women gather. In a young wife's first few years in the community, she can expect to have her mother-in-law's side of any disagreement given fuller weight than her own—her mother-in-law has, after all, been a part of the community a lot longer. However, the discussion itself will serve to curb many offenses. Even if the older woman knows that public opinion is falling to her side, she will still be somewhat more judicious about refusing her daughter-in-law's next request. Still, the daughter-in-law who hopes to make use of the village forum to depose her mother-in-law or at least gain herself special privilege will discover just how important the prerogatives of age and length of residence are. Although the women can serve as a powerful protective force for their defenseless younger members, they are also a very conservative force in the village.

Taiwanese women can and do make use of their collective power to lose face for their menfolk in order to influence decisions that are ostensibly not theirs to make. Although young women may have little or no influence over their husbands and would not dare express an unsolicited opinion (and perhaps not even a solicited one) to their fathers-in-law, older women who have raised their sons properly retain considerable influence over their sons' actions, even in activities exclusive to men. Further, older women who have displayed years of good judgment are regularly consulted by their husbands about major as well as minor economic and social projects. But even men who think themselves free to ignore the opinions of their women are never free of their own concept, face. It is much easier to lose face than to have face. We once asked a male friend in Peihotien just what "having face" amounted to. He replied, "When no one is talking about a family, you can say it has face." This is precisely where women wield their power. When a man behaves in a way that they consider wrong, they talk about him—not only among themselves, but to their sons and husbands. No one "tells him how to mind his own business," but it becomes abundantly clear that he is losing face and by continuing in this manner may bring shame to the family of his ancestors and descendants. Few men will risk that.

The rules that a Taiwanese man must learn and obey to be a successful member of his society are well developed, clear, and relatively easy to stay within. A Taiwanese woman must also learn the rules, but if she is to be a successful woman, she must learn not to stay within them, but to *appear* to stay within them; to manipulate them, but not to appear to be manipulating them; to teach them to her children, but not to depend on her children for her protection. A truly successful Taiwanese woman is a rugged individualist who has learned to depend largely on herself while appearing to lean on her father, her husband, and her son. The contrast between the terrified young bride and the loud, confident, often lewd old woman who has outlived her mother-in-law and her husband reflects the tests met and passed by not strictly following the rules and by making purposeful use of those who must. The Chinese male's conception of women as "narrowhearted" and socially inept may well be his vague recognition of this facet of women's power and technique.

The women's subculture in rural Taiwan is, I believe, below the level of consciousness. Mothers do not tell their about-to-be-married daughters how to establish themselves in village society so that they may have some protection from an oppressive family situation, nor do they warn them to gather their children into an exclusive circle under their own control. But girls grow up in village society and see their mothers and sisters-in-law settling their differences, to keep them from a public airing or presenting them for the women's community to judge. Their mothers have created around them the meaningful unit in their fathers' households, and when they are desperately lonely and unhappy in the households of their husbands, what they long for is what they have lost. . . . [Some] areas in the subculture of women . . . mesh perfectly into the main culture of the society. The two cultures are not symbiotic because they are not sufficiently independent of one another, but neither do they share identical goals or necessarily use the same means to reach the goals they do share. Outside the village the women's subculture seems not to exist. The uterine family also has no public existence, and appears almost as a response to the traditional family organized in terms of a male ideology.

Male and Female in Hopi Thought and Action

Alice Schlegel

Alice Schlegel holds a Ph.D. from Northwestern University, awarded in 1971. Currently a professor in the Department of Anthropology at the University of Arizona, she has carried out fieldwork in the southwestern United States among Native Americans; her research specialties include cross-cultural methods, adolescence, and gender.

When traditional Hopi women are asked "Who are more important, women or men?" a common reply is "We are, because we are the mothers," with the qualification that men are important, too, as the messengers to the gods.

This paper will examine some of the assumptions that have been made about female reproduction, separation of the sexes, and the position of women. In recently published literature on female status, the universally secondary position of women in society has been asserted, and it has been accounted for by women's role in bearing and rearing children (Chodorow 1974; Ortner 1974; Rosaldo 1974). It is furthermore implied that this secondary position becomes one of subordination when the sexes operate within separate domains, the public for men and the domestic for women (Rosaldo 1974, pp. 39–40). These assertions are contradicted by data from traditional Hopi society, where the sexes are divided into two domains of action, and women's role in the reproduction and maintenance of life is the conscious justification for the position of equality they enjoy.

We shall examine the separation of activity between the domestic organization of the lineage and household, under the control of a female head, and the religious and political organization of the village, under the control of male community leaders. We shall also note the level of the clan, midway between household and community, in which authority is shared between a brother and sister pair. We shall look at the Hopi concept of sexual interdependence—between male and female actors in the social scene and between principles of maleness and femaleness in ideology.

"Male and Female in Hopi Thought and Action" by Alice Schlegel, from *Sexual Stratification*, Alice Schlegel, ed. © 1977 Columbia University Press. Reprinted with permission.

The key word here, I believe, is *balance*. Many societies operate with underlying concepts of ideological dualism. A widespread form of dualism either focuses upon or includes male-female relationships. Such notions are found both in tribal societies . . . and in literate civilizations such as China, where *yin-yang* is a core symbol for a range of binary oppositions. But dualism does not necessitate balance, or equality between the parts. It would require a lengthy excursion into Hopi metaphysics and cosmology to treat adequately the concept of balance as applied to man's nature and the universe, and that is beyond the scope of this paper. But the Hopi relationship of equality between the sexes, each with its own nature and social roles, will be examined in this light.

DOMESTIC LIFE

The Women in the Household

When a Hopi child is born, it is assured of a place within the matrilocal household and the matrilineal clan. If it is a boy, he will become a companion and helper to his father, who will teach him to farm, hunt, and herd. He is a potential heir to any of the religious-political positions held by his "uncles," or mothers' brothers. If it is a girl, she is welcomed as a source of continuity of the household and the clan. When she grows up, she or one of her sisters will inherit her mother's house and be responsible for the maintenance of her aged parents. As a mother and sister, she will have responsibility for many of the ceremonial objects used by her sons and brothers. She will "feed" the sacred masks by sprinkling them with cornmeal, thus assuring continual life and power to these necessary features of certain ritual performances. When asked, the Hopi insist that they wish for sons and daughters equally; however, women state that "you raise up a daughter for yourself, but you raise up a son for somebody else." Daughters remain at home, whereas sons are sent out upon marriage to become the providers and progenitors in the households of other women.

When a girl marries, she brings her husband into her household to work under the direction of her father and the ultimate authority of her mother. If she is not the heiress to the house, her husband will build her a house of her own, adjacent to or near her mother's house. Although he builds the house, it belongs to her and she can request him to leave at any time. Furthermore, all household goods, except the personal property of men, belong to her. Her husband farms fields assigned to her through her clan, and when the produce is brought in and she has formally thanked him, it is hers to allocate or dispose of as she sees fit. Of course, her husband is free to leave and move in with another woman or return to the house of his mother or sister, but in any event he lives in a house controlled by a female head. He moves into his wife's house as a stranger, and it is only after he has proven his worth through providing for her family that he earns a position of respect within it. The Hopi recognize this by saying that "a man's place is outside the house." All the long hours of labor in this dry and uncertain climate go to benefit a household and clan over which he has no authority beyond the authority he exerts over his young children, and his domestic satisfaction lies in the love and respect he earns as a good father and provider.

As might be expected, young men are none too eager to marry. To a woman, however, marriage is essential, as she needs a provider for herself and her children. While illegitimate children are not looked down upon, they are at a disadvantage in that they have no father to provide for them. A man who never married the mother of his child, or who has left her, is expected to contribute to his child's support, but rarely does so to the extent of fathers living in the home. A woman can turn to her brothers for some help, but this is usually burdensome for these men who have enough to do just taking care of their own families.

As a girl matures, she is under parental pressure to bring a husband into the house, for her father is eager for the help a son-in-law can give. In addition, her marriage is necessary for her life in the Afterworld: the wedding robes that her husband's male relatives weave for her become her shroud and the vehicle by which her spirit is transported into the world of the dead.

The boy, however, is under no such pressures. He enjoys his relatively carefree life as a young bachelor and is somewhat reluctant to take on the heavy responsibilities of marriage. Marriages are normally not arranged, and the burden of finding a spouse falls mainly upon the girl. Girls initiate a marriage by making the proposal, which may or may not be accepted. The transfer of labor and loyalty to the wife's household is symbolized by a ceremonial prestation [payment of money] of cornmeal to the groom's household, conceptualized by the Hopi as "paying for him," and by the short period of groom service that the bride performs by grinding corn and cooking for her husband's household while her wedding robes are being woven.[1] Once the wedding rituals are completed, the groom moves into the bride's house and "goes over to her side." Few men beyond their mid-twenties remain bachelors in spite of reluctance to marry, for the good Hopi is one who accepts the heavy duties of community responsibility, and fatherhood, highly valued by the Hopi, is one of the ways a man can contribute to the village.

Unlike the woman, the Hopi man has his responsibilities divided between two social units. To the household of his wife he owes his labor and his protectiveness as a father and a husband. However, he also owes loyalty to his natal household and clan. When clan matters arise, such as the assignment of clan lands or clan participation in ceremonies, male clan members are expected to take part. If a man holds a religious-political position, inherited through the clan, he must train one of his young clan mates, usually his sister's son, to succeed him. To a man who holds such a position, life is doubly busy—not only must he fulfill his domestic duties but he must also spend a great deal of time involved in ceremonial activities. Most of these leaders are middle-aged and old men, who are likely to have one or more sons-in-law in the house to help with farming and herding.

Women have no such potential conflict of loyalties. Once they have succeeded in marrying and bearing children, particularly daughters, they are established as responsible adults in the eyes of the clan and the community. They have produced life, and their role lies in the maintenance of physical life through feeding their families and others, and spiritual life through feeding the sacred objects. Most of this activity goes to benefit their own house and clan. Toward their husbands' natal house and clan they owe little beyond some contributions of food during periods of ceremonial activity, and a relationship of respect exists between them. Their greatest duties to households other than their own revolve around their roles as grandmothers and "aunts," or father's sisters, to the children of their sons and brothers, with whom they have an amiable joking relationship.

Hopi women appear to be in an enviable position when compared to women in male-dominant societies. Indeed, when the system works as it is designed to, these women are self-assured and confident of their place in the world. However, their very strength is also the source of their vulnerability. While they can make the final household decisions, they are dependent upon those men who have married into the house. They must have a husband or a son-in-law to provide for them. Fathers grow old and unable to work, brothers are busy with their own families, and sons marry and move out. It is critical for a woman to get and keep a husband, while men always have the alternative of moving in with their mothers or sisters. If a woman and her husband separate, her relatives are likely to urge her to forget the quarrel and take him back, saying: "One of your own people might be willing to plant for you, but only a husband will give you meat and clothes" (Forde 1931, p. 382). The Hopi emphasize the need for tact in marital relations, for they believe that love and the willing acceptance of responsibility cement the marital bonds. Even infidelity, said to be the most common cause of marital trouble, should be overlooked if possible, or at least dealt with by appealing to the errant partner's sense of marital and parental responsibility.[2]

The Woman and Her Male Kin

A woman is not under the authority of her husband, nor is she under the authority of her brother or mother's brother, as is the case in some other matrilineal societies (Schlegel 1972). It is true that an uncle (mother's brother) must be listened to with respect, and children are expected to obey him; and if parents are having difficulty with a recalcitrant child, the uncle will be called in to remonstrate or ultimately to punish him or her. Nevertheless, upon reaching adulthood the individual becomes his own master, and the uncle can only advise and remonstrate. While uncles are treated respectfully, this respect is tempered with a good deal of humor, and there is considerable reciprocal teasing and mild joking. . . .

Brothers and sisters are equals; if the brother has the right to criticize or advise his sister, so has she the right to do the same to him. Furthermore, although it is acceptable for a man to move into his sister's house upon separation from his wife, she can always refuse his request if she feels justified in doing so. In one case, the sister refused because she did not approve of her brother's reasons for leaving his wife (Nagata 1970, pp. 280–81).

In general, women are thought of as more emotional and headstrong than men, and therefore women are believed to be in need of advising by men more than men are by women. The role of adviser to a woman generally falls upon her close male kin—father, mother's brother, and brother. Husbands are reluctant to advise wives, and they should do it tactfully, as wives are thought likely to take offense. However, women do not hesitate to speak out and criticize or advise their fathers, uncles, and brothers if they feel the need to do so. They may point out to the kinsman that he is not behaving in proper fashion and thereby is not setting a good example for their own conduct. (Men may say the same to their fathers and uncles.) Older people of both sexes should be listened to respectfully by younger men and women, but they must earn this respect through their own good behavior.

Unlike many matrilineal societies, the mother's brother is not the kinsman who receives the greatest respect in this society. Rather, it is the *mö'wi*, or female in-law, the wife of a son, brother, or mother's brother. She is both addressed and referred to by this term, which connotes respect and deference, and there is the belief that using her name might bring harm to the one who does so. At the very least, using her name would be disrespectful. For no other status, kinship or otherwise, is the use of the name prohibited. The *mö'wi* is always treated with special courtesy by all those who address her husband as "son," "brother," or "uncle." The explanation given for this respect is that "she cooks for us [while her wedding robes are being woven] and brings food when she comes to visit." This is but one example of the high value placed upon women as feeders.

COMMUNITY LIFE

While most female authority is exerted within the sphere of household activities, women are not barred from participation in or influence over community activities. By withholding support they can informally exert the power of the veto (for an example, see below), although they rarely do so; for most of the community activities engaged in by men are for the benefit of women as much as for the benefit of men.

While household and community operate to a large degree as two separate areas of activity, they are not conceived of by the Hopi as two separate domains. The model of the house underlies the conception of the village; so to understand community authority and responsibility, one must understand the transformations of the concept of the house.

The house is, above all, the actual or symbolic structure that shelters the individual, that places and identifies him, and within which he is safe, whether in this life or the Afterworld. All creatures have houses, and to be without a house, as the spirit of the deceased is during his passage from the world of the living to the world of the dead, is to be in a state of danger to oneself and possibly others.

Each Hopi has a symbolic house, drawn for him when he is a newborn infant. One of the first actions of the Mudhead Clowns upon entrance into the plaza during ceremonial dances is to draw themselves a house upon the ground, for they are representing newly emerged beings.

The house of the family and matrilineage is the actual structure into which every Hopi is born and Hopi men marry. These are places for family privacy, and any adult caught spying into another house is believed to be up to no good, probably a witch looking at his or her victim. It is within these houses that women exert authority and men take a secondary place, as we have seen.

Each clan also has a house, one that is both actual and symbolic. It is actual in that it is the house belonging to the leading lineage of the clan, the lineage to which the Clan Mother and her brother the Clan "Big Uncle" belong. It is in this house that clan-owned ceremonial property is stored, and it is a duty of the Clan Mother to care for it. We can also think of the Clan House as symbolic, as the focal point of the entire clan under the joint leadership of a brother and sister pair. It is in the clan house in this sense that men and women share authority, in their roles as Mother and Big Uncle.

Finally, the entire village is conceived of metaphorically as a house: the term for village chief is *kikmongwi*, or leader of the house, the stem for house being *ki* and the word for leader being *mongwi*. The *kikmongwi* is addressed by all the villagers as "father," and his wife is addressed as "mother." It is at this level that authority over the "house" lies in male hands, the *kikmongwi* and his council. While an authority, the *kikmongwi* is by no means authoritarian; rather, like a father, his principal duty is to care for his children so that they may thrive. The father does this by providing food and clothing for them; the *kikmongwi* does this by acting as principal communicant with the rain-bringing, life-giving supernatural beings. It is through his prayers, coming from a pure heart and an untroubled mind, that the forces of blessing are released.

Women in Community Political Activity

While the political system can be studied as a structure of formal authority, it can also be examined as the process by which decisions are made that affect community life, and this must include noninstitutionalized power and influence as well as authority. This point of view is the more appropriate for the Hopi political system, in which authority over community action is dispersed rather than concentrated and decisions are appropriately arrived at by consensus rather than by decree. . . .

The Hopi do have a village chief, the *kikmongwi*, but his principal role is to maintain harmony between the village and the spiritual world. His council, composed of men who inherit their positions through their clans (having been selected and trained by the previous incumbent), serves more as an advisory group than as a legislative or judicial body. The focus of community life is the ceremonial system, and the individual ceremonies are under the control of *mongwi*, or leaders, who inherit their positions through their clans. (Some of these *mongwi* are on the council.) While some clans are more important than others, in that they "own" the more important ceremonies, there is no rigid hierarchy. As we have seen in the discussion of domestic life, authority is not a principle of social interaction of kin; similarly, it is not a principle of social interaction within the community. The principles that are discussed by the Hopi and observable in action are the acceptance of duty and cooperation toward common goals. Whatever authority is exerted by community leaders is directed at the coordination of effort, not at enforcement of unilateral decisions. Resolution of conflicts is essentially a private matter between the parties involved; and conflicts that cannot be handled privately either break the village apart, as happened when Oraibi split in 1906, or simply persist for years or even generations.

To say, therefore, that women have no positions in the formal authority structure is to say very little.[3] As the mothers, sisters, and wives of men who make community decisions, the influence of women cannot be overestimated. These women, after all, control the houses that the men live in; and the man's position in the home is to a large extent dependent upon his relationship to its female head. Women do not hesitate to speak their minds, whether in the privacy of the home to male kin and their visitors or in public meetings. One example illustrates what is in effect the veto power of women: in one village the chief and his sister were divided over a political issue concerning the village, and she refused to play her role in the Soyal ceremony, led by the chief, until he capitulated. As Hopi men readily admit, women usually get their way.

Each village is politically autonomous, and alliances with other Hopi villages or with communities from other tribes exist only on an ad hoc basis. Trade is conducted between individuals; women do not generally go on trading parties, but they participate actively in any exchanges that occur when outsiders come into the village for that purpose. They also control any proceeds gained from trade goods, such as corn products or pottery, that they have processed or manufactured.

The one community activity from which women were excluded in earlier times, before the *pax Americana*, was warfare. For both practical and ideological reasons, war was a male activity. However, if a raid occurred when men were away on long-distance hunts, the women of necessity helped defend the village and the nearby fields. One of the favorite legendary figures in Oraibi is Hehe'wuhti, or Warrior Woman, who was in the process of pulling up her hair when the village was attacked. She led the women's defense with her hair up on one side, flowing down on the other, and thus is she portrayed.

Women in Community Ceremonial Activity

The Hopi have a complex ceremonial system, and it is the cycle of ceremonies that provides the rhythm of the yearly round. All children are initiated into the Kachina Society sometime between the ages of five and ten, after which they can take part in activities surrounding the kachina dances,[4] although only men actually dance as both male and female kachinas. In addition, some boys and girls are initiated at this time into the Powamu Society, which has the responsibility of caring for the kachinas.

In their late teens or early twenties, all men are initiated into one of the four men's fraternities: Wuwucim and Tao, which have a benevolent character concerned with reproduction and agriculture, and Al and Kwan, which have a fiercer character concerned with hunting (Al) and war (Kwan).

The ceremonial cycle contains four great ceremonies of village-wide involvement and some lesser ones put on by specific ceremonial groups. With the exception of the women's societies, control of all ceremonies is in the hands of male ceremonial leaders and most of the participants are men. Nevertheless, women play a vital role in ceremonial life. They grind the sacred cornmeal, the symbol of natural and spiritual life, that is a necessary ingredient in almost all ceremonies. When masked dances are held, the dancers are sprinkled with cornmeal by female members of the Powamu Society. Women provide the food that feeds the participants; in some of the ceremonies, this is distributed among onlookers, and this feeding is highly valued. Women as well as men may sponsor a kachina dance by providing, with the aid of their male and female relatives, the large quantity of food for the dancers to eat and to distribute to the audience. On such dance days the sponsor is said to "stand above the *kikmongwi*."

Women's Ceremonies

While most of the ceremonial societies are controlled by men, although they may have women members, there are three women's societies—Marau, Lakon, and Oaqül. These are optional: a woman need not enter any, or she can join any or all of them, although most women who belong to any belong only to one. Initiation can occur at any age, but most join as children or young girls or are brought in as infants by their mothers or other female kin. Each women's society has several male members as well, who act as assistants to the head priestess and make the *pahos*, or prayer sticks, required by the ceremonies. Like other societies, each women's society is "owned" by a clan, and

the chief priestess and her male assistants belong to the owning clan.

The women's societies hold their major public ceremonies in the fall, after the termination of the men's portion of the ceremonial cycle in late summer.[5] All of them last for nine days, although in Hopi thinking they are eight-day ceremonies, as the first day is considered to be the last day of the preceding time of preparation rather than part of the ceremony itself. The major public performances are held on the last day. Most of the ceremonial activity takes place in a *kiva*, or ceremonial building, borrowed from the men who use it daily.[6] The chief priestesses move in for the duration of the ceremony, with other members spending as much time there as they can spare from their household duties.

While each of the women's societies has its own ritual and symbols, there are certain common elements. All include some representation of Muingwa, the god of germination and the protector of all wild and domestic plants. All use corn, actual or depicted, as the major ritual element. (It is a major ritual element in most other ceremonies as well.) All initiate new members by placing them inside a kind of hoop made of yucca, raising and lowering it four times to the accompaniment of prayers and blessings. The symbolism of birth is very clear.[7] In all the dances, the women form a semicircle with their backs to the spectators, while various activities occur within the circle. This is in contrast to the men's dances in which the dancers form straight lines. In the women's dances, unlike the men's dances, only the participants with special roles are dressed in costume, while the dancers in the semicircle wear traditional Hopi dress.

The most complex of these ceremonies is Marau, and it is the one with the most overtones of the male portion of the ceremonial cycle. Marau women are said to be "sisters" to the men of Wuwucim (and perhaps Tao), and there is much good-natured and bawdy bantering between these "siblings" at the time of the Marau dances. Three nights of burlesque plaza performances are included in the Marau ceremony, with women mocking the men's kachina dances and singing obscene or humorous songs about their "brothers."

The Marau ceremony itself contains elements that bring to mind elements of Wuwucim, the great winter ceremony of the four fraternities. (It takes its name from the Wuwucim Society, the largest of the fraternities.) As in Wuwucim, offerings are made to all the dead, and departed members of the society are called back to the ceremony. In the plaza performance on the last day, elements are included that seem to reflect some of the basic features of Wuwucim. After the dancers have formed their circle and begun dancing, two pairs of women in short men's kilts and headdresses come toward the circle. These are called *Marautaka,* or "Marau men." The first pair hold bows and arrows, and as they proceed they shoot the arrows into bundles of vines that they throw before them. These arrows are spoken of as "lightning arrows," and they symbolize fertilization, as lightning is thought to fertilize plants. Thus, they exhibit the benevolent, life-giving character of Wuwucim and Tao fraternities. However, by shooting arrows these women are also performing acts characteristic of hunting and warfare, related to the nature of the Al and Kwan fraternities. That this shooting has to do with more than germination is indicated by the fact that after the ceremony the arrows are deposited at the shrine of the war gods. The arrows, then, are a key symbol of two major, and contradictory, principles of Hopi relationship to their world—benevolence and predation. In the Wuwucim ceremony these principles are separated by allocating them differentially to two pairs of fraternities. In Marau, they are brought together.

The second pair of major performers carry long poles and rings wrapped in old buckskin, which is said to have come from the clothing of enemies slain long ago. As they proceed, they toss the rings to the ground and throw the poles at them. These poles bring to mind the lances carried by the Kwan society, and the association with enemies and the clothing of the dead parallel aspects of the Kwan society rituals. Thus, Marau seems to unite into a single set of rituals those rituals, and the principles underlying them, performed separately by men's groups during Wuwucim. It seems to be a condensation and transformation of the major symbolic elements of the men's ceremony.

Lakon and Oaqül are very much alike. They are both called basket dances because at the termination of each dance set in the major public performance, decorated baskets are thrown to the spectators. Men in the audience try to get them, shouting, pushing other men aside, and even grabbing them from each other's hands. Women and children, wisely, stand to the rear. At the end of the grabbing, both men and baskets are likely to emerge somewhat battered. It is said that all this aids men in their hunting, for the shouting attracts the curious deer and brings them close to the village.

There are symbolic and ritual features of Lakon that relate to hunting. Primary among these is the "sibling" relationship between Lakon women and Al (and possibly Kwan) men. Here again, as in Marau, male and female elements are brought together. This is most vividly depicted in the headdress worn by the two central performers in the Lakon dance, which has a bunch of feathers attached to the right side and a horn protruding from the left. These elements have been interpreted by one Hopi as representing masculinity (the horn) and femininity (the feathers as a replacement for flowers) (Titiev 1972, pp. 99–100, 293). There is a subtle relationship between women and game animals, especially antelopes (the major type of hunted game), that crops up in various rituals and even in jokes about

extramarital sexual adventures: men talk about "hunting for two-legged deer." Outside of marriage, males are believed to be the sexual aggressors, and the predatory nature of male sexuality is revealed in the notion that a woman should be "paid" with a gift if she acquiesces. This is not prostitution but rather reflects the idea that one should give something in return for whatever has been taken.

Lakon and Oaqül seem to be harvest festivals as well, for effigies or other representations of Muingwa form an important element in the private kiva rituals, and seeds are used as a part of the altars in the kivas. Decorated baskets, when not adorning the walls, are used for prestations of food at weddings and during Powamu, the spring festival of germination, so their use in these ceremonies seems to emphasize the feminine role of corn grinder and feeder. Oaqül, a recent introduction, is not so well integrated into the system as are the other two ceremonies.

The female portion of the ceremonial cycle, then, has a double role in the cycle. First, it emphasizes the distinctiveness of women by bringing in elements, such as baskets, that are specific to female activities. The birth-giving nature of the act of initiation is the most dramatic of these elements. Second, by incorporating, uniting, and transforming major elements that appear in male ceremonies, it transmits the message that women, like men, contribute to the Hopi community and universe. Men and women are separate and have distinctive functions and even characters, but they are both part of the total Hopi world and they work together for common goals. Through the women's ceremonies, the necessary interdependence of male and female is expressed.

MALE AND FEMALE IN HOPI IDEOLOGY

If we consider the women's ceremonies discussed above within the context of the total ceremonial cycle, particularly in relation to the men's ceremonies that immediately precede and follow them, we gain some insight into the way that male and female principles are conceptualized by the Hopi.

The major cycle, involving almost total village participation, ends in July with Niman, or the Home Dance. The kachinas, who made their first appearance shortly before Soyal in December, go after this dance to their home in the San Francisco Peaks, the sacred mountains to the southwest of the Hopi villages. In August, preceding the women's portion of the cycle, two men's ceremonies are held in alternate years. These are the Snake-Antelope Ceremony, conducted by the Snake and Antelope Societies, and the Flute Ceremony, conducted by the Flute Societies. They involve only the members of these societies and the clans that "own" them. These ceremonies can be thought of as complementary to one another, representing the two contradictory aspects of the masculine principle, benevolence and predation.[8]

The Flute Ceremony is replete with symbols of plant reproduction and the elements that foster it, such as water and the sun. This, I believe, is expressive of the male role as the germinator. As the farmer to his fields, the husband and father to his wife and children, the *kikmongwi* to his village, and the Great Spirit to his people, the male is needed to activate and care for life. In contrast, the Snake-Antelope Ceremony represents the predatory nature of males, who must also kill if life is to be maintained. Snake dancers wear war costume and refer to the snakes that they handle as "warriors." According to information given to Stephen (1936, p. 714) in 1843, the Snake Society members were the actual warriors in olden times, while the Antelopes were the old men who stayed home praying in the kivas for success. The duality of masculinity is represented in these two ceremonies, as it is represented in the two pairs of men's fraternities, Wuwucim and Tao, and Al and Kwan.

The Lakon ceremony, which is the first of the women's ceremonies, can be regarded as representing the different natures of male and female. Females are related to the elements that grow out of Mother Earth—edible plants in their natural form or as a medium of exchange, symbolized by baskets, and game animals. Males stand to females both as the farmer stands to his crops, a benevolent and protective relationship, and as the hunter stands to game animals. While this latter relationship is most obviously predatory, it contains an element of benevolence as well; for a hunter performs rituals that placate the dead animal by sending its spirit back to the animal world and thereby ensuring the perpetuation of animal life. Men must activate the life force and they must protect it, but in protecting it they must also kill, both animals for food and enemies for safety. Women, however, do not partake of this dual role of life givers and life destroyers: their single nature is to give and keep life.

The Marau ceremony, which follows Lakon, can be regarded as the female counterpart to Wuwucim, as we have discussed above. The burlesque elements so prominent in this ceremony, which occur to a lesser degree in the Wuwucim ceremony, can be regarded as signifying the tension underlying the ambiguous relationship between men and women. On the one hand they are separate and have different characters; on the other they are the same, as members of the moral in contrast to the natural and supernatural worlds. That this joking is related to men and women as males and females is shown by the explicitly sexual nature of the songs and jokes exchanged and the vivid depictions of genitals used in the joking portions of the ceremonies.

Wuwucim, the first ceremony in the male cycle, takes place in November.

The last of the women's ceremonies to be held is Oaqül, which is similar to Lakon. It seems to be the least important of the women's ceremonies and restates the message transmitted in Lakon.

The great cycle, involving four major community ceremonies plus a number of kachina dances, begins with Wuwucim and ends with Niman. This cycle expresses Hopi beliefs about the natural and social world and the progress of the Hopi people through time. The little cycle, which takes place between Niman and Wuwucim, consists of men's and women's society performances and transmits different messages. Taken all together, it is in part a symbolic statement about the nature of male and female and their roles in social life. It contrasts the double nature of men with the single nature of women. If I am correct in considering Marau to be a feminine transformation of Wuwucim, then this ceremony brings together the duality into an expression of unity.

THE FEMALE AS THE SOURCE OF LIFE

As the opening sentence of this paper indicates, Hopi women perceive their importance as lying in their reproductive role, and a good part of the role of men is to protect the women so that they can fulfill this role. When they act as guardians of the women and advisers to them, they are making it possible for women to have the physical and spiritual safety required if children, and the Hopi people, are to thrive. Health and life itself depend upon keeping harmony with other people and the spirit beings, and a troubled mind makes it impossible for a woman to care for herself and her children properly. If a woman is disturbed, she and her children are in danger.

Societal maintenance through the production and perpetuation of life is an important goal of any society, but it may become secondary if the immediate need of the society is focused around warfare or other specifically male activities. For the Hopi, who consider the taking of life in hunting and warfare a necessary evil, warfare is played down; productivity is the major social goal.[9] When the Hopi dance, they say that they are praying for rain; but this has to be understood not only realistically, as a desperate need in this dry climate, but also metaphorically. Rain, which the men induce through their harmonious relation with the spirit world, is a major symbol for the power that activates life. This power can also be dangerous—the lightning that fertilizes the fields can also kill, or torrential rains can wash away the young plants. The other major symbol of life activation, the sun, is potentially dangerous as well, for it can burn the delicate plants unless they receive the rain. So, the task of men is to control the life-activating force and permit it to operate beneficently through the bodies of women and within Mother Earth. Both sexes fulfill their necessary tasks within the natural and spiritual domains of promoting life.

The woman as the source of life itself is expressed by the feminine nature of corn, the dominant symbol of life and an ingredient in almost all ritual activity. Each newborn infant is given a perfect ear of corn, its Corn Mother, which will protect it as the symbolic house drawn for the infant protects it. It is not surprising that the god of plants, including corn, is a male, Muingwa, for it is a masculine duty to care for corn and all female life.

The life-giving nature of women is encapsulated in one of the Hopi witchcraft beliefs. In order to gain worldly power, a person bargains away his life, or "heart." In order to survive, he or she must magically steal the hearts of others, thus killing them. Children, being young and pure of heart, are the favored victims. It is said that the heart of a boy will give the witch four more years of life. The heart of a girl, however, will allow him or her to live eight more years.

CONCLUSION

We have examined some of the features of social organization and the ideological system that are related to the high evaluation of women among the Hopi and the equality they enjoy with men. In this integrated network of activities and beliefs, the social and subsistence roles of men and women form a model for the beliefs about masculinity and femininity. In turn, these beliefs provide the sense of "rightness" with which the Hopi perform their domestic and community activities. At every point along the path through life, traditional Hopi look to their beliefs to guide and justify their daily conduct, and the way in which they perform their daily activities influences their relationship with the spiritual world. When he tends his plants, or when he fulfills his marital and paternal duties, a Hopi man is not only performing subsistence and social activities but he is contributing to the maintenance of life as well; and his contribution takes on a sacred quality that permits him to stand in good relation to the spiritual world. When a Hopi woman grinds corn, she does so with the knowledge that she is providing food for her children and the people, and the very substance she handles is the sacred element of life. Corn grinding should not be regarded as the onerous and time-consuming task it would appear to be; rather, it is a sacred duty of women, to be done with a pure heart and untroubled mind. Women sing corn-grinding songs as they work to lighten the task and express its life-giving contribution.

Male and female are interdependent and equally important principles of Hopi social life and ideology. These principles are complementary rather than similar. The female sphere of activity is the household, and the male sphere of activity is the community. Men and women control different portions of the ceremonial cycle. Each sex has its own tasks—only men hunt, only women grind corn—although both may come together in caring for the fields or herds, even though this is primarily the duty of men. But the dichotomy of masculine and feminine that separates the sexes is bridged in their necessary interdependence at each point in the social and ideological systems. The separation of the sexes does not cause the subordination of one and superordination of the other; rather, it permits each sex to fulfill its necessary and equally valued role in the maintenance of the society. Where the ideological focus of a culture is life, and both sexes are believed to be equally necessary to the promotion of life, devaluation of either sex is unlikely. . . .

NOTES

1. For a discussion of wedding customs and the pressure on girls to marry, see Schlegel 1973.
2. One wonders why infidelity is at the same time so deplored and so common. It probably provides one of the few escapes from the tight regulation of social life, and even vicarious enjoyment of infidelity is apparent in the teasing and joking that goes on about "private wives" and "hunting for two-legged deer." Men are usually the initiators of sexual activity (although women sometimes do initiate sexual affairs), so infidelity may also be a means by which men express covert resentment against their wives for their relatively insecure position in the home. Furthermore, as there are strong sanctions against the overt expression of anger between men, the seduction of another man's wife may be a way of expressing hostility toward him.
3. Actually, there is one case in which women do enter the formal authority system: if a *mongwi* dies without naming an heir, it is up to the Clan Mother to name his replacement. . . .

   Today, there is even a woman who claims chieftainship of Oraibi, on the grounds that her brother, the designated chief, has not kept to the traditional Hopi way. There is considerable controversy over this: some Hopi claim that she is not a real chief, since, never having been initiated into a ceremonial fraternity, she cannot perform the chiefly rituals (see below); while others support her on the grounds that she has stepped in to provide necessary leadership. There is an earlier case of a woman chief of Moenkopi, a daughter village to Oraibi. Her position was never one of a true *kikmongwi*, as Moenkopi was included in the Oraibi ceremonial cycle: rather, she seems to have been a liaison between Moenkopi and the Anglo authorities in the nearby town of Tuba City. . . .
4. The term *kachina* refers both to a supernatural being whose primary role is to bring rain and to the man who impersonates him in the kachina dance. It is believed that when the dancer puts on the kachina mask, the spirit of the kachina enters his body and he becomes a kachina. There are well over 100 different kachina forms, some more popular than others.
5. Shorter ceremonies are held in winter months for the women's societies discussed here and the other societies discussed below.

The major ceremony in each case is held in summer or autumn, and it is these ceremonies that are discussed in this paper.

6. Marau had its own kiva, owned by the Lizard Clan which owns Marau. In 1901 it was rebuilt and taken over by the men, who have since loaned it to the Marau Society for its ceremonies. Lakon and Oaqül use a different kiva, borrowed from the men. In addition to their ceremonial use, kivas serve as men's houses.

7. The hoop is used only for women's society initiation and the initiation of children into the Powamu and Kachina Societies, which are held in Marau Kiva at Oraibi. It is not used for initiation into other societies or the men's fraternities, even though the concept of rebirth is made explicit in the latter by treating the fraternity initiates like newborn infants.

8. Flute and Snake-Antelope ceremonies are complementary to one another in timing, and, as I indicate, in symbolic expression. According to Parsons (1940), there is archaeological and ethnohistorical evidence that the ceremonies were once the same ceremony, or at least more closely related than they are today. Momtcit, a war ceremony comprising two sets of dancers like the Snake-Antelope Ceremony, is now defunct. Perhaps Momtcit was to Snake-Antelope as Oaqül is to Lakon, a restatement of the same message (see the discussion below).

9. Warfare themes are not central to the great cycle of ceremonies, even though they appear in the little cycle of summer and fall ceremonies. The Hopi have played down the prominence of warfare, and it was not the means by which manhood was achieved or validated—initiation into a fraternity accomplished that. Prowess in warfare was respected only in that it provided defense for the village and allowed the physical and spiritual activities dedicated to the maintenance of life to be pursued.

REFERENCES

Chodorow, Nancy. 1974. "Family Structure and Feminine Personality." In *Women, Culture, and Society,* ed. by M. Z. Rosaldo & L. Lamphere, pp. 43–66. Stanford, CA: Stanford University Press.

Forde, C. D. 1931. "Hopi Agriculture and Land Ownership." *Journal of the Royal Anthropological Institute of Great Britain and Northern Ireland* Vol. 61:357–405.

Nagata, Shuichi. 1970. *Modern Transformations of Moenkopi Pueblo.* Urbana: University of Illinois Press.

Ortner, Sherry B. 1974. "Is Male to Female as Nature Is to Culture?" In *Woman, Culture, and Society,* ed. by M. Z. Rosaldo & L. Lamphere, pp. 67–88. Stanford, CA: Stanford University Press.

Parsons, Elsie Clews. 1940. "A Pre-Spanish Record of Hopi Ceremonies." *American Anthropologist* Vol. 42:541–42.

Rosaldo, Michelle Zimbalist. 1974. "Woman, Culture, and Society: A Theoretical Overview." In *Woman, Culture, and Society,* ed. by M. Z. Rosaldo & L. Lamphere, pp. 17–42. Stanford, CA: Stanford University Press.

Schlegel, Alice. 1972. *Male Dominance and Female Autonomy: Domestic Authority in Matrilineal Societies.* New Haven, CT: Human Relations Area Files Press.

Schlegel, Alice. 1973. "The Adolescent Socialization of the Hopi Girl." *Ethnology* Vol. 12:449–62.

Stephen, Alexander M. 1936. *Hopi Journal of Alexander M. Stephen,* ed. by E. C. Parsons. New York: Columbia University Press.

Titiev, Mischa. 1972. *The Hopi Indians of Old Oraibi: Change and Continuity.* Ann Arbor: University of Michigan Press.

9

Sex, Age, Common Interest, and Stratification

In all human societies, kinship and residence are important for the organization of people into various groups. These are not the only **organizational principles,** however; others that are frequently used include sex, age, common interest, and stratification. In all societies some division of labor by sex exists. In some societies this division is relatively flexible, in that tasks normally performed by one sex may be performed by the other, as circumstances dictate, without "loss of face." This is the case among the Bushmen, where many tasks are shared between men and women. In some other societies, though, the sexes are rigidly separated in what they do, as among the Iroquoian peoples of what now is New York State. Among them the tasks of men took them away from their villages for purposes of hunting, warfare, and diplomacy (in the twentieth century, for high-steel work in urban areas), while the work of women was carried out in and near the villages.

Grouping by age involves the concepts of **age-grades** and **age-sets,** categories to which one belongs by virtue of age, and cohorts of individuals who move through a series of age-grades together. The concepts are familiar to college students: A particular "class" (of '98, '99, or whatever) constitutes an age-set whose members pass through the first year, sophomore, junior, and senior age-grades together. Age-grades, with or without age-sets, are found in many human societies, with important ritual activity often marking the transition from one age-grade to the next.

Common-interest groups, formed for a specific purpose and to which one belongs by virtue of an act of joining (as opposed to automatic assignment by virtue of descent, age, sex, and so on), are particularly characteristic of urban industrial societies, although they may be found in traditional agrarian societies as well. In the United States they exist in profusion, ranging all the way from street gangs to civic groups like the Lions or Elks clubs. Common-interest associations are especially well suited to industrialized and developing societies, where new needs are constantly arising, around which new associations can form.

Grouping by sex, age, or common interest may or may not involve a degree of inequality; after all, groups may exist for different purposes without being ranked as inferior or superior to one another. Among the Iroquoians, for example, the rigid separation of sexes was *not* associated with subordination of one sex to the dominance of the other. Rather, the tasks assigned each sex were regarded as of equal value, and neither sex could impose its will on the other. By contrast, stratification *always* involves inequality, as whole categories of people **(social classes)** are ranked high versus low relative to one another. **Stratification,** one of the defining features of **civilization,** is backed by the power of the state, which may use force to maintain the privileges of those most favored by the system. Needless to say, those in the uppermost class, the **social elite,** have prior claim to basic resources, whereas those at the bottom of the scale must make do with whatever those of higher rank leave them.

Although one may speak of sex, age, common interest, and stratification as if they were always discrete organizational principles, the reality is not nearly so clear-cut. The first article in this chapter is a particularly good illustration of this; in the southeastern United States, sex, age, and common interest all are significant for enrollment in the military college that is the subject of Abigail Adams's paper. Enrollment in this institution is a matter of choice but is restricted to men. The young men who choose to enroll are of essentially the same age, and they will pass through the institution together. As is typical of age-grading, full admittance as a "member of the corps" follows initiation rites that separate the initiate from "ordinary" society for a period of time, before being readmitted (in this case, "reborn") into society in a new status.

The ultimate transition from one age-status to another is from life to death, and in some societies, death may mark the transition to a fourth age-grade, that of ancestors. In his article, Olatunde Lawuyi looks at obituaries published in Nigerian newspapers, which along with congratulatory advertisements, serve the economic and political interests of the social elite in Niger-

ian society. Because they are costly to publish (they are an important source of revenue for the media), the notices indicate by their mere existence the wealth and power of their subjects. They further serve to advertise the particular concerns, interests, and accomplishments of the elite and allow other individuals to broadcast their association with prominent individuals.

The last article, by Brett Williams, neatly illustrates social stratification in action. Two of the ways in which social classes are manifest is through **symbolic indicators**—activities and possessions indicative of one's status—and patterns of interaction—who interacts with whom, and in what way. "Elm Valley" affords good illustrations of both and highlights the misunderstandings that stem from somewhat different worldviews held by members of different social classes.

Dyke to Dyke

Ritual Reproduction at a U.S. Men's Military College

Abigail E. Adams

Abigail E. Adams is a lecturer at Hollins College in Virginia and a Ph.D. candidate at the University of Virginia. She has a Masters in Latin American studies from Stanford University. Her current research is on evangelicals in the highlands of Guatemala and in the United States. She also continues to research the issues presented in this article, following military-style colleges, men's and women's roles in them, and their relationship to private and public life.

The U.S. military now trains women combat pilots (and even closeted homosexuals), but two military colleges are in court to defend their right as state institutions to accept only heterosexual men. This article examines the resistance to enroll women at one of these colleges, which I will refer to as "South East Military Institute" (SEMI), by analysing the institution's rituals known as the "Ratline" and "Break Out."

SEMI is one of two remaining state-supported men's colleges in the United States, both of which are Southern "military" schools, although not official U.S. armed service academies (which have been coeducational since 1976). SEMI and its state's government were ordered by U.S. federal courts to either admit women, cut state funding, or create a SEMI-style program elsewhere in the state. The U.S. Supreme Court refused in May [1993] to consider SEMI's appeal, and SEMI's governing board this Fall will announce the plan that complies with federal courts—but keeps women from enrolling (Associated Press, 8 August 1993).

SEMI had won an initial 1991 case against the U.S. Department of Justice when a district federal judge accepted SEMI's argument that it provides valuable diversity for the state's higher education: "Excluding women is substantially related to this mission . . . [SEMI] has set its eye on the goal of the citizen-soldier, . . . and I will permit it to continue to do so."

The decision was an innovative application of political correctness, but was condemned by SEMI's opponents as the work of an "anachronistic" yet "pow-

erful old boys' network" (Goodman, 1991), devoted to keeping women out of business, politics and the military. Yet the issue was not about excluding women generally—just excluding them from SEMI. One cadet (student) wrote me, "Why do women want to open all doors closed to them? . . . Women belong in the military but not at 'SEMI.'"

"The very thing that women are seeking would no longer be there" if women were admitted, said SEMI's 1992 senior class president. Alum were more adamant: "The first moment any woman enters [SEMI], she will be fooling herself—because SEMI will cease to exist."

I stumbled into SEMI's controversy while teaching anthropology at a nearby women's college. My students mentioned SEMI when we studied Melanesian rites of passage. SEMI's Commandant of Students sent our class a videotape of SEMI's freshman or "Rat" year, and later visited as our guest informant. I found he shared "the anthropological romance with initiation rites" (Herdt, 1982:xvi). SEMI had won its first case the day before, and both the Commandant and I were intrigued by what ritual analysis would reveal about SEMI's "uniqueness." The Commandant asked me to lecture on ritual process at SEMI, and to attend SEMI's major ritual, Break Out. I welcomed the opportunity to leave the armchair—as far as my gender would permit—and study this ineffable "thing" that women would destroy at SEMI.

SEMI's opponents and supporters have also focused on SEMI's famous regime of "bizarre psychological and physical ordeals," as distinctive as the cadets' crisp uniforms and buzz cuts (Yoder, 1991). As I watched Break Out in 1993, the ritual seemed less of a "bizarre ordeal" than a metaphorical birth, an impression which the SEMI cadets corroborated when we analysed the ritual later. I was further struck, not by the

"Dyke to Dyke: Ritual Reproduction at a U.S. Men's Military College" by Abigail E. Adams, from *Anthropology Today*, Vol. 9, No. 5, 1993, pp. 3–6. Reprinted with permission of the Royal Anthropological Institute of Great Britain and Ireland.

intensity of "hazing," but by the tenderness of the seniors, who are called "dykes." Why, at a school dedicated to heterosexual men, would its major ritual recall childbirth and its central role, female homosexuality?

MEN'S RITUALS: HERE, THERE BUT NOT EVERYWHERE

My students were right: SEMI's "Ratline," Break Out, and "dyke" system fit perfectly with Van Gennep's tripartite scheme of separation, liminality and re-aggregation (1960). SEMI's method for creating the "citizen-soldier" includes three missions of military discipline, academics and athletics, but at its heart is the Ratline. In SEMI parlance, the Ratline is "the longest distance between two points," exaggerated routes around campus that freshmen had to follow, but in general it refers to the seven months of initiation they must endure to become cadets.

The question of why men need and participate in initiation rituals has re-emerged along with the "men's movement." Previously, arguments centered on the psychoanalytic, such as the thesis that these rites break boys from identifying with and depending on mothers (Whiting et al., 1967), or Bettelheim's idea that men express and resolve "womb envy" by culturally creating ritual analogies of what women do "naturally": create people (1954).

Why then don't *all* societies have male cults? Robert Bly (1990) suggests that U.S. men particularly need initiation rituals in post-World War 2 society, because as fathers left the home for work, boys lost their male role model.

It was the early literature on the male cults of Melanesia and Amazonia that initially reminded my students of SEMI's rituals. These writings described these societies as having unilineal descent systems that emphasize sexual polarities, in which one sex forms the core of a local group, and the Other sex are the affines, aliens, spies, possibly enemies (Murphy, 1959; Allen, 1967). SEMI was conceived of in 1834, the beginning of the Victorian era, certainly a period of sexual polarities. The antebellum upperclassmen took pride in winnowing out the "weak" and creating manhood for the survivors, claiming, "Give us your boy and we'll send you a man." They also invented some of the harshest hazing methods of the Ratline: the "company room," a nightly session of corporal punishment and exercise; "sweat parties," a company room conducted in a steam-filled shower room; "straining" and "finning out," which are taxing postures that Rats must hold; and "fagging," or menially serving upperclassmen (Wise, 1978).

It was only after the World War 2 era that Break Out was created as a formal culmination to the Ratline experience. Originally it was called "Bloody Sunday," and Rats had to run a gauntlet of the bodies and fists of upperclassmen, including seniors. Later classes of Rats "ran the stoops," fighting their way up the barracks' flights of steps over mattresses, juniors and sophomores, but aided by seniors.

Today, by contrast with the Melanesian and the Victorian era SEMI cults, secrecy and cruelty are not so important (President Reagan starred in a 1938 Hollywood movie about SEMI, *Brother Rat*). Many of the techniques resemble Outward Bound, EST and other "New Age" consciousness-raising programs. However, like other male cults, the predominating metaphors of SEMI's Ratline still emphasize and transform sexuality, childhood and family.

SEPARATION: SEMI'S UNIQUE METHOD

From the first day "in barracks," the entering class is separated from previous life, but also from SEMI as "rats" (the epitome of a liminal animal), "the lowest form of life . . . but still higher than anything *outside*," stated a cadet. They enter an upside-down world of unpredictable rules, space and time. The Ratline is administered by the upperclassmen in the barracks: the four floors of unlocked, spartan dormitory rooms, organized in balconies, outside staircases and communal bathrooms around a central courtyard, which are ranked by class from the ground floor of the senior class to the fourth floor of [the] entering class. This is "home" for 1,300 cadets. Right away the new students find it is *not* like home:

> When the class of 1980 arrived in August, it was greeted by veterans [who] were polite and friendly and put the new [students] to bed that night without introducing them to the rat system. But that same night they hauled them out of bed . . . (Wise, 1978).

The rats are stripped of young manhood and infantilized: put to bed, yelled at in baby talk, told how to eat, how to bathe, how to walk, how to talk. Like babies, their bodies are not their own. They are reduced to the "sucklings" that Victor Turner described in *The Ritual Process*.

The "suckling" imagery is used as well by SEMI cadets to subordinate. Classmates resist and insult each other and lowerclassmen with "You suck" or "Suck it in." Another tradition is called the Rape of the First Sentinel. When the first rat marches "guard detail," he is attacked by the seniors, who rip off parts of his clothing, spray him with shaving cream, and throw days-old food and used chewing tobacco on him. Said 1990's rat sentinel, "*It* sucked" (emphasis mine), successfully externalizing the "rape." His accosters reported, "Pretty good rat. He took it like a man" (*The Cadet* 1990).

Before "Break Out," some one-third of the entering class has left, either dropping out or not meeting the requirements. Those who remain have dissolved into the mass of "good rats ... low profile, subservient, doesn't stand out." This is the epitome of the highly valued "Rat Unity," a bonding and levelling said to be essential for survival. But each also has a special Rat Daddy or "dyke," a senior who serves as his mentor and advocate. The rat/aide helps his senior "dyke (deck) out" or dress, and previously, did "light fagging such as running a few errands," making the dyke's bed, shining his shoes. The rat receives advice and haven from his senior dyke, whom he has the privilege of visiting "informally" (Wise, 1978: 298).

LIMINALITY: BREAK OUT

Break Out is announced during the last month of winter. After morning classes end, the upperclassmen "resurrect" Rat discipline, and have one hour to "purge" themselves using the harsher measures. Juniors and sophomores taunt the Rats, while the seniors encourage them: "You'll make it." The Rats are marched to an auditorium where the senior class president tells them to do well, because after graduation, "all we leave behind is you." Then they run to Break Out field, on the "outskirts" (Nelson, 1993) of the campus, which the town's firetruck has sprayed to create a medium of mud.

The Rats crawl on their bellies through the mud some 50 yards to a first 10-foot high bank. As they crawl, upperclassmen of juniors and sophomores attack them, shout at them, push them to their bellies, sit on them, pull them back by their legs, fill their faces and clothes and "all orifices" with the mud. By the time the Rats reach the first bank, their eyes and ears are filled with mud, and they can barely grope their way along. Many Rats have lost their pants. They cannot tell who is friend, fellow rat or foe. At the base of the bank, they scramble over each other towards the top, but are pushed down by sophomores and juniors. Some Rats try to help each other in an effort at "Rat Unity"; however, it is largely their seniors who help them up. At the top of the first bank, the sophomores and juniors toss the Rats into a water ditch, pull them out and push them up another bank of brush.

INTEGRATION: DYKE TO DYKE

Only when they have gotten to the top of the second bank is the ordeal over. The seniors rush to greet them, tenderly wash the mud out of their eyes and ears, and wrap them in their own blankets. At this point, dykes embrace each other, take photos and pose for the professional video cameraman. The rats run back to the rear of barracks, where their dykes hose them down *en masse,* and give them dry clothes. According to my ca-

det informants, the moment when the seniors wash away the Rats' mud is their "incorporation" into the corps of cadets.

Several alumni and parents anxiously wait on the path returning from Break Out field, although they are urged not to attend. "Go get 'em, Killer!" shouts one. Upperclassmen lead them in cheers and exercise chants about impregnating local women. As night falls, the entire "corps of cadets" assembles in the barracks' courtyard. Each class gives their cheer, including the freshmen. They are no longer called Rats, except Brother Rat by classmates. They are "part of the SEMI *corps* of cadets," but not until graduation will they become "SEMI men."

ENGENDERINGS: MONSTROUS MOTHERS AND DYKE FATHERS

Break Out struck me as a birth from which the newborn emerges blinded and covered by birth fluids, to be cleaned up and blanketed. One observer commented how the rats in their belly-scramble across the mud field resemble the cartoon sperms in the old health class movies, competing to overcome the vagina's obstacles, penetrate the egg and conceive life. Given the metaphor of the ritual as birth rather than conception, one could almost see the ritual as a Super-birth, in which all the sperms have won and all the babies are born. The Super-birth has an accelerated gestation of seven months and delivery of one to two hours. In the Super-womb of SEMI (always referred to as "She"), the Super-foetuses are actively conditioned and will "labour" their way to their daddies, after "breaking the water" of the ditch.

Break Out also transforms the Ratline's gender benders in which the Rats are sterile, effeminate, and subordinate: babies, dyke "wives," and "passive" homosexuals. Immediately after their birth, they become virile, active, even "Killers," whose first feeding will be a special steak dinner from their Rat Daddies.

If the seniors are the fathers, who are the mothers? The mud identifies them: the juniors and sophomores who become one with the womb/field, as their bright yellow sweats become caked with the medium created by the phallic fire-engine spray that the seniors have arranged. I suggest that the Rat "line" symbolizes ties with mothers, or at SEMI, with the juniors and sophomores, who deliver most of the hazing. It is the umbilical cord connected to monstrous mothers, who rule over a childhood of rules one doesn't write, punishment one doesn't deserve, and a hierarchical enmeshment that one can't break.

The upperclassmen also use the imagery of rapists: sexual, sterile, but powerful. Ethnographers have documented how the threat of homosexual rape sets hierarchies in all-male settings like prisons and fraternities

(Sanday, 1990; Blake, 1971). But juniors and sophomores lose their power in Break Out, their ability like mothers or rapists to hold "the corps"/the body from manhood. They will only regain power by becoming "dykes" as seniors.

"Dyke" refers to SEMI's dress uniform, and to the rat himself. "A rat often takes on the traits of his dyke," (Wise, 1978). For Break Out, many rats shave into their buzz cuts their class year and the year of their senior dykes. The term "dyke," then, is a clear example of teknonymy,[1] in which the reciprocal term denotes how the Rat and the Senior create each other.

"It is the first classmen's most important relationship," stated a former Commandant of Students, "until they are married and have children of their own" (Wise, 1978). In fact, a senior told the SEMI counsellor that being a dyke "is like having my own child." "They feel a paternal instinct towards them," the counsellor concluded. In 1990, when a group of rats attacked a rival school's mascot at an off-campus football game and broke several spectators' bones, the senior class took full responsibility like parents for minor children (*The Cadet*, 1990).

The parenting may be paternity, but it is also ambiguous. Rat Daddy is in fact "a *combination* of your mother, father, and older brother" (*The Bullet*, 1990). The Rat Daddies' role in Break Out is both the doctor's work of delivery, and the nurses' "dirty" work of washing and eventually feeding the newborn (Ortner, 1974).

The role's ambiguity is highlighted by the term, "dyke," which since the 1920s commonly refers to homosexual women (Mills, 1989). In fact, this current usage may derive from the military term, and the domestic nature of the military officer's aide. One may argue that the word doesn't carry the modern—and negative—connotation within SEMI's tradition-laden world of meanings. But a "dyke" may also be seen as someone who can bear and nurture children, participates in same-sex relations, and does not have subordinate or subordinating sexual relations with men.

Perhaps the seniors are best seen as "dyke midwives" in the ritual, mediating between the transforming three parallel series of sexual roles: infant/mother/father; cocksucker/homosexual rapist/dyke; wife/mother/midwife. The dyke midwife is the powerful mediating point, who creates "mothers" out of wives, and their own redeeming "dyke" paternity. SEMI cadets "matriculate" into wifehood and motherhood and graduate into 'SEMI manhood' and grandpaternity.

RITUAL REPRODUCTION AND UNILINEAL DESCENT

The question still remains: why can't women attend SEMI? SEMI does socialize its cadets to be "gentlemen" with explicit instructions on how to treat "ladies." Cadets are taught to set women apart, rather than to mentor, lead or work with women. This paternalism infuriates those who view SEMI as a patriarchal institution. In fact, given SEMI's emphasis on creating mentors out of teen-agers, women might do quite well, given their head start in relational skills.

The most informative statement was from the thoughtful cadet who stopped telling me what women could or couldn't endure and said simply "*I could never do 'it'* [the hazing?] *to a woman.*" At SEMI, a "gentleman does not so much as lay a finger on a lady," states the Rat Bible. Instead, SEMI's procreation is monosexual, establishing a patrilineal descent kinline through an inversion of childbirth, in which the foetus and father can take control of the generating body. Women are peripheral to SEMI and have no maternal rights, although they are necessary to establish the cadets' heterosexuality. In Ring Figure, the formal dance when the juniors receive their class rings, the cadets and their dates (no one attends "stag," alone) create the "figure" of their class year on the dance floor.

I propose that the fight is not over keeping women out of men's domains; there *is* a "woman" (in fact several) in SEMI's body/corps (cf. Martin, 1987) and rituals. SEMI has created a unilineal descent system of fictitious kin through its alliance with the state. But now SEMI's men are fighting for their reproductive rights and family welfare, even after being turned down by the Supreme Court in 1993. In an interesting twist, SEMI and the old boys have joined the pro-choice battle.

NOTE

1. Teknonymy: the custom of identifying a person with a name which marks him/her as parent of a child.

REFERENCES

Allen, Michael. 1967. *Male Cults and Secret Initiations in Melanesia.* Melbourne: Melbourne U.P.
Bettelheim, Bruno. 1954. *Symbolic Wounds: Puberty Rites and the Envious Male.* New York: Collier.
Blake, James. 1971. *The Joint.* New York: Doubleday.
Bly, Robert. 1990. *Iron John. A Book about Men.* Reading, MA: Addison-Wesley.
The Bullet. 1989. "South East Military Institute."
Goodman, Ellen. 1991. *Washington Post* 22 June.
Herdt, Gilbert H. (Ed.). 1982. *Rituals of Manhood: Male Initiation in Papua New Guinea.* Berkeley: University of California Press.
Kiser, Judge Jackson L. 1991. 17 June decision.
Martin, Emily. 1987. *The Woman in the Body: A Cultural Analysis of Reproduction.* Boston: Beacon Press.
Mills, Jane. 1989. *Womanwords: A Dictionary of Words about Women.* New York: Free Press.
Murphy, Robert F. 1959. "Social structure and sex antagonism." *Southwestern Journal of Anthropology* Vol. 15, No. 2, 89–98.
Nelson, Diane. 1993. "Rigoberta Menchu Jokes." Paper presented at 13th International Congress of Anthropological and Ethnological Sciences, Mexico City.

Ortner, Sherry. 1974. "Is Female to Male as Nature is to Culture?" in *Woman, Culture and Society*, ed. by M. Z. Rosaldo & L. Lamphere. Stanford, CA: Stanford University Press.

Sanday, Peggy Reeves. 1990. *Fraternity Gang Rape: Sex, Brotherhood, and Privilege on Campus*. New York: New York University Press.

Turner, Victor. 1969. *The Ritual Process*. Chicago: Aldine.

Van Gennep, Arnold. 1909 (1960). *The Rites of Passage*. Chicago: Chicago University Press.

Whiting, John et al. 1967. "The Function of Male Initiation Ceremonies at Puberty," in *Personality and Social Life*. ed. by R. Endelman. New York: Random House.

Wise, Henry A. 1978. *Drawing Out the Man*. Charlottesville: U. of Virginia.

Yoder, Edwin. 1991. *Washington Post*, 22 June.

Advertised Self in Obituaries and Congratulations in Some Nigerian Dailies

Olatunde Bayo Lawuyi

Olatunde Bayo Lawuyi received his Ph.D. in anthropology from the University of Illinois in 1985. He is now senior lecturer in social anthropology in the Department of General Studies at Oyo State University of Technology, Ogobomoso, Nigeria.

A conspicuous feature of the Nigerian dailies is the obituary[1] and congratulation advertisements. These advertisements, which altogether often take up more than a page, are considered to be among the less serious, less substantial and less important features of the dailies. Nevertheless, the advertisements—especially in papers with a wide circulation—appear to arouse considerable interest among the reading public. Some readers regard them, especially the obituaries, as "obnoxious" (Saro-Wiwa, 1990), as "junk journalism" (Abu, 1990) befitting a depraved society, as a form of communication (Obijiofor, 1989) or as money-making business (Dare, 1985a). These criticisms are related, no doubt, to the fact that the advertisements enter into popular culture as forms which relate the advertised with their socio-political community: specifically with its biography and personages and with its present social relations and members (Lawuyi, 1990).

The biographical approach helps to elucidate the complex ways by which self-definitions can be "translated" into public professional influence (Ben-Ari, 1987). But then it also dovetails into a larger framework of ceremonial and symbolism that pervades the lives of the elite in all sorts of situations meant to create or augment their status (Cohen, 1976; 1981). The ceremonial includes funeral ceremonies, chieftaincy title conferment festivities, and social parties where praise-music is played. These contexts are characterised by their special style of life (accent, dress, manners, patterns of friendship, exclusive gathering, and ideology) and by their symbols, which are either traditional but not popular, or popular but not traditional (Barber, 1987).

The identification with traditional symbols of status is not so much because the elite accept their values

(Aluko, 1970; Achebe, 1966) as because they conceive of them as an adaptive, utilitarian tool in the mobilisation of support for their role. As Barber (1987) argued, the most important attribute of traditional symbols is not the power to communicate but the power to locate the elite within a specific social universe which is the ground of existence. Such symbols as are adopted therefore tend to be conservative, escapist or merely vacuous; "and in this way they work against the real interests of the people, accepting and reinforcing the values that maintain the *status quo*. They are instruments of ruling class hegemony in the Gramscian sense" (Barber, 1987: 7).

The expression "hegemony" means that the ruling class has shared values. But these values are not constant, they shift; each hegemony has a unique character of its own, and the process of making historical sense of them is inevitably hazardous—especially since we are dealing with vacuous symbols. If we wish then to approach the problem in a historical/anthropological fashion, "we have to identify processes that exemplify paradigm—transcendence, trains of events that open closed universes of meaning and make them comparable and accessible to each other" (Larsen, 1987: 4).

This article is concerned with the analysis of elite culture and the way it articulates the particular and the universal within an heterogeneous, stratified and dynamic system. The focus is on elite values in obituary and congratulation advertisements in the *Daily Times* (Lagos) and *Daily Sketch* (Ibadan), but careful consideration has been given to other newspapers. A remarkably similar pattern of publication is found nationally within Nigeria and regionally along the West African coast. Even elite residents abroad, with limited access to their national dailies, patronise regional publications like *West Africa* to advertise their concerns, interests and achievements. The accent is on the personal and institutional processes involved in the creation and

"Advertised Self in Obituaries and Congratulations in Some Nigerian Dailies" by Olatunde Bayo Lawuyi, from *Africa,* Vol. 61, No. 2, 1991. Reprinted with permission.

maintenance of communities: for instance, career making, mobilisation of resources and personnel, and interaction of personalities. The thesis is that the obituary and congratulation advertisements are not only about power but are also attributes of status. Specifically, the power order and the economic order that inform their construction form a dialectic the essential manifestation of which is selfhood (Cohen, 1976). This selfhood, as a social construct, brings out not only the public nature of success, but also how it may be altered to define a new situation or status.

The analysis that follows is based on the examination of copies of the *Daily Times* (and *Sunday Times*) and the *Daily Sketch* (and *Sunday Sketch*), published since 1966 and stored, in the library of Obafemi Awolowo University—itself established in 1962. In addition, various interviews were conducted with the business managers of the *Daily Sketch* and the Broadcasting Corporation of Oyo State, with the *Guardian* (Lagos) and *Daily Times* correspondents in Ile-Ife, and with the newspaper vendors and advertisement agents in Ile-Ife. The interviews were conducted at various times between February 1989 and March 1990 on various issues which ranged from the history of the Nigerian press and the media's marketing strategy to public opinions about the publications. Still on public opinion, I conducted a survey of the "social marketing of the dead" by selecting three biographies of the deceased written in their "Order of Funeral Service"[2] for an analysis of how attitudes to criteria of success vary among the Yoruba according to religion, social origin and sex. The three biographies were selected on account of their "shortness," so that the respondent should not be subjected to a long essay that could be construed as a waste of time and hence discourage a positive response. Each of the three biographies was selected from the categories of (1) the uneducated, (2) public school teachers and (3) university lecturers. The only category left out in my collection of thirty "Orders of Funeral Services' is that of the businessmen and women—their write-ups are usually long.[3] The survey was administered to fifty lecturers who are Yoruba on the campus of Obafemi Awolowo University. The sample size was stratified by religion, urban/rural roots and sex. The survey was self-administered. The individual respondents were to identify significant events in each of the deceaseds' lives, to rate the events in the order they considered them significant, and to mention aspects which they thought were missing in the biographies but ought to be emphasised.

The analysis is organised in four sections: (1) an historical survey highlighting the evolution of marketing strategies; (2) a section on the structure of the obituary publications, highlighting career paths and social network; (3) a focus on the similarities and differences in obituary and congratulation publications, so as to present a consensual framework on the elite construction of selfhood, especially as mediated by forms of economic and political development; (4) the mode of celebrating the successes which inform the selfhood construction.

It would be difficult to appreciate the death symbolism, which is the central focus of attention, without understanding the emergence of modern individualistic morality and the new cultural premises that have resulted. Hence the attention paid to the merchant culture.

THE PRESS AND THE MERCANTILE CULTURE

The first newspapers in Nigeria were established in the 1850s and '60s. The aim was to increase the level of literacy; the emphasis was on literary content, politics was secondary. The early newspapers patterned their contents and style after the Sierra Leonean and Gold Coast (Ghana) papers, which were themselves products of British commercial influence. The *Sierra Leone Gazette*, published in Freetown during the first quarter of the nineteenth century, probably blazed the trail for others to follow. The decisive factor was to promote competence in the English language, though, in later years, the understanding of English was to serve the evangelical missions of the European Christian missionaries (Omu, 1978).

The foreign papers had obvious attractions for Nigerian readers. One was the increasing consciousness of the value of Western education. Another was the opportunities for trade and employment which the newspapers provided by their advertisements. Quite often jobs in Lagos were advertised in these foreign papers and the recruitment that followed provided incentives for the educated Nigerians of the diaspora to come to Lagos and exploit the opportunities for upward mobility and wealth. So great was the attraction of homecoming that Fred Omu noted:

> The trade of Lagos was characterised by what a newspaper was to call "suicidal competition among merchants." Business establishments which had begun to grow from the 1850s now proliferated and, in the absence of local newspapers, a few of these advertised their wares in the London-based *African Times*. The importance of the commercial situation lies not only in the fact that it stimulated further emigration but also because it heightened the demand for the type of news (shipping intelligence and market conditions, for example) that had fostered newspapers in England and other European countries. [1978: 22]

The advertisements made references to skills, education and experience. While these references do not essentially define success, they nevertheless enter into public discourse and arts as symbolic complexes which underlie and structure people's intellectual, academic and social careers. With their introduction the old and new symbols met, each competing for the attention of the public. The colonial intervention in local history, for instance, succeeded in transforming such symbols as education, Western dress, professional identity and property development into characteristics of the elite. But the Islamic and Christian interventions gave rise to symbols which include refinement of decorum, conspicuous piety, sympathy for the poor, and self-construction for job opportunities. These symbols mirror status differences, and found their way into the press in various modes of publication and advertisement.

How much revenue the early newspapers realised from advertisements is difficult to learn, as most publishers were reluctant to disclose the information (Omu, 1978). But Omu's work suggests that advertisements featured less prominently in the newspapers between 1880 and 1920. Many of the papers survived on the competence and managerial ability of their editors, on their political appeal, on the capital outlay of the publishers or on official patronage by local administrators. The *Nigerian Daily Times*, for example, survived through its ability to present a strong, healthy and vigorous public opinion (Omu, 1978: 61). But it had the advantage of being a "foreign capital supported daily" (Omu, 1978: 63). The *Nigerian Daily Times* had a virtual monopoly of European commercial advertising, and the revenue strengthened its ability to attract experienced technical staff who introduced popular techniques of presentation and general improvements in typography and distribution (Omu, 1978). All these enabled it to achieve a wide appeal and to undergo a process of expansion at a time when other papers were folding.

Between 1923 and 1930 no newspaper realised as much as £500 from sales. Quite a number depended on subscribers who often did not pay their dues, and on advertisers. The newspapers were forced to depend more on advertisers because, while they openly scolded subscribers for not paying (Omu, 1978), they could at least insist that advertisers should pay in advance. The space given over to advertisements fluctuated between 50 and 70 per cent of the type area of the newspapers. Indeed, in the 1920s some papers even averaged between 90 and 99 per cent. Very little portion of the advertisement pages was taken up by obituary or congratulation messages; most of them were on merchandise, household provisions and luxury goods, news of ships' movements and the activities of local administrators. Notable patrons were Paterson Zochonis, Pickering & Berthhould and Miller Brothers.

The proceeds from advertisements were still quite small. By the 1940s, conscious of the slow development of indigenous advertising, the press threw in a little

bait to raise the revenue base (Dare, 1985b). Some introduced the cheap, but well patronised, classified advertisements common in British tabloids which rarely extended for more than a page or two and were charged per word. They were usually without the photographs of the advertised product. Others appealed to national sentiment which had built up since the nationalist movements began in the 1920s and consequently led to the birth of such politically motivated papers as the *West African Pilot* in 1939 and the *Nigerian Tribune* in 1949. In the attempt to broaden their revenue base the papers gave much space to personality profiles. In addition, obituaries took a more picturesque form with the display of passport size or full-length photographs indicating wealth (by dress and size of publication) and power (by insignia of the office the deceased held). The patrons were the civil servants, the private medical doctors and the businessmen.

The 1950s and '60s witnessed the establishment of many government newspapers such as the *Nigerian Outlook* (1960), *Morning Post* and *Sunday Post* (1961), *Daily Sketch* (1964) and *New Nigerian* (1966). It was an era that also saw the introduction of radio and television into the community (Dare, 1985b). Those who dominated the media advertisements were the government officials and the politicians canvassing for electoral support or haranguing the people to demonstrate their backing for ethno-regional interests and development. It was clear that:

> not only does the ruling elite make the news, it is the news—as endless verbatim reports of politicians' speeches, accounts of elite weddings and birthday parties, and the pages and pages of expensive obituaries testify. And if the poor are invisible, the very poor are a downright nuisance—some regimes have treated them literally as rubbish. [Barber, 1987: 3]

Governments, through their political activities and actors, were the major financiers of the papers, radio and television into the 1970s and early '80s. The patrons of advertisements widened, though, with the oil boom of the 1970s and the upward mobility fostered by it. By the late '80s, however, the total expenditure approved by the authorities for their papers and radio had taken a downward turn owing to a slump in the price of oil. The total expenditure for Federal Radio Corporation of Nigeria (FRCN) for 1988, for instance, was N13,147,392 as against N33,400,368 in the previous year. In 1986 the amount had been N51,182,056. "Without commercialisation and with the dwindling funding we are getting from the government," said Saka Fagbo, the director of commercials at Nigerian Television Authority (NTA), "we would have gone under" (*Newswatch*, 1989: 46). As of 1989 the FRCN had achieved 100 per cent of its targeted commercial activities, while the Broadcasting Corporation of Oyo State

(BCOS) raised its revenue from a little over a million naira in 1988 to over 4 million naira in 1989.[4]

It is difficult to determine how much the Obituaries and Congratulations contributed to the companies' profits, since the authorities are unwilling to give the information.[5] But it is clear that the two advertisement forms represent a large chunk of the revenue. Most of the media (including the ones mentioned above) solicit congratulation messages and In Memoriams of famous people. They do so through their field agents, who receive a commission of between 5 and 15 per cent of sales, depending on the level of technical production involved, the nature of the advertised products (as shop windows or coverage of ceremony) and the variety of advertisements the agency can handle.[6] The rivalry also involves discounts on "group messages" especially for celebrated personalities on their installation as community heads or chiefs, on the award of honorary degrees at local and foreign universities, and on their birthdays. The discounts extend to paid advertisements to welcome the President, the governor of the state, or his officials, when on a visit to communities.

Generally, as in many cultures, it is felt to be somewhat distasteful to solicit obituaries. Yet "if you raise the price of obituary advertisements three-fold, there would always be takers" (Saro-Wiwa, 1990: 7). The patrons are the elite and they are served by a press unwilling to promote the sale of cadavers but nevertheless interested in advertising the achievements of the elite. The restrictions the media place on any advertisement depend upon the target audience. For instance, the *Concord* newspapers would not publish any advertisements of alcohol, since the religion of the publisher, a Muslim, forbids the sale of alcohol. Similarly, the *Guardian* newspaper once refused to publish any obituary advertisements. But by April 1989 the policy had changed as attempts were made to broaden the revenue base.[7] The company has since published obituaries of the wife of Professor A. E. Afigbo and of the wife of the proprietor, Chief M. Ibru. The focus is on the elite, in a paper that now says with pride that it is "the medium for Nigeria's top consumers, for the affluent and the influential, for the decision makers and opinion leaders, for those who value quality, and who spend money on themselves, families and homes" (*Guardian*, 11 November 1989: 4).

All papers in Nigeria now advertise the elite through their dead ones. In an attempt at calculating the revenue such publications could have yielded for the *Daily Times* and *Daily Sketch* in 1989, I noticed that the *Times* published an average of seven obituaries daily (ranging between four and ten) while the *Sketch* published an average of two obituaries (ranging between one and four). Of those published, there were more quarter-page advertisements than full-page or half-page ones in the two papers.[8] Most of the patrons

were members of the business community and professional people. Generally, the *Times* had more full-page advertisements than the *Sketch*; in fact the full-page advertisements came to nearly a third of the total number published daily.

Between 1989 and January 1990 the *Daily Times* increased its charges by 10-20 per cent, while the *Sketch*'s charges rose by 10-15 per cent. I calculated that, on the basis of the total publications for the month of December 1989, the *Daily Times* achieved a revenue of not less than N750,000, while the *Sketch*'s total collection would amount to not less than N100,000. Further estimates for November 1989 and January 1990 (when the price rose) indicate that December 1989 brought in about 10 per cent less than November, but about 13 per cent more than January (i.e., apart from increase in price, there were more notices published). The margin of error would be plus or minus 5 per cent.

Radio and television are also involved in the business of marketing the elite. Their prices differ greatly for obituaries and congratulations, being much lower than those in the print media. The Broadcasting Corporation of Oyo State charges N30.00 for a radio announcement, N50.00 for a television announcement without a picture, and N60.00 for a television announcement with picture.[9] Generally, the various media tap the sentiments and financial abilities of various categories of people. The very wealthy patronise all the media. Those of middling income go for the use of the radio and the television. Those less well-off still patronise the radio mostly. Clientage differs because, firstly, the audio-visual media air their announcements within a few hours of the time the notices are put in. In contrast, most papers would require at least two weeks' notice. As a result the poor, who cannot afford mortuary costs for two weeks, or the Muslims, who are enjoined to bury their dead quickly, cannot use the print media. Secondly, the audio-visual media can be listened to or viewed by the illiterates, since some of the personal-paid announcements are in local, indigenous, languages. Thirdly, apart from their cheap prices, the audio messages do reach all the nooks and crannies of the nation.

The point, however, is not about obituaries and congratulations as documents contrived to portray wealth or somehow to order the complex reality in which Nigerians live and to give meaning to their lives. Rather, I suggest that an understanding of these publications entails taking into account a cultural context of commercial development and the definition of success.

THE STRUCTURE OF OBITUARY PUBLICATIONS

The obituaries are of two types: the "Obituary/Transition" released immediately after death and clearly similar to the "Notices" often pasted on house walls and electricity poles in rural and urban centres, and the "In Memoriam" which commemorates the duration of transition. The "In Memoriam" is reckoned in days, months or years and, with it, we examine textual phenomena as constitutive of social action (Mulkay, 1984: 547; Ben-Ari, 1987: 66), i.e., as reflexive of how people organise the social and cultural orders of their experience. An obituary goes thus:[10]

With great feelings of loss but in total
submission to the will of God, we announce
the transition into immortality of a
wonderful sister and mother

Mary Scott
which event occurred on Thursday—
28th December, 1989
Burial Arrangements
Funeral Mass at St. Dominic's Catholic Church, Yaba
at 12.00 on Friday, 05 January, 1990
Interment at Ikoyi Cemetery immediately after.
May Her Gentle Soul Rest In Peace
John A. V. Scott
for the family

[*Daily Times*, 3 January 1990: 19]

Contrast this with an In Memoriam which appeared in the same publication and on the same page:

In evergreen memory of our late
Father and Grandfather
Chief Amose Olatumbi Bamtefa
(The Baba Ijo of St. Peter's Anglican Church,
Sonyindo Sagamu)
who rested in the Lord on 3rd January, 1989
"To live in the hearts of those whom we love is never
to die"

Our most sincere appreciation goes to:
The Bishop of Remo Diocese, Chief (Mrs.)
H. I. D. Awolowo, Iya Ijo St. Saviour Church,
Ikenne, Chief (Mrs.) T. Ogunlesi, Iya Ijo
St. Paul's Church, Sagamu; Archdeacon Sewo,
Archdeacon Adewale, Canon Dr. & Mrs. Odumuyiwa
and the numerous well-wishers whose names we
cannot all possibly mention here for their
support and kindness during the funeral ceremony.
We thank you all
By Children and Grandchildren

[*Daily Times*, 3 January 1990: 19]

In the In Memoriam the writers allude to sources of support during bereavement and express their appreciation; they also convey their feelings on the role of the deceased in the development of self or collective

maturity. There is, in addition, a photograph of the deceased and an indication of his social status as Baba Ijo (father of the congregation). As the day the deceased died is mentioned, we are thus afforded a glimpse of the mourning period. Elsewhere I have estimated that the mourning can last over fifty years (Lawuyi, 1988).

An "appreciation section" features In Memoriams published a year after death. All In Memoriams have a list of survivors or bereaved; some even mention their qualifications and place of residence. There is a hint of the genealogical link with the dead—as son, daughter, nephew, cousin, etc. The line-up is indicative of seniority in the family structure. Thus even the deceased children of the deceased are not ignored; they are listed and assigned a proper rank. As an example of the list of survivors, the following children appeared as the bereaved of Mrs. Christiana Omoge Akagbosu:

Chief (Dr.) Joseph T. Akagbosu—(Son), Chairman/
Managing Director
Mr. Casimir T. Akagbosu—(Son), Commissioner of
Police, Benin State Command
Mr. Paul T. Akagbosu—(Son), Sales Manager,
Leventis Motors, Lagos

[*Daily Times*, 6 February 1986: 9]

The identification of surviving kin and their status is not uncommon for the relative ranking of the deceased's status within the community, especially among his peers. It is also important in order to establish the right of inheritance in situations where the deceased could possibly have begotten "illegal" children (e.g. those born by concubines). However, the practice of identifying kin and rank is much more common with the Bendelites and the Igbo than with the Yoruba. It is suggested that the Yoruba's overriding concern with malevolent forces, or *aye*, could have inhibited similar self expression.[11]

Within the obituary, attention is paid to such criteria of identity as the sex, age and place of birth of the deceased. These criteria are linked with references to a "career path," to the trajectory of self-promotion programmes which originate in a certain community and ethnic group and traverse various institutions of training and career development.

The criteria are distinct from, yet are linked to, the "appreciation" directed towards the elite by those below them: chiefs, military governors, politicians, academics, diplomats, service chiefs, bishops, etc. Mentioning these people clearly has to do with activities which underlie and structure the deceased's career. The elite career, heavily laced with opportunities for mobility and resource allocation and appropriation, consists of an inventory of roles which individuals have built up over time and is expressed in a small, but significant, reference to the emotions of those involved:

Your 1/6d [15k] school fees loan to your needy pupil in 1935 has already yielded abundant dividends from which many scholars today draw knowledge.

[*Daily Times*, 17 January 1986: 15]

Or:

Babe-Oke, we are grateful for the legacy of a good name, good education, exemplary upbringing and proud family tradition you have left for us; the imperishable services you gave to your community in inspiring the education of children and your generous disposition not only to your family, the less privileged within your community but also all those whose paths crossed yours!!

[*Daily Times*, 9 January 1990: 14]

In these descriptions of a "career" the individual is shown as having tried as much as possible to educate himself, his family and acquaintances. Within this career path role performance shifts from parenthood, community leadership or professional expertise to membership of religious organisations. The institutions to which the individuals are linked provide the recruitment area for their social networks. Hence for one who attended St. Peter's Anglican Church, Sonyindo, most of his friends had to come from his church, from Sagamu or from the Ijebu Yoruba (since Sonyindo is an Ijebu community). Similarly, for someone who served as director general of the department of local government in the military governor's office, Lagos State, the social network is urban in character:

In particular we will remain forever indebted to His Excellency, Colonel Raji Rasaki the military governor of Lagos State; the entire members of the Lagos State Executive Council; the Honourable Commissioners of Lagos State; his former colleagues the Director-General of the various ministries and departments in Lagos State . . .

[*Daily Times*, 6 January 1990: 17]

The individual as director general, as religious leader, as school principal or as army officer, would, while alive, have served in capacities in which he/she helped to recruit, to pay for and to contribute to the advancement of opportunities and jobs of others. Several roles do, of course, coexist in his/her network so that operationally emphasis must be placed on the institutional settings in which the network originated and was maintained.

Yet, even then, the individual's career on the one hand and the characteristic, both morphological and interactional, of the social network on the other are also related to obligations stemming from services previously rendered to the individual by his friends, relations and professional colleagues. In essence a multi-stranded network usually prevails, especially in a situation where the individual has enough room to manipulate the rules

and situations to draw to himself a coterie of friends who could benefit from the manipulation. One then finds that a multi-stranded network is more distinctive of urbanites, and of public/private office holders, in contexts in which power relations are relatively unequal. In contrast, single-stranded networks characterise the relations of those without important public/private offices and who are rurally based: here, unlike in the urban centres, the individual is not involved in a loose-knit network organised by different ethnic, professional and national groups. He is intimately bounded to rurally oriented loyalties and quite often those mentioned in the advertisement would be from the same rural background.

COMPARISON WITH THE CONGRATULATION PUBLICATIONS

But why publish congratulations? The answer lies in precisely the same thrust which motivates the publication of obituaries. In both attention is drawn to the achievements of a single individual with whom the writers identify. The preface to both texts begins with an "I," a "We" or a "The." For instance:

The Chairman, Board of Directors and entire Staff of Jacco Pharmacy International Limited heartily rejoice with . . .

[*Daily Sketch*, 19 March 1988: 14]

"The" projects a collective identity and so differs from "I":

I, Architect J. A. Agunbiade On Behalf Of My Colleagues . . .

[*Daily Sketch*, 5 March 1988: 13]

In dealing with the relationships constituted by the obituary or congratulation we should stress that the exercise of power by some people over others enters into all of them, on all levels. Certain economic and political relationships are crucial in that no matter what other functions the publication may perform, it must acknowledge the organisation of knowledge in a social unit, and then lead the reader to an uncomplicated appreciation of the social reality of debt and gratitude. This means that all interpersonal and intergroup relations projected in the publications must at some point conform to the dictates of economic or political power. Let it be said, however, that these dictates of power are but aspects of group relationships, mediated in this case through the forms of an economic or political organ.

Indeed, the congratulation advertisement merely expands on the economic process, on man and the relatively scarce resources available to him (Cohen, 1976: 22). It is about patronage, about economic power ultimately maintained by reward and deprivation. The advertisement celebrates a birthday (*Daily Times*, 8 January 1990: 23), the opening of a new business centre (*Daily Sketch*, 19 March 1988: 14), the conferment of a chieftaincy title (*Daily Times*, 24 January 1990: 11) or the receipt of an honorary degree (*Daily Times*, 13 January 1990: 19), to mention a few. In securing people's attention the writers focus on control of crucial resources and on those that exercise control, as well as on service to the nation, community or group. In one instance, it is appropriate to wish the celebrant:

> more success in (his) contribution to the Pharmaceutical Industries in Nigeria and more years of service to the nation's health care system.
>
> [*Daily Sketch*, 19 March 1988: 14]

In another instance the celebrant is wished more contributions to national development:

> National Oil joins his (Major-General Hassan Usman Katsina's) admirers, family and friends in wishing him many more years of meaningful contribution to the development of one Great Nation.
>
> [*Daily Times*, 20 January 1990: 4]

While undoubtedly underscoring a patronage relationship, the congratulation text, like that of the obituary, is heavily dependent on the social context in which men's ideas seek paradigmatic status (Darnell, 1971: 101, Ben-Ari, 1987: 67). Hence the promotion of the person of the advertiser and his business is not uncommon. This may be viewed as a strategy for gaining attention.

> The Board, Management and Staff of
> Globe Motors (Nig.) Limited
> Rejoice with a bosom friend
> Mr. Ime S. Umanah
> On the award of an honorary doctorate degree
> of Laws by the University of Calabar,
> On the 13th of October, 1990
> An apt acknowledgement of
> your humble contributions
> to finance and industry.
> We are proud to be associated
> With you.
>
> [*Daily Times*, 13 January 1990: 19]

With the logo of the firm,[12] the address of the advertiser's place of business and the acknowledgement of a social debt the congratulation is used to improve the advertiser's economic chances. Usually an invitation goes to the reader to patronise the advertised and the advertiser's business. The strategy is one of using a stone to kill two birds: you praise, flatter, advertise your important client or boss, and improve your business or status as a result. Two things here are all-important: the first is that a person is not absolutely an individual. He is a means to an end. He is a "you" in a framework in which the "I," "We," "The" that mark the beginning of the texts are interchangeable and designate consuming interest. The second is that the "you" circle of society (however widely or narrowly this phrase may be understood) is a sort of loosely compacted person. Therefore, there are varied references to it in forms of age, place of birth, network of friends, and family structure and roles. This portrait of the self (as a flexible one) appear ideally suited to those who seek power and recognition outside their local communities in that they must learn to operate in an arena of continuously changing friendships and alliances, which form and dissolve in competition for scarce resources. This boils down to the fact that, as in obituaries, the individual must learn to function in a complex society by judicious manipulation of social ties and resources.

THE SYMBOLISM OF SUCCESS

The individuals who are able to operate both in terms of community-oriented and economically oriented expectations then tend to be selected out for mobility. They become the economic and political "brokers" of group-community relations: a function which carries its own reward within the merchant culture as increased publicity. The publicity is a delicate index of attitude, as the nature and style can reveal an underlying ideological orientation or significant changes.

So, how does death come into the picture? Ordinarily, death is not passed off as an achievement, as a success. But it nevertheless is one. In Nigeria it has become a more visible feature of social life when elevated in a burial ceremony or as an anniversary. A constellation of factors has produced this visibility. First, the political upheavals which marked the end of the First Republic in 1966 and involved arson, thuggery, mass destruction of life and property. These portrayed death as a symbol of power, as a victory for the destroyer (Achebe, 1966). Both the government and the opposition forces needed this power to legitimate their claims of superiority. They saw death not as a unifying symbol but as an expression of struggle either against injustice, inequality and exploitation or against lawlessness, unbridled ambition and arrogance. Death within this scheme was seen in terms not of self-completion or of the creation of symbolic immortality (as is critically bound into the way of dying in Japan: Litton, 1979). The deaths did not create a community of national heroes/heroines (Settar, 1989). Rather, the social response to these politically motivated deaths tends to imply that people see living/dying as a dynamic process characterised by competition (Togonu-Bickersteth, 1986).

Second, by the time of the oil boom, inequality within society had become distorted. The elite class had widened so rapidly and haphazardly that the symbolic line between rich and poor became blurred (Barber, 1987). There were more vehicles on the road and gradations within commercial culture were manifested in type of private vehicle and driving style, as well as in the profit motive. Careless driving, uncontrolled consumption of alcohol, speeding, and lack of expansion and maintenance of the transport routes caused accidents (Falola and Olanrewaju, 1986). On the roads were (and still are) damaged vehicles, burnt-out chassis, and lying as litter the bodies of men and animals. The universe of which driving is a part joins that of dynamism and power in being rooted in new-found wealth and guided by competition.

There is a third point. While occasions of death do provoke, in some instances, a sober mood, they are also in other instances the context for the celebration of success and competition. They create a joyful mood because the rites that follow exhibit structural features, symbolic motifs and performative patterns that recur in the same way that politicians celebrate their success over the opposition; i.e., the intention is to consume all that one had or use the celebration to demonstrate what one is not by adopting styles which contrast with everyday experience.

The demonstration of success may not, of course, be commonly shared within the heterogeneous, fluctuating conglomeration of ethnic, religious and class groups that make up Nigerian society but it is nevertheless linked with the world market economy to which every group is obliged to respond. Several objects used at burial ceremonies are thus the insignia of civic and political notables. These include garments or ornaments, the rare or laboriously produced materials of which symbolically distinguish the elite from the poor, the person of higher from those of lower rank or accomplishments. Among the Yoruba, these include expensive *aso oke*, lace materials and costly items of food and drink. Among the Igbo a Western-tailored suit shows class. With the Hausa-Fulani the individual is expensively dressed in "Babbarriga." In some ceremonies the entire family or a group of friends may even choose to wear the same colour and dress. But then there are subtle distinctions which mark status—for example, one type of lace material is cheaper than another. The symbolism of solidarity and independence (and, presumably, of dominance

and hostility as well) between social ranks pervades the entire ceremony, even in the manner of conspicuous consumption. For food and drink are supplied in accordance with status and even here the rank of the receivers as well as that of the givers is granted recognition according to a minutely scrutinised order of precedence.

The obituary publications serve the useful purpose of calling people to such a "potlach." The specificity as well as generality of the response to the invitation is not only economically motivated (making it more apt for the merchant culture and its capacity to transmit messages and values across geographical, ethnic and even national boundaries) but also cultural.

The publicity given to the list of survivors, to the age of the deceased and to his/her social status accords well with the traditional Yoruba criteria of success which, according to Akiwowo (1983: 13–14), include: *ire aiku* (the value of good health till old age), *ire owo* (financial security) or *ire oko-aya*, the value of intimate companionship and love (*ire ife*), *ire o'mo'* (the value of parenthood) and *ire abori o'ta* (the value of assured self-actualisation). The same publicity taps into the Igbo emphasis on individuality, achievement and status. A successful man in Igbo society is identified by the number of his children and wives, his social titles, his knowledge of other places, and the property he has accumulated (Uchendu, 1965). In addition, the publications convey values that are not in conflict with the Christian symbols of success, education, status mobility and professionalism. Most southern Nigerian Christians of the middle and upper classes, therefore, patronise them.

But while the northern Christians from Kwara, Benue, Plateau, Kaduna and Kaduna States also advertise the dead, their Muslim friends may not. Their objections touch on many factors, including *Mutumin Kirkii*, the concept of the good man (Kirk-Greene, 1974). Firstly, a *Mutumin Kirkii* highlights the outward civilities of human relations (patience, propriety, generosity, respect) of a kind not projected in the obituary or congratulation publications. Secondly, as Muslims bury their dead rather quickly, their demands for publication space cannot be sufficiently rapidly met. Thirdly, some Muslims would object to reproducing images of living or dead persons.

Essentially, variations do exist in ethno-regional attitudes to the publications. But there are also intra- and inter-group objections. Survey samples indicate that variations exist within the middle-class university community along lines of religion, social root and sex. This is because each group emphasises different criteria of success: the Christians focus on educational attainment (70 per cent of the sample, n = 20), and the Muslims on service to the community (60 per cent of the sample, n = 10). Those raised in urban centres highlight the fact that the obituaries serve as an inspiration to others (55 per cent of the sample, n = 30), while a considerably smaller number of those born in a rural community (40 per cent of the sample, n = 20) agree that it has inspirational value. More males (72 per cent) than females (65 per cent) think that such publications speak to success. Indeed, the females who were interviewed generally considered the obituary vulgar. Their opinion merges with that of Saro-Wiwa (1990), who actually believes that a paper should sell on the strength of its news coverage, its features, the quality of its editorial and the breadth and depth of coverage of social problems.

There is a general tendency among the educated to lay emphasis on the social responsibility theory of the press, assuming that the elite should not rule but serve. Their views of what the press should be are well summarised by Peterson (1979: 74), who has articulated the following features of the social responsibility theory: (1) service the political system by providing information, discussion and debate on public affairs; (2) enlighten the public so as to make it capable of self-government; (3) safeguard the rights of the individual by serving as a watchdog against government; (4) service the economic system, primarily by bringing together buyers and sellers of goods and services through the medium of advertising; (5) provide entertainment; (6) maintain its own financial self-sufficiency so as to be free from the pressures of special interests.

Obituaries and congratulations serve functions (4) and (6). The answer of the media to objections that they are promoting, through the vacuous symbol of death, the economic foundation of elitism is to argue for distinguishing between promoting the sale of death and the marketing of elitism.

CONCLUSION

The argument of this article is that obituary and congratulatory notices are part of the national culture but that attitudes to them vary across ethnic, religious and class groups. The acceptance or rejection of these publications is informed by cultural notions of success. Thus the material found in both obituaries and congratulations harp on the economic process and on the power created by reward and deprivation. Indeed, the construction of selfhood within each one of the publications is but an aspect of social relationships, mediated in this case through the various forms of economic or political development in Nigeria. The successful person, a member of the elite, is one who advances his career to a point that needs to be publicly acknowledged or celebrated. Death is just part of a symbolic complex of achievements that can be advertised.

NOTES

1. The word "obituary" is used here rather loosely to designate its various manifestations as "Transition," "In Memoriam," "Notice" or "Obituary." It is thus all-embracing and does not refer only to the specific form of the Obituary.

2. These are small pamphlets containing the order of worship both in the church and later at the burial ground. They contain the hymns to be sung, the prayers to be said and the Bible passages to be read on the occasion. Few of these "Orders of Funeral Services" contain biographies; many people consulted on the issue thought it either unnecessary or expensive—adding to the cost of production. The inclusion of a biography in the "order" is itself a recent phenomenon dating to the early 1970s. But it should be added that the Muslims also have their own pamphlets giving the Order of the Funeral Service. These rarely contain biographies, for the same reasons as those stated above.

3. The shortest in my collection has three pages of biographical sketch while the longest has five pages. The longest belongs to Chief S. Akinola, the Sawe of Ilesa, 1896–1988.

4. A radio announcement on BCOS in January 1990.

5. Neither Mr. Fola Awonusi, the advertisement manager of the *Daily Sketch*, nor Mr. Alawale, the Controller of Sales, BCOS, was willing to give information on this issue. In the case of Mr. Alawale it was because his company lumps together revenue from obituaries with that realised from other types of "Shop Windows" (birthday announcements, changes of name and adverts on the launch of a business). The effort to collect information on how much revenue the *Daily Times* realised failed too, despite the intervention of my friend Dr. Soremekun, a *Daily Times* columnist and former employee.

6. The BCOS agent in Ile-Ife supplied this information in an interview. The agent also mentioned that the individual advertiser inputs his material at the lithograph and typesetting stages, but that agents can write for illiterates who may not be familiar with the requirements of the media. The interview was conducted on 29 March 1990 in Oranmiyan shopping complex, shop B2.

7. I would like to thank the *Guardian* correspondent in Ile-Ife (name withheld on request) and Mr. Ayodele Jegede, also of the *Guardian*, for their useful insights into why the *Guardian* changed its stand. However, incidentally and ironically, the paper has been in the forefront of the debate on the value of the obituary advertisement to the publishers and to the reading public (see the references in the text).

8. In the *Daily Times* there are at least ten categories of advertisement. These are full-page, half-page, 13 in. × four columns, 13 in. x three columns, 6 1/2 in. x four columns, 6 1/2 in. x three and a half columns (i.e. quarter-page), 6 1/2 in. x three columns, 15 cm. x two columns, 7.5 cm. x two columns and "SCI." The cheapest is "SCI." It is about one-ninth the price of the full page.

9. All prices are relative to 1989. Information was supplied by Mr. Alawale, who also hinted at the value attached to the various media. Mr. Gbenga Fayemiwo, the editor of *Kowe*, an Ejigbo-based newspaper, was also of much help in discerning the attitudes of the public to the obituary and congratulation publications.

10. Those broadcast on radio and television contain the same information as published in the print media.

11. Dr. Toyin Falola, personal communication, 15 February 1990.

12. The logo is placed either at the top or at the bottom of the advertisement. In addition there would be a picture of the celebrant or advertiser, and not just a photo of the person being celebrated.

REFERENCES

Abu, Sully. 1990. "All the News That's Fit for the Trash-Can," *Guardian*, 4 March, p. 7.

Achebe, Chinua. 1966. *A Man of the People*. London: Heinemann.

Akiwowo, Akinsola. 1983. *Ajobi and Ajogbe: Variations on the Theme of Sociation*. Ile-Ife: University of Ife Press.

Aluko, T. M. 1970. *Chief the Honourable Minister*. London: Heinemann.

Barber, Karin. 1987. "Popular Arts in Africa," *African Studies Review*, Vol. 30, No. 3, 1–78.

Ben-Ari, Eyal. 1987. "On Acknowledgment in Ethnographies," *Journal of Anthropological Research*, Vol. 43, No. 1, 63–84.

Cohen, Abner. 1976. *Two-Dimensional Man*. Berkeley: University of California Press.

Cohen, Abner. 1981. *The Politics of Elite Culture*. Berkeley: University of California Press.

Dare, O. 1985a. "The Art of the Obituary," *Guardian*, 22 October, p. 9.

Dare, O. 1985b. "Press: 126 Years of Patchy Service," *Newswatch* (Lagos), October.

Darnell, R. 1971. "The Professionalization of American Anthropology: A Case Study in the Sociology of Knowledge," *Social Science Information*, Vol. 10, 85–103.

Falola, T., & Olanrewaju, S. A. 1986. *Transport Systems in Nigeria*. Syracuse, N.Y.: Syracuse University Press.

Kirk-Greene, A. H. M. 1974. *Mutumin Kirkii: The Concept of the Good Man in Hausa*. Bloomington: Indiana University Press.

Larsen, Tord. 1987. "Action, Morality, and Cultural Translation," *Journal of Anthropological Research*, Vol. 43, No. 7, 1–28.

Lawuyi, Olatunde B. 1988. "Obituary and Ancestral Worship: Analysis of a Contemporary Cultural Form in Nigeria," *Sociological Analysis*, Vol. 48, No. 4, 372–79.

Lawuyi, Olatunde B. 1990. "The Story about Life: Biography in the Yoruba Obituaries," *Diogenes*, forthcoming.

Litton, R. J., et al. 1979. *Six Lives, Six Deaths: Portraits from Modern Japan*. New Haven, CT: Yale University Press.

Mulkay, M. 1984. "The Ultimate Compliment: A Sociological Analysis of Ceremonial Discourse," *Sociology*, Vol. 18, No. 4, 531–49.

Obijiofor, Levi. 1989. "Obituaries as Communication," *Guardian*, Vol. 8 April, p. 9.

Omu, Fred. 1978. *The Press and Politics in Nigeria, 1880–1937*. London: Longman.

Peterson, Theodore. 1979. "The Social Responsibility Theory," in *Four Theories of the Press*, ed. by F. S. Siebert et al., pp. 73–103. Urbana: University of Illinois Press.

Saro-Wiwa, Ken. 1990. "In Pursuit of Excellence," *Daily Times*, 11 February, p. 7.

Settar, S. 1989. *Inviting Death: Indian Attitudes towards the Ritual Death*. New York: Brill.

Togonu-Bickersteth, F. 1986. "Obituaries: Conception of Death in the Nigerian Newspapers," *Ife Social Sciences Review*, Vol. 9, No. 1–2, 83–93.

Uchendu, V. C. 1965. *The Igbo of South-Eastern Nigeria*. New York: Holt, Rinehart and Winston.

Owning Places and Buying Time
Class, Culture, and Stalled Gentrification

Brett Williams

Brett Williams is professor of anthropology and director of American studies at American University, Washington, DC. She received her Ph.D. from the University of Illinois in 1975. Her fieldwork has been done in the United States, among migrant workers of Mexican descent from Texas (see Chapter 8), in a mixed ethnic neighborhood of a northeastern city, and among waitresses. She has also written about southern folklife and on the African-American hero John Henry. Her research interests include poverty, the media, folklore, and politics and culture.

Gentrification allows ethnographers a rare glimpse of the interplay of class and culture in everyday life. But because dramatic displacement generally follows, we seldom find the chance to observe this process in detail. In the last few years, however, economic hard times have stalled gentrification, so that people who may not have intended to be neighbors have come to share problematic communities. They bring to these communities different resources, visions of neighborhood, expectations for neighbors, and patterns of everyday interaction. The limits and opportunities of class shape varied neighborhood traditions at the same time that these traditions stretch and enliven the constraints of class. Stalled gentrification thus makes everyday life a rich arena for exploring the interaction of passions, economics, habits, and ways of carving out a life.

My research, six years of participant-observation and structured interviews, took place in a neighborhood that I will call Elm Valley, where class divisions tend to coincide with renting and owning. A streetcar suburb in a northeastern city, Elm Valley lost many of its white residents in the 1950s and 1960s. After a period when its population was mostly Black American, Elm Valley—like other areas undergoing gentrification—has been rediscovered by white middle-class settlers (Allen, 1980; Goldfield, 1980; Hennig, 1982; McCaffrey, 1982). Other new immigrants have come as well, able, because of the city's strict rent control laws, to crowd into small apartments. Today the population

of this neighborhood of about 5000 people is approximately 50% Black American, 20% Latin American, 20% white, and 10% immigrants from other parts of the world, especially Southeast Asia, East Africa, and the Caribbean. If the gentrification that began in the mid-1970s had continued, most of the Black owners would have been displaced by higher taxes and pressure from speculators; the tenants, too, would have been forced out by renovations and condominium conversions. Instead, city legislation and high interest rates have, since 1980, stalled gentrification. Thus, Elm Valley is surprisingly diverse, and home ownership crosses lines of race. Black families make up the majority of both owners and renters. Almost all non-Anglo immigrant groups rent, however; and most of the young, newer, white residents own their homes.[1]

In spite of the disruption of gentrification and displacement, the neighborhood might be a model of class and cultural integration. Distinctly bounded by a park and two avenues, it has a lively main street and many small businesses that allow neighbors to build contacts (Jacobs, 1961). The architecture of Elm Valley stresses the front porch, and its wide, deep alleys encourage informal, disclosing interaction from kitchens, around gardens, and over clotheslines out back. Finally, the Black families who bought houses in the 1950s, together with the core of white families who chose to stay, have given Elm Valley an unusual cross-racial bridge that until recently stretched out a tradition of civic activism.[2]

These neighborhood qualities have shaped passionate attachments to Elm Valley, but with gentrification these attachments have failed to cross the barriers of social class. Neighborhoodwide organization has folded after 100 years. New owners wage an escalating memo and bulletin war against the men on the street. In the large apartment buildings that preserve Elm Valley's class diversity, tenants discriminate among themselves as they negotiate with their landlords about renovation and control. Elm Valley is a crumbling community of lost possibilities, even though people there are trying to resist chaotic change and take control of their lives. Yet they bring to these efforts disparate, sometimes distracting visions of neighborhood and of neighbors. This article explores the conflicts that have erupted from those perceptions, as well as the clues those conflicts hold to the interaction of class and culture.

RENTERS FACING OWNERS

On one block in Elm Valley a large dilapidated apartment building that I call The Manor faces attractive rowhouses across the street. Renters and owners do not enter one another's homes, but looking across the street allows them glimpses of others' lives. Renters see owners engaged in optional, honorable tasks such as carpentry, painting, and gardening. This renovation and tinkering ironically mirrors the deterioration of The Manor. In addition, most of [the] tenants' domestic duties are defensive, fighting back filth in their overcrowded apartments. When families postpone washing dishes, let food sit out overnight, or fail to mop their floors after meals, they invite pests that are especially problematic if the families sleep where they eat. Many one-bedroom apartments shelter from four to a dozen people, who sleep in the living/dining room area and, for example, store their shoes under the coffee table. Such intensive use means recleaning the same small space each day to reap the largely negative rewards of relatively fewer roaches and mice. The puttering, *offensive* tasks renters observe across the street cast these circumstances into sharp relief.

These same tasks also signal to tenants owners' control over the physical facades of their houses. By contrast, tenants feel strongly their own lack of control over a facade. For example, they are not allowed to use the grass in front of their building to play games or mind children. If they do, the resident manager may emerge from the building with a shrill public reprimand. This lack of control is obvious in other ways as well. Tenants would like a say about such strategic decisions as installing a security system, controlling pests, permanently repairing the elevator and the boiler. Many feel at the mercy of machines that swallow money more reliably than they dispense goods and services. The erratic support system of The Manor makes everyday life a gamble: A person might return home loaded with groceries and a child in a stroller to discover a

broken elevator and face a four-floor walkup, or put off washing his or her hair until morning only to find that there will be no hot water for three days. The laundryroom is a source of special indignities; residents have to stand in line for the few machines that work, jealously defend their places between loads, and negotiate the treacherous transition from washers to even scarcer, often cold driers.

Even when tenants are inside their apartments, conversations and quarrels, the smell of meals, and the sounds of music and television seep through the walls and out into the halls; embarrassing substances drip through the floors and ceilings. As one woman put it, "I know everybody hears our little family things." And they did: This woman's husband was a notorious drinker who enjoyed playing Dr. King's "I Have a Dream" speech at top volume when high. Other families' secrets erupted as well, as a bathtub might overflow, smoke filter out, or a woman chase her husband into the hall.

Finally, tenants find telling the places where they see owners—outdoors but in charge, on their porches, in their yards, shovelling the snow from a small patch of sidewalk. These transitional spaces highlight the easy movement outdoors and back inside that tenants lack, for they must negotiate buffer zones such as hallways, elevators, and stairwells. Although they enjoy meeting neighbors in these places, tenants feel vulnerable there as well (Jacobs, 1961; Reed, 1974). The annexes to a house also bear witness to greater space inside (which families can use to separate eating, sleeping, and recreational activities), and to a more negotiable domestic organization (as families can divide themselves up in ways that parents who must lug small children with them to the laundry room cannot). Thus, these glimpses of owners' lives reflect varied features of life in a house and the rights and privileges that accompany owning one: easy access, choices about tasks and companions, negotiable space, taking the domestic offensive, and orchestrating a flexible family.

When owners look across the street at the dwellings of tenants, they see an impersonal shared facade with no options for outdoor tasks beyond fixing and washing cars. Some complain that the building blocks the sun. Some comment on what they consider to be an astonishing parade of foot traffic and a great deal of hauling. Rather than cars, most tenants depend on the multipurpose pull-along cart that is a centerpiece of low-income urban life. Those tenants who prefer the public laundromat to The Manor's whimsical machines join others who tow groceries and small children. All of these sights seem embarrassing as they testify to a less-controlled presentation of self, a perception shared by some tenants who complain about having to display their dirty laundry and who line their carts with plastic garbage bags to preserve what privacy they can. Finally, from the vantage point of owners, renters seem to engage in widespread, inappropriate use of the outside, a matter at the center of conflict in Elm Valley. Because owners know little beyond what they see at places like The Manor, the people who use the street seem to have become emblematic of renters. Their activities outdoors testify to contrasting strategies for living in a neighborhood.

THE WORK OF THE STREET

Elm Valley's tenants choose tremendous financial sacrifice to stay in a neighborhood they prefer to those suburbs rapidly swelling with the displaced poor. Some do not see this as a choice, citing the "time and trouble it takes to move" or "the money we'd spend commuting back into town," and claiming "I'd be back over here every day anyway." Others, however, are explicit about opting for a neighborhood. What I will call "the work of the street" reflects, encourages, and rewards that decision to stay.

The work of the street reflects in part the small, hot apartments, in which people feel they cannot entertain, and the sparse financial resources that prevent renters from traveling freely. Although women use the street freely during the day, and although there are women on the street and linked to the street at night as well, they do not gather there in the clear and dramatic ways that men do. Their networking strategies seem more varied and more likely to be inside, whether at work, at church, or inside their buildings. The work of the street seems to be largely the preserve of men.

On the street men bolster family economies. They network and they pool. They swap services such as rides, repairs, and hauling; exchange goods such as clothing, small appliances, furniture, food stamps, and things from work such as crabs, tostados, pesticides, and cleaning fluids. Men often trade goods for favors— souse meat or "gas money" for a ride; pirated or home-grown vegetables for babysitting; playing a number in exchange for "a taste"; help with moving in exchange for a crib; homemade soup for a watch. Sometimes men organize small cooperatives for a trip to a suburban farmers' market to shop in bulk. The pooling and swapping that is so important to the poor and so often the concern of women is in this situation an activity that men also share.

Some men earn their living by streetwork. One man owns a truck, which he uses for harvesting the surplus vegetables of suburban gardeners, moving furniture, delivering appliances, and salvaging trees to sell for firewood. Another man sells dresses, coats, and jewelry on the street and is generally available there to sweep and run errands for shopkeepers, help mind

children for passersby, or deliver them to nursery school. Men like these two are conscientious and self-conscious custodians of the street, keeping careful track of what goes on during the day and often sharing information and delivering messages and warnings.

Other men do not live from streetwork but look to it to solve routine problems: to find information about a city bureaucracy, to look for jobs, to have appliances repaired, to locate help with moving, to fill ordinary, everyday needs. The street as *work* looms large in family negotiations; men stress its financial benefits when they bargain for time away from their homes: "I have to try to run into Ben so that I can tell him Maria needs firewood"; "I have to deliver these greens to Harper so that I can tell Jimmy to come around and fix the stereo"; "How do you expect me to find a job if you won't let me go to the tavern?" But the men of Elm Valley, like their counterparts in other cities, love the street (Hannerz, 1969; Liebow, 1967; Suttles, 1968; Williams, 1981). It is fruitless to untangle the financial benefits of streetwork from the other attractions of streetlife, and the men of Elm Valley would not do that, for finances are interwoven with a great deal of trust and talk, lasting social relationships, and the detailed knowledge that works just as well to manage stigma as to cook up deals.

In the intricate world of the street men do all they can to understand the details of one another's biographies. Because they memorize others' reputations, they tolerate a great deal of deviance and diversity. I was first struck by this early one morning when a slightly tipsy man approached me with a big sharp chisel. I was grateful when another man chorused, "Just getting off work, Curly?" and proceeded to tell me that Curly worked all night cleaning and repairing office buildings. I particularly appreciated this exchange because the second man had tried to make me feel safe on the street, but there are many other examples. One man is well liked but known to be a pickpocket; those whose pockets he picks generally blame themselves because they know, and know that he knows they know he does that. Another man is known as a soft touch but a terror "when he's drinking," yet another as a soft touch when he's drinking. Others are known to be "not drinking," a personal career linked to problems of health, family conflict, alcoholism, or probation.

The street is also an arena for preserving the culture of the Carolinas, through foodways (souse meat, greens, and many parts of the pig, including tails, ears, and knuckles); remedies (junction weed boiled with a penny for chicken pox, wild onion roots boiled with butter and Calvert whiskey for a cold, ear wax for chapped lips); expressions (to be pleasantly tipsy on Calvert is to be "high as a Georgia pine"). Men also identify real friends as "from Carolina" or "from my home town." On the street they share urban lore as well, organizing complicated neighborhood lotteries around football games, sharing stories about the numbers, playing strategies, lucky wins, narrow losses ("That's how the numbers get you"). Many residents agree that the more dire their straits, the more obliged they are to play. Beyond financial possibilities, however, numbers strategies and lore are much more than work; one's regular number, evolving tactics for choosing one and deciding where to play it, biography of wins and narrow losses are important parts of personal identity. Each person is a complex weave of vivid everyday detail acted out on the street.

The world of the street draws in its shopkeepers and muddles divisions between shopper and seller. One man, for example, claims that in 18 years he has done no shopping outside Elm Valley. He has long-term relationships with some of the older shopkeepers, relations which may involve credit or part-time employment. As new stores open, he entrenches himself in each, coming to be known by name and to entangle and complicate relationships, crossing all the usual boundaries of urban consumption. He arranges layaway at the drugstore, barter at the thrift shop (whose owner watches for and saves clothes that fit him and his family), charitable contributions for his children's nursery school from the new grocery store. He defines his needs so that they can be satisfied in Elm Valley and then redefines and stretches what it offers.

It is on the street that we see most clearly the passion for texture that is central to the renters' neighborhood world, a passion that emerges from the interplay of financial constraints and cultural traditions. This passion for texture is much like the thick description valued by folklorists and ethnographers (see Geertz, 1973). It includes a decided preference for depth over breadth, an interest in rich, vivid, personal, concrete, entangled detail. It involves repetition, density, mining a situation from many faces and angles. A joke, a story, a teasing line can be retold and rephrased many times, as long as the emphasis varies just slightly. Inside apartments I saw a love of texture in a desire to fill empty spaces with artifacts and objects and to manage the density of domestic life by weaving through it the sounds and colors and rhythms of television. It emerged in renters' interest in programs such as *Dallas* and *Dynasty*, which offer vivid, concrete, detailed entanglements. It is clear in many residents' preference for local over national news, for stories that can be followed from beginning to end. It is clearest on the street in the intimate knowledge men build of one another, in the ways that roles, institutions, and relationships are complicated and rewoven, the formal and informal sectors muddled, interaction intimate and multifaceted.

THE METROPOLITAN VISION

Owners have also chosen a community in the face of other options. New owners' reasons for choosing Elm Valley vary. Some like the convenient commute, but keep more cosmopolitan personal attachments; some are fond of the lovely streetscapes and fine, historic architecture; some are nostalgic, even utopian in their hope of rooting themselves in an old-fashioned urban neighborhood; some are activists tackling international problems there. Many value the personal growth that they feel accompanies confronting diversity. Their perceptions of neighborhood life generally differ from renters, and these perceptions again reflect some of the complex class cultures, including varied resources for travel and indoor activities as well as radically different visions of what a neighborhood offers and how it should be used.[3] Looking at some of [the] owners' strategies for handling family needs should make this difference clear.

As a result of stalled residential gentrification, the commercial gentrification of Elm Valley is also incomplete (see Hennig, 1982). Although the commercial strip boasts an art and an antique store, there is no PLANTS, Etc. or California Café. Thrift shops, dry cleaners, and liquor stores rely on large numbers of clients rather than wealthy ones. Most owners find them uninteresting and inadequate and therefore shop outside the neighborhood, often while driving to and from work.

For child enrichment, many owners look outside Elm Valley for pools, schools, playgrounds, violin and ballet lessons. Few owners avoid the neighborhood completely; most use mixed strategies.[4] One woman, for example, devoted many hours of volunteer time to a local nursery school, for she felt that it offered her daughter an important multicultural experience. Now, however, she sends her child to elementary school outside the neighborhood. A strong advocate of hiring local people for domestic work, repairs, and childcare, she shops in remote parts of the metropolitan area and does not walk through Elm Valley because she considers it unsafe. (To some extent gender crosscuts class in limiting women's movement at night; however, cars do provide shells of sorts for metropolitan travel for those who own them.)

Another woman, active in a bid to have Elm Valley named a historic district, has led a fight to stop the local Korean grocery store from placing advertising leaflets under windshield wipers. It developed during a meeting on the topic that she had no idea that this store underpriced local supermarket chains, or that the owner had hired all local workers ("winos" in some versions) to cement neighborhood relations. It had not occurred to her to shop there. Her assumptions would be incomprehensible to many tenants; they had learned as much as they could about the new store as soon as it had opened, in part through the new workers, who gave the owners an immediate pipeline to the street.

Other owners juggle buffering and involvement in a number of ways; but strategies that may be appropriate for families can create problems for the community. Elm Valley already houses institutions inherently segregated by class: buses, church basement daycare centers, laundromats. Other places that might jumble people across class lines and encourage small contacts are segregated by default (see Jacobs, 1961; Love, 1973; Merry, 1980, 1981; Molotch, 1969). These range from the local elementary school to shops, taverns, and parks. That owners leave the neighborhood to find more elaborate toddler parks is especially hard on female tenants with small children. Women work parks to build contacts with other parents so that they can organize play groups, carpools, babysitting coops, birthday parties and everyday friendships (see Swartley, 1983). Most women are wary of Elm Valley's one rather inadequate park, which therefore remains in the hands of men, many of whom do take their children there, but most of whom hardly need another arena for building contacts.

Thus, the greater financial resources, shopping, and child enrichment strategies as well as the more metropolitan vision of many new owners deprive them of access to the street. To just hint at the complex interplay of race, ethnicity, and residence here, the more extended and established Black households are nearly always tied through at least one male member to the street. The few longer-term white residents of Elm Valley either work the streets or the alleys. Those tenants in group houses or small apartments, even if they are white and new to Elm Valley, are less likely to own cars, more likely to walk and to know at least some of the shopkeepers who are tied into street talk. But few of the newer white owners pursue these arenas.[5]

"HOW CAN WE GET THE BUMS OFF THE STREET?"

The various groups involved perceive one anothers' strategies differently. One day several men prominent on the street explained their vision of the situation: The newer owners are different from the older, "racial whites," who are "stuck in (Elm Valley) with its cheap beers and cheap (Black people) because they're too old or too poor to move." The newer residents "move in but don't associate." In part they may be afraid: "They hear a lot of garbage when they go outside the neighborhood to associate." This "garbage" is not challenged because those who hear it do not get to know the details of their neighbors' personalities. But mostly they do not associate because "they just don't know

how—they weren't raised up that way." Although these men feel strongly that the newer residents should "learn how to speak on the street," their assessment is fairly benign in its stress on cultural background.

Their attention to detail also contributes to these men's feelings about the new owners. Some of the men on the street cite neighborhood history as a reason to feel benign: Whites have always lived in Elm Valley; integration was fairly painless; prejudiced individuals stand out and can be known. Some of these individuals, however, are regarded with affection simply because they are known. For example, one of the tavern owners is an 82-year-old native Kentuckian who freely uses racial epithets, organized hard for John Connelly's presidential campaign, and tries to persuade Blacks that they should support the party of Lincoln. She is widely considered a cheap and temperamental employer and a vindictive, erratic hostess. Nonetheless, many details of her life are known: Her concern for alcoholics; her personal rescue of a popular retarded man; the joy she takes in children. (Her case demonstrates, I believe, the extent to which a passion for detail and texture is ultimately a forgiving world view.)

Other men cite the fallout effects of class privilege as grounds for their relatively benign feelings toward the new owners. Property owners demand and receive decent city services, so that Elm Valley's streets, traffic lights, and curbs are better repaired and its trash more reliably hauled away than in the past. New owners also bring volunteer time, money, and knowledge to neighborhood activities; they organize block parties, renovate the local library, and heal the elm trees.[6]

Owners for the most part do not reciprocate this good will; their feelings seem to vary from indifference to tolerance or compassion to vague unease or active dislike. They lack many of the tenants' inclinations to build detailed cross-class portraits: Tenants (and certainly not the men on the street) do not bring tangible class resources into Elm Valley life; new owners do not call on neighborhood memories in evaluating biographies; many have a broader, more metropolitan vision rather than an eye for local detail. In any event, new owners are not often motivated to explore the texture of Elm Valley life. Their feelings toward tenants in general are not at issue here; my concern, like theirs, is the way in which some owners' more extreme feelings about the men on the street (as standing for tenants) are splitting Elm Valley apart.

Late in 1983 a cluster of angry residents organized a committee they called "Elm Valley's Corridor Committee." During their early months they distributed memos and handbills attacking the men on the street and citing particular abuses such as loitering, littering, drinking and using profanity. "What can we do about public urination?" queried one flier. Eventually this group circulated a letter to Elm Valley households with a list of demands, including one for foot patrols with guard dogs.

The city's charter establishes for each neighborhood an elected neighborhood council, composed of five members representing small districts within the neighborhood. Hearing murmurs of support for the Corridor Committee, this council invited city officials to a public meeting to air the complaints. The Corridor Committee's chair set the tone, asking in her introductory remarks, "How can we get the bums off the street?"

The committee's paper war had gone unnoticed by tenants, for it occurred outside the social system of personal exposure and talk which they see as structuring neighborhood life. The meeting was another matter. Few tenants attended, for they feel that the neighborhood council is a property owners' preserve. What most considered to be the vicious contents of the letter, however, had leaked out. Several of the more central and flamboyant men from the street therefore attended the meeting out of anger and curiosity. Also, the more politically active but usually distracted residents came to argue against what they saw as racist rabble-rousing, as did some of the men from established Black households with ties to the street. For the first time Elm Valley had a forum where people could talk and interpret acts across class.

At the meeting the owners made momentary alliance with feminists who did not want to be harassed on the street. Trying to reconcile these two interests, a white renter who also works as a nursery school social worker suggested that when walking the street a person "salute each man." She argued that the men on the street feel that they make it safer, because they watch out for their friends and they also know what goes on. They know who is likely to mug, and after the mugging they will hear about it. Some of the Black householders commented that outdoor toilets might address the public urination problem and that large trash cans might help with litter. A Latino leader argued that the men on the street "don't have homes." The only man to talk from the street complained that "the police always come down on us but not the Spanish people." The outcome of this long, angry and complicated meeting was the triumph of a liberal solution: Elected officials repeated their reluctance to "enforce manners"; the police chief cited "people's right to use the street"; beat officers explained the difficult logistics of arresting someone urinating outdoors; and the council was charged to explore available social services.

The wide appeal of the Corridor Committee is puzzling, however, especially since it grew among people who had chosen to live in a varied urban community. To some extent class cultures can help to explain this appeal: We have seen that the interplay between traditions and resources that expresses class

cultures encourages owners to choose breadth over depth in everyday life. The virtues of this choice are obvious, as these families preserve access to those facilities that they feel enrich and broaden their lives, and that offer them continuing advantages in school and at work. Yet probing for depth, texture, and intricacy seems to be a more successful strategy than buffering and juggling density if one wants to carve out a comfortable life in Elm Valley. Grasping the neighborhood's texture depends on a rich public life of inspection and exposure for at least the male members of renting families. Yet this occasion for building and exploring texture stigmatizes those who have figured out how well it works to build a community.

"YOUR BUILDING IS GOING DOWN, DOWN . . ."

The second arena of conflict is between landlords and renters irritated by the deterioration of their buildings. The Manor provides one example: A network of women tenants began to organize in winter, a time of intense sociability within the building and a time when tenants felt the building's problems more harshly. The women were angry about the malfunctioning machines, the erratic heat and hot water, and especially concerned about the stairs and hallways, which were emerging as popular places to socialize, smoke, and drink. They initiated a campaign of petition signing and letter writing. The most telling feature of the women's written complaints was the way they were framed. These frames reveal a sense of having paid with rent money and time for a home, a place where one belongs and feels secure. These women added a moral dimension as they called up a relationship between building a home and the kinds of people they are. They cited personal qualities to legitimize their requests. For example, each woman noted in her letter how long she had lived in The Manor: "I have lived here for 18 years," or "This is the first time in 13 years I have had to complain," or "We have been here 8½ years and have cooperated with the Agency in every way." This matter of ethos seems crucial in legitimizing their demands. The women asked for more say about transitional places and the mechanical support system. Their demands did not appeal to universal human rights or even to local law. They demanded particular privileges because they were particular sorts of people: moral, concerned, and settled. Ironically, the glimpses they have managed of owners' lives seem to have encouraged them to identify with owners as a kind of people.[7]

These personal letters offered details of the women's everyday lives ("I am often home alone in the afternoons and it is very cold") and tried out names rumored to attach to officers of the management corporation. The corporation response, however, was a less personal, masterful mass memo. Beginning "Dear Tenant," it mentioned the tenants' complaints as well as the grievances of owners across the street about litter on the lawn. It grouped hallways, stairwells, the laundry room, and the lawn as "public areas," and used them as evidence that tenants of the Manor were *not* like homeowners after all: They dumped trash on the floor, they left graffiti in the laundry room, they used the stairwell as a bathroom. Tenants should improve themselves, for "It's your home." Lumping all tenants denies the exceptional homeowning qualities the women attributed to themselves. The message is that these kinds of discriminations are inappropriate; while the women had invoked the cultural attributes surrounding connections and commitments to a place, management responded by lumping them by class.

Tenants offered varied explanations for the rapid and distressing decline of the building. One theory held that management was allowing it to deteriorate on purpose so that long-term tenants would leave. Turnovers allowed the landlords to raise rents; and if the building deteriorated enough to be condemned, the owners could gut it and convert into condominiums. Few of the renters believed that management would collaborate in the building's decline; many felt that owners would want to keep homeowning-like people in the building and would certainly want to keep the property up.

Another view suggested that a recent change in resident managers was responsible. Like many other mediators, resident managers give owners a face; they personalize landlords to tenants at the same time that they are known as tenants themselves. In theory they are neutral and fairly powerless mediators, there as go-betweens for owners and tenants to everyone's mutual benefit. In practice they are rarely neutral enough to jeopardize their jobs. As one manager put it (in response to a tenant's complaint that his negligence had meant that her friend's ceiling had collapsed and almost killed a baby), "I only got one friend and that's the man who gave me my job."

This manager, Mr. Ironsides, was a problem drinker who rarely responded to tenant requests for repairs. Coincident with stalled gentrification and the movement of Latino tenants into the building, he had died. He was replaced by a woman who proved to be competent and prompt at managing repairs. Mysteriously, tenants began to mutter within a few weeks that she was "too nice," "too weak," and "too soft." Mr. Ironsides reemerged in the public memory as a hero, a man who "roamed the halls with a blackjack" keeping order. Ms. Johnson's unpopularity was partly a matter of timing and partly a matter of gender. Some of the hostility reflected ethnicity—a Jamaican labeled "African" by

the custodial staff, she was seen as too lenient toward other "foreigners." This hostility that Black renters felt toward her illuminates the third divisive arena in Elm Valley.

"THE DO DROP IN" OR HOME AS SANCTUARY

Many Black renters placed the bulk of the blame for the building's problems on the "Spanish people," a half-dozen extended families recently arrived from El Salvador. The complaints of women and men tenants against these families varied in revealing ways. Women tenants complained many times that "Spanish people use the hall like a porch." The young men liked to congregate in the halls, and they often failed to manage the stigma of public life in time-honored local ways, for example, by moving discreetly away from a woman approaching or by offering a wholesome-sounding greeting to signal benevolent intent. In addition, they cheerfully broke bothersome rules: One group, for example, simply commandeered the service elevator whenever the one designated for tenants was stuck somewhere else.

Most striking about Black women's antagonisms toward these young Latino men, however, was their use of labels emphasizing ethnicity rather than gender and age. Most of us are leery of groups of young men hovering in an ambiguous place, but what tenants stressed in encoding these groups was that they were "Spanish." Perhaps the stress on ethnicity reflected Latino families' general transformations of domestic life space. As large, extended families in desperate straits, they crowded many people into their small apartments. Other tenants claimed that "one might sign the lease and then they sneak all kinds of others in." Not knowing exactly who or how many occupied a unit disoriented other tenants, and their confusion was compounded by irritation at the efficient dispersal of Latino family members to manage tasks such as laundry. Those tenants who had developed ways to beat the laundry room rush soon found that there was never a time when several elderly Latinas were not in the laundry room minding infants and washing many loads of clothes. Even more annoying was the house-like use to which Latino families transformed their apartments. On two floors domestic networks spread out over several apartments, but because they shared many tasks and responsibilities, the families flowed between these units, left their doors open, and encouraged their children to play in the halls. They did, in fact, use the hall as a porch.

A hall is the closest thing to a porch that tenants have. It is an important transitional area for storing trash on the way to the trash room, packing urban carts, and chatting. Informal dress and even night clothes seem to be acceptable in the hall (see Reed, 1974). Latino families were drawing a fairly appropriate analogy between hall and porch that was consistent with the living arrangements most had known at home. But to other tenants this use of the hall as porch highlighted all its contradictions: This great, shared, indoor porch in which there was neither privacy nor say so demanded some sort of cooperation in limiting interaction. Families who used it detracted from others' right to have it not used.

Women saw these behaviors as proof that the Latino tenants were not like homeowners. Some were concerned about the preponderance of men in these families, and argued, "Women make an apartment more like a home." Others stressed transiency: "They think this is the 'Do Drop In,' they're like college students; they don't care about keeping it up because they don't want to make it a home."

Men phrased the problem a little differently. Many male tenants felt that Latinos "use the hall like the street," and that they did not make the appropriate overtures for sharing public space. In turn, they attributed all anonymous troubles to Latinos, including the trash room fires that grew common during the winter of 1983 and one episode in which 50 tires were slashed. As one man put it, "Spanish people only come out at night, because they think they're white then. Black people do what they want during the day."

There is an irony in this process that seems to parallel what is happening outdoors. Black renters' passion for texture and detail is thwarted by a language and set of customs they do not understand. Most of the refugees define home differently than Elm Valley's long-term tenants because they have radically different priorities for it. Many want to offer shelter to fellow refugees and, in fact, to use the promise of shelter to encourage kin and friends to migrate. They are not so interested in keeping up the property or necessarily in building ties. They want to use home as a sanctuary. Even those who may want more privacy soon face a choice between cutting off fellow refugees and doubling up. Their desperation has created scenes in several apartments featuring rows of cots and numbers of depressed and displaced people.

None of these things is particularly clear to other tenants, who know little of the circumstances in Central America that have propelled these refugees north. The theory they have built to explain The Manor's decline relies heavily on the immediate and concrete details of building life that they can observe every day. Whenever one family moves out, it is replaced by another of lesser quality. This gradual substitution of good tenants by worse ones means that the building inevitably deteriorates. Management is complicit "be-

cause they don't screen new tenants," but the problem is essentially one of tenant mobility. If tenants move out, there is likely to be something wrong with the building anyway; those who come in are by definition not settled or committed, and if they are willing to move into a declining building, they are doubly suspect. Speaking a different language and bringing culturally distinct and inappropriate traditions for inhabiting space further complicate the problem. In The Manor women argue that by settling in and taking an active, moral interest in a building one can act like a homeowner. This ethos then frames the rhetoric through which they demanded particular privileges and services. The frame turns out to be a divisive one that leads to blaming other tenants for problems with the landlord and for the decline of the building.

CONCLUSION

Stalled gentrification brings together residents who ordinarily would not be neighbors and who have disparate options, constraints, perceptions, and traditions that are expressed in varied, easily misunderstood strategies for urban life. New owners buy a piece of a place and feel that through property they have put down roots in the community. Acquiring the responsibility and concerns attached to property values makes them less sympathetic to the men on the street, who seem to endanger those things. Their more cosmopolitan attachments and broader visions place them to some extent outside Elm Valley's cultural system.

Unable to buy houses, Elm Valley's renters have bought time and used that time to dig in and build ties. Entangled in a rich weave of local ethnographic detail, renters have expressed their anger over the threat of displacement in part through efforts to align themselves with the qualities that seem to characterize owners: settledness, commitment, connections, control. They have thus built difficult divisions among themselves. Owners distance themselves from the characteristics that seem to stick to renters: inappropriate display, misuse of public space and time, immersion in immediate time and place.

Ironically, a rich, diverse community with many possibilities for truly intricate integration is torn apart by conflicts rooted in the constraints of class, the traditions through which people link themselves to ethnic and racial groups, and the playing out of those constraints and traditions in everyday life strategies.

NOTES

1. For many reasons that will become apparent, the name of this neighborhood is a pseudonym, the location disguised, the statis-

tics rounded out, and the description of my research abbreviated. The research has involved a complicated constellation of residential patterns and community organizing activities as well as formal research strategies such as taped interviews and participant observation. Because I was the mother of two infants during the research, I have been worried about distorted findings, particularly regarding male-female relations and in describing such arenas as the laundry room. I have found Rosaldo's (1984) discussion of "the positioned observer" reassuring.

2. Some of these friendships continue on the integrated residential blocks. Because they are cross-racial and longstanding, they are an important kind of neighborhood glue.

3. To stress the circumstances of renting and owning is not to deny the importance of race and ethnicity. There is some evidence that the passion for texture has deep roots in Black culture, seen, for example, in urban street epics, children's clapping, rhyming and jumprope games, and blues music. The circumstances of renting thus encourage and bolster the emergence of a cultural form that has been expressed in other times, places, and media as well. It is significant in Elm Valley that many Black householders seem to entexture their alley communities or residential blocks and to link themselves to the street through at least one male family member. However, renting as a class constraint is still important in encouraging people to probe for depth. White renters are generally much more tied to the shops, schools, and sidewalks of Elm Valley than their counterparts who own. It is too soon to tell exactly what the strategies of the new, renting refugees from Southeast Asia and Central America will be: Early observations indicate that Latin men have begun to embrace the life of the street; Southeast Asian families may be building a public life around one apartment building.

4. In one unusual but representative situation, two men with two toddlers apiece grew to know each other when one was assigned to be the other's doctor and noted from his patient's file that they were neighbors. The children began to play together, but their paths soon split. The doctor had bought a house in Elm Valley before it was fashionable and he enjoys its international variety. He was, however, determined that his children not suffer culturally because of his decision. When the doctor was in charge of the children, they went to a park in a wealthy neighborhood, to swimming lessons in the suburbs, or to a museum. The patient minded his own children frequently, but he saw their early developmental tasks differently. Although he took them regularly to Elm Valley's seedy park, he also let them play right on the sidewalk while he talked to his friends, and he took them shopping and into taverns with him. He patiently herded them to the store, allowing them to inspect every plant and animal specimen, vehicle, pothole, stairwell, and construction site that caught their attention along the way. He taught them to greet and joke with all the shopkeepers, bus drivers, and people on the street. He wanted them to learn details, nicknames, reputations, stories and histories, what to expect and predict, how to capture texture for themselves.

5. Many of the owning families do seem to seek texture in particular places, revisiting, for example, a special park, a small museum, or the downtown dinosaurs. They bring to these places the same ethnographic affection that for many renters is an encompassing, definitive strategy for living in a neighborhood.

6. Hennig (1982) writes of gentrification that although planners expected it to boost cities' financial resources by increasing tax revenues and decreasing demand for social services, this has not been the case. New owners demand more, back up those demands, and dislike contributing to the public sector in exchange for services they are more likely to find elsewhere. This appreciation of class privilege in a multicultural situation is similar to what Rosen (1977, 1980) found in his research at a preschool:

Middle-class parents stressed a desire to expose their children to cultural differences; poorer parents stressed the status of a school that middle-class children attended and a desire to reap the benefits in skills and resources that would help their children excel in schools later on.

7. The house is a well-worn centerpiece of the American Dream, in which it usually stands for happiness and success. Constance Perrin's (1978) interviews with people in the housing and banking industries revealed that they read a great deal into houses and in particular into owning one. Her informants easily painted owners as more independent, responsible, and rooted than tenants, whom they believed to be poor providers and decision makers, socially marginal, and uncommitted to a community. The mortgages that banks grant owners certify that they are properly climbing the ladder of life; and owning a house further encourages good character and valued behaviors, in part by liberating residents from the problematic relations that stem from tenants' shared use of common facilities. Realtors seem to have carried these associations even further, as their promotional materials refer to houses as "homes." "Home" to stand for even an empty house has crept into popular usage almost metaphorically, with all the nuances of connections, commitments, and roots that "home" used to pose in contrast to house.

REFERENCES

Allen, I. 1980. "The Ideology of Dense Neighborhood Development." *Urban Affairs Q.* Vol. 15, No. 4: 409–428.

Geertz, C. 1973. *The Interpretation of Cultures.* New York: Basic Books.

Goldfield, D. 1980. "Private Neighborhood Redevelopment and Displacement." *Urban Affairs Q.* Vol. 15, No. 4: 453–468.

Hannerz, U. 1969. *Soulside.* New York: Columbia University Press.

Hennig, J. 1982. *Gentrification in Adams Morgan.* Washington, DC: George Washington University Press.

Jacobs, J. 1961. *The Life and Death of Great American Cities.* New York: Random House.

Liebow, E. 1967. *Tally's Corner.* Boston: Little, Brown.

Love, R. 1973. "The Fountains of Urban Life." *Urban Life and Culture* Vol. 2, No. 2: 161–209.

McCaffrey, P. 1982. "The Gentry are Coming." *Perspectives* (Winter): 22–27.

Merry, S. 1980. "Racial Integration in an Urban Neighborhood." *Human Organization* Vol. 39, No. 1: 59–69.

Merry, S. 1981. *Urban Danger: Life in a Neighborhood of Strangers.* Philadelphia: Temple University Press.

Molotch, H. 1969. "Racial Integration in a Transition Community." *Amer. Soc. Rev.* Vol. 34: 878–893.

Perrin, C. 1978. *Everything in Its Place.* Princeton, NJ: Princeton University Press.

Reed, P. 1974. "Situated Interaction: Normative and Nonnormative Bases of Social Behavior in Two Urban Residential Settings." *Urban Life and Culture* Vol. 2, No. 4: 460–487.

Rosaldo, R. 1984. "Grief and a Headhunter's Rage," in *Text, Play, and Story,* ed. by E. Bruner. Washington, DC: AES.

Rosen, D. 1977. "Multicultural Education: An Anthropological Perspective." *Anthropology and Education Q.* Vol. 8: 221–226.

Rosen, D. 1980. "Class and Ideology in an Innercity Preschool." *Anthro. Q.* Vol. 53: 219–228.

Suttles, G. D. 1968. *The Social Order of the Slum.* Chicago: University of Chicago Press.

Swartley, A. 1983. "If This Were Any Other Job, I'd Shove It." *Mother Jones* Vol. 8 (May): 33–55.

Williams, M. 1981. *On the Street Where I Live.* New York: Holt, Rinehart & Winston.

10

Political Organization and Social Control

The concepts of **political organization** and **social control** are about the ways power is distributed and embedded in society. Power is found in all social relationships. Even in seemingly innocuous places like Disney World, Clifford Shearing and Philip Stenning show the subtle and not so subtle ways in which people are controlled. Power is not about physical force alone, as was shown by the way the ayatollah Khomeini defeated the Shah of Iran with neither troops nor equipment or, more recently, by the dramatic collapse of the Soviet Union. This is what makes the study of power so fascinating. An insightful perspective on these events can be gained from the world traditionally studied by anthropologists.

The events of the Colonial Era, the short but intense period from about 1884 to 1960 when the industrialized European powers acquired large amounts of colonial real estate in Africa and Asia, set the parameters for the political structures under which the poor majority of the world's population live. Elizabeth Eames's essay is a representative study of how this colonial intrusion had an impact on "traditional" society. She shows how **colonialism** undermined women's traditional autonomy and argues that colonial authorities were largely oblivious to what they were doing because the way in which they saw the world and asked questions was shaped by their Victorian outlook. To consolidate their position, the British and the other colonizers used remarkably similar strategies. They created a class of **subalterns**, local indigenes who were propelled into positions of petty power and who ruled on the colonizers' behalf.

In this they were aided by missionaries who provided the subalterns with the minimal educational skills and who played a further important role in legitimating colonial rule. At the same time, missionaries also provided the seedbed for the later anticolonial movements. Legitimacy, with its rich invocation of symbols, is a key concern in the politics about power.

Eames's study provides a graphic illustration of the process that concerns Jason Clay, namely, warring among **nations** and **states.** Most of the states in the contemporary world are the product of colonialism, and rather than simply accept them as necessary, we need to ask some probing questions about their nature. Why is it that states are so often controlled by people of one nation, who use their power to suppress the rights of other nationalities living within the same state?

The subaltern warrant chiefs and clerks described by Eames became the source of the Third World elite or *petite bourgeoisie* who often wind up using the state to enrich themselves. As Archie Mafeje, a leading African anthropologist, put it: "They think that the way to fish is by emptying the pond." There are a number of reasons for such a predatory worldview, which is intimately tied into how they view the state. Certainly they do not see the state the way Western political theorists see it, as some sort of neutral umpire protecting and caring for its citizens in exchange for taxes. As a Papua New Guinean said to one of this book's editors: "The State is a money box in a tent which is controlled by the senior officials." This intellectual legacy is still very much with us and indeed will probably grow as Africa and the other Southern Hemisphere countries become increasingly marginalized and hence less subject to public scrutiny.

Many anthropologists see autonomy and how **cultural pluralism** is tolerated within the state as the major issues facing the close of this century. This view is perhaps overstated to make the point. Consider Papua New Guinea as an example: It is a country of some 3,000,000 people with over 700 different nations of which the largest language group has fewer than 200,000 speakers. Ask any Papua New Guineans what they regard as the major achievement of their Australian colonizers (Papua New Guinea rather reluctantly became an independent state in 1975), and they will say the creation of **law** and order. They will say that prior to colonization everyone fought, but the Australians brought peace to the country. Papua New Guineans are renowned for their **egalitarian ethos.** Politically they have no strongly developed **hierarchies** with chiefs or kings. This meant that if they had a dispute, they

had to settle it between themselves, largely through warfare and related compensation payments. The Australians brought peace by creating overarching third-party dispute management forums for hearing disputes. In short, they said, if you have a problem, do not make a war but bring it to the District Commissioner. This principle of **dispute management** was not new. Indeed, it forms one of the rationales for the creation of the World Court of International Justice. What is important, though, is why were these triadic structures successful during the colonial heyday but not in the post-independence era? Many commentators have interpreted the new "lawlessness" confronting many parts of the globe as a resurrection of "primitive" or "tribal warfare." That the matter is not so simple is well argued in the essay by Neil Whitehead and Brian Ferguson.

Say "Cheese!"

The Disney Order That Is Not So Mickey Mouse

Clifford Shearing and Philip C. Stenning

Clifford Shearing is a criminologist at the University of Toronto currently attached to the Community Law Center at the University of the Western Cape, South Africa.

One of the most distinctive features of that quintessentially American playground known as Disney World is the way it seeks to combine a sense of comfortable—even nostalgic—familiarity with an air of innovative technological advance. Mingled with the fantasies of one's childhood are the dreams of a better future. Next to the Magic Kingdom is the Epcot Center. As well as providing for a great escape, Disney World claims also to be a design for better living. And what impresses most about this place is that it seems to run like clockwork.

Yet the Disney order is no accidental by-product. Rather, it is a designed-in feature that provides–to the eye that is looking for it, but not to the casual visitor—an exemplar of modern private corporate policing. Along with the rest of the scenery of which it forms a discreet part, it too is recognizable as a design for the future.

We invite you to come with us on a guided tour of this modern police facility in which discipline and control are, like many of the characters one sees about, in costume.

The fun begins the moment the visitor enters Disney World. As one arrives by car one is greeted by a series of smiling young people who, with the aid of clearly visible road markings, direct one to one's parking spot, remind one to lock one's car and to remember its location and then direct one to await the rubber-wheeled train that will convey visitors away from the parking lot. At the boarding location one is directed to stand safely behind guard rails and to board the train in an orderly fashion. While climbing on board one is reminded to remember the name of the parking area and the row number in which one is parked (for instance, "Donald Duck, 1"). Once on the train one is encouraged to protect oneself from injury by keeping one's body within the bounds of the carriage and to do the same for children in one's care. Before disembarking one is told how to get from the train back to the monorail platform and where to wait for the train to the parking lot on one's return. At each transition from one stage of one's journey to the next one is wished a happy day and a "good time" at Disney World (this begins as one drives in and is directed by road signs to tune one's car radio to the Disney radio network).

As one moves towards the monorail platform the directions one has just received are reinforced by physical barriers (that make it difficult to take a wrong turn), pavement markings, signs and more cheerful Disney employees who, like their counterparts in other locations, convey the message that Disney World is a "fun place" designed for one's comfort and pleasure. On approaching the monorail platform one is met by enthusiastic attendants who quickly and efficiently organize the mass of people moving onto it into corrals designed to accommodate enough people to fill one compartment on the monorail. In assigning people to these corrals the attendants ensure that groups visiting Disney World together remain together. Access to the edge of the platform is prevented by a gate which is opened once the monorail has arrived and disembarked the arriving passengers on the other side of the platform. If there is a delay of more than a minute or two in waiting for the next monorail one is kept informed of the reason for the delay and the progress the expected train is making towards the station.

Once aboard and the automatic doors of the monorail have closed, one is welcomed aboard, told to remain seated and "for one's own safety" to stay away from open windows. The monorail takes a circuitous route to one of the two Disney locations (the Epcot Center or the Magic Kingdom) during which time a friendly disembodied voice introduces one briefly to the pleasures of the world one is about to enter and the methods of transport available between its various locations. As the monorail slows towards its destination one is told how to disembark once the automatic doors open and how to move from the station to the entrance gates, and reminded to take one's possessions with one and to take care of oneself, and children in one's care, on disembarking. Once again these instructions are reinforced, in a variety of ways, as one moves towards the gates.

It will be apparent from the above that Disney Productions is able to handle large crowds of visitors in a most orderly fashion. Potential trouble is anticipated and prevented. Opportunities for disorder are minimized by constant instruction, by physical barriers which severely limit the choice of action available and by the surveillance of omnipresent employees who detect and rectify the slightest deviation.

The vehicles that carry people between locations are an important component of the system of physical barriers. Throughout Disney World vehicles are used as barriers. This is particularly apparent in the Epcot Center, . . . where many exhibits are accessible only via special vehicles which automatically secure one once they begin moving.

Control strategies are embedded in both environmental features and structural relations. In both cases control structures and activities have other functions which are highlighted so that the control function is overshadowed. Nonetheless, control is pervasive. For example, virtually every pool, fountain, and flower garden serves both as an aesthetic object and to direct visitors away from, or towards, particular locations. Similarly, every Disney Productions employee, while visibly and primarily engaged in other functions, is also engaged in the maintenance of order. This integration of functions is real and not simply an appearance: beauty *is* created, safety *is* protected, employees *are* helpful. The effect is, however, to embed the control function into the "woodwork" where its presence is unnoticed but its effects are ever present.

A critical consequence of this process of embedding control in other structures is that control becomes consensual. It is effected with the willing cooperation of those being controlled so that the controlled become, as Foucault has observed, the source of their own control. Thus, for example, the batching that keeps families together provides for family unity while at the same time ensuring that parents will be available to control their children. By seeking a definition of order within Disney World that can convincingly be pre-

sented as being in the interest of visitors, order maintenance is established as a voluntary activity which allows coercion to be reduced to a minimum. Thus, adult visitors willingly submit to a variety of devices that increase the flow of consumers through Disney World, such as being corralled on the monorail platform, so as to ensure the safety of their children. Furthermore, while doing so they gratefully acknowledge the concern Disney Productions has for their family, thereby legitimating its authority, not only in the particular situation in question, but in others as well. Thus, while profit ultimately underlies the order Disney Productions seeks to maintain, it is pursued in conjunction with other objectives that will encourage the willing compliance of visitors in maintaining Disney profits. This approach to profit making, which seeks a coincidence of corporate and individual interests (employee and consumer alike), extends beyond the control function and reflects a business philosophy to be applied to all corporate operations (Peters and Waterman, 1982).

The coercive edge of Disney's control system is seldom far from the surface, however, and becomes visible the moment the Disney-visitor consensus breaks down, that is, when a visitor attempts to exercise a choice that is incompatible with the Disney order. It is apparent in the physical barriers that forcefully prevent certain activities as well as in the action of employees who detect breaches of order. This can be illustrated by an incident that occurred during a visit to Disney World by Shearing and his daughter, during the course of which she developed a blister on her heel. To avoid further irritation she removed her shoes and proceeded to walk barefooted. They had not progressed ten yards before they were approached by a very personable security guard dressed as a Bahamian police officer, with white pith helmet and white gloves that perfectly suited the theme of the area they were moving through (so that he, at first, appeared more like a scenic prop than a security person), who informed them that walking barefoot was, "for the safety of visitors," not permitted. When informed that, given the blister, the safety of this visitor was likely to be better secured by remaining barefooted, at least on the walkways, they were informed that their safety and how best to protect it was a matter for Disney Productions to determine while they were on Disney property and that unless they complied he would be compelled to escort them out of Disney World. Shearing's daughter, on learning that failure to comply with the security guard's instruction would deprive her of the pleasures of Disney World, quickly decided that she would prefer to further injure her heel and remain on Disney property. As this example illustrates, the source of Disney Productions' power rests both in the physical coercion it can bring to bear and in its capacity to induce co-operation by depriving visitors of a resource that they value.

The effectiveness of the power that control of a "fun place" has is vividly illustrated by the incredible queues of visitors who patiently wait, sometimes for hours, for admission to exhibits. These queues not only call into question the common knowledge that queuing is a quintessentially English pastime (if Disney World is any indication Americans are at least as good, if not better, at it), but provide evidence of the considerable inconvenience that people can be persuaded to tolerate so long as they believe that their best interests require it. While the source of this perception is the image of Disney World that the visitor brings to it, it is, interestingly, reinforced through the queuing process itself. In many exhibits queues are structured so that one is brought close to the entrance at several points, thus periodically giving one a glimpse of the fun to come while at the same time encouraging one that the wait will soon be over.

Visitor participation in the production of order within Disney World goes beyond the more obvious control examples we have noted so far. An important aspect of the order Disney Productions attempts to maintain is a particular image of Disney World and the American industrialists who sponsor its exhibits (General Electric, Kodak, Kraft Foods, etc.). Considerable care is taken to ensure that every feature of Disney World reflects a positive view of the American Way, especially its use of, and reliance on, technology. Visitors are, for example, exposed to an almost constant stream of directions by employees, robots in human form and disembodied recorded voices (the use of recorded messages and robots permits precise control over the content and tone of the directions given) that convey the desired message. Disney World acts as a giant magnet attracting millions of Americans and visitors from other lands who pay to learn of the wonders of American capitalism.

Visitors are encouraged to participate in the production of the Disney image while they are in Disney World and to take it home with them so that they can reproduce it for their families and friends. One way this is done is through the "Picture Spots," marked with signposts, to be found throughout Disney World, that provide direction with respect to the images to capture on film (with cameras that one can borrow free of charge) for the slide shows and photo albums to be prepared "back home." Each spot provides views which exclude anything unsightly (such as garbage containers) so as to ensure that the visual images visitors take away of Disney World will properly capture Disney's order. A related technique is the Disney characters who wander through the complex to provide "photo opportunities" for young children. These characters apparently never talk to visitors, and the reason

for this is presumably so that their media-based images will not be spoiled.

As we have hinted throughout this discussion, training is a pervasive feature of the control system of Disney Productions. It is not, however, the redemptive soul-training of the carceral project but an ever-present flow of directions for, and definitions of, order directed at every visitor. Unlike carceral training, these messages do not require detailed knowledge of the individual. They are, on the contrary, for anyone and everyone. Messages are, nonetheless, often conveyed to single individuals or small groups of friends and relatives. For example, in some of the newer exhibits, the vehicles that take one through swivel and turn so that one's gaze can be precisely directed. Similarly, each seat is fitted with individual sets of speakers that talk directly to one, thus permitting a seductive sense of intimacy while simultaneously imparting a uniform message.

In summary, within Disney World control is embedded, preventative, subtle, co-operative and apparently non-coercive and consensual. It focuses on categories, requires no knowledge of the individual and employs pervasive surveillance. Thus, although disciplinary, it is distinctively non-carceral. Its order is instrumental and determined by the interests of Disney Productions rather than moral and absolute. As anyone who has visited Disney World knows, it is extraordinarily effective.

While this new instrumental discipline is rapidly becoming a dominant force in social control . . . it is as different from the Orwellian totalitarian nightmare as it is from the carceral regime. Surveillance is pervasive but it is the antithesis of the blatant control of the Orwellian State: its source is not government and its vehicle is not Big Brother. The order of instrumental discipline is not the unitary order of a central State but diffuse and separate orders defined by private authorities responsible for the feudal-like domains of Disney World, condominium estates, commercial complexes and the like. Within contemporary discipline, control is as fine-grained as Orwell imagined but its features are very different. . . . It is thus, paradoxically, not to Orwell's socialist-inspired Utopia that we must look for a picture of contemporary control but to the capitalist-inspired disciplinary model conceived of by Huxley who, in his *Brave New World*, painted a picture of consensually based control that bears a striking resemblance to the disciplinary control of Disney World and other corporate control systems. Within Huxley's imaginary world people are seduced into conformity by the pleasures offered by the drug "soma" rather than coerced into compliance by threat of Big Brother, just as people today are seduced to conform by the pleasures of consuming the goods that corporate power has to offer.

The contrasts between morally based justice and instrumental control, carceral punishment and corporate control, the Panopticon and Disney World and Orwell's and Huxley's visions is succinctly captured by the novelist Beryl Bainbridge's observations about a recent journey she made retracing J. B. Priestley's celebrated trip around Britain. She notes how during his travels in 1933 the centre of the cities and towns he visited were defined by either a church or a centre of government (depicting the coalition between Church and State in the production of order that characterizes morally based regimes).

During her more recent trip one of the changes that struck her most forcibly was the transformation that had taken place in the centre of cities and towns. These were now identified not by churches or town halls, but by shopping centres; often vaulted glass-roofed structures that she found reminiscent of the cathedrals they had replaced both in their awe-inspiring architecture and in the hush that she found they sometimes created. What was worshipped in these contemporary cathedrals, she noted, was not an absolute moral order but something much more mundane: people were "worshipping shopping" and through it, we would add, the private authorities, the order and the corporate power their worship makes possible.

REFERENCES

Bainbridge, B. 1984. Television interview with Robert Fulford on *"Realities"* Global Television, Toronto, October.

Foucault, M. 1977. *Discipline and Punish: The Birth of Prison.* New York: Vintage.

Peters, T. & R. H. Waterman, Jr. 1982. *In Search of Excellence: Lessons from America's Best-Run Companies.* New York: Warner.

Priestley, J. B. 1934. *English Journey: Being a Rambling But Truthful Account of What One Man Saw and Heard and Felt and Thought During a Journey through England the Autumn of the Year 1933.* London: Heinemann and Gollancz.

Why the Women Went to War

Women and Wealth in Ondo Town, Southwestern Nigeria

Elizabeth A. Eames

After undertaking extended fieldwork in west Africa, Elizabeth Eames obtained her Ph.D. at Harvard. She currently teaches at Bates College in Lewiston Maine.

... Guided by an optimistic western feminism, I had chosen to live and work with Yoruba women—renowned for their economic independence and their almost total association with the public arena of the marketplace ... [My] expectations [of the domination of the Yoruba women in trade] were essentially confirmed during my years on the scene. Yoruba farmers are generally male, traders female. Not only are all traders women, but most women are traders: 97% of the women I surveyed traded, two thirds of them at official town markets.

Specifically, I lived and worked in Ondo Town, a hinterland city currently home to perhaps a quarter-of-a-million. Ondo is an ancient city-state whose political history has been overshadowed and markedly influenced by such famous empires as Benin, Ife, and Oyo (see, for example, Forde and Kaberry 1967). I chose Ondo, however, to confirm my suspicion that a certain constellation of circumstances had enhanced the position of its women: Ondo was founded by a woman, whose female and male descendants still reign; Ondo rules of descent and inheritance are significantly more bilateral than those of other major Yoruba sub-groups; historically, trade was relatively more important than military conquest to Ondo's dominance over surrounding peoples. I suggest that all of these factors are implicated in the foundation and the maintenance of Ondo's solidly dual-sex political system (Okonjo 1976), the functioning of which I explore below.

During my first field trip, I had focused most of my attention on the economic responsibilities of ordinary women. But in an effort to document the annual women chiefs' festival (for the god of wealth), I was

"Why the Women Went to War: Women and Wealth in Ondo Town, Southwestern Nigeria" by Elizabeth A. Eames, from *Traders Versus the State Anthropological Approaches to Unofficial Economies* ed. by Gracia Clark, 1988, pp. 80–97. (Boulder, CO: Westview Publishing. Reprinted with permission of Elizabeth A. Eames, Bates College.)

funded for a brief return in 1985. As I witnessed the unexpected events recounted here—the Ondo Market Women's War—I came to realize the significance of political linkages between ordinary women's lives, their voluntary market associations, and the hierarchy of women chiefs. These events forced me to re-cast my previous work in the light of Ondo women's political roles.

I took a second look at the riddle posed by the position of *Olobun*, woman king, owner-of-markets, priestess-of-profit. Up to that point, I had unwittingly absorbed the official (male) view that the *Olobun* position was merely a ritual title, the holder of which was so hemmed in by taboos and prohibitions that she could have no importance in the political realm. I had failed to contemplate her significance for the structure as a whole.

In light of my analysis of the women's war, I can state with confidence that the position of *Olobun* is of crucial symbolic significance, and serves as the ritual/symbolic/ideological capstone legitimizing (yet circumscribing) women's place in the arena of political power. Along with the usual characterization of Yoruba politics as a redistributive/big-man system, I would argue that there is a legitimate place for the big-woman in Ondo Yoruba society, a prescribed route for her to follow, and a clear mechanism for the redistribution of her resources via bartering wealth into honor. Moreover, it is the highly revered, dangerous and mysterious title of Woman King, surrounded by so many prohibitions and taboos, that makes possible a this-world power struggle over access to the—seemingly lesser—position of *opoji*, or woman chief.... I must emphasize for the reader unfamiliar with West Africa that these organizations were formerly governmental in nature. Rather than an index of women's informal power, they were the locus of wholly legitimate authority. Please note, moreover, that I use the term "woman king" advisedly—she is neither the wife of a king (they are called *olori*), nor is she a ruler by default, that is for lack of a male heir. Her epithet, *Oba Obinrin*, means *woman king*.

An instance of women's public political role and mobilization for action is documented here in an attempt to rectify their chronic invisibility in public historical and political records. But the women's war also raises other issues: How are "traditional" symbols used to communicate "modern" messages? More specifically, messages critical of the functioning of a formal state structure. By going to war, the women's organizations publicly demonstrated their power and thereby asserted their legitimacy in the peoples' eyes, even in the face of non-recognition by the central government. Herein lies, perhaps, political anthropology's contribution to recent political science discussions of the so-called "soft state" in Africa.

Let me begin by describing the Women's War in Ondo in 1985. I will then compare the gender symbolism employed during this demonstration of female solidarity with that of the famous Aba Women's War of 1929, wherein sixty Igbo and Ibibio women lost their lives at the hands of colonial troops (Perham 1937). The role of these women's institutionalized protests within the traditional state structure will lead us directly into a discussion of their role within modern state structures.

THE ONDO WOMEN'S WAR (IJA OBINRIN ONDO)

On November 11, 1985, the streets of Ondo Town, southwestern Nigeria, were transformed into a sea of bobbing headties. I had been in the kitchen area with Mama Bayo and a handful of children, gossiping as usual while she washed vegetables and I picked through rice. As the ordinary rumble of street noise rose to a crescendo, my companion grasped its significance and darted outside, exclaiming in Yoruba, "It's women's war, no market today!"

It turned out that she was only slightly off the mark—the war lasted *ten* days. Ten days of escalating civil disorder, economic disruption, ritual invocation, curses and counter-curses. To the common folks of Ondo it spelled turmoil, and even hunger. I must admit, however, that for a foreign feminist doing fieldwork it was a thrilling sight indeed!

What government policies and practices had led up to this strike? In an effort to tap into revenues circulating in the so-called informal sector, Ondo state had four days earlier instituted a substantial levy on all women[1]—and only women—based on the essentially accurate assumption that all Yoruba women sell something. The military governor's office had not dealt directly with the town council of women chiefs,

the *opoji*, but had notified the king about the state's decision.

The relationship between Nigeria's federal and state government, its civil service, and its "natural rulers" is complicated and tense. In stark contrast to military governors, who rule by "might" over essentially arbitrary geographical units, divine kings and high chiefs maintain their special legitimacy through their sacred relationship to the land. Kings are consulted by office-holders, their blessing is courted by office-seekers, and their salaries are paid by the state. They have political and judicial jurisdiction in civil (though no longer in criminal) matters occurring within their borders.

Ondo Town's dual-sex political institutions have always been invisible to those in charge of Nigeria's state apparatus; hence no direct lines of communication existed between the governor and the women chiefs. So, the *Osemawe* (king) of Ondo informed the *opoji*. They, in turn, convened a meeting of the heads of each market trading association at the Rex Cinema house,[2] where they drafted letters to various community leaders and officials.

When their letters of protest were ignored, they began the process of mobilizing for a fight by informing a certain set of three surrounding villages that they had a grievance. As these villages are responsible for the burial of a deceased king's body parts, this seems to be a way of warning them that they soon may have a dead king on their hands. Indeed, if such a war escalates and remains unresolved, the kingmakers should persuade a king to commit suicide.

What followed was structured and orchestrated. At first, the women simply closed down the market as if a king had died and marched in ranks according to what they sold, parading their protest in song. The next day, they paraded *en masse* to inform each male chief and the Chief of Police of their woes.

Their terms soon escalated. They carried symbolically potent objects (*akoko* leaves and brooms), violated the recesses of the palace, removed their wrappers and cursed the king. While no local women opened their stalls during the war, male traders from the North who continued to sell potatoes and beans in the marketplace reported to the townswomen that the Ondo king had been spotted performing a ritual "turning of the curse" back on the market itself. At this, the women threatened their ultimate weapon. This supernatural sanction, to be explained in detail below, was known as "making a market at *Iparuku*" and it would certainly mean the king's demise. On that day—the 9th day of the *ija obinrin*—the matter was settled: only those women who owned their own cement buildings were to pay the tax. The following day, the women chiefs performed a ritual cleansing of the market and the king made a costly sacrifice to counteract the curse born of his townswomen's ill-will.

Of the narrative so-far presented, the salient image to keep in mind is the highly condensed and multivocal symbolic action of *making a market at Iparuku.* This non-descript but ritually potent spot is where the prospective king is transformed into a divine being by partaking of a cannibal stew made of the heart of his predecessor, cooked and served to him by the *Olobun,* the woman king, head of the women chiefs, and, literally translated, "owner of the region's markets."

The West African colonial record documents other such women's wars of resistance in nearby Eastern Nigeria and Western Cameroon. Recent feminist scholarship has, not surprisingly, salvaged these incidents from the heap of colonial history, and re-analyzed the accounts to illustrate colonial attitudes as well as indigenous practices. In their discussions of the Aba Women's War of 1929 and the Anlu Rebellion of 1958, Van Allen (1972; 1976), Ifeka-Moller (1975) and Ardener (1975) have each argued that the gender symbolism employed associated women above all with fecundity, fertility and the "wild." Ifeka-Moller, especially, argues that in the Igbo and Ibibio cases, where women were associated with subsistence farming, their trading wealth was seen as illegitimate and threatening. Ifeka-Moller explicates the chain of cultural associations thusly: as women moved into trade from farming, their womanhood was threatened because their fertility was threatened because their link with the land was dissolving.

Although at first glance the Ondo women seem to be employing similar symbolic language—leaves, threat of nakedness, insult, etc.—I hope to demonstrate the primary and wholly *legitimate* association expressed was woman as office-holder and wielder of wealth. In short, Woman-As-Trader was primary, and fecundity was secondary.[3] For instance, the *akoko* leaves held in their hands were symbolic of legitimate political voice, invoked in this case against a king who was perceived as betraying his legitimate role. *Akoko* leaves are associated with title-houses, title-taking ceremonies and with the foundation of the kingdom out of chaos. Leaves communicating the message of wildness would have been palm fronds, and these leaves are indeed used during rites of passage and rites of rebellion and the chaotic half of the annual festival of cosmic ordering (dedicated to *Ogun*).

Clearly, then, *Ija Obinrin* is neither an uncontrolled riotous outpouring of rage nor a rite of rebellion providing catharsis for the masses while leaving the political order essentially intact. I did witness these two alternatives during fieldwork: Ondo's 1983 post-election riots included looting, arson and lynching. The widespread civil strife of this period culminated in General Buhari's New Year's Eve coup. Secondly, a

textbook example of a "rite of rebellion" takes place every September in Ondo. During the *Opepee* festival, the masses spend all night roaming the town, hurling insulting songs at king and chiefs. But the women's war was something else: By going to war, the women were exercising their rights as political subjects, expressing their political voice through the proper channels—the woman king, her council of women chiefs, and the heads of their market associations. Only when this went unheeded did the protest shift into high-gear—all the while remaining within the customary political boundaries of insult, obscenity, and curse.

It has oft been stated that among the Yoruba-speaking people, all status was achieved, and all personal power was based, on maintaining a large loyal following. As with all other positions of prominence in this wealth-in-people system (Bledsoe 1980), so too with the king. Though divine, he was not an absolute ruler, but merely the premier member of the council known as the kingmakers because they chose the king from among the candidates lobbying for the seat. But one might add, they could be king-breakers. To them was given the power and the right to order a king to commit suicide or, if necessary, to actually administer poison to the ruler. Ondo's kinglist includes information on forty-two past rulers, and according to my calculation, twelve (or almost 30%) were recorded as having been dethroned in this way. The practice has apparently persisted for almost three centuries. Even the regional strife of the late nineteenth century entailed only a slight rate increase. Within living memory, three kings have been deposed, in 1901, 1925, and 1942. Among them is included the father of the present king.

The first and paradigmatic case of deposing a king was Bajumu, the tenth king of Ondo, who supposedly ruled from 1702–1711. It is crucial to note that he stands accused in the chronicle of way-laying market women and seizing their goods (Bada of Saki 1940). His only other recorded offense was waging an unjust war with an unnamed neighboring town. He was warned by his people, it is said, but turned a deaf ear to their cries. It would seem from this sketchy history that Bajumu offended the ordinary citizens, both female and male, by disrupting their lives and their livelihoods. As Bajumu marauded wayfarers and incited military hostilities in pursuit of booty for his own coffers, he would have disrupted both women's trade and men's agricultural routine and labor supply.

All this becomes relevant when one realizes that in 1985, Nigeria's military rulers stood accused and condemned of similar offenses in the eyes of its citizens. Nigeria's national economy had suffered tremendous blows in the last few years, as the result of a worsening export market, but also as a result of years of inefficiency and graft. Prices of local produce had doubled that year, and I recorded a ten-fold price increase for imported essential commodities. . . . The government wreaked havoc when brutally interfering with market women—they banned the sale of a wide range of imports, confiscated contraband or hoarded goods right out of market stalls, enforced sale at unrealistic controlled prices, and even razed roadside markets during their misguided "War Against Indiscipline" (known locally as WAI, pronounced "WHY?").

On top of these hardships, Ondo's cocoa farmers suffered a terrible blow in 1985. Their entire crop and a sizable portion of their mature trees were lost, due to the state-run cocoa marketing cooperatives' failure to distribute insecticide. This was viewed as almost willful incompetence since the year's supply had reportedly been in Lagos port awaiting distribution for the preceding six months.

Austerity was biting everyone, but most especially the average male cocoa farmer and the average woman food or provisions seller. The new tax decree followed an increase in school fees for supposedly free education, increased hospital charges for ostensibly free health care, a newly announced mandatory contribution to the "Ondo State Development Fund," as well as the perpetual income taxes, which are costly to dodge and costlier to pay.

Moreover—and this was the crowning blow—it was rumored that the king had reported to the Governor that Ondo women were an untapped source of income, his evidence being that they built buildings of their own. Ondo wives are well aware that their men are acutely sensitive on the subject of women building houses. In the wider Nigerian society where women are not primarily associated with revenue from trade, this building of houses by Ondo women is taken as proof-positive that Ondo women make "uppity" wives.

All this led up to Monday, November 11, 1985, when the Ondo women's war began. Ranks and ranks, tens of thousands of women, and only women, marched from the market to the palace to the police station chanting and singing, registering their protest and demanding satisfaction, proceeding in turn to each prominent male chief's residence, reporting their difficulty. They carried certain commonplace objects with ritual potency—two pieces of broomstick and a certain kind of leaf. Both are used by the woman king during the installation of a new king, and their use in this instance implied that a new installation ceremony would soon be necessary.

Their songs escalated from mere manifestos of tax resistance, to insult ("Out of thirty/Itiade scored zero"), to obscenity ("He takes tax/Like he takes our private parts"), to songs reserved for times of war ("There is trouble/If you see grass burning"), to implicit threats against the king's life (singing songs mourning a dead chief), to explicit threats on the king's life ("Itiade turns into a goat/We kill and eat him"). . . .

They stormed the palace, violating the section forbidden to all women. They demonstrated their grief and their extreme emotional turmoil in the culturally prescribed way of parading in their slip but without their outer wrapper. Not only is nakedness or a disheveled appearance associated with deep mourning or the last stages of mental breakdown, but it is in this context also potent behavior: the most powerful curse of all is that of a naked woman. By parading in their slips alone, they were implying such a curse, explained to me as displaying in front of the king his own "mother's secrets."

While superficially non-violent (though highly energetic and boisterous), the protestors' words and actions served to register a vote of no confidence in the king, thereby threatening not only the king's tenure in office, but his very life. In a very real sense his life was at stake—the curses would have set in motion the process called euphemistically "making the king sleep." It is unclear if actual poison is in King Itiade's future. But supernaturally potent actions were taken which he had to counteract at great expense, much to the delight of the women I knew.

THE STRUCTURAL CENTRALITY OF OLOBUN

Unfortunately for its womenfolk, Ondo is no longer a city-state, but a city in the state of Ondo, southwestern Nigeria. The highly formalized dual-sex political structure has been dealt a series of severe blows, beginning with the colonialists' unwillingness to deal with women. To a series of foreign ethnographers they remained invisible. Even more distressing, Yoruba chroniclers of their own culture and history have perpetuated the dominant male ideology—casting a mere passing glance in the direction of Ondo's woman king and her cabinet of women chiefs, allotting at most a paragraph of text to Ondo's unique political configuration (Adeyemi 1935, Ogunshakin 1976, Ojo 1976). Olupona (1983) is the first to pay any attention to the institution, but it remains tangential to his analysis. For all these reasons and probably many more, recorded political history of Ondo ignores women's voice. . . .

The title [of woman king] is hereditary through the female descendants of the female founder of the town. The post is highly ritualized, dangerous, mysterious and revered. Her single most important function is to cook and serve a stew made of the dead king's heart during the installation of the new king. This seems to be the origin of the title's danger and mystery. You will recall that the most potent threat used during the women's war was to make a market at *Iparuku*. Iparuku is the very place this ritual transformation occurs.

She has no clout, this old woman without temporal/secular power, yet carries tremendous ritual significance. Her legitimization and validation function is very real, since her duties include ceremonial installations of title holders and the opening of new markets. She might also be called something on the order of the "high priestess of profit."

Hence, the *Olobun* embodies Woman as Mother, Trader, Domestic Laborer, and, yes, even Witch:

- Mother: Ritual "mother" of the king; elder; to be taken care of by her symbolic son

- Trader: Controls the founding of markets and the god of prosperity/profit

- Domestic Laborer: Taboos surrounding her person emphasize household cleanliness and efficiency (e.g., she must not set foot on an unswept floor, she must not eat yesterday's stew, etc., etc.)

- Witch: Dealer in supernatural; giver and taker of life; cooking that cannibalistic feast for a new king further associates women with cannibal witches, wherein the source of power is "eating" human flesh, in this case, literally.

Only the *Olobun* and her cabinet of *opoji* may propitiate *Aje*, that is, Profit. It is this cabinet of women chiefs who have real political, judicial and economic roles to perform—settling quarrels, voicing women's interests in the king's council, leveling market tolls, etc. It is among the women chiefs of her council that we find the struggle for power, where amassing wealth can lead through generosity to gaining a following and contesting a title. In this re-distributive economy, where women have independent incomes and networks, here is the way for a woman to barter her opportunity to make a fortune in the marketplace into honor and status. This is to everyone's advantage, since title-holders spread wealth around, yet titles also bring with them new sources of income.

In the past, the bases of these women's power included such things as: successful trade, a large number of dependents, membership in voluntary societies, inheritance, land, craft specialization, slaves, pawns, medicine, etc. Any and all of these could lead to social reputation.

Of course, in this century, Ondo's political integration has been torn asunder by such things as re-aligned trade routes, new products, new need for as well as new sources of cash, enforced peace, abolition of slavery and tolls, and the disruption of tributary and judicial payments. At the same time, a new status system based on personal fortune or western education has altered the social bases of the political system. By shoring up the faltering political structure they considered crucial to indirect rule, the British irrevocably altered its form.

Only the senior male (*eghae*) chiefs' judicial role has been enhanced by the colonial and post-colonial governments. No longer are their positions subject to the vagaries of ordinary citizens' shifting loyalties, but find their foundation in an external source of power.

The female chiefs have suffered in very much the same way as have the male chiefs below the *eghae* level. Bereft of any officially recognized judicial function, deprived of the government salary due chiefs, and with real political decisions made elsewhere than the king's council, the women chiefs' power has been on the wane.

But in November 1985, they fought back. And the government did have to modify their policy. Shrewdly, they singled out cement stalls and left alone those with tables in the open air.

One question with which we are left, then, is how can extant women's organizations be marshalled for decision-making at the national level? I hope that the preceding analysis will highlight their *potential* for mobilization. The case of the *Ija Obinrin Ondo* does support March and Taqqu's conclusion in *Women's Informal Associations in Developing Countries: Catalysts for Change?* that rotating credit associations provide the most solid foundation upon which to build equitable planned change (1986). But the sad truth is that not one of Nigeria's myriad lively newspapers picked up this story, and the government's divide-and-rule tactic served its purpose all too well.

NOTES

1. Except those paying income tax directly out of government salary.
2. The irony of this appellation must have escaped them.
3. The cultural association of children with wealth makes this separation between trade and motherhood less clear-cut.

REFERENCES

Adeyemi, Reverend. 1935(?). *History and Culture of the Ondo*. Unpublished Master's thesis. (on deposit at Harvard's Tozzer Library).

Ardener, Shirley. 1975. "Sexual Insult and Female Militancy." In *Perceiving Women*, ed. by Shirley Ardener. New York: Wiley.

Bada of Shaki. 1940. *Iwe Itan Ondo*. Ondo: Igbehin Adun Press.

Bledsoe, Caroline. 1980. *Women and Marriage in Kpelle Society*. Stanford, CA: Stanford University Press.

Forde, Daryll, & P. M. Kaberry (Eds.). 1967. *West African Kingdoms in the Nineteenth Century*. London: Oxford.

Ifeka-Moller, Caroline. 1975. "Female Militancy and Colonial Revolt: The Women's War of 1929, Eastern Nigeria. In *Perceiving Women*, ed. by Shirley Ardener. New York: Wiley.

March, Kathryn S., & Rachelle L. Taqqu. 1986. *Women's Informal Associations in Developing Countries: Catalysts for Change?* Boulder, CO: Westview.

Mintz, Sidney. 1971. "Men, Women and Trade." *Comparative Studies in Society and History* Vol. 13: 247–268.

Ogunshakin, Patrick. 1976. *Ondo: The People, Their Customs and Traditions*. Lagos: Inway.

Ojo, Jerome O. 1976. *Yoruba Customs from Ondo.* Vienna: Institut fur Volkerkunde der Universitat Wien.

Okonjo, Kamene. 1976. "The Dual-Sex Political System in Operation: Igbo Women and Community Politics in Midwestern Nigeria." *Women in Africa.* ed. by Hafkin & Bay. Stanford, CA: Stanford University Press.

Olupona, J. O. Kehinde. 1983. *A Phenomenological/Anthropological Analysis of the Religion of the Ondo-Yoruba of Nigeria.* Unpublished Ph.D. dissertation, Department of Religion, Boston University.

Perham, Margery. 1937. "The Aba Market Women's Riot in Nigeria, 1929." In *Native Administration in Nigeria.* London. (Reprinted in *The Africa Reader: Colonial Africa,* ed. by Cartey & Kilson. New York: Vintage.)

Van Allen, Judith. 1972. "Sitting on a Man: Colonialism and the Lost Political Institutions of Igbo Women." *Canadian Journal of African Studies* Vol 6:2.

Van Allen, Judith. 1976. "Aba Riots or Igbo Women's War? Ideology, Stratification and the Invisibility of Women." In *Women in Africa,* ed. by Hafkin & Bay. Stanford, CA: Stanford University Press.

What's a Nation? Latest Thinking

Jason W. Clay

After receiving his Ph.D. from Cornell in 1979, Jason Clay became an associate in social anthropology at the Peabody Museum, Harvard University. His primary position was research and editorial director for Cultural Survival, Inc., an advocacy group for indigenous people founded by David Maybury-Lewis (see Chapter 2). Clay was also director of marketing for Cultural Survival and played a major role in developing markets for goods produced in sustainable ways by indigenous peoples (Rain Forest Crunch is one example). He has published extensively on issues involving the rights of indigenous peoples and currently is an independent consultant.

Eastern Europe's revolts and the Soviet Union's unraveling are part of a worldwide call to redefine the relationship of the *state* to the *nations* each contains.

There are about five thousand nations in the world today. What makes each a nation is that its people share a language, culture, territorial base, and political organization and history. The Kayapó Indians are but one nation within the state called Brazil. The Penan people of Sarawak are but one nation within the state called Malaysia. To nation peoples, group identity matters well beyond state affiliation. The five thousand nations have existed for hundreds, even thousands of years. The majority of the world's 171 states have been around only since World War II. Very few nations have ever been given a choice when made part of a state. Some states have far better records than others, but overall, no ideology, left or right, religious or sectarian, has protected nations or promoted pluralism much better or worse than any other. In fact, the twentieth century has probably seen more genocides and ethnocides than any other.

All modern states are empires, and they are increasingly seen as such by nations. From Lithuania to Canada, the movement by nations pushing for power sharing and autonomy demands that the world evolve a creative new kind of geopolitics—call it "decentralized federalism"—or be gripped by worse and worse cycles of violence.

Clearly, the Palestinians who live within Israel's borders will not soon identify themselves as Israelis.

But did you know that the Oromos in Ethiopia have more members than three-quarters of the states in the United Nations, and that they do not think of themselves as Ethiopians? The twenty million Kurds don't consider themselves first or foremost Turks, Iranians, Iraqis, or Syrians. The Efe Pygmies barely know what Zaire is. There are about 130 nations in the USSR, 180 in Brazil, 90 in Ethiopia, 450 in Nigeria, 350 in India. That so many nations are squeezed into so few states is, in fact, the nub of the problem.

Three-quarters of the 120-odd shooting wars in the world today are being fought between nations and the states that claim to represent them. With very few exceptions, these wars are not about the independence of nations, but rather their level of autonomy: who controls the rights to resources (land, water, minerals, trees), who provides local security, who determines the policies that affect language, laws, and cultural and religious rights. While states can exist regardless of the answer to these questions, nations cannot.

In most states, power is in the hands of a few elites, who operate by a simple credo: Winner take all. They control foreign investment and aid, and use both to reinforce their power. They set local commodity prices, control exports, and levy taxes. The result, on average, is that powerless nations provide most state revenues and receive few services in return. "Development" programs usually allow a state to steal from its nations, whether it be Indian land throughout North and South America, Penan timber in Malaysia, pastoralists' land throughout Africa, or oil from the Kurds in Iraq. Naturally, most nations attempt to resist this confiscation of their resources, which leads to open conflict.

"What's a Nation? Latest Thinking" by Jason W. Clay, from *Mother Jones*, Vol. 15, No. 7, 1990, pp. 28–30. Copyright © 1990 by Mother Jones. Reprinted with permission of the publisher.

Nearly all debt in Africa, and nearly half of all other Third World debt, comes from the purchase of weapons by states to fight their own citizens. Most of the world's 12 million refugees are the offspring of such conflicts, as are most of the 100 million internally displaced people who have been uprooted from their homelands. Most of the world's famine victims are nation peoples who are being starved by states that assimilate them while appropriating their food supplies. Most of the colonization, resettlement, and villagization programs are sponsored by states, in the name of progress, in order to bring nation peoples to their knees.

A vicious circle forms. The appropriation of a nation's resources leads to conflict, conflict leads to weapons purchases, weapons purchases lead to debt, and debt leads to the appropriation of more resources—and the cycle intensifies.

As the cold war ends, new relationships will evolve, not only between the United States and the USSR, but also among their allies and the nonaligned states. Seeing fewer Third World countries as proxies in an ideological war, the superpowers are pulling back on aid. That means cutting the umbilical cords of Third World elites. The consequent weakening of their power may unleash more struggle between state rulers and nations who sense an opportunity to win more control over their futures. The number of shooting wars in states is likely to increase, at a time when arms makers and NATO and Warsaw Pact countries are trying to dump obsolete weapons and find markets for new ones. Nation-state conflicts, when intensified, will spawn legions of refugees—*this* is likely to be the growth field of the 1990s.

Yet it is clearer in 1990 than in recent decades that cultural identity is alive and well. In Africa, for example, to justify dictatorships and one-party rule, local elites and foreign interests have long proclaimed the evils of tribalism. Lately, some self-described "liberators for life" have apparently concluded that they can only survive by opening up their political systems. Dictators in Benin, the Ivory Coast, Zaire, and Zambia have moved to allow opposition parties and elections. But simply allowing tribes to form political parties won't necessarily defuse pressures, because it won't change the fact that these are nations within states. There is intriguing talk in Uganda of a confederation of tribes, based on the League of Iroquois, where local power would be left to the tribes and state politics would be decided by a joint council in which each tribe, regardless of size, has an equal vote. Under such a system, larger tribes are likely to resent not being able to wield proportional power. Yet it does address the vulnerability of small nations, which insist that they have the right to exist, as long as they do not deny others those same rights.

If nations and states are to find a peaceful coexistence, a system of decentralized federalism will have to evolve. By this I mean a political system that is built from the bottom up, one that gives autonomy and power to nation peoples, who in turn empower the state to act on their behalves.

Beyond this guiding principle, there is no one model. Weak states with strong nations may break themselves into new states. Newly independent nations, after trying to make a go of it for a while, may later decide it is to their advantage to be part of a larger political unit. Many nations may use independence as a negotiating stance and settle for more local control within a state. To date, because the political processes in most states are not open, the only way nations have been able to push for their rights is to take them by force. The next twenty years will likely be bloody if the world cannot find a new and better way to answer the demands of its now emboldened nations.

Deceptive Stereotypes about "Tribal Warfare"

Neil L. Whitehead and R. Brian Ferguson

Neil Whitehead is an Oxford D.Phil. He has specialized in historical anthropology, especially of lowland South America and the Caribbean. He teaches at the University of Wisconsin in Madison.

R. Brian Ferguson teaches in the Department of Sociology, Anthropology and Criminal Justice, Rutgers University, Newark. He has long been interested in warfare and has published extensively on the subject.

Who would have imagined the current nostalgia for the cold war? We lived with the threat of imminent nuclear destruction for decades, but at least the battle lines seemed clear. East versus West, Communism versus capitalism. Any brushfire war, anywhere in the world, could be forced into this mold. To be sure, this interpretation blinded us to many realities, but at least it was tidy.

That sense of order is missing today. The great polarity has evaporated, and we are left with proliferating local conflicts that seem to be getting more savage all the time. Groping for a framework to make sense of the carnage, pundits and politicians are tapping into old ideological currents about "tribal warfare." These explanations, however, are contradicted by much recent research. Rather than illuminating the wellsprings of violence, they only muddy the waters.

The human species is held to be inherently tribalistic. We are said to cleave to others like "us" and to react with unreasoned fear and hostility to "them." Humans form tribes, it is said, and the relations between tribes are hostile. Applied to recent outbreaks of violence around the world, the concept of tribalism suggests that a weakening of control by central governments allows an upsurge of primal antagonisms. The violence seems to erupt from the people themselves.

These views are based on mistaken, but deeply ingrained, ideas about the origin and nature of tribes. "Tribe" itself is a loaded term. In the rhetoric of Euro-

"Deceptive Stereotypes about 'Tribal Warfare'" by Neil L. Whitehead and R. Brian Ferguson, from *The Chronicle of Higher Education*, November 10, 1993. Reprinted with permission of N. L. Whitehead, Assoc. Professor, Dept. of Anthropology, University of Wisconsin-Madison and R. B. Ferguson, Assoc. Professor, Dept. of Anthropology, Rutgers University.

pean expansionism during the heyday of colonialism, it was used as a disparaging label for indigenous peoples whose political organization did not exhibit the hierarchical, centralized authority of a state. In this pejorative sense, *tribal* was contrasted with *civilized*.

But tribe also refers to a genuine kind of polity, a group that anthropologists describe as being bounded and distinct from its neighbors to some degree, capable of a measure of coordinated political action, yet lacking a stratified central structure. Many indigenous peoples do not exhibit this cohesion, their highest sovereign units being families or more extended groups of kin.

But true tribes often were created in the areas that European colonialists governed, in response to a gradual process of colonial expansion during the past 500 years. For example, the Mohegans emerged out of Algonquian populations in New England to become a distinctive tribe by taking sides in 17th-century colonial wars.

Frequently, tribal peoples have engaged in brutal, horribly destructive wars, a direct inspiration for Hobbes's "war of all against all." The loudly trumpeted mission of Europe's colonialists was to put a stop to such carnage, to "pacify the savages."

The problem with this interpretation is that, in cases from all over the world, comparing the *earliest* reports of European contact with indigenous peoples to later reports shows that tribal warfare sometimes was absent when the Europeans first arrived, or at least was much less intensive than it was after they appeared. Perhaps more astonishing, the tribes that are so prominent in later accounts often were unrecognizable as tribes when the Europeans initially arrived.

The central point in the volume that we recently edited, *War in the Tribal Zone* (School of American Research Press, 1992), is that both the transformation and intensification of war, as well as the formation of tribes, result from complex interactions in an area that we call "the tribal zone." The zone begins at the points where centralized authority makes contact with peoples it does not rule. In tribal zones, newly introduced plants, animals, diseases, and technologies often spread widely, long before the colonizers appear. These and other changes disrupt existing sociopolitical relationships, fostering new alliances and creating new kinds of conflicts.

Thus, life and war on the American Great Plains took on an entirely new cast when smallpox, horses, guns, and displaced peoples arrived from distant frontiers. The arrival of priests, traders, soldiers, and settlers in a tribal zone always complicated circumstances and often encouraged new kinds of wars (for example, as various tribes took different sides against rival colonial powers), along with new patterns of trade and political alliances. The new people who arrived had trouble dealing with the lack of boundaries and the independence of the native peoples that they encountered, so they encouraged the formation of politically unified groups—tribes. Even without such direct encouragement, the extreme conflict frequently generated by the arrival of colonialists promoted tribalization, as local people were compelled to band together just to survive.

To be sure, both warfare and tribes have existed for a very long time in human history. But the often horrifying tribal bloodshed that was, and continues to be, used to justify the expansion of European control in most cases was a reaction to a colonial presence. Thus, research done by one of us shows that the formation of a distinctive Carib people in northern South America, and the devastating warfare reported in the region, was a response to the initial bloody colonization by rival Spanish and Dutch powers from the 16th through the 18th centuries.

Research by the other author on the Yanomani of the remote borderlands of Brazil and Venezuela, who often are said to be one of the most violent peoples on earth, shows that their violence is tightly connected in timing, targets, and intensity to changes in the presence of Westerners stretching back for centuries.

How is this relevant to contemporary conflicts? We are in danger of allowing our misunderstanding of tribal conflict, a misunderstanding that is a product of our own cultural history, to prevent us from grasping the real causes of contemporary violence in various countries.

To speak of "ancient tribal hatreds," as many observers of conflicts in Somalia and in the former Yugoslavia have done, invokes an image of timeless, unchangeable political oppositions. In fact, tribal boundaries are highly changeable; they can arise, dissolve, or shift as a result of diverse circumstances. Labeling current conflicts as tribal also promotes the idea that violent conflict is a predictable outgrowth of cultural differences between groups. In fact, tribes often are from identical cultures, and cultural difference itself is a very poor predictor of violent conflict—just as cultural homogeneity is not necessarily a predictor of peace. Consider the fact that Somalia is one of the most culturally homogeneous states in all of sub-Saharan Africa.

To invoke tribal warfare in areas such as the former Yugoslavia is especially misleading. The essence of tribal political organization and of real tribal warfare is that it is based on extensive discussion and consensus among local leaders. In the Balkans, authoritarian leaders give the orders. If the fighting has become increasingly polarized along cultural lines, it is because self-aggrandizing heads of state have deliberately played on existing cultural differences. When soldiers who have been encouraged to think of themselves as defenders of one ethnic group are ordered to rape women of another, ethnic hatred will grow. It is clear that ancient animosities do exist in the culture of the region, but these seeds of violence only blossom when they are cultivated by politicians.

Another danger is that we may accept the stereotypical assumption that tribal warfare is irrational, perhaps even an expression of atavistic biological impulses. In contrast, close study of the decision making involved in genuine tribal warfare usually reveals canny strategizing about very tangible interests. Moreover, the main circumstances shaping tribal military decisions are rarely purely local, as is often claimed, but instead involve the connections between local groups and the outside world. Very frequently, the fighting is about who will benefit more or suffer less from ties to colonial power centers. Thus, from the 17th-century Mohawk Indians to the 20th-century Yanomani, wars have been fought to gain monopolistic control over the physical space around Western colonial outposts and missions.

These observations suggest how we should understand war in places such as Somalia. A variety of power bases exist, growing out of the local organization of subsistence and exchange, but also shaped by a long history of political interactions with foreign governments. The ruling groups in Somalia were supported by the superpowers during the cold war, then abandoned. United Nations forces now have become entangled in this political web, becoming identified with one side against another in a conflict where the sides themselves are defined largely by the nature of their relationship with outside powers. For example, in this complex political field, Ali Mahdi Mohammed has been the most prominent leader aligned with United Nations forces, and Mohammed Farah Aidid has been painted as the U.N.'s foe, even though earlier he had also cooperated with and benefited from the U.N. presence.

A broad-ranging debate over the newly elevated principle of "humanitarian intervention" is just beginning. The issue will be with us for years, if not in Somalia or Bosnia, then somewhere else. It is a con-founding issue, and each case will be disquietingly unique. But our understanding will always be clouded if we view local wars as eruptions of primitive tribal animosities. A better conception is that violence emerges and is structured by the intersection of local and external forces. Any act of humanitarian intervention will itself become a part of that interplay. If such interventions continue in Somalia or elsewhere, we must recognize and continually monitor their effects—and that means avoiding deceptive stereotypes about tribal wars.

11

Religion and Magic

What does it mean to be religious? Is belief rational? Can we have faith in science? Why do we wear appropriate clothing on ritual occasions? What foods go with which meals? The greater part of our existence is devoted to making sense of the world rather than telling the truth about it. Indeed, French anthropologist Claude Lévi-Strauss argues that the distinctive characteristic of humans is precisely our capacity to make meanings in order to make sense of ourselves. In such projects, he argues, humanity has an **a priori** classification system that is ingrained before practical utilization of knowledge. The reason why we eat certain food on certain occasions and dress appropriately for certain rituals or activities is based on this classification system. The analysis of this deeply embedded system is by **structural analysis.** The more basic this system of classification, the more difficult it is for us to reconcile activities involving mutually incompatible categories. For example, the distinction between human and animal is fundamental, and this would explain why bestiality is still viewed with horror in most societies.

Our day-to-day knowledge, then, is built upon and supported by a prior system of knowledge that is gratuitous (in opposition to the Western notion that systems of thought always have practical ends in view). This is why in our day-do-day life we operate on a mass of assumptions and partial understandings and accept the authority of our society as mediated through physicians, electricians and lawyers. Actions are based on a mixture of faith and experience. If we fail to achieve our ends, then we might seek alternative explanations. Thus the failure of a light bulb might eventually be attributed to "Chance," which would be the structural equivalent of "God" in another society.

One of the ways we accentuate difference between ourselves and others is by exaggerating their propensity to have "weird" beliefs and practices in contrast to our own eminently rational and logical beliefs and actions. They are always held to be guided and influenced by "sorcery" and "superstition." Nowhere is this expressed more strongly than in the realm of **magic and religion.** Most of us have a strong faith in the "technological fix" for solving our problems. The problems of famine, starvation, and even AIDS, we believe, rhetoric notwithstanding, will be solved by science. Science will provide us with the technological means of neutralizing the problem, thereby freeing us from the necessity of changing our behavior.

Tanya Luhrmann shows how witches are alive and active as a subculture even in highly industrialized countries like Britain and the United States. Her article shows how they construct "tradition" to legitimize their activities and points to the fallacy that "we" are so different from "them."

That our beliefs frequently override technology is shown in Silvia Rodgers's paper in which she subjects ship-launching ceremonies to a classic structural analysis. She shows how the religious beliefs (superstitions?) of sailors (including even senior officers), their symbolic classification of the ship, the extensive reincarnating power of a ship's name, and the relationship between women and ships all play an important role in how sailors believe and act. Furthermore, these are sailors with high educational qualifications and experience, who literally control earth-shattering means of destruction in the form of nuclear weaponry.

In his paper, David Lewis-Williams gives us a look at a type of religious experience that is (and has been) common in many (probably most) of the world's societies. This is the phenomenon of **trance,** an altered state of consciousness individuals enter in order to make contact with supernatural beings and powers. One reason it is common is that all humans are capable of entering trance, because they all have the same type of nervous system—in a very real sense they are "hard wired" for the experience. In spite of this, there are cultures that deny this reality by regarding trance behavior as "abnormal." The United States is a good example; individuals entering altered states of consciousness are apt to be regarded as "mentally unbalanced," and if hallucinogenic substances are involved, the individual may be jailed for illegal activity. By contrast, other societies accept the neuropsychological reality of trance and "explain" it by imbuing it with sacred meaning. Especially in societies in which one finds **shamans**—individuals especially skilled at making contact with and manipulating supernatural beings and forces—the ability to enter altered states plays a prominent role in ritual activity.

The last article in this section serves as a bridge to the next (Chapter 12) on culture change. All around the world today, wars waged for a variety of political and ideological reasons are a cause of substantial change, and the question arises: How to heal the wounds of psychological, emotional, and cultural violence that is potentially more devastating than physical violence? In Mozambique, people are turning to traditional healers, for whom the effects of violence have been added to the roster of "diseases" they must deal with.

The Goat and the Gazelle
Witchcraft

Tanya Luhrmann

Tanya Luhrmann received her Ph.D. in 1986 from Cambridge University, England, and then took a position as associate professor at the University of California in San Diego. Her regional interests lie in England and India, while her topical interests include psychological anthropology, rationality, and morality. Her work in psychological anthropology won her the prestigious Sterling Award for best paper in this field.

Full moon, November 1984. In a witches' coven in northeast London, members have gathered from as far away as Bath, Leicester and Scotland to attend the meeting at the full moon. We drink tea until nine—in London, most rituals follow tea—and then change and go into the other room. The sitting room has been transformed. The furniture has been removed, and a twelve-foot chalk circle drawn on the carpet. It will be brushed out in the morning. Four candlesticks stake out the corners of the room, casting shadows from the stag's antlers on the wall. The antlers sit next to a sheaf of wheat, subtle sexual symbolism. In spring and summer there are flowers everywhere. The altar in the centre of the circle is a chest which seems ancient. On top an equally ancient box holds incense in different drawers. On it, flowers and herbs surround a carved wooden Pan; a Minoan goddess figure sits on the altar itself amid a litter of ritual knives and tools.

The high priestess begins by drawing the magic circle in the air above the chalk, which she does with piety, saying, "Let this be a boundary between the world of gods and that of men." This imaginary circle is then treated as real throughout the evening. To leave the circle you slash it in the air and redraw it when you return. The chalk circle is always drawn with the ritual knife; the cakes, wine and the dancing always move in a clockwise direction. These rules are part of what makes it a witches' circle and they are scrupulously observed. On this evening a coven member wanted us to "do" something for a friend's sick baby. Someone made a model of the baby and put it on the altar, at the Minoan goddess's feet. We held hands in a circle

around the altar and then began to run, chanting a set phrase. When the circle was running at its peak the high priestess suddenly stopped. Everyone shut their eyes, raised their hands, and visualized the prearranged image: in this case it was Mary, the woman who wanted the spell, the "link" between us and the unknown child. We could have "worked" without the model baby, but it served as a "focus" for the concentration. Witches of folklore made clay and waxen effigies over which they uttered imprecations—so we made effigies and kept a packet of plasticene in the altar for the purpose. By springtime, Mary reported, the child had recovered, and she thanked us for the help.

Modern witchcraft was essentially created in the forties—at least in its current form—by a civil servant, Gerald Gardner, who was probably inspired by Margaret Murray's historical account of witchcraft as an organized pre-Christian fertility religion branded devil-worship by the demonologists, and more generally by the rise of interest in anthropology and folklore.[1] Gardner had met Aleister Crowley, knew of the Golden Dawn, and may have been a Freemason. (Indeed his rituals show Crowleyian and Masonic influence.[2]) In the early fifties, Gardner published fictitious ethnographies of supposedly contemporaneous witches who practised the ancient, secret rites of their agrarian ancestors and worshipped the earth goddess and her consort in ceremonies beneath the full moon.[3] He claimed to have been initiated into one of these groups, hidden from watchful authorities since the "burning times."[4] In his eyes, witchcraft was an ancient magico-religious cult, secretly practised, peculiarly suited to the Celtic race. Witches had ancient knowledge and powers, handed down through the generations. And unlike the rest of an alienated society, they were happy and content. This paragraph gives the flavour of his romanticism:

> Instead of the great sabbats with perhaps a thousand or more attendants [the coven] became a small meeting in private houses, probably a dozen or so according to the size of the room. The numbers being few, they were no longer able to gain power, to rise to the hyperaesthetic state by means of hundreds of wild dancers shrieking wildly, and they had to use other secret methods to induce this state. This came easily to the descendants of the heath, but not to the people of non-Celtic race. Some knowledge and power had survived, as many of the families had intermarried, and in time their powers grew, and in out of the way places the cult survived. The fact that they were happy gave them a reason to struggle on. It is from these people that the surviving witch families probably descend. They know that their fathers and grandfathers belonged, and had spoken to them of meetings about the time of Waterloo, when it was an old cult, thought to exist from all time. Though the persecution had died down from want of fuel, they realized that their only chance to be left alone was to remain unknown and this is as true today as it was five hundred years ago.[5]

The invention of tradition is an intriguing topic: why is it that history should grant such authority, even in so rational an age? Witches speak of a secretive tradition, hidden for centuries from the Church's fierce eye, passed down in families until the present generation. There is no reason that such claims could not be true, but there is very little evidence to support them. The most sympathetic scholarship that speaks of an organized, pre-Christian witchcraft has very shaky foundations[6]—although there is more recently work that suggests that there were at least shared fantasies about membership in witch-related societies.[7] But those accused of witchcraft in early modern Europe were very likely innocent of any practice.[8]

Witches have ambivalent attitudes towards their history. . . . They share, however, a common vision of their past, differing only on whether this past is myth or legend. Many of them say that the truth of the vision is unimportant: it is the vision itself, with its evocative pull, that matters. The basic account—given by someone who describes it as a myth—is this:

> Witchcraft is a religion that dates back to paleolithic times, to the worship of the god of the hunt and the goddess of fertility. One can see remnants of it in cave paintings and in the figurines of goddesses that are many thousands of years old. This early religion was universal. The names changed from place to place but the basic deities were the same.
>
> When Christianity came to Europe, its inroads were slow. Kings and nobles were converted first, but many folk continued to worship in both religions. Dwellers in rural areas, the "Pagans" and "Heathens," kept to the old ways. Churches were built on the sacred sites of the old religion. The names of the festivals were changed but the dates were kept. The old rites continued in folk festivals, and for many centuries Christian policy was one of slow cooptation.
>
> During the times of persecution the Church took the god of the Old Religion and—as is the habit with conquerors—turned him into the Christian devil. The Old Religion was forced underground, its only records set forth, in distorted form, by its enemies. Small families kept the religion alive and in 1951, after the Witchcraft Laws in England were repealed, it began to surface again . . .[9]

It is indeed an evocative tale, with secrecy and martyrdom and hidden powers, and whether or not witches describe it as actual history they are moved by its affect.

Witchcraft is meant to be a revival, or re-emergence, of an ancient nature-religion, the most ancient of religions, in which the earth was worshipped as a woman under different names and guises throughout the inhabited world. She was Astarte, Inanna, Isis, Cerridwen—names that ring echoes in archaeological texts. She was the Great Goddess whose rites Frazer and Neumann—and Apuleius—recorded in rich detail. Witches are people who read their books and try to create, for themselves, the tone and feeling of an early humanity, worshipping a nature they understand as vital, powerful and mysterious. They visit the stone circles and pre-Christian sites, and become amateur scholars of the pagan traditions behind the Easter egg and the Yule log.

Above all, witches try to "connect" with the world around them. Witchcraft, they say, is about the tactile, intuitive understanding of the turn of the seasons, the song of the birds; it is the awareness of all things as holy, and that, as is said, there is no part of us that is not of the gods.[10] One witch suggests a simple exercise to begin to glimpse the nature of the practice:

> Perhaps the best way to begin to understand the power behind the simple word *witch* is to enter the circle. . . . Do it, perhaps, on a full moon, in a park or in the clearing of a wood. You don't need any of the tools you will read about in books on the Craft. You need no special clothes, or lack of them. Perhaps you might make up a chant, a string of names of gods and goddesses who were loved or familiar to you from childhood myths, a simple string of names for earth and moon and stars, easily repeatable like a mantra.
>
> And perhaps, as you say those familiar names and feel the earth and the air, the moon appears a bit closer, and perhaps the wind rustling the leaves suddenly seems in rhythm with your own breathing. Or perhaps the chant seems louder and all the other sounds far away. Or perhaps the woods seem strangely noisy. Or unspeakably still. And perhaps the clear line that sepa-

rates you from bird and tree and small lizards seems to melt. Whatever else, your relationship to the world of living nature changes. The Witch is the change of definitions and relationships.[11]

The Goddess, the personification of nature, is witchcraft's central concept. Each witch has an individual understanding of the Goddess, which changes considerably over time. However, simply to orient the reader I will summarize the accounts which I have heard and have read in the literature. The Goddess is multifaceted, ever-changing—nature and nature's transformations. She is Artemis, virgin huntress, the crescent moon and the morning's freshness; Selene, Aphrodite and Demeter, in the full bloom of the earth's fertility; Hecate and axe-bearing Cerridwen, the crone who destroys, the dying forests which make room for new growth. The constant theme of the Goddess is cyclicity and transformation: the spinning Fates, the weaving spider, Aphrodite who each year arises virgin from the sea, Isis who swells and floods and diminishes as the Nile. Every face of the Goddess is a different goddess, and yet also the same, in a different aspect, and there are different goddesses for different years and seasons of one's life.

The Goddess is very different from the Judaeo-Christian god. She is in the world, of the world, the very being of the world. "People often ask me whether I *believe* in the Goddess. I reply, 'Do you believe in rocks?'"[12] Yet she is also an entity, a metaphor for nature to whom one can talk. "I relate to the Goddess, every day, in one way or another. I have a little chitchat with Mommy."[13] Witches have talked to me about the "duality" of their religious understanding, that on the one hand the Goddess merely personifies the natural world in myth and imagery, and that on the other hand the Goddess is there as someone to guide you, punish you, reward you, someone who becomes the central figure in your private universe. I suspect that for practitioners there is a natural slippage from metaphor to extant being, that it is difficult—particularly in a Judaeo-Christian society—genuinely to treat a deity-figure as only a metaphor, regardless of how the religion is rationalized.[14] The figure becomes a deity, who cares for you.

Gardner began initiating people into groups called "covens" which were run by women called "high priestesses." Covens bred other covens; people wandered into the bookstore, bought his books and then others, and created their own covens. By now there are many types of witchcraft: Gardnerian, Alexandrian, feminist, "traditional" and so forth, named for their founders or their political ideals. Feminist covens usually only initiate women and they usually think of themselves as involved with a particularly female type of spirituality. Groups stemming from Gardner are

called "Gardnerian," Alexandrian witchcraft derives from Alex Sanders' more ceremonial version of Gardnerian witchcraft. Sanders was a charismatic man who deliberately attracted the attention of the gutterpress and became a public figure in the late sixties. Some of those who read the sensationalistic exposés and watched the television interviews were drawn to witchcraft, and Sanders initiated hundreds of applicants, sometimes on the evening they applied. Traditional witches supposedly carry on the age-old traditions of their families: whether by chance or otherwise, I met none who could substantiate their claim to an inherited ritual practice.

Covens vary widely in their style and custom, but there is a common core of practice. They meet on (or near) days dictated by the sky: the solstices and equinoxes and the "quarter days" between them, most of them fire-festivals in the Frazerian past: Beltane (1 May), Lammas (1 August), Halloween (31 October), Candlemas (2 February). These are the days to perform seasonal rituals, in which witches celebrate the passage of the longest days and the summer's harvest. Covens also meet on the full moons—most witches are quite aware of the moon's phases—on which they perform spells, rituals with a specific intention, to cure Jane's cold or to get Richard a job. Seasonal ritual meetings are called "sabbats," the full moon meetings, "esbats."[15] Membership usually ranges between three and thirteen members, and members think of themselves—or ideally think of themselves—as "family." In my experience, it usually took about a year of casual acquaintance before someone would be initiated.[16] The process took so long because people felt it important that a group should be socially very comfortable with each other, and—crucially—that one could trust all members of the group. As a result, covens tended to be somewhat socially homogeneous.[17] In the more "traditional" covens, there are three "degrees." First-degree initiates are novices, and in their initiation they were anointed "witch" and shown the witches' weapons.[18] Second-degree initiates usually take their new status after a year. The initiation gives them the authority to start their own coven. It consists in "meeting" death—the initiate acts the part of death if he is male; if she is female, she meets death and accepts him. The intended lesson of the ritual is that the willingness to lose the self gives one control over it, and over the transformations of life and death. Third-degree initiation is not taken for years. It is essentially a rite of mystical sexuality, though it is sometimes "symbolic" rather than "actual." It is always performed in privacy, with only the two initiates present.[19] Behind the initiation lies the idea that one becomes the Goddess or God in one of their most powerful manifestations, the two dynamic elements of the duality that creates the world.

Witchcraft is a secretive otherworld, and more than other magical practices it is rich in symbolic, special items. Initiates have dark-handled knives they call "athames," which are the principal tools and symbols of their powers: they have special cups and platters and incense burners, sometimes even special whips to "purify" each other before the rite begins. There is always an altar, usually strewn with herbs and incense, with a statue of the Goddess, and there are always candles at the four directions, for in all magical practice the four directions (east, south, west, north) represent the four ancient elements (air, fire, water, earth) which in turn represent different sorts of "energies" (thought; will power; emotion; material stability).[20] Then, another symbol of the secrecy and violation of convention, most covens work in the nude. This is ostensibly a sign of freedom, but probably stems from the evocative association of witchcraft and sexuality, and a utopian vision of a paradisial past. There are no orgies, little eroticism, and in fact little behaviour that would be different if clothes were being worn. That witches dance around in the nude probably is part of the attractive fantasy that draws outsiders into the practice, but the fantasy is a piece with the paganism and not the source of salacious sexuality. Or at least, that seemed to be the case with the five covens I met.

I was initiated into the oldest of these witches' groups, a coven which has remained intact for more than forty years. It was once Gardner's own coven, the coven in which he participated, and three of the current members were initiated under his care. It pleases the anthropologist's heart that there are traces of ancestor worship: the pentacle, the magical platter which holds the communion "mooncakes," was Gardner's own, and we used his goddess statue in the circle.

The coven had thirteen members while I was there. Four of them (three men and one woman) had been initiated over twenty-five years ago and were in their fifties: an ex-Cambridge computer consultant, who flew around the world lecturing to computer professionals; a computer software analyst, high priest for the last twenty years; a teacher; an ex-Oxford university lecturer. The high priestess was initiated twenty years ago and was a professional psychologist. Another woman, in her forties, had been initiated some ten years previously. She joined the group when her own coven disbanded; another man in his fifties also came from that coven. He was an electronic engineer in the music industry. By the time I had been in the group several months, Helga and Eliot's coven had disbanded (this was the coven associated with the Glittering Sword) and Helga at any rate preferred to think of herself as a Nordic Volva rather than as a Celtic witch. So she abandoned witchcraft altogether, though she became deeply engaged in the other magical practice, and Eliot and another member of his coven, the

young Austrian who was also in the Glittering Sword, joined the group. The rest of the younger generation included a woman in her thirties who was a professional artist but spent most of her time then raising a young child. Another member was a middle-level manager of a large business. He was in his late thirties and was my "psychic twin": we were both initiated into the group on the same night. Another man, thirtyish, managed a large housing estate. The computer consultant and the teacher had been married twenty-five years, the high priest and high priestess had lived together for twenty. Four other members had partners who did not belong to the group, but two of them belonged to other magical groups. Three members of the group were married to or closely related to university lecturers—but this was an unusually intellectual group.

This coven, then, had a wide age range and was primarily composed of middle-class intellectuals, many of whose lovers were not members of the group. This was not particularly standard: another coven with whom this group had contact had nine members, all of whom were within ten years of age, and it included three married couples and three single individuals. A Cambridge coven had a similarly great age span, and as wide a range of professions. But one in Clapham was entirely upper working class, and its members were within about fifteen years of age. For the meetings, the group relied upon a standard ritual text. Gardner (with the help of Doreen Valiente, now an elder stateswoman in what is called the "Craft") had created a handbook of ritual practice called the "Book of Shadows," which had supposedly been copied by each initiate through the ages. ("Beltane special objects: jug of wine, earthenware chalice, wreaths of ivy . . . High priestess in east, high priest at altar with jug of wine and earthenware chalice . . .") The group performed these rites as written, year in and year out: they were fully aware that Gardner had written them (with help) but felt that as the original coven, they had a responsibility to tradition. In fact, some of them had been rewritten by the high priest, because Gardner's versions were so simple: he felt, however, that he should treat them as Gardner's, and never mentioned the authorship.

The seasonal rituals were remarkable because in them, the priestess is meant to incarnate the Goddess. This is done through a ritual commonly known as "drawing down the moon." The high priestess' ritual partner is called the "high priest," and he stands opposite her in the circle and invokes her as the Goddess; and as Goddess, she delivers what is known as the "Charge," the closest parallel to a liturgy within the Craft. Gardner's Book of Shadows has been published and annotated by two witches, and it includes this text.

The high priest: Listen to the words of the great Mother; she who of old was called among men Artemis, Astarte, Athene, Dione, Melusine, Aphrodite, Cerridwen, Dana, Arianhod, Isis, Bride, and by many other names.

The high priestess: Whenever ye have need of anything, once in the month, and better it be when the moon is full, then shall ye assemble in some secret place and adore the spirit of me, who am Queen of all witches. There shall ye assemble, ye who are fain to learn all sorcery, yet who have not won its deepest secrets; to these will I teach things that are yet unknown. And ye shall be free from slavery; and as a sign that ye be really free, ye shall be naked in your rites; and ye shall dance, sing, feast make music and love, all in my praise. For mine is the ecstacy of the spirit, and mine is also joy on earth; for my law is love unto all beings. Keep pure your highest ideal; strive ever towards it; let naught stop you or turn you aside. For mine is the secret door which opens up the Land of Youth, and mine is the cup of the wine of life, and the Cauldron of Cerridwen, which is the Holy Grail of immortality. I am the gracious Goddess, who gives the gift of joy unto the heart of man. Upon earth, I give the knowledge of the spirit eternal; and beyond death, I give peace, and freedom, and reunion with those who have gone before. Nor do I demand sacrifice; for behold, I am the mother of all living, and my love is poured out upon the earth.

The high priest: Hear ye the words of the Star Goddess; she in the dust of whose feet are the hosts of heaven, and whose body encircles the universe.

The high priestess: I who am the beauty of the green earth, and the white Moon among the stars, and the mystery of the waters, and the desire of the heart of man, call unto thy soul. Arise and come unto me. For I am the soul of nature, who gives life to the universe. From me all things proceed, and unto me all things must return; and before my face, beloved of Gods and men, let thine innermost divine self be enfolded in the rapture of the infinite. Let me worship be with the heart that rejoiceth; for behold all acts of love and pleasure are my rituals. And therefore let there be beauty and strength, power and compassion, honour and humility, mirth and reverence within you. And thou who thinkest to seek for me, know that seeking and yearning shall avail thee not unless thou knowest the mystery; that if that which thou seekest thou findest not within thee, thou wilt never find it without thee. For behold, I have been with thee from the beginning; and I am that which is attained at the end of desire.[21]

The nature-imagery, the romantic poetry, the freedom—this is the style of language commonly heard within these ritual circles. The point of this speech is that every woman can be Goddess. Every man, too, can be god. In some Gardnerian rituals—like Halloween—the high priestess invokes the stag god in her priest, and he gives similar speeches.

When the coven I joined performed spells, no ritual form was prescribed because no spell was identical to any other. The idea behind the spell was that a coven could raise energy by calling on their members' own power, and that this energy could be concentrated within the magical circle, as a "cone of power," and directed towards its source by collective imagination. The first step in a spell was always to chant or meditate in order to change the state of consciousness and so have access to one's own power, and then to focus the imagination on some real or imagined visual representation of the power's goal. The most common technique was to run in a circle, hands held, all eyes on the central altar candle, chanting what was supposedly an old Basque witches' chant:[22]

> Eko, eko, azarak
> Eko, eko, zamilak
> Eko, eko, Cernunnos
> Eko, eko, Aradia[23]

Then, the circle running at its peak, the group suddenly stopped, held its linked hands high, shut its eyes and concentrated on a prearranged image.

Sometimes we prefixed the evening with a longer chant, the "Witches' Rune":

> Darksome night and shining moon
> East, then South, then West, then North;
> Hearken to the Witches' Rune—
> Here we come to call ye forth!
> Earth and water, air and fire,
> Wand and pentacle and sword,
> Work ye unto our desire,
> Hearken ye unto our word!
> Cords and censer, scourge and knife,
> Powers of the witch's blade—
> Waken all ye unto life,
> Come ye as the charm is made!
> Queen of Heaven, Queen of Hell,
> Horned hunter of the night—
> Lend your power unto the spell,
> And work our will by magic rite!
> By all the power of land and sea,
> By all the might of moon and sun—
> As we do will, so mote it be;
> Chant the spell, and be it done![24]

The tone of the poem captures much about witchcraft; the special "weapons" with special powers, the earthly power and goddess power used within the spell, the dependence of the spell upon the witches' will.

Most of the coven meetings I attended in England—in all I saw the rituals of some six Gardnerian-inspired groups—were similar in style. However, there were also feminist covens, a type of witchcraft relatively rare in England but quite important in the States. Witchcraft appeals to feminists for a number of reasons. Witches are meant to worship a female deity rather than a male patriarch, and to worship her as she was worshipped by all people before the monotheistic religions held sway: as the moon, the earth, the sheaf of wheat. Members of feminist covens talk about witchcraft and its understanding of cyclic transformation, of birth, growth and decay, as a "woman's spirituality," and the only spirituality in which women are proud to menstruate, to make love, and to give birth. These women (and sometimes also men[25]) are often also compelled by the desire to reclaim the word "witch," which they see as the male's fearful rejection of a woman too beautiful, too sexual, or past the years of fertility. The witches of European witch-craze fantasies were either beautiful young temptresses or hags.

Feminist covens emphasize creativity and collectivity, values commonly found in that political perspective, and their rituals are often quite different from those in Gardnerian groups. Perhaps I could offer an example, although in this example the women did not explicitly describe themselves as "witches" but as participating in "women's mysteries."

On Halloween 1983 I joined a group of some fifteen women on top of a barrow in Kent. One of the women had been delegated to draw up a rough outline of the ritual, and before we left for the barrow she held a meeting in which she announced that she had "cobbled together something from Starhawk and Z Budapest [two feminist witchcraft manual authors]." (Someone shouted, "don't put yourself down.") She explained the structure of the rite as it stood and then asked for suggestions. Someone had brought a pot of red ochre and patchouli oil which she wanted to use, and someone else suggested that we use it to purify each other. Then it was suggested that we "do" the elements first, and people volunteered for each directional quarter. The person who had chosen earth asked if the hostess had any maize flour which she could use. We talked about the purpose of the rite. The meeting was like many other feminist organization meetings: long on equality, emotional honesty and earthiness, short on speed.

When we arrived on the barrow some hours later, we walked round in a circle. Four women invoked the elements, at the different directions, with their own spontaneously chosen words. It was an impressive midnight: leafless trees stark against a dark sky, some wind, an empty countryside with a bull in the nearby field. Then one woman took the pot of red ochre and drew a circle on the cheek of the woman to her left, saying, "May this protect you on Halloween night," and the pot passed around the circle. Then the woman who had drafted the ritual read an invocation to Hecate more or less taken from Starhawk, copied out in a looseleaf binder with a pentacle laminated on the front:

> This is the night when the veil that divides the worlds is thin. It is the New Year in the time of the year's death,

when the harvest is gathered and the fields lie fallow. The gates of life and death are opened; the dead walk, and to the living is revealed the Mystery: that every ending is but a new beginning. We meet in time out of time, everywhere and nowhere, here and there, to greet the Death which is also Life, and the triple Goddess who is the cycle of rebirth.

Someone lit a fire in a dustbin lid (the cauldron was too heavy to carry from London) and each of us then invited the women that we knew, living or dead, to be present. We then chanted, the chant also taken from Starhawk, in which we passed around incense and each person said, "x lives, x passes, x dies"—x being anger, failure, blindness, and so forth. The chorus was: "It is the cold of the night, it is the dark." Then someone held up a pomegranate (this was found in both Starhawk and Z Budapest) and said, "Behold, I show you the fruit of life." She stabbed it and said, "Which is death" and passed it around the circle, and each woman put a seed in the mouth of the woman to her left, saying, "Taste of the seeds of death." Then that woman held up an apple—"I show you the fruit of death and lo"—here she sliced it sideways, to show the five pointed star at its centre—"it contains the five pointed star of life." The apple was passed around the circle, each woman feeding her neighbour as before and saying, "Taste of the fruit of life." Then we passed a chalice of wine and some bread, saying, "May you never be hungry," pulled out masks and sparklers, and danced around and over the fire. Many of these actions required unrehearsed, unpremeditated participation from all members present, unlike the Gardnerian coven, where those not doing the ritual simply watch until they are called to worship or to take communion (members often take turns in performing the rituals, though). There was also the sense that the group had written some of the ritual together, and that some of the ritual was spontaneous.

There are also "solo" witches, individuals who call themselves witches even though they have never been initiated and have no formal tie to a coven. I met a number of these women (they were always women). One had an organization she called "Spook Enterprises" and sold candles shaped like cats and like Isis. Another called herself a witch but had never been initiated, although she was well-established in the pagan world. Another, the speaker at the 1983 Quest conference, gave talks on "village witchcraft": on inquiry, it appeared that she had been born in Kent, and was an ex-Girtonian.[26]

Mick, the woman of this sort whom I knew best, owned a Jacobean cottage where she lived alone on the edge of the Fens, the desolate drained farmland outside Cambridge. She managed a chicken farm. She told me that she discovered her powers at the age of ten, when she "cursed" her math teacher and he promptly broke his leg in two places. It was clear that witch-craft was integral to her sense of self, and she took it seriously, albeit with theatre. She called her cottage "Broomstick Cottage," kept ten cats and had a cast iron cauldron near the fire place. In the corner of the cottage she had a small statue of Pan on an altar, alongside a ritual knife stained with her own blood. Many of the villagers knew her and in Cambridge I heard of the "Fen witch" from at least four different sources. Once, when I was sitting in her garden (her Elizabethan herb garden), two little boys cycled past. One shouted to the other, *"That's* where the witch lives!" Mick got "col-lected" for her personality, she told me: people seem to think it exotic to have a witch to supper. And this may have been one of the reasons she cherished her claims. She was a very funny, sociable woman, always the cen-tre of a party, but a bit lonely, I think, and a bit roman-tic: witchcraft served a different function for her than fervent Christianity might have done, but like all reli-gions, the witchcraft reduced the loneliness, lent charm to the bleak landscape, and gave her a social role.

There is a certain feel to witchcraft, a humour and an enthusiasm, often missing in other groups. Witch-craft combines the ideal and the mundane. It blends spiritual intensity and romanticism with the lovable, paunchy flaws of the flesh. Fantasies of elfin unicorns side comfortably with bawdy Pans. The high priest of the coven I joined described this as "the goat and the gazelle": "all witches have a little of each." Part of this is the practice itself. People can look slightly ridiculous standing around naked in someone's living room. One needs a sense of humour in order to tolerate the prac-tice, as well as enough romanticism to take it seriously. And witches are perhaps the only magicians who in-corporate humour into their practice. Their central invocation, the declamation of the priestess-turned-goddess, calls for "mirth and reverence." Laughter of-ten rings within the circle, though rarely in the rites. One high priestess spontaneously explained to me that "being alive is really rather funny. Wicca [another name for witchcraft] is the only religion that captures this."

NOTES

1. *In Witchcult in Western Europe* (1921), Murray argued—much influenced by Frazer—that an organized pre-Christian fertility cult lay behind the witchcraft persecutions. The religion centred on the cycle of the seasons and their crops, and deity was incar-nate in a horned male god, who had a female form, Diana. Mur-ray proposed that the male god had superseded the female deity, and that the Inquisition had twisted the symbolism into a cult of devil-worship. Murray described her researches as an-thropological, and compared witches to shamans: just as sha-mans understand themselves to leave their bodies, so witches believed themselves to leave their bodies to "fly"—when they participate in certain rituals. It was a commendable approach, because it interpreted the witchtrials as concerning genuine popular belief—not as the collective delusion historians often assumed.

Other influential books in the development of modern witchcraft were Leland (1899) *Gospel of Aradia;* Frazer (1890; the twelve volumes were slowly published, and the abridged volume appeared in 1922, when Frazer's influence was at its peak—Cohn (1975: 107) *The Golden Bough;* Evans-Wentz (1911) *The Fairy Faith in Celtic Countries;* and later, Graves' (1968; first edition 1948) *The White Goddess.*

2. There seems to be no hard evidence that Gardner actually was a Mason. However, there are some striking similarities in ritual structure between the two practices: an initiatory hierarchy of three "degrees" (Masonry of course has many higher degrees in addition to the three basic ones); an initiation ceremony in which an initiate is presented blindfolded, with a garter around one leg, then presented to the different directional quarters, and presented both the "weapons" or "tools" of what is known as the "Craft."

3. He claimed that he had only published then because of the re-peal of the Witchcraft Laws in 1951, which proclaimed the prac-tice of witchcraft illegal. They were replaced by the Fraudulent Mediums Act. See Farrar and Farrar (1984: 277).

4. Gardner may well have been initiated into a practising group. He claimed that he had been initiated in 1939 by one Dorothy Clutterbuck. Some members of the group I joined had actually known him, and one at least—the most senior member—was persuaded that the group had existed, and that "Old Dorothy" was not a fictitious character. Gardner talked about her, he said, as if she had been alive. Valiente, Gardner's close associate, was also persuaded of this woman's reality, and searched for the traces of her in county records. She produced evidence of a Do-rothy Clutterbuck born and buried at a suitable time, in suitable places. See appendix in Farrar and Farrar (1984: 283–300). How-ever, there is no reason to suppose that if such a group existed, it necessarily predated the publication of Murray's book.

5. Gardner (1954: 46).

6. While the attempt to examine the sixteenth- and seventeenth-century witchcraft persecutions as the product of popular belief was laudable, Murray took the apparent beliefs of the accused for their actual practice, and she drew her evidence from literary accounts of trials and from confessions exacted under torture. Certainly many confessions attest to the existence of sabbats, flying and the like, and there were those who believed that they were witches and confessed freely. However, there is little evi-dence to indicate the existence of an organized pagan fertility cult. Macfarlane, for example, found no evidence for an under-ground pagan religion in his thorough study of witchcraft pros-ecutions in Essex, nor did the language of the prosecutions include descriptions of the sabbat, the diabolic contract, and so forth (1970: 10). Thomas, drawing on a formidable knowledge of the period, concludes that "in England there can be little doubt that there was never a 'witch-cult' of the type envisaged by contemporary demonologists or their modern disciples" (1971: 516). The "Murrayite thesis" is rarely taken seriously, in its full form, today.

7. The relative ease with which people confessed to practice in itself indicates a widespread popular belief in witchcraft: what-ever political purpose the persecution may have served, it de-pended upon common folk belief. In addition, there seems to have been popular medieval European belief in a Diana (Hero-dias, Holda) figure, who travelled through the night accompa-nied by souls of the dead and by female devotees. These "ladies of the night" visited households with benevolent care; there were also beliefs of "night-witches," cannibalistic women who devoured babies (Cohn, 1975: 206–19). Ginzburg presents evi-dence from late sixteenth-century Friuli of a belief in the

"benandanti," "good walkers," who left their bodies at night and, armed with fennel stalks, set out to battle witches over the crops, the livestock, or other desired goods. This fantasy seems to have its roots in a pre-Christianity fertility religion. However, it is not clear that the benandanti ever met in the flesh, or that the fantasy was anything but that. "On the basis of the available documents, the existence or non-existence of an organized set of witches in fifteenth- to seventeenth-century Europe seems to be indeterminate" (Ginzburg, 1983: xiv). Further evidence of a pre-Christian belief in witchcraft is given by Le Roy Ladurie (1987).

8. Explanations of the "witchcraft craze" of early modern Europe are rife. Accounts include: Trevor-Roper (1956), Cohn (1975), Thomas (1971), Macfarlane (1970), Henningsen (1980), Ginzburg (1983), Larner (1981, 1984), Estes (1983), Le Roy Ladurie (1987), Ben-Yehuda (1980). Accounts of the Salem trials include Boyer and Nissenbaum (1974) and Demos (1982). The corpus of this work is one of the best illustrations of the complex causality of any particular historical events, for the different accounts—admittedly handling different events in varied contexts—point to the interdependency of psychological fantasy, small-scale social tension, and larger political and economic developments: the fear of a being who subverts the fertility of body and land, with unrestrained perverted sexuality, the cannibalistic, incestuous "bad mother"; the child-rearing customs particular to a given society; the availability of criminal proceedings which made prosecutions available; the rise of a commercial ethic, a new individualism and the demise of the small face-to-face community; the collapse of a magic-like Catholicism for a stern, unforgiving Protestantism and the rise of a post-Galenic medicine, able to differentiate between the natural and non-natural cause for a disease; the political tensions within a given community; and then, Reformation and Counter-Reformation tensions, the rise and tenure of a notion of the "godly state" in which Christianity held political significance. This blend of personally salient fantasy, cognitive shift, and political ideology probably precipitated the outbreak of witchcraft fear as Europe crossed the boundary from early modernism into secularized nation-states, heightening and creating social tension in its wake. But it is a phenomenon with many explanations and many causes, a typically messy transformation.

The accounts of African witchcraft are as numerous, but tend to be more homogeneous in their explanation, pointing primarily to witchcraft's role in relieving social tension—a social "strain gauge," as one author puts it. Nevertheless, authors sometimes mention the psychodynamic elements of witchcraft fantasy, and point to some of the larger political elements of a rash of witchcraft accusations. The primary collections of essays, which include papers or book-excerpts from most of the scholars in the area, include: Marwick (1970), Douglas (1970), Middleton and Winter (1963), and Middleton (1967).

9. Adler (1986: 45–6).

10. This is a phrase taken from Crowley's Gnostic Mass (1929: 345–61). It sometimes appears in witchcraft rituals or in writings about the practice.

11. Adler (1986: 43–4).

12. Starhawk (1979: 77).

13. Witch, Z. Budapest, quoted in Adler (1986: 105).

14. Gombrich's (1971) study of Sinhalese Buddhism draws a related conclusion, that devotees tend to treat the Buddha-figure as a god, not—as doctrine would have it—an enlightened man.

15. The terms are probably drawn from Margaret Murray, although "esbat" appears in a sixteenth-century French manuscript (Le Roy Ladurie, 1987: 7). "Sabbat" is a standard demonologist's term.

16. I was fortunate: there was a feeling in the group I joined that my time in the country might be limited, and certainly that my stay in London was relatively brief (fifteen months). In consequence

I was initiated only six months after my initial contact with the members.

17. This may be an exaggeration. Social ease with the applicant was clearly pertinent to the coven's decision to initiate someone, and personality style seemed more crucial than socioeconomic standing. I knew an applicant turned down by one coven, despite the fact that he was of a similar age and background as most of the members, and despite the fact that their coven needed more men to have an even balance of the sexes—which is thought desirable. This was probably because he seemed too independent to the high priestess; there was at least some personality conflict between them.

18. As already mentioned, this portion of the ritual resembles the first degree initiation in Freemasonry.

19. The role and nature of this "third-degree" initiation has been, not surprisingly, a source of some controversy within witchcraft, and different participants have differing views about whether it should be "actual" or "symbolic" or held at all.

20. Air, earth, water and fire were recognized constitutive elements in the ancient world and their role and nature was a matter of considerable debate. The attribution of directional definition and human capacity may be a later accretion.

21. Farrar and Farrar (1981: 42–3).

22. Pennethorne Hughes corroborates this attribution, but it is not clear that other historians would substantiate the claim.

23. Farrar and Farrar (1984: 17).

24. Farrar (1971: 20).

25. There was at least one group of this ilk that was mixed: they would probably argue for the importance of integrating the male divine principle into a goddess-centred religion, and so justify the men's presence in a context usually focused on "women's mysteries."

26. Girton is the oldest women's college at Cambridge.

REFERENCES

Adler, M. 1986. *Drawing Down the Moon.* Boston: Beacon.

Ben-Yehuda, N. 1980. "The European Witch-Craze of the 14th to 17th Centuries: A Sociologist's Perspective." *American Journal of Sociology,* Vol. 86, No. 1, pp. 1–31.

Boyer, P., & S. Nissenbaum. 1974. *Salem Possessed.* Cambridge, MA: Harvard University Press.

Cohn, N. 1975. *Europe's Inner Demons.* New York: New American Library.

Crowley, A. 1976 [1929]. *Magick in Theory and Practice.* New York: Denver.

Demos, J. 1982. *Entertaining Satan.* Oxford: Oxford University Press.

Douglas, M. (Ed.). 1970. *Witchcraft: Confessions and Accusations.* London: Tavistock.

Estes, L. 1983. "The Medical Origins of the European Witch-Craze." *Journal of Social History,* Vol. 17, Winter, pp. 271–84.

Evans-Wentz, E. 1911. *The Fairy Faith in Celtic Countries.* Oxford: Oxford University Press.

Farrar, J., & S. Farrar. 1981. *Eight Sabbats for Witches.* London: Hale.

Farrar, J., & S. Farrar. 1984. *The Witches' Way.* London: Hale.

Frazer, Sir J. G. 1922. *The Golden Bough* (abridged). London: Macmillan.

Gardner, G. B. 1982 [1954]. *Witchcraft Today.* New York: Magickal Childe.

Ginzburg, C. 1983 [Italian 1966]. *The Night Battles,* trans. by J. Tedeschi & A. Tedeschi. Baltimore, MD: Johns Hopkins University Press.

Gombrich, R. 1971. *Precept and Practice.* Oxford: Clarendon.

Graves, Robert. 1968 [1948]. *The White Goddess.* New York: Farrar, Strauss and Giroux.

Henningsen, G. 1980. *The Witches' Advocate: Basque Witchcraft and the Spanish Inquisition (1609–1614)*. Reno: University of Nevada Press.

Larner, C. 1981. *Enemies of God*. Oxford: Blackwell.

Larner, C. 1984. *Witchcraft and Religion*. Oxford: Blackwell.

Le Roy Ladurie, L. 1987. *Jasmin's Witch*. Aldershot: Scolar Press.

Leland, C. 1899. *Aradia: Gospel of the Witches*. New York: Weiser.

Macfarlane, A. 1970. *Witchcraft in Tudor and Stuart England*. New York: Harper and Row.

Marwick, M. (Ed.). 1970. *Witchcraft and Sorcery*. Harmondsworth, England: Penguin.

Middleton, J. (Ed.). 1967. *Myth and Cosmos*. Austin: University of Texas Press.

Middleton, J., & E. H. Winter (Eds.). 1963. *Witchcraft and Sorcery in East Africa*. London: Routledge and Kegan Paul.

Murray, M. 1921. *The Witchcult in Western Europe*. Oxford: Oxford University Press.

Starhawk, 1979. *The Spiral Dance*. New York: Harper and Row.

Thomas, K. 1971. *Religion and the Decline of Magic*. New York: Scribner's.

Trevor-Roper, H. R. 1956. *The European Witchcraze*. New York: Harper and Row.

Z. Budapest, quoted in Adler, M. 1986. *Drawing Down the Moon*. Boston: Beacon, p. 105.

Feminine Power at Sea

Silvia Rodgers

Silvia Rodgers was awarded her doctorate in anthropology at Oxford University for her research on "the symbolism of ship launching in the Royal Navy."

The ceremony that accompanies the launch of a Royal Navy ship is classified as a state occasion, performed more frequently than other state occasions and to an audience of thousands. But until now it has never been the subject of research, either historical or anthropological.

If the ceremony of launching looks at first sight like the transition rite that accompanies the ship as she passes from land to water, it soon becomes clear that the critical transition is from the status of an inanimate being to that of an animate and social being. From being a numbered thing at her launch, the ship receives her name and all that comes with the name. This includes everything that gives her an individual and social identity, her luck, her life essence and her femininity.

My research into the ceremony sheds light not only on the nature and development of the ceremony itself but also on the religious beliefs of sailors, on the symbolic classification of a ship by sailors, on the extensive and reincarnating power of the ship's name, and on the relationship between women and ships and mariners. It is the last aspect on which I want to concentrate here.

Most of us know that sailors refer to a ship by the feminine pronoun. But the extent of the metaphor of the ship as a living, feminine and anthropomorphic being is not, I think, appreciated. Furthermore, it is this metaphor that shows up the quintessential and extraordinary nature of the launching ceremony. I say "extraordinary" because this ceremony is unique in our society and any of its auxiliary societies in that it symbolically brings to life an artefact. It looks more like a case of animism than of personification. Its status in the Royal Navy as a state occasion makes all this even more remarkable, particularly as it is accompanied by a service of the established Church.

There are of course other new things that are inaugurated by secular or sacred means. But in none of these instances does the artefact acquire the properties of a living thing, let alone a feminine person. There is the proclivity to personify virtues and institutions in the feminine, but these are not conceptualized as living and human beings. Personal articles are given human attributes, with a name and even a gender. But this is not a social rule, nor a rule of grammar, as in the case of the personified ship. Nor is life, name and gender instilled through the public enactment of a prescribed ceremony.

Members of the Royal Navy, and indeed the merchant navies, talk about a ship as having a life, a soul, a spirit, a personality and a character of her own. These notions are not necessarily differentiated, and the terms are used interchangeably. Whether the word "soul," "life" or "spirit" is used depends on the informant. What is constant is the gender of the ship. In the English language, which allows gender only to human beings and animals of determinate sex, it is the rule to refer to a ship as "she" or "her." While reflecting the strength of the metaphor, the rules of grammar also indicate its limit. The linguistic boundary lies in the region of the relative pronoun. According to Fowler it is correct to say: "The ship that lost her rudder" and the "*Arethusa* that lost her rudder" or "*Arethusa* who lost her rudder." Sailors frequently drop the "the" in front of the name of a ship. They explain that if I went to see a friend I would not say "I am going to see the Sally" but "I am going to see Sally" and that this applies to a ship.

The image of the ship as a fictive woman is established in diaries and chronicles, is legally encoded in naval and legal documents, and celebrated in poetry and prose. It survives masculine names, figureheads and the labels East-Indiamen and men-of-war. In the

"Feminine Power at Sea" by Silvia Rodgers, from *Royal Anthropological Institute News*, Vol. 64, 1984. Royal Anthropological Institute. Reprinted with permission.

current Royal Navy, as I have indicated, the metaphor is as strong as ever. But what kind of woman is she? A ship is represented as possessing the attributes of more than one category of woman. All are stereotypes that are idealized by sailors. Two images predominate: the all-powerful mother who nurtures and offers womb-like protection; and the enchantress of whom a man can never be certain. Other images intrude, but all inspire romantic and consuming love, awe and constant devotion. When Conrad writes of "the mysteries of her (the ship's) feminine nature" and how the love of a man for his ship "is nearly as great as that of man for a woman, and often as blind" he expresses the sentiments of modern sailors.

Conrad not only depicts vividly the ship as a woman, but brings out the whole environment of being at sea. My informants frequently explain to me, with some emotion and with interesting detail, the reality at sea. It is disorienting, frightening as well as awe-inspiring. This environmental context is crucial when we look for reasons for the feminine nature of the ship. In an environment which is not the natural habitat of human beings, a man may feel himself to be especially vulnerable if as a species he is incompletely represented. That vulnerability could well account for the partnership of an all-male crew with a feminine ship. It is significant that the male and secular principle is complemented not by a secular and natural woman, but by her metaphysical and metaphorical manifestation. Needham has gathered enough ethnographic evidence from diverse and land-based societies to suggest that the complementary opposition men: women: temporal:mystical is widespread if not archetypal. It is easy to understand that the oceanic environment exacerbates the need for mystical protection that emanates from women. In addition, in circumstances where uncertainty and the likelihood of sudden death is increased, the symbol of rebirth in the form of the mother would be particularly welcome. Nor should we omit to look at the metaphor from the point of view of the archetypal figure of the mother and the mother goddess which according to Neumann is deep within the human psyche. Neumann (1974) also explains how the ship has served as the symbol of the mother, of rebirth, and salvation for many cultures over many periods; and not only for people that go to sea.

It comes as a surprise to find that unlike the life essence of the ship, the universality of the ship as a symbolic woman is undermined by some ethnographic data. Nevertheless it is very widespread and historical, and cross-cultural material helps to underline the supernatural power of women in the oceanic domain. Hornell finds that from the Mediterranean to the Pacific Ocean, and from Ancient Greece to that the 20th century, "ships are generally considered to be feminine." He believes the feminine principle is often introduced when the ship is dedicated to her tutelary goddess at the launch. He describes such cases from the coast near Madras. Hornell points out that sometimes there is an identifiable icon of the deity. Malinowski relates how the Trobriand canoes are closely associated with the Flying Witches, whose Power is on occasion concentrated in the carvings at the prow.

In western societies, from the coasts of Preclassical Mediterranean to Catholic Europe, patron saints of mariners are usually feminine. Figureheads, now no longer extant on British ships, were particularly efficacious if the image was a woman, especially if she was bare-breasted (Kemp 1976). There is some ground for concluding that this icon symbolized the mother who suckled the infant god, and that this made her a powerful intercessor especially against the devil. However one hardly needs this evidence to recognize the existence of a special relationship between women, ships and mariners in British fleets.

First and foremost is the irrefutable feminine nature of the ship. Then there is the launch at which the two most important personages are both feminine: the ship and her sponsor. It is the role of the sponsor, a woman of high rank by ascription, to exercise her mystical powers to imbue the ship with luck and life by naming her in strict adherence to the ritual detail: the bottle must move, the ship begin to move, the name (the generator of the luck and life) be pronounced—all at the same moment. Anything else augurs bad luck for the ship. Unfortunately, a ship at her launch is hypersensitive towards her sponsor and may react with self-destructive wilfulness to any lapse by the sponsor in her manner of dress or rendition of the formula. There are many accounts of instances when a ship has refused to move or moved too soon, making it impossible for the bottle to break at the right moment. When a ship behaves in this way she puts her own luck at risk, but it is always the sponsor who is blamed. The sponsor's power to bless has inadvertently turned into the power to curse.

There are several ethnographic examples where positive power coexists with negative power in one and the same person: a coexistence that had been spotted earlier by Jacob Grimm (in Briffault 1927). But negative power, where ships of the Royal Navy are concerned, usually emanates from ordinary women. Strict taboos attempt to restrict this harmful influence. A woman on board a ship at night is regarded with particular misgiving. She is bound to bring bad luck, and sophisticated technology is no proof against this. On the contrary, it may itself be a target. This is nicely demonstrated by the true story of the Rolls-Royce engine of a destroyer that blew up when a woman computer programmer had spent the night on board. It was perfectly true that the manufacturers had omitted to drill a critical hole, and the engine could have blown up at any time. But why, the officers wondered, had it blown up on the one night that a woman was on board? (The reasoning is Azande, the granary is waterborne.) The taboos excluding women from critical areas extend to the part of the dockyard where ships are under construction. We know that equivalent taboos are described in a host of ethnographies. They also operate on oil rigs and down coal mines in Britain, and are very stringent in fishing communities here and across the world.

With modern technology no match for the vicissitudes of luck, it is not surprising to find that the ceremony of the launch is as indispensable as ever, and part of the regulations of the Royal Navy. Nor is it surprising that it is still believed that if the bottle fails to break at exactly the right time, the fate of the ship is in doubt.

At the launch of a destroyer in 1975, a distinguished naval officer was alarmed when he thought that the sponsor had failed to break the bottle across the bow. "After all," he told me, "I might be in command of her one day." The role of the sponsor has if anything increased. Advanced technology has made it possible for her to be seen to control not only the mystical but also the technical part of the launching. From 1876, engravings in the *Illustrated London News* portray Royal sponsors setting the ship in motion and releasing the bottle with just a touch of the finger. It may have been coincidental that this overall control mechanism was installed at the same time as the Christian service was added to the ceremony.

But the very existence of a Christian service presents a puzzle. The critical part of the launching ceremony is concerned with imbuing the ship, an artefact, with luck and the soul and personality of a feminine entity—hardly in accord with Christian doctrine. Although this naming ritual has always been called a "christening," the term is misleading: the subject of the ritual is not a human being but an artefact; the liquid is not water but wine; the celebrant is neither ordained nor male. The duties of the sponsor (or godmother as she is sometimes referred to) are in any case not consistent with that of a Christian godmother, apart from the secular obligations that start after the launch.

The puzzle comes no nearer to solution when one looks at the varying attitudes of ministers of the Church to this ceremony. Some clergymen in the 19th century voiced strong disapproval of the naming ritual and of its being called a baptism. Today, incumbents of parishes local to the shipyards are happy to conduct the service at a launch. The only aspect that continues to baffle them is that no higher ranking ministers are ever invited to officiate, not even when the Queen Mother is the sponsor. Although the service was inaugurated by the Archbishop of Canterbury in 1875, since then it has been the rule for the local incumbent to

conduct it. But if the ceremony of the launch seems to bother the main body of the Church, for naval chaplains the problem is even more complicated. Among the duties of the Chaplain of the Fleet is the keeping up to date of the launching service, and approving the minister chosen to conduct it. Yet, as a senior naval chaplain was at pains to point out to me, according to the Naval Chaplaincy no naval chaplain should himself ever take part in a launching. Incidentally, this same chaplain shares, and with conviction, the view of sailors that the ship is a living and feminine entity, though he does deny the ship her soul, that hallmark of a Christian being.

To understand the religious beliefs of sailors one has to look beyond the tenets of Christianity. The power of a ship's name, the naming ceremony, the metaphor of the ship as a fictive woman, the taboos relating to women: all are part of the beliefs of sailors which they themselves call "superstitious." It is well known in our own society that sailors are superstitious. What is not appreciated is that when sailors describe themselves as being superstitious, and they do so frequently, it has none of the usual pejorative connotations. They explain it as a natural consequence of life at sea, which makes them see things in a different way. An acceptable part of their syncretic religion, it comes near to the sense that adhered to *superstitio* in early Classical Rome: a valued and useful quality (Benveniste 1973).

Historical investigation shows that this so-called superstition has always existed in British navies, though specific manifestations may have changed. A ceremony to mark the launch of a new ship seems to have been imperative for centuries. But it has undergone such transformations that it is unrecognizable from, for example, the one performed in Pepys's time. The ship has always been feminine, but the relationship between women and ships had shifted over time. That the power of women has remained confined to the supernatural plane will come as no surprise.

With so much emotion invested in a ship, one may well ask why the demise unlike the launch, of a Royal Navy ship, is marked only by routine, and not by ritual. The answer must surely lie in the name through which the life, luck and personality survive the body of any one ship. The choice of names is vast, but the same names recur time and again: the present *Ark Royal* is the fifth ship of that name; the first belonged to Elizabeth I. If a name is outstandingly lucky and illustrious, it is reincarnated more frequently than others. The name as the keeper of life, as integrator into society and its history, has ethnographic parallels. Mauss draws on North American Indian material to show that the name of a person is part of the stock of the tribe, and that it reincarnates the original ancestor (. . . , 1979). When Gronbech describes the power or the names in *The Culture of the Teutons* (1931) he could be writing about names of Royal Navy ships. But unlike the societies studied by Mauss and others, the Fleet, or the society of Royal Navy ships, consists entirely of feminine personages.

REFERENCES

Benveniste, Emil. 1973. *Indo-European Language and Society*. London: Faber.

Briffault, Robert. 1927. *The Mothers: A Study in the Origins of Sentiments and Institutions*. 3 vols. New York.

Conrad, Joseph. 1960. *The Mirror of the Sea*. London: Dent.

Gronbeck, V. 1931. *The Culture of the Teutons*. London: Oxford University Press.

Hornell, James. 1946. *Water Transport*. Cambridge, England: Cambridge University Press.

Kemp, Peter. 1976. *The Oxford Companion of Ships and the Sea*. London: Oxford University Press.

Malinowski, Bronislaw. 1932. *Argonauts of the Western Pacific*. London: Routledge.

Mauss, M. 1979. (1950). *Sociology and Psychology*, trans. by B. Brewster. London: Routledge.

Needham, Rodney. 1980. *Reconnaissances*. Toronto: Toronto University Press.

Neumann, E. 1974. *The Great Mother*, trans. by R. Manheim. Princeton, NJ: Princeton University Press.

Reality and Non-Reality in San Rock Art

J.D. Lewis-Williams

J. David Lewis-Williams began his study of Bushman rock art in 1959 and received a Ph.D. from the University of Natal, South Africa, in 1977. He is now professor of cognitive archaeology and director of the Rock Art Research Unit at the University of Witwatersrand. His research on Bushman beliefs and application of the findings of neuropsychological research into altered states of consciousness has radically revised our perception of the rock art of southern Africa and elsewhere.

For many years, it was thought that San rock art was principally decorative or narrative; that the so-called "artists" worked simply to please themselves and their viewers. At first glance there is much to support this view. The painted animals in particular seem to have an aesthetic sensitivity that does not readily point to arcane or symbolic interests. Then there are those compositions that appear to depict scenes from daily life—dances, hunts and so forth. But in the 1970s we came to realize that this view can be sustained only by ignoring what we know about art in small-scale societies: if the San artists were as naive as the traditional view suggests, they were unique, because people in small-scale societies are not like Western artists who, in another popular myth, are said to produce art simply for the sake of art. On the contrary, so-called "primitive" artists have quite specific purposes in mind, and their pictures have specific and often very complex meanings.

An even more important point is that the traditional view of San rock art as a narrative of daily life can be sustained only by ignoring what we know about the San themselves. It was believed that we had no independent records of the beliefs and interests of the artists. Everything, it was thought, had to be inferred directly from the paintings. In fact, we have a great deal of San ethnography. Much of it comes from the last century and is thus contemporary with the last painters and engravers. Contrary to general belief, some of it includes direct comments on specific paint-

Adapted from "Reality and Non-Reality in San Rock Art" by J. D. Lewis-Williams, delivered 6 October 1987 as the 25th Raymond Dart Lecture; © Witwatersrand University Press 1988; printed in the Republic of South Africa by The Natal Witness (Pty) Ltd, Pietermaritzburg. Used with permission of J. D. Lewis-Williams.

ings (see, for example, Orpen 1874). In addition, we have a rich collection of material from the San presently living in the Kalahari Desert (see, among others, Marshall 1976; Tobias 1978; Lee 1979; Silberbauer 1981). These non-painting people are not descendants of the now-extinct artists. For one thing, they speak different languages. But detailed comparison of their beliefs and rituals with those of the nineteenth-century San show that, despite regional variations, the San over much of southern Africa shared a broad belief system (Lewis-Williams 1980, 1981).

When we started to take all this information seriously we discovered somewhat unexpectedly that, far from being simply narrative or decorative, the rock art was associated with the activities of San medicine people, or shamans, who today number about half the men and a third of the women in any camp. These people entered a state of trance at a medicine dance or in more solitary circumstances and, in that condition, cured the sick, went on out-of-body journeys, made rain, and controlled the movements of antelope herds (for accounts of San shamanism see Lee 1968; Marshall 1969; Katz 1982). Both paintings and engravings depict these activities, the hallucinations of San medicine people and also symbols of the supernatural potency they activated in order to enter the world of trance experience (Lewis-Williams 1981, 1983, 1987).

But recognition of the essentially shamanistic nature of the art is the beginning not the end of research. It merely gives us a general understanding. We now have the task of trying to "decode" the art and to elucidate its structure and the meanings of its elements. We are at a stage of research that is in some ways comparable with that reached many decades ago with stone artifacts. Once it was conclusively shown that handaxes were man-made, work did not stop. That was just the beginning of a long research programme. So it is with rock art. New and exciting avenues are now opening up that will lead to better understanding of southern African rock art.

———————

In the last few years we have started to explore one of these new avenues, one that helps to clarify why there are more geometric forms among the engravings than among the paintings. This new avenue is neuropsychological research on altered states of consciousness and, more particularly, the trance-like states associated with shamanism. We know that under these circumstances the human mind produces a range of hallucinations. Visual hallucinations are the most popularly known, but there are also auditory, physical, and olfactory hallucinations. In fact, all the senses—not just vision—can hallucinate.

The conditions that induce an altered state of consciousness in which these hallucinations are experienced are extremely varied. They include the use of hallucinogens, sensory deprivation, intense concentration, rhythmic movement, hyperventilation, hunger, pain, and even migraine (Siegel and West 1975; Siegel 1977; Winkelman 1986). San shamans seldom use hallucinogens; they enter trance by hyperventilation, rhythmic movement and music, and intense concentration, but their experiences seem very similar to those induced by LSD, peyote and other hallucinogens (Winkelman 1986).

Once it was realized that much trance experience is controlled by the nervous system and that the nervous system is common to all people, it became necessary to gain a better understanding of the human nervous system's entrance into and progression through trance states, so that we could assess the art in these terms. I must emphasize that I am now talking about neuropsychological research conducted without any knowledge of or reference to rock art. Because this research makes sense of certain important aspects of San art, it provides an independent line of evidence, over and above the strong ethnographic evidence, that the art was associated with altered states of consciousness—in other words, that it was essentially shamanistic. Neuropsychology enables us to distinguish three broadly conceived stages in the sequence of mental imagery during altered states of consciousness (Lewis-Williams and Dowson 1988).

In the first stage subjects experience entoptic phenomena (Siegel and Jarvik 1975:111; Siegel 1977:132). These are luminous visual percepts that take geometric forms such as grids, zigzags, dots, undulating lines, nested catenary curves and spirals. All these shapes are experienced as incandescent, shimmering, moving, ro-

Entoptics	N.W. Cape	Magaliesberg

Table 1 Entoptic phenomena compared with rock engravings from the north-western Cape and Magaliesberg.

tating, and sometimes enlarging patterns, and they are independent of light from an external source. They are experienced with the eyes open or closed and tend to be located at reading distance. Sometimes a bright light in the centre of the field of vision obscures the forms, but peripheral images can be observed. Another bewildering factor is the rapidity with which the phenomena change. Laboratory subjects new to the experience find it difficult to keep pace with the rapid flow of imagery, but, significantly, training and familiarity with the experience increase their powers of observation and description (Siegel 1977:134). People who experience migraine will be familiar with at least some entoptic phenomena. The seven shapes illustrated in the first column of Table 1 were extracted from the reports of a large number of subjects in experiments conducted under laboratory conditions: they are the most common types. They are created, in ways not yet fully understood, by the actual physical, neurological structures of the eye, the optic nerve or the cortex.

These entoptic phenomena have also been observed among living peoples. For instance, the Tukano people of the Amazon Basin, who regularly take the hallucinogen *yajé*, say that in the first stage of their trance experience they "see" what are clearly combinations of or variations on the forms established by laboratory experiments, and they draw them on their houses, drums, and other objects (Reichel-Dolmatoff 1972). Reichel-Dolmatoff (1978) then discovered that they attached specific meanings to these shapes. For instance, nested U-shapes are said to represent the rainbow or the Sun Father's penis. Horizontal undulating lines represent "the thought of the Sun Father." Chains of small dots, also undulating, are the Milky Way, which is the first goal of the ecstatic flight of narcotic trance. Reichel-Dolmatoff's research shows without doubt that people in at least one small-scale society who enter certain altered states of consciousness experience the same entoptic phenomena as those experienced by laboratory subjects in Los Angeles and New York.

The relevance of this initial stage of altered consciousness to our problem will now be clear. But let us recapitulate for a moment. We know from the ethnography that San shamans went into trance. We know, again from ethnography, that at least some art depicts their hallucinations. From neuropsychological research we know that San shamans would have experienced geometric entoptic phenomena because the nervous system is a human universal, and it automatically produces these forms in certain altered states. Now we come to the final question: do the engraved geometric forms look at all like entoptic phenomena? Let us make some comparisons between them and the forms established by laboratory research.

In the second and third columns of Table 1 there are rock engravings from two regions of southern Africa. The parallels are certainly striking: most of the seven types were depicted by the engravers in each region. This is not to say that each kind of entoptic is equally represented among the southern African engravings. Some forms are more common than others, and not all sites have the same range of entoptics. This is because shamanistic societies tend to concentrate on and attach meaning to a limited, standardized range of entoptics and to ignore others, in the same way that they select certain animal species for symbolic purposes and depiction. Knowing a priori that the art derives, at least in part, from altered states, we can therefore easily accept that San rock engravers depicted their entoptic phenomena on the rocks just as the Tukano paint theirs on their houses. Note that we are not simply identifying any squiggle as an entoptic phenomenon. We are showing that a set of seven distinct forms, the very ones we should

expect to find in a shamanistic art, are indeed present.

If I am correct in identifying these engravings as entoptic phenomena, I have merely compounded the problem posed by the differences between paintings and engravings because we know that the paintings are also shamanistic and associated with altered states of consciousness. In fact, some of the most striking depictions of hallucinations are painted rather than engraved. Why, then, do these entoptic forms not appear as commonly among the paintings? To answer this question, we must move on to consider the second stage of trance experience.

In stage two subjects try to make sense of their entoptic phenomena by elaborating them into something recognizable (Horowitz 1964:514; 1975:177, 178, 181). In a normal state of consciousness the brain receives a constant stream of sense impressions. A visual image reaching the brain is decoded by being matched against a store of experience. If a "fit" can be effected, the image is "recognized." In altered states the nervous system itself becomes a "sixth sense" (Heinze 1986) that produces a variety of images including entoptic phenomena. The brain attempts to recognize, or decode, these forms even as it does impressions supplied by the nervous system in a normal state of consciousness. Horowitz (1975:177) links this process of making sense to the disposition of the subject: "Thus the same ambiguous round shape on initial perceptual representation can be 'illusioned' into an orange (if the subject is hungry), a breast (if he is in a state of heightened sexual drive), a cup of water (if he is thirsty) or an anarchist's bomb (if he is hostile or fearful)."

This description of what happens in the second stage of altered states provides the first part of an answer to our problem. San shaman artists who went far enough along the continuum of trance experience elaborated the basic entoptic forms into objects on which their general beliefs about trance experience placed some particular value. In other words, they construed the basic geometric forms as something they hoped or expected to see in the spirit world. Let us examine two examples of this process of construal in the art; the first is engraved, the second painted.

A common entoptic form in the art is a grid that may be rectangular or rather like a honeycomb. Figure 1 shows two grids engraved on a single rock; each is enclosed by a perimeter line. Such lines are probably also entoptic, for subjects report boundaries of lines so thin that it may be impossible to say whether they are black or white (Klüver 1942:177). Between the grids is a giraffe, its body markings echoing the grids. We can see at once that the entoptic grid reminded the artist of the pattern on a giraffe, and he construed it as, or elaborated it into, a giraffe. In fact, the juxtapositioning of the grids with the giraffe seems to point to a stage-two

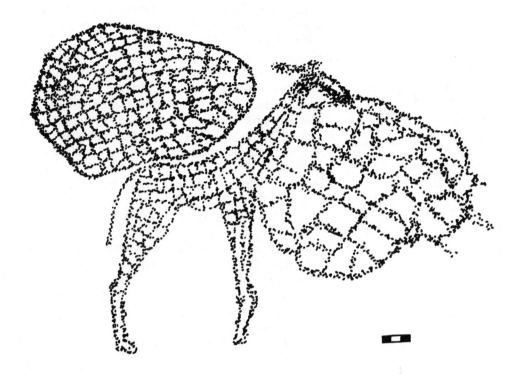

Figure 1   Rock engraving of two bounded grids and a giraffe. (After Sherz 1975.) The scale in this and subsequent illustrations is in centimetres.

vision. Most depictions of giraffes are, of course, not conveniently accompanied by grids as is this example, but it seems highly probable that, in San beliefs about trance experience, the entoptic grid was closely associated with the giraffe and that some shamans in stage two elaborated their vision of the grid into that animal.

But why would they associate the grid with a giraffe rather than, say, a tortoise? The answer to this question is to be found in San beliefs about supernatural power. When a shaman enters trance he or she activates an invisible potency that the !Kung call *n/um* and the now-extinct southern */Xam* San called *!gi:*. Marshall (1969) has likened it to electricity: harnessed it can be beneficial, but out of control it is dangerous. This potency is named after a range of "strong" things, such as big game animals. The eland has more *n/um* than any other animal, but also prominent among the powerful animals is the giraffe. In the Kalahari today the San still dance giraffe potency (Biesele 1975).

Something of what the "giraffe experience" is like comes through in an account of trance an old, experienced !Kung shaman gave to Biesele (1979:55). He started his account by saying,

Just yesterday, friend, the giraffe came and took me again. Kauha [god] came and took me and said, "Why is it that people are singing, yet you're not dancing?"

When he spoke, he took me with him and we left this place. We travelled until we came to a wide body of water. It was a river. He took me to the river. The two halves of the river lay to either side of us, one to the left and one to the right.

There is a great deal of interest in this account of San non-reality, but we can note only three points. Notice first how the giraffe "took [him] again." The power of the giraffe overwhelmed him, and he was in its thrall. Then notice that he does not draw a careful distinction between god (Kauha) and giraffe. Both came and "took" him. Finally, he is taken to a river into which he plunges. Being under water is a San metaphor for trance experience (Lewis-Williams 1980:472), and that plunge was his entry into non-reality. An account such as this gives us some insight into how San viewers may have responded to an engraved grid. It spoke to them of overwhelming giraffed power and the spirit world.

Now let us turn to a painted example of stage-two construal. Another common entoptic form comprises nested U-shapes or catenary curves. This was construed by the San painters in various ways (Lewis-Williams, n.d.), but we shall examine just one. In the wild, honeycombs naturally assume the form of nested catenary curves. It was this fact that enabled Pager

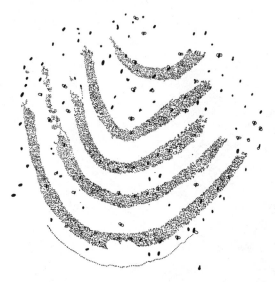

Figure 2   Rock painting of honeycombs and bees. Natal Drakensberg. (After Pager 1971:figs. 387, 86.)

(1971:151, 347–352) to identify certain paintings as bee-hives. Some also have bees individually and minutely drawn, each with a pair of white wings (Figure 2). Today we can go further and suggest that the U-shapes have an entoptic origin. People in trance saw the U-shapes and elaborated them into honeycombs (Lewis-Williams, n.d.). It is also possible that construal of entoptic catenary curves as hives may have been partially suggested to the San by a humming sound often heard by people in altered states of consciousness (Harner 1973:119; Halifax 1979:49; Bootzin 1980:343). The Amahuaca trancers of the Amazon Basin interpret this sound as cicadas, crickets and frog calls (Halifax 1979:144), while other people hear it as wind, trickling water or rain (Munn 1973:119; Christie-Murray 1978; Halifax 1979:32, 74, 97). Auditory hallucinations are therefore open to different interpretations, though cross-culturally their structure remains constant because, like entoptic phenomena, they are produced by the human nervous system. The San, it seems, construed their aural hallucinations as the buzzing of bees and so linked them to their visual hallucinations of U-shaped entoptic phenomena.

The reason some San construed nested U-shaped entoptics as honeycombs comes from Kalahari San ethnography. The !Kung consider bees to have a great deal of potency, and they like to dance when bees are swarming because they believe they can harness the bees' power (Wilmsen, pers. comm.) as they harness the power of other "strong" things. A painting in the northeastern Cape shows a line of figures, some of whom bleed from the nose and carry flywhisks, dancing beneath a swarm of bees and a hive. It is a convincing depiction of the association between bees and the trance dance (Lewis-Williams 1983:fig. 16). At least

some artists thus construed their combined visual and aural hallucinations as visions of a very powerful shamanistic symbol.

We are now beginning to see how entoptic phenomena can be "disguised," as it were, by the people who see and depict them. Indeed, if the construal is greatly elaborated the entoptic raw material may be completely swamped. The two examples I have described preserve the basic entoptic forms (grids and U-shapes), but that is not always the case. More radical changes to entoptic forms are experienced in the third and last stage of altered consciousness.

As subjects move from the second stage into the third, marked changes in imagery occur (Siegel 1977: 132). Many laboratory subjects report experiencing a vortex or rotating tunnel that seems to surround them, and there is a progressive exclusion of perceptual information (Horowitz 1975:178). The sides of the vortex are marked by a lattice of squares like television screens. The images on these 'screens' are the first spontaneously produced hallucinations; they eventually overlie the vortex as entoptics give way to images of people, animals, monsters, houses and so forth (Siegel and Jarvik 1975:127, 143; Siegel 1977:136). These *iconic images* appear to derive from memory and are often associated with powerful emotional experiences (Siegel and Jarvik 1975:111). This shift to iconic imagery is also accompanied by an increase in vividness. Subjects stop using similes to describe their experiences and assert that the images are indeed what they appear to be. They "lose insight into the differences between literal and analogous meanings" (Siegel and Jarvik 1975:128). Nevertheless, even in this essentially iconic stage, entoptics may persist: iconic imagery is "often projected against a background of geometric forms" (Siegel 1977:134). This is the stage of true hallucination, and the subject, in deep trance, inhabits a bizarre world of non-reality.

My first example of a painting from this stage preserves a distinction between entoptic and representational elements. To understand it we must recall that in 1873 J. M. Orpen and W. H. I. Bleek were told that shamans of the rain entered trance at a medicine dance and that, in trance, they captured a so-called rain-animal, the *!kwa-ka xoro* (Orpen 1874; Bleek 1933). When they killed this animal its blood and milk became rain. All this was, of course, an hallucination experienced in trance and, even though the hallucinatory element has not always been recognized, paintings of it have been known since the last century (for a fuller account of San rainmaking see Lewis-Williams 1981: 103–116). In fact the first accounts of this kind of rainmaking were given by San after being shown Orpen's copy of a painting of rain-animals. Another such painting (Figure 3) shows entoptic phenomena very clearly associated with hallucinatory rain-animals. It has been

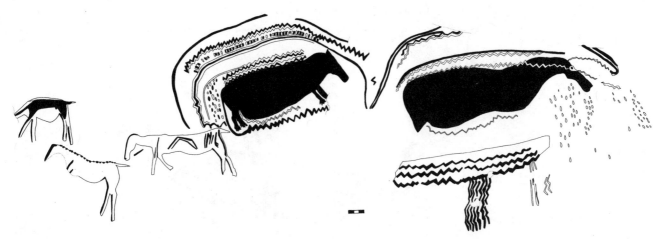

Figure 3 Rock painting of rain-animals and entoptic phenomena. Eastern Orange Free State.

suggested that the zigzags here represent a pool of water, but closer inspection of the painting seriously questions an entirely literal reading. To the right a zigzag crosses the rain-animal's neck, merges with its eye, and then proceeds farther to the right. At the left, the rain-animal's tail turns into a zigzag, and another zigzag emerges from or enters into its body. Rather than the zigzags being a simple depiction of water, it seems much more probable that what we have here are two hallucinatory rain-animals seen through an entoptic haze. Exactly what the San understood by the surrounding entoptics is, however, not yet clear.

My next stage-three examples bring us to what seems to be the principal reason for the apparent absence of entoptics from southern African rock paintings. The reason is that in this stage entoptic forms become intimately combined with hallucinations of animals and people (Klüver 1942:177; Siegel 1977:134). This was vividly described by a laboratory subject experiencing the grid entoptic. He reported that his arms, hands and fingers turned into fretwork—as he called it. Eventually he exclaimed, "The fretwork is I" (Heringer cited by Klüver 1942:182).

This striking report recalls a drawing made by one of Katz's (1982:237) !Kung San informants who was an experienced trancer. Asked to draw his conception of himself, he drew a zigzag that, he said, was his spine, and then seven separate zigzags that, he said, were the rest of his body. . . . From this we know that San shamans combine entoptic forms with hallucinations of the human body. When we turn to rock paintings of men with zigzag necks and legs we are no longer puzzled. . . . They are painted stage-three hallucinations of people integrated with zigzag entoptics—just as is reported by laboratory subjects.

The next example (Figure 4) comes from the eastern Orange Free State, where George William Stow copied it in the 1870s. Surely one of the most remark-

able of all San rock paintings, it takes us directly into the bizarre, arcane world of trance experience. The animal here was identified by one of Bleek's nineteenth-century informants as a "black rain" (Stow and Bleek 1930:pl. 58). The southern San spoke of female and male rain. The female rain was the soft, soaking rain that left wide splashes in the sand. The male rain was the fierce, black thunderstorm that stirred up the dust and left sharp footprints in the sand. Controlling a male rain, or a rain-bull, was difficult and it could break the thong thrown over its head and escape. The shamans held out buchu, sweet smelling herbs, to it, for it loved the scent of buchu and would go quietly along. Even so, capturing such a rain-animal demanded all the power and all the skill of the shamans of the rain.

This rain-bull has a zigzag painted on it (Stow's copy shows two). As with the others we saw surrounded by zigzags (Figure 3), this zigzag emerges from or enters into its eye. The animal also has white dots painted on it. Zigzags are also associated with most of the shaman figures surrounding the rain-bull. In some cases the zigzags leave the shamans' bodies and are therefore clearly not body paint. One of the shamans is comparable to a figure from the northeastern Cape (Figure 5). In both instances the zigzag curves away from the figure. As Figure 5 shows, these curving zigzags are very like a common entoptic form. Many of the figures have appendages on their outstretched arms that probably represent feathers. Flight, as in many cultures, was another metaphor for trance experience. In some of the southern San myths, the Mantis, who was himself a shaman, "gets feathers" when he enters trance and flies away (Lewis-Williams 1983:45–48).

Another painting (Figure 6) shows a different integration of entoptic phenomena with a rain-animal. Here a rather loose grid has been painted over the

Figure 4   Rock painting of a rain-animal and shamanistic figures. Eastern Orange Free State. (Copied by T. A. Dowson with additions from G. W. Stow's copy (Stow and Bleek 1930:p1. 58.) The containing line represents the slab of rock preserved in the National Museum, Bloemfontein.

body of the animal. Closely associated with the grid are the ubiquitous white dots. Of particular interest is the white ring that seems to form part of a bridle. This may not be too farfetched an interpretation because the San of the last century were expert riders, and there are paintings of horses with bridles and reins. In addition, there is evidence that suggests a connection between bridles and reins and rain-animals. Some accounts of rainmaking tell of a thong being thrown over a rain-animal's head in order to control it. This idea seems to

have been combined with the concept of reins. One of Bleek's (1933: 305) informants said that shamans of the rain "rode the rain, because the thongs with which they held it were like the horses' reins, they bound the rain. Thus they rode the rain, because they owned it." At the head of the "bound" rain-animal a man holds out an object that may be a flywhisk or buchu. Both of these would be indications of control. This painting is thus a complex combination of trance and "real" elements. An entoptic grid and dots have been integrated with an hallucinatory rain-animal in such a way as to suggest control and a bridle. In other words, this is exactly what we would expect to find in a stage-three hallucination.

My last painted example (Figure 7) is the most complex of all. Notice first that three men in this panel have their arms in a rather awkward backward position. This posture is widely painted and it was a puzzle for a long time. Clearly it meant something—but what? The answer came during a discussion with a !Kung shaman. He told me various things about the trance dance, and then, unprompted, he stood up and adopted this posture. He explained that some San shamans hold their arms like this when they ask god to put more potency into their spines. The posture is, in fact, a clear indication that we are looking at depictions of shamans.

Notice too the eared serpent's tusks. They are repeated on the eland, and one of the arms-back men has one as well. At present we do not know exactly what these tusks mean, but they are commonly painted on people in trance (Vinnicombe 1976:figs. 232, 233, 237, 247, 249; Lewis-Williams 1983:58). This leads to the conclusion that the serpent and the eland are transformed shamans. Moreover, eared snakes are often painted coming out of the rock face and with trance

Figure 5   a. Navicular entoptic phenomenon.
b. Shamanistic figure from north-eastern Cape.

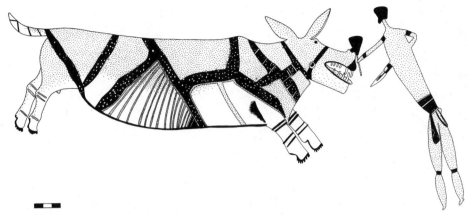

Figure 6   Rock painting of a rain-animal. North-eastern Cape.

features such as nasal blood (Lewis-Williams 1981:fig. 23). Entering and leaving the rock face may be particularly significant because shamans go into the ground on their out-of-body journeys. They travel underground and then come up again to see where they are. Old K"xau told Biesele (1979: 56) that his teacher had said that when he learned how to trance he would enter the earth: "That [he] would travel far through the earth and emerge at another place." This is, of course, just what snakes do. Snakes are in this way analogous to shamans.

Like snakes, eland are also sometimes painted with unusual features. In addition to the grid, this one has tusks and red lines on its face, as do some of the shamans accompanying it. It too may thus be a shaman who in his own or another's hallucination is transformed into the animal whose power he is appropriating. Transformation into an animal is a common trance hallucination. One of James's subjects described such a transformation: "I thought of a fox, and instantly I was transformed into that animal. I could distinctly feel myself a fox, could see my long ears and bushy tail, and by a sort of introversion felt that my complete

anatomy was that of a fox" (Siegel and Jarvik 1975: 105). It is by no means impossible that we have here shamans who thought of an eland or a snake because those two creatures are an integral part of San beliefs about trance, and were, like James's subject, transformed into those animals.

Having established the visionary nature of the painting, we can now approach the entoptic elements: they are a grid, dots, a zigzag, and a U-shape. The grid has been integrated with the eland . . . ; the dots cover most of the painting; and the zigzag is boldly depicted. The U-shape is particularly interesting because it has been construed as a snake coming out of a step in the rock face. The flickering periphery of the entoptic raw material has been retained in a series of curving red lines.

In examining San rock paintings and engravings we have been reconnoitring a mysterious no man's land between reality and non-reality—strange and bizarre for us, but not so much for the shaman-artists who regularly explored the most distant purlieus of the mind and then fixed their visions and understandings of the spirit world on the rocks of southern Africa.

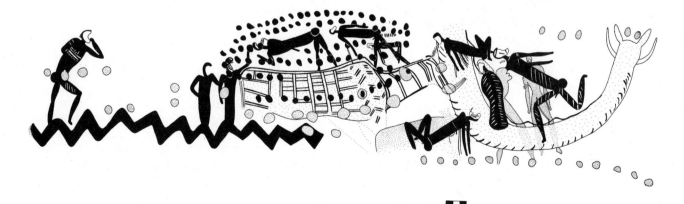

Figure 7   Rock painting of complex hallucinatory elements. North-eastern Cape.

When we look at these strikingly beautiful depictions, it is sometimes hard to accept that they were conceived not in serene artistic contemplation but in the turmoil, terror and power of an overwhelming experience. Later, having returned from that experience to the world of reality, the San shaman-artists recollected and depicted their excursions into the spirit world. As Wordsworth, in his Preface to *The Lyrical Ballads*, wrote of poetry, San rock art is powerful "emotion recollected in tranquility."

REFERENCES

Biesele, M. 1975. *Folklore and Ritual of !Kung Hunter-Gatherers*. Ph.D. thesis. Harvard University.

Biesele, M. 1979. "Old K"xau." In J. Halifax (Ed.), 1979, pp. 54–62.

Bleek, D. F. 1933. "Beliefs and Customs of the /Xam Bushmen." *Bantu Studies* Vol. 7: Part V, The rain, pp. 297–312; Part VI, Rain-making, pp. 375–392.

Bootzin, R. R. 1980. *Abnormal Psychology*. New York: Random House.

Christie-Murray, D. 1978. *Voices from the Gods*. London: Routledge and Kegan Paul.

Halifax, J. (Ed.) 1979. *Shamanic Voices: A Survey of Visionary Narratives*. Harmondsworth, England: Penguin.

Harner, M. J. 1973. "The Sound of Rushing Water." In *Hallucinogens and Shamanism*. ed. by M. J. Harner. New York: Oxford University Press, pp. 15–27.

Heinze, R. J. 1986. "More on Mental Imagery and Shamanism." *Current Anthropology* Vol. 27: 154.

Horowitz, M. J. 1964. "The Imagery of Visual Hallucinations." *Journal of Nervous and Mental Disease* Vol. 138: 513–523.

Horowitz, M. J. 1975. "Hallucinations: An Information-Processing Approach." In Siegel, R. K. & West, L. J. (Eds), 1975, pp. 163–195.

Katz, R. 1982. *Boiling Energy: Community Healing among the Kalahari !Kung*. Cambridge, MA.: Harvard University Press.

Klüver, H. 1942. "Mechanisms of Hallucinations." In *Studies in Personality*, ed. by Q. McNemar & M. A. Merrill. New York: McGraw Hill, pp. 175–207.

Lee, R. B. 1968. "The Sociology of !Kung Bushman Trance Performance." In *Trance and Possession States*, ed. by R. Prince. Montreal: R. M. Bucke Memorial Society, pp. 35–54.

Lee, R. B. 1979. *The !Kung San: Men, Women and Work in a Foraging Society*. Cambridge, England: Cambridge University Press.

Lewis-Williams, J. D. 1980. "Ethnography and Iconography: Aspects of Southern San Thought and Art." *Man* Vol. 15: 467–482.

Lewis-Williams, J. D. 1981. *Believing and Seeing: Symbolic Meanings in Southern San Rock Art*. London: Academic Press.

Lewis-Williams, J. D. 1983. *The Rock Art of Southern Africa*. Cambridge, England: Cambridge University Press.

Lewis-Williams, J. D. 1987. "Paintings of Power: Ethnography and Rock Art in Southern Africa." In *The Past and Future of !Kung Ethnography: Critical Reflections and Symbolic Perspectives: Essays in Honour of Lorna Marshall*, ed. by M. Biesele, R. Gordon & R. B. Lee. Hamburg: Helmut Buske Verlag, pp. 231–273.

Lewis-Williams, J. D. n.d. "Seeing and Construing: An Entoptic Phenomenon in San Rock Paintings." Unpublished ms.

Lewis-Williams, J. D., & T. A. Dowson. 1988. "The Signs of All Times: Entoptic Phenomena in Upper Palaeolithic Art." *Current Anthropology* Vol. 29: 201–245.

Marshall, L. 1969. "The Medicine Dance of the !Kung Bushmen." *Africa*, Vol. 39: 347–381.

Marshall, L. 1976. *The !Kung of Nyae Nyae*. Cambridge, MA: Harvard University Press.

Munn, H. 1973. "The Mushrooms of Language." In M. J. Harner (Ed.), 1973, pp. 86–121.

Orpen, J. M. 1874. "A Glimpse into the Mythology of the Maluti Bushmen." *Cape Monthly Magazine* (N.S.) Vol. 9: 1–13.

Pager, H. 1971. *Ndedema: A Documentation of the Rock Paintings of the Ndedema Gorge*. Graz: Akademische Druck- u. Verlagsanstalt.

Reichel-Dolmatoff, G. 1972. "The Cultural Context of an Aboriginal Hallucinogen: *Banisteriopsis caapi*." In *Flesh of the Gods: The Ritual Use of Hallucinogens*, ed. by P. T. Furst. London: Allen and Unwin, pp. 84–113.

Reichel-Dolmatoff, G. 1978. *Beyond the Milky Way: Hallucinatory Imagery of the Tukano Indians*. Los Angeles: University of California, Los Angeles, Latin America Center.

Scherz, E. R. 1975. *Felsbilder in Südwest-Afrika. Teil II*. Cologne: Bohlau Verlag.

Siegel, R. K. 1977. "Hallucinations." *Scientific American* Vol. 237: 132–140.

Siegel, R. K., & M. E. Jarvik. 1975. "Drug-Induced Hallucinations in Animals and Men." In R. K. Siegel, & L. J. West (Eds), 1975, pp. 81–161.

Siegel, R. K., & L. J. West (Eds), 1975. *Hallucinations: Behavior, Experience and Theory*. New York: Wiley.

Silberbauer, G. B. 1981. *Hunter and Habitat in the Central Kalahari Desert*. Cambridge, England: Cambridge University Press.

Stow, G. W. 1905. *The Native Races of South Africa*. London: Swan, Sonnenschein.

Stow, G. W. & D. F. Bleek. 1930. *Rock Paintings in South Africa*. London: Methuen.

Tobias, P. V. (Ed.) 1978. *The Bushmen*. Cape Town: Human and Rousseau.

Van Riet Lowe, C. 1956. *The Distribution of Prehistoric Rock Engravings and Paintings in South Africa*. Pretoria: Archaeological Survey.

Vinnicombe, P. 1976. *People of the Eland*. Pietermaritzburg: University of Natal Press.

Wilmsen, E. N. Personal communication.

Winkelman, M. 1986. "Trance States: A Theoretical Model and Cross-Cultural Analysis." *Ethos* Vol. 14: 174–203.

Treating the Wounds of War
The Culture of Violence

Carolyn Nordstrom

Carolyn Nordstrom received her Ph.D. in 1986 from the University of California, Berkeley, where she is now on the faculty of the Department of Peace and Conflict Studies. Her areas of interest include South Asia as well as southern Africa, where she carried out four seasons of fieldwork in Mozambique between 1988 and 1991 in conjunction with the Ministry of Health. Her topical interests range beyond peace and conflict studies to culture theory as well as medical and political anthropology.

I use these tin cans when I do my healing ceremonies. I take an empty can and put in some rocks and then seal it. I shake the can when I am working, and the rocks clatter—it makes quite a noise. This can with the rocks in it, that is what someone's head is like when they have been affected by war.

—Traditional medical practitioner, Mozambique

With the October 1992 ceasefire, the 15-year war in Mozambique is over. Or is it? There is more to consider than ongoing military control in a country trying to reconstruct order from chaos. Cultures of violence and trauma are legacies of an extremely brutal war. To understand them, it is necessary to look back at the fighting that marked the war in Mozambique during the 1980s.

Mozambique's "internal" war was developed and guided externally. It began when Frelimo (Frente de Libertação de Moçambique) came to power after Mozambique achieved independence from Portugal in 1975. Rhodesia and then South Africa instigated and led the rebel group RENAMO (Resistência Nacional Moçambicana) in an attempt to undermine the model that a black majority Marxist-Leninist-led country offered to resistance fighters of other countries. Although RENAMO supporters and opportunists do exist in Mozambique, essentially the rebel group has little popular support. With destabilization, rather than any coherent political ideology, as the defining factor in forming RENAMO, dirty war tactics—using terror in the targeting of civilian populations—predominated. Its human-rights violations have been among the worst in the world.

The extent of the violence in Mozambique can be captured in a few statistics.

- More than one million people, the vast majority of them noncombatants, lost their lives in the war.
- The war orphaned over 200,000 children. (Some estimates are much higher.) Adequate assistance is more a wish than a reality in a country where one-third of all schools and hospitals were closed or destroyed by RENAMO and only a single orphanage operates.
- The war displaced nearly a quarter of the 15 million people in Mozambique from their homes. More than half of all Mozambicans were directly affected by the violence, famine, and destruction unleashed by the war.
- Ninety percent of Mozambicans live in poverty, 60 percent in extreme poverty. Forty percent are malnourished, and in the last year of the war more than half of the country's inhabitants were in need of direct food aid. Famine, limited resources, inadequate infrastructure, and fighting hindered aid efforts and took the lives of many.
- We can only guess at the numbers who were raped; beaten, tortured, and maimed; burned out of villages and homes; kidnapped by RENAMO for forced labor and concubinage; or forced into fighting—not to mention those who were forced to watch this happen to loved ones.

"Treating the Wounds of War" by Carolyn Nordstrom, from *Cultural Survival Quarterly*, Summer 1993, pp. 28–30. Reprinted with permission.

DEFINITIONS OF VIOLENCE

The people who theorize about and wage war tend to try to control its definitions. These definitions, however, are narrow ones that focus predominately on military engagements and troop interactions. Even if civilians and communities are recognized casualties of a war, the military apparatus, and by extension the war itself, is seen as something apart from the ebb and flow of everyday life and cultural vitality. The Mozambicans cited in this article challenge the traditional assumption of political and military science that war's violence applies only to soldiers, political ideologies, and governments. Violence comes unbidden and unexplained into the heart of the civilian population, the center of war's destructiveness.

Since World War II, when civilian wartime casualties began to far outpace combat casualties, modern wars have only vaguely resembled the formal "textbook" definitions of war. This is nowhere more apparent than in an armed conflict such as Mozambique's, in which the use of terror against noncombatants—as a way to enforce political acquiescence—was a primary strategy of warfare. Civilian life and society not only become the battleground in these wars, they become the targets. Violence spills out across the social and cultural landscape to affect the country's entire population.

It is the abhorrent brutality that has most captured the attention of those investigating RENAMO's war of terror: journalistic reports, government analyses, and international nongovernmental organizations (NGOs) all focus on physical acts of brutality, especially RENAMO's. Stories that most violate notions of human decency—gruesome mutilations, rapes, murders—tend to circulate most widely.

Yet when I listened to average Mozambicans discuss the war, these barbarous accounts, although present, weren't the focal point of the violence. People were concerned with a deeper, more enduring type of violence: the destruction of home and humanity, of hope and future, of valued traditions and community integrity. Psychological, emotional, and cultural violence rank equally with, and in many cases outrank, physical violence.

Consider the words of an old traditional healer in a town in the center of Zambezia Province that had been the site of intense conflict for several years:

> Wounds [from the war] can be easily treated. That is, the physical wounds. Some of these kids have wounds because they have seen things they shouldn't see, that no child should have to see—like their parents being killed. They change their behavior. This is not like being mad; that we can treat. No, this is from what they have seen: it is a social problem, a behavioral problem, not a mental problem. They beat each other, they are disrespectful,

they tell harsh jokes and are delinquent. You can see it in their behavior toward each other: more violence, more harshness, less respect—more breaking down of tradition.

Mozambicans consistently pointed out that not all severely disruptive wounds stem from direct physical violence:

> The war brings many types of violence, and some we can deal with better than others. The physical mutilation and massacres are horrible: the women raped, the ears and lips cut off, the friend chopped to death with a machete. . . . There is no excuse for this, no easy solution to the suffering it causes. But you want to know what I think is the worst thing about this war? It is sleeping in the bush at night. [Because RENAMO often attacked at night, many people slept in the bush.] Animals live in the bush, not humans. My marriage bed is the center of my family, my home, my link with the ancestors and the future. This war, the *Bandidos Armados* ["armed bandits"—RENAMO], have broken my marriage bed, and with that they try to break my spirit, break what makes me who I am, make me an animal. This is the worst violence you can subject someone to.

The war also kills hope and any sense of normality. One day I was speaking to a child of five or six who had walked hundreds of miles with his family after RENAMO had attacked and burned his village. He had the countenance of an adult and the weakened body of a child half his age, and he spoke about the violence he had witnessed with a detached seriousness, much as an old man might speak. Asked about a small wound on his leg, the type of injury children are prone to get, he answered:

> The wound? I will die of it. We walked here many days, and we had nothing while we walked. I watched my brother starve to death during that time. We had to leave our home because the bandits attacked it, and I saw them kill my father. Now we are here and I watch my mother dying slowly, because we have nothing. I will die too.

These forms of violence are only marginally recognized in traditional conflict studies, and solutions to these types of problems are seldom even broached. Among those most affected by war, however, finding solutions to these kinds of violence are paramount. This is not only because violence is so crippling to the sustainability of life, limb, and community, but because Mozambicans who have seen violence first hand recognize the dangers of the growth of a culture of violence. Virtually every Mozambican I spoke with agreed with the wisdom captured by the healer who said:

> People have just seen too much war, too much violence—they have gotten the war in them. We treat this,

we have to—if we don't take the war out of the people, it will just continue on and on, past RENAMO, past the end of the war, into the communities, into the families, to ruin us.

The idea that violence can, as one person said, "stick on a person like a rash on the soul" is pervasive in Mozambique.

HEALING WAR'S WOUNDS

What is fairly unique about Mozambicans is their conviction that cultures of violence that can be built up can also be broken down. In fact, in many heavily affected areas, people asked that every new arrival touched by the war's violence—including those who had seen people die of starvation—be treated by a traditional healer who specialized in war trauma to "take the violence out of them."

Traditional healers have incorporated conflict resolution into their healing arts. They counsel marginalized or renegade soldiers (predominately RENAMO) to give up fighting and return to their communities and a peaceful way of life. The healers focus on severing the person from the soldier mentality. They act to reintegrate the person into community life, and they can teach community members to accept the ex-soldier (who may well have committed atrocities there). Healers have even encouraged others to kidnap RENAMO soldiers to "help them get over the war." Conversely, many citizens criticize UN schemes to demobilize soldiers and move them to camps isolated from the community—a situation that could continue the cycle of violence.

Average citizens on the front lines are far more involved in the mitigation of conflict than outsiders might suspect. Granted, the situation at the local level is complex and often contradictory. There are people working in the political, military, and economic spheres who seek to benefit from the fractures caused by war. Others, like the traditional healers, are trying to solve the inequalities, injustices, and abuses caused by war and those who exploit violence for their own gain. These positive forces include local-level political groups (both legal and proscribed) who meet across conflict lines to defuse tensions; traders who carry goods, messages, and refugees across no-man's-lands; religious leaders who sponsor peace talks in the thick of the battle; teachers who work with traumatized children in battle-scarred villages.

Ongoing narratives weaving violence, isolation, treachery, and hope are often at the heart of discussions by average civilians as they search for better solutions to the culture of violence wrought by the war. These discussions, unlike those concerned only with the physical destructiveness of violence, emphasize the long-term problems, those that will last well beyond ceasefires, that can grow out of the current conflict.

The reverberating effects of violence on uncertain futures are nowhere more evident than with women who have been kidnapped and raped by soldiers, and who have, in many instances, borne children from these assaults. As Joaguim Segurada, a Portuguese anthropologist working with a private organization in Mozambique, noted:

> So what happens when these women go back to their homelands? Still they are missing their husbands, their families, and who will want them? Maybe they return to find their lands missing—that they have lost the rights to them when they lost their husband, or maybe some avaricious person or enterprise has taken their land over, and the women have no means, no strength to fight this. But worse than that, they will have lost "normalcy": the context of their family and home can never be the same again—it has been irreparably destroyed. Healthy culture, as they knew it, is gone.

Women working for the Organization for Mozambican Women in Zambezia, one of the provinces most severely affected by the war, were more graphic in assessing this problem. They frequently lamented the many times women forced to have sex with soldiers returned home to find husbands who had taken other wives or who despised them for having been with other men, families who marginalized them for having lived with the enemy, and communities who called the children produced by rapes *lixo* (garbage).

In Mozambique, many educators, religious and community leaders, healers, and citizens recognize that violence is "formative," that it shapes people's perceptions, self-images, and outlooks on life. That this situation need not exist motivates the work of many who want to change the reality of the front lines.

Local solutions attempt to deal not only with immediate traumatization, but with disrupted social and cultural systems that can linger long after the last bullet has been fired. Many people at the epicenter of a war realize it is often cyclic: it deposits seeds of conflict that will germinate at a later date. But many are optimistic that specific actions can break this cycle of violence. Few accept that conflict is natural to humans. They have seen that a few soldiers can wreak brutal havoc on an entire society.

RESOLUTION AND TRANSFORMATION

One of the most unfortunate barriers to healing cultures of violence is the fact that national and international agencies too often neither support nor recognize much of the local-level work conducted to identify and treat the legacies of violent conflict. These agencies lose the insights of those at the "ground" level, dooming good intentions to failure as local people go without the sponsorship that could carry their ideas to fruition on a large scale. As one old Mozambican villager, recently burned out of his home and village, summed up, "If the governments and all those other outsiders who think they know what is going on would just get out of this, we could cure this country in no time."

As the destructive legacies of cultures of violence become recognized, the wounds of war that can spark new conflicts over time can be healed. The old Mo-zambican quoted above might be encouraged by some of the programs the government is instituting. In the hope of curtailing the reverberations of war's violence. The Ministry of Education has begun a program to assist traumatized youth in primary schools, and the Mozambican Women's Organization has projects to help women who are grappling with the effects of rape, dislocation, and chronic poverty. And, as of 1989, the government has elected to incorporate indigenous healers into the health-care system to benefit from the range and depth of healing knowledge they offer—knowledge that heals societies as well as bodies.

12

Culture Change

Cultures change all the time, but the most dramatic instances are to be found in the confrontation between small-scale and large-scale societies. By 1900, hardly any autonomous tribal people were left on the globe because most had been conquered and subjugated by powerful forces of Western technology and ideology. This takeover changed political relationships profoundly. It was not Western culture per se that confronted these people, but a worldwide economic system that made use of this inexpensive labor administered usually by some form of colonialism (see Maybury-Lewis's article, this chapter). It was in this **economic exploitation** that these people were transformed.

The results of this transformation were hardly uniform. Industrialization or colonialism did not shape new household or other cultural forms; rather, any new forms were the product of how so-called tribal people *interpreted* their colonial experiences and acted on the basis of these interpretations. Some cultures are clearly more amenable to culture change than others, and explanations of culture change have been sought in a variety of interlocking factors including relative deprivation, exploitation and economic inequality, and congruence of cultural elements. Frequently culture change is manifested in terms that are the antithesis of the colonial situation. Thus, for example, if the colonized are treated hierarchically, the culture change movement might stress **egalitarianism.** This is known, in terms formulated by the anthropologist Victor Turner, as a form of antistructure or **liminality.**

Perhaps the most dramatic form of these movements are those known as **cargo cults** or **Millenarian movements**—typically religiously based movements that promote social change. They are also movements

to make sense of what is a bewildering and frustrating experience for many of the colonial underdogs. Much interesting work has been done on this subject, and some anthropologists have even gone so far as to apply these models to their own society. The rise of Christianity, for example, shows many similarities with Melanesian cargo cults (see Chapter 2). Both are very much the products of an oppressive colonial system and both led to the formulation of an alternative lifestyle and ideology. The major difference is, of course, that Christianity went on to become a successful movement, whereas most of these movements are rather short-lived.

What one makes of these movements depends on whose point of view is taken. The Mau Mau, for example, was a movement in Kenya that the colonial authorities saw as a terroristic movement that used "sick" rituals like the slaughter of goats and people to intimidate the local populace. Later analyses, however, showed it to be not a fanatical cult but a highly effective anticolonial movement. Outsiders' preoccupation with the esoteric and their inability to communicate because of language barriers have often resulted in outsiders projecting their own fantasies onto such movements—a situation abetted by the need of such movements to maintain some secrecy.

After gaining independence, many Southern Hemisphere countries were given massive foreign aid to help in their development. Much of this aid is believed to be misplaced. When financial aid was originally provided to these countries, anthropologists were rarely consulted, for a number of reasons: They were believed to favor "traditional culture" and thus were against change; moreover, they took too long to do their studies since they insisted on fieldwork. But after some particularly dismal failures of foreign aid, anthropologists are increasingly being called upon to provide the local perspective, because they are believed to be well qualified to serve as bridge personnel who understand both the worlds of the local people and that of the planners. They are supposed to help identify the unanticipated consequences of large development projects. Such consequences can often be disastrous for the local people, as A. L. Spedding's case study of the coca eradication project in Bolivia, part of President Reagan's War on Drugs, shows.

Anthropologists are by no means unanimous as to what their role should be in these social engineering projects. Their attitudes range from seeing them as simply another form of recolonization, to disillusionment, to damage control—accepting that such projects are inevitable. James Brain's and James Ferguson's papers point to the truth of Walt Kelly's character Pogo's adage that "We have met the Enemy and he is us." Brain's concern is more with the anthropology of the development expert, while Ferguson asks a more basic question: What does development do? Of course, aid is not only provided to promote development, but often is a response to war, famine, or other disasters, raising questions that Alex de Waal examines in his article. The role of the anthropologist in culture change and the necessity to "study up" are well demonstrated in David Maybury-Lewis's historical overview.

Coca Eradication

A Remedy for Independence?—With a Postscript

A. L. Spedding

A. L. Spedding did fieldwork in Bolivia between 1986 and 1988 for her London School of Economics Ph.D. She now works as a free-lance writer, novelist, and researcher.

. . . Tratar de quitar la coca es querer que no haya Peru . . . es, finalmente, imaginacion de hombres que por sus intereses, pensando que hacen algo, destruyen la tierra sin la entender.

. . . To try to get rid of coca is to wish that there be no Peru . . . it is, finally, the dream of men who for their interests, thinking they are doing something, destroy the earth without understanding it.

—Juan de Matienzo (1567) *Gobierno del Peru*

If development is something which occurs in programmes funded by aid, there is not much development in Bolivia. The region of Bolivia I am concerned with is Sud Yungas, a section of the eastern slopes of the Andes, with a subtropical climate and an economy based on the cultivation of coca by Aymara peasant farmers. By local standards, it is a long way from being a backward area; since the price of coca began to rise in the 1970s, branch roads have been constructed into most districts, there is considerable commercial activity, many communities have piped water supplied to all houses except those next to springs, and some have even installed a domestic electricity supply, tapping into the network carrying hydroelectricity from a distant dam. All this has been achieved through self-help and community labour projects, organized by the peasants themselves, and using the windfall profits of the great coca boom which ran from about 1970 and took off between 1980 and 1986. The only programme funding economic development, as opposed to medical aid, is the UN's Agroyungas project. Its aim is development through crop substitution, which is a euphemism for coca eradication. Yet the properties of coca make it a development economist's dream. So why does it have to be eradicated and replaced by coffee for the export market?

Coca is a woody, slow-growing shrub, with a straggling habit of growth and a maximum height of about 1.50m. The part of the bush which is harvested is its leaves, borne in pairs, bright green, resembling bayleaves but smaller and thinner. If they are not stripped off the bush, after three or four months they turn brown and fall off, to be replaced by a new crop. In practice the leaves are harvested before they turn brown, dried in the sun and packed into sacks for transport and sale. Many adults in Bolivia consume coca, as an infusion or by "chewing" it. In fact the leaves are not chewed, but placed in the side of the mouth between gum and cheek, with a small quantity of *llujta*, an alkaline paste made from vegetable ashes. In combination with saliva, this releases some of the fourteen alkaloids which the leaves contain. The consumer sucks on the wad from time to time to absorb them in the juice it produces.

The effect is rather like a strong cup of coffee, without the tremors and headaches overindulgence in caffeine can produce. Swallowing the coca juice suppresses appetite and reduces thirst. It contains appreciable quantities of vitamin A, and the llujta provides calcium. An accustomed chewer can extract enough stimulants from it to stay awake all night, so it is used not only for all-night rituals but by long distance lorry and bus drivers. An infusion of coca is a cure for the stomach problems due to high altitude, and coca tea is consumed by upper and middle class Bolivians, although chewing it is restricted to people considered ethnically Indian, most of whom are peasants. Coca is an ingredient in a variety of herbal cures in the Andean medical system, and is essential in indigenous ritual and divination.[1]

Until the collapse of tin prices in the 1980s, mining was the principal export sector of the Bolivian economy, as it had been when Bolivia was the province of Upper Peru in the Spanish Empire. The first great coca boom occurred in response to the sixteenth-century

mining boom. The Spanish provided Indian forced labourers with coca because it meant they could work
longer hours with less food, but even had the shifts
been short, people would have refused to mine without coca. A mine lies in the territory of the earth spirits
and coca is indispensable as offering to and protection from them.[2] Spaniards bought up coca estates
and dominated the lucrative trade which supplied the
mines; they had a vested interest in preserving coca.[3]
The Catholic Church, however, recognized coca chewing as a rite of indigenous religion, and combated its
use. The quote which heads this essay is from a Spanish colonial administrator of the sixteenth century; it is
plain that the debate between those who benefit from
coca, and those who want to eradicate it, was already
active in 1567.

Opponents of coca claim that it damages the health
and renders the habitual user thoughtless and apa-
thetic. Coca use is thought to be a consequence of poverty: people cannot afford food and chew coca to dull
their hunger. This, in turn, is thought to stupefy them
so that they are even less able to overcome their disadvantages. It is true that—for instance—a homeless
person in the Bolivian capital, or a poor peasant parent
with seven children to feed, will obtain an ounce of
coca to keep themselves going while they give what
food they have to their children; but I encountered just
as many habitual, and even heavy, users of coca among
the rich peasants who had plenty to eat. The true importance of coca is religious and ritual; it is an essential
mediating agent in Andean culture. The exploitation
which native Andeans have been subjected to has produced a situation where many of the people most committed to the Andean cultural tradition are very poor,
but coca is not used because of poverty, although it
does provide a much appreciated solace in the lives of
the dispossessed; if people give up coca when they become rich, this is because the social system obliges
middle class people to shun Andean customs. In this
sense any attack on coca amounts to a direct attack on
the Andean tradition, and this is exactly why the Catholic Church opposed its use. The recent use of coca to
produce a prohibited drug has only provided secular
grounds for this continuing assault on indigenous
values.

From the point of view of a peasant family, coca is
a superb crop. It grows at altitudes up to 2,000m above
sea level (which is rather low in Andean terms), needs
no irrigation, resists drought and disease, and provides
three harvests a year. In Yungas it is planted in terraces
of pounded earth, which require a huge investment of
labour to create, but once the field has been planted, it
will start to yield in its second year. If it is well maintained it will go on yielding three harvests a year for
thirty years or more. It needs weeding regularly, and
the harvest is extremely labour-intensive, but it can be

harvested by anyone aged eight to eighty, and labour
is the one resource which the peasant family can produce in ample supply. In Sud Yungas, every peasant
man is expected to make a coca field when he marries.
By the time the coca is in full production, the children
will be old enough to start helping with the harvest.
This new coca is called *wawa kuka*, "child coca."

When yields start to decrease, the plants are
pruned back to stumps and allowed to regenerate.
This can be repeated almost indefinitely, although the
plants start to thin out after a while. Each harvest is
called *mita*. This comes from the Inka term *mit'a*, a turn
in the state labour draft. It was adapted as *mita* by the
Spaniards to provide drafts of labourers for mines,
weaving shops, and public service. The mature coca is
called *mit'ani*, "owns a mita"; during the days of labour
service on the hacienda, the mit'ani was the woman
obliged to perform domestic services in the landlord's
house. As the coca plants die off, they are replaced by
manioc, then citrus saplings and coffee, and the field
eventually becomes a mixed plot of these and other
crops. If wished it can be made over into another coca
field. By this time the couple who planted the original
field will be dead or in retirement, and a new generation will be working the land. If any coca plants from
the old field still survive, they are not grubbed out
when the land is cleared, but left sticking out of the
new terraces. They are called *awicha*, "grandmother";
the integration of coca into the cycle of the domestic
group is paralleled in the names it receives at various
stages.

During times when coca is in boom, as it was in
the sixteenth as well as the twentieth century,[4] it is
planted in fields carved directly out of the forest. The
usual use of these fields is for subsistence crops, such
as maize, walusa (an Andean variety of taro), beans
and vegetables. After some years of repeated cropping
the soil is "tired," and it is at this point that coca should
be planted, it responds well on exhausted soils. Bolivian consumers prefer the small-leaved and aromatic
coca which grows on the hillsides of degraded red slate
which is all that is left in the traditional coca regions,
some of which have been producing coca in the same
place since the fifteenth century and earlier.[5] These
regions lie between 1,000 and 2,000m above sea level.
In recent years people from the Andean highlands
have migrated in number to the colonization schemes
in the tropical lowlands (below 600m above sea level).
The soil in these areas is very poor once the forest has
been cleared, and people do not hold enough land for
them to be able to clear a new field every two years as
the original indigenous population did. They fell and
burn the forest, sow maize the first year and rice the
next; after this the soil is good for nothing, so they
plant coca, which will grow when nothing else will.[6] In
these conditions it provides four harvests a year, bear-

ing big leaves which have a bitter taste when chewed and are unusable for divination. The alkaloid content, however, is the same (some sources claim that it is higher than the mid-altitude product, but my evidence does not support this) and this lowland coca is mainly used for processing into cocaine base. Badly planned colonization projects have thus given a major fillip to the cocaine trade. Sud Yungas, however, is an old-established (Inka and before) coca region, and most of its production is of a quality suitable for the "traditional" Bolivian market.

The complex process by which cocaine is extracted from the leaves (some four hundred pounds of which are needed to provide a pound of relatively pure cocaine) was discovered in 1880, but cocaine only became the "drug of choice" for extensive sectors of the US bourgeoisie from about 1975 onwards. It has gone out of fashion in the middle classes of California (whose preferred diversion is now going to Narcotics Anonymous meetings) but the British government continues to predict an avalanche of "snow" and its new derivative, crack, which, it claims, is about to swamp Britain's cities. Crack appears to be cocaine carbonate, very similar in properties to cocaine sulphate, the crude base produced in primitive forest "factories" for later conversion to the soluble (and hence snortable) cocaine hydrochloride.

Like crack, this base can be mixed with tobacco and smoked. It is highly addictive. Yungas peasants who go to work treading coca in these "factories" are given it as part of their wages. If they use it at all (many just sell it) it is to "quit oneself the drunkenness" so as to prolong even further the sessions of festive drunkenness which are indispensable to every ritual and social occasion in the Andes. They use base in the same way as they use alcohol: smoke or drink to excess, pass out, suffer a hangover and go back to work, with no further recourse to intoxicants—apart from the daily chew of leaves—till the next special occasion. A few individuals do develop a habit, but most have relatives and friends who soon put a stop to it. Most of the people who manufacture or deal in base in Bolivia do not consume it, which contrasts with the situation in the West, where the majority of cocaine dealers became involved in the business as consumers. I was familiar with various small-scale peasant base makers, but their activities did not lead to violence, theft, or addiction; the social structure of the rural community is strong enough to restrain anti-social activities.

Contrast this to the ravages reportedly wrought by cocaine and crack addiction in the United States: for the proletarian there who takes up crack, the drug provides a direct escape from boredom and an urban environment which is all too often hideous and decaying. Crack and cocaine dealing offer a chance to make money, not only to those whose race and class restricts

their access to the formal job market, but also to financiers prepared to take a risk for high gain; while the proprietor of a Bolivian base factory barely makes a living, the individuals who finance international smuggling can reap vast rewards. The potential benefits of the drug trade are not combated by effective means such as punitive damages for banks found to be laundering funds, while the activity of government agencies supposed to be combating the trade are at times equivocal; witness the evidence in the recent Cuban cocaine smuggling trial that US agents had infiltrated the operation, but allowed it to continue shipping drugs into the States because this could be used to smear Cuba.[7] Hysterical denunciations of "the pushers," who usually come from disadvantaged and disaffected social groups, provide an excuse for more expenditure on mechanisms of social control, not only domestic police and customs but extending to military and paramilitary incursions in producing countries, under the guise of attacking the problem at its source. Support for neoliberal economic policies is often combined with demands for political and economic interference in this form. No-one suggests that the answer to alcoholism is uprooting the vineyards of France and California, but the answer to cocaine addiction is military campaigns in the Andes, aerial spraying with poisonous herbicides (which is now being carried out in Peru), and programmes such as Agroyungas.

Agroyungas began to function in Sud Yungas from 1985 onwards. It is funded by the UN, with contributions from Italy and other EEC countries including Britain (Conservative politician Timothy Raison visited Bolivia in 1987). The UN appointed a Spaniard as overall director, backed up by other international technocrats. The salaries of this directorate and the staff in project's funds [sic]. A second portion is absorbed by the rather lower salaries paid to Bolivian engineers, agronomists, and sociologists, who are the active interface between the technocrats and the peasants. Their pay is generous by local standards, but they resent being paid less than the "gringos" on the senior staff. Some crumbs are left to pay the local people hired as cooks, drivers and field assistants. All this money is paid out as salaries, not loans, and the recipients are free to do what they like with it; which is not the case with the funds disbursed to peasant producers.

The UN makes available US$2,000 dollars per hectare of coca eradicated. This is a loan, not a payment. Most peasants do not have as much as one hectare under coca, and receive correspondingly less. The money is paid out over a period of three years. Just as the poor in the United States are given part of their welfare benefits in food stamps to prevent them spending money on anything else, only a part is disbursed in cash, at a level calculated to cover the day-wages for extra labour needed to fulfill the project's demands. The rest of the payment is in the form of tools and seedlings for the crop which is to replace coca. This is an improved form of coffee known as catura coffee. In return the peasant has to deposit some kind of land title as security for the loan. If the loan is not repaid, this will be used to seize the land—which sounds brutal, but this sanction is the only one strong enough to get most peasants to pay back loans to someone not personally known to them. It has to be paid back within seven years, plus interest of three to five per cent on the outstanding sum. This is very cheap, since ten per cent a month is considered a fair rate of interest on loans from local moneylenders.

When Agroyungas arrived in Sud Yungas, it was headed by an enthusiastic engineer who I will call "Guillermo." He ran around making all sort of promises; apart from improved coffee, people would have roads built into every recess of their communities, and would receive help with chicken and duck breeding, mules for transport and better water supply so that they could grow irrigated vegetables. None of these promises ever materialized, apart from catura coffee and the roads. Road building consisted of driving a JCB through the community—in at least one case, undermining the foundations of a house which collapsed as a result—and calling the resulting earth track a road. People were initially attracted by these offers and by the cheap loans. Guillermo played down the coca eradication aspect—"it depends on you," he would say. Actually uprooting coca is unthinkable within the customary system of land use, and people were encouraged to sign up for the project without its being emphasized that if they did they would in due course have to pull up their coca. The sociologists who were working on the project in 1987 said that Guillermo had made a lot of careless promises and had eventually been dismissed, after which things had proceeded more sensibly. The peasants' explanation of his over-enthusiasm and subsequent dismissal is rather different:

> That engineer Guillermo? My cousin used to drive his jeep for him. He was a dealer! When they drove to the capital they had to stop a few kilometres before the police checkpoint. The base was hidden in the engine. Guillermo opened it up and sprinkled it with petrol so that it wouldn't smell, then they just drove on through.

Agroyungas is part of the Bolivian government's Three Year Plan to do away with the *narcotrafico*. The inception of this plan coincided with the arrival of US troops in Bolivia in July 1986. 1986–7 was to be the year of Voluntary Eradication, 1987–8 of Forcible Eradication, and 1988–9 of Interdiction, with the construction of new prisons for unregenerate growers and traffickers. The first years of Agroyungas, then, corresponded to Voluntary Eradication; clients of the programme

were shocked when, in 1987, the project started to demand that they actually dig up their coca, since the catura coffee was supposed to be coming into production to replace it.

Coffee does have advantages as a smallholding crop. Its disadvantages are, firstly, it needs either reasonably good soil or fertilizers in order to yield well, and secondly, it only gives one harvest a year. Since the nineteenth century coffee has been a secondary cash crop in Sud Yungas. The local variety is an arabica known as criollo coffee; it has adjusted to local soils and climate and though it does not bear much, what it does yield is better quality than catura coffee. Like coca, when it gets too straggling it can be pruned back to a stump and then regrows. It is cultivated in a mixed plot of citrus, bananas and other crops, protected by tall shade trees which are also pollarded for firewood. In these conditions it yields adequately and seeds itself within the thicket; to grow more coffee one simply transplants these young plants. Catura coffee plants fruit loaded with berries and look wonderful when they stand next to the sparse criollo coffee. However they do not seed themselves, need a special nursery, and must be fertilized and sprayed if they are to realise their superior potential. After a number of years they are exhausted and must be replaced; apparently they do not survive pruning. The coffee harvest is already the worst labour bottleneck of the year and were there to be still more coffee produced it would be even harder to get enough people to pick it: I have seen catura coffee left unharvested, admittedly when its owners were not peasants, for this reason. People are used to coca, which provides money almost all year round from a series of small fields with staggered harvests, and do not want to depend on a large once-a-year harvest with the inevitable period of penury preceding it.

Annual harvests also encourage debt bondage to buyers who advance money in the months before the crop comes in. In addition people are not used to investing much time or money in coffee—in contrast to coca. Coca does not self-sow and has to be propagated in a nursery for up to two years before it can be transplanted; at this stage it is still only six inches high. It is the only crop for which firebreaks are constructed round its fields, and the only one for which insecticides are used. It is not sprayed, since the grower expects to be able to chew it, but ground insecticides are used against root infestation and leaf-cutter ants. Coca has a symbolic value which means that people are prepared to go to all this trouble for it, since they take a lot of pride in producing a crop which is considered desirable according to the traditional criteria. It should have small leaves, of a size to fit comfortably in the mouth, and be "sweet"—contain a large amount of oil of wintergreen and other aromatics. These aromatics, rather than the alkaloid content, are what coca chewers value. The crop should have regularly shaped leaves, without discolouration or misshapes, and be carefully dried so that it preserves a good green colour: discoloured coca signifies disease in the system of divination, and has an unpleasant taste. Coca growers dispense quantities of coca to their guests on ritual occasions and there is a lot of prestige to be lost if one dispenses a poor quality coca. Conversely, there is no prestige at all to be gained if one produces a good crop of catura coffee.

During boom years, new coca fields are created everywhere, but when prices collapse, as they did in 1986, these speculative fields are rapidly abandoned to bush. The mechanisms of the global market—which is now saturated and declining—will deal with the excess production generated in response to the temporary fashion for cocaine in the West. Coca eradication is measured by area cleared, not the fall in production, so a huge field with a few exhausted plants in it counts for more than a small but highly productive one. Most of the fields offered for eradication are already choked by weeds or are too old to be of any value. At times the grower takes the loan for eradicating such a field and uses it to plant a new coca field in an area out of sight of the authorities, but the growers who do this are peasant farmers for whom coca is the only practical cash crop; speculators who got into coca when its price was rising no longer find it economic, the low price does not pay for the labour necessary. The fields which continue in cultivation are those managed by peasant families who cannot afford to abandon their investment, have to occupy their family members somehow, and do not find catura coffee an adequate alternative.

The directors of Agroyungas also failed to take into account the structure of the peasant community. Each family owns several plots, usually scattered throughout the extension of the community, and may also exploit plots in common land; in the latter case these plots are used for subsistence annuals, not for perennial crops. If legal titles are held, they give the owners the standing of smallholder; although in Peru the peasant community is a legal entity, communal landholding has no standing in Bolivian law. In practice, however, the *sindicato* (gathering of household heads) exercises jurisdiction over the community as a whole. It acts as guarantor of land titles, decides disputes over boundaries, and decides if outsiders shall be allowed to cultivate or buy land within the community. This jurisdiction extends to deciding if a new crop which would alter the system of land use—as would the replacement of coca by catura coffee—should be introduced. If it is to be introduced, then a majority of the community will do so at the same time.

Agroyungas was misled by the formal status of peasant communities as bundles of smallholders and approached individuals to see if they would join the project. The more united communities discussed this in the syndicate and in the majority of cases decided not to join; their members abided by this decision. Some communities were already divided, however, and certain individuals joined the project while others did not (it seems that there were no cases of entire communities which decided to abandon coca). In at least one such community the subsequent activities of Agroyungas exacerbated the divisions to the point where those who were with the project violently assaulted those who were not. The peasant commentary on this interprets it as a sign that those who had joined the project, when they found that they did not just get money to grow coffee but had to pull up their coca, realized that they were losing out. Out of jealousy they attacked those who had stayed with the customary economy based on coca. This only encouraged the communities which had not yet joined the project to stay out of it. By 1987 Agroyungas would only take on new clients if they subscribed in groups of at least twelve households. Most communities in Sud Yungas have between thirty and sixty households, so if twelve are prepared to come out in public for Agroyungas, it is likely that they will be able to drag a sufficient majority in their wake. Agroyungas admitted that they had entered the area totally ignorant of local conditions and that much of the project had failed as a result.

This relative lack of success is the only really good thing about Agroyungas: it didn't do much harm because it didn't do much anyway, at least for the peasantry. Another example which I encountered during fieldwork was a European-based "appropriate technology" group, represented by several young people on generous EEC grants. They spent a year climbing Andean peaks and canoeing down tropical rivers, as well as consuming "Bolivian marching powder,"[8] and then, when they realised that they had not actually done anything to justify their grant, wrote a laudatory report on a series of "appropriate technology" water pumps designed by an engineer with a grant from Oxfam. They did not actually sponsor the installation of any of these pumps, which could be used in irrigation and small-scale mining. Meanwhile the peasants continue "scratching the earth" (as they themselves describe it) with implements which have not changed since the eighteenth century. Should they decide independently to produce a new crop instead of coca, they receive no support. One man in Sud Yungas had the idea of producing strawberries, a luxury crop which enjoys a high price in the city, but which needs specially prepared fields and a lot of care. He had heard on the radio that the government offered loans to petty producers, so he applied to the local branch of the Banco Agrafio for a loan, only to be repeatedly fobbed off with the claim that they had not received authorization from the capital. In the end he planted a few strawberries with family labour and the help of an old woman working in *ayni* (mutual aid); with a loan he would have been able to employ wage labourers and plant an area large enough to be profitable, and when he made money from it the demonstration effect would have encouraged many other people to try the new crop. A government which was sincerely interested in coca eradication should have jumped at the chance to support local initiatives like this.

How would it benefit the people of Sud Yungas if, instead of coca, they depended on coffee as their main cash crop? Aymara came to Sud Yungas perhaps in the twelfth century, to grow coca, cotton, hot peppers and tobacco, to send up the mountain to the Altiplano (around 4,000m above sea level) where their political capital was and is. In return they received supplies of meat, fish and dried tubers which they could not produce in Yungas. This interchange continues to be the basis of the economy in Sud Yungas. The recent insertion of coca producers in the international economy via clandestine trade has introduced merely superficial changes in the region. The same traders who buy coca for the traditional market also buy it for base makers. Many intermediaries compose the chain between peasant producer and the barons who ship coke to Miami, and this insulates growers to some degree. After the inflated prices of the boom collapsed in 1986 (in response to the arrival of US troops in the lowlands and the simultaneous departure of the major drug traffickers) the market returned to the annual cycle determined by regional supply and demand. This market is static, but reliable, and allows some of the surplus value generated to be retained within the region. Not so with coffee.

The three export houses which sell Bolivian coffee abroad have depots in Sud Yungas, which buy coffee direct from producers or from local intermediaries. The 1987 price offered to producers was a quarter to a third of the price which had been paid two years before. This was due to the breakup of the world coffee cartel which had maintained prices. Coffee prices are subject to speculation and depend on the state of negotiations between the major consumer, the USA, and the major producers, Brazil and Colombia. The Brazilian harvest is a major determinant of price in the South American region. If the peasants were to depend on coffee for their cash income, they would be tied directly to these unpredictable fluctuations in the world coffee market, which have no relation to the state of their own harvests or anything else in their regional or national economy. The religious and ritual uses of coca are attacked in the Bolivian press with claims that *aculli* (traditional coca chewing) is "drug addiction," "one of the most basic signs of the backwardness of our peasant population" and a cause of "introversion, submission, cowardice, lesser mental and physical development."[9]

This barely veiled racism typifies the attitude of the upper classes in Bolivia towards the rural Andean masses. These upper classes are already dependent on US aid handouts and the fluctuations of world commodity markets; perhaps this is why they see the destruction of the still resilient peasant economy through "development" as a form of progress.[10]

POSTSCRIPT

The current escalation of violence in the Colombian "drug wars" and the concomitant announcement of "further increases in US spending on drug-control programmes in the Andean countries" (Guardian, 6.9.89) has brought particular salience to the subject of this article. It is depressing to see that much of this spending will be in the form of "military aid" and the provision of aircraft and vehicles to assist the armed repression of the cocaine trade, when it is well known that repression only weeds out the small and unprotected traders while encouraging the large "cartels" to purchase more arms and militarize their operations. Commentators admit that "there has been less violence in Bolivia, where . . . governments have resisted US pressure to begin forcible eradication of coca fields" (Guardian, 5.9.89) while in Peru the government's heavy-handed tactics in the coca region of the Huallaga valley have led to coca growers accepting the presence of Sendero Luminoso guerillas, who regulate the trade, levying a "revolutionary tax" and obliging buyers to pay a fair price to local producers of coca and base.

The Bolivian government has not so much resisted US pressure as been too weak to do anything to prevent coca growing, but even there the militarized narcotics force known as the "Leopardos" has been extending its operations throughout 1988 and 1989. The only way to reduce the amount of coca grown in the Andes—given that the demand for cocaine in the West does not seem to be decreasing—is to fund a programme of genuine capital investment in the local economy.

In Sud Yungas, one possibility would be the construction of large-scale irrigation systems allowing people to cultivate crops requiring quantities of water: coca does not need irrigation. In other regions, the building of roads would allow people to produce crops which need motor transport to be brought to the cities: coca has a high value per unit weight and is not very perishable, so it is one of the few cash crops that can be grown in places with poor communications. It is to be hoped that the publicity being given to coca will provide an opportunity to consider the many alternatives to armed repression.

NOTES

1. An account of the many uses of coca is given in Carter, William and Mauricio Mamani, *Coca en Bolivia*, La Paz, 1986. As well as being "chewed," coca is burnt or buried in ritual offerings, ap-

plied as a plaster or an infusion in medicine, and used for divination, where the leaves are scattered and the patterns they fall into observed. Apart from the medical use as tea, all these uses of coca are strongly associated with Indian ethnicity and serve as one of the diagnostic markers of ethnic affiliation.

2. Nash, June. 1979. *We eat the mines and the mines eat us: dependency and exploitation in Bolivian tin mines.* New York.
3. Ruggiero, Romano, & Genevieve Tranchard, 1983. Una encomienda coquera en los yungas de La Paz (1560-6) HISLA 1.
4. Matienzo, Juan de. 1967. *Gobierno del Peru.* [1567]. Paris.
5. Albo, Xavier. 1978. El mundo de la coca en Coripata, Bolivia. *America Indigena 38.4.*
6. Flores, G., & Blanes, F. 1084. ¿Donde va el Chapare? La Paz.
7. *The Independent,* 4 July 1989.
8. McInerney, J. 1985. *Bright Lights, Big City.* New York.
9. Quotes from *Documento Responsibilidad,* a sensational magazine devoted to cocaine scandals: issue 2, La Paz, May 1987.
10. Galeano, Eduardo. 1973. *Open Veins of Latin America. Five Centuries of the Pillage of a Continent.* New York and London, 1973.

REFERENCES

Albo, Xavier. 1978. "El mundo de la Coca en Coripata, Bolivia." *America Indigena.*
Carter, William, & Mauricio Mamani. 1986. *Coca en Bolivia.* La Paz.
Flores, G., & F. Blanes, 1984. "¿Donde va el Chapare?" La Paz.
Galeano, Eduardo. 1973. *Open Veins of Latin America. Five Centuries of the Pillage of a Continent.* New York and London.
Matienzo, Juan de. 1967. *Gobierno del Peru.* [1567]. Paris.
McInerney, J. 1985. *Bright Lights, Big City.* New York.
Nash, June. 1979. *We Eat the Mines and the Mines Eat Us: Dependency and Exploitation in Bolivian Tin Mines.* New York.
Quotes from *Documento Responsibilidad,* a sensational magazine devoted to cocaine scandals: Issue 2, La Paz, May 1987.
Ruggiero, Romano, & Genevieve Tranchard. 1983. Una Encomienda Conquera en los Yungas de La Paz (1560) HISLA 1.
The Independent, 4 July 1989.

The Ugly American Revisited

James L. Brain

James Brain first experienced Africa, where he has done fieldwork, as a welfare officer for the British Colonial Service. He went on to study anthropology at Syracuse University, which granted him a Ph.D. in 1968. He is now emeritus professor of anthropology at the State University of New York College at New Paltz, and his research specialties include social organization, social change, sex roles, and Swahili.

In 1958 the publication of the novel *The Ugly American* by William J. Lederer and Eugene Burdick caused a great furor. In that year alone there were twenty printings. Its emotional and political impact were instrumental in the founding of the Peace Corps and perhaps the establishment of the National Defense Education Act. A sense of shame and dismay was aroused among most liberal-minded educated Americans by the idea that our State Department representatives abroad could be so naive and gullible, so isolated in a cocoon of air-conditioned American technological culture, so lacking in any knowledge of alien cultures and languages, that they would do more harm than good to American real interests. Many of us felt guilty and even outraged that the ignorance and ethnocentrism of our aid administrators were getting us hated in the world.

Many people never read the novel and assumed from its title that it was about the ugliness of the American image abroad; indeed, it became common to say "He's a real ugly American." In one sense this idea correctly identified the message of the book; in another, it is ironic that one of the book's few heroes was the person referred to: a small ugly modest man who understood the real needs of the people and wanted to initiate schemes such as the construction of simple water pumps using a bicycle as the power unit. The snag that the little man discovered was that such schemes were of no interest whatever to anyone in the State Department. The reasons can be simply stated and they are just as strong today: (1) they are not spectacular even though they might revolutionize people's lives; (2) they would only cost a few thousand dollars;

nothing that costs less than several millions is even considered; (3) no American institution—companies, contractors, universities—would make a big profit.

I recently saw the book in a flea market, bought it and re-read it. It was horribly resonant to me as I recently worked for US AID on a two-year contract in Tanzania. I resigned after one year filled with dismay. Nothing has changed: we are still making the very same mistakes, spending huge sums of our tax money, and getting ourselves cordially hated for it.

Tanzania has been the recipient of perhaps more non-military aid than any other country in Africa, taking it from all kinds of sources, both east and west. Like every Third World country, its economy has suffered severely from the massive rise in oil prices and from the low prices for the kind of crops on which it depended in the past for its foreign exchange—coffee, cotton, sisal, tobacco. At the same time it is very shocking for someone like myself who went there first some 32 years ago to see the depths of poverty, inefficiency, and squalor to which it has been reduced. The reasons are many and complex. Chief among them are undoubtedly: (1) the nationalization of the wholesale and retail sector of the economy: shops have virtually nothing in them most of the time; bare requirements of sugar, flour, rice, cooking oil, etc. arrive at irregular intervals—sometimes weeks or months apart—and are sold out immediately (the majority of the people live by subsistence agriculture so although they can no longer get any luxury goods (sugar, margarine, luxuries!) they don't starve, otherwise the country would collapse in a month); (2) the nationalization of the highly effective producer cooperative movement started under the British in the nineteen fifties: the government is now the sole buying agent and pays poor prices, pays late, or even in IOUS; (3) the omnipresent party which really runs the country and which together with the huge bureaucracy constitutes an exploitative regime that makes the former colonial period look benign indeed; (4) the policy of compulsory "villagization" carried through in the seventies which has left a legacy of bitterness, cynicism, and passive resistance among the peasants.

Leaving this all aside—hard but just possible if we really want to help the people—what sort of things are being done in the way of international aid? There seems to be a correlation between the size of the country and the effectiveness of its aid program: the smaller the better; the larger, the poorer—with us, of course, the largest. For instance, Norway trains forestry experts—essential for a country with no other fuel resources as yet tapped. Denmark trains veterinarians—crucial for a country that has millions of cattle, sheep and goats, yet where meat and dairy products are almost unobtainable. Even the Republic of Ireland has a useful little scheme running a carpet factory to make carpets from the sisal it is hard to sell (the man running it was a gem: he had started a darts club at the local bar and was totally one of the boys). If you visit the West German aid organization you will find it very modest, yet it is doing an excellent job and is very popular. The Dutch have a good scheme constructing small village wells and pumps. There is no Dutch aid office; it is part of the embassy.

Contrast this with the United States. The AID office occupies two air-conditioned floors of a large office block and is considerably larger than the embassies of most countries. The U.S. Embassy is some three miles away in a mini-fortress (originally made for the Israelis until they had to leave the country) inconveniently located for everyone except perhaps the ambassador. Outside the AID office is a large sign which includes the logo of two clasped hands. It used to have one black hand and one white—the latter representing the United States—until someone finally realized that all Americans are not white and all aid recipients are not black. The hands are now both the same neutral color. (Incidentally, a few blocks away is the USIS office which has everything captioned in English for a population of whom perhaps ten percent know English. Why? "We are only interested in the educated elite," I was told by the officer in charge. As far back as 1965 I was protesting to the ambassador that American projects had notice boards describing them to the public only in English, and even volunteered to translate them into Swahili, which is known to the entire population, unlike most African countries where there is a multiplicity of languages. When the Chinese were giving aid to Tanzania a few years ago all their projects had large signs in Chinese, English and Swahili. In that same year, I now recall, a highly intelligent young woman whom I had trained in Swahili

and who came out as an officer in the information service, was hurriedly removed to another country after pressure from the State Department community who were outraged that she should be friendly with one of the most important Tanzanian ministers. She was white.)

Inside the AID office one is met by a massive photograph of the incumbent president, the floors are carpeted, a pretty receptionist and glamorous secretaries all add to the impression of a huge organization. The impression is only too correct. Two busy floors of highly salaried officers are dreaming up six-million-dollar schemes. Nothing less is ever considered—as someone once said: "The paper work alone costs that much."

The process goes something like this. Someone has an idea for a project. Since it is going to be very expensive a lot of work has to go into preparing it. The preparation of a contract can take a long time and the final resultant document has all the size of a family bible. All kinds of congressional conditions have to be met—many of them concerned with certifying that the country to whom the aid will be given is not hostile to the U.S. It is very easy to evade these conditions, but the amount of paper required is almost incredible. Doubtless some of the schemes proposed and which have been carried out in the past have been of value to Tanzania; many have not. Why, one might ask, does a country like Tanzania accept such schemes? The answer, as one might expect, is that there is something in them for a lot of people. Usually every scheme will mean some free vehicles, some new buildings, salaries for some staff positions, and perhaps most importantly, some scholarships for Africans to go to the U.S. for advanced degrees. Why do we get involved? The answer is much the same: there is something in it for a lot of people.

When a scheme has been processed through Washington and agreed to by the country concerned, it is put out for tender—perhaps the most bizarre system of any aid system. The bidders are usually land-grant universities. They claim to make no profit out of such a deal; on the other hand, many of their faculty members get free trips out as consultants, salaries for faculty and staff members at the home university are met, other faculty members can be shipped off for a few years at the government's expense (who will then become "experts"), and the university will get the students who have been awarded scholarships. One might question the value of involving agricultural institutions in this country committed to an "agribusiness" approach in the agriculture of countries at a largely subsistence level; or the sense of sending students to such institutions where they will learn almost nothing of any practical value to them at home. Moreover, one often wonders what on earth anyone from, say, Colorado or Utah has to contribute as a consultant on a three-week visit.

The persons recruited to go out for two or three years (like myself) are called "contract staff." They are the second-class citizens of the AID hierarchy. The real mandarins are the career officers of the State Department—and I hasten to add that many of them are decent, hardworking people, but caught in a system that is absurd. As I said, their job is to dream up new schemes—never less than six million dollars, remember—and, of course, to be "project officers" to keep a vague eye on the hatched chicks that actually make it through the astounding jungle of regulations in Washington. To do this they received—in 1981—a minimum salary of $50,000 plus a substantial post allowance, commissary privileges (including duty-free liquor), travel allowances for home leave annually for themselves and their families, a large house surrounded by a chain-link fence and guards. In effect they live at a level far above what most would expect in jobs in this country, far, far above the level of any of the previous colonial service officers. They are totally out of contact with the ordinary people. None that I met spoke more than a few words of any local language. Their social contacts are confined to the upper elite of the government and the diplomatic corps. Many of them are able to retire in their forties on a pension. As I said before, many of them are good, kind people, but they are trapped into a crazy, expensive, wasteful and largely useless system that gets us no credit and a lot of hatred.

Not only are most of the career officers totally out of contact with the people of the countries in which they are working; they are also astonishingly ignorant of the cultures of those countries. Peace Corps Volunteers usually get a good training in the language, history, political development and culture of the country. They are only there for two years. Career officers of the State Department are often in a country for many years but know nothing of it beyond the capital and the game parks.

To someone like myself who was involved in the Peace Corps from its first inception, the ironies of contrast are constant. Whereas Peace Corps Volunteers really know a lot about the country where they are going and have to have some proficiency in the language, AID personnel have no preparation other than a pamphlet about the cost of living and what to take. There is no language requirement on them even though they may stay in a country for several years. Peace Corps Volunteers live not too differently from the local people, travel by local transportation, have to speak the language. They have done a great deal to change the image of rich Americans. Even contract AID officers (and this included me) are supplied with a large house, a refrigerator and large freezer, have to purchase a car, and have salaries considerably larger than they would

get in the U.S.—enormous by local standards. Perhaps it is necessary to get qualified people; volunteers are just starting their careers; most AID contract officers are taking an unpaid leave of absence. There is usually some antagonism between the Peace Corps and the AID organization—the former feeling sometimes a little holier than thou and the latter feeling guilty about the stark contrast between themselves and the local people.

What kind of schemes am I talking about? Let us take a couple: first, the one with which I was connected. I have to backtrack a little to explain my connection. I worked in extension work in Tanzania and Uganda from 1951–63. In 1971, as an anthropologist, I returned for the summer to do research on belief systems. The dean of the agricultural college, who had known me for many years, instantly coopted me to give a series of lectures to the students on extension work because nowhere in their technically-oriented syllabus did they learn how to put over what they had learnt. It seemed to me to be a very useful idea and so in 1980 I applied for and was to be given a Fullbright fellowship to do this for a whole year. At this juncture I was approached by AID and asked wouldn't I like to do the same thing for two years at a high salary ($36,000 as compared to the $16,000 of the Fullbright)? Greed won out and I turned down the Fullbright: a decision I deeply regret. To my astonishment I found that the college had gone from the sublime to the ridiculous, with the establishment of an entire academic department devoted to agricultural education and extension. My idea is that students need perhaps two courses: an introduction to cultural anthropology to help them to understand how communities function, and a course on how to teach a practical subject. They certainly do not need courses on the philosophical and psychological foundations of education. Part of the scheme was to supply three faculty members, part to send Tanzanians to the States to do doctorates, part to build a large training center for courses, workshops, conferences and the like. Admirable, one might think, but there are dozens of idle buildings around where one could do any of these things without spending a large sum of money.

As I was about to leave, a new project was shaping up in which a big western state university would send out about twenty researchers with Ph.D.s to carry out research on the latest buzz-word—farming systems. Obviously, such a scheme will be very costly—each officer in the field costs $100,000 a year for a start—and I constantly voiced two major criticisms. First, most of the information required is already well known if someone were to do a little reading of the archives. Second, it would be quite possible for a trained anthropologist with a good knowledge of Swahili to obtain all that is needed in a few weeks at most; in many cases a few days would be enough. To bring in American farming experts with no background in East Africa, with no knowledge of the language or culture, unfamiliar with the history, is like throwing American taxpayers' money down the drain. But, of course, the university concerned will make a lot of money, all kinds of lucrative contracts will result, instant experts will be created—and then they will be able to be called in to advise on similar problems elsewhere.

In Africa in general and Tanzania in particular one major cultural matter of supreme importance has so far escaped the experts' notice, just as it escaped the notice of the colonial regimes of the past: that the farmers of Africa are usually the women. At the very least the women work on the farms as much as the men—they also fetch the water, cut and fetch the firewood, pound corn in a mortar, do the cooking, take care of the children. The only politician in all Africa to realize this fact is the often maligned Hastings Banda of Malawi, one of the only countries in Africa to be self-supporting in food. How? Dr. Banda invites the women from a particular area to the capital, gives them a big dance with lots of beer and food and a present, and then exhorts them to go back home and do everything the extension officers tell them.

The impression that I constantly got was that most AID people mentally perceived a "farmer" to be a tall white man, wearing blue jeans, boots and a Stetson staring out over his wide acres. Ronald Reagan receiving the Queen of England at his ranch would be a good model. The idea that a farmer might be a woman was not something that had really sunk in. Given the sharply divided sex roles of African society, a man cannot deal with women; on the other hand, a well-educated woman—African or American—can be accepted by both men and women. Plainly, we should send women experts and train more African women.

What should we do then? We might take a lesson from the smaller countries and think small. Abolish the wasteful AID offices and their career persons whose task it is to produce these expensive and largely useless schemes. One or two officers attached to the embassy should be entirely sufficient to act as liaison with the government and the contract workers. Get involved in small-scale schemes which don't need large buildings

and vehicles. The kind of training that extension workers might get in India, Egypt, Israel, or even China would be of far more use than anything they could get in this country. Must we always make a profit? Would it be too much to pay for people to go elsewhere, to admit that we don't have all the agricultural answers, especially for small-scale peasant agriculture that is likely to remain the mode for the foreseeable future? If the millions poured into the present schemes were channelled into research in intermediate technology it would be much more useful. Simple hand grinding machines and small-scale wells and pumps could make life less burdensome for the real producers of food—the women.

An even more radical idea was propounded in 1966 by Charles Hynam when he wrote an article with the intimidating title of "The Disfunctionality of Unrequited Giving." He pointed out that long ago in anthropology it was noticed that the principle of reciprocity is one of the most basic in human social organization. If you continually give things to someone which he cannot return he will feel a sense of obligation to you which in time will inevitably turn to dislike, hatred even. The application of this to the international aid scene is obvious. The more aid we give the more we shall be hated. His solution is one of supreme simplicity. Instead of all the bilateral aid agreements, everyone should channel funds to the World Bank which would then set up local branches all over the Third World like savings and loan associations. One of the major hindrances to development is often lack of initial capital on a small scale. By having a local bank it would be possible for individuals, or even cooperatives or whole villages, to obtain loans to finance projects which would be repaid with reasonable rates of interest. No one would be obligated to anyone and a lot of development would result. The beauty of the idea is that it does not prescribe a capitalist mode of development or a socialist one but could assist both individuals or groups.

It is sad enough that we should be wasting such astronomical sums on crazy weapons. Should we not make sure that the money we do spend to help Third World countries does in fact help them?

The Anti-Politics Machine

"Development" and Bureaucratic Power in Lesotho

James Ferguson (with Larry Lohmann)

James Ferguson is a political and economic anthropologist who specializes in southern Africa. He teaches at the University of California, Irvine.

In the past two decades, Lesotho—a small landlocked nation of about 1.8 million people surrounded by South Africa, with a current Gross National Product (GNP) of US$816 million—has received "development" assistance from 26 different countries, ranging from Australia, Cyprus and Ireland to Switzerland and Taiwan. Seventy-two international agencies and non- and quasi-governmental organizations, including CARE, Ford Foundation, the African Development Bank, the European Economic Community, the Overseas Development Institute, the International Labour Organization and the United Nations Development Programme, have also been actively involved in promoting a range of "development" programmes. In 1979, the country received some $64 million in "official" development "assistance"—about $49 for every man, woman and child in the country. Expatriate consultants and "experts" swarm in the capital city of Maseru, churning out plans, programmes and, most of all, paper, at an astonishing rate.

As in most other countries, the history of "development" projects in Lesotho is one of "almost unremitting failure to achieve their objectives."[1] Nor does the country appear to be of especially great economic or strategic importance. What, then, is this massive and persistent internationalist intervention all about?

CONSTRUCTING A "DEVELOPER'S" LESOTHO

To "move the money" they have been charged with spending, "development" agencies prefer to opt for standardized "development" packages. It thus suits the agencies to portray developing countries in terms that make them suitable targets for such packages. It is

not surprising, therefore, that the "country profiles" on which the agencies base their interventions frequently bear little or no relation to economic and social realities.

In 1975, for example, the World Bank issued a report on Lesotho that was subsequently used to justify a series of major Bank loans to the country. One passage in the report—describing conditions in Lesotho at the time of its independence from Britain in 1966—encapsulates an image of Lesotho that fits well with the institutional needs of "development" agencies:

> Virtually untouched by modern economic development . . . Lesotho was, and still is, basically, a traditional subsistence peasant society. But rapid population growth resulting in extreme pressure on the land, deteriorating soil and declining agricultural yields led to a situation in which the country was no longer able to produce enough food for its people. Many able-bodied men were forced from the land in search of means to support their families, but the only employment opportunities [were] in neighbouring South Africa. At present, an estimated 60 per cent of the male labour force is away as migrant workers in South Africa . . . At independence, there was no economic infrastructure to speak of. Industries were virtually non-existent.[2]

THE INVENTION OF "ISOLATION"

To a scholar of Lesotho, these assertions appear not only incorrect but outlandish. For one thing, the country has not been a "subsistence" society since at least the mid-1800s, having entered the twentieth century as a producer of "wheat, mealies, Kaffir corn [sic], wool, mohair, horses and cattle" for the South African market.[3] Nor were the local Basotho people isolated from the market. When they have had surpluses of crops or livestock, the people have always known how to go about selling them in local or regional markets. According to *The Oxford History of South Africa*:

"The Anti-Politics Machine: Development and Bureaucratic Power in Lesotho" by James Ferguson (with Larry Lohmann), from *The Ecologist*, Vol. 24, No. 5 (Sept./Oct. 1994). Reprinted with permission of the publisher.

In 1837 the Sotho of Basutoland . . . had grain stored for four to eight years: in 1844 white farmers "flocked" to them to buy grain. During 1872 (after the loss of their most fertile land west of the Caledon) the Sotho exported 100,000 *muids* [185-lb bags] of grain . . . and in 1877 when the demand for grain on the diamond fields had fallen, 'large quantities' were held by producers and shopkeepers in Basutoland.[4]

Livestock auctions, meanwhile, have been held throughout the country since at least the 1950s, and animals from central Lesotho have been sold by the Basotho as far afield as South Africa for as long as anyone can remember. Far from being "untouched" by modern "development" at the time of independence, colonial rule had established a modern administration, airports, roads, schools, hospitals and markets for Western commodities.

The decline in agricultural surpluses, moreover, is neither recent nor, as the Bank suggests, due to "isolation" from the cash economy. More significant is the loss by the Basotho of most of their best agricultural land to encroaching Dutch settlers during a series of wars between 1840 and 1869. Nor is migration a recent response of a pristine and static "traditional" economy to "population pressure." As H. Ashton, the most eminent Western ethnographer of the Basuto, noted in 1952, "labour migration is . . . nearly as old as the Basuto's contact with Europeans"[5]—indeed, throughout the colonial period to the present, Lesotho has served as a labour reservoir exporting wage workers to South African mines, farms and industry.

Large-scale labour migration, moreover, preceded the decline in agriculture by many years and may even have contributed to it. Even in years of very good crop production, from the 1870s on intermittently into the 1920s, workers left the country by the thousand for work. In the early stages, it seems, migration was not related to a need to make up for poor food production but to buy guns, clothing, cattle and other goods, and, from 1869, to pay taxes.

LESOTHO REALITY

In fact, far from being the "traditional subsistence peasant society" described by the Bank, Lesotho comprises today what one writer describes as "a rural proletariat which scratches about on the land."[6]

Whilst the World Bank claims that "agriculture provides a livelihood for 85 per cent of the people,"[7] the reality is that something in the order of 70 per cent of average rural household income is derived from wage labour in South Africa, while only six per cent comes from domestic crop production.[8] Similar myth-making pervades a joint FAO/World Bank report from 1975, which solemnly states that "about 70 per cent of [Lesotho's] GNP comes from the sale of pastoral products, mainly wool and mohair." A more conventional figure would be two or three per cent.[9]

Also false is the "development" literature's picture of Lesotho as a self-contained geographical entity whose relation with South Africa (its "rich neighbour") is one of accidental geographic juxtaposition rather than structural economic integration or political subordination, and whose poverty can be explained largely by the dearth of natural resources within its boundaries, together with the incompleteness with which they have been "developed." If the country is resource-poor, this is because most of the good Sotho land was taken by South Africa. Saying, as USAID does in a 1978 report, that "poverty in Lesotho is primarily resource-related" is like saying that the South Bronx of New York City is poor because of its lack of natural resources and the fact that it contains more people than its land base can support.

REARRANGING REALITY

A representation which acknowledged the extent of Lesotho's long-standing involvement in the "modern" capitalist economy of Southern Africa, however, would not provide a convincing justification for the "development" agencies to "introduce" roads, markets and credit. It would provide no grounds for believing that such "innovations" could bring about the "transformation" to a "developed," "modern" economy which would enable Lesotho's agricultural production to catch up with its burgeoning population and cut labour migration. Indeed, such a representation would tend to suggest that such measures for "opening up" the country and exposing it to the "cash economy" would have little impact, since Lesotho has not been isolated from the world economy for a very long time.

Acknowledging that Lesotho is a labour reserve for South African mining and industry rather than portraying it as an autonomous "national economy," moreover, would be to stress the importance of something which is inaccessible to a "development" planner in Lesotho. The World Bank mission to Lesotho is in no position to formulate programmes for changing or controlling the South African mining industry, and it has no disposition to involve itself in political challenges to the South African system of labour control. It is in an excellent position, however, to devise agricultural improvement projects, extension, credit and technical inputs, for the agriculture of Lesotho lies neatly within its jurisdiction, waiting to be "developed." For this reason, agricultural concerns tend to move centre stage and Lesotho is portrayed as a nation of "farmers," not wage labourers. At the same time, issues such as structural unemployment, influx control, low wages, political subjugation by South Africa, parasitic bureaucratic elites, and so on, simply disappear.

TAKING POLITICS OUT OF "DEVELOPMENT"

One striking feature of the "development" discourse on Lesotho is the way in which the "development" agencies present the country's economy and society as lying within the control of a neutral, unitary and effective national government, and thus almost perfectly responsive to the blueprints of planners. The state is seen as an impartial instrument for implementing plans and the government as a machine for providing social services and engineering growth.

"Development" is, moreover, seen as something that only comes about through government action; and lack of "development," by definition, is the result of government neglect. Thus, in the World Bank's view, whether Lesotho's GNP goes up or down is a simple function of the current five-year "development" plan being well-implemented or badly-implemented: it has nothing to do with whether or not the mineworkers who work in South Africa get a raise in any particular year. Agricultural production, similarly, is held to be low because of the "absence of agricultural development schemes" and, thus, local ignorance that "worthwhile things could be achieved on their land." In this way, an extraordinarily important place is reserved for policy and "development" planning.[10]

Excluded from the Bank's analysis are the political character of the state and its class basis, the uses of official positions and state power by the bureaucratic elite and other individuals, cliques and factions, and the advantages to them of bureaucratic "inefficiency" and corruption. The state represents "the people," and mention of the undemocratic nature of the ruling government or of political opposition is studiously avoided. The state is taken to have no interests except "development": where "bureaucracy" is seen as a problem, it is not a political matter, but the unfortunate result of poor organization or lack of training.

Political parties almost never appear in the discourse of the Bank and other "development" institutions, and the explicitly political role played by "development" institutions such as Village Development Committees (VDCs), which often serve as channels for the ruling Basotho National Party (BNP), is ignored or concealed. "The people" tend to appear as an undifferentiated mass, a collection of "individual farmers" and "decision makers," a concept which reduces political and structural causes of poverty to the level of individual "values," "attitudes" and "motivation." In this perspective, structural change is simply a

matter of "educating" people, or even just convincing them to change their minds. When a project is sent out to "develop the farmers" and finds that "the farmers" are not much interested in farming, and, in fact, do not even consider themselves to be "farmers," it is thus easy for it to arrive at the conclusion that "the people" are mistaken, that they really are farmers and that they need only to be convinced that this is so for it to be so.

In fact, neither state bureaucracies nor the "development" projects associated with them are impartial, apolitical machines which exist only to provide social services and promote economic growth. In the case of the Canadian- and World Bank-supported Thaba-Tseka Development Project, an agricultural programme in Lesotho's central mountains. Sesotho-language documents distributed to villagers were found to have slogans of the ruling Basotho National Party (BNP) added at the end, although these did not appear in any of the English language versions. Public village meetings conducted by project staff were peppered with political speeches, and often included addresses by a high-ranking police officer on the "security threat" posed by the opposition Basutoland Congress Party. Any money remaining after project costs had been repaid went to the BNP's Village Development Committees—leading one villager to note caustically, "It seems that politics is nowadays nicknamed 'development.'"

Tellingly, when I interviewed the Canadian Coordinator of the Thaba-Tseka Project in 1983, he expressed what appeared to be a genuine ignorance of the political role played by VDCs. The project hired labour through the committees, he stated, because the government had told them to. "We can't afford to get involved with politics," he said. "If they say 'hire through the Committees,' I do it."

It seems likely that such apparent political naivete is not a ruse, but simply a low-level manifestation of the refusal to face local politics which, for institutional reasons, characterizes the entire "development" apparatus.

INEVITABLE FAILURE

Because the picture of Lesotho constructed by the Bank and other "development" agencies bears so little resemblance to reality, it is hardly surprising that most "development" projects have "failed" even on their own terms. Thus after years of accusing local people of being "defeatist" or "not serious" about agriculture, and even implying that wage increases at South African mines were "a threat" to the determination of farmers to become "serious," Thaba-Tseka project experts had to concede that local people were right that little besides maize for local consumption was going to come out of their tiny mountain fields, and that greater investment in agriculture was not going to pay handsome rewards.[11]

Casting themselves in the role of politically-neutral artisans using "development" projects as tools to grab hold of and transform a portion of the country according to a pre-determined plan, "development" officials assumed that the projects were givens and all they had to do was "implement" them.

In the case of the Thaba-Tseka project, for example, planners assumed that it would be a relatively simple matter to devolve much of the decision-making to a newly constituted Thaba-Tseka district, in order to increase efficiency, enable the project to be in closer touch with the needs of "the people" and avoid its becoming entangled in government bureaucracy. But what the planners assumed would be a simple technical reform led—predictably—to a whole range of actors using the reforms for their own ends.

The project's Health Division, for example, was partly appropriated as a political resource for the ruling National Party. Power struggles broke out over the use of project vehicles. Government ministries refused to vote funds to the project and persisted in maintaining their own control over their field staff and making unilateral decisions on actions in the district. An attempt to hire a Mosotho to replace the project's expatriate Canadian director was rejected, since as long as the programme's image remained "Canadian," there could be no danger of bringing about a real "decentralization" of power away from Maseru, Lesotho's capital.

Instead of being a tool used by artisans to resculpt society, in short, the project was itself worked on: it became like a bread crumb thrown into an ant's nest. Plans for decentralization were thus abandoned in 1982. Yet Thaba-Tseka's planners continued to insist that the project's failure resulted somehow from the government's failure to understand the plan, or from the right organizational chart not having been found. Needing to construe their role as "apolitical," they continued to see government as a machine for delivering services, not as a political fact or a means by which certain classes and interests attempted to control the behaviour and choices of others.

A DIFFERENT KIND OF PROPERTY

Another example of "failure" stemming from the "development" discourse's false construction of Lesotho is that of livestock "development."

"Development" planners have long seen Lesotho's grasslands as one of the few potentially exploitable natural resources the country possesses,[12] and the country's herds of domestic grazing animals as an inertia-ridden "traditional" sector ripe for transformation by the dynamic "modern" cash economy. What is required, according to planners, is to develop "appropriate marketing outlets," control grassland use to optimize commercial productivity through destocking and grazing associations, introduce improved breeds, and convince "farmers to market their non-productive stock."[13]

Far from being the result of "traditional" inertia, however, the Basotho's reluctance to treat livestock commercially is deeply embedded in, and partly maintained by, a modern, capitalist labour reserve economy. In Lesotho's highly monetized economy, an item such as a transistor radio or a bar of soap may be subject to the same market mechanisms of pricing, supply and demand as it is anywhere else. Cattle, goats and sheep, however, are subject to very different sorts of rules. Although cash can always be converted into livestock through purchase, there is a reluctance to convert grazing animals to cash through sale, except when there is an emergency need for food, clothes, or school fees.

This practice is rooted in, and reinforced by, a social system in which young working men are away in South Africa supporting their families for ten or eleven months of the year. (Mines hire only men, and it is very difficult for women from Lesotho to find work in South Africa.) If a man comes home from the mines with cash in his pocket, his wife may present him with a demand to buy her a new dress, furniture for the house or new blankets for the children. If, on the other hand, he comes home with an ox purchased with his wages, it is more difficult to make such demands.

One reason that men like to own large numbers of livestock is that they boost their prestige and personal networks in the community, partly since they can be farmed out to friends and relatives to help with their field work. They thus serve as a "placeholder" for the man in the household and the community, symbolically asserting his structural presence and prestigious social position, even in the face of his physical absence. After he has returned to the household because of injury, age or being laid off from the South African mines to "scratch about on the land," livestock begin to be sold in response to absolute shortages of minimum basic necessities. Grazing animals thus constitute a sort of special "retirement fund" for men which is effective precisely because, although it lies within the household, it cannot be accessed in the way cash can.

Hence a whole mystique has grown up glorifying cattle ownership—a mystique which, although largely contested by women, is constantly fought for by most men. Such conflict is not a sign of disintegration or crisis; it is part of the process of recreating a "tradition" which is never simply a residue of the past. If the cultural rules governing livestock in Lesotho persist, it is because they are made to persist; continuity as much as change has to be created and fought for.

Investment in livestock is thus not an alternative to migrant labour but a consequence of it. If livestock sellers surveyed by "development" experts report no source of income other than agriculture, this does not mean that they are "serious stock farmers" as opposed to "migrant labourers"; they may simply be "retired."

However useful and necessary they may be, moreover, livestock in Lesotho is less an "industry" or a "sector" than a type (however special) of consumer good bought with wages earned in South Africa when times are good and sold off only when times are bad. The sale of an animal is not "off-take" of a surplus, but part of a process which culminates in the destruction of the herd. A drop in livestock exports from Lesotho is thus not, as the "development" discourse would have it, a sign of a depressed "industry," but of a rise in incomes. For instance, when wages were increased in South African mines in the 1970s. Basotho miners seized the opportunity to invest in cattle in unprecedented numbers, leading to a surge in import figures from 4,067 in 1973 to 57,787 in 1978. Over the same period, meanwhile, cattle export figures dropped from 12,894 to 574. A boom in exports, on the other hand, would be the mark of a disaster.

Not surprisingly, attempts to "modernize" Lesotho's "livestock sector" have met with resistance. Within one year of the Thaba-Tseka project attempting to fence off 15 square kilometres of rangeland for the exclusive use of "progressive," "commercially minded" farmers, for example, the fence had been cut or knocked down in many places, the gates stolen, and the area was being freely grazed by all. The office of the association manager had been burned down, and the Canadian officer in charge of the programme was said to be fearing for his life.

This resistance was rooted in more than a general suspicion of the government and the "development" project. To join the official "grazing association" permitted to use the fenced-in land, stock owners were required to sell off many poor animals to buy improved ones, ending up with perhaps half as many. Such sales and restrictions in herd size were not appealing for most Basotho men. Joining the association not only meant accepting selection, culling and marketing of herds. It also meant acquiescing in the enclosure of both common grazing land and (insofar as any Mosotho's livestock are also a social, shared domain of wealth) animals. It thus signified a betrayal of fellow stock-owners who remained outside the organization, an act considered anti-social. Prospective association members also probably feared that their animals—which represent wealth in a visible, exposed, and highly vulnerable form—might be stolen or vandalized in retaliation.

THE SIDE EFFECTS OF "FAILURE"

Despite such disasters, it may be that what is most important about a "development" project is not so much what it fails to do but what it achieves through its "side effects." Rather than repeatedly asking the politically naive question "Can aid programmes ever be made really to help poor people?", perhaps we should investigate the more searching question, "What do aid programmes do *besides* fail to help poor people?"

Leftist political economists have often argued that the "real" purpose of "development" projects is to aid capitalist penetration into Third World countries. In Lesotho, however, such projects do not characteristically succeed in introducing new relations of production (capitalist or otherwise), nor do they bring about modernization or significant economic transformations. Nor are they set up in such a way that they ever could. For this reason, it seems a mistake to interpret them *simply* as "part of the historical expansion of capitalism" or as elements in a global strategy for controlling or capitalizing peasant production.

Capitalist interests, moreover, can only operate through a set of social and cultural structures so complex that the outcome may be only a baroque and unrecognizable transformation of the original intention. Although it is relevant to know, for instance, that the World Bank has an interest in boosting production and export of cash crops for the external market, and that industrialized states without historic links to an area may sponsor "development" projects as a way of breaking into otherwise inaccessible markets, it remains impossible simply to read off actual events from these known interests as if the one were a simple effect of the other. Merely knowing that the Canadian government has an interest in promoting rural "development" because it helps Canadian corporations to find export markets for farm machinery, for example, leaves many of the empirical details of the Canadian role in Thaba-Tseka absolutely mysterious.

Another look at the Thaba-Tseka project, however, reveals that, although the project "failed" both at poverty alleviation and at extending the influence of international capital, it did have a powerful and far-reaching impact on its region. While the project did not transform livestock-keeping, it did build a road to link Thaba-Tseka more strongly with the capital. While it did not bring about "decentralization" or "popular participation," it was instrumental in establishing a new district administration and giving the government a much stronger presence in the area than it had ever had before.

As a direct result of the construction of the project centre and the decision to make that centre the capital of a new district, there appeared a new post office, a police station, a prison and an immigration control office; there were health officials and nutrition officers and a new "food for work" administration run by the Ministry of Rural Development and the Ministry of Interior, which functioned politically to regulate the power of chiefs. The new district centre also provided a good base for the "Para-Military Unit," Lesotho's army, and near the project's end in 1983, substantial numbers of armed troops began to be garrisoned at Thaba-Tseka.

In this perspective, the "development" apparatus in Lesotho is not a machine for eliminating poverty that is incidentally involved with the state bureaucracy. Rather, it is a machine for reinforcing and expanding the exercise of bureaucratic state power, which incidentally takes "poverty" as its point of entry and justification—launching an intervention that may have no effect on the poverty but does have other concrete effects.

This does not mean that "the state," conceived as a unitary entity, "has" more power to extract surplus, implement programmes, or order around "the masses" more efficiently—indeed, the reverse may be true. It is, rather, that more power relations are referred through state channels and bureaucratic circuits—most immediately, that more people must stand in line and await rubber stamps to get what they want. "It is the same story over again," said one "development" worker. "When the Americans and the Danes and the Canadians leave, the villagers will continue their marginal farming practices and wait for the mine wages, knowing only that now the taxman lives down the valley rather than in Maseru."[14]

At the same time, a "development" project can effectively squash political challenges to the system not only through enhancing administrative power, but also by casting political questions of land, resources, jobs or wages as technical "problems" responsive to the technical "development" intervention. If the effects of a "development" project end up forming any kind of strategically coherent or intelligible whole, it is as a kind of "anti-politics" machine, which, on the model of the "anti-gravity" machine of science fiction stories, seems to suspend "politics" from even the most sensitive political operations at the flick of a switch.

Such a result may be no part of the planners' intentions. It is not necessarily the consequence of any kind of conspiracy to aid capitalist exploitation by incorporating new territories into the world system or working against radical social change, or bribing national elites, or mystifying the real international relationships. The result can be accomplished, as it were, behind the backs of the most sincere participants. It may just happen to be the way things work out. On this view, the planning apparatus is neither mere ornament nor the master key to understanding what happens. Rather than being the blueprint for a machine, it is a *part* of the machine.

WHAT IS TO BE DONE? BY WHOM?

If, then, "development" cannot be the answer to poverty and powerlessness in Lesotho, what is? What is to be done, if it is not "development"?

Any question of the form "What is to be done?" demands first of all an answer to the question "By whom?" The "development" discourse, and a great deal of policy science, tends to answer this question in a utopian way by saying "Given an all-powerful and benevolent policy-making apparatus, what should it do to advance the interests of its poor citizens?"

This question is worse than meaningless. In practice, it acts to disguise what are, in fact, highly partial and interested interventions as universal, disinterested and inherently benevolent. If the question "What is to be done?" has any sense, it is as a real-world tactic, not a utopian ethics.

The question is often put in the form "What should *they* do?," with the "they" being not very helpfully specified as "Lesotho" or "the Basotho." When "developers" speak of such a collectivity what they mean is usually the government. But the government of Lesotho is not identical with the people who live in Lesotho, nor is it in any of the established senses "representative" of that collectivity. As in most countries, the government is a relatively small clique with narrow interests. There is little point in asking what such entrenched and often extractive elites should do in order to empower the poor. Their own structural position makes it clear that they would be the last ones to undertake such a project.

Perhaps the "they" in "What should they do?" means "the people." But again, the people are not an undifferentiated mass. There is not one question—What is to be done?—but hundreds: What should the mineworkers do? What should the abandoned old women do? and so on. It seems presumptuous to offer prescriptions here. Toiling miners and abandoned old women know the tactics proper to their situations far better than any expert does. If there is advice to be given about what "they" should do, it will not be dictating general political strategy or giving a general answer to the question "what is to be done?" (which can only be determined by those doing the resisting) but answering specific, localized, tactical questions.

WHAT SHOULD WE DO?

If the question is, on the other hand, "What should *we* do?," it has to be specified, which "we"? If "we" means "development" agencies or governments of the West, the implied subject of the question falsely implies a collective project for bringing about the empowerment of the poor. Whatever good or ill may be accomplished by these agencies, nothing about their general mode of operation would justify a belief in such a collective "we" defined by a political programme of empowerment.

For some Westerners, there is, however, a more productive way of posing the question "What should we do?." That is, "What should we intellectuals working in or concerned about the Third World do?" To the extent that there are common political values and a real "we" group, this becomes a real question. The answer, however, is more difficult.

Should those with specialized knowledge provide advice to "development" agencies who seem hungry for it and ready to act on it? As I have tried to show, these agencies seek only the kind of advice they can take. One "developer" asked my advice on what his country could do "to help these people." When I suggested that his government might contemplate sanctions against apartheid, he replied, with predictable irritation, "No, no! I mean development!" The only advice accepted is about how to "do development" better. There is a ready ear for criticisms of "bad development projects," only so long as these are followed up with calls for "good development projects." Yet the agencies who plan and implement such projects—agencies like the World Bank, USAID, and the government of Lesotho—are not really the sort of social actors that are very likely to advance the empowerment of the poor.

Such an obvious conclusion makes many uncomfortable. It seems to them to imply hopelessness; as if to suggest that the answer to the question "What is to be done?" is: "Nothing." Yet this conclusion does not follow. The state is not the only game in town, and the choice is not between "getting one's hands dirty by participating in or trying to reform development projects" and "living in an ivory tower." Change comes when, as Michel Foucault says, "critique has been played out in the real, not when reformers have realized their ideas."[15]

For Westerners, one of the most important forms of engagement is simply the political participation in one's own society that is appropriate to any citizen. This is, perhaps, particularly true for citizens of a country like the US, where one of the most important jobs for "experts" is combating imperialist policies.

This article is a summary of some of the main arguments of *The Anti-Politics Machine: "Development", Depoliticization and Bureaucratic Power in Lesotho* by James Ferguson, published by the University of Minnesota Press, 1994.

NOTES

1. Murray, C., *Families Divided: The Impact of Migrant Labour in Lesotho*. New York: Cambridge University Press, 1981, p. 19.
2. World Bank. *Lesotho: A Development Challenge*. World Bank. Washington, DC, 1975, p. 1.
3. "Basutoland." *Encyclopedia Britannica*, 1910.
4. Wilson, M. & L. Thompson (Eds.) *The Oxford History of South Africa.* (vol. 1). New York: Oxford University Press, 1969.
5. Ashton, H., *The Basuto: A Social Study of Traditional and Modern Lesotho* (2d ed.) New York: Oxford University Press, 1967, p. 162.
6. Murray, C., op. cit. 1.
7. FAO/World Bank, *Draft Report of the Lesotho First Phase Mountain Area Development Project Preparation Mission,* Vols. I and II), FAO. Rome, 1975. Annex 1, p. 7.
8. van der Wiel, A. C. A., *Migratory Wage Labour: Its Role in the Economy of Lesotho*. Mazenod: Mazenod Book Centre, 1977.
9. FAO/World Bank. op. cit. 7. Annex 1, p. 7.
10. World Bank, op. cit. 2. p. 9.
11. See "Appraisal of Project Progress During the Pilot Phase and Review of Plans to Expand Agricultural Programs in Phase II of Project Operations." Ottawa: CIDA, 1978, p. 39.
12. See, for example, FAO/World Bank. op. cit. 7, Annex 1, pp. 10–12. For a related South African history of government intervention into "traditional" livestock keeping, see W. Beinart, & C. Bundy. "State Intervention and Rural Resistance: The Transkel, 1900–1965." In *Peasants in Africa* ed. by M. Klein. Beverley Hills, CA: Sage, 1981.
13. CIDA, op. cit. 11.
14. Quoted in Murphy, B., "Smothered in Kindness." *New Internationalist*. No. 82. 1979, p. 13.
15. Foucault, M., "Questions of Method: An Interview." *Ideology and Consciousness*. Vol. 8. 1981, p. 13.

In the Disaster Zone

Anthropologists and the Ambiguity of Aid

Alex de Waal

Since taking his doctorate at Oxford, Alex de Waal has been involved with numerous NGOs (nongovernmental organizations) concerned with human rights, disaster relief, and development in Africa. He is the author of a definitive study on the Sudanese famine and co-director of the organization African Rights.

A decade ago, a researcher investigating the languages of northern Uganda came upon an anthropological first: the subjects of an ethnographic monograph asked him for advice in taking legal action against the author of a book. The Ik, made notorious as the cultureless villains of Colin Turnbull's *The Mountain People* (1972), wanted to sue for libel.

Turnbull's description of life and death among the Ik is a harrowing account of how, under the stresses of chronic famine, a people apparently abandoned all their social norms in favor of totally selfish and wantonly aggressive behavior—some of it directed against their unhappy ethnographer. Turnbull described it as a society mutilated beyond recognition. The only approach to ritual he noted consisted of throwing cow dung against a tree. Turnbull concluded that the Ik "were driven to survive against seemingly invincible odds, and they succeeded, at the cost of their humanity." He recommended that the community should be dispersed.

According to the information gathered by the linguist Bernd Heine and published in the journal *Africa* in 1985, the Ik would have had a strong legal case against Turnbull; at the very least, they could probably have obtained a court injunction banning further sales of the book. Judging by the critical reaction to *The Mountain People*, most professional social anthropologists would have testified in favor of the Ik, though perhaps admitting to an apprehensive tremor as to what other litigation the case might unleash.

Called to account in the furor that followed publication of *The Mountain People*, Turnbull responded in a letter in the journal *Cultural Anthropology* that "there was no culture to kill." In the 1970s, he might have

escaped with such a comment; his critics had few comparative ethnographics of disaster with which to compare his book. There is no doubt that today *The Mountain People* would be rejected as unpublishable, though it remains on the reading lists for many undergraduate courses in anthropology. With the benefit of a decade's worth of research on the subject, anthropologists know increasingly well how people react under such stresses, and it is not as Turnbull describes. Like the media images of Beirut and Mogadishu, such descriptions tell us more about the disturbed psyche of their author than the social realities of disaster.

The Ik homeland lies a few hundred miles south of the Upper Nile Valley where British social anthropology came of age. Since the classic texts of the 1940s and '50s were written, the peoples of the region have undergone a succession of calamities with few parallels in the modern world. Only now is the discipline catching up with what has happened to some of its most important subjects.

The Nuer of the southern Sudan, for example, became celebrated as a result of Edward Evans-Pritchard's series of monographs, based on field-work done in the 1930s. Nuer pastoralists became the archetypal stateless society. In the seamless anthropological present of Evans-Pritchard's writings, stories of cosmic turmoil were located in a mythical past, even though the Nuer had at that time only just emerged from decades of hunger, bloodshed and resistance to Arab and European colonialism. Indeed, it was the very recalcitrance of the Nuer in the face of the first attempt at colonial administration that was the spur to Evans-Pritchard's investigation. His field-work was conducted on the anthropological front line.

In retrospect, periods of peace in southern Sudan appear as intervals in a cycle in which upheaval and violence alternate with relative tranquility. The region

"In the Disaster Zone: Anthropologists and the Ambiguity of Aid" by Alex de Waal, from *Times Literary Supplement*, July 16, 1993. Reprinted with permission.

returned to war in 1963, soon after independence. This has wreaked havoc on southern Sudanese societies, but it kept the anthropologists away. War itself was not seen as a suitable subject for investigation. Peace came in 1972, but such are the slow rhythms of academe, anthropologists only began to return to the area at the end of the decade—just in time for the second civil war which broke out ten years ago. To today's ethnographers of Sudan, there can be nothing mythical about stories of global chaos: the apocalypse is now.

One such ethnographer, Sharon Hutchinson, revisited the Nuer in the 1970s, forty years after Evans-Pritchard. Nuer society, she found, was still overwhelmingly pastoral and largely acephalous, but important elements had been transformed by ready access to firearms. Among the Nuer, guns have now become part of bridewealth payments; communal ownership of them demarcates social groups; people adorn themselves with images of firearms and use cartridges as jewelry. Killing with rifles has a wholly different set of connotations to killing with spears; it involves less skill and effort, and is depersonalized; it is difficult or impossible to trace the trajectory of a bullet from rifle to victim.

During the current civil war, the Nuer have suffered famine, displacement and massacre at the hands of the government army and rival southern factions. Some of this is in reprisal for the carnage inflicted by the Nuer militia on their enemies—as major protagonists in the war, Nuer fighters have earned a fearsome reputation. So the Nuer survive, though their numbers may be depleted.

The convulsions of north-east Africa present greater perils for smaller and less well-armed peoples like the Mursi of the Ethiopia-Sudan borderlands. The Mursi are a small pastoral society, numbering perhaps 6,000, who have found themselves victims of both guns and a lack of rain. In 1971–73 there was severe drought and famine among the Mursi. Many died—most from disease and hunger, some violently and a few from suicide by starvation. The anthropologist David Turton witnessed the famine. In a paper for the specialist journal *Disasters* that he now edits, Turton wrote that the Mursi "came through this experience with their social and economic institutions intact and an undiminished sense of their cultural identity."

More recently, the Mursi were again victims, this time of a massacre. They had the misfortune to be neighbors to a people whose very name indicates the centrality of modern automatic weapons to their life. Formerly known as Nyam-Etom ("Elephant-Eaters"), this group now calls itself Nyang-Atom ("Carriers of New Guns"). The Nyangatom were given Kalashnikovs by the Sudan government in order to fight against southern rebels; the Mursi had only a few aging rifles. In February 1987, between 600 and 800 Mursi were

killed in a surprise Nyangatom attack: a devastating demographic loss, but, equally importantly, a profound break in the pattern of inter-communal relations in the region. The Mursi were compelled to evacuate the southern part of their territory. At considerable risk of suffering another massacre, they began to plan what they themselves called a "return match" to even the score. Fortunately for the Mursi, the Nyangatom fell foul of the Kenyan government when they murdered two policemen in a cattle raid: the Kenyans fought the second leg of this encounter with helicopters and armored cars, and the Nyangatom withdrew with 200 fighting men dead.

David Turton found himself in an increasingly common position for members of the discipline: defending the integrity of a people threatened with the demise of their way of life, even the extinction of their society. This is a new and more brutal version of the familiar phenomenon of ethnographers trying to protect their subjects from the onslaught of commercial interests embodied in development-oriented nation states. This time, however, international organizations are commonly seen as the savior rather than the threat. Western relief operations are regarded as necessary, but also recognized to be late, inefficient, and culturally insensitive. Social anthropologists are finding a new niche: advocating more and improved aid to "their" peoples, and simultaneously making international aid programs more effective and appropriate.

Nobody can oppose increased and better lifesaving assistance. But putting anthropology in the front line of the relief encounter has its hazards. Aid agencies waver between being representatives of the Humanitarian International and the vanguard of a new philanthropic imperialism. The Pharanonic projects of the 1960s and '70s—the dams and resettlement schemes that are now so reviled—were the result of similar benevolent developmentalism. In future decades, surveying the economic and social ravages brought to the African continent by an over-supply of food aid, we may condemn today's advocates of emergency humanitarianism as equally misguided.

This is the dilemma of disaster sociology: do social scientists have enough faith in the fundamentals of their discipline to hold to them when lives are in the balance? Common sense tells us that academic principles should be abandoned when giving food rations that might save children from death—but good sociology regularly debunks common sense.

It is one step from recognizing that peoples can survive disasters with their social fabric intact to arguing that they do in fact survive them better without external intervention of any kind. Certainly, Turton ascribed the Mursi's resilience in the face of the 1970s famine in part to the fact that the international community did not come to their aid. A few sacks of food were left by the Ethiopian Relief and Rehabilitation Commission at the border of Mursi territory, and the Mursi allocated the food as they saw fit. Doubtless a feeding program devised by nutritionists could have saved more lives, but the Mursi, even if they had had that option, would probably have preferred benign neglect.

The closer one comes to a people suffering famine, the less effective international interventions appear. Almost every detailed investigation of a famine has concluded that it is a moot question whether food aid did more good than harm. Those who recommend simple, externally provided solutions do so only from a distance. The antidote to such simplistic thinking is detailed field-study. But conducting field-work in a famine raises a range of practical and ethical difficulties. What is "participant observation" in a famine? Observing starvation is one thing, participating in it is something entirely different. Perhaps a social anthropologist might want to endure hunger in order to gain a better understanding of the trauma of famine. Raymond Firth had no option but to do this on his second stay in Tikopia in 1952–53, when a combination of drought and hurricane devastated the crops and caused famine. Few modern anthropologists are exposed in this way, however, and none have actually gone so far as to deliberately get life-threateningly undernourished as part of their field-work.

Investigating wars is still more problematic. Participating in a war for research purposes would certainly raise eyebrows at the ethics committee of the Economic and Social Research Council. It would also be hazardous: the Geneva Conventions, even were they respected, do not draw a distinction between sociological investigators and spies. Glynn Flood, a young anthropologist studying the Ethiopian Afar pastoralists, was murdered in 1975, almost certainly by the Ethiopian security forces, who were planning a military campaign against the people he was studying.

Wars are also different from famines in that "survival strategies" like gathering wild food—now something of a *cause celebre* in the literature on famine—are often simply impossible. People who try them may be shot or blown up. Certainly there are traditional rules of warfare in many societies, and established mechanisms for protection of civilians. In Somalia, for example, religious communities have provided sanctuary for civilians of the "wrong" clan caught up in the fighting, and some clans have negotiated neutrality in the conflicts. Where there is a history of reciprocal raiding between neighboring peoples, if there is an approximate balance of armaments, a negotiated truce is likely.

However—particularly since the advent of automatic firearms, with their capacity for industrialized carnage, and pocket-sized antipersonnel landmines, which cannot distinguish fighter from villager—such solutions are precarious at best. There is no traditional method of clearing minefields, save stepping on the mines.

Modern warfare shows both the value and the limits of anthropological method. A social anthropologist may be well placed to understand a conflict, but that does not automatically lead to identifying solutions. It is fashionable to advocate the use of international forces to intervene in civil conflicts and "save" the suffering civilians. Some Somali social scientists advocated this last year. In turn, the US military tried to enlist anthropological expertise in formulating its post-invasion policies. Here is another dilemma: should an anthropologist collaborate with an occupying military force?

In an ironic manner, front-line anthropology is returning the discipline to its early role as an intelligence system for the administration of native peoples. The avowedly humanitarian motives for the operations made the ambiguities scarcely less comfortable. With relief organizations providing one of the few growth areas in employment opportunities for anthropology graduates, this situation is unlikely to change.

Much of the current anthropological corpus already consists of "grey literature," chiefly consultants' reports for aid agencies. Typically, an agency wants a social and economic assessment of an area where its relief operations are running into unexpected difficulties. These reports are researched and written under severe time constraints, for an audience of even more time-pressed managers of relief programs, and with specific administrative or logistical goals in mind. Perhaps from a visceral loyalty to the discipline, the authors of these reports often include far more sociological detail than their institutional readers will ever appreciate. Sometimes typed in the field, usually Xeroxed and with only a dozen copies extant, such documents are rarely archived in academic libraries. None the less, grey literature is probably the richest sociological source material for many parts of Africa today.

At its best, anthropology in the service of the relief agencies can snatch specific remedies for individual communities. The protection and resettlement of Sudanese Uduk refugees in Ethiopia by the United Nations High Commission for Refugees, at the behest of their long-time ethnographer Wendy James, is an excellent example of this. At its worst, such activities can provide a liberal gloss for a new humanitarian imperialism. Having called for the US Marines to invade Somalia, the American relief agency CARE has been actively recruiting social scientists to make its programs more user-friendly. Should the United Nations forces in Somalia become a party to the conflicts, anthropological analyses will undoubtedly feature in their counter-insurgency manuals.

With a few notable exceptions, exemplified by Conrad Reining's *The Zande Scheme,* anthropologists have been reluctant to subject the "aid" industry to the same critical scrutiny as the supposed beneficiaries of its largesse. Enough trained anthropologists have participated in its machinations for there to be a formidable reserve of material; anecdotes suggest that many have observed their colleagues with a critical sociological eye as well. This second front for disaster sociology may prove vital for the health of the discipline. By making the monsters of concern more accountable, it might even assist the well-being of the disaster-stricken, aid-recipient peoples of Africa and elsewhere.

A New World Dilemma: The Indian Question in the Americas

David H. P. Maybury-Lewis

David H. P. Maybury-Lewis received his D.Phil. degree from Oxford University in 1960. He has carried out fieldwork in Central Brazil among the Shavante and Sherente, whose experience he has followed from independence to their current status as minorities within the Brazilian state. A professor of anthropology at Harvard, he is also president of Cultural Survival, Inc., an organization he founded to defend the interests of indigenous peoples and to help them retain their identity within countries in which they exist.

At the beginning of his remarkable quartet, *Memories of Fire*, the Uruguayan novelist Eduardo Galeano gives this vivid description of the invasion of the Americas:

> He falls on his knees, weeps, kisses the earth. He steps forward, staggering because for more than a month he has hardly slept, and beheads some shrubs with his sword.
>
> Then he raises the flag. On one knee, eyes lifted to heaven, he pronounces three times the names of Isabella and Ferdinand. Beside him the scribe Rodrigo de Escobedo, a man slow of pen, draws up the document.
>
> From today everything belongs to those remote monarchs: the coral sea, the beaches, the rocks all green with moss, the woods, the parrots, and these laurel-skinned people who don't yet know about clothes, sin, or money and gaze dazedly at the scene. Luis de Torres translates Christopher Columbus's questions into Hebrew: "Do you know the kingdom of the Great Khan? Where does the gold you have in your noses and ears come from?"
>
> The naked men stare at him with open mouths, and the interpreter tries out his small stock of Chaldean: "Gold? Temples? Palaces? King of kings? Gold?"
>
> Then he tries his Arabic, the little he knows of it: "Japan? China? Gold?" The interpreter apologizes to Columbus in the language of Castile. Columbus curses in Genovese and throws to the ground his credentials, written in Latin and addressed to the Great Khan. The naked men watch the anger of the intruder with red hair and coarse skin, who wears a velvet cape and very shiny clothes.

This was arguably the most extraordinary meeting in the history of humankind. It reunited two por-

tions of humanity that had been separated for forty thousand years, ever since the inhabitants of the Americas had lost touch with their Asiatic forebears. The world—both the New World and the Old World—was dramatically changed forever.

Clearly, the quincentenary of such an extraordinary event should be remembered and marked, but how? In my view the event deserves to be remembered as an occasion for sober reflection rather than celebration, much as the holocaust in Nazi Europe is something we are constrained to remember without celebration. The analogy comes to mind not because the invaders set out to massacre the indigenous inhabitants of the Americas (sometimes they did, sometimes they did not) but because the immediate consequences of the European invasion constituted the greatest demographic disaster in human history.

We know that the Europeans brought with them a gold fever that astounded the Indians and a ruthlessness that many of the indigenous peoples discovered too late, but they also brought worse. They let pestilence loose in the Americas. In the words of a Maya chronicler, "Before . . . they [the Indians] had no sickness; they had no aching bones; they had no burning chest; they had no abdominal pain; they had no consumption; they had no headache. At that time the course of humanity was orderly. The foreigners made it otherwise when they arrived here." The writer continues in despair, "Let us therefore die! Let us therefore perish! For our Gods are already dead!"

Many of the Indians did die. It is estimated that by the end of the sixteenth century the indigenous population of the Americas had been cut in half. The survivors faced a future of slavery, serfdom, or forced labor,

"A New World Dilemma: The Indian Question in the Americas" by David H. P. Maybury-Lewis, from *Symbols*, Fall 1993, pp. 17–23. Reprinted with permission of Cultural Survival, Cambridge, MA.

unless they were remote enough to defend themselves at the margins of European settlement.

The Spaniards were only the first of the European invaders to set about enslaving the Indians, and they did so with occasional misgivings. Bishop Bartolomé de las Casas was so appalled by the cruelties of the conquerors and the decimation of the indigenous populations that he devoted his life to the Indian cause. His monumental *Historia de las Indias* was a searing indictment of the conquistadors and is often thought to have been the work that first exposed the *leyenda negra,* or black legend, of Spanish cruelty in the New World.

Many people feared that the quincentenary of Columbus's arrival in the Americas would reopen the debate over the *leyenda negra,* with Spanish celebration of their heroic exploits being countered by indigenous insistence on the cruelties of the conquest. Fortunately, that debate has been largely avoided, and I do not propose to renew it here. I see little point in arguing over the relative cruelty of these as opposed to those conquerors. The whole process was shot through with cruelty and injustice, with suffering and, yes, heroism. That is what makes it so difficult to evaluate or even to treat dispassionately. Yet I have just called for sober reflection on the conquest, and this is what I shall try to give you.

It seems to me that an important and essential aspect of that reflection has to be a consideration of what has happened to the indigenous peoples of the Americas since 1492. They tend to be the forgotten peoples of the New World. How often are they mentioned in the news stories that most of us read? In all our current preoccupation with Mexico, how often do we read about the large indigenous population of that country? When the US administration was focusing on Central America, we learned little about the circumstances of the indigenous populations of the region. Even the indigenous majority in Peru received scant attention in our newspapers until it was mistakenly reported that the *Sendero Luminoso* (Shining Path) movement was an Indian uprising.

Yet the treatment of indigenous peoples since the conquest is more than the Americas' original sin, which can now be conveniently forgotten. It is a matter of more consequence that has at times profoundly influenced the nature of modern American societies. At the very least it is intimately related to, and diagnostic of, the forces that have shaped those societies. Consider, for example, the colonial debates over the treatment of Indians. The Spanish and Portuguese monarchs occasionally passed laws protective of the Indians and their communities. Such laws usually resulted from a combination of factors. The arguments of people like Las Casas or the Marquess of Pombal, who sought to abolish Indian slavery in Portuguese America, were in the ascendant. At the same time the Iberian monarchs wanted to keep control of Indian communities and Indian labor. If these were controlled instead by powerful colonists, then a kind of feudalism was established on the other side of the Atlantic that challenged the power of the kings themselves. In fact, when the crown passed laws protective of the Indians, the colonists regularly flouted them. They could and did rebel if deprived of forced Indian labor. On one celebrated occasion, the Spanish colonists were so outraged by royal attempts to protect the Indians that the king's representative had to travel to New Spain in disguise in order to offer the royal compromise that averted outright rebellion. Similarly, when the Marquess of Pombal decreed the abolition of Indian slavery in Brazil, the colonists refused to comply. They did not see why the Jesuits should be allowed to gather Indians in their mission communities while the colonists were deprived of Indian slaves. The Marquess sent his brother to Brazil to enforce the edict, but his brother listened to the colonists and advised Pombal to abolish the Jesuits instead, which he duly did. This led to what Osvaldo Hurtado, a modern Ecuadorian writer and president of his country, referred to as the "institutionalized illegality of Spanish colonial society." It has much to do with a tradition that has bedeviled a number of Latin American countries: passing beautiful laws with little expectation that they will be enforced or observed.

The independence movements of the late eighteenth and early nineteenth centuries did not change this, nor did they do much for indigenous peoples. The constitutions adopted by the newly independent republics were eloquent about the rights of man but silent about the Indians. In countries with sparse indigenous populations, such as the United States, Indians were considered to have no place in the new nations. They were thought of as the peoples beyond the frontier, in "Indian territory," a notional territory that was pushed steadily westward until it was swallowed up altogether at the end of the nineteenth century. In countries with significant indigenous populations, conservatives and liberals fought civil wars over the length and breadth of the Western Hemisphere. Their clashing visions of the future paid scant attention to Indian concerns. The conservatives demanded freedom from the mother country in order to manage their own affairs and to go on exploiting the Indians. The liberals demanded freedom for all, including the Indians, but what they meant by this for the Indians was the freedom to cease being Indian altogether. They considered *Indio* a derogatory word and Indianness a stigma—a kind of royalist, conservative, ecclesiastical device for maintaining indigenous peoples in a state of savagery. In the liberal vision of the future there would be no more Indians; the very word would be prohibited. The new constitutions therefore promised freedom and equality for all, with no mention of the Indians and no special provisions for them. It was assumed that they would disappear into the mainstream.

That hope was not fulfilled. In 1821 Simón Bolívar said at the Congress of Cúcuta that lands alienated from the Indians in Gran Colombia (corresponding roughly to modern Venezuela, Colombia, Panama, and Ecuador combined) during the tumultuous years leading up to independence should be returned to them "as soon as circumstances permit." Circumstances never did, however, either in Gran Colombia or anywhere else. On the contrary, the nineteenth century was an era of such intense pressure on the indigenous peoples of the hemisphere that it could well be referred to as the time of the second conquest.

In countries with large indigenous populations, conservatives encroached on Indian lands and maintained Indian communities in poverty as a source of labor. Liberals, on the other hand, sought to break up traditional landholdings in the interest of modernization. They therefore moved to break up the estates of the great landowners and the Church. They also moved to break up the lands held by indigenous communities. Hoping to force the Indians to abandon their traditional ways and to enter the modern labor market. Both policies placed heavy burdens on the Indians, who were treated as a less than fully human labor force.

The details are revealing. In Ecuador, for example, the new constitution adopted in 1852 excluded Indians (the majority of the population) from citizenship. In 1857 slavery was formally abolished, so that black Ecuadorians were emancipated. At the same time the system of *concertaje* was institutionalized. This was the Ecuadorian version of a system that proliferated throughout the Americas. It enabled labor contractors to enter into a *concierto*, or arrangement (elsewhere referred to less euphemistically as the *enganche*, or hook) with Indians. Under this system Indians were tricked or forced into accepting contracts that they did not understand and often tried unsuccessfully to repudiate— contracts that obliged them to work for long periods of time for miserable wages or for payment in kind.

Peru relied less on such arrangements and more on taxes levied in cash and in labor directly on the indigenous population. Indians, for example, were required to work without payment to build roads and were then obliged to pay tolls to use them, although non-Indians could use the same roads at no charge. The government discovered that it could not manage the economy without exacting "the Indian tribute," as it was called. The tribute was nevertheless abolished at regular intervals throughout the nineteenth century. It had to be abolished repeatedly because each abolition was more theoretical than real, and Indians went on being forced to pay.

In Guatemala and El Salvador, the countries with the largest indigenous populations of Central America, the modernization policies of liberal-party dictators at the end of the nineteenth century forced Indians to carry passbooks showing that they had performed the legally required number of days of labor. Indians were thus obliged to work for starvation wages on the coffee plantations. This system has continued almost to the present day in some places, and the effects of it on Indian individuals and families are harrowingly described in the story of her life as told by Rigoberta Menchú, winner of the 1992 Nobel Peace Prize.

The classic example of liberal legislation that was put into effect with modernizing intent and had extremely painful consequences for indigenous populations was the Reform Law in Mexico. This was enacted by President Juárez, himself part Indian and proud of it, in 1856. It aimed to break up the great *haciendas*, the large landholdings of the Church, and the communal landholdings of the Indians. Juárez's intention was to modernize the country and especially to modernize Mexican agriculture. The result of his initiative, however, was that under Porfirio Díaz and his group of advisors, known as the *científicos* (scientists), these lands were reconcentrated in the hands of large agribusinesses, while the Indians and the rural poor sank deeply into poverty and peonage. The extraordinary concentration of land and the ever-widening gap between rich and poor were clearly two of the most important factors that caused the Mexican Revolution that broke out in 1910.

Throughout the nineteenth century, then, conservative policies squeezed the Indians, while liberal policies sought to destroy their communities. In fact, the Americas since the conquest have been a vast laboratory for the eradication of indigenous cultures. As one studies the record, one cannot help being struck by the effort and ingenuity devoted by the conquerors to this task. They attacked indigenous religions. They imposed forced labor of various kinds. They invented a whole series of ways to lure or trick those not already forced to work into peonage through debt (the debt could only be worked off—and only with difficulty). Here and there they simply abolished Indians by a stroke of the pen and followed that up by trying to break up indigenous communities. They took Indian children away from their parents, sometimes by force, to be educated in alien schools that taught them to despise the ways of their peoples and discouraged them from speaking their own languages. The assault on indigenous landholding makes for the most remarkable reading of all: it is clear that the invaders not only coveted and seized Indian lands whenever they could; they were also affronted by those peoples and communities that held their lands in common. The Europeans considered that concept the very essence of savagery, for it departed from the ideas of private property and individual title to land that were considered central to Western civilization. It was thus with a convenient conviction of moral superiority that the invaders constantly tried to break up the communal landholdings of the Indians.

The relentless effort to destroy indigenous communities led to constant Indian rebellions throughout the hemisphere. The rebellions sometimes achieved considerable local success but, being local, were invariably defeated when the imperial power had gathered sufficient force to strike back at the locality. The colonists realized that the attack on indigenous landholding was a perennial and festering source of discontent, but they persevered anyway. Thus, an edict issued in 1834 in Gran Colombia made it clear that "in no tribunal or court will complaints be heard, whose sole object is to request that Indian lands not be divided."

Indigenous peoples, then as now, clung fiercely to their lands and communities. Their societies had been decapitated, so their communities constituted the basis of their culture and their dignity. The alternative that the enveloping society tried to force them to accept was not very attractive. They were urged to abandon their languages and cultures and to enter the mainstream of "civilization," though in that mainstream they would be stigmatized and treated as slaves, serfs, directed workers, or peons. In the light of this history and of the five-hundred-year effort to eradicate the indigenous cultures of this hemisphere, their resilience is quite remarkable.

The effort to destroy these cultures (ethnocide) was sometimes accompanied by an attempt to destroy the indigenous populations themselves (genocide). This was an option only in the regions or countries with the sparsest indigenous populations. The classic example is Argentina, where Araucanian Indians, splendid horsemen with vast herds of cattle, dominated the pampas in the nineteenth century. In 1879–80 General Roca's campaign, known in Argentine history books as the Conquest of the Desert, was expressly intended to annihilate the Araucanians and to seize and redistribute their lands. In fact, the Araucanians were not actually annihilated, but they were thought to be. They ceased to exist socially and culturally for nearly a century. Meanwhile, real genocide was committed in the far south, where small populations of nomadic Ona and Yaghan were hunted down and killed like animals by the local sheep farmers. Most of those farmers were British expatriates, which shows (if such a demonstration is still needed) that colonial brutality is not the special preserve of any one nationality. All of this was justified in the name of civilization, progress, and the manifest destiny of Argentina to extend its rule to the southern tip of the South American continent.

A similar push to the south in Chile at the same time and for the same reasons led to the final defeat of the Chilean Araucanians. These Indians, who had stopped the Spanish conquest at the Bio-Bio River and had retained their independence through the three subsequent centuries, were defeated by the army's modern weaponry and reduced to penury and starvation. We rarely hear about them now, although there are one million of them in a total Chilean population of about fourteen million.

At the same time the United States was engaged in its own push to the West, in pursuit of its own vision of manifest destiny, and with similarly drastic consequences for the indigenous inhabitants of the "Indian territory" that was to be Indian no longer. In his book *The Winning of the West*, Teddy Roosevelt justified the conquest of the Indians in terms that probably represented the prevailing attitude of the invaders as they moved westward after the Civil War: "The settler and the pioneer have at bottom had justice on their side. This great continent could not have been kept as nothing but a playground for squalid savages."

This attitude and this process were not peculiar to the Americas. All over the world indigenous peoples were being conquered and dispossessed in the name of civilization. Because this was held to be a matter of right triumphing over wrong, no accommodation with the conquered populations was thought to be desirable, and none was sought. At best they were to be corralled and made over as despised and counterfeit copies of their conquerors; at worst they were simply to be annihilated. Meanwhile, the evolutionism and racism of the conquerors made the whole process seem inevitable.

Similar attitudes persist in our own times. They lie behind the plausible falsehoods of conventional wisdom that are still subscribed to today by otherwise reasonable people. According to such views, "tribal" or "traditional" societies are obsolescent. They cannot adjust to the modern world. They are doomed by the march of progress and must inevitably disappear. These views conveniently conceal from us the facts that these societies have shown a remarkable tenacity and resilience, and that if they are destroyed, it is not by abstract laws of history or nature but by the political choices of the powerful, by our willingness to overpower them, and by our unwillingness to live and let live.

In the Americas we, and particularly the Native Americans among us, are still coping with the consequences of the oldest European imperialism. These consequences can be seen in the contemporary circumstances and concerns of modern American states. Consider, for example, the contrasts between Mexico, Guatemala, and Peru, all countries with large indigenous populations.

In Mexico, after the revolution of 1910–20, an attempt was made to connect the Indians and the rural poor with the corporate state, to link them through the PRI (the Institutional Revolutionary Party) to the national life. An official ideology of *indigenismo* guided national policy toward indigenous peoples. The ideology is now much criticized by Mexican anthropologists for being paternalistic and assimilationist, something imposed by the state on the Indians. Nevertheless, in spite of its shortcomings, it produced a long period of comparative social stability in the Mexican countryside—a stability that is even more remarkable if we compare it with the experience of other American nations.

Peru, for example, had its own brand of *indigenista* ideology. Started in something like the spirit of *Uncle Tom's Cabin* in writers who called attention to the sufferings of the Indians, it was given forceful expression by figures such as Jose Carlos Mariategui, the theorist of Peruvian socialism, and Haya de la Torre, the leader of the APRA party (the American Popular Revolutionary Alliance). They spoke of an indigenous future, not just for Peru but for the Americas. Their rhetoric was rejected and their party suppressed, while the indigenous bulk of Peru's population continued to be systematically marginalized. This accounts for the extraordinary success of the Shining Path movement. It is successful not because it is an indigenous uprising (it is not) but because it has brought Peru to the brink of chaos, due to the fact that the country had never made a sustained effort at national mobilization.

Guatemala, on the other hand, has dealt with its Indian question in a different way: through repressive violence in defense of the status quo. This serves as an object lesson, showing what can happen in a country where there has been no social revolution and little social mobilization, and where the elites harbor a fear of the Indian masses, who must therefore be terrorized in order to be kept in their place.

What is the contemporary significance of the Indian question in countries where indigenous peoples are an insignificant fraction of the total population? Consider the case of Brazil, whose indigenous inhabitants live scattered throughout the interior and constitute less than 0.5 percent of the total population. Why are their concerns treated as a matter of national security? Ostensibly, the national security doctrine has been put forward by the military to protect Brazil's extensive frontiers. We are asked to believe that peoples like the Yanomami, ten thousand strong and outnumbered and outgunned by the miners who have invaded their territory, might wish to link up with their less numerous brethren in Venezuela and form a separate state. Alternatively, the national security doctrine is said to be needed as a defense of Brazilian sovereignty because there has been wild talk in various places about internationalizing the Amazon in order to protect its ecology for the world.

In fact, the defense of indigenous rights is subversive in a different sense. When Indians protest about what is being done to them in the interior of the country, they are classed with smallholders, the landless poor, and other "troublemakers" who call into question the Brazilian model of development and call attention to the glaring injustices in Brazilian society. Meanwhile, the insistence of indigenous peoples on being allowed to maintain their own cultures is also considered subversive, for it undermines Brazil's self-image as a melting pot. In effect, Brazil's indigenous peoples are held to threaten and undermine the state simply by wishing to be themselves, by being reluctant to evaporate into the mainstream. It was therefore quite logical that until recently the Brazilian government had an official policy of "emancipating" the Indians. They were not held in servitude but were considered wards of the state. The only way the Indians could be emancipated, therefore, was if they legally gave up being considered Indian and were thus deprived of their indigenous identity.

It is one of the many ironies of the American experience that the invaders created the category of Indians, imposed it on the inhabitants of the New World, and have been trying to abolish it ever since. Brazil's effort to "emancipate" its Indians is only the latest in a long line of measures devised to accomplish similar ends. In many countries it was decreed that Indians would no longer be referred to as *Indios* but would instead be called *campesinos* (peasants); Indianness was thus abolished by a stroke of the pen. In Chile, General Pinochet's government tried to destroy the identity of the large Mapuche (Araucanian) minority by forcing them to divide their lands into privately owned lots. Even the Alaska Native Claims Settlement Act, which is widely thought to be one of the more generous settlements made with indigenous peoples, was drafted to turn Indian communities into corporations and their members into stockholders. Future members of the community will not acquire stocks unless stocks are bequeathed to them by those who originally received them. Meanwhile, stocks can soon be given, willed, or sold to people who are not members of the communities. The effect of the act, if not its intention, is to provide a mechanism for phasing out the native communities altogether.

Such measures have been justified over the centuries by arguments that are still used today. We must make hard choices between the rights of indigenous peoples and the good of the state, between stagnation and development, between progress and pluralism. Indeed, in the United States as well as in Brazil, many people are alarmed by any challenge to the idea that their nation is a melting pot. In this country the demands of indigenous peoples for the right to maintain their own cultures without being relegated to second-class citizenship are deemed deeply subversive, for it is feared that satisfaction of those demands will contribute to the tribalization of American society.

Such tribalization is held to be dangerous for two reasons: it is thought to undermine American society and culture, and it is thought to lead to interethnic conflict. The United States, the argument runs, has avoided such conflict, which we now see raging in other parts of the world, and should continue to do so by insisting on its own melting-pot tradition.

Ethnic conflict is a great and legitimate fear, but it is important to see ethnic conflict, and indeed all violence in the modern world, in context. Violence in our time—and we live, arguably, in the most violent century yet—is not especially associated with ethnic divisions that undermine the state. That kind of violence obviously does take place, but violence may also be visited by the state on its citizens. Nazi Germany, the Soviet Union, and Pol Pot's Cambodia are only the most glaring examples. Alternatively, violence in a country may be comparatively unrelated to ethnic divisiveness. The United States, for example, has an extraordinarily high level of interpersonal violence in comparison with other developed countries. Canada, by contrast, has a much lower level of interpersonal violence, yet that nation's ethnic divisiveness is often held up as an example of the kind of conflict that the United States must at all costs avoid.

I think we tend to idealize the peace and social order maintained by the unitary state and to exaggerate the danger to this vision presented by permitting cultural distinctiveness or local autonomy to indigenous peoples or ethnic groups. In fact, much of the violence in the world today comes from the suppression (or attempted suppression) of ethnicity in the name of the unitary state. Two years ago a survey carried out by Cultural Survival revealed that about 120 shooting wars were going on in the world, 90 of which involved states that were attempting to suppress ethnic minorities.

Yet even if we concede that the suppression of ethnicity can lead to as much bloodletting as its expression, ethnic divisiveness is still a legitimate concern. The issue was recently and powerfully addressed by Arthur Schlesinger, Jr., in his book *The Disuniting of America*. Schlesinger admits that the traditional canon of American culture has reflected the traditions of only part of the country's population, excluding others and making them feel like second-class citizens. He argues, however, that the cure for this state of affairs proposed by the multiculturalists is worse than the disease. That cure includes such measures as the tendentious rewriting of history, the introduction of curricula whose main purpose is to make minorities feel good, the denial of

any merit to Western civilization, the insistence on adherence to inane standards of political correctness, and the espousal of an anything-goes relativism. Schlesinger asserts, therefore, that the United States should combat multiculturalism, virtually in defense of its own sanity, and that it should insist on its own common culture, taught to its citizens through a curriculum suitably modified to be less exclusionary than before.

I agree with Schlesinger's diagnosis and his convincing exposé of the absurdities of the extreme multiculturalists. But there is no reason to throw the baby out with the bathwater because of those absurdities. I agree that the proper corrective to the traditional exclusiveness of the American canon should not be an ethnic chauvinism that replies in kind with chauvinistic countercultures. It need not, however, be a renewed insistence that the expression of ethnicity is divisive and that it should be superseded or suppressed by American civic culture. A third solution is possible: what I call serious multiculturalism. This corrective is based on a presumption of tolerance and a desire for mutual understanding and mutual accommodation among subcultures. Such accommodation has to be taught and learned, and it depends on a serious effort to make multicultural, multiethnic systems work. Incidentally, serious multiculturalism would require as much effort from minorities that feel they have been wronged as it would from the majority that is accused of excluding them.

Is this a hopeless utopian vision? No more so, I suggest, than the idea of democracy. Yet we feel it is realistic to try and make democracy work. We do not give up on democracy because the Germans once elected Adolf Hitler or because of any of the other crimes that have been committed in its name. I use the analogy deliberately, for it seems to me that the countries with the best chance of making serious multiculturalism work are those that are relatively wealthy and have traditions of democracy, tolerance, and openness—countries, in fact, like the United States and Canada and Australia.

Is all this a long way from the Indian question? I do not think so. The New World dilemma was how the invaders were to deal with the indigenous populations of the hemisphere. This presented at the time of the conquest, and still presents today, a challenge to every country in the Americas. The challenge is, What kind of a country is ours? What kind of a country do we want it to be?

Nations, as Benedict Anderson so rightly put it, are imagined communities. The indigenous challenge to the United States is to make a further leap of the imagination beyond the ideals of democracy and egalitarianism; to imagine a nation that can tolerate indigenous cultures within its pluralism; to imagine a nation that does not need to extinguish the traditions that nourish it, because it inspires in its citizens a commitment to a transcendent Americanism.

If any country in the Americas could achieve this, it would be the best possible tribute to the civilization that was imposed on the hemisphere five hundred years ago, for it would show that Western civilization was not exhausted (as its critics claim) by the waning of European hegemony. It would show instead that Western civilization is capable of renewal, of using its democratic traditions to lead the way into the multi-ethnic future that awaits us all.

13

The Future of Humanity

The philosopher Kierkegaard once wrote that there are two ways—one way is to suffer and the other is to be a professor of another's suffering. In this sense we are all potential professors. Anthropologists, drawn largely from the affluent middle class, have made a career out of studying "others" who are typically less privileged, and they especially have an obligation to profess.

The fact is that the "others" have suffered in the past, are suffering now, and will continue to suffer in the future. Sometimes the suffering is so unpleasant that we do not want to hear about it. This is one reason why **genocide** is a topic hardly ever discussed. Yet its implications for understanding the banality of evil are awesome. It is for this reason that Jared Diamond's short article on genocide is included in this chapter. It is also the reason the piece on **AIDS** by Ronald Frankenburg is included. The horrors of present-day genocides (Rwanda's Tutsis being a well-known recent example) do not stay at the forefront of reporting and concern for long, and AIDS runs the risk of becoming similarly "invisibilised," even though it continues to spread in all parts of the world. Some of the most dramatic reports of its recent spread come from Asia, a continent where there were once few reported cases.

It is important to address these issues. Before World War II, anthropologist Everett C. Hughes had studied a small German village that was so close to one of the concentration camps that the villagers could literally see the smoke from the smokestacks. After the war, Hughes returned to the village, and he discovered that the villagers had hardly been touched by their proximity to the death camps. He wrote a classic essay entitled "Good People and Dirty Work" on how people could symbolically tune out such disturbing aspects of their lives. In our increasingly interdependent global "village" we cannot afford such luxuries. Part of the problem is not that we do not want to see, but that we do not know *how* to see.

One of the key ways we see and understand phenomena is by use of metaphor. For example, medical doctors did not know how the heart functioned until a pneumatic pump was invented; then, by using the pump as metaphor, they could start understanding how the heart functioned. It is for this reason that we include the essay by Gernot Köhler entitled "Global Apartheid." Köhler takes **apartheid** as a metaphor and applies it to global society. Whether we agree with it or not, the metaphor enables us to view the world differently. It also provides us with a recipe for possible action.

Since Köhler wrote his paper, important and encouraging changes have occurred in South Africa, but globally the situation has become much worse. The gap between rich and poor and between white people and people of color has increased substantially. In 1960 the wealth of the richest 20 percent was some 30 times greater than that of the poorest 20 percent. By 1989 the gap had increased to 60 times, and by 1992 it was estimated to be over 150 times greater. In the 1990s, it is estimated that the rich (predominantly white) countries, which have about only one-quarter of the world's population, consume more than 70 percent of the world's energy, 75 percent of its metals, 85 percent of its wood, and 60 percent of its food.

Even among countries receiving aid from industrialized countries, there are major discrepancies: The richest 40 percent of Southern Hemisphere countries, for example, receive more than twice as much aid as do the poorest 40 percent. This proves the adage that development aid is like champagne: In success you deserve it, and in failure you need it. And, like the South African government that was accused of providing the more affluent Zulus of Chief Buthelezi with weaponry, we find that countries that spent heavily on arms—more than 4 percent of their gross national product—received twice as much aid as did more moderate military spenders (*Weekly Mail*, 1992).

In an era when "Yuppiedom" has elevated selfishness and egoism to a virtue, it is important to take **global interdependency** not as a source of potential shame but as a source of moral responsibility. The political philosopher Robert Goodin (1985) has developed a comprehensive theory of responsibility based on the concept of vulnerability. More people are vulnerable to us—individually or collectively—than we have made commitments to in any sense, but we have the same sort of strong responsibilities toward all those who are vulnerable to our actions and choices. While we should try to protect the vulnerable, we should also strive to reduce their vulnerability. This approach fits particularly well with anthropology precisely because the people we "traditionally" study are especially vulnerable.

There are many ways we can protect and aid the vulnerable on this globe. One collective form of protective action is that of **anthropological advocacy groups** like Cultural Survival, but there is also the possibility of individual, personal action. One anthropologist who is involved in personal advocacy is Megan Biesele, who is working with those whom we label the Bushmen. The Bushmen are famous in the anthropological literature for exemplifying the original "affluent society," insofar as they did not have to work much to achieve a satisfactory level of subsistence. Their image has been further influenced by the surprise hit movie *The Gods Must Be Crazy*. Much of this mystique and our fascination with them has been fed by **ethnographies,** which have been misinterpreted by a public eager to project our own fantasies onto another people. The truth of the matter is that, far from being some band of "Beautiful People," the Bushmen have been the most brutalized and exploited peoples in southern Africa's bloody history and have almost been genocided out of existence. Biesele provides a thought-provoking contemporary account of Bushman society (focused on the place where *The Gods Must Be Crazy* was filmed) based on extended field participation and linguistic fluency. She lets her people largely speak for themselves. Such forms of self-critical advocacy ethnography, we are convinced, are one of the most important waves of the future.

AIDS and Anthropologists

Ronald Frankenberg

Ronald Frankenberg is the director for medical social anthropology at the University of Keele in the United Kingdom. His research has been carried out in such diverse places as Zambia, Tuscany, and Wales.

Some years ago, a commission was formed for urgent anthropology, and Claude Lévi-Strauss and others sought to save Amazonian groups who were not merely threatened here and now but whose whole future was in jeopardy. AIDS requires urgent anthropology on an even greater scale, for if the pandemic is not checked it is as capable of virtually destroying human life on earth as nuclear radiation or other ecological disasters. However, there is every hope of checking its progress, and for once there is no argument but that, as has slowly come to be realized, anthropology (social, ecological and through the study of the culture of risk) could and must be of major importance in stopping all three separate but related epidemics which WHO has recognized as making up a global pandemic.

AIDS itself is not a disease but a complex of symptoms and diseases which some (up to now about 80,000 known to WHO) if not all of the persons (between five and ten million worldwide—Mann 1988) infected with a virus called HIV are no longer able to resist because of damage to their immune system. ("HIV may cause neurological disease in infected patients in whom immune defence remains intact. This observation raises the possibility that neurological features may eventually come to dominate the clinical perception of HIV related disease." OHE 1988.) There is as yet no cure nor vaccine against HIV in sight and even the most optimistic predictions of either—ten years' time—would be too late to avert catastrophe. Prevention is not merely better than cure, it is the cure: prevention of transmission of the virus (epidemic one), prevention of the development of the AIDS syndromes which HIV makes possible (epidemic two) and prevention of unnecessary suffering for the general population includ-

"AIDS and Anthropologists" by Ronald Frankenberg, from *Anthropology Today*, Vol. 4, No. 2, 1988. Royal Anthropological Institute. Reprinted with permission.

ng the HIV seropositive and people with AIDS caused, not by biological, but by socially determined factors (epidemic three).

HIV is spread worldwide in the same ways through sexual intercourse (homosexual or heterosexual), through transfer of blood (transfusions, sharing or re-use of injection needles), and from mother to child (Acheson 1988).

THE FIRST PATTERN

Industrial West, Australia, Latin America

As is now well known, AIDS was first identified as a problem amongst Gay men in certain cities in the United States who began to present to medical institutions with rare cancers and a form of pneumonia. [Because of] the presence and often co-presence of these conditions, it gradually became apparent (despite institutional resistance from those, especially in the National Institutes of Health, opposed to transmission theories of malignant disease—Shilts 1987), [that they] must arise from damage to the immune system and from a transmissible virus disease. Gay men paid and continue to pay a terrible price for this knowledge; but everyone, Gay or not, is given the possibility of salvation by the chance of the virus's identification among those people at that place and at that time. For the United States, despite all the faults of its health care system, has a medical infrastructure which makes it possible quickly to identify new medical disorders and to discover the categories of people affected and thus to identify causative mechanisms and modes of transmission and what needs to be done to prevent or cure them. Given the political will, it also has the financial means to cope with new epidemics. Second, there is in San Francisco a self-conscious, more or less solidary, articulate and politically active Gay community, which, after an unsurprisingly faltering beginning (Shilts 1987), took stock of the situation and demonstrated to other Gays and to the rest of the world what could be done humanely to care for those already infected, and to slow down or stop further transmission. Unfortunately, through no fault of theirs, it was already too late for many of their friends and lovers. Professor M. W. Adler, one of Britain's leading experts, has pointed out that the symptomless nature of HIV infection, and the long latent period (5–8 years) before its effects, including those on the immune system, become apparent, meant that the first cases of AIDS emerged in 1980 when nearly a quarter of a cohort of Gay men were HIV seropositive (*The Independent* 17 February 1988). Also unfortunately Gays elsewhere in the world were less well-placed to respond, although self-help organizations like the Terrence Higgins Trust and Body Positive did a major task in Britain; and non-Gays were not disposed to listen or to learn from people whom at best they saw as other than themselves and at worst feared and hated for the challenge they seemed to represent to accepted social and family order and their own hardly (in both senses) suppressed temptations and desires. Even anthropologists failed to react constructively; as I reported in my A. T. article (February 1987) on the 1986 AAA meetings, AIDS was left to the Gay Caucus and put at the most unpopular time. When, at last, it became a prominent topic at the 1987 meetings, many still saw it as a purely Gay issue. Despite the negative reactions, we now know—as Hafdan Mahler, Director of WHO, has forcibly pointed out—that it is possible to check the spread of even an intractable and insidious disease by health promotion at a societal or communal level even when biological methods seem to offer little help. This knowledge, where before was merely hope, holds out new and exciting potentials for what is coming to be called social epidemiology, epidemiology reciprocally enriched by the social and cultural understandings of anthropology and sociology.[1]

The tendency to associate modes of transmission by means of body fluids with "risk groups," instead of the more epidemiologically useful "risk behaviours," led to "drug addicts"—as, in popular parlance, non-legitimated intravenous drug users are unhelpfully called—being added to Gays as scapegoats. The wish to see AIDS as a problem for the other, non-respectable, the out-of-control, was intensified. It was further reinforced by the notion of the "innocent victim," the haemophiliac infected with Factor 8 and the HIV-positive baby. Thus the Pope showed his rational lack of fear of biological contagion by embracing a person with AIDS; to the approval of some Catholics and the dismay of others, his message was made ambiguous in relation to the fear of moral contagion by the fact that he chose a child with haemophilia. I felt that he might have reassured my Orthodox Jewish aunt who, when I was a child, warned me against Christianity whose Founder's best friend Mary Magdalene, she said, was a prostitute. Especially since, as in earlier epidemics of sexually transmitted disease (Brandt 1987), prostitutes and the promiscuous (people with more sexual experience than us) were singled out for blame together with people from outside the metropolitan Industrial West.[2]

THE SECOND PATTERN

Africa and the Caribbean

The reaction to the discovery of AIDS and HIV infection among Gay men and intravenous drug users was, as I have already suggested, at best distanced but reproving pity. They had scored an "own goal" as Princess Anne put it, more in sorrow than in anger, and at worst a theologically perverse, at least by New Testament standards, theory of divine anger and retribution was favoured in Britain by some Chief Constables and Rabbis. The reaction to the discovery in one part of Africa of developed AIDS, and of widespread HIV positivity spread for the most part heterosexually and therefore equally prevalent among men and women, only just escaped from being catastrophic. Western ignorance of geography, and stereotypes of African promiscuity, together with hasty suggestions of still greater immigration and travel control over black (and sometimes poor) Africans in sharp contrast to the absence of such suggestions in relation to white (and often rich) Americans led, at first, understandably to outright denial of the problem. Careful diplomacy by WHO and others and the good sense and experience of African politicians and statesmen, with President Kaunda characteristically giving a courageous lead, very quickly overcame this denial.[3]

Particularly in urban areas of South Central Africa, up to 25% of the population between 20 and 40 years old may be HIV positive, and in some areas also 5–15% or even more of pregnant women are. The implications of these figures are staggering. The urban elite, on whom further development and national economic recovery depend, may be more than decimated. The productive and skilled workers and educators may be rendered ineffective and a whole generation made virtually unable to reproduce itself. Orphans and the elderly may be left without support, and achievements in the field of health may be made impossible to maintain. This is also a danger in poor areas of Southern Europe and in parts of Latin America, and even ultimately Asia.

THE THIRD PATTERN

In Asia, most of the Pacific, the Middle East and much of Eastern Europe, there are very few cases of AIDS, and even HIV seems to have appeared more recently than in other parts of the world. In most of these countries it is believed that HIV came from outside either from sexual intercourse with foreigners or by the import of infected blood products. However there is now evidence of internal transmission in the usual ways, and even if these nations succeed, in fact, in carrying out the policies of isolation and control to which some of them, including India, China and the Soviet Union are, in part, committed, they will not entirely halt the spread of HIV. Fortunately despite their reservations they attended the recent WHO summit and are signatories of the London Declaration and thus pledged to world co-operation.

THE ROLE OF ANTHROPOLOGY

The first objective of WHO's Global AIDS strategy is to prevent HIV infection, but this cannot be done in isolation from, or with indifference towards either the development of AIDS among those already infected or the social experience of people, rightly or wrongly, believed to be at special risk, as well as the HIV seropositive and persons with AIDS.

Surprisingly little is known about specific individual sexual behaviours or about culturally approved practices of groups and subgroups. Straightforward questionnaire techniques are difficult to apply and produce data of arguable validity. Among British sociologists, Coxon (1988) has developed an ingenious self-reporting diary technique to study sexual behaviour of Gay men. Social or cultural anthropologists have already specialist knowledge of, as well as the necessary skills to discover, patterns of sexual behaviour in different societies and sub-groups. They are unlikely even to be tempted to the view that *"we* have our regulated sexual patterns, *you* are a bit odd but understandable, *they* are just promiscuous." They can understand the social circumstances in which desires become practices and in turn symbolic markers of either individual or cultural and social identity. Their knowledge and study of other kinds of behaviour change can help them to see how changes of practice can be instituted from within a society in such a way as to leave cultural and personal identity unthreatened.

How valuable such a skill may be and how urgent its application is can be demonstrated by the difference between say Danish and British television advertising aimed at young people, which deserves comparative analysis. The British seems based on an assumption that the culture of young people can be at once ignored and condemned as bad or at least amoral, and that decisions (about risk-taking for example) are purely personal or at most dyadic. Even if the disco culture portrayed has been researched and is accurate, the wider social context of sought-for approval and avoidance of disapproval by important others, especially among peers and coevals, is just not there. The Danish advertising, on the other hand, begins by accepting that there are adolescent hedonistic values, and while leaving the choice of fundamental change open to young people themselves, shows how existing patterns can be modified to make them safer. An even sharper contrast may be seen between the Australian Government's "fear of death based" TV campaign, which was aimed at the whole population, and that (presented as an example of "how to do it" at the London Summit) which Aboriginal health promoters devised in co-operation with local people and which aimed not at instilling terror but at the enhancement of life with reduced danger. Clearly, involving groups in self-help health promotion is one of the more effective strategies for preventing the transmission of HIV, and one in which anthropologists have much to offer as facilitators.

Anthropologists have sometimes been criticized in the development field for being better at analysing failure than helping to create success. As regards AIDS, this may be a useful fault. Health educators are aware that while smoking in Britain, for example, has in general decreased, smoking amongst working-class young people and women has risen. Anthropologists again have the skills, both theoretical and practical, to examine the meanings and practices which make such crucial differences occur.

There is a world of difference between talking of a disease that has hitherto mainly affected Gays, and talking of a "Gay disease," or still more if "queer" or even "homosexual" is substituted for Gay. Anthropologists have learned what they may not themselves even recognize as being a rare sensitivity to partly concealed linguistic elisions like using Lapp for Sami, or Eskimo for Inuit, which may be perceived by those named as adding a latent symbolic communication of lack of esteem to the use of surface signs.

Anthropologists study *disease* as manifested in its particular social context of *sickness* as well as carrying an individual meaning of *illness*. They are thereby both less surprised and better prepared to analyse situations where danger and sickness are attributed prematurely or even falsely to those identified as being at risk. The knowledge that healing, whether by shaman, surgeon or sacerdote, is a social process, laden with specifiable cultural meanings, gives anthropologists an important possible role in understanding and investigating how, for example, traditional healers may be encouraged within their own society and culture to do the sick no harm and to continue to protect the well. The anthropological literature on natural and especially body symbolism (Douglas 1973) has prepared its students to understand such cultural taboos and non-taboos as the ability of British television audiences to tolerate (even before nine in the evening) the pictorial representation of the unnatural breach of body boundaries by (illegitimate) needles in contrast to the impossibility of the explicit depiction (unlike elsewhere in Northern Europe) of, not necessarily per se disapproved, sexual penetration.

Furthermore, anthropological study of the myriad different cultural meanings of death (Frankenberg 1987, Bloch et al. 1982) puts its practioners in a strong position to help in the social adjustment already faced by many Gays and their relatives to a changing demographic pattern in which people are dying in their reproductively, productively and socially most active years, an actual and potential shift in the modal age of death upwards in the developing world, downwards in industrial society.

The advent of HIV and its mode of transmission have taken not only medicine and epidemiology by surprise, but have also found both the social and cultural anthropology of risk perception and behaviour, and cultural ecology theories in anthropology, as yet insufficiently developed. Health promotion is central in countering the pandemic arising from HIV infection as well as future global pandemics. There is also a renewed realization of the social implications of measured mortality in terms of both changing age distributions of individual dying and the possibility that the future of human society is once again in question through potential ecological disaster. These developments have given a new potential importance not just to virology and immunology within core medical specialties, but also to the study of anthropology in general and medical anthropology within it. When WHO gathered together more Health Ministers than ever before at the London Summit in January [1988], the handful of invited independent observers included at least three anthropologists, and anthropologists also played a prominent part at the First International Conference on the Global impact of AIDS in March. We are presented with a challenge which we are despite our deficiencies uniquely qualified to meet, and which for our own sakes and for the sake of the general good we cannot afford to shirk.

NOTES

1. For examples in other fields see the work on developing societies of Patrick Vaughan, Carol MacCormack, Kris Heggenhougen and others at the London School of Hygiene and Jean La Fontaine's recent report on Child Abuse in Britain for ESRC (see *Anthropology Today*, October 1987, p. 1).
2. The London fieldwork and comparative analysis of LSE anthropologist Sophie Day has shown how simplistic and unjust this is in relation to prostitute women.
3. As is so often the case there remain contrary views; see Chirimuta and Chirimuta 1987 and *The Guardian* 5 February 1988 for a favourable review of this book which in my personal view is wrong. It has also been argued, without evidence strong enough to convince most epidemiologists or WHO, that both African and Gay prevalence of AIDS are synergistically affected by other sexually transmitted diseases. Poverty is, of course, even more prevalent in Africa.

REFERENCES

Acheson, Sir D. 1988. *Modes of Transmission: The Basis of Prevention Strategies.* Paper to World Summit of Ministers of Health for AIDS Prevention. London WHO/UKG, January.

Bloch, M., & J. Parry. 1982. *Death and the Regeneration of Life.* Cambridge University Press.

Brandt, A. 1987. *No Magic Bullet,* with additional chapter on AIDS. Oxford University Press.

Chirimuta, R. C., & R. J. 1987. *AIDS, Africa and Racism.* Chirimuta, Bretby, Derbyshire.

Coxon, A. P. M. 1988. "The Sexual Diary as a Research Method in the Study of Sexual Behaviour of Gay Males." *Sociological Review.* Vol. 36, No. 2, May (forthcoming).

Douglas, M. 1970 (1966). *Purity and Danger.* Penguin.

Douglas, M. 1973 (1970). *Natural Symbols.* Penguin.

Frankenberg, R. 1987. "Life: Cycle, Trajectory or Pilgrimage? A Social Production Approach to Marxism, Metaphor and Mortality." Chapter XII, pp. 122–140 in *Rethinking the Life Cycle,* ed. by Alan Bryman et al. Macmillan.

LaFontaine, J. 1988. *Child Sexual Abuse.* An ESRC Research Briefing.

Mann, J. 1988. *Global AIDS: Epidemiology, Impact, Projections and the Global Strategy.* Paper to World Summit . . . (as under Acheson above).

Office of Health Economics. 1980. HIV and AIDS in the United Kingdom. Briefing no. 23, January, London.

Shilts, R. 1987. *And the Band Played On.* Penguin.

In Black and White

Jared Diamond

Jared Diamond teaches physiology in the medical school of the University of California, Los Angeles, but has spent much time studying birds in New Guinea. Although not an anthropologist, he frequently writes on anthropological topics for such magazines as *Natural History* and *Discover*.

How have ordinary people so often throughout human history, brought themselves to commit genocide?

While the anniversary of any nation's founding is taken as cause for its inhabitants to celebrate, Australians have special cause in this, their bicentennial year. Few groups of colonists faced such obstacles as those who landed with the first fleet at the future site of Sydney in 1788. Australia was still terra incognita: the colonists had no idea of what to expect or how to survive. They were separated from their mother country by a sea voyage of 15,000 miles, lasting eight months. Two and a half years of starvation would pass until a supply fleet arrived from England. Many of the settlers were convicts who had already been traumatized by the most brutal aspects of brutal eighteenth-century life. Despite those beginnings, the settlers survived, prospered, filled a continent, built a democracy, and established a distinctive national character. It's no wonder that Australians feel pride as they celebrate their nation's founding.

Nevertheless, one set of protests has marred the celebrations. White settlers were not the first Australians. Australia had been settled at least 40,000 years before by the ancestors of the people now usually referred to as Australian aborigines and also known in Australia as blacks. In the course of English settlement, most of the original inhabitants were killed by settlers or died of other causes, leading some descendants of the survivors to stage protests this year. The bicentenary celebrations focused implicitly on how Australia became white. This column focuses instead on how Australia ceased to be black and how courageous English settlers came to commit genocide.

Lest white Australians take offense at this piece, I should make it clear at the outset that I am not accusing their forefathers of having done something uniquely horrendous. My reason for discussing the extermination of the aborigines is precisely because it isn't unique: it's a well-documented example of a common event in human history. Genocide is such a painful subject that either we'd rather not think about it at all or else we'd like to believe that nice people don't commit genocide, only Nazis do. But our refusing to think about it has consequences: we've done little to halt the numerous episodes of genocide since World War II, and we're not alert to where it may happen next. Hence I'll indicate briefly how frequent it is, why people do it, and what I learned from a friend of mine who joined in a genocidal massacre thirty years ago. Let's begin by recalling the founding of white settlement in the state of Tasmania.

Tasmania, an island slightly larger than West Virginia, lies 200 miles off Australia's southeast coast. When it was discovered by Europeans in 1642, it supported about 5,000 hunter-gatherers related to the aborigines of the Australian mainland and with perhaps the simplest technology of any modern peoples. Tasmanians made only a few types of simple stone and wooden tools. Like the mainland aborigines, they lacked metal tools, agriculture, livestock, pottery, and bows and arrows. Unlike the mainlanders, they also lacked boomerangs, dogs, nets, knowledge of sewing, and ability to start a fire.

Since the Tasmanians' sole boats were rafts capable of only short journeys, they had had no contact with any other humans since the rising sea level cut off Tasmania from Australia 10,000 years ago. Confined to their private universe for hundreds of generations, they had survived the longest isolation in modern human history—an isolation otherwise depicted only in science fiction. When the white colonists of Australia finally ended that isolation, no two peoples on earth were less equipped to understand each other than were Tasmanians and whites.

The tragic collision of these two peoples led to conflict almost as soon as British sealers and settlers arrived in about 1800. Whites kidnapped Tasmanian children as laborers, kidnapped women as consorts, mutilated or killed men, trespassed on hunting grounds, and tried to clear Tasmanians off their land. Thus, the conflict quickly focused on Lebensraum, which throughout human history has been among the commonest causes of genocide. As a result of the kidnappings, the native population of northeast Tasmania in November 1830 had been reduced to seventy-two adult men, three adult women, and no children. One shepherd shot nineteen Tasmanians with a swivel gun loaded with nails. Four other shepherds ambushed a group of natives, killed thirty, and threw their bodies over a cliff remembered today as Victory Hill.

Naturally, Tasmanians retaliated, and whites counter-retaliated in turn. To end the escalation, Governor Arthur in April 1828 ordered all Tasmanians to leave the part of the island already settled by Europeans. To enforce this order, government-sponsored groups called roving parties, and consisting of convicts led by police, hunted down and killed Tasmanians. With the declaration of martial law in November 1828, soldiers were authorized to kill on sight any Tasmanian in the settled areas. Next, a bounty was declared on the natives: five British pounds for each adult, two pounds for each child, caught alive. "Black catching," as it was called because of the Tasmanians' dark skins, became big business pursued by private as well as official roving parties. At the same time a commission headed by William Broughton, the Anglican archdeacon of Australia, was set up to recommend an overall policy toward the natives. After considering proposals to capture them for sale as slaves, poison or trap them, or hunt them with dogs, the commission settled on continued bounties and the use of mounted police.

In 1830 a remarkable missionary, George Augustus Robinson, was hired to round up the remaining Tasmanians and take them to Flinders Island, thirty miles away. Robinson was convinced that he was acting for the good of the Tasmanians. He was paid 300 pounds in advance, 700 pounds on completing the job. Undergoing real dangers and hardship, and aided by a courageous native woman named Truganini, he succeeded in bringing in the remaining natives—initially by persuading them that a worse fate awaited them if they did not surrender, but later at gunpoint. Many of Robinson's captives died en route, but about 200 reached Flinders, the last survivors of the former population of 5,000.

On Flinders Island Robinson was determined to civilize and christianize the survivors. His settlement—at a windy site with little fresh water—was run like a jail. Children were separated from parents to facilitate the work of civilizing them. The regimented daily schedule included Bible reading, hymn singing, and inspection of beds and dishes for cleanness and neatness. However, the jail diet caused malnutrition, which combined with illness to make the natives die. Few infants survived more than a few weeks. The government reduced expenditures in the hope that the natives would die out. By 1869 only Truganini, one other woman, and one man remained alive.

These last three Tasmanians attracted the interest of scientists, who believed them to be a missing link between humans and apes. Hence when the last man, one William Lanner, died in 1869, competing teams of physicians, led by Dr. George Stokell from the Royal Society of Tasmania and Dr. W. L. Crowther from the Royal College of Surgeons, alternately dug up and reburied Lanner's body, cutting off parts of it and stealing them back and forth from each other. Crowther cut off the head, Stokell the hands and feet, and someone else the ears and nose, as souvenirs. Stokell made a tobacco pouch out of Lanner's skin.

Before Truganini, the last woman, died in 1876, she was terrified of similar postmortem mutilation and asked in vain to be buried at sea. As she had feared, the Royal Society dug up her skeleton and put it on public display in the Tasmanian Museum, where it remained until 1947. In that year the museum finally yielded to complaints of poor taste and transferred Truganini's skeleton to a room where only scientists could view it. That, too, stimulated complaints of poor taste. Finally, in 1976—the centenary year of Truganini's death—her skeleton was cremated over the museum's objections, and her ashes were scattered at sea as she had requested.

While the Tasmanians were few in number, their extermination was disproportionately influential in Australian history because Tasmania was the first Australian colony to solve its native problem and achieve the most nearly final solution. It had done so by apparently succeeding in getting rid of all its natives. (Actually, some children of Tasmanian women by white sealers survived, and their descendants today constitute an embarrassment to the Tasmanian government, which has not figured out what to do about them.) Many whites on the Australian mainland envied the thoroughness of the Tasmanian solution and wanted to imitate it, but they also learned a lesson from it. The extermination of the Tasmanians, carried out in settled areas in full view of the urban press, had attracted some negative comment. Hence the extermination of the much more numerous mainland aborigines was effected at or beyond the frontier, far from urban centers.

The colonial governments' instrument of this policy, modeled on the Tasmanian government's roving parties, was a branch of mounted police termed Native Police, who used search-and-destroy tactics to kill or drive out aborigines. A typical strategy was to surround a camp at night and to shoot the inhabitants in an attack at dawn. White settlers also made widespread use of poisoned food to kill aborigines. Another common practice was roundups in which captured aborigines were kept chained together at the neck while being marched to jail and held there. The British novelist Anthony Trollope expressed the prevailing nineteenth-century British attitude toward aborigines when he wrote, "Of the Australian black man we may certainly say that he has to go. That he should perish without unnecessary suffering should be the aim of all who are concerned in the matter."

These tactics continued in Australia long into the twentieth century. In an incident at Alice Springs in 1928, police massacred thirty-one aborigines. The Australian parliament refused to accept a report on the massacre, and two aboriginal survivors (rather than the police) were put on trial for murder. Neck chains were still in use and defended as humane in 1958, when the Commissioner of Police for the state of Western Australia explained to the *Melbourne Herald* that aboriginal prisoners preferred being chained.

The mainland aborigines were too numerous to exterminate in the manner of the Tasmanians. However, from the arrival of British colonists in 1788 until the 1921 census, the aboriginal population declined from about 300,000 to 60,000.

Today the attitudes of white Australians toward their murderous history vary widely. While government policy and many whites' private views have become increasingly sympathetic to the aborigines, other whites deny responsibility for genocide. For instance, in 1982, *The Bulletin*, one of Australia's leading news magazines, published a letter by a lady named Patricia Cobern, who denied indignantly that white settlers had exterminated the Tasmanians. In fact, wrote Ms. Cobern, the settlers were peace loving and of high moral character, while Tasmanians were treacherous, murderous, warlike, filthy, gluttonous, vermin infested, and disfigured by syphilis. Moreover, they took poor care of their infants, never bathed, and had repulsive marriage customs. They died out because of all those poor health practices, plus a death wish and lack of religious beliefs. It was just a coincidence that, after thousands of years of existence, they happened to die out during a conflict with settlers. The only massacres were of settlers by Tasmanians, not vice versa. Besides, the settlers only armed themselves in self-defense, were unfamiliar with guns, and never shot more than forty-one Tasmanians at one time.

I have already mentioned that the fate of Australian aborigines was typical of many episodes of genocide throughout human history in having been precipitated by a conflict over Lebensraum. In addition, Ms. Cobern's letter is a classic example of the usual response of a people charged with genocide. Typically, killers deny most responsibility for group murders; invoke self-defense or provocation, insofar as they acknowledge any responsibility at all; attribute ultimate responsibility to the victims, and denigrate the victims as sub-humans implicitly deserving of death, whatever death's actual cause.

To appreciate that the fate of the Australian aborigines was hardly unique, we have only to recall our own not-quite-complete extermination of American Indians, another struggle over Lebensraum. History books usually portray this struggle as a series of military conflicts in our distant past between groups of armed adult males: the U.S. Army versus mounted Indian warriors. In fact, much of the struggle consisted of sneak attacks and isolated murders in which white civilians killed Indians of any age and either sex. It was only in 1916 that the last "wild" Indian in the United States (the Yahi Indian known as Ishi) died, and frank and unapologetic memoirs by the killers of his tribe were still being published as recently as 1923. For instance, a rancher named Norman Kingsley explained how, in shooting a group of more than thirty unarmed Yahis that he had cornered in a cave, he exchanged his .56 caliber Spencer rifle for a .38 caliber revolver when it came to shooting the babies, because "the rifle tore them up so bad." When Robert Anderson wrote about his dawn attack on a Yahi village, he mentioned that his friend Hiram Good suggested sparing the women while killing every man or well-grown boy, but "it was plain to me that we must also get rid of the women," who were then killed with some particular savagery not described in detail.

It used to be thought that humans were unique among animals in killing members of their own species. However, recent field studies have documented murder or group murder by many other species, including ants, hyenas, wolves, lions, monkeys, gorillas, and chimpanzees. Genocide by humans is at least as old as the oldest preserved written records. We all know the biblical account of how the walls of Jericho came tumbling down at the sound of Joshua's trumpets. Less often quoted is the sequel: Joshua obeyed the Lord's command to slaughter Jericho's inhabitants, as well as those of Ai, Makkedah, Libnah, Hebron, Debir, and many other cities. This was considered so ordinary that the Book of Joshua devotes only a phrase to each slaughter, as if to say: of course he killed all the inhabitants, what else would you expect? The sole account requiring elaboration is of the slaughter at Jericho itself, where Joshua did something really unusual: he spared the lives of one family (because they had helped his messengers).

We find similar episodes in accounts of the wars of the ancient Greeks, Crusaders, Pacific islanders, and other groups. Obviously, I'm not saying that slaughter of the defeated irrespective of sex has always followed crushing defeat in war. But that outcome, or else milder versions like the killing of men and the enslavement of women, happened often enough that they must be considered more than a rare aberration in our view of human nature. Since 1950 there have been nearly twenty episodes of genocide, including two claiming more than a million victims each (East Pakistan in 1971, Cambodia in the late 1970s) and four more with more than a hundred thousand victims each (the Sudan and Indonesia in the 1960s, Burundi and Uganda in the 1970s). A few cases attracted some international attention, but who protested the slaughter of Zanzibar's Arabs in 1964 or of Paraguay's Aché Indians in the 1970s?

What are the situations in which genocide is most likely? Historically, perhaps the commonest situation has involved one people attempting to usurp another people's Lebensraum, as exemplified by the fate of Australian aborigines and Native Americans. Another common type of situation involves power struggles within a pluralistic society, as when Rwanda's Hutu people killed Tutsi people in 1962–63 and when Burundi's Tutsi killed Hutu in 1972–73. As for scapegoat killings of a helpless minority blamed for frustrations of their killers, one immediately thinks of slaughters of Jews by many peoples over many centuries and of Stalin's killings of several ethnic minorities in Russia at the height of World War II. Most of these types of genocide also involved racial or religious persecution.

All human societies have sanctions against murder, which must somehow be overcome for genocide to happen. Overriding principles commonly invoked include self-defense, revenge, manifest rights to land, and possessing the correct religion or race or political belief. These are the principles that fan hatred and transform ordinary people into murderers. A further universal feature of genocide is an "us/them" ethical code that views the victims as lower beings or animals to whom laws of human ethics don't apply. For instance, Nazis regarded Jews as lice; French settlers of Algeria referred to local Moslems as *ratons* (rats); Boers called Africans *bobbejaan* (baboons); educated

northern Nigerians viewed Ibos as subhuman vermin; and Ms. Cobern expressed a low opinion of Tasmanians.

Many books have been written on the psychology of genocide. It's hard not to go numb while reading them. It remains hard to imagine how we, and other nice ordinary people that we know, could bring ourselves to look helpless people in the face while killing them. I came closest to being able to imagine it when a friend whom I had long known told me of a genocidal massacre at which he had been a killer.

Kariniga is a gentle Tudawhe tribesman who worked with me in New Guinea. We shared life-threatening situations, fears, and triumphs, and I like and admire him. One evening after I had known Kariniga for five years, he described to me an episode from his youth. There had been a long history of conflict between the Tudawhes and a neighboring village of Daribi tribesmen. Tudawhes and Daribis seem quite similar to me, but Kariniga had come to view Daribis as inexpressibly vile. In a series of ambushes the Daribis finally succeeded in picking off many Tudawhes, including Kariniga's father, until the surviving Tudawhes became desperate. All the remaining Tudawhe men surrounded the Daribi village at night and set fire to the huts at dawn. As the sleepy Daribis stumbled down the steps of their burning huts, they were speared. Some succeeded in escaping to the forest, where Tudawhes tracked down and killed most of them during the following weeks. But the establishment of Australian government control ended the hunt before Kariniga could catch his father's killer.

Since that evening, I've often found myself shuddering as I recalled details of it—the glow in Kariniga's eyes as he told me of the dawn massacre; those intensely satisfying moments when he finally drove his spear into some of his people's murderers; and his tears of rage and frustration at the escape of his father's killer, whom he still hoped to kill some day with poison. That evening, I thought I understood how at least one nice person had brought himself to kill. The potential for genocide that circumstances thrust on Kariniga lies within all of us. As the growth of world population sharpens conflicts between and within societies, humans will have more urge to kill each other, and more effective weapons with which to do it. To listen to first-person accounts of genocide is unbearably painful. But if we continue to turn away and to not understand it, when will it be our own turn to become the killers—or the victims?

Global Apartheid

Gernot Köhler

Gernot Köhler was connected to the Center of International Studies at Princeton University at the time he wrote this article in 1978.

The concept of apartheid has significance far beyond the situation in South Africa which coined the term. Indeed, the concept can be generalized to apply to the present world situation. It provides both a better understanding of the present human condition and more effective guidelines to change it. The processes of interdependence, interpenetration and intercommunication in the present era have made the entire humanity into one global society. The present nation-state system, which obscures the appearance of this society, fails miserably in responding to the concerns and needs of the global community. The concept of global apartheid provides a more realistic and comprehensive view of the world and suggests appropriate ways of so acting as to make a beginning toward realizing a just, participatory, peaceful and humane global society.

This paper presents the view that Global Society is an apartheid system. The purpose of this paper will be to define and describe global apartheid, analyse some of its most striking features, and suggest some broad strategy lines for overcoming its worst aspects.

STRUCTURAL SIMILARITIES WITH SOUTH AFRICAN APARTHEID

It would be useful for our present discussion to distinguish between apartheid as a policy and apartheid as it is practiced within specific societies. Policies of apartheid are programs or measures that aim at the creation or maintenance of racial segregation. Supporters of such policies claim that segregated development of two racial groups does not imply dominance of one over the other. Apartheid, in this view, permits the possibility of separate but equal, or equivalent, life chances for each of the separated races. The logic of this argu-

ment apart, its validity has been disproved in fact wherever such a policy has been professedly tried. Apartheid policies just cannot be pursued and sustained except in the context of structural apartheid.

When we speak of apartheid as a structure, we refer to the social, economic, political, military, and cultural constitution of a society. Whenever a minority race dominates a majority composed of other races in a society, that society exhibits a structure of apartheid.

South Africa is a classic example of this. In South Africa, the dominance of the white minority over the black majority takes different forms—from the denial of political representation to the black majority to brutal repression to an enormous differential in living standards to many others.

Condemnation of South African apartheid has been almost universal. The UN General Assembly has condemned racism and apartheid in South Africa on numerous occasions, with majorities bordering on unanimity, despite the well-known reluctance of member-states to have the organization intervene in the domestic jurisdiction of any state. If on few issues in international politics there has been such a massive agreement, it is because policies of racial segregation, which ensure the dominance of the white stratum of society, flagrantly violate the aspirations of a majority of humanity for liberation from dominance and are in sharp conflict with the norms of equality of all human beings, and because apartheid constitutes the most repugnant form of human rights violation.

It is argued below that the apartheid structure of the global society has important similarities with that of South Africa. Indeed, the global society is a mirror reflection of South African society. One can go a step further and say that global apartheid is even more severe than South African apartheid. There seems to be no other system that is more "apart," in the sense in which apartheid is. Let us, then, look at the macrostructure of the global society.

THE STRUCTURE OF GLOBAL SOCIETY

The world is commonly seen as a multitude of countries or nation-states. World politics and world economics are commonly understood as a set of relations between sovereign nation-states. This view, though not wrong, is limited. It is true that nation-states issue passports and visas, show national flags, organize military forces, make national laws, conduct foreign policy, make trade agreements with other nation-states, and so on. World affairs can be comprehended by what nations and their governments do to each other, be it in the military, economic, cultural, or other domains. Such intergovernmental and interstate exchanges and relations today seem all-important, although their importance in relation to the activities of non-governmental actors and in relation to supranational organizations are changing. In recent years, an increasing awareness of interdependence has led to some questioning of the manner in which the nation-state system operates. Numerous observers have become sensitive to the phenomenon of transnationalism, which implies a diminution in the sovereignty of individual states. Nevertheless, the prevailing view still is that the most useful way of understanding global politics is through the prism of the nation-state system.

Without questioning the validity of these views, we now propose an alternative—namely, to view the world as a macrosociety. This view is reinforced by pictures of the earth as seen from outer space, by an increased sense of economic interdependence between countries, by the emergence of world conferences for the airing of views on diverse subjects of global interest, by intellectual endeavors and scientific models which treat the world as a single system. The notions of meeting the basic needs of four to eight billion people, establishment of minimal levels of decency with regard to civil and political liberties of all individuals and groups, notions of pollution and resource depletion and of quality of life are becoming more commonplace in the rhetoric of academics, policy-makers and knowledgeable and responsible individuals around the globe. Perhaps the most forceful illustration of this approach is a recent article by Nathan Keyfitz in which he analyzes the social structure of the world as if the globe was a single society.[1] We believe that these trends capture a part of reality not adequately comprehended by the paradigm of the nation-state system, and it is in that spirit that we wish to speculate about world society.

When we view the world society as a macrosociety, we begin to ask questions that we normally ask only with regard to national societies—e.g. is it nice to live there? What is the political system of this society? What is its economic system and how does the world society allocate its resources? How is this society stratified? What is the role of women in world society? How does world society treat its children? What are the race relations in the world society? How does the world society protect its members from murder and mass murder? How does it provide for social security? Is it a happy society? These questions are different from those dealt with in the study of international politics and international economics, if only because they relate to the world society rather than to the nation-state.

The literature that comes closest to dealing with global structure in this sense is to be found in the writings on imperialism, dependency, and center-periphery relations. These see the world society as a highly stratified macrosociety which is characterized by exploitation and relations of political, economic, military, and psychological domination and dependence between the center and the periphery of the world. This modern world system, which emerged in the fifteenth and sixteenth centuries, transcends national boundaries, cripples the economic circuits of peripheral societies, generates artificial underdevelopment, and affects both center and periphery countries in various domains other than economic.

While this mode of analysis is very valuable, it could be even more so if it stressed the important fact of racial stratification on a world scale and the attendant racist attitudes and behaviors, which are still with us although the formal empires have all but withered away. We therefore propose to use the concept of "global apartheid" for the interpretation and analysis of the present structure of world society.

As indicated above, our contention is that the structure of the world is very similar to the structure of South Africa and that both are equally appalling. The similarity manifests itself in all major dimensions of analysis—political, economic, military, cultural, psychological, social, racial and legal. A formal definition of "global apartheid" though capturing only the skeleton of a concept, might read thus: Global apartheid is a structure of world society which combines socioeconomic and racial antagonisms and in which (i) a minority of whites occupies the pole of affluence, while a majority composed of other races occupies the pole of poverty; (ii) social integration of the two groups is made extremely difficult by barriers of complexion, economic position, political boundaries, and other factors; (iii) economic development of the two groups is interdependent; (iv) the affluent white minority possesses a disproportionately large share of world society's political, economic, and military power. Global apartheid is thus a structure of extreme inequality in cultural, racial, social, political, economic, military and legal terms, as is South African Apartheid.

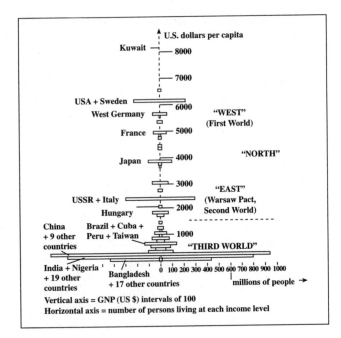

Figure 1   World income tree

Source: Ruth Legot Sivard, *World Military and Social Expenditures 1976* (Leesburg. Virg. WMSE Publications), pp. 21–31. The grouping of data by intervals of $100.00 per capita was done by the author.

SOME DATA ON GLOBAL APARTHEID

In South Africa, the population ratio between the non-white majority and the white minority is about 4.7 to 1. In the world society, about two-thirds of the population is nonwhite and one-third white. Both in South Africa and in the world society, being "white" and belonging to the upper stratum tend to go together, although there are also poor whites and rich non-whites. The upper stratum—both in South Africa and the world—is not a homogeneous group. There exist linguistic-ethnic-cultural cleavages within this stratum (notably, Afrikaner versus English in South Africa and "West" versus "East" in global society). The whites in South Africa and in the world alike enjoy a higher standard of living and have more power than the non-whites. The world income tree (Figure 1) . . . shows the economic stratification of the world. It shows the rich countries at the top and the poor countries at the bottom according to their per capita gross national product, and countries with similar wealth are grouped together. The length of the bars shown in the figure indicates how many people belong to each income group. Figure 1 thus shows how about two-thirds of humanity live at, or close to, the bottom, of the socio-economic pyramid of the world, while one-third of humankind live in middle and top positions. The West (or, the "First World") and the East (i.e. the "Second World") occupy the top and middle ranks of this tree.

Table 1   Income Shares

Segment of population	Bulgaria	USA	India	South Africa	World
	Percentages of gross national product (or gross global product) received by the three segments of population				
Top 20%	33.2	38.8	52.0	58.0	71.3
Middle 40%	40.0	41.5	32.0	35.8	23.5
Lowest 40%	26.8	19.7	16.0	6.2	5.2

Sources: 1. Roger D. Hansen, *The U.S. and World Development: Agenda for Action 1976* (New York: Praeger, 1975), pp. 148–149 for Bulgaria (1962), USA (1970), India (1964), and South Africa (1965); 2. World Bank, *Population Policies and Economic Development* (Baltimore, MD: Johns Hopkins University Press, 1974), p. 37 for World (1971).

They happen to be predominantly "white," Japan being the major exception. They are the upper crust of the world society in much the same way as Afrikaner and English whites in South Africa are the upper stratum of that society.

When we treat the world as a single society and compare its inequality to situations of inequality *within* certain countries, we find that *global* inequality of income is even more severe than the income inequality within national societies (Table 1).

As Table 1 shows, the income inequality of the world is even worse than that of South Africa. In South Africa, the poorest 40% of the population receive only 6.2% of the national product, while the poorest 40% of the world receive an even smaller share (5.2% of the world product). At the other end of the spectrum, the richest 20% of South Africa's population take 58.0% of the income, while the richest 20% of the world take even more (71.3% of the world income.)

Life expectancy is also an index of global apartheid. The members of the affluent, predominantly white societies of the "North" live longer than the members of the poor, predominantly nonwhite societies of the Third World (see Figure 2). It shows that life expectancy is lowest for the poorest countries and tends to rise in proportion to a country's wealth until a certain threshold is reached. Above that threshold of wealth, life expectancy tends to change very little. The countries of the "North" enjoy a similar, high life expectancy. Eastern Europe is, in this respect, as privileged as the Western affluent societies.

It should be noted, too, that most of the world's weapons of mass destruction are owned by the white societies of the "North"—the United States, USSR, France, and England. World Wars I and II and the possibility of a future nuclear war between the United States and the Soviet Union have so much occupied the minds of some of us in the affluent countries that we

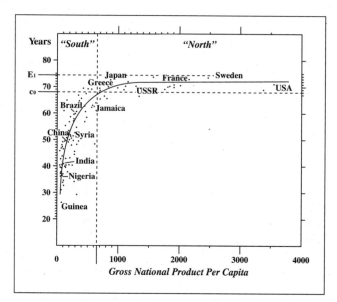

Figure 2 Relationship of life expectancy with per capita GNP

Source: Adapted from G. Köhler and N. Alcock, "An Empirical Table of Structural Violence." *Journal of Peace Research*, Vol. 13, No. 4, 1976.

Table 2 The Inequality of Global Violence

A. Estimated world totals, 1965 deaths from:

international violence	11,500–23,000
civil violence	92,000
structural violence	14,000,000–18,000,000

B. Distribution of violent deaths, 1965 (World = 100% in each category)

Affluent "North"	population	30.6%
	international violence	9.1%
	civil violence	.1%
	structural violence	4.2%
Poor "South"	population	69.4%
	international violence	90.9%
	civil violence	99.9%
	structural violence	95.8%

Source: Gernot Köhler and Norman Alcock, "An Empirical Table of Structural Violence," *Journal of Peace Research*, Vol. 4. The percentages for structural violence are based on the so-called Swedish Model.

fail to see that actual international violence (resulting from international wars and intervention) and *actual* civil violence (from revolutions, riots, massacres, etc.) and actual structural violence[2] (from miserable socioeconomic conditions) are all related to global apartheid. Estimates for the year 1965 show how all three forms of large-scale violence are unequally distributed in a manner that is consistent with global apartheid (see Table 2).

Table 2 shows the enormous inequality of death and suffering from war and other forms of violence. If violence were equally distributed, the North, with 30% of the world's population, would suffer 30% of all forms of violence and the South, with 70% of world population, would suffer 70% of all violent deaths. The data indicate, however, that the South has suffered much more than "its fair share" of violent death—namely, over 90% in all categories—and that the North has had correspondingly low shares.

While comparable up-to-date estimates are not available, preliminary calculations suggest the following developments since 1965:

a. The world total of deaths due to structural violence seems to have declined slightly despite the rise in world population. It can be assumed that the distribution of fatalities between the North and the South remains as unequal since 1965 as it was in 1965.

b. The world total of deaths due to large-scale armed violence, both international and domestic, does not ex-

hibit a steady trend but fluctuates considerably from year to year and period to period. Between 1965 and 1976, a peak was reached in 1971 when the Pakistan-Bangladesh-India war and the war in Vietnam sent the annual world total of deaths in this category to about 1.5 million or more. From 1973 to 1976, the corresponding world figure may have been around 100,000 deaths, with the inequality between the North and the South remaining undisturbed.[3]

THE NEED FOR REFORM OF THE INTERNATIONAL SYSTEM

Most observers agree that the international system is currently in a phase of major changes although there is a wide range of views both on the nature and on the most desirable direction of this transformation. In our view, the world society, structured like global apartheid, clearly requires reforms in order to make the society more suitable for living in for most of its members. Just as the world community opposes apartheid in South Africa, it should also oppose global apartheid. Ideally, reform should lead to the abolition of global apartheid. This is not merely a moral demand; for two-thirds of this world society, it is urgent and necessary to enable this multiracial majority to live a life of dignity.

For the more affluent societies of the North, the abolition of global apartheid may not seem urgent, but it is in their own interest no less than in the interest of the South to actively press for a world without apartheid. This view is dictated by political and economic prudence. As the examples of Zimbabwe (Rhodesia) and South Africa amply illustrate, the maintenance of an apartheid system is costly in political, military, social, economic, and psychological terms.

But as long as the apartheid system is not challenged from below, the self-interest of the upper stratum, defined in narrow wealth and power terms, is tied to the perpetuation of the status quo. As soon as it is effectively challenged from below, the costs of maintaining it begin to rise. When the lower stratum of the system becomes highly self-assertive and permanently "unruly" in the perspective of the predominantly white upper stratum, the self-interest of the upper stratum is no longer served by the defense of the status quo. Prudent upper-stratum statesmanship then feels inclined to doubt its usefulness in terms of the costs of maintaining apartheid. The following is a short list of such costs.

1. *Economic health.* The world economy cannot unfold its full productive potential because global apartheid impedes the productivity of the Third World and, thereby, keeps the North's income from trade with the South far below what it could be. This, in turn, contributes to slow growth, inflation, and unemployment in the North.

2. *Economic security.* The affluent countries require oil, minerals, and other goods from the Third World. Lack of North's responsiveness to Third World interests increases South's inclination to disrupt oil and resource flows to the North.

3. *Military security.* Deep economic conflicts in the world system contribute to the world's military instability. This is dangerous for the affluent countries in view of the fact that even those armed conflicts which are seemingly "peripheral" from the viewpoint of the North can lead to a breakdown of deterrence and to a large-scale war between the two major alliances of the North, as World War I illustrated.

4. *Liberty.* Massive poverty breeds authoritarianism of the Right or the Left. To the extent that the affluent countries cherish the world-wide presence of liberty, the lack of liberty in the world, linked to global apartheid, must be counted as a cost.

5. *Human growth.* For many people in the affluent societies who have a humanistic or spiritual orientation, the present world situation which stunts human growth and development on such a large scale is a cost.

The development of race relations in the United States provides an interesting illustration both of the opportunities and of the difficulties encountered in the abolition of an unfair racial situation. It shows that it is quite possible that major segments of the dominant white stratum come to support desegregation policies.

On the other hand, the example also shows that progress in this direction is slow and that, even after the society's attitudes and laws on race have begun to change, the problem continues in terms of class differences.

MAJOR DIMENSIONS OF REFORM

It is not enough to set out to abolish global apartheid; there ought to be a fair idea of where to go—i.e. there ought to be an image of an alternative world structure. Such an alternative would, in my opinion, have to satisfy the following criteria: (1) basic needs for all individuals are satisfied and abject poverty is eradicated; (2) racial discrimination is eliminated; and (3) international and intranational income differences are significantly reduced.

For this purpose, it is necessary to make a realistic assessment of the present structure and its dynamics. As noted above, there are two competing paradigms which claim to provide an accurate view of the world: the classical nation-state paradigm and the center-periphery paradigm. It is now generally recognized that a pure nation-state paradigm does not sufficiently correctly conceptualize the enormous economic and racial stratification of the world. The center-periphery paradigm, on the other hand, though a valuable contribution to the understanding of the dynamics of the global political economy, is found to be rather constrictive when attempts are made to apply it to political and social action in all the regions of the world. The example of South Africa is very instructive in this regard. When we apply the center-periphery analysis to the South African situation, all members of the white minority have to be considered as members of the "center," and all members of the black majority as members of the "periphery." While this interpretation seems plausible, one of its inferences does not hold for South Africa. The center-periphery analysis assumes or predicts that all members of the center have an interest in maintaining the unfair status quo. In South Africa, however, as Steve Biko pointed out, white opposition to the status quo has been at times very strong and was, on occasion, stronger than the black opposition to it.[4] The center-periphery analysis is thus—for the South African situation—not as "realistic" as one might think. I am contending that, at the global level, the center-periphery paradigm is likewise too rigid and less realistic.

At the world level, we find many members in the "center of the center," i.e. elites in the North, who oppose global apartheid and global militarism. We also find many elites in the Third World who do not behave as lackeys of the global center, as assumed or predicted by the center-periphery theory. Furthermore, the "periphery of the center," i.e. workers, housewives, employees, etc. in the countries of the North, do not unequivocally support the "center of the center" in efforts to maintain the global status quo. The activities of the lay members of churches in North America and Europe in voluntary aid to the Third World and in opposition to South African apartheid are a clear illustration of this point. Nor do the "masses" in Third World countries necessarily oppose collaboration between their leaders and Northern countries. In short, the center-periphery paradigm is partly true, but it is far from an accurate description of the reality.

If we view the world as structured on the lines of global apartheid, the role of the Northern, white opponent to global apartheid—"elite" or "mass"—makes sense. Similarly, the Southern, nonwhite moderate collaborator with the North—"elite" or "mass"—can be seen under the paradigm of global apartheid, as a shrewd politician on behalf of underdog interests or a traitor to those interests—depending on circumstances and behavior—whereas he is made out to be invariably a traitor of underdog interests in the center-periphery paradigm.

The world is thus most realistically depicted as a society which is "apart" and stratified, i.e. global apartheid, and which encompasses armed nation-states as administrational districts. Policies for world reform can mobilize support not only in the "periphery of the periphery," as center-periphery analysis assumes, but throughout the North and the South, both among "elites" and "masses." As in any large-scale political movement, different sectors of the movement may support even a drastic reform movement for somewhat different reasons and on the basis of a combination of different interests.

Socioeconomic issues are obviously central to the abolition of global apartheid. At the same time, other dimensions—military, political-legal, ecological, and cultural-psychological—are related to the socioeconomic issues and must undoubtedly be attended to in any attempt to abolish that system. Thus, we believe that it can be shown that the prospect of progress toward disarmament would be vastly improved by a movement directed toward abolishing global apartheid. Similarly, modification of the institutional structures at the global level (e.g. in the World Bank, international commodity markets, and others) should be enhanced to permit racial balance and fair representation of the world's multiracial majority. Thirdly, ecological considerations might be given serious attention by persons in the Third World if the movement for an ecologically sane world took recognition of the world's apartheid. Finally, in the cultural-psychological realm, we must learn cognitions and attitudes which combine positive communal and national identifications with positive attitudes toward a common world society

and which entail a respect for common global concerns and interests as opposed to particularistic national interests.

TOWARD A JUST, PARTICIPATORY, PEACEFUL AND HUMANE GLOBAL SOCIETY

It is generally recognized that social theory and the major concepts of an era arise out of, and respond to, the underlying material and social conditions which have a bearing on political action and the establishment of normative orders. Thus, for example, both Adam Smith and Karl Marx would probably agree that the notions of the marketplace and of class antagonism were products of empirical situations which favored the use of such concepts and the values they imply. Concepts which are able to combine a grasp of the ongoing behavioral world and provide a normative thrust become the basis, then, for determining what is considered as "knowledge," "information," and "data" about the world, and how we are to behave towards it. We have attempted to articulate the concept of global apartheid because we believe that the processes of interdependence, interpenetration, and the communicative era in which we live are making the planetary dimension of human society the most significant new prism through which to view social processes and the social organization of humanity. We believe further that the state system fails miserably in meeting the concerns and needs of this emerging global community. It is our contention that the concept of global apartheid—even in the limited form in which we have presented it here—provides us with a more comprehensive and realistic way of viewing the world, and thus enables us to suggest ways of behaving and acting in the political, economic and social realm so as to begin to realize a just, participatory, peaceful, and humane global society.

NOTES

1. Nathan Keyfitz, "World Resources and the World Middle Class," *Scientific American* 235, 1, July 1976, pp. 28–35.
2. "Structural violence" is a term used in contemporary peace research and is to be distinguished from armed violence. While armed violence is violence exerted by persons against persons with the use of arms, structural violence is violence exerted by situations, institutions, social, political and economic structures. Thus, when a person dies because he/she has no access to food, the effect is violent as far as that person is concerned, yet there is no individual actor who could be identified as the source of this violence. It is the system of food production and distribution that is to blame. The violence is thus exerted by an anonymous "structure." The measurement of the number of persons killed through structural violence uses statistics of life expectancy. By comparing the life expectancy of affluent regions with that of poor regions, one can estimate how many persons died in the poor region on

account of poverty and poverty-related conditions (e.g. lack of doctors, clean water, food, etc.), which can be interpreted as "structural violence."

3. Trends in global structural and armed violence in the twentieth century are being investigated by William Beckhardt and Gernot Khler. The research is in progress.

4. An interview with Steve Biko, conducted by Bernard Zylstra and published in the *Christian Science Monitor*, 10 November, 1977, pp. 18–19, contains the following passages.

> *Question:* What is black consciousness?
>
> *Biko:* By black consciousness I mean the cultural and political revival of in oppressed people . . . So black consciousness says: "Forget about colour!" But the reality we faced 10 to 15 years ago did not allow us to articulate this. After all, the continent was in a period of rapid decolonization, which implied a challenge to black inferiority all over Africa.
>
> This challenge was shared by white liberals. So for quite some time the white liberals acted as the spokesmen for the blacks . . .
>
> . . . Society as a whole was divided into white and black groups. This forced division had to disappear; and many nonracial groups worked toward that end. But almost every nonracial group was still largely white, notably so in the student world . . . So we began to realize that blacks themselves had to speak out about the black predicament . . .
>
> At this time we were also influenced by the development of a black consciousness movement in the United States . . .

REFERENCES

Keyfitz, Nathan. 1976. "World Resources and the World Middle Class," *Scientific American* 235, 1, July, pp. 28–35.

Zylstra, Bernard. 1977. "An Interview with Steve Biko." *Christian Science Monitor*, 10 November, pp. 18–19.

The Bushmen of Today

Megan Biesele

After receiving her Ph.D. in anthropology from Harvard in 1975, Megan Biesele worked in Botswana on land rights and economic self-determination. She taught at both the University of Texas and Rice University, but since 1987 has been foundation director and project director of the Nyae Nyae Foundation of Namibia. With Stephen A. Tyler she edited *The Dialectic of Oral and Literary Hermemeutics,* published in 1986 by the American Anthropological Association.

Until the 1950's several thousand Bushman people were still hunting large game with poisoned arrows and gathering wild food in the westward extension of the Kalahari basin in Namibia. This area provided a last refuge for the Bushman people, hunted as vermin since the first arrival of Dutch settlers at the Cape in 1652. In the Kalahari basin they were able to continue their ancient way of life, living in small, mobile bands of about 40 people, each one centered on and supported by the resources of a *n!ore,* the Ju/'hoan Bushman word meaning "the place to which you belong," or "the place which gives you food and water." Bushmen have lived around these *n!ores* for as long as 40000 years, practicing one of the most ancient and simple human technologies on earth.

In the past 40 years, however, life has changed drastically for Namibia's Bushmen. In the mid-1960's the Odendaal Commission recommended to the South West African government that the West Caprivi and Bushmanland be designated as "homelands" for all the people classified as "Bushman" in Namibia. Ironically the proclamation of "homelands" has meant the loss of vast areas of land traditionally used by the Bushmen. The process of "legal" dispossession, which predates the decision to establish homelands, signalled the end of the hunter-gatherer way of life for the vast majority of Namibian Bushmen. Beginning in the 1950's the Department of Nature Conservation began to expropriate large sections of the traditional hunting lands for game and nature reserves. The process began with the Hai// 'om Bushmen being driven from their lands to make way for the Etosha Game Reserve. Around the same

time the Kxoe Bushmen lost their land on the Kavango River when it was proclaimed a nature reserve. In 1968 the Department of Nature Conservation expropriated the West Caprivi for a game reserve. About 6000 Ju/ 'hoan people were evicted from the land they had lived on for centuries.

In 1970 Bushmanland was established. For the Ju/ 'hoan Bushmen it meant the loss of 90% of their traditional land of Nyae Nyae, and all but one of their permanent waterholes. Southern Nyae Nyae, about 32000 sq km, was expropriated by the administration and given to the Herero as Hereroland East.

Northern Nyae Nyae, about 11000 sq km was first incorporated into the Kavango homeland and then proclaimed the !Kaudum Game Reserve in 1982. One of the last acts of the Interim Government of National Unity was to confirm the expropriation of the !Kaudum Game Reserve.

Today 33000 people classified as "Bushman" in Namibia have no land on which to hunt, gather or produce food and are increasingly without work. Without land they have resorted to employment in the army or to ill-paid work for white and black farmers. The vast majority who have been unable to get employment squat near places of work, dependent on the wage earners. This has been the pattern for so long now that new generations have grown up without the skills to hunt and gather. Malnutrition and disease led to a 5% decline in the population classified as "Bushman" in the 1970's. . . .

The Ju/'hoan people of Eastern Bushmanland, called Nyae Nyae, have been more fortunate. Some 3000 out of the total population of 33000 Bushmen have retained ties to a fragment of their land. For the past generation they have been the only people in

"The Bushmen of Today" by Megan Biesele, from *Shaken Roots,* Environmental and Development Agency.

Namibia who have hunted and gathered for their living while learning new farming skills. They are also the only people classed as "Bushman" who still have real residential ties to their foraging territory.

Nyae Nyae stretches north to south along the Namibia-Botswana border between the Kavango River and the Eiseb Valley. Originally it extended over approximately 50000 sq km. Hunter-gatherers need more than 37 sq km per person to sustain a stable population in this area. An uplift in the rock formation brings water to the surface in Nyae Nyae. Clearly visible on a geological map, the uplift makes Eastern Bushmanland rise like an island in a sea of sand. Twelve permanent and nine semi-permanent waterholes make the communal land habitable. . . .

In contrast to Nyae Nyae, Western Bushmanland—two thirds of the homeland created in 1970—lies in the deep sand sea. Water must come from deep boreholes requiring expensive pumping engines. The cost of fuel for pumping makes subsistence farming impossible. Bush foods and game are scarce. *Gifblaar,* a plant poisonous to cattle, is very common.

It was in Western Bushmanland that the South African Defence Force (SADF) chose to locate its "Bushman" battalion headquarters and bases. Bushmen from Namibia and those displaced by the Angolan civil war were recruited into the army as trackers and infantrymen for the offensive against Swapo in Angola. Thousands of Bushman people lived in Western Bushmanland until the elections in November 1989, supported by the relatively high salaries of war. Now with the war over, people have nowhere to turn. Some are reportedly trying to eat grass in a desperate struggle to survive. . . .

Most of the Bushmen who made a career of army life over the last decade are Barakwengo, Hai//'om and Vasekela people from the northern areas and from Angola. Now, as the wages of war dry up the soldiers and their families squat in a kind of numbness. They have no land and no homes.

"My future?" one man said, "I don't see a future."

Other ex-soldiers are more fortunate. Ju/'hoan Bushmen from Eastern Bushmanland around Tium!kui have land to return to, and families who have stayed on the land to develop and possess it. /Kaece /Kunta, whose people live at the permanent waterhole at /Aotcha settled by Oma Stump, welcomed the end of life in the army when the war ended. /Kaece /Kunta has no regrets as he recalls his war experiences.

"They told us we would be getting on a plane in Rundu. We had to fly at night because when you fly into Angola in the daytime they shoot you down. The flight is about 1000 km. When we arrived there, they told us to be very careful of going out in the open, because planes were flying over and shooting from the air. It was here that we saw fighter planes for the first time in our lives. The white people lined us up and we stood there and looked at them. Then the white people said, 'Hey, Bushmen, you must watch out for those planes: if they see you they'll shoot you dead—'and after that we knew.

"When we were on the ground later, we were very much afraid, because the planes were searching for us up in the sky above. They shot at us terribly, pursuing us relentlessly. . . .

"People were also throwing handgrenades. These bombs are certain death and even to speak of them is to speak badly. The only reason we lived through it is we were taught how to be careful. If this had not happened, none of us Bushmen would have returned. All our thoughts were put to living through it.

"We saw the villages of the dead, those who had been killed, and their dead children. We saw the skulls of dead people, and those of children who had died. When you walked through these villages, you were stepping on death, the corpses of dead people. It was horrible. You had to step on them and they just crumbled to dust.

"If hunger gripped your middle while you were on these 'ops' and you hadn't seen food for three days, and then you had a chance to eat, you couldn't eat the food because it all tasted like death. If you were too weak to work, they'd prick your one shoulder with a needle, then prick your other shoulder, so you'd have strength to work well. . . .

"My parents didn't agree when I first wanted to go into the army. But I went in anyway—I thought it was just plain work. It was only later that they began killing people. The whole time I was in Angola, all I thought about was staying alive long enough to get back to my family."

DEATH BY MYTH

> There are two kinds of films. One kind shows us as people like other people, who have things to do and plans to make. This kind helps us. The other kind shows us as if we were animals, and plays right into the hands of people who want to take our land.
>
> —Tsamkxao ≠Oma

One of many pernicious myths about Bushman people, exacerbated by films like "The Gods Must Be Crazy," is that they still live in a desert never-never land without unfulfilled desires. The reality is that all but about 3% of the Bushman people in Namibia are completely dispossessed and must struggle unremittingly to survive. Whether they do so on white-owned farms, on Herero or Kavango cattle posts, squatting at the edges of towns, or living in dependence on police or the army, their ability to control their own lives is very limited. As a people with a long history as hunter-gatherers, everything in their background conditions them for dependency on people they perceive as stronger.

Traditionally, the Bushmen had no leaders, believing that a person who set himself up as better than another was without shame and harmful to group life. Nurturant and undemanding of their children, they promoted tolerance and downplayed ambition. Thus they suffer today not only from exploitation at the hands of more arrogant peoples, but also from the social legacy of a life that once worked when land was limitless and competing people few. Bushman people can be fairly characterized as those who have again and again stood aside as stronger forces muscled in. . . .

A n!ore IS A PLACE YOU DO NOT LEAVE

The trees are ours, and the elephants are ours. This is our land. Our things we make and wear come from it—our ostrich beads, our bows and arrows.

We Ju/'hoansi are people who have lived in our *n!oresi* for a long time. We didn't know the thing called a horse, and we made fires and did all our work without burning the tortoises and other tiny things. There were no white people's trucks driving around in our *n!ore*, here on our land. When these things came, their people saw us as nothing-things. So they shut off the land with fences and the eland died against the fences so that today our children are dying of hunger. There are no eland left, the wire has killed them all. And that fence between here and Botswana has also killed many animals. This was the work of governments. We once had our own government which kept us alive but this new government which has come in has killed us.

—/Kaece Kxao, N//haru≠'han, Eastern Bushmanland

Isolation from the outside world ended abruptly for the Ju/'hoansi when Native Administration of their area began in 1960. There was a migration of all bands to a single administrative centre called Tjum!kui, where they were given a school, a clinic, a church, a large jail, and some small jobs.

Some 900 Ju/'hoan people believed the administration's promises to teach them gardening and subsidize stock-raising, and an area which once supported 25 people by hunting and gathering was overwhelmed. A government-subsidized bottle store, unemployment, and the local disappearance of bush foods under heavy human pressure combined to turn Tjum!kui into a rural slum. The Ju/'hoansi called it "the place of death."

In the late 1970's a movement began among some families in Tjum!kui to return to the *n!oresi* from which they came. Tsamkxao ≠Oma and his father ≠Oma "Stump" took their people back to /Aotcha, location

of the only permanent waterhole now left within the shrunken borders of Bushmanland. Black /Ui took his family to N≠aqmtjoha, and Kxao "Tekening," the artist, took his to Nanemh. They began to work in earnest to hold onto their land. Now 25 new communities have returned to their families' old places. "We must lift ourselves up, or die!" people tell each other.

The Ju/'hoansi in Nyae Nyae have started a new life as farmers. They still rely a great deal upon hunting and gathering as they make the difficult transition to small-scale stock-raising. But they know the land left to them does not permit a return to hunting and gathering alone. Life in such a transition is not easy and they struggle against many things: against lions that kill their cattle, and elephants that trample their gardens and wreck their water pumps; against unhelpful or hostile officials who believe them incapable of development. They also struggle within themselves to adapt the cultural rules and values that underwrote the old foraging way of life to the very different one of agriculture.

Ju/'hoansi know that without more intensive food production they are doomed to remain wards of some government, dependent and vulnerable. Tsamkxao Oma is the chairperson of the newly-formed Nyae Nyae Farmers' Cooperative, a body which ties all the communities together to support the farming effort. Since 1986 Tsamkxao and the representatives from the 25 new communities have worked to make the cooperative a democratic organization responsible for many decisions about development. But as Tsamkxao said, "The Farmers' Coop is coming into government things much later than everyone else: the Boers took hold of things first. Now it's very late and we have to get going." . . .

At the time of the November 1989 election in Namibia, the Nyae Nyae Farmers' Cooperative was ratifying its first constitution, ≠Hanu a N!an!a'an. Representatives from the 25 villages travelled the rutted dirt tracks of Eastern Bushmanland to hold informational meetings and explain the new document. Written by a committee of Ju/'hoansi and hired scribes in English and the Ju/'hoan language, the constitution is intended to inject legal strength into ancient Ju/'hoan concepts of communal land holding. . . .

Representatives of the Farmers' Cooperative know that media coverage of what they are now trying to do is essential. They want to make the point in Southern Africa that there are similar groups of people in other parts of the world. Australian Aborigines, and North and South American Indians are also struggling for land rights and self-determination. Tsamkxao ≠Oma, the coop chairman welcomed a journalist recently saying, "We're glad you're here because newspapers are very important to us. I went to a conference in Cape Town last year and I found that many people there had never even heard about us. Newspapers will help us inform people, and they may be a way to help end discrimination. These days we cannot accept that our children have to hear words like 'bobbejaan' and 'kaffir.'"

Easily mythologized, Bushman people have captured the interest of popular media like film, TV, and glossy magazines. But their real voices have been obscured by the loud clamour of the myths in which they are enshrined. Silenced by the voice-overs, not only of film narrators, but also of neighbours and governments and even of well-meaning friends, they have gone on communicating to each other but not to the world outside. Bushmen have been seen both as a sort of fairy-folk, floating over the landscape with no concept of property and no need for solid resources, and as blood-thirsty poachers with a killer instinct. Romanticisation and denigration can amount to the same thing in the end, a kind of death by myth . . . or by misinformation.

The Nature Conservation forces of what was once the South West African government were succeeding in taking Bushman land right up until the last days before UN Resolution 435 was implemented. Dreaming of a future revenue-generating tourist industry, the conservationists have sequestered huge swatches of what once was the well-known and reliably productive *n!ores* of the Ju/'hoan and Kxoe Bushmen. Tsamkxao spoke of an area of Nyae Nyae where Ju/'hoansi have lived for as long as anyone can remember, the permanent waterhole of Gura, where Nature Conservation and the Department of Government Affairs have joined forces to promote safaris and trophy hunting at the expense of Farmers' Coop plans for the area.

"Something we've known for a long time is that the antelopes of Gura were ours, our fathers' fathers' sustenance. And the water there has been our source of life. Even I, when I was small, washed myself at Gura and drank the water there when I was thirsty. At that time I didn't know of a single European or Afrikaner who had been there. This government which calls itself 'Bushmanland' is talking about my things! Why should other people make money here from our animals? We have been here a long time: don't the Nature Conservation officials know they are just small children?"

Officials do seem to be neglecting an important source of information about the environment by not listening to the Ju/'hoan hunters. These people, with their long history of stability in the area have a great deal to contribute to conservation planning. Many generations of information about animal and plant species and their interactions should not be discounted simply because they have been passed on orally. The written tradition of scientific study in this area is young by comparison, and could profit from an infusion of older wisdom. Bushman folklore and religion contain evidence of a very ancient and healthy respect for natural resources, and an ethic of conservation which is thorough-going and socially sound. In fact, seeing these people as natural conservators may be a good way to appreciate what they can contribute. As a /Gwi Bushman, Compass Matsoma, of neighbouring Botswana said recently, "We are the only ones who can live with animals without killing them all."

Not only tourists and hunters but also eager pastoral peoples now wait at the shrunken borders of "Bushmanland" for opportunities to move in. Descendants of survivors of the German Herero Wars at the beginning of this century, when General Von Trotha issued his famous genocide order to kill all men, women and children, have been living as refugees in Botswana. With the coming of independence, many now hope to return across the border and settle on the rich pastures and relatively abundant waters of the Nyae Nyae area, one of the last areas not yet overgrazed in Namibia.

But the Nyae Nyae people say "People shouldn't think they can ruin one area by grazing too many cattle and then move onto someone else's land and ruin that too. We will keep the numbers of our cattle small. We think not only of today but of tomorrow and the day after that."

As new cattle herders, Ju/'hoansi face many challenges. The primary one is the confrontation with their own tried-and-true means of organizing their work. While hunting with poisoned arrows is a most individualistic pursuit, sharing of all food was customary. Keeping cattle and planting dryland gardens involves a new negotiation of labour processes and products. Ju/'hoansi spend a lot of time talking about this.

A dark side coexists with the exultation and excitement of new beginnings. Alcohol undermines Ju/'hoan spirit as it does that of so many African communities. People in Eastern Bushmanland do not seem to be chronic alcoholics at this stage. Distance from bottle stores and poverty have protected most of them. But many brew beer from sugar and yeast on pension day, and when the bottle store was still open in Tjum!kui it caused immense social disruption.

Just after the independence election, Ju/'hoan people took their first public stand acknowledging that excessive drinking is a community problem. At a meeting of the Nyae Nyae Farmers' Cooperative, strong feeling arose over the issue of the social disruption caused by home-brewed beer.

"Those who drink are the ones who cause anger and fighting. Those who don't drink just sit quietly . . . We're not saying don't drink at all, but just drink slowly and wisely . . . I think we should say to ourselves, I have work to do before I drink. First I'm going to do my work.

"When you drink, you shouldn't go around thinking like a Boer and telling people that you are a big shot. If you do that, someday people will become angry with you and their hearts will grow big against you. You don't go saying you're a chief. Instead, you sit together and understand each other. None of us is a chief, we're all alike and have our little farms. So when you drink, just think clearly about it and talk to each other about being careful. We've been told now, so let's be smart about drinking. Let's not fight. Let's start today to talk to each other about drinking and help each other." (Dabe Dahm.)

The bottle store at Tjum!kui, which once did big business on army pay day, has been closed.

Back on their land after living in town with the problems of alcoholism and unemployment, Ju/'hoansi can once more be dignified examples for their children. "We are people who have our work," they say. Children see their mothers and fathers engaged again in productive activities they know well.

A sense of purpose again pervades life in Eastern Bushmanland. Enthusiasm to take part in building a new Namibia runs through the meetings of the Nyae Nyae Farmers' Coop. . . .

NOT KNOWING THINGS IS DEATH

The importance of knowledge in obtaining a living is very much present in the minds of the Ju/'hoan Bushmen. Once they had to be able reliably to tell the difference between poisonous and non-poisonous plants and to judge the likelihood of crossing paths with a worthwhile animal at a given season of the year. They had to know how to make riems, rope, string, sinew thread, carrying bags and nets, stamping blocks, aerodynamically effective arrows, and much more, all from natural materials. The word for "owner" (kxao) in Ju/'hoan most deeply means "master," in the sense of one who knows, or knows how to use. To own property is to be its steward; to own an area of land, a n!ore, is not to possess it exclusively but to use it well.

"A big thing is that my food is here and my father taught me about it. I know where I can drink water here. My father said to me, 'These are your foods and the foods of your children's children.' If you stay in your n!ore you have strength. You have water and food and a place." . . .

When things change greatly in one generation, sometimes older people teach children, and sometimes children are in a position to teach adults. Kxao/Ai!ae of N≠anemh says to his boys that the way to keep your n!ore is to develop it.

"I hold my cattle in my left hand, and my garden in my right hand, and together they give me life.". . .

New ideas and new concepts have flooded into Nyae Nyae in one generation. Has there been enough time for Ju/'hoansi themselves to change sufficiently to participate in the coming independence? Events like UN Resolution 435 and free elections and the final end of apartheid have suddenly overtaken them with many of them not knowing what is really in store.

Like other Namibians, Ju/'hoan Bushmen have had their geographical isolation deepened by the apartheid policies of South Africa and before that, as long as a century ago, by the original German colonial administration of *Südwest*. They have lived through decades of administrations whose communications have somehow missed them because, being egalitarian, they did not have identifiable chiefs. . . .

Suddenly, now, Ju/'hoansi face both the challenge and the opportunity of taking part in a political process watched eagerly by the eyes of the world. But can a small minority with a hunting and gathering heritage, a recent history of isolation and exclusion from affairs that concern them, and a problematic present situation of economic underdevelopment and militarization transform itself quickly enough? Can the Ju/'hoansi hold on to what remains of their ancient territory and also take advantage of the new opportunities of freedom? An egalitarian culture which has always underplayed leadership is faced with the necessity of selecting leaders to participate in the new politics. As at the South African Cape three centuries ago, when leaders were called into being among Bushman groups warring for their lives with the Dutch colonists, Ju/'hoansi are now creating leaders to meet the challenges of the present. . . .

In 1988, news of the implementation of UN Resolution 435 and the promise of free elections in 1989 startled the Ju/'hoansi into a realization of the magnitude of possible changes. Since September of 1988 the Nyae Nyae Farmers' Cooperative, a grassroots community organization in Eastern Bushmanland, has been holding informational meetings about Namibian independence at far-flung villages. Black /Ui at N≠aqmtjoha welcomed the arrival of the discussion team: "I thank you all. I thank you for this talk which comes from far away to us. But one thing that gives me pain is that long ago I never heard anything like this, but only today am hearing it. Today my heart is happy with what I have heard. News is life."

Before the effects of the UN election information process were felt in Bushmanland, the Farmers' Coop tried to explain elections to people who had no word for them in their language. Many had never even heard the Afrikaans word *verkiesing*.

"An election means to come to an understanding about a n!ore."

"An election means that you give praise to the person who will sit in the chair of leading, the head person."

"An election is where you plant your feet and stop."

The talks about elections and other democratic concepts were held in villages of grass or mud houses with no protected public gathering place. The sun beat down at the edges of whatever patch of shade could be found large enough to shelter the village people and the bakkie-load of travellers. Children bounced on their mothers' laps and people of all ages sat close together, often with their legs crossing those of their neighbours. The chairperson of the Farmers' Cooperative, Tsamkxao Oma, constantly encouraged others besides himself to speak.

Issues as small as how to keep tourists from swimming in the drinking water dams to ones as large as securing legal title to their land have been under long discussion at these meetings.

The Nyae Nyae area communities are preoccupied with how to ensure that they are included in talks about conservation and other issues concerning them. Great resentment is felt toward government officials who travel all the way from Windhoek to Tjum!kui, a distance of 750 kilometres, ostensibly to consult with the Ju/'hoan communities, but actually only to meet with the white officials at the comfortable Nature Conservation rest camp, and then go home. The public nature of communication has become a vital issue, and it came to a head in early March 1989 with the arrival of an SADF public relations team at /Aotcha.

Huge armoured vehicles swept into the tiny village of mud houses. Uniformed men with submachine guns silenced the usual hubbub. The army was pulling out of northern Namibia, campaigning as it went for the Democratic Turnhalle Alliance (DTA), Swapo's main opposition. "Watch out for the Hyena" (Swapo) and "Vote for the Eland" (DTA) were the condescending folktale slogans the soldiers offered. "The eland is the animal without deceit: you are the eland."

The Ju/'hoan hunters' sign for eland antelope horns is a "V" made with the first and second fingers. This also happens to be the adopted hand sign for the DTA. In a further twist of irony, which the soldiers couldn't have known about, but which made an even harder puzzle for the Ju/'hoansi to unravel, "Eland" is an ancient clan name for many Ju/'hoansi in the area. Hyenas, on the other hand, are thought of as outcast animals who are always up to no good. Some people were taken in by this overwhelming symbolism, but others remained skeptical. "Swapo has never done anything to us; why should anyone call them hyenas before hearing what they have to say?" said one man.

Ultimately, the public relations meeting at /Aotcha was a bit of a rout because the officer in charge refused the people's request to tape the session. The message brought by the SADF that day was hardly secret, but since it could not be taped, the people regarded the communication as a "theft." Unfortunately for the army it didn't know that the Ju/'hoansi call tape cassettes xusi, their word for oracle disks. Oracle disks are thrown down on the ground like dice and are said to reveal the future by the pattern they make. These disks

are traditionally made from eland hide and are thus associated with the eland's herd sociability and supposed guilelessness.

Playing with strong symbolism can ultimately backfire, as it did resoundingly during the last feverish days of election campaigning in Bushmanland. Dabe Dahm, a Farmers' Cooperative representative at the village of //Auru, had thought for a year about the DTA's use of the eland to represent its party. Having observed violent drunkenness and clear intimidation of potential voters by the DTA campaigners, he said, "Today my shame is piled high. My people's name from long ago, 'the people of the eland,' has been rubbed in the dirt and stolen by politicians who will never do anything for us. All they want is to give other people our land."

The same day at Dabe Dahm's village people spoke of the loss of the actual eland on which they once depended. Many adults remembered a time when eland were abundant in their area.

Most Ju/'hoansi believe that the drastic reduction in eland numbers is due to the game fences. . . . Regardless of their decline in numbers, eland live in folklore and inhabit people's minds and a move to try eland domestication in Nyae Nyae is gaining support. Ju/'hoansi see eland farming as a sensible alternative to the kind of abuse of grazing resources they have seen destroy the productivity of adjacent areas such as Eastern Hereroland. The eland is adapted to the area, it does not suffer from the effects of *gifblaar,* and it can sustain itself on water-bearing plants such as desert cucumbers and juicy roots when water is scarce. Some Ju/'hoan people have worked on the farms of Afrikaner people in the Grootfontein area who keep eland and other game on their farms, and they know what a fine candidate the eland is for management as a herd animal. . . .

"Trucks with hunters shooting from them have chased away the animals we had here, trucks and the fences that have been built. Long ago you saw all the animals here, even eland. But today there's not a single eland. Even ostrich eggs you don't see, because the ostriches too are stopped by the fences. We don't want this, we want the fences taken down so that wild animals will come back and be close to us as before."

"If Ju/'hoansi had strength, maybe they could think of catching lots of eland, and maybe roan antelopes, and farming with them. But until after the election we will have no strength. The white people still have all the strength in this land. Maybe after the election we could do it . . . Long ago the eland used to cross Nyae Nyae according to the season, but one season the fence was closed on them and on their calves, and they haven't returned."

It's clear that the policies of the South West African state with their paternalism and emphasis on separation have angered the Ju/'hoansi for a long time. In particular they resent being left out of communications. Ju/'hoansi call themselves "the owners of argument," and "the people who talk too much." For them, it's important that issues be discussed and debated by everyone so that ill-will doesn't fester in someone left out of the talk. . . .

The idea of representation for their voices in government is catching on among the Ju/'hoansi at the same time as they are realizing the power of the printed word. As Tsamkxao told one group meeting under a thorn tree, "One problem is that we have no scribe. We have no-one who is the 'owner of the mail.' So let the children help us. Let the children go to school, learn, and know. Let's make a plan. Let's let everyone know that we have someone with a writing-stick. Let's have a scribe, a writer, a translator. Let's not be without these."

None of the language of democracy, in fact, seems terribly new among the Ju/'hoansi, rather it is age-old. These are the people who gravely said to anthropologist Richard Lee over a decade ago: "We have no headman, each one of us is a headman over himself." The concept of "one person, one vote" fits right in with Ju/'hoan ideology, and among these sexually egalitarian people one doesn't even have to add, as would be necessary in many parts of the world, "and a woman's vote is just like a man's."

Tsamkxao illustrated democracy at one meeting, at a place called //Xa/oba, talking about collective strength and the responsibilities of the people's representatives: "I thank the old people who have spoken, but we also need to begin to hear from the young people about their n!ores. Everyone must work together. Do you see these sticks in my hand? If you pick up lots of sticks, you can't break them. But one stick alone breaks easily. So we want things from now on to be done on paper, legally, beginning with meetings where everyone comes together to listen. We don't want a Ju/'hoan representative who just stuffs news into his own ears and doesn't speak to us. If you speak for a group of people to a government, and if you speak badly, it doesn't just affect one person. It affects everyone. When you do something, all your people should have a way of learning about it. Political parties are for letting people know things."

One of the things Ju/'hoansi are letting people know now is that they suggest legal institutionalization of something like their old n!ore system. They know it has been successful over a long span of time, and see it as the basis for something that could work in Namibia's future. It would mean a new kind of survival for them, too, not the traditional one, but a creative one, their own special contribution to nation-building.

In 1989 Namibia had good rains. By March, Bushmanland was lush and green. One evening, as lilac-breasted rollers tumbled after insects against cumulus clouds lit with a pink glow by the setting sun, an historic meeting began at Nyae Nyae. After generations without meaningful talk with outside political forces, representatives of the Nyae Nyae Farmers' Coop met with officials of Swapo, the party which will construct the Namibian land tenure systems to come. With the two groups sitting on the grass in a rough circle of about forty people, including onlookers, the Coop presented a document stating its goals with regard to land and representation. Written in the Ju/'hoan language and translated into English, the statement calls for a democratic national system with regional autonomous government in Nyae Nyae based on current and long-term residence.

Ju/'hoansi know they are the last Bushman people in Namibia to have an unbroken contact with even the small fragment of land that is still theirs. And they know these ties to land are their main resource: "Where your mother and father are buried is where you have your strength."

The Ju/'hoansi of Eastern Bushmanland are the lucky ones. But they are planning carefully to share their land and a chance to make an independent living with other Bushmen in Namibia. The election and the talk that preceded it has begun to give these isolated people a sense of the altruism needed to create a nation.

"I said to the Administrator General, 'Will you help us since our n!ore is small? Hereros have taken part of it and !Kaudum is another part gone.'

"I also told him, 'The people who once worked in the army today have no work and no other strength. How will we help those people?'

"I said, 'The people called Vasekela—we still haven't met together to talk with them. I understand that they may be allowed to stay in Western Bushmanland and make gardens. We must ask how they are going to do that without water.'

"We want to help everyone we can. It's important that we who are the Ju/'hoansi have our own government and do our own work. We have only a small place, but we want to go to the Gobabis farms and find our people who long ago were taken away. We want to get them and bring them here. Can we find a way to help everyone?

"We have received money from the 'owners of helping' [aid funds] and we have dug boreholes for more water in our small land. The !Kaudum people are many, and many others are on police-posts that will now die, or in Gobabis. We who are representatives of the Nyae Nyae Farmers' Cooperative are like people planting a tree. We should realize that we are not just one small thing but are starting something big. The work will go on, even beyond our deaths. The boreholes will be there." (Tsamkxao ≠Oma.)

Appendix

An Anthropologist's Guide to the Internet

David Houston

Currently studying anthropology and complex systems at the University of Vermont, David L. R. Houston also works as the client services coordinator in the university's division of computer and information technology. His work and study take him on regular excursions into cyberspace, where he takes a critical look at the Internet, a fascinating component of a newly emerging global culture.

It's likely that most aspiring anthropologists have seen or heard of things like "e-mail" or "Mosaic" or "Internet," but it's not a given that everyone in this group has any actual hands-on experience with this new and rapidly expanding medium of information exchange. The growth of Internet resources of interest to anthropologists is stunning, and it is a challenge to the new user that—though daunting at first—is well worth the reward.

This paper is an introduction to the Internet: what it is and what it can offer to the practicing (or armchair!) anthropologist.

WHAT IS THE INTERNET?

Most people have probably seen or used a personal computer (or PC) for some purpose, perhaps producing nicely finished written works using a word processor. The development of the personal computer has come on the heels of other information systems development—that of the mainframe computer. The rapid advances of technology have been particularly stunning for the PC, however, and now the power locked inside this simple desktop machine often exceeds that of the mainframe computer of 10 years ago.

Printed by permission of David Houston.

One result of these technical advances was the implementation of a method of computer communication called ARPANET. This was an effort by the U.S. Department of Defense to facilitate rapid forms of communications among an elite group of scientific researchers. These researchers needed a means to share their findings quickly and efficiently. As this technology grew, it produced a curious and unstoppable side effect: the associated communications network grew ever larger. This growth was a direct result of the primary goal of the network—scientific research—and in the 1980s it took a significant step forward with the addition of the National Science Foundation project, NSFNET. This led to the need for even better, faster, and more widespread communications, producing an ever widening sphere of influence. The growth of this network became very nearly inevitable, for as the range of communications spread and brought more and more people under its sway, the resultant pressure led to the improvement of the entire process.

The result, with which we work today, is called the Internet. It includes all of the original "players"—the military and industrial segments of pure research—but has now brought into the picture most institutions of higher learning. In addition, the original "local community" that extended throughout the United States is now, by any measure, worldwide.

WHAT CAN BE DONE WITH THE INTERNET?

The use of the Internet originally began with the express intent of exchanging research information, and that use holds true today. The addition of features not imagined by its original designers has made the Internet a powerful and fascinating research tool. While there are a wide variety of communications methods presently available to users, the simple exchange of electronic messages is probably the most extensively utilized part of the Internet. It is called e-mail.

E-mail

E-mail allows you to be in instant communication with many of your peers and a whole host of other institutions (universities, libraries, etc.) world-wide. What you need for e-mail is pretty straightforward: a computer, an account on a local "host" system (described at the end of this article), and either a direct connection to that host or a modem. Software for the process is nearly always included in the installation of the host connection card or the modem. If you don't have any of these things, start by contacting the local Computing Center on your campus. This same organization can probably refer you to the people responsible for setting up host accounts. If you are not attached to any university, there are many viable and low-cost ways to get on the information highway. Inquiring at a computer store or center is a good place to start.

If you do nothing else at all on the Internet, I'd strongly encourage you to use e-mail. The opportunities and benefits there are substantial: contact with colleagues, access to libraries at other institutions, and a means of staying in touch on trips and fieldwork opportunities. Most campuses offer good introductory sessions on e-mail use. These are usually free and a great way to get started.

Lists

If you have or are planning to use e-mail, then the next easy step up is called a list. A list is actually a special kind of e-mail address. A list has a large number of "subscribers" who all send and receive "postings," or messages, to the list. The numbers of topics covered by lists are staggering, and the number that are of interest to anthropologists are many. Getting "subscribed" to a list is relatively easy: you simply send a message to a piece of software called a "listserv" or "listproc," include the *subscribe* command, the name of the list, and your full name. One fairly common mistake that new users make is to send such requests to the actual list itself—whereby everyone on the list gets this same message! If you really cannot find any correct address for the listserv of a list, then it is generally acceptable practice to send a message to the list itself and specifi-

cally ask its membership to provide such information. If you are pleasant and respectful about it, you won't be chided for this sort of request. After you send your subscription request to the listserv, the very first thing you'll get back is a set of instructions for that list. It's important to save this message.

Once you have subscribed to a list, you will start receiving all of the "postings" that its membership submits. Depending upon the list, this can range from one or two such messages a month (even less, in some cases) to 100 or more messages per day! If you find that you are overwhelmed, then it might be best to unsubscribe. The introductory document sent to you will tell you how to do this. One small caveat here: it is essential to send unsubscribe requests from the exact same address that you sent the subscribe request, or you will not be removed from the list.

Lists are a common and very interesting way to communicate with a large group of peers that share a common interest. Many lists are quite specialized, and while the vast majority are "public" (which means anyone can subscribe), there are a few "private" ones as well. In the former type, it's possible that there will be a few subscribers who may not be too serious about the topic. In most cases, brazenly obnoxious behavior results in annoyed responses from list members. The end of this paper offers a few ways to access "lists of lists" to help you make some choices as regards subject matter.

UseNet News

The UseNet news is a huge array of specialty "topic areas" that resemble lists only in that users send postings to a particular group. The UseNet news is not something that you can subscribe to—you have to have a "newsreader" on the host system and actually go in and read the postings. Because the news groups are wide open to anyone, the kind of audience varies a great deal. Not surprisingly, topics of interest to anthropologists on the UseNet news also are home to some unusual points of view! This tends to constrain interest as regards special topics, but there are a few less frequented areas that can be interesting. Lest one come away with the impression that UseNet news is home to the fringe element only, I'll emphatically add that one very useful way to use the news is for technical help. There are hundreds of groups whose focus is computing—software, hardware; anything that has anything to do with computing probably has a newsgroup associated with it. This includes many commercial products. The result is that if you have any sort of question about some aspect of computing, you can often get very good results by looking at the UseNet. In fact, it is often better, when dealing with commercial products, to try the frequenters of the UseNet first. It is highly likely that you'll get the answer to a problem very quickly, and it won't cost you the exorbitant fees that many software vendors will charge.

You'll need to have a newsreader on your host system: some of the common ones include tin, vn, and nn. If you are not sure if your host system has a newsreader, ask your system administrator.

Gopher

Gopher is a special, easy-to-use information "browser" that nearly all host systems support. To use gopher, you simply need access to your host account. In most installations, typing 'gopher' at your host "prompt" (where you are after you first log on to the system) will start the gopher software program. You don't need to subscribe or send any e-mail at all, and most institutions have some gopher files that are useful.

Gopher lets you "tunnel" through the Internet through a series of simple menus. When you first start gopher, you'll be looking at the "root" menu or the top level of that particular host's gopher server. The menu structure is pretty straightforward: you use the arrow keys on your computer to move up and down until you are positioned in front of a numbered menu item, and then either hit the return key or the right arrow to "enter" that directory area.

While the use of gopher is declining a bit (due to the enormous popularity of Mosaic), it is still a strong and very viable information-gathering tool. It's not likely to go out of date soon, so don't stay away just because it's not "high tech" or flashy. There are still a large number of institutions using and actively supporting gopher, and as a result, some of the really useful resources are still to be found in the various gopher sites worldwide. Some of the more useful ones are listed at the end of this article, but one that deserves special note is Scott Yanoff's list of special Internet connections. This particular list is notable both because of its longevity and its scope: it contains more than 15 pages of subject entries that range from Agriculture to World Wide Web sites and is a great way to find a starting point on the Internet.

The best and most effective way to get something out of gopher is really to just go ahead and do it. You can't hurt anything, and the process of actually browsing is a great way to uncover more resources.

FTP

Of the many things you do on the Internet, there will almost certainly be times when you discover a particular file or a piece of software that you want to copy to your own computer. There are millions of offerings to be had, and the process of getting them from the remote site, or host, to your local PC is called *downloading*. FTP, or File Transfer Protocol, is the technique that enables you to accomplish this.

The most popular method of using FTP is called *anonymous ftp*. It is referred to as anonymous because you are actually "logging in" to other systems as a guest; you rarely own an account on such systems. FTP sites have established special directories that permit any user to log in as the user named "anonymous." In this type of transfer a specific location is chosen by the user (see the end of this article for examples). On nearly every large host system that you will use is a piece of software called, not surprisingly, ftp. To access this software, you simply type the letters *ftp* followed by a space and the exact name of the target site. If your objective was the Anthropology network FAQ, for example, you would simply enter:

ftp lucy.ukc.ac.uk

at your host system prompt. Note there is a growing selection of software that can be used directly on your PC, however, and the host system ftp is by no means the only method in use. Specific instructions for using these software packages are best obtained from your campus computer department.

After you are "connected" to the target site, the next steps vary only with the type of software used. Thus, logging into any anonymous ftp site is always the same: one enters the word *anonymous* at the "login" prompt, and enters his or her personal e-mail address as the password for purposes of identification and courtesy.

Once connected, the next step involves "navigating" to the precise directory where the files that interest you are stored. Most references to ftp sites or particular files will include a complete directory entry as well. At this point the file is retrieved using either the "get" command or the specific software feature that "downloads" the software. It's not nearly as complex as it might seem.

There is a lot more that can be done with ftp—"getting" software and files as well as "putting" files out for others. It is suggested that you read one or more books (several good ones are listed at the end of this article) about the process of file transfer to get the most out of it.

The World Wide Web and Mosaic

The World Wide Web (www) is the new, graphically oriented information browser for the Internet. The emphasis—and the strength—of the World Wide Web approach lies in the integration of text, graphics, color, and even sound in the delivery of information. There are several ways to approach World Wide Web navigation.

The pioneering "browser" is a software product called Mosaic. Developed at the University of Illinois, Mosaic has the longest history in www browsers. In general, you should not expect to be able to use Mosaic with a modem. Some institutions have what is called SLIP support, which does allow this, but most of the time you will find that it is only possible to use Mosaic (and several other browsers) with a direct Internet connection. Mosaic is a free software product, and if you try it out you'll probably become hooked rather quickly! NetScape is another popular browser. Similar in function to Mosaic, it is also free, but is produced by a private organization. There is also the lesser-known browser, MacWeb. All these browsers operate similarly on any of the two major computer "platforms." You simply start the application and in a moment you are connected to the Internet. Most institutions that offer access to the Internet have probably preconfigured the browsers to "point" to the "home page" of that institution, but it is a simple matter to jump right to a specific location.

As mentioned above, most of the graphically based browsers really require a direct Internet connection to use, but it's possible that your site has a piece of host software called *Lynx* that allows you to navigate the entire world wide web in a text-only mode. While not nearly so dramatic as its colorful cousins, it is nevertheless a very useful tool to have available, if only for the purpose of rapidly navigating the plethora of sites using only a modem.

What separates the www approach from the existing suite of Internet tools is, as noted, the inclusion of so many nontextual components in the presentation of selected information. While this might not seem to be such an important criterion at first glance, a brief tour of one or two sites will rapidly demonstrate otherwise. The ability to display pictures of locations, artifacts, people, or works of art on the same page that carries descriptive text makes the process of using the information available on the Internet that much more compelling.

SO MANY TOOLS . . . NOW WHAT?

Outlined above have been some of the more accessible and usable tools for navigating the vast sea of information that is the Internet. But after all is said and done about these tools, one might well ask—"What do I get from the Internet?" Obviously, what one gets will vary a great deal, depending, for example, on the area of particular interest. It's very easy to waste time on the Internet—there is so much information that it's a very simple matter to get lost in the ocean. The trick is to have some idea of what you are interested in before you actually start. For anthropologists, this simplifies the matter a bit. It's relatively straightforward to find a large number of "pointers" to the topic of your choice.

It's also helpful to have some idea of what is out there; not a detailed working directory, but a more generalized sense of what you can and cannot find on the Internet. Libraries and library access, for example, are one thing that you are certain to find quickly. Something as specialized as the Human Relations Area Files (HRAF), though, is not a likely candidate for inclusion. Where do you start? It's helpful to spend some time in gopher. This single resource can show you the extent of things that are out there. Gopher resources will "point" you to other resources—not the actual text content, perhaps—but the locations. Simply looking at the gopher menus will give an idea of what's there. Using gopher also gets you to the "list of lists," which will be a boon to specialized disciplines.

Starting out with the more sophisticated tools such as Mosaic is fun, but it's easy—almost too easy—to get swallowed up in the whole process! I'd suggest that these tools be approached after you have a good idea of how to get around, what's where, and what some of these resources mean.

WHAT THE FUTURE HOLDS

The Internet is expanding rapidly, and the debate as to issues such as cost, access, security, and privacy will no doubt linger for quite some time. The use of the Internet will certainly increase dramatically in the years ahead. Some pretty spectacular things have shown up on the Internet lately, and a few of these have some far-reaching significance to the field of anthropology in general.

Late in 1994, a new cave site of stone age art was discovered in southern France. First reports indicated that it was more spectacular than Lascaux, but that, like that site, access would be strictly limited. Within about a month, several researchers in French universities had placed both text and full-color, photographic-quality images of this site on the world wide web. Aside from the breathtaking beauty of these works, this is significant in that it permits a very wide range of persons *virtual* access to these caves while preserving the actual site itself.

The Mayan Epigraphic Database Project (MED), located in Virginia, is an outstanding example of how the efforts by a dedicated group can be of real, tangible benefit to all. Opened to the "public" in late 1994, this project is an experiment in "networked scholarship" and is attempting to enhance Classic Mayan Epigraphic research. The goal is to produce an Internet-accessible relational database of primary and secondary resources in this subject. Although still under development, it's clear that the benefit of this kind of shared research holds real promise.

The aforementioned examples are but a tiny sample of the ever growing resource base. I've included them as two outstanding examples of the strength of the Internet as a communications medium. At the end of this article is a list of additional interesting resources that are well worth trying.

It may seem that the Internet, computers, and the World Wide Web are intimidating to try and understand: many may shy away from using these tools. But, in the end, these things will push relentlessly onward as more and more professional anthropologists, teachers, students, and others learn to use and exploit these tools to their advantage. It's easy to stay away, drum up excuses, and say "I can't do that" or "it takes too much time, and time is what I don't have," but the fact is that you can do it, you can find the time, and you can get a lot out of it. Many will no doubt hang on to the excuses, stay away, and in a few more years will look over the shoulders of others and wonder what they're missing. Don't be shy—jump in and get your feet wet!

HIGHLY RECOMMENDED FOR NEW USERS

The following resources are strongly suggested as a good suite of places and things to start with.

Listservs—Try these for a while, at least (Unsubscribe if you don't like what you see.)

ANTHRO-L: Anthropology—send subscribe requests to listserv@ubvm.cc.buffalo.edu

ARCH-L: Archaeology—send subscribe requests to listserv@tamvml.tamu.edu

JWA: Journal of World Anthropology—send subscribe requests to listserv@ubvm.cc.buffalo.edu (back issues available via buffalo gopher; see below)

Gopher servers—always a good source of information

Buffalo Gopher server: Gopher to: wings.buffalo. edu select "Academic & Departmental Information," then "Academic Departments and Research Centers" then "Anthropology Department" ("Worldwide E-mail Directory of Anthropologists" back issues of "Journal of World Anthropology," etc.; also available via ftp)

Electronic Journals & Archives

World Systems Archive (announcements, documents, data, biographical, and publications information)—ftp to csf.colorado.edu and connect to directory 'wsystems'.

World Wide Web Servers

Archaeological Field Work Opportunities—Server http://durendal/cit.cornell.edu/TestPit.html

Archnet (Prehistoric archaeology of the northeast) (also via gopher) Server http://spirit.lib.uconn. edu/HTML/archnet.html

Gopher Resources

Gopher Jewels: gopher to: cwis.usc.edu:70

Internet Assistance:
gopher to: peg.cwis.uci.edu
select 13: Accessing the Internet
then select 9: PEG: a peripatetic, eclectic gopher
then select 7: INTERNET ASSISTANCE.
The Scott Yanoff list is near the end of the menu structure.

General Resources

Internet Resources of Interest to Anthropologists: Intended for those who have some working knowledge of Internet tools, this list is regularly updated and maintained. It contains a large number of resources of interest to both anthropology and archaeology. It is presently archived in several locations and formats.

via Anonymous ftp:
ftp. neosoft.com
(pub/users/claird/sci.anthropology/Anthropology_network_FAQ);
ftp.anatomy.su.oz.au (/danny/anthropology/ net-faq);
lucy.ukc.ac.uk (/pub/Anthropology_network_ FAQ) Gopher

via Gopher:
ArchNet: gopher to spirit.lib.uconn.edu

via WWW:
http://lucy.ukc.ac.uk/afaq.html
http://www.anatomy.su.oz.au

GOING FURTHER

There's a lot more to learn about the Internet, and more tools to use. The following books are great additions, and they offer good opportunities for learning more methods and finding more information.

Krol, Ed. *The Whole Internet: User's Guide and Catalog.* O'Reilly & Associates.
LaQuey, Tracy. *The Internet Companion, A Beginner's Guide to Global Networking.* Addison-Wesley.

Glossary

a priori In logic, working from the general to the particular; deductive reasoning.

age-grade A category determined by age; each person goes through many categories of age during life.

age-sets A group of persons initiated into an age-grade at the same time and who move together through successive age-grades thereafter.

agrarian society One in which food is produced by farming the land.

AIDS Acquired immunodeficiency syndrome; a fatal disease transmitted sexually, through contaminated blood products, and from a mother to child during pregnancy and/or through breast milk. Now pandemic.

anthropological advocacy group Group formed to advance the rights of indigenous peoples.

anthropological perspective The practice of viewing customs and institutions in their holistic and evolutionary context.

anthropology The study of humankind, in all times and places.

apartheid The separation of races within a single society, with whites monopolizing positions of power and having favored access to valued resources.

applied anthropology The use of anthropological techniques and knowledge in order to solve "practical" problems.

autonomy Self-government.

balanced reciprocity Where goods are exchanged, those that are given and those that are received are of equal value.

cargo cults A type of revitalization movement common in parts of the Pacific; adherents believe the ancestors will arrive in a ship loaded with white peoples' cargo and will drive whites out.

civilization A type of society marked by the presence of urban settlements, social inequality, and a state type of political organization.

clan A noncorporate group in which each member claims descent from a common ancestor without necessarily knowing the genealogical links to that ancestor.

code switching The process of changing from one level of language to another.

colonialism The unilateral assertion of political jurisdiction over a people and their territory by some other people.

common-interest group A group formed for a specific purpose with membership based on an act of joining, rather than age, kinship, marriage, or territory.

communication The transmittal of information from one individual to another, whether it be a hunger cry from an infant, words of a language, or flirtatious behavior.

cultural anthropology The branch of anthropology concerned with human behavior (as opposed to physical, also known as biological, anthropology).

cultural arrogance The ethnocentric notion that one's own culture is superior to another.

cultural pluralism Interaction socially and politically within the same society of people with different ways of living and thinking.

cultural relativism The necessity to suspend judgment in order to understand a custom in its cultural context; essential for understanding other peoples' practices.

culture The values and standards of a people that enable them to make sense of the world and to shape every aspect of their behavior.

dependence training A way of raising children that promotes compliance in performance of assigned tasks and dependence on the domestic group, rather than personal independence.

development economist An economist who studies or works with peoples or cultures whose lives are in the midst of cultural change.

dispute management How a society handles disagreements such as ownership of land, marital rights, or dowry.

economic exploitation Exploitation of one population's labor and resources by another population for the latter's benefit, at the expense of the former.

economics The study of the production, distribution, and consumption of goods and commodities.

egalitarian ethos The expectation that all should share equally in valued resources and have an equal say in making important decisions.

egalitarianism A social system in which as many valued positions exist as there are persons capable of filling them.

egalitarian redistribution The redistribution of resources so that all members of the society share equally.

enculturation The process by which a people's culture is transmitted from one generation to the next.

endogamy Marriage within a specified category of individuals.

ethnocentrism The belief held by all people that one's own culture is superior in every way to all others.

ethnographies Studies of particular cultures based on firsthand observation.

ethnology The study of cultures from a comparative or historical point of view.

exchange The reciprocal giving of things, whether it be camels for wives, bananas for meat, money for manufactured goods, or whatever.

exogamy Marriage outside of a specified group.

extended family A family composed of two or more married couples with their dependent offspring, the core members of which are related by ties of blood, who live together in one household.

family A residential kin group minimally composed of a woman, her dependent children, and at least one adult male joined through marriage or blood relationship.

fieldwork The study of a society, or some segment thereof, carried out in that society itself.

foraging The finding of food in nature, as opposed to food production through farming or herding.

generalized reciprocity Exchange in which the value of the gift is not calculated nor is the time of repayment specified.

genocide The extermination of one people by another, either as a deliberate act or as the accidental outcome of activities carried out by one people with little regard for their impact on others.

global interdependency The interdependency between all of the peoples of the world that has come to exist in the twentieth century.

globalization The development of global interdependency; the process by which the world's peoples become increasingly interdependent.

hierarchy An organizational structure in which high-ranking elements subsume lower-ranking ones.

historical linguistics The study of linguistic change and the relationships between different languages.

holistic perspective A perspective by which anthropologists view things in the broadest possible context, in order to understand their interconnections and interdependence.

homosexuality A sexual preference for members of one's own, rather than the opposite, sex.

hunter-gatherer One who lives on foods either hunted or gathered in the wild; preferred term now is *food-forager*, which incorporates hunting, gathering, fishing, and scavenging.

incest Sexual relations between individuals, normally declared "off-limits," usually between parents and children or siblings of opposite sex; in some cultures, however, other relationships may be considered incestuous.

independence training A way of raising children that promotes independence, self-reliance, and personal achievement.

kindred The maternal and paternal relatives of a particular individual to whom he or she can appeal for assistance and who gather together on important occasions in the life of the individual.

kinesics "Body language"; system of postures, facial expressions, and body motions that convey messages.

language Communication by means of sounds that are put together in meaningful ways according to a set of rules.

law Social norms, the neglect or infraction of which is regularly met by the threatened or actual application of physical force on the part of an individual or group possessing the socially recognized authority to do so.

liminality Being at the point of change, from one status to another.

lineage A corporate group, membership in which is based on demonstrable descent from a common ancestor.

linguist One who studies languages, their structure, and use.

linguistic anthropology A branch of cultural anthropology that studies the linguistic behavior of humans.

magic The idea that there are ritual formulas that, if followed precisely, manipulate supernatural powers for desired ends.

male initiation rite See Rite of passage.

market exchange The buying and selling of goods and services with prices set by forces of supply and demand. In non-Western societies, usually occurs in a marketplace.

marriage A transaction and resulting contract by which a woman and a man establish continuing rights of sexual access to one another and in which the woman involved is eligible to bear children.

matrilineal descent Ancestry traced to a common ancestor exclusively through women.

matrilineal society A society in which matrilineal descent is an important organizing principle.

millenarian movement In a colonial or multicultural society, a revitalization movement that attempts to resurrect a group, with its own subcultural ideology, that has long suffered in an inferior social position.

multiculturalism The doctrine that accepts the validity of groups within a larger society operating according to their own distinctive standards and values.

nation A people who share a common language, culture, territorial base, political organization, history, and (often) religion.

natural selection An evolutionary process by which individuals with characters best suited to a particular environment survive and reproduce with greater frequency than do those without them.

negative reciprocity Contrasts with balanced reciprocity in that one party to the exchange tries to get the better of it.

nuclear family Consists of husband, wife, and dependent children, living together in a single household.

Oedipus complex In psychoanalysis, the term for the child unconsciously being attracted to the parent of the opposite sex while being hostile to the same-sex parent.

organizational principle A principle, such as descent from a common ancestor, by which individuals are organized into groups within a society.

pandemic Epidemic over large regions; for example, AIDS is pandemic globally.

paralanguage The extralinguistic noises such as grunts, cries, or laughter that accompany language.

patrilineal descent Ancestry traced to a common ancestor exclusively through men.

patrilineal society A society in which patrilineal descent is an important organizing principle.

physical anthropologist An anthropologist who studies humans as biological organisms.

poison oracle The use of poison to summon the supernatural to find the truth of a matter.

political organization The means by which decisions are made, conflicts resolved, and order maintained within a society.

polygamy A form of marriage in which one may have multiple spouses, that is, one man with two or more wives (polygyny) or one woman with two or more husbands (polyandry).

prehistorian One who studies ancient societies for which there are no written records.

psychoanalytic theory The theory of personality developed in the late nineteenth century by Sigmund Freud.

psychological anthropology The branch of cultural anthropology that studies the interface between culture and the individual.

redistributive exchange The collection of goods by some central agent, be it a "big man" or the state, for subsequent redistribution.

religion Rituals, with explanatory myths, that mobilize supernatural powers for the purpose of achieving or preventing transformations of certain events.

revitalization movements Social movements, commonly of a religious nature, that seek to totally reform a society.

rite of passage A ritual that marks changes in the lives of individuals, such as birth, puberty, marriage, and death.

shaman An individual especially skilled at contacting and manipulating supernatural beings and powers, usually by entering a state of trance.

social anthropologist An anthropologist who studies the social life of human beings.

social class In a nonegalitarian society, a class of individuals who enjoy equal or nearly equal prestige according to the system of evaluation.

social control The control exerted on individuals by the institutions of their society.

social elite In a nonegalitarian society, those who occupy important positions of power and have preferred access to valued resources.

social engineering project A project designed specifically to change some aspect of a society.

social group Any socially recognized group within a society.

society A people who share a common territory and who share common cultural traditions.

sociolinguistics The study of how language is used in particular social settings.

state A country with a centralized political system having the power to coerce.

stratified redistribution A system of redistribution in which the redistributor withholds his or her own labor, retains the largest share, and ends up with more material wealth.

stratified society The division of society into two or more groups of people (social classes) who do not share equally in the basic resources that support life, influence, and prestige.

structural analysis Analysis of the underlying structure of a myth or activity.

structural linguistics The scientific study of the structure of a language.

subaltern Subordinate.

subculture The standards and values of a group of people within a larger society.

subsistence Means of support of way of life.

symbolic indicator Activities and positions indicative of one's position in a class-structured society.

trance An altered state of consciousness in which one's nervous system generates images that the individual perceives as real.

variable Something that changes; in science, a factor that is varied while all others are held constant.

Index